Direct Compositionality

OXFORD STUDIES IN THEORETICAL LINGUISTICS

PUBLISHED

1 *The Syntax of Silence Sluicing, Islands, and the Theory of Ellipsis*
by Jason Merchant

2 *Questions and Answers in Embedded Contexts*
by Utpal Lahiri

3 *Phonetics, Phonology, and Cognition*
edited by Jacques Durand and Bernard Laks

4 *At the Syntax–Pragmatics Interface: Concept Formation and Verbal Underspecification in Dynamic Syntax*
by Lutz Marten

5 *The Unaccusativity Puzzle Explorations of the Syntax–Lexicon Interface*
edited by Artemis Alexiadou, Elena Anagnostopoulou, and Martin Everaert

6 *Beyond Morphology Interface Conditions on Word Formation*
by Peter Ackema and Ad Neeleman

7 *The Logic of Conventional Implicatures*
by Christopher Potts

8 *Paradigms in Phonological Theory*
edited by Laura Downing, T. Alan Hall, and Renate Raffelsiefen

9 *The Verbal Complex in Romance*
by Paola Monachesi

10 *The Syntax of Aspect: Deriving Thematic and Aspectual Interpretation*
edited by Nomi Erteschik-Shir and Tova Rapoport

11 *Aspects of the Theory of Clitics*
by Stephen Anderson

12 *Canonical Forms in Prosodic Morphology*
by Laura J. Downing

13 *Aspect and Reference Time*
by Olga Borik

14 *Direct Compositionality*
edited by Chris Barker and Pauline Jacobson

15 *The Oxford Handbook of Linguistic Interfaces*
edited by Gillian Ramchand and Charles Reiss
[Published in association with the series]

Direct Compositionality

Edited by
CHRIS BARKER AND PAULINE JACOBSON

OXFORD
UNIVERSITY PRESS

OXFORD
UNIVERSITY PRESS

Great Clarendon Street, Oxford OX2 6DP

Oxford University Press is a department of the University of Oxford.
It furthers the University's objective of excellence in research, scholarship,
and education by publishing worldwide in

Oxford New York

Auckland Cape Town Dar es Salaam Hong Kong Karachi
Kuala Lumpur Madrid Melbourne Mexico City Nairobi
New Delhi Shanghai Taipei Toronto

With offices in

Argentina Austria Brazil Chile Czech Republic France Greece
Guatemala Hungary Italy Japan Poland Portugal Singapore
South Korea Switzerland Thailand Turkey Ukraine Vietnam

Oxford is a registered trade mark of Oxford University Press
in the UK and in certain other countries

Published in the United States
by Oxford University Press Inc., New York

First published 2007

British Library Cataloguing in Publication Data
Data available

Library of Congress Cataloging in Publication Data
Data available

Typeset by SPI Publisher Services, Pondicherry, India
Printed in Great Britain
on acid-free paper by
Biddles Ltd. www.biddles.co.uk

ISBN 978–0–19–920437–3 (Hbk)
ISBN 978–0–19–920438–0 (Pbk)

1 3 5 7 9 10 8 6 4 2

Contents

General Preface

The theoretical focus of this series is on the interfaces between subcomponents of the human grammatical system and the closely related area of the interfaces between the different subdisciplines of linguistics. The notion of 'interface' has become central in grammatical theory (for instance, in Chomsky's recent Minimalist Program) and in linguistic practice: work on the interfaces between syntax and semantics, syntax and morphology, phonology and phonetics etc. has led to a deeper understanding of particular linguistic phenomena and of the architecture of the linguistic component of the mind/brain.

The series covers interfaces between core components of grammar, including syntax/morphology, syntax/semantics, syntax/phonology, syntax/pragmatics, morphology/phonology, phonology/phonetics, phonetics/speech processing, semantics/pragmatics, intonation/discourse structure as well as issues in the way that the systems of grammar involving these interface areas are acquired and deployed in use (including language acquisition, language dysfunction, and language processing). It demonstrates, we hope, that proper understandings of particular linguistic phenomena, languages, language groups, or inter-language variations all require reference to interfaces.

The series is open to work by linguists of all theoretical persuasions and schools of thought. A main requirement is that authors should write so as to understood by colleagues in related subfields of linguistics and by scholars in cognate disciplines.

In this volume, Chris Barker and Pauline Jacobson have brought together a focussed collection on the syntax–semantics interface. The issue under consideration is architectural: what are the implications of the idea that the syntactic and semantic systems work in tandem (Direct Compositionality)? Barker and Jacobson argue in their introduction to the volume that Direct Compositionality places strong constraints on the syntax semantics interface, and the following chapters explore this in detail, bringing into play both the validity of theoretical assumptions and the force of empirical challenges.

David Adger
Hagit Borer

1

Introduction: Direct Compositionality

CHRIS BARKER AND PAULINE JACOBSON

The papers collected in this volume grew out of a workshop "Direct Compositionality: A Workshop" sponsored by NSF Grant BCS-0236462 and held in June 2003 at Brown University. In addition to the eleven papers published here, the workshop featured three additional papers: by Daniel Büring, Alexis Dimitriadis, and Danny Fox. Moreover, all of the contributors here plus the three mentioned above served as discussants for one of the other workshop papers. The quality of the discussant comments, the contribution of this aspect of the conference to the workshop, and the influence of the discussant comments on the final papers was quite extraordinary, and thus we would like to acknowledge the contributions of all of the conference participants. Space unfortunately precluded the inclusion of the specific discussant comments, but each paper has been revised in light of these comments. We would therefore like to thank everyone who attended the workshop, as well as NSF for their support.

1.1 What is Direct Compositionality?

In its simplest formulation, the hypothesis of direct compositionality can be summed up with the following slogan:

The syntax and the semantics work together in tandem.

At the very least, this slogan imposes a certain discipline on the syntax–semantics interface; it requires, for example, that for every syntactic operation there must be a corresponding semantic operation. Of course, this by itself may not seem like a requirement with considerable consequences, since the relevant semantic operation could be as trivial as the identity function on meanings. But indeed this does have a significant consequence: for it ensures that the input to every syntactic operation—or, put differently, every expression which is computed in the syntax—actually does have a *meaning.* And therein lies one of the major differences between direct compositionality and some other views of the organization of the grammar where interpretation is "postponed" until a later stage in the grammatical computation; we will return to this point below. Thus direct compositionality names one of the core principles of Montague's *Universal Grammar,* and the fragment in Montague's (1973) 'The Proper Treatment of Quantification in Ordinary English' (PTQ) stands as one of the first and most influential directly compositional analyses of a significant portion of English grammar. (Indeed, this remains one of the most influential semantic analyses of any sort.)

Of course, direct compositionality is a type of compositionality, where (roughly) a theory of grammar is compositional if the meaning of an expression can be reliably computed from the meanings of its parts. Many discussions of compositionality concern themselves with the extent to which natural language is or is not compositional; the papers in this volume for the most part assume that natural language *is* predominantly or essentially compositional, and consider instead the following question: when natural language is compositional, is that compositionality direct or not?

As with any discussion of compositionality, there will always be some who question whether direct compositionality is "merely" a methodological preference, or whether there are genuine, testable empirical consequences that follow from the claim that natural languages are directly compositional. At the very least, direct compositionality makes concrete empirical predictions about which linguistic objects *have* meanings. To illustrate with a concrete example, consider the standard, non-directly compositional analysis of quantifier scope construal: a verb phrase such as *saw everyone* fails to have a semantic interpretation until it has been embedded within a large enough structure for the quantifier to raise and take scope (e.g., *Someone saw everyone*). On such an analysis, there is no semantic value to assign to the verb phrase *saw everyone* at the point in the derivation in which it is first formed by the syntax (or at any other point in the derivation, for that matter). A directly compositional analysis, by contrast, is forced to provide a semantic value for any expression that is recognized as a constituent in the syntax. Thus if there are good reasons to believe that *saw everyone* is a syntactic constituent, then a directly compositional analysis must provide it with a meaning.

Clearly, then, whatever the naturalness and appeal of direct compositionality, it cannot be taken for granted. By no means do all respectable approaches adhere to direct compositionality. In fact, as noted above, any formalism fails to be directly compositional that postpones interpretation until a level of Logical Form. This includes, of course, any theory that relies on Quantifier Raising, which is by far the dominant paradigm in the field today. The papers in this volume explore the correctness of the hypothesis of direct compositionality, arguing in some cases against it, and in some cases trying to show that apparent challenges to the hypothesis can be met. Moreover, the question of whether or not (and to what extent) direct compositionality can be maintained is relevant to a wide range of formal frameworks. Indeed, the papers in this volume discuss this hypothesis in the context of type-logical grammars (Barker, Dowty), variable-free approaches (Barker, Bittner, Dowty, Jacobson, Shan), and combinatory grammars that rely heavily on type-shifting (Jacobson, Winter). The question of whether or not interpretation is directly readable off the "surface" level or involves instead a certain amount of hidden material and/or reconstruction is addressed from different perspectives in Bhatt and Pancheva, Caponigro and Heller, Romero, and Sharvit. The papers also address a variety of empirical phenomena; often extending the discussion to domains which have not been "standard fare" in previous discussions (see especially Bittner and Potts). Although each of these papers bears directly on the feasibility of direct compositionality, the arguments given by the authors in this volume do not always favor direct compositionality. Our hope, then, is that this volume will help provide a better understanding of the issues and the trade-offs, rather than a resolution to the question.

In the remainder of the introduction we will first map out the position of direct compositionality within the modern theoretical landscape, and then provide more detailed descriptions of the specific contributions of the papers included in the volume.

1.2 The Organization of the Grammar

One way to appreciate the constraints imposed by direct compositionality is by outlining some of the views which have been taken in the literature for the last thirty-five years or so about the way in which the syntax and semantics interact. In so doing we hope to illustrate a bit more what sorts of systems are directly compositional, what sorts are not, and the latitude concerning syntactic operations which is feasible while still maintaining a theory of direct compositionality. Some of this discussion is elaborated on in Jacobson (2002).

Jacobson (2002) defines the notion of "strong direct compositionality" which (as opposed to weaker versions of direct compositionality) is really a claim about what sorts of syntactic operations are allowed. Thus strong direct compositionality (like all varieties of direct compositionality) claims that each syntactic expression has a meaning, but also imposes the following constraint on the syntax: there can be no reference to syntactic (or semantic) structure internal to a constituent—and so from this it follows that the only syntactic combination operation allowed is concatenation. Type-shifting is allowed. An example would be any context-free syntax with rule-to-rule interpretation (such as the fragment in Gazdar *et al.* (1985)); one could perhaps augment this or a similar system using Hendriks' (1993) type-shifting system for handling quantifier scope. Certain kinds of Categorial Grammars (depending on the range of syntactic operations that they allow) are also strongly direct compositional.

One of the main features of strong direct compositionality is that the grammar never needs to refer to the internal structure of any expression, and hence no such structure need be "kept track" of as syntactic expressions are computed. But many practitioners of direct compositional approaches do not maintain such a strong requirement on the syntax. At the other end of the spectrum would be the practice taken in classical Montague grammar in which the syntax allowed for a variety of operations including substitution rules (as in Montague's famous Quantifying-In rule) in which the grammar must be able to locate the first occurrence of an indexed pronoun within a syntactic structure. Montague's grammar is, nonetheless, directly compositional: each expression has a meaning (and each syntactic rule has a corresponding semantic operation). We can call any theory which relaxes the prohibition against reference to internal structure in the syntax a theory with "weak direct compositionality".

In between pure strong direct compositionality and the variety of weak direct compositionality in Montague's PTQ is a theory where there is just one other operation besides concatenation: an infixation operation. In the Categorial Grammar literature this has gone under the rubric of "Wrap"—see, for example Bach (1979, 1980), as discussed in some detail by Dowty in this volume. Thus Dowty considers cases in which a complex-transitive verb is allowed to "wrap" itself as a circumfix around its direct object (see the references in Dowty for the exploration of this in a variety of Categorial Grammar literature). If Wrap is permitted, then the grammar must keep track of *some* amount of internal structure, for it needs to "know" where to place the infixed material. This kind of direct compositional theory, however, makes use of no other structural information than just that. (Adding Wrap to a grammar that otherwise would have only context-free generative capacity increases expressiveness to the level of so-called mildly context-sensitive generative capacity; see, e.g., Vijay-Shanker and Weir (1994).)

There is another kind of direct compositional theory which one can imagine and which is close to (although not exactly like) the classical theory of Generative Semantics (see, e.g., McCawley 1970; Lakoff 1971). In this view we have a set of rules building expressions and in tandem assigning them a meaning—but there are syntactic rules which are allowed to "adjust" the syntactic structure before pronunciation. (This of course means that the grammar will indeed need rules in the syntax referring to the internal structure of expressions because such rules are always stated on structures rather than just on strings: these rules are the classic "transformations" of classical transformational grammar.) While the rules adjusting the structure do not "change meaning", we can nonetheless associate them with a corresponding semantic operation (the identity function). The important part is that each expression still receives a meaning, and the rules computing the initial structure of the transformational derivation are like the rules in a strong direct compositional theory: they "build" syntactic expressions and assign each a meaning. As mentioned above, this is similar to—although not exactly—the theory of Generative Semantics; the reason for the difference is that Generative Semantics did not (at least in general) actually posit an explicit model-theoretic interpretation for its "Logical Forms" (the representations computed by the initial syntactic rules). Had it done so, however, it would have been a direct compositional theory in this sense.

But now let us compare all these with a different kind of view about the organization of the grammar—the view that we can call "Surface-to-LF". This is like the Generative-Semantics view taken above, except it is "backwards": in the first phase, syntactic rules build an uninterpreted complex structure, in a second phase syntactic rules adjust that structure to produce a Logical Form, and only then does the semantics apply (compositionally, bottom-up) to interpret the subexpressions of LFs. This is the view which has been taken in much of the semantics literature associated with "Extended Standard Theory", Government-Binding Theory, and the Principles and Parameters Theory (see, e.g., Chomsky 1976; May 1977), and is the view in the system which is codified in Heim and Kratzer (1998). Unlike all of the views above, this is not directly compositional: here there are expressions referred to in the syntax and which form the input to many syntactic operations which have no meaning; they are interpreted only "later" in the grammatical computation. So take, for example, the case of in-situ quantification, in which a generalized quantifier can be inserted into direct object position of a transitive verb despite having an incompatible semantic type, in which case semantic interpretation must wait until a later operation of Quantifier Raising produces an interpretable LF.

1.3 What Direct Compositionality is Not (Necessarily)

To elaborate further on just what is (and is not) entailed by the hypothesis of direct compositionality, let us at this point mention some notions that are typically associated with direct compositionality but which are nevertheless logically independent of it.

1.3.1 *The Rejection of Movement*

Much work that discusses direct compositionality rejects movement on methodological grounds. This makes a certain amount of sense: if you believe that the constituency you see in the syntax is exactly the constituency you see in the semantics, and *vice versa*, you might be less likely to postulate the kind of hidden syntactic structure that characterizes many movement-based analyses.

Nonetheless, there are movement approaches that are still compatible with at least some form of direct compositionality. For example, as noted above, Generative Semantics-style approaches certainly contained movement rules—but it is still the case that each expression has an interpretation. And, as mentioned above, Montague's PTQ fragment is certainly directly compositional, yet the rules governing quantification require lowering of a quantificational noun phrase into a position formerly occupied by an indexed pronoun. While technically speaking this need not be thought of as "movement" (it is actually a kind of substitution operation), it certainly has much the same effect, and one might well argue that it is simply a different metaphor for the same thing. For a second example, in this volume Dowty discusses motivation for the operation of Wrap. Again technically this is not quite the same as "movement" in the standard approach, but it has much the same effect. Thus there is no conflict in principle between "movement" (and its relatives) and direct compositionality, as long as each syntactic operation has a well-defined semantic effect (or, put differently, each syntactic expression has an interpretation). The kind of movement that *would* be disallowed by the hypothesis of direct compositionality is movement needed in order to "create" interpretable structures. After all, direct compositionality insists that all syntactic expressions are interpretable (and indeed do have a meaning), so postponing interpretation until "after" the application of certain movement rules would be at odds with this.

1.3.2 *Variable-Free*

Much work—especially recently—that discusses direct compositionality also rejects the essential use of variables in favor of so-called variable-free approaches (see, e.g., Szabolcsi 1987; Dowty 1992; Jacobson 1999; among many others). However, the relationship between direct compositionality and variable-free analyses is indirect, and the two are not logically linked. The fragment in, for example, Montague's PTQ relies heavily on variables and assignment functions and yet is directly compositional; meanings are computed at each step relative to an assignment function but are still computed in tandem with the syntactic composition. Of course empirical facts may lead to the conclusion that direct compositional analyses can be *facilitated* in a variable-free account, but the hypothesis of direct compositionality does not a priori commit one to the rejection of variables and assignment functions.

1.3.3 *Type-Shifting*

Much work discussing direct compositionality makes heavy use of type-shifting operators. Type-shifting is a natural tool for building directly compositional analyses, since type-shifting operators are always presented as having a precisely defined semantic effect, often in conjunction with a change of syntactic category. (Of course, type-shifting is also routinely used in analyses that are not directly compositional, and in these analyses there generally is no associated change of syntactic category.) But again, while empirical facts might suggest that direct compositional analyses can be facilitated with the use of type-shifting, the two are logically independent. While it is not easy to find a directly compositional analysis that does not rely on type-shifting in one form or another, Montague's PTQ (yet again) provides a key example. Although it has now become common to think of the principle ultrafilter meaning for a proper name (where $[[\text{John}]] = \lambda P[P(j)]$) as derived from the individual j through a process of type raising (as in, e.g., Partee and Rooth 1983), this was not the strategy taken in PTQ. There, all noun phrases, including proper names, uniformly denote generalized quantifiers without any shifting back and forth. And we might further note that one can always trade in a "type-shift" rule for a "silent expression" in the syntax whose meaning is such that it performs the type-shift function (these have generally gone under the rubric of empty or silent operators), and so type-shifting operations can be recast in this way if desired. The issue of type-shifting is taken up in much more detail in Winter's contribution to this volume, which discusses some complex and empirically interesting relationships between the syntax and the semantics of type-shifting.

1.4 Descriptions of Individual Papers

Each of the papers in this volume carefully explores the predictions of direct compositionality within a different empirical domain. These domains include binding and anaphora (Barker, Bittner, Jacobson, Dowty, Shan); quantification (Barker, Dowty, Bittner, Shan); comparatives, superlatives, and equatives (Bhatt and Pancheva, Sharvit); scope in *wh*-constructions (Sharvit); copular sentences (Caponigro and Heller, Romero); adverbial meaning (Bittner, Dowty); and *de se*, reported, and quoted discourse (Bittner, Potts).

We have grouped the papers in this volume into three broad sections. But we caution the reader to keep in mind that these divisions are, to some extent, arbitrary; we chose them to help give some organizing principles to the discussion. Thus the first is a group of papers dealing with some general issues about what direct compositionality is, exploring some of the formal consequences and choices available, and locating this hypothesis and relevant techniques within broader theoretical contexts. This group includes the papers by Dowty, Barker, Shan, and Winter. The second group of papers focuses on a range of empirical phenomena which have traditionally been quite central in the debates both about direct compositionality and about the organization of the grammar. This includes the papers by Caponigro and Heller, Romero, Jacobson, Bhatt and Pancheva, and Sharvit. (Again we would like to note that the papers in the first group also deal with a rich range of empirical phenomena such as quantifier scopes, adverbial modification, the analysis of plurals, and so forth, but these papers are perhaps more programmatic in their primary focus. And the second group of papers also, of course, deal with programmatic issues, but spend more time illustrating this with respect to some areas that are "traditionally" seen as the testing ground for direct compositionality.) The third group of papers broadens the empirical domain(s) of the debate by looking at constructions (and languages) which largely have not factored into the discussion. This includes the papers by Bittner and by Potts; both of which also consider implications of direct compositionality for theories of discourse understanding, and *vice versa.*

1.4.1 *Part 1: Some Programmatic Issues*

We open the volume with **David Dowty**'s paper "Compositionality as an Empirical Problem", which consists of three parts. First, Dowty argues that since we have no a priori definition of compositionality, we should rather focus on discovering principles which can be empirically motivated concerning the ways natural languages actually do compose meaning, and then construct a theory of compositionality based on those. Dowty proposes that the notions of "compositional transparency" and "syntactic economy" can be used as ways to choose among competing compositional analyses. After a survey of the space of possible compositional theories, Dowty argues that an important but overlooked issue is that "compositionality" is a meaningless constraint in the absence of a theory of what sorts of objects meanings can and cannot be, and of what operations a compositional interpretation rule may and may not perform on meanings.

The second part illustrates this program with the problem of "adjunct accessibility" (which adjuncts can have semantic access to which NP arguments of the verb). Dowty argues that with a constrained theory of "proposition", "property", and (curried) "relation"—one in which these meanings lack internal structure (as in possible worlds semantics)—the resulting constraint on compositional interpretation predicts a wide range of syntactic properties of adjuncts. Appealing to his recent theory of complements as reanalyzed adjuncts, Dowty shows that the frequently observed distinctions between subject-control complement verbs (*promise*) vs. object-control verbs (*persuade*) are explained by the same compositional constraints seen with other adjuncts.

In the third part, Dowty addresses long-distance compositional interpretation (and anaphoric binding in particular), where a more complex account of compositional interpretation would seem to be inevitable. He argues that using compositional transparency and syntactic economy as metrics to evaluate competing theories, it turns out that free-variable-binding (co-indexing) with Quantifier Raising theories of bound anaphora are demonstrably less motivated than combinatory (i.e. variable-free) accounts of anaphoric binding. (The latter group includes Jacobson's (1999) analyses as well as other formulations of combinatory binding, such as one Dowty explores in this paper that employs Moortgat's scoping type constructor.)

Whether a particular formal analysis is directly compositional often depends on the choice of grammatical framework. Montague's Universal Grammar (in particular, the analysis in PTQ), as well as most varieties of Combinatory Categorial Grammar, notably as developed by Steedman, Jacobson, and others, are directly compositional by construction. In contrast, analyses that rely on Q-Raising and a level of Logical Form distinct from surface structure are not directly compositional. **Chris Barker**, in "Direct Compositionality on Demand", considers the status of Type-Logical Grammar (TLG) with respect to direct compositionality. He concludes that Type Logical grammars are not necessarily directly compositional; however, they can be if the grammar as a whole satisfies a property that he calls Direct Compositionality on Demand.

Barker concentrates on two main problem domains that have traditionally provided the most compelling motivation for non-directly compositional approaches, namely, binding and quantifier scope construal. Barker proves that a TLG analysis of binding due to Jaeger is directly compositional in an unusual way: not every derivation is directly compositional. In particular, binding can be non-local, allowing an NP to affect the interpretation of some other NP that is not its immediate sibling. However, for every derivation provided by the grammar, there is guaranteed to be some derivation that is syntactically and semantically equivalent (in a certain precise sense) and that is strictly directly compositional. Barker goes on to show how one standard TLG approach to quantifier scope construal (due to Moortgat) can be extended to provide an analogous guarantee for quantifier scope construal. The result is a grammar that can provide the convenience and perspicuity of coindexation and quantifier-raising techniques, at the same time as it also provides a natural way to decompose long-distance operations into strictly directly compositional local increments.

Chung-chieh Shan's contribution, "Linguistic Side Effects", compares certain semantic phenomena with what are known as *side effects* in the theory of computer programming languages. For instance, he shows how in-situ quantification (*John saw everyone*) can be implemented by means of programming constructs called "shift" and "reset". Other semantic phenomena discussed in some detail in the paper include binding, *wh*-question formation, and their interactions. These phenomena, of course, are some of the central problem domains for testing the theory of direct compositionality. On the programming language side of the comparison, Shan suggests that these phenomena can be analyzed in terms of input, output, and control operators (this is "control" in the sense of "control over the order of execution" of the elements of a program).

This paper in effect proposes an ambitious research program for exploring deep connections between computer science and linguistics. In addition to providing an intuitive motivation of the main ideas, Shan provides sketches of a number of concrete analyses. The overall picture is that each of the semantic phenomena discussed can be analyzed in terms of a single computational concept known as a continuation. Shan shows how this can not only explain each individual phenomenon within a uniform directly compositional framework, but it can also elegantly account for interactions among the phenomena, here exemplified by the interaction of *wh*-fronting with binding, as in the weak crossover violation **Who$_i$ did his$_i$ mother see?*

Many directly compositional analyses make heavy use of type-shifting. In fact, in "Type-Shifting with Semantic Features: A Unified Perspective", **Yoad Winter** points out that many type-shifting analyses are motivated to some degree by considerations of direct compositionality (although type-shifting now enjoys considerable acceptance even within approaches which do not necessarily adhere to direct compositionality). In Partee and Rooth's original work on type-shifting, type-shifting was seen as a device applying only to resolve mismatches between the semantic types of two expressions which were allowed to combine in the syntax but whose types—without adjustment—would not allow for any method of semantic combination. (Note that it has become popular in recent work to phrase this idea within a non-direct compositional architecture in which the syntax first "computes" representations and then "sends them" to the semantics. But the notion of the syntax allowing two expressions to combine while the semantics (running in tandem) does not without some type-shifting is also quite possible in a direct compositional architecture, as is illustrated in Winter's paper.) Winter provides a formal fragment giving a precise characterization of what it would mean for a grammar to use type-shifting only in order to repair a mismatch between an expression's syntactic context and its semantic type. Partee and Rooth offered empirical arguments in support of the "last-resort" view, yet despite its appeal ("leave all categories as simple as possible"), more recent treatments tend to allow type-shifting freely when they allow it at all.

Winter then reviews a number of arguments involving the semantics of plurals that suggest that at least some type-shifting operators cannot be viewed as applying only when the combinatory syntax creates mismatches between two combining expressions. To give the flavor of the arguments, consider that the historically accurate reading of the claim that *Dylan and Simon and Garfunkel wrote many hits in the 1960s* requires collectivizing *Simon and Garfunkel*, since they were a songwriting team. If collectivization is accomplished by a type-shifting operator, its application certainly cannot be motivated by any syntax/semantics mismatch involving the nature of the predicate, since *Simon and Garfunkel* are a proper subpart of the subject, and thus do not constitute an argument of the verbal predicate.

Winter then provides a second fragment with a more finely articulated set of syntactic categories and semantic types. In particular, categories indicate morphological number (singular vs. plural), and types indicate semantic number (atomic individuals vs. sets of individuals). If an expression has a syntactic number feature that does not match its semantic number feature, type-shifting operators can resolve the discrepancy. Thus Winter recasts the opposition between "resolving mismatch" type-shifting vs. freely applied type-shifting as an opposition between *externally motivated* type-shifting, in which the semantic types of functor and argument do not match, vs. *internally motivated* type-shifting, in which the syntactic category and the semantic type of a single expression requires resolution. The paper ends with a uniform account of the two kinds of shifting.

1.4.2 *Part 2: Case Studies*

The second group of papers are focused on additional case studies and on studies of domains which have traditionally figured quite heavily in debates about direct compositionality and related questions concerning the organization of the grammar. Thus **Pauline Jacobson**'s paper "Direct Compositionality and Variable-Free Semantics: The Case of 'Principle B' Effects" addresses one of the most pressing challenges to direct compositionality. "Principle B", in its usual formulation, prohibits "coindexing" a pronoun with a c-commanding NP within the same local domain (where the local domain is usually NP or S). One reason why this is a challenge to direct compositionality is that it suggests that the interpretive possibilities of a pronoun depend on features of some element not yet visible at the point at which the pronoun in question combines to form a larger constituent. For instance, in **Bush*$_i$ *defeated him*$_i$, we must guarantee that the pronoun *him* cannot have the same index as *Bush.* But according to the hypothesis of direct compositionality, we must commit to all details of the interpretation of *him* by the time we form the verb phrase *defeated him.* Even worse, if we adopt the variable-free approach to binding advocated in, for example, Jacobson (1999), pronouns uniformly denote the identity function, so it is far from obvious how we could account for Principle B effects at all; there are no indices to help regulate the interpretation of pronouns.

Jacobson proposes a strategy that is partly syntactic and partly semantic. Her starting point distinguishes pronouns from other types of NPs syntactically. For instance, she gives the category of *him* as NP[p], the category of a pronominal NP. By assumption, lexical verbs subcategorize for only normal NPs. In order to allow a pronoun to occur in, say, direct object position, Jacobson provides a category-shifting operator that explicitly allows a direct object of category NP[p]. Crucially, the type-shifting rule simultaneously adjusts the denotation of the predicate in such a way that it denotes a function that is defined only for pairs of distinct individuals. Then if we attempt to bind a pronominal direct object to the subject position, as in **Bush*$_i$ *defended him*$_i$, although there will be a well-formed syntactic analysis, the corresponding semantic denotation will be undefined. Jacobson shows that this analysis automatically makes good predictions involving paycheck pronouns. In addition, it automatically accounts for well-known problems for the standard account of Principle B effects such as **Every candidate*$_i$ *thinks that he*$_i$ *should say that he*$_i$ *will praise him*$_i$. Jacobson's paper ends with discussion of the existence of Principle B connectivity effects in specificational copular sentences (see the next two papers for further discussion of this general issue). She argues that once one has a local account of the Principle B effect then connectivity effects are automatically accounted for without the use of abstract representations, at least in this case.

The correct account of connectivity effects and of specificational copular sentences in general is taken up in much more detail in the next two papers. Connectivity effects are shown in, for example, *What John is is proud of himself*, where a reflexive is licensed despite (on the surface) not being c-commanded by a local "binder". Many accounts have posited an abstract representation at which the relevant condition is met. Although there are variants of this, most are incompatible with at least a strong version of direct compositionality. In their paper "The Non-Concealed Nature of Free Relatives", **Ivano Caponigro** and **Daphna Heller** focus primarily on two major implementations of the question–answer approach to specificational sentences and the implications of these approaches to the direct compositionality debate. The first is an approach due originally to Ross, and more recently championed by den Dikken *et al.*, in which the pre-copular constituent of a specificational sentence is analyzed as a question and the post-copular constituent as its answer. Thus in *What John is is proud of himself*, the idea is that *what John is* is a question—it can, after all, occur in an embedded question position, as in *I know what John is.* If the pre-copular material were indeed a question, then the post-copular material could be its answer, and if we assume that answers are full sentences (denoting propositions) then we would conclude that the full answer is a full sentence, with portions deleted (or simply not pronounced). This would explain the licensing of the reflexive, and similarly for other connectivity effects. Because this analysis posits silent (or deleted) material, it would pose a challenge for most versions of direct compositionality. More seriously, since the identity condition on such a deletion could not be determined locally, it would be difficult to reconcile with direct compositionality in general.

Caponigro and Heller argue that the pre-copular constituent indeed cannot be an ordinary embedded question but is, rather, a free relative (as argued originally in Higgins, 1973). To show this, they consider a variety of languages (Macedonian, Hungarian, Wolof, and Hebrew) in which free relatives and questions are morphosyntactically distinct. In all cases the unambiguously free relative can occur in specificational sentences and—most importantly—show connectivity effects. From this Caponigro and Heller conclude that the simple question + (partial deletion of) answer theory cannot be the right account of connectivity. But this still leaves open the possibility of another analysis: that the pre-copular constituent is a free relative but behaves like a *concealed question.* This theory has been championed recently by Schlenker and, in this volume, by Romero. Note that this poses essentially the same challenge to direct compositionality as does the "ordinary question + deletion of a full answer" analysis; the post-copular constituent would still require additional abstract (or silent) structure whose identity conditions could not be determined locally.

Caponigro and Heller go on to argue further against the concealed question analysis, arguing that these behave neither syntactically nor semantically like concealed questions. They further show that some languages (Macedonian) allow specificational sentences (with connectivity) but in fact have no concealed questions. They thus conclude that the question–answer approach to specificational sentences faces serious problems when applied cross-linguistically, and that an (as yet incomplete) directly compositional analysis remains a contender.

Maribel Romero's paper, "Connectivity in a Unified Analysis of Specificational Subjects and Concealed Questions", comes to exactly the opposite conclusion, and argues that the concealed question + (partial deletion of the) answer theory has the fullest range of coverage of the competing accounts. Building on her previous work, she argues first that the subjects of specificational copular sentences (such as the underlined material in *The price of milk is $1.29*) are indeed concealed questions, just like the underlined material in *John knows the price of milk*) and hence the two should receive a unified treatment. There are a number of ways in which these two behave alike. For example, she notes a hidden ambiguity in *John knows the price that Bill knows:* either John knows a price (so-called reading A), or John knows which price Bill knows (reading B). The same ambiguity shows up in the pre-copular constituent of specificational sentences. Romero's paper brings to the table a variety of additional arguments to the effect that the pre-copular constituent is a question rather than having an "ordinary" DP meaning; these center on exhaustivity implications, pronominalization constraints, and coordination phenomena.

Given this, Romero considers two alternatives to the concealed question + deletion account of connectivity effects. One is a movement account; she shows a number of problems with this account. The second is the "as is" account. In particular, she considers the possibility that the pre-copular constituent is indeed a concealed question, but the answer part contains no deletion (after all, the connectivity debate centers primarily on the analysis of the post-copular constituent). While the past literature does contain accounts of various kinds of connectivity effects ("bound variable" connectivity and opacity connectivity), none systematically consider these in the context of the A vs. B readings discussed above. Romero argues that once the full range of effects is considered, the concealed question + deletion analysis has the fullest coverage and is thus to be preferred over the more obviously direct compositional "as is" approach.

Rajesh Bhatt and **Roumyana Pancheva** offer perhaps the most direct arguments against direct compositionality in their paper "Degree Quantifiers, Position of Merger Effects with their Restrictors, and Conservativity". Building on past work of their own, the first part of their paper is concerned with explaining three puzzles. The first is why the complements of degree heads always show up in extraposed position (**John is more than Flora is suspicious* vs. *John is more suspicious than Flora is*). The second is an observation due originally to Williams that the surface position of the complement of the degree head marks the scope of the entire degree expression (even when the head is embedded further). Thus *John is required to publish fewer papers this year than six to get tenure* is only a report of an unusual tenure policy that punishes over-publishing, while *John is required to publish fewer papers this year to get tenure than six* is a report only about the minimum requirement on publication. The third puzzle is that usually only adjuncts extrapose. Their explanation rests on the interaction of several devices: raising the degree head at LF to mark its scope; "late merger" which allows its complement to be introduced only after it has been raised; and the copy theory of movement which would require a copy of this complement in the lower position were it merged earlier. These, taken together with the fact that the quantifier here is non-conservative, would lead to a contradiction if the complement of the degree head appeared in non-extraposed position, or appeared in a higher extraposed position. (See also Fox 2001 for related observations concerning ordinary relative clauses.)

One might think that the fact that the complement has scope where it appears on the surface would favor a direct compositional analysis, but Bhatt and Pancheva's analysis mitigates against this conclusion. For crucial to the account is the fact that the degree head has to raise at LF and is thus interpreted in a position other than where it "enters into" the syntax. The full explanation also rests on other assumptions incompatible with at least a strong direct compositional architecture, such as the copy theory of movement, which posits that in other cases things which "move" in the syntax actually have interpretive effects in both their original and their moved positions. But the story does not end here, for Bhatt and Pancheva show that the same facts hold for equatives and the above explanation (based in part on the non-conservativity of degree phrases such as *more than*...) will not explain the pattern with *as (tall as)*. To this end, then, they speculate on two different (not mutually exclusive) additional principles to extend the analysis to equatives. Both are incompatible with the hypothesis of direct compositionality; these principles restrict the application of certain syntactic operations (in this case, early merger) on the basis of the ensuing semantics of other applications of early merger. Thus, for example, they hypothesize that the system is "intelligent", and might block early merger for degree complements in general since in some cases it will result in a contradiction. The intricate argumentation in this paper—combined with some interesting observations and speculations about the meaning of *as*—provides a thought-provoking challenge to direct compositionality, as well as providing an account of a number of apparently disparate puzzles by use of techniques incompatible with direct compositionality.

Yael Sharvit's contribution, "Two Reconstruction Puzzles", critiques other work of Bhatt, advocating a "reconstruction" analysis of superlative constructions such as *The longest book John said Tolstoy had written was Anna Karenina.* At issue is the interpretation on which the book in question was merely said by John to have been written by Tolstoy (and may have in fact been written by someone else). If we reconstruct *longest book* into the trace position within the relative clause (perhaps by means of a copying mechanism), we get the desired interpretation. But of course reconstruction is inimical to direct compositionality, since it requires interpreting material in some displaced position other than its surface syntactic position.

Sharvit observes that a closely parallel interpretation is available for *wh*-interrogatives, such as *John knows which books Tolstoy wrote.* After careful consideration of strong vs. weak interpretations of *wh*-interrogatives, quantificational variability effects, and the interaction with presupposition (the so-called Donald Duck problem), Sharvit concludes that the relevant interpretation for *wh*-interrogatives stems from an independently motivated quasi-quotational analysis on which *books* is interpreted relative to John's belief worlds. In fact, argues Sharvit, recourse to a reconstruction analysis is not only not necessary, but reconstruction gives incorrect predictions.

Given the parallel between the superlative examples and the *wh*-interrogative examples, this result calls into question the claim that the relevant interpretation of the superlative examples involves reconstruction. Nevertheless, Sharvit argues that a reconstruction analysis makes good predictions in the superlative case, and furthermore that even the best non-reconstruction analysis available has severe disadvantages.

The resulting picture is a challenge for everyone: reconstructionists must try to explain why reconstruction seems to be blocked in *wh*-interrogatives, and advocates of direct compositionality must confront the arguments that superlatives (at least) require reconstruction.

1.4.3 *Part 3: New Horizons*

The two papers in the third part of this volume have in common that they push towards the discussion completely new horizons and into domains that have not been discussed before in these terms. Both are concerned in part with modeling reported discourse—an area whose consequences for the organization of the grammar has heretofore received little attention. Both papers attempt to tackle areas which are seemingly especially baffling under a direct compositional view, and argue that with some new tools as part of the semantic apparatus, these areas can be accounted for.

Maria Bittner, in "Online Update: Temporal, Modal, and *de se* Anaphora in Polysynthetic Discourse", evaluates direct compositionality in the context of *de se* reports and adverbial quantification in Kalaallisut (Eskimo-Aleut), the national language of Greenland. In the standard approach, *de se* and adverbial quantification would each involve movement at LF in order to explicitly indicate the relative scope of the aspectual and modal operators. Furthermore, the polysynthetic nature of the language under study increases the difficulty of arriving at a directly compositional treatment, since the operative morphemes are embedded within words in a way that does not transparently reflect their relative scope (quite the contrary).

Yet Bittner argues that a directly compositional analysis is not only possible, but superior to an LF or index-based account. Building on Muskens' compositional treatment of tense and aspect as a species of anaphora, and on the centering theory of Grosz *et al.*, Bittner implements the idea of prominence-based anaphora using a pair of stacks: one for topical discourse referents, and one for background referents. Since discourse referents are added to each stack in a strictly local manner, modal and aspectual operators can have anaphoric access to times and events without relying either on LF manipulations or on long-distance coindexation.

In order to allow for *de se* report, the texts for interpretation present a son's discussion of the chess playing of his father, with glosses such as "The next day, he often says 'I won'." Indeed, on Bittner's analysis, the formal representation of a developing discourse unfolds rather like a chess game itself, in that the contribution of each aspectual element richly depends on the effects of the previous discourse moves.

Christopher Potts' paper, "The Dimensions of Quotation", is also concerned with discourse, and builds a directly compositional fragment that handles the semantics of several types of direct quotation (e.g. *Lisa said "Maggie shot Burns"*). He argues that utterances (consisting of a phonological, a syntactic, and a semantic representation) form a syntactic category that can enter into larger syntactic derivations. In order to allow semantic composition, Potts enrolls expression markers in the domain of discourse, so that, for instance, Lisa can stand in the utterance relation to the utterance marker for *Maggie shot Burns.* In addition, he argues that the semantics must sometimes deal with the normal semantic content of the quoted expression, and his fragment provides flexible access to such meanings. The result is a multidimensional theory of meaning on which expressions describe the world, and simultaneously describe aspects of the speech situation, including who said what. Not only does the developing discourse keep track of what was said, but who said what, and how they said it.

Potts develops a number of applications of this fragment. His comments on ellipsis are especially important for the hypothesis of direct compositionality, since Potts' framework provides a way to require that an instance of ellipsis must have an overt antecedent in previous linguistic discourse, a popular approach to ellipsis that has heretofore been beyond the reach of traditional directly compositional approaches. In a second application that goes beyond any formal treatment (directly compositional or otherwise), Potts proposes what may be the first compositional treatment of metalinguistic negation.

References

Bach, E. 1979. 'Control in Montague grammar', *Linguistic Inquiry*, 10: 515–31.

—— 1980. 'In defense of passive', *Linguistics and Philosophy*, 3: 297–341.

Chomsky, N. 1976. 'Conditions on rules of grammar', *Linguistic Analysis*, 2: 303–51.

Dowty, D. 1992. 'Variable-free syntax, variable-binding syntax, the natural deduction Lambek calculus, and the crossover constraint', in *Proceedings of the 11th Meeting of the West Coast Conference on Formal Linguistics.* Stanford, CA: CSLI Lecture Notes.

Fox, D. 2001. 'The syntax and semantics of traces', handout of November 2001 talk at the University of Connecticut.

Gazdar, G., Klein, E., Pullum, G. K., and Sag, I. 1985. *Generalized Phrase Structure Grammar.* Oxford: Blackwell.

Heim, I. and Kratzer, A. 1998. *Semantics in Generative Grammar.* Malden, MA: Blackwell.

Hendriks, H. 1993. *Studied Flexibility.* Amsterdam: ILLC Dissertation Series.

Jacobson, P. 1999. 'Towards a variable-free semantics', *Linguistics and Philosophy*, 22: 117–84.

—— 2002. 'The (dis)organization of the grammar: 25 years', *Linguistics and Philosophy*, 25: 601–26.

Lakoff, G. 1971. 'On generative semantics', in D. Steinberg and L. Jakobovits (eds), *Semantics.* Cambridge: Cambridge University Press. 232–96.

McCawley, J. 1970. 'Where do noun phrases come from?', in R. Jacobs and P. Rosenbaum (eds), *Readings in English Transformational Grammar.* Waltham, MA: Ginn. 166–83.

May, R. 1977. 'The Grammar of Quantification'. Ph.D. dissertation, MIT.

Montague, R. 1970. 'Universal grammar', *Theoria*, 36: 373–98. Reprinted in Thomason (ed.), 1974, 119–47.

—— 1973. 'The proper treatment of quantification in ordinary English', in K. J. J. Hintikka, J. M. E. Moravcsik, and P. Suppes (eds), *Approaches to Natural Language.* Dordrecht: Reidel. 221–42. Reprinted in Thomason (ed.), 1974, 222–46.

Partee, B. H. and Rooth, M. 1983. 'Generalized conjunction and type ambiguity', in R. Bäuerle, C. Schwarze, and A. von Stechow (eds), *Meaning, Use, and Interpretation of Language*. Berlin: de Gruyter. 361–83.

Steedman, M. 2000. *The Syntactic Process*. Cambridge, MA: MIT Press.

Szabolcsi, A. 1987. 'Bound variables in syntax (are there any?)', in J. Groenendijk, M. Stokhof, and F. Veltman (eds), *Sixth Amsterdam Colloquium*. Amsterdam: Institute for Language, Logic and Information, University of Amsterdam. 331–53.

Thomason, R. (ed.) 1974. *Formal Philosophy: Selected Papers of Richard Montague.* New Haven, CT: Yale University Press.

Vijay-Shanker, K. and Weir, D. J. 1994. 'The equivalence of four extensions of context-free grammars', *Mathematical Systems Theory*, 27: 511–46.

Part I

Some Programmatic Issues

2

Compositionality as an Empirical Problem

DAVID DOWTY

2.1 Why Be Interested in Compositionality?

Gottlob Frege (1892) is credited with the so-called "principle of compositionality", also called "Frege's Principle", which one often hears expressed this way:

Frege's Principle (so-called) "The meaning of a sentence is a function of the meanings of the words in it and the way they are combined syntactically."

(Exactly how Frege himself understood "Frege's Principle" is not our concern here;[1] rather, it is the understanding that this slogan has acquired in contemporary linguistics that we want to pursue, and this has little further to do with Frege.) But why should linguists care what compositionality is or whether natural languages "are compositional" or not?

2.1.1 *An "Empirical Issue"?*

Often we hear that "compositionality is an empirical issue" (meaning the question whether natural language is compositional or not)—usually asserted as a preface to expressing skepticism about a "yes" answer. In the most general sense of Frege's Principle, however, the fact that natural languages *are* compositional is beyond any serious doubt. Consider that:

- Linguists agree that the set of English sentences is at least recursive in size, that English speakers produce sentences virtually every day that they have never spoken before, and that they successfully parse sentences they have never heard before.

[1] Janssen (1997) maintains that the label "Frege's Principle", as understood in recent linguistics research, is inappropriately ascribed to Frege himself.

- If we accept the idealization that they do understand the meanings of the sentences they hear, obtaining the same meanings from them that others do, then:
- Since the meanings of all sentences obviously cannot be memorized individually, there must be some finitely characterizable procedure for determining these meanings, one shared by all English speakers.
- As the sentences themselves can only be enumerated via derivations in the grammar of the language, then inevitably, the procedure for interpreting them must be determined, in some way or other, by their syntactic structures as generated by this grammar (plus of course the meanings of the individual words in them).

What does not follow from this, of course, is just *how* meaning depends on syntactic structure: as far as this argument goes, the dependency could be simple or complex: it could be computable in a very direct way from a fairly "superficial" (or mono-stratal) syntactic derivation, or computable only in a very indirect way that depends, perhaps in as yet unsuspected ways, on many aspects of a total syntactic derivation, including possibly multiple syntactic levels of derivation simultaneously.

Here, for example, is a semantic rule that is "compositional" by this broad definition: "If the maximum depth of embedding in the sentence is less than seven, interpret the whole sentence as negative; if it is seven or more, interpret it as affirmative". Or again, "If the number of words in the sentence is odd, interpret the scope of quantificational NPs from left to right; if it is even, interpret scope from right to left". Such rules as these *are* ways of "determining (a part of) the meaning of a sentence from its words and how they are combined syntactically",[2] but no linguist would entertain rules like them for a moment. The UNCONSTRAINED COMPOSITIONALITY that a broadly stated "Frege's Principle" encompasses is most likely not what linguists really have in mind when they question whether language is or is not "compositional". Clearly, something more specific is intended by the term *compositional*—something not so broad as to be trivially true, not so narrow as to be very obviously false. But do we really need to worry about formulating the proper, non-trivial definition of "compositional"? Hasn't somebody done that already?

[2] I am assuming that "how they are combined syntactically" means the same as "their syntactic mode of combination", or even "the syntactic rules by which they are derived" if by the latter we mean applying those rules to their inputs in a particular way, i.e. we don't count *John loves Mary* and *Mary loves John* as having the same mode of combination.

2.1.2 *An Irrelevant Issue?*

Alas, various writers have claimed to show, in one way or another, that compositionality can only be a vacuous claim, or trivially false one, or one that is otherwise uninteresting—given the particular understanding of it they offer, that is. Janssen (1986) purports to have demonstrated that any kind of meaning at all can be assigned by a compositionally interpreted grammar—if there is no limit on how abstract a syntactic analysis can be. Zadrozny (1994) claims that—under certain assumptions as to what denotations can be—a compositional semantic analysis can always be constructed for any given syntactic analysis. On the other hand, Pelletier (1994) argues that the very fact that (non-lexical) semantic ambiguity can exist where there is no obvious evidence of syntactic ambiguity (the quantifier scope ambiguity in *Every linguist knows two languages* for example) shows that natural language is clearly "not compositional" (so, presumably, the subject should be considered closed). For discussion, see Janssen (1997), Westerstähl (1998), Dever (1999), and Barker (2002).

Janssen's (1997) long treatise on compositionality (which is, by the way, to be recommended highly) begins in a way that seems to presuppose that there does exist a (specific, unique) principle of compositionality which has been the subject of much discussion ("The principle of compositionality is a well-known issue in philosophy of language", "The principle is often adhered to in programming languages", etc. (Janssen 1997: 429). Yet he soon notes that this principle "contains several vague words which have to be made precise in order to give formal content to the principle" (p. 426), so he proceeds to construct "a mathematical model of compositionality" (pp. 447–53), and only in terms of that model does he try to address the results of Zadrozny (1994) and Janssen (1986) and the question whether compositionality is a non-trivial matter in light of those. If saying something concrete that has "formal content" depends on his mathematical model (or a similar one like Montague's (1970)), what exactly have philosophers, linguists, and others who do not know those models been arguing about? Is the concept of compositionality a Platonic ideal, which we have been discussing for a long time, even though we did not understand what it was (and did not realize that)?

I believe that there is not and will not be—any time soon, if ever—a unique precise and "correct" definition of compositionality that all linguists and/or philosophers can agree upon, such that we can meaningfully expect to determine empirically whether natural language does or does not have that property. A major source of difficulty, an insurmountable one at least for the present, is that exactly what "compositionality" (as a property of natural language) means inevitably depends on exactly how "syntactic mode of combination", "meaning", and "a function on meanings" should be given precise definitions. For example, as a foundation to build his formal model of compositionality on, Janssen has to lay down nine pre-theoretic assumptions about the nature of grammar and meaning, but certainly not everyone who has claimed that natural language is compositional, or argued that it is not, would be willing to accept all of these—for example, one of his assumptions rules out "some variants of Transformational Grammar, with a series of intermediate levels between the syntax and the semantics". Another is that "all expressions that arise as parts have meaning." (Does this mean we must either agree that *to* in *I want to go* has a meaning in itself or else that *to* is not really a "part" of the sentence?) And he responds to Pelletier's position on syntactic ambiguity by distinguishing between *syntactic structure* and *syntactic derivation*; he requires that "ambiguous expressions must have different derivations", although the derivations may result in the same structures. To some linguists this may seem an acceptable response,[3] but it may strike others as merely begging the question. (I cite Janssen here, out of a number of possible illustrations of my points, not because his treatment is any more susceptible to objection than that of anyone else who has tried to be exact, but because he is particularly clear about what he is assuming.) Among linguists, "syntactic mode of combination", etc. are the subject of ongoing investigation and debate, which no one expects to be completely resolved in the near future. But an equally great source of difficulty in "testing" some particular definition of compositionality is the question of exactly what meanings are.

So what is to be done? Clearly, the meanings of natural language sentences *can* be figured out on the basis of their syntax somehow or other: we don't yet know exactly how this works, but as empirical linguists we would like to be able to find the most interesting generalizations we can discover about the process, whatever these turn out to be. If these do not exactly qualify as "strictly compositional" on this definition or on that definition, that is too bad, but we would like to understand as well as we can what principles natural language does follow for constructing the meaning of a full sentence. In other words, I propose:

Compositionality really should be considered "an empirical question". But it is not a yes–no question, rather it is a "how"-question.

[3] In fact, I advocate a distinction like this in §2.5.3 below: the difference is that I am putting it forward as an empirical hypothesis with a particular kind of motivation, not an assumption we must accept before we can define *compositionality*.

The objection to approaching this task by first debating which exact definition of compositionality is correct, then arguing over alleged counterexamples to it, is that this has focused too much attention on validating or falsifying a claim about one particular definition, generating rounds of criticisms and rebuttals, while many other important questions about compositionality in natural language semantics tend to be ignored. (Suppose one day we actually could agree on a proper definition of "compositionality" and then eventually determined that natural language was in fact not "compositional" in that sense. Would we at that point forget about compositionality in natural language altogether and turn our attention to something else?) The larger goal that we as empirically oriented linguists should aim for is distinguishing the class of possible semantic interpretation procedures found in natural languages from those that are not found—just as we try to address the corresponding questions in syntax, phonology, etc.[4]

2.2 Redefining the Compositionality Problem

To put the focus and scope of research in the right place, the first thing to do is to employ our terminology differently. I propose that we let the term NATURAL LANGUAGE COMPOSITIONALITY refer to *whatever strategies and principles we discover that natural languages actually do employ to derive the meanings of sentences, on the basis of whatever aspects of syntax and whatever additional information (if any) research shows that they do in fact depend on.* Since we do not know what all those are, we do not at this point know what "natural language compositionality" is really like; it is our goal to figure that out by linguistic investigation. Under this revised terminology, there can be no such things as "counterexamples to compositionality", but there will surely be counterexamples to many particular hypotheses we contemplate as to the form that it takes.

Given that formulation of the goal, the next question is: what criteria should we use to evaluate the hypothesis that this or that proposed compositional rule is correct (or this or that principle about compositional rules in general). I suggest we can do that in the same way as for any linguistic analyses of any other kind: which one is simpler, more comprehensive, which one fits generalizations about compositionality we have good evidence for up to now.

[4] This is not to say that the research strategy of studying the consequences of various formal definitions of "compositional" has no value for linguistics: it most certainly does. The concern is rather that it—much like the issue of whether all natural language syntax is weakly context-free—should not be blown out of proportion to its real significance and should not divert efforts away from other equally important questions in mathematical linguistics.

And we should try to find empirical data that argue for our conclusions whenever possible.

This conception of the task should be distinguished from the similar-sounding position that Janssen (1997) finally endorses at the end of his article: that "compositionality is ... a methodology on how to proceed", that it has "heuristic value", and it has "improved" analyses. But we need to do more: we need to ask *why* it should be a good methodology to be "more" compositional, if it is, and ask what "more compositional" means in natural language. And, given the lack of agreement on what natural language syntax is like, plus also the areas of syntax that syntacticians of all schools would agree we understood incompletely, how can we ask meaningful questions about compositionality in the face of this indeterminacy and of the unclear interdependence between syntax and semantics?

2.2.1 *Why Expect Compositionality to be Transparent?*

The multitude of cases where natural language semantics is transparently compositional on the basis of its constituent structure alone are so familiar and ubiquitous that we are likely to discount them. Even the simple fact that in *The small dog chased the large cat, small* semantically restricts *dog* (but not *cat*) while *large* affects *cat* (but not *dog*) would not necessarily be expected if compositional semantics did not proceed constituent by constituent. (Otherwise, we might expect that proximity, for example, would be as significant as constituent structure, but in fact it misleads as often as not: in *The brother of Mary arrived*, it is the brother that arrives, not Mary.) Only a Roger Schank could possibly question the relevance of the manifest constituent structure for a great majority of the steps in computing a sentence's interpretation. It is only when matters are analyzed that are by comparison fairly esoteric (such as details of anaphoric binding and quantifier scope) that puzzles about the exact syntactic sources of compositional interpretation arise. The issue we face is not whether natural language semantics is compositional on the whole in a straightforward way (overwhelmingly, it is), but where exactly transparent compositionality *stops* (if it does) and how compositionality works from there on. This prevalence of straightforwardly compositional linguistic data is a reason to take as our default assumption, when we investigate a new construction, that its interpretation will be compositional in a more obvious than obscure way.

Although speculation that some properties of natural language take the form they do because of the greater utility of those forms (so-called *functional explanations*) is notoriously difficult to test and has historically often led linguistic science off course, one fundamental fact about the existence of language is undeniable: the ability to acquire and use a language communally is an adaptive trait for humans because it enables humans to convey the benefit of their experiences to other humans who have not had those experiences personally, to engage in complex cooperative behavior, etc.: in short, language is adaptive because it conveys meaning.

Recursively formed syntactic structure is obviously necessary to make it possible to create an unlimited variety of linguistic messages. At a minimum, for each way of forming a syntactic unit there must be a way to determine the meaning of the unit from the meanings of its parts. But, why should a biologically adaptive language-using capacity result in meanings that are created by syntactic structure in a significantly more obscure way than they actually need to be? Conversely, if the whole point of syntax is to construct messages recursively, then why should we not expect syntax itself to be no more complicated than is needed to convey expeditiously the range of messages that languages do convey?

To be sure, certain things immediately come to mind which cloud that a priori argument. For example, there seems to be a cross-linguistic tendency to avoid embedding a full clause in the middle of a matrix clause, most likely because center-embedded clauses are harder to parse for some reason, so extrapositions of a clause to the periphery of a sentence are common, as in *A woman just arrived who nobody knows*. But does the discontinuous syntax not make the compositional rule for linking up the meaning of the distant modifier with that of its head more complicated than we would have thought it needed to be?

A second complication is one quite familiar to historical linguists: a sequence of historical developments in a language can result in more irregular patterns than one would expect to find otherwise, patterns that make sense only when this history is understood: this phenomenon clearly happens in morphology and syntax, so it probably also occurs in compositional semantics as well.[5]

Still, there is reason to hope that these factors can be identified, and many instances have been already, so that their effects on syntax and compositional interpretation in particular cases can be isolated. With what remains, I propose that it should be our DEFAULT assumption that *the form that compositional interpretation takes is no more complicated than what the syntax most simply projects, and the form syntax takes is no more complicated than it needs to be to project meaning transparently*.

[5] A further possible reason for the existence of compositional semantic rules that seem unnecessarily complicated is discussed in §2.6.9.

2.2.2 *Compositional Transparency and Syntactic Economy*

Given this formulation of the goal of investigation, how should we evaluate various hypotheses about natural language compositionality? Two properties immediately become relevant:

Compositional transparency: the degree to which the compositional semantic interpretation of natural language is readily apparent (obvious, simple, easy to compute) from its syntactic structure.

Syntactic economy: the degree to which the syntactic structures of natural language are no more complicated than they need to be to produce compositionally the semantic interpretation that they have.

The two properties are distinct, because a syntactic construction could be highly transparent, yet be more complicated than it really needs to be to convey the meaning it has. Conversely, a syntactic construction could be economical, but so much so as to be hard to parse or ambiguous. To imagine what it could mean for syntax to be "too" economical, consider Polish parenthesis-free notation for statement logic (e.g. (1*a*)) as compared with the more familiar "infix" notation (e.g. the equivalent (1*b*)):

(1) (*a*) *CAKpqNrs* (*b*) $((p \wedge q) \vee \neg r) \rightarrow s$

The former syntax is more economical than the latter in that most complex formulas have fewer symbols in them, yet for purposes of human parsing, most people find that this extra economy makes parenthesis-free formulas harder to grasp than with infix notation (though not necessarily harder for computers of course).

The a priori arguments in this section imply that, all other factors being equal, we should expect that the combination of syntax and compositional semantics that natural languages employ will tend to maximize compositional transparency and syntactic economy.

A third property, which will be examined at length in §2.4.2 below, is the semantic counterpart of syntactic economy:

Structural semantic economy: the degree to which the meanings and operations on meanings used during compositional interpretation to build up complex meanings out of simpler meanings are no more complicated than they need to be to derive, in stepwise fashion, all the complete sentence meanings that natural languages in fact express.

Note that these measures need not imply that we literally judge individual analyses on "functional" grounds: rather, we can appraise the "closeness of fit" between syntax and semantics in a strictly formal way, using the same criteria theoretical linguists always apply: which of two analyses of some part of the syntax–semantic interface is simpler, applies to more data, is consistent with general properties of that interface that we already have much evidence for, etc.?

Obviously, these properties can be assessed only in a preliminary and impressionistic way at present, although as more and more general principles of compositional interpretation become well-understood, more concrete substance can be given to them. At present, though, it will often be possible to compare two specific analyses and decide, with some confidence, which is the less complicated in these three ways. And that is what we need for now.

The form of arguments based on these properties, which will be used extensively in this paper, is this: "If syntactic analysis A together with semantic analysis A′ were in fact the correct analyses, then this natural language would have turned out to be more compositionally transparent (syntactically economical, etc.) than it would be if syntactic analysis B, together with semantic analysis B′, were the correct one. This is one argument favoring the combination of A and A′ over B and B′."

Just as obviously, trade-offs among these properties will arise in comparing analyses of particular cases: of two analyses under consideration, one might allow us to achieve greater syntactic economy and/or transparency at the expense of greater semantic structural complexity—or *vice versa*. For example, I will argue in §2.5.2.1 that introducing a specific non-context-free operation (Wrap) into English syntax is justified by enabling a family of related far-reaching generalizations about English compositional semantics to be maintained, resulting in greater transparency. As an example of the opposite kind of conclusion, Kubota (2005) argues that a variety of compositional semantic phenomena involving a class of deverbal noun constructions in Japanese can all be made consistent with reasonable generalizations about syntax in Head-driven Phrase Structure Grammar (HPSG) only if a modification is made in our assumptions about compositional interpretation.

What is methodologically novel here (to some anyway) is the idea that in evaluating an analysis of a particular linguistic problem we should take into account (i) the generality (vs. complexity and idiosyncrasy) of the compositional syntax–semantics interface that the analysis in question would commit us to, *quite independently of* (ii) evaluating the syntactic part of the analysis on purely syntactic grounds, and (iii) evaluating the accompanying semantic analysis on purely semantic grounds. What has been more typical of past research practice is proposing and defending syntactic analyses on syntactic grounds, then asking afterwards what we can infer about compositional semantics under those analyses—or similarly, proposing/defending semantic hypotheses on solely semantic grounds, then asking later, if at all, what kind of compositional connection with syntax is consistent with them. All three aspects of syntactic/semantic analysis should have potentially equal weight. For the strategy I am proposing to lead to genuinely novel results, it would have to be pursued without biases about syntax or about semantics held over from theories developed on the basis of only one side of the picture.

2.3 Some Empirical Questions about Natural Language Compositionality

In the rest of this section (§2.3), I will try to survey the possible dimensions of the study of natural language compositionality as an empirical problem: these are of four kinds: (i) *questions about general features of the correspondence between syntax and semantics* (for example, is the Fregean homomorphism model of Frege's Principle the right place to start?); (ii) *questions about which aspects of syntax are relevant to compositional semantics* (for example, do the syntactic categories of constituents determine some aspects of how they are interpreted?); (iii) *questions about meanings themselves,* (what are they, exactly?), about *possible operations on meanings* (for example, the context-free semantics issue in §2.4.2), and about *external information accessed in compositional interpretation*; (iv) finally, there are *methodological questions about the inquiry* (for example, how do we evaluate compositional transparency properly?).

A recurring theme in this survey is that some kinds of compositional rules which at first seem to be excluded by a certain contemplated constraint on compositionality can, upon closer inspection, be reformulated as rules that satisfy the constraint. But this does not imply that the search for a better articulated theory of natural language compositionality is futile. Rather, it challenges us to look closer and decide whether (i) the two formulations should be treated as equivalent for our present purposes, or (ii) there are other motivated principles that imply that only one of the formulations should be allowed.

In the second part of this paper (§2.6), I will look at a case study where assuming a conservative version of compositionality, together with syntactic and compositional principles inherent in Categorial Grammar (henceforth CG), predicts a kind of syntactic distinction that is independently supported in a variety of cases, but can also be applied to other cases where direct syntactic evidence is not available: in other words, a case where attention to aspects of compositionality predicts useful facts about syntax. In the last portion of the paper (§2.7), I turn to one of the most debated domains of compositional interpretation, long-distance anaphoric binding, and compare two kinds of compositional theories (variable-binding vs. combinatory) from the point of view of the methodology proposed in this paper.

Issues surrounding natural language compositionality have of course already been treated a large number of times, for example in Partee (1984), Janssen (1997), Jacobson (2002), and others already mentioned; see the numerous references cited in Szabó (2000) for others. My focus in this article is on issues that are largely complementary to their concerns, so I refer you to those articles to obtain a wider perspective on the subject of compositionality.

2.3.1 *The Core of Frege's Principle: Semantics as Homomorphism*

What seems to be the core notion that all writers on the subject have taken Frege's Principles to suggest was described in probably the most general possible way by Montague in the comprehensive linguistic meta-theory found in his paper "Universal Grammar" (Montague 1970), henceforth UG.[6] We are to begin by viewing syntax as consisting of some collection of basic expressions (words or the like) and some group of syntactic operations which can map one, two, or more expressions (either basic ones or ones already derived) into new derived expressions; these operations reapply recursively. Within the branch of mathematics called *universal algebra*, a syntactic system is seen as an algebra $\langle A, F_\gamma \rangle_{\gamma \in \Gamma}$, where A is the set of all expressions, basic and derived, and each F_γ is a syntactic operation (Γ is simply a set of indices to identify the syntactic operations); A is closed under the operations F_γ $_{\gamma \in \Gamma}$. Note that this, by design, says nothing further about the nature or form of syntactic expressions (they might be strings, trees, smoke signals, prime numbers, aardvarks, etc.) or what the operations actually do to them when they "combine" them (e.g. concatenate them, add words or morphemes to them, merge them, delete the first and reverse the word order of the second, etc.). Second, there is to be a structurally similar algebra of meanings $\langle B, G_\gamma \rangle_{\gamma \in \Gamma}$: B is the set of basic and derived meanings, and G_γ is a set of operations forming complex meanings from simpler ones. But as with syntax, nothing is assumed as to what sort of things meanings are or about the ways in which they can be affected by these operations. The syntactic and meaning operations are to match up, that is for each n-place syntactic operation F_γ there is a unique n-place semantic operation G_γ—that is, G_γ is to interpret semantically what F_γ forms syntactically. A *semantic interpretation for a language* is then defined

[6] As Janssen (1997) notes, that formalization is very similar to Janssen's own. Both are of course described more precisely and in more detail than I have space to discuss here.

as some HOMOMORPHISM from $\langle A, F_\gamma\rangle_{\gamma\in\Gamma}$ to $\langle B, G_\gamma\rangle_{\gamma\in\Gamma}$; that is, the semantic interpretation of a language is viewed as a function h construed as follows: for each n-place syntactic operation F_ι and its uniquely corresponding n-place compositional semantic operation G_ι (its "function of the meaning of the parts"),

$$h(F_\iota(\alpha_1, \ldots \alpha_n)) = G_\iota(h(\alpha), \ldots h(\beta_n))$$

To illustrate with the instance of this schema where F_ι is a binary syntactic operation (2*a*), we could instantiate the symbols in this formula in a way that makes it paraphrase Frege more literally, as in (2*b*):

(2) (*a*) $h(F_\iota(\alpha, \beta)) = G_\iota(h(\alpha), h(\beta))$

(*b*) *meaning-of*(SYNTACTIC-COMBINATION$_\iota$-OF(**Fido, barks**)) = SEMANTIC-FUNCTION$_\iota$-OF (*meaning-of*(**Fido**), *meaning-of* (**barks**))

(Once we fix the part of h that assigns meanings to the basic expressions (words) in A, the way that semantic operations match up with syntactic operations ensures that every complex expression in the language receives a unique meaning, that is the compositional interpretation procedure determines all the rest of h.) The difference between this homomorphic definition of compositionality and the broad interpretation allowed by a literal reading of Frege's Principle lies in what the homomorphic definition rules out: the latter makes all semantic interpretation "strictly local"—it says in effect that the meaning of any syntactic construction is determined by the meanings of its *immediate* constituents and *only* by those meanings—for example, there can be no "long distance" interpretive procedures that involve steps in syntactic construction that are not immediately adjacent, nor any transformation-like interpretive procedures that modify or add to interpretations of constituents once they are formed. (We will scrutinize this view at length below.)

Note that having a compositional interpretation of this form is one straightforward way to ensure that every one of the infinitely many possible syntactic structures of a language will receive a well-defined interpretation (though this may not be the only way). Also, it might seem that a theory in which the only compositional semantic rules are the strictly homomorphic ones ought to achieve a high degree of compositional transparency, syntactic economy, and semantic structural economy—possibly, we might conjecture, a higher degree than one with other kinds of compositional rules. But we should not assume in advance that natural languages have exactly this form of syntax–semantic interface, nor that this format will necessarily yield higher values on these scales.

2.3.2 *Is the "Homomorphism" Model the Right Starting Point?*

To be sure, there are possible ways of interpreting a language that depart significantly from a homomorphic one: Janssen (1997) cites some examples from computer languages. Probably the "pattern-matching" UNIFICATION procedure employed to match up syntactic form and semantic representation (and/or "F-structure") in Lexical-Functional grammar (Kaplan and Bresnan 1982) should be viewed this way. Whether a proposal actually departs from the homomorphism model is a harder question in other cases, such as the TYPE-DRIVEN TRANSLATION of Klein and Sag (1985) and in a similar proposal by Jacobson (1982), in which the interpretation of a constituent is determined by trying different ways of putting together the interpretations of its constituents by certain semantic operations (functional application, etc.) and checking whether each is type-theoretically well-formed, then possibly modifying the results until a well-formed one is produced. Is this consistent with homomorphic compositional semantics? Bach (1980) introduced the term SHAKE-AND-BAKE SEMANTICS for that theory (the metaphor here is that the input meanings are shuffled around into all possible combinations until one happens to fit), and he contrasted this with RULE-TO-RULE SEMANTICS, his term for homomorphic semantics à la Montague, where each semantic (translation) operation seems to be algorithmic in a "non-branching" way. But does such an interpretive rule necessarily fail to be homomorphic? If we agree with Bach that this violates the spirit of some desirable view of compositionality, it is necessary to be more specific about just why it does.

2.3.3 *Kinds of Non-Homomorphic Semantic Rules*

We can distinguish two kinds of not-strictly-homomorphic rules. I will use *free semantic rule* to refer to compositional rules which are not tied to the application of any one particular syntactic rule: proposals in this category include *type-shifting rules*, one version of which is introducing certain combinators. In some proposals, the application of such a rule (or combinator) is in effect necessarily "triggered" when a certain kind of situation arises in the course of a derivation, although no particular syntactic rule explicitly invokes it. The two steps in Cooper Storage (Cooper 1983) could be viewed as free interpretive rules (not obligatorily triggered ones): a semantic rule (NP-STORAGE) can optionally produce additional meanings for any NP meaning that appears in a derivation. The second rule, (NP-QUANTIFICATION), can be applied, also non-deterministically, at any one of several subsequent points.

One kind of proposal we do not seem to find in the literature, as far as I know, is a rule which "un-does" or "re-does" an interpretation that has already been formed; a hypothetical example would be an analysis in which the second quantifier scope reading of a sentence like *Someone loves everyone* is produced, optionally, by unpacking the reading already formed and putting it back together in a different way.

2.3.4 *Rule-to-Rule Input with Delayed Effects*

Another possible kind of interpretive rule is one that is Fregean (homomorphic) in all respects except that it also affects meaning one or several steps later in the derivation. Call this a *delayed-effect rule*. For example, you could take a different view of the Cooper Storage analysis (or on some other "scoping-out" proposals) as a single, delayed-effect interpretive rule, which could (if desired) be associated with the syntactic formation of NPs but has an effect that is only fully realized at some later stage, for example using the quantificational meaning of an NP later in the derivation to bind a deeply embedded variable at the site where the NP was originally introduced. (The type-logical scoping analysis in §2.8.3 is of this kind, but without true variable-binding in the second step.)

Evaluating free and delayed-effect compositional rules is sometimes complicated by the possibility of recasting them so as to fit within the homomorphic format. Note that nothing said so far would rule out a syntactic rule, applying to a single constituent, that had no "visible" effect on its input (i.e. its syntactic operation is the identity function) and did not change its syntactic category. If this is allowed, then we could replace some kinds of free syntactic rules with "correctly" homomorphic rules that achieved the same effects. On both the viewpoints described above, Cooper Storage would be a non-homomorphic rule, but it can also be formalized so as to be homomorphic (and one of the ways Cooper (1983) formalized it, it was). First, following Cooper, we expand the formal definition of a *meaning* to become a *set of sequences of meanings* of the original kind found in Montague Grammar: these sequences consist of the original kind of meaning found in Montague Grammar, plus "stored NP meanings", tagging along behind, as it were. NP-Storage could be treated as a null-effect syntactic rule (taking a single NP as input and giving the identical NP as output), but its associated compositional rule would replace the NP meaning with a variable and put the NP meaning "in storage". NP-Scoping could be fitted into the homomorphic format in the same way. (Some theoretical frameworks would rule out null-effect syntactic rules altogether, and NP-Storage and NP-Scoping can of course be treated as free semantic rules instead.)

Consider now compositionality: with no Quantifier-Raising/Lowering or other movement rules (or null-effect rules) the syntactic analysis of English has been greatly simplified, vis-à-vis Montague's quantifying-in analysis, making the resulting theory rank higher in syntactic economy. On the other hand, the formal characterization of a "meaning" has been greatly complicated, vis-à-vis Montague's or other traditional analysis of the semantics of quantification, and the further complexity in the semantic operations required for NP-Storage and NP-Quantification are at least as extreme: semantic structural economy suffers, since either a variable-binding or combinatory (cf. 8.1.2) account of binding and wide-NP scope could have given us the same ultimate sentence meanings in a far simpler way. It is odd that the very significant amount of semantic complexity introduced by Cooper Storage has never received much comment in the literature, nor has the trade-off between storage and other accounts in syntactic vs. semantic complexity been explicitly weighed (insofar as I am aware).

Compare this with the opposite extreme: the theory of Type-Logical Grammar (TLG) (discussed below) necessarily includes syntactic rules which do not visibly affect the appearance of a constituent, although rules always must alter its syntactic category in some way. However, a compositional rule of the complexity of Cooper Storage would be ruled out unequivocally in that theory. Like movement (and/or quantifying-in) theories of quantification, this one has high syntactic complexity, but as we will see below, the type-logical framework has a very highly "streamlined" compositional semantics.

The point to be made here is not that a compositionality-sensitive methodology can tell us (at this point anyway) definitely which is the better kind of analysis. Rather, the advantage is that it allows us to better pinpoint where the trade-offs in complexity lie and forces us to confront the task of motivating one choice over another in where to put the complexity. Cooper's Quantifier Storage has been seen as a great advance by some who seem to see simplification in syntactic analysis as an overriding concern but apparently do not worry too much about the significant additional complexity in the semantic theory Cooper Storage entails. The suggestion here is that a one-sided view of such an issue as quantification should no longer be tolerated.

2.3.5 *Type-Shifting*

The term "type-shifting" (or "type-lifting") covers a deceptive variety of kinds of analysis, ranging from homomorphic no-visible-effect category-changing rules with strictly determined compositional effects to free semantic rules which may or may not have a fully predictable effect (or maybe not a logically definable one). For this reason, trying to survey and compare the various proposals from the point of view of compositional transparency and syntactic economy would take us very far afield, even though these questions are important ones to address. If you want to try to evaluate compositional transparency here, I can only urge you to try to determine very carefully just what syntactic and compositional relationships each analysis involves, when you read this literature. Jacobson (2002) surveys type-shifting as it appears in "Direct Compositionality" analyses; Partee and Rooth (1983) have a very different proposal in mind, one that intentionally dispenses with a category-to-type correspondence, and at the other extreme, the TLG account can be found in Carpenter (1997) and Moortgat (1997).

2.3.6 *Imposing a Uniform Category-to-Meaning Mapping*

Further conditions on compositional interpretation which have been adopted in some theoretical frameworks are two kinds of semantic consistency with respect to syntactic category:

- All expressions in the same syntactic category have the "same kind of meaning" for their interpretations ("same kind" is often "same logical type").
- All syntactic constructions having the same syntactic input and output categories are interpreted by the same compositional semantic rule.[7]

The second of these would normally be taken to presuppose the first, but not *vice versa*. Note that these constitute a *strengthening* (constraint on) homomorphic semantics as described up to now. Whether achieving such consistency should matter to us is clouded by lack of agreement on what "same syntactic category" or "same kind of meaning" should mean here; sameness of logical type is the usual criterion, but other possibilities are imaginable.[8] All else being equal, such consistency would seem to increase compositional

[7] Montague's PTQ exemplifies this in its specification of a mapping g from syntactic categories of English to types of intentional logic, and use of the same semantic operation (translation rule), namely the one mapping $\langle \alpha', \beta' \rangle$ to $\alpha'(^\wedge\beta')$ for all "functional application" syntactic rules. However, PTQ does not use this form of translation for all its compositional semantic rules, nor does all category-to-type mapping follow from g. The Universal Grammar theory (Montague 1970) does not require that there be any particular pattern at all to the relationship between syntactic rules and compositional rules, except that all expressions of a category must have interpretations of the same logical type; this helps ensure type-theoretic well-formedness.

[8] For example, mass nouns have been analyzed as denoting elements in a non-atomic join semi-lattice, count nouns as denoting sets of discrete individuals. Various writers have argued that nouns and verbs have consistently different kinds of denotations, even though no distinction between their denotations is made in standard logic and model-theory. "Kind of meaning" here might be treated as a difference in logical type or a *sortal* difference.

transparency, in comparison to theories without it. (And syntactic economy is not necessarily decreased by it.)

Such consistency has sometimes been viewed as very desirable in the past: many linguists considered it an important achievement of Montague's that his theories permitted proper names, quantificational noun phrases, and bound pronouns—all of which are alike in syntactic category and syntactic behavior across many languages—to be interpreted uniformly in their compositional semantics (which entailed in his theory that their meanings had the same logical type), differing only in their "lexical" meanings.[9] This treatment of NPs set the stage for the theory of generalized quantifiers, which in turn permitted the first successful systematic treatment of the semantics of coordination and negation across all syntactic categories (Keenan and Faltz (1985) is perhaps the most developed of a field of research initiated by John Barwise and Robin Cooper). The unified compositional interpretation of intensional and extensional verb meanings in PTQ (which depends on and interacts with Montague's NP semantics) was also viewed in the 1970s and 1980s as an improvement over earlier heterogeneous treatments of intensional contexts—cf. Partee's arguments that the earlier idea of "decomposing" *seek* as *try to find* (to account for its intensionality) failed to have the motivation usually ascribed to it—leaving Montague's analysis as the better solution.

But more recently, advocates of discourse representation theory (DRT) argued that it was better not to assimilate names and pronouns to the same kind of interpretation as quantificational NPs (perhaps type-raising them "on the fly" only when necessary in certain contexts). Doubts have also arisen about the wisdom of collapsing the two kinds of transitive verbs into the same semantic type (Zimmermann 1993). Barbara Partee, for example, applauded Montague's achievement of these uniform category-to-meaning correspondences in the 1970s, but by the 1990s derided his commitment to this consistency as "generalizing to the worst case" (that is, what always permits the unification of heterogeneous kinds of readings is assimilating expressions requiring only the lower logical type into the higher type needed by others, not *vice versa*, even if there are more words of the former class than the latter; so, for example, extensional verbs had to be moved to the higher type of the intensional ones, although there are far fewer of the latter.) But why, exactly, does achieving category-to-type consistency—and thereby a more systematic compositional semantics—by employing a higher logical type uniformly for all the words that belong to a natural language syntactic category constitute "generalizing

[9] Or "word internal meanings," if you think it matters that the classical determiners, **be**, **necessarily**, etc. were decomposed using only the "logical words" of predicate logic.

to the worst case"? Why was this a good thing to do in 1970 but a bad one in 1990? After all, finding an analysis that encompasses seemingly exceptional data under a broader generalization is a hallowed paradigm of argumentation in linguistic theory. One facile answer is that a higher logical type is worse than a lower logical type because it is "more complicated", but why exactly is that so? It has always been recognized that model-theoretic constructs cannot be identified with units of psychological processing (we do not carry around infinite sets of possible worlds in our heads when we grasp propositions or generalized quantifier denotations when we understand NPs), nor can translations into a formal language that serve as the (dispensable) intermediary correspond to what is in the head either; ultimately the only empirical test of a model-theoretic account of natural language semantics is the characterization of *entailments among sentences* it gives, and the higher-order IL formula $\lambda P[P(j)](\mathbf{walk}')$ necessarily has exactly the same entailments as the logically equivalent first-order $\mathbf{walk}'(j)$. Treating the denotation of an extensional verb like *find* as a third-order relation that can be equivalently expressed via a first-order relation will get you no more and no fewer entailments than treating its denotation as a first-order relation. It follows from the role of the concept of *logical equivalence* in logical systems that a longer formula cannot be considered "better" than a logically equivalent shorter one in any sense other than for pedagogical or other extra-logical considerations (such as saving processing time in computational uses of formulas). So we are in need of a better justification of avoiding a "worst case" analysis than we have so far (perhaps also a better definition of "worst case" before we should take this epithet seriously). Perhaps Partee's change of heart came about after she had observed several instances where adoption of a consistently higher type assignment throughout a linguistic category turned out, upon closer inspection, to lead to certain difficulties that a heterogeneous category–type correspondence would have avoided. But unless it is shown that there really is some common property of such situations that is responsible for this apparent pattern, we have no reason to expect that we will inevitably encounter such problems sooner or later with analyses that generalize to a higher common type.

2.3.7 *"Curry-Howard" Semantics, "Radical Lexicalism", and Type-Logical Syntax*

One particularly strong version of category-consistent compositionality and severely constrained compositional semantic operations is described as the "Curry-Howard Isomorphism" (Carpenter 1997: 171–5; van Benthem 1983), which I will here simply refer to as "Curry-Howard Semantics".

This approach is today almost always adopted in categorial theories based on the Lambek Calculus, notably TYPE-LOGICAL SYNTAX (or TYPE-LOGICAL GRAMMAR (henceforth TLG): I use these terms interchangeably) (Carpenter 1997; Moortgat 1997). In the (associative) Lambek Calculus, the only syntactic rules are essentially these two:[10] (i) *Slash-Elimination* (or $/$-E)—from the sequence 'A/B B', derive A, and (ii) *Slash-Introduction* (or $/$-I)—if a sequence of categories having B at its right end can be combined so as to produce category A, then if you remove the B, what remains will have category A/B. According to the Curry-Howard correspondence, the Elimination rule is always compositionally interpreted as FUNCTIONAL APPLICATION (of the meaning of the expression in A/B to that in B), the Introduction rule as FUNCTIONAL ABSTRACTION (over the argument position represented by the missing B). There are no other compositional rules in the Lambek Calculus apart from these two[11] (or if you like, other than them and other rules derivable logically from them, such as functional composition and type-lifting). This idea derives ultimately from Curry and Feys' (1958) observation of the isomorphism between pure terms of the lambda calculus and proofs in implicational statement logic (of which the associative Lambek Calculus is a linearized instance, that is $/$-E is the rule of Modus Ponens and /-I is the rule of Conditional Proof (Hypothetical Reasoning, $\rightarrow$ *–Introduction*). Van Benthem (1983) called attention to the relevance of the correspondence to semantically interpreting the Lambek Calculus. Although it might appear to be too restricted, this system is actually powerful, in that many of the familiar combinatory rules in Combinatory Categorial Grammar (henceforth CCG) follow as theorems, as do their desired compositional interpretations, from just these two syntactic rules. For example, for functional composition (of A/B with B/C to give A/C), the interpretation in a Curry-Howard interpretation is easily proved to be $\lambda v[\alpha(\beta(v))]$, where α and β are the interpretations of the A/B and B/C expressions respectively. Type-lifting, where A becomes $B/(A\backslash B)$, will necessarily have the interpretation $\lambda v[\alpha(v)]$; the Geach derivation from A/B to $(A/C)/(B/C)$ must be $\lambda v_1 \lambda v_2[\alpha(v_1(v_2))]$, and so on.

Taking this approach seriously in natural language semantics leads to a theory of the kind Lauri Karttunen once characterized as RADICAL LEXICALISM: with case grammars (CGs) in general, but even more strictly under Curry-Howard semantics, all "construction-specific" compositional meanings

[10] Actually an exaggeration but not a relevant one here: see Moortgat for an official formulation of the Lambek Calculus.

[11] The program of Type-Logical Syntax does usually augment the Lambek Calculus with additional TYPE CONSTRUCTORS, both unary and binary, but the Lambek Calculus (usually the non-associative version) still plays the role of the "logical core" of the system.

(perhaps all "interesting" ones for that matter) must be analyzed as packed into the meaning of some lexical item(s) in the construction: there can be no special "constructional meaning" specific to some syntactic configuration, since functional application and functional abstraction are the only compositional possibilities. (Since in a CG all of the syntactic structure as well is ultimately generated by the categories that lexical words are assigned, the term "radical lexicalism" applies to syntax as well as to semantics.)

What is perhaps surprising about (semantic) radical lexicalism to those who encounter it for the first time is how often it can be made to work well. Almost all "syntactic constructions" turn out to have an identifiable lexical head, and since the head takes the other elements in the construction as its syntactic complements (arguments), a meaning can almost always be assigned to that head that produces the desired semantic relationships among the pieces. With many cases of constructional meanings that do not at first blush seem to involve a lexical head of an appropriate category, evidence can usually be found that one word is actually "lexicalized" as head, that is has undergone a lexical rule giving it an additional subcategorization frame and a specialized meaning for that frame, alongside its more familiar frame and meaning. For example, it might seem that *Mary hammered the metal flat* has a causative constructional meaning, but it has been noted (Dowty 1979) that this construction is lexically and semantically idiosyncratic in ways that depend on the choice of the transitive verb (e.g. we have *John knocked the boxer unconscious* but not **John socked (hit, smacked) the boxer unconscious*, and whereas *hammer the metal flat* has about the same meaning as *flatten the metal by hammering it, squeeze the orange dry* does not mean the same at all as *dry the orange by squeezing it*). That is, in addition to category *TV*, *hammer* should be analyzed as having the additional lexical category *TV/AdjP* (see Dowty (1979) for the lexical rule in question).

A few apparently recalcitrant cases still exist: whereas the relative pronoun in an ordinary relative clause (such as a *man whom we met yesterday*) can be analyzed as the head of the construction in such a way as to be solely responsible for the relative clause syntax and meaning, this is not so plausible in complementizerless relative clauses such as *a man we met yesterday*, as no alternative "lexicalized" categorization for some word is easily motivated (although some way or other of treating this under radical lexicalism can still be construed).

A theory in which only two compositional rules are possible, with even the choice between them always predictable from the shape of the names of the category involved, should in theory increase compositional transparency. But as with category-to-type uniformity, if achieving radical lexicalism involves what looks like a significant "complication" of many lexical meanings, is that really a bargain? The dilemma about "generalizing to the worst case" arises here again, and finding a good answer will eventually be necessary before we can be sure how to respond to a framework that streamlines compositional semantics to the maximum extent.

2.4 Context-Free Semantics

2.4.1 *Meaning Algebras: How are Operations on Meanings Computed?*

Something that is easy to overlook in the highly general definition of compositional semantic interpretation Montague gave in UG, as a homomorphism between algebras, is that in his algebraic model nothing was said about *how* the result of applying a compositional semantic operation might be "computed" from its operands. Indeed nothing in these definitions entails that that had to be computable at all. Perhaps at the level of abstraction that is of interest at that point, this question should not matter, but for both syntax and semantics for natural languages, where the domains of these operations are infinite yet the operations are taken as a theory of a system that can be used by humans or computers, we must obviously require that there be some algorithm to determine what the result of applying any operation F_i to its argument(s) $\alpha, \beta, \ldots$ will be (and as Janssen (1997) notes, today it is standard in the field of universal algebra to require that the operations of an algebra be *computable.*)[12]

In syntax this is always taken as self-evident, for example we do not expect to find a natural language syntactic operation F_i such that F_i (**walk, slowly**) = **cows eat grass** or F_i(**Mary, walk in the garden**) = **happier than an ostrich**, but rather operations that can be computed in a systematic way. That should be just as true for semantic operations.

My reasons for bringing up this point are, first, to emphasize how easy it is to fail to notice assumptions about compositionality we are taking for granted even when we read a definition such as §2.3.1, but, second, to focus attention on the question of *how* a constituent's meaning is to be computed from the meanings of its parts. When $G_\gamma(\alpha, \beta)$ is computed, what aspects of α and β can be manipulated by G_γ? Consider an analogous question in syntax: when the syntactic operation is the simplest possible one, concatenation, then the operation needs to "know" no more than the phonological forms of its inputs. But if we want to define the operation F_j such that F_j(**Bill, be awake**) = **Bill is awake** and (F_j(**they, be awake**) = **they are awake**), etc., then

[12] Perhaps Montague took this for granted and failed to notice he had not specified it explicitly—as Janssen also mentions, universal algebra was then a fairly new field—or perhaps not.

computing the result requires at least the information as to what the head of the second expression is and what its inflectional paradigm is. All linguistic theories, of course, include a detailed, well-motivated theory of what syntactic and morphological properties of natural language expressions are needed to compute the required syntactic operations on them. But a correspondingly comprehensive account of which properties of meanings are needed to carry out compositional semantic operations is lacking, although actually just as relevant.

2.4.2 *What is Context-Free Semantics?*

One aspect of compositional interpretation that I believe often underlies discussions and disagreements about "strict compositionality" among linguists, but is not very clearly recognized for what it is, is a constraint on semantic operations that can be termed CONTEXT-FREE SEMANTICS;[13] it could also be called STRICTLY LOCAL COMPOSITIONALITY (in the sense of "strictly local" used in HPSG, cf. Levine and Meurers (2005)). In Montague's linguistic metatheory, the (more general) theory of "Meaning" does not actually require semantics to be context-free, as noted above, but the (more specific) theory of reference[14] (which includes sense, denotation, and truth, and which is an instantiation of the general theory of meaning) does observe context-free semantics, as does the semantics of intensional logic used to illustrate this theory (with the one exception discussed below), and as do other formal logical languages (mostly).

I suggest that context-free semantics is at present the most relevant starting point from which to explore a theory of natural language compositionality, and I will try to show that it can have unexpected consequences for syntactic analysis as well as for semantics if its implications are pursued fully. Note I am not arguing that context-free compositionality definitely *is* the correct theory of all aspects of natural language interpretation. Context-free semantics is prima facie a form of compositional interpretation that would seem to maximize compositional transparency and structural semantic economy.

To say in a simple way what "context-free semantics" is, I start by turning the familiar definition of context-free phrase structure rules upside down. We

[13] I have found no written precedent for this term, although I have occasionally heard it in conversations since at least 1996.

[14] That is, the section titled "3. Semantics: Theory of Meaning" gives the "bare" algebraic-homomorphism characterization I discussed above, and this is general enough that not only what is subsequently defined in "4. Semantics: Theory of Reference" but also the "theory of translation" and of "interpretation induced by translation" are formally all instances of it. Within the "Reference" section, the term *meaning* also appears, but here it refers to a function from {possible worlds} × {contexts} to denotations, while *sense* refers to a function from (solely) possible worlds to denotations.

all know that for syntactic rules to be CONTEXT-FREE means that whether the node C can be expanded to D E in the tree (3) below may not depend on the presence of a node of category B (or anything B dominates), but only on properties of the node C (i.e. its node label). In the more modern terminology of "constraint-based" phrase-structure theories, STRICT LOCALITY (Levine and Meurers 2005) requires that the constraints constituting a grammar can only be stated in terms of local trees, that is subtrees consisting of a mother node and one or more daughter nodes that it immediately dominates.

(3) (*a*)

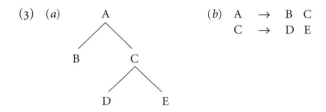

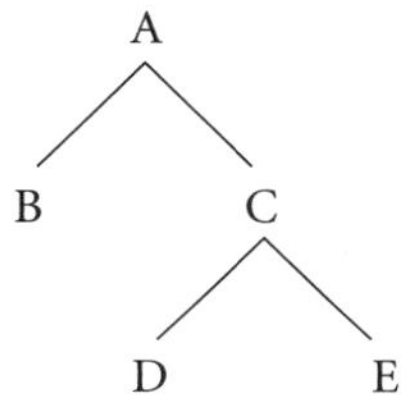

(*b*) A $\rightarrow$ B C
C $\rightarrow$ D E

If you "invert" PS rules to make them into recursive formation rules, building structure from the bottom up (e.g. the kind of recursive formation rules used for formal logical languages), the context-free requirement (locality) amounts to saying that whether B and C can be put together to form A may not depend on what the nodes D and E are that C dominates (or anything below D and E), but only on the identity of the node C itself.

The requirement of *context-free semantics* is parallel—with this important difference: I will now talk about *derivation* trees (like Montague's "analysis trees") in which the tree's node labels are *meanings, not* syntactic categories (as they are in a phrase-structure tree) and not *categories* of meanings, but meanings themselves (really).

The context-free constraint is that when you put together meanings α and β by some semantic operation G, $G(\alpha, \beta)$ may depend only on what α and β are, each "taken as a whole", but may not depend on the meanings that α and β were formed from by earlier semantic operations.

2.4.3 *The Problem with "the Meaning as a Whole"*

But the notion of "the meaning taken as a whole" is more problematic than it might seem: whether that restriction has any real consequences depends on just what meanings are and how you think about them.

If you think of meanings as "semantic representations" or "logical forms at LF", that is as like formulas in some formal language, then this constraint is puzzling: if meanings have this form, then consider that if representations

α and β differ at any point whatsoever, no matter how deeply "embedded" the difference may be, then α and β are ipso facto not the same semantic representation. But, if a semantic rule can depend on what a meaning *is*, and if no subpart of that formula should be exempted from helping to determine *what* that meaning is, why should a semantic rule be prohibited from being sensitive to all the details of it? What would it mean for a semantic operation to see only the "whole meaning" *without* ever taking any of the parts of it into account? Now, if a compositional rule G applying to α and β deleted some subpart of one of these in producing $G(\alpha, \beta)$, then obviously that part would be no longer accessible in the result $G(\alpha, \beta)$. But in formation rules for logical languages, and formation rules for the semantic representations of linguists, complex expressions are built up monotonically; the expression produced at any step contains as subparts all the expressions produced at all earlier steps. The source of the difficulty here is thinking of a meaning as nothing *but* a "semantic representation".

But consider a semantic theory in which the meaning of a sentence, a proposition, is a set of possible worlds. A set of worlds has no internal structure—it has no subject, no object, no Agent, and no Patient; it has no main connective, no quantifier scopes. It might have been derived from the meanings of its parts by intersecting one set of worlds with another, but you cannot recover the original sets just from the intersection itself. A context-free semantic operation applying to a proposition has nothing to go on, so to speak, but the set of worlds it has in front of it. In this theory, therefore, a context-free semantic operation must be a set-theoretically definable operation you can perform on the kind of set-theoretic object(s) that was/were just given to you as denotations of the syntactic inputs.

I should make it clear that I am not making the claim here that a set of possible worlds *is* the most appropriate theoretical construct to serve as a proposition (although the theory based on this idea has been very productive in the past and continues to be). This view of propositions, and the view of properties and relations that goes with it, is useful for expository purposes, as it can help us think of meanings as "black boxes" when it is useful to do so, in order to sharpen our understanding of just what context-free semantics entails.

But, even in theories that do take all meanings to be set-theoretic objects, formulas of a formal language are usually used as "intermediate" representations, following the precedent of the translations into intensional logic in Montague's work. How could one tell, by looking at some semantic operation applying to some complicated formula, whether it is context-free or not? Fortunately, there is an easy way to do this (at least if the answer is affirmative) within Montague's general definitions of MEANING (and DENOTATION) and of MEANING INDUCED BY TRANSLATION in "Universal Grammar" (Montague 1970):

- Whether the translation language (the formal language into which English is initially translated) has a context-free model-theoretic semantics can be determined by examination of (i) the definitions of a *model* and types of possible denotations in it, and (ii) the recursive interpretation rules for this language (with respect to such a model). In the case of Montague's IL—with some caveats to be mentioned in §2.4.6 below—it is.
- Montague precisely defines an allowable translation rule to be a certain kind of combination of the syntactic rules of the translation language (called a *polynomial operation over syntactic operations* (of a syntactic algebra $\langle A, F_\gamma \rangle_{\gamma \in \Gamma}$), (Montague 1970: 232)). Put simply, a translation rule may build up a complex formula using its input translations by putting things together in just the ways that one or more IL formation rules can put things together, in one or more steps. (Also, they can add in basic symbols from IL, such as a particular variable.) But they cannot take apart the input formulas to alter the smaller formulas from which they were formed, because no IL syntactic rule does that. Nor can what a rule does in a given case depend on "peeking inside" one of the input formulas to see what kind of smaller formulas it was formed from in previous steps: no IL rule does this either.
- This has the consequence that any translation rule meeting these conditions will produce context-free interpretations if all the syntactic rules of the translation language have context-free interpretations.
- As the semantic interpretation of English is defined to be the composition of the translation function (from English to IL) with the interpretation function of IL (from IL formulas to their denotations in a model), it will follow that the semantic interpretation of English will be context-free as long as these conditions are met.[15]

Since it is easy to learn what a "legal" translation rule is,[16] then as long as you confine yourself to legal rules, you can be sure that your semantic interpretation will be context-free, even though these meanings are represented by formulas with internal structure.[17]

[15] I take this to be a fairly safe conjecture, and one that is obvious from the relevant parts of Montague (1970), but I won't try to prove it here.

[16] Janssen (1997) cites an example of a translation rule violating this constraint, taken from the early Montague Grammar literature.

[17] Don't be misled by the status of beta-reduction steps ("lambda-conversions") that you usually see applied to Montague-style translations after the compositional assembly of complete translations

2.4.4 *Catches and Escape Hatches*

What might seem at this point to be a relatively clear distinction between context-free and non-context-free compositional operations is muddied by various things which may look like "escape hatches", technically complying with context-free semantics while perhaps escaping it in spirit.

2.4.5 *"Direct Compositionality" vs. Free Variable Denotations*

Jacobson (2002) advocates a version of compositional interpretation which she calls Direct Compositionality. This is a kind of rule-to-rule view ("coupled with each syntactic rule is a semantic rule specifying how the meaning of the larger expression is derived from the meanings of the smaller expressions"). But in her characterization, direct compositionality is also to be associated with some of the amendments to R-to-R semantics mentioned above, viz., type-shifting rules are to be added (in one or another version), wide-scope quantification might be handled via Cooper Storage or possibly by Hendriks' account, which is a special variety of type-shifting. To this extent, "Direct Compositionality" refers to a collection of alternatives defined by the group of linguists Jacobson includes under that name; it is not completely delimited by a unifying definition of a version of compositionality.

But in any event the most central feature for Jacobson is the HYPOTHESIS OF LOCAL INTERPRETATION, which is that "every constituent has a meaning," a condition Barker (2002) phrases as "each linguistic constituent has a well-formed and complete denotation that does not depend on any linguistic element external to that expression." (Note free semantic rules and delayed-effect rules may not necessarily be excluded by this.)

However it is stated exactly, the main thrust of the hypothesis of local interpretation is to exclude the standard Tarskian semantic treatment of free and bound variables: the complaint is that the denotations of variables are indeterminate when they are first introduced into a derivation and depend on quantifiers introduced later on.

This objection does not necessarily hold.[18] Although the traditional way of giving semantics for predicate logic begins by defining formulas as true or false only *relative to* some assignment of values to variables (equivalently,

has taken place. These manipulations are not a part of compositional interpretation as properly understood: the "reduced" and "unreduced" versions of the translation stand for exactly the same proposition or other denotation in a model. The reductions serve only to make the translations into something easier for the linguist to read.

[18] Only after writing this section did I notice that Janssen (1997) contains a very similar explanation of this same alternative formulation of Tarski semantics, in order to make a similar point. See his article for more details on technical aspects of it.

says when an assignment *satisfies* a formula), an alternative but equivalent specification of Tarskian semantics takes the denotation of a formula to be a SET OF VARIABLE ASSIGNMENTS—where to satisfy a qualm in (Jacobson 1999)[19] we take an "assignment" to be simply an infinite sequence of individuals. Then the semantic rules are stated in this fashion: using for simplicity one-place predicates to illustrate the rule for atomic formulas, "$\delta(x_n)$" denotes the set of all assignments (sequences) in which the n-th member of the assignment is in the denotation of the predicate "δ" in the model in question.[20] Semantic rules for the connectives specify, for example, that $[\![[\phi \wedge \psi]]\!]^M$ is the intersection of the set of assignments $[\![\phi]\!]^M$ with the set $[\![\psi]\!]^M$, and similarly for other connectives. Then $[\![\exists x_n[\phi]]\!]^M$ is the set of all assignments differing (possibly) from one in $[\![\phi]\!]^M$ only in the n-th member. It will follow in this method that a formula which has all its variables bound will denote either the set of all assignments or the empty set; the former case we call "true", the latter "false". Notice that nowhere in this process does a free variable lack a denotation, it is rather always associated with a set of individual denotations, and that denotation for the variable itself does not change during the semantic derivation of the sentence.

Of course, one price you seem to pay for this change is that the denotation of a formula is now not a simple truth value but an infinite set of functions, each of which has an infinite domain (if one assumes, as is usually done, that the supply of distinct variables should be denumerably infinite). Of course, it was never really a truth value in the first place, and this version is not obviously much worse (if worse at all) than the more familiar formulation, since literally evaluating the Tarskian semantic rules for the quantifiers would require "checking" an infinite number of (infinite) assignment functions for the value assigned to certain variables at each compositional step inside the quantifier. But if this is the objection, then stipulating that "each constituent must have a complete interpretation independent of any external expression" is not the way to implement it successfully: rather, you should simply object to the Tarskian account of bound variables directly—which, as Jacobson herself has shown, is something we have other good motivation to do. (More possible reasons are suggested in §2.7.)

[19] Jacobson worries that assignments as usually described are functions that have variables as their domain, hence in themselves are not purely objects in the model. But a familiar alternative formulation treats assignments simply as sequences of individuals (individuals from the model's domain): instead of referring to "the value of the assignment function g for the argument x_n", we can speak of "the n-th member of the sequence g".

[20] If you want to think of the variable by itself as having a denotation, independently of the rule for atomic formulas, you could, for example, let x_n denote the integer n).

2.4.6 *Intensions, Extensions, and 'Tensions*

Montague's PTQ grammar makes much of the observation that in many functor-argument constructions in English, getting the correct semantics for the combination demands access to the *intension* of the argument term, rather than simply its traditional *denotation*. For example, determining the denotation of *former senator* requires not merely the denotation of *senator* at the current index but its denotation at earlier times, and that is recoverable from its intension. PTQ is explicitly constructed so as to let expressions in those contexts "denote" their senses—via the $^\wedge$ and $^\vee$ operators that complicated his intensional logic significantly (and the headaches of students trying to master it). Pace Montague, there are points in his intensional logic itself when a semantic rule requires "intensional" information not "denoted" by the input to the rule. One case is the modal operator $\Box$, which combines with a formula ϕ, denoting a truth value, and gives a new formula $\Box\phi$, also denoting a truth value. But the meaning of $\Box$ is not a function on truth values: to get the truth value for $\Box\phi$ at some index $\langle w, t\rangle$, you need to know the truth value of ϕ at all other indices $\langle w', t'\rangle$ as well. (The tense operators **F** and **H** need to know their argument's truth values at other times.) To be sure, this rule actually does receive a determinate interpretation, because the semantic rules for IL recursively define denotations with respect to *all* indices at once (just as they recursively define denotation with respect to all possible variable assignments), it is just that the required information is not in the *denotation* at the "current" index. The case of $\Box$ is easily rectified by redefining $\Box$ to combine with a proposition-denoting expression rather than one denoting a truth value (e.g. $\Box^\wedge[\mathbf{walk}'(j)]$ would be well-formed). Alas, the semantic rule for $^\wedge\alpha$ itself also has this feature: it does not derive the denotation of $^\wedge\alpha$ at an index from the denotation of α at that index; it needs α's denotation for all other indices as well. And this case cannot be "corrected" as $\Box$ can (though here again, the appropriate semantics is fixed within the system as a whole). Hence Montague's insistence on using $^\wedge\alpha$ alongside α (perhaps so as to be able to formalize literally Frege's notion of "indirect denotation") cannot be carried out with complete consistency by means of the formal distinction he invented for this purpose. If Montague had based his recursive semantic definitions on *senses*, and defined *denotation* secondarily from that—rather than *vice versa* as he did in PTQ—the problem would have been avoided. But David Lewis argued that adherence to the supposedly important distinction between intension and extension is unnecessary for a satisfactory theory of possible-worlds semantics, in an article aptly titled "'Tensions" (Lewis 1974). Most formal semanticists have agreed with Lewis. All of Montague semantics can be reformulated to make it literally context-free semantically if desired: the reformulation called "Ty_2" (Gallin 1975) is the most general and best-known implementation.

2.4.7 *Contextual Parameters*

Another escape hatch is the multiplication of *contextual parameters* to which denotations are commonly relativized in model-theoretic semantics, such as time (of utterance), speaker, hearer, etc.[21] The invention of *two-dimensional tense logic* in Hans Kamp's dissertation (Kamp 1968) is a nice illustration. Standard monadic "Priorian" tense operators combine with formulas to produce new formulas recursively, as for example ϕ, $\mathbf{P}\phi$, $\mathbf{F}\phi$, $\mathbf{PP}\phi$, $\mathbf{FPF}\phi$, etc. Although the interpretation of the outermost tense operator depends on the context of utterance, the standard interpretation of embedded ones is context-free, in that each such operator "shifts" the interpretation to a new point in time, but after a second or further tense operator has been added, it is not always possible to recover the relationship between the times (time range) indicated by embedded tense operators and the contextually interpreted "speech time". For example: if the formula $\mathbf{PF}\phi$ is true at time t_0, then we know that the embedded formula $\mathbf{F}\phi$ must be true at some t_1 earlier than t, and we know that ϕ itself is true at some t_2 later than t_1, but it is indeterminate whether t_2 is earlier than, equal to, or later than t_0. However, Kamp observed that there is a difference between these two English sentences:

(4) (*a*) A child was born who would be king.

(*b*) A child was born who will be king.

In (4*a*), we cannot tell whether the time of the child's being king has already come about, as of the time this sentence is spoken (just as with the standard interpretation of $\mathbf{PF}\phi$), but in (4*b*), that time is placed unambiguously *later* than the time of utterance: this is something that an embedded standard tense operator cannot ensure.

Kamp's proposal was to introduce a second temporal parameter into the recursive semantic definitions, creating a *two-dimensional tense logic*: this functioned intuitively somewhat like Reichenbach's (1947) *reference time*, in relation to which the original temporal index corresponded to *speech time*. Then the rules for the two tense operators $\mathbf{F}_{wd}$ ("would") and $\mathbf{F}_{wl}$ ("will") are as follows, where i is the "reference-time" and j is the "speech time".

[21] Janssen (1997) also discusses the issue that deictic (context-dependent) expressions present for compositionality but makes a slightly different point about Kamp's analyses.

(5) $[\![\mathbf{F}_{wd}\phi]\!]^{M,i,j} = 1$ iff $[\![\phi]\!]^{M,i',j} = 1$, for some $i' > i$.

$[\![\mathbf{F}_{wl}\phi]\!]^{M,i,j} = 1$ iff $[\![\phi]\!]^{M,i',j} = 1$, for some $i' > j$.

That is, $\mathbf{F}_{wl}$ still anchors to the actual speech time j, no matter how many tense operators it is embedded within.

As it has turned out, a semantics for tense with two contextual time indices seems to be completely appropriate for natural languages, not really because of phenomena like (4*a*, 4*b*) but because for English tenses, "reference time" does seem to be an important independent contextual parameter: past tense most often identifies a time mentioned in the previous sentence (or one immediately afterward) or one otherwise implicit in the context (Hinrichs 1986), and not the indefinite "some-earlier-time-or-other" that the standard past operator introduces. The point I want to call attention to, however, is a methodological one: adding an additional contextual parameter allows us to produce a kind of interpretation that would not be possible with a context-free semantic interpretation of embedded tenses. (The really challenging empirical problem with indexicality in language is distinguishing semantically "hard-wired" dependence on context (e.g. *yesterday, tomorrow* are clear examples) from "non-semantic" dependence on context, which must be figured out by the hearer by unspecified "pragmatic" information. Genitives, and especially the Russian genitive, are (just) one particularly troublesome instance of the dilemma: see Barbara Partee's appendix to Janssen (1997) for discussion.)

In summary: The three cases of potential "violations" of the *hypothesis of local interpretation* just discussed—denotations for free variables, operators with covert access to denotations at other possible worlds, and interpretation of context-dependent aspects of meaning—can all be made to satisfy the local-interpretation hypothesis (and also the context-free constraint on semantic interpretation) by the same strategy:

If you have been assuming meanings to be a certain kind of thing (call this the *a*-type), but discover that compositional interpretation needs access to some unanticipated "external" type of information *b*, that *a* does not supply, you can circumvent the problem by redefining your notion of "meanings" to be functions from *b*-type things to *a*-type things.

2.4.8 *A Bottom Line: What* are *Meanings, Really? And What are Possible Operations on Meanings?*

One important lesson is to be drawn from the above considerations:

We cannot pin down more specifically what compositionality really involves until we can decide more specifically (i) what meanings really are, and (ii) what semantic operations can be performed on meanings.[22]

If we assume a possible-worlds semantics, some limits are thereby set on the theoretically possible compositional semantic operations, if our semantics is to be context-free, that is: these are operations definable on sets (for operations on formulas), and for the type of set-theoretic constructs out of these that we choose as denotations for other categories (e.g. functions from entities to sets of worlds), only operations that are set-theoretically definable on each of these are possible.[23] But different semantic analyses will require operations of a wide range of complexity. I can illustrate the point by comparing some alternative models of denotations and asking in each case (i) what sorts of things meanings must be, and (ii) exactly what a semantic operation has to be able to do in order to get the desired semantics in a context-free way.

In extensional statement logic, "meanings" are just the two truth values, and the semantic operation needed to produce the interpretation of $[\phi \wedge \psi]$ is merely a binary truth function. To interpret this same formula in a propositional intensional semantics, sentences must denote sets of worlds, and the operation of set intersection is now the appropriate one.

Consider the account of Tarskian variable-binding semantics discussed in §2.4.5 (in an extensional semantics now) on which formulas denote sets of sequences of objects (one method for constructing "assignment functions" for variables). Here the semantic operation for producing $\llbracket [\phi \wedge \phi] \rrbracket^M$ needs to be able to form the intersection of the two sets $\llbracket \phi \rrbracket^M$ and $\llbracket \psi \rrbracket^M$, but doing that does not depend on any particular properties of the objects in the two sets.

However, the semantic operation for producing $\llbracket \exists x_n [\phi] \rrbracket^M$ from $\llbracket \phi \rrbracket^M$ in this same system needs to be able to examine each sequence in a set of sequences and determine what all the other possible sequences are that are exactly like it except for the n-th member of that sequence. That of course is a

22 Dever (1999: 321–22) likewise concludes "systematicity is not the route to real constraints on the range of available meaning theories. What we need instead are constraints on what meanings are assigned to component parts. Without such constraints, both compositionality and systematicity are always available."

23 In theories of meaning in which propositions are not sets of worlds but primitive entities (e.g. Thomason 1980), the limits (if any) are presumably imposed by the type of algebraic operations on propositions that the theory allows. On the other hand, we could also move to wider characterizations—as we are urged to do by proponents of "structured meaning" theories, theories which still employ the kinds of meanings found in possible-worlds semantics, but for meanings of complex expressions, construct tree-like structures that have ordinary possible-worlds-semantics meanings at each node. This opens the possibility that any well-defined operation on a "meaning tree" could count as a possible natural language semantic operation, unless further constraints were imposed.

more complicated operation, and it does depend on specific properties of the things in $[\![\phi]\!]^M$ that the previous operation did not.

Now consider Cooper Storage: to be able to characterize Storage and Scoping within the algebraic model of Montague's "Universal Grammar", Cooper (1983) must treat all meanings as sets of sequences of sequences; then the semantic operation corresponding to NP-scoping must be able to examine such a meaning and determine whether a sequence that is the non-initial element of a sequence of sequences in that set is (one translated as) $\langle x_i, \alpha \rangle$ (as opposed to $\langle x_j, \beta \rangle$, etc.), then use α and the head of the sequence, ϕ, to construct a formula of the form $\alpha(\lambda x_i [\phi])$. Is this a context-free operation? Insofar as the "primary" (head) part of a sentence meaning (the part corresponding to a Montagovian meaning) is not decomposed to identify parts which were assembled by earlier compositional operations, the operation may still be technically context-free. Whether you really want to count it as context-free may be pointless hair-splitting, but a more important observation to make is that this must be a (much) more complicated unpacking semantic operation, on a meaning that has a more complex structure, than any model-theoretically defined account of natural language meaning ever proposed before.

2.5 How Compositionality Depends on Syntactic Analyses

2.5.1 *The Syntactic Level(s) at Which Compositional Interpretation Takes Place*

In syntactic theories with multiple levels of syntactic structure, the form of compositional interpretation that will be required obviously depends on the level or levels that are interpreted, as well as other assumptions specific to those theories of syntax. The picture of compositional interpretation that will emerge in such theories will be quite complicated. In this paper, I can better focus on the foundational and methodological issues in characterizing compositionality by presupposing a mono-stratal syntactic theory such as CG or HPSG. I refer you to Jacobson (2002) for extensive discussion of "where" compositional interpretation has been situated within multi-level as well as single-level syntactic/semantic theories from the 1970s to the present, and the repercussions of the choice of level(s) that are to be interpreted.

2.5.2 *Compositional Transparency vs. (Non-)Context-Free Syntax and the Significance of Wrap*

The issues surrounding context-free compositionality would be clearer if natural language syntax were always completely context-free. Things almost surely cannot be that simple, however, once compositional interpretation is made a serious concern. One obvious recalcitrant problem (already cited above) is the numerous rightward extrapositions in English, such as the postposed relative clause in (6):

(6) A woman just came into the room *who we met at the station earlier.*

While this presents some kind of syntactic problem or other for any monostratal theory such as HPSG or CG, it becomes a very awkward challenge if compositional semantics is to be kept transparent—as long as the syntax must be literally context-free, that is.

At this kind of juncture, some advocates of a CG theory have proposed adding certain non-context-free syntactic operations to an otherwise context-free syntax. In the case of extraposition, for example, a syntactic operation might be suggested that combines the NP *a woman who we met at the station earlier* with the VP *just came into the room* and results in (6), rather than *A woman who we met at the station earlier just came into the room.* With this tactic, a context-free compositional interpretation of the sentence is still unproblematic. A non-concatenative syntactic operation that has in fact been proposed repeatedly in CG is (Right) Wrap (Bach 1979, 1980; Dowty 1996), introduced below.

The argument for such a move is that the nature of the compositional semantics of the language as a whole can be kept much more systematic and exception-free, at the expense of this one reduction in Syntactic Economy. Thus what is gained on the one side significantly outweighs what is lost on the other.

This move would be less ad hoc (and would in fact give support to the methodology this paper advocates) if the necessary non-concatenative operation could be motivated by more than keeping compositional semantics simple and context-free. Otherwise, compositional transparency has been trivialized. Consequently, only compelling independent motivation should be a sufficient reason for adopting Wrap or other non-context-free operations. For Wrap, this justification has been demonstrated, although this is not widely appreciated, even in some arenas of CG research.

2.5.2.1 *The Significance of Wrap for English Syntax and Compositionality: The Categorial Theory of Argument Structure* First, if admitted as a possible operation, Wrap would be motivated at multiple points in English syntax and has common (morpho-)syntactic characteristics across all of them; these wrap sites include (i) combining direct object NPs with phrasal transitive verbs; note that wrapping is postulated not only for *persuade Mary to leave* but uniformly for *all* cases of verbs that take a direct object plus some additional complement, for example *hammer the metal flat* results from combining the phrasal *TV hammer flat* with *the metal*, and *give a book to John* results from combining the *TV give to John* with *a book*, as well as for *TVs* containing a *TV* adjunct—an adjunct type that will be motivated in §2.6.2 below. Since the combination of a simple transitive verb with its object can be treated as a (trivial) instance of Wrap, the grammar of English can simply specify once and for all that when any constituent of category TV combines with its argument, Wrap is the syntactic operation used. Wrap is also motived (ii) in complex PPs such as *without John present*; (iii) as noted by Bach (1984), in constructions such as *too hot to eat, easy person to please*; and (iv) to produce Aux-inverted clauses—*Where has Mary gone?, Never have I seen such a catastrophe, Had she been aware of the error, she would have corrected it.* A property all these cases share, observed by Arnold Zwicky, is that a pronoun in the position of a wrapped-in NP is obligatorily cliticized to the head (which will necessarily immediately precede it); cf. (Dowty [1992] 1996).

The pay-off to postulating Wrap is that it allows us to maintain three kinds of general syntactic and compositional principles simultaneously, each of which would otherwise come apart; these all ultimately follow in part from the highly general CATEGORIAL THEORY OF ARGUMENT STRUCTURE which is something that arises automatically from the way multi-place predicates have to be treated in CG, viz. as "curried" functions. These are the following: (i) the steps by which "curried" multi-place verbs (predicates) combine with their arguments supplies us with a definition of *(grammatical) subject, direct object, oblique object*, and *X-complement* ("X-complements" being PPs, AdjPs, other PredPs, infinitive complements, *that*-complements),[24] viz. the argument that combines last with the predicate (the subject NP) ranks the highest, the penultimate argument to combine with it (the direct object NP) is next highest, and so on. It is via this classification that: (i.a) CG realizes the necessary basic morphosyntactic generalizations about agreement and government, for example making nominative, accusative, etc. the (default) inflection for subject, object, etc., in a consistent way for one-, two-, and three-place predicates; (i.b) general rules for word order among subject, object, etc. are stated; and (i.c) the correlation with different coordination possibilities/properties are then correctly predicted. The curried, step-wise argument structure puts these grammatical functions in a (correct) *obliqueness hierarchy* (the hierarchy *subject, object, indirect/oblique object, other complement*) which is relevant for two kinds of grammatical organization: (ii) the generalizations about properties of so-called "relation-changing" operations (Passive, Raising (to subject and

[24] Actually, the hierarchy is a bit more fine-grained, as it can be extended to distinguish two different types of infinitive complement, one higher and one lower than an NP direct object argument, see §2.6.9.

to object), Dative-Shift, other diathesis shifts) which were documented across a very wide range of languages in research in Relational Grammar;[25] finally (iii) the hierarchical constraints on anaphoric binding, extraction, and scope which are correlated with *c-command* in other theories (the corresponding syntactic/semantic relationship has been called "F-command" in CG, cf. Bach (1980)) are determined by this same hierarchical assembly of arguments (and verbal adjuncts). It is probably also significant that this hierarchy corresponds to the default precedence (left–right) order of arguments in English, for example, various scope and binding relationships that satisfy both precedence and F-command sound better than those that satisfy either alone.[26]

Without using Wrap, that is if verbs were always combined with their arguments by linear concatenation, then direct objects would consistently fail to obey any of the generalizations about grammatical function in (i)–(iii) that are determined by the argument hierarchy, for example in *Mary gave a book to John, a book* would necessarily be an oblique object, not a direct object (thus not predicted to behave grammatically in a way parallel to *a book* in *Mary read a book*). NB there is no way to redefine things so as to "reverse" parts of these associations yet still preserve the rest at the same time. (Note renaming the penultimate NP argument "Oblique Object" and the ante-penultimate "Direct Object" does no good, because it is the grammatical behavior that follows from being the penultimate NP that matters, not the label you give to this position, nor does simply altering the compositional semantics help.) Thus the explanatory power of the categorial account of argument structure with respect to many syntactic phenomena would almost entirely collapse without Wrap.

Quite aside from English, considerable cross-linguistic motivation for Wrap as a mode of combination comes from "Wackernagel" phenomena, cases in which a certain morpheme or syntactic unit is required to occupy "second position", where "second position" may be determined at the word, morpheme, or phoneme level (Hoeksema and Janda 1988). A recent proposal that includes Wrap within a parameterized universal theory of word order is found in Kruijff (2001) for a combinatory categorial grammar framework.[27]

[25] Relational Grammar (Perlmutter and Postal 1984) had limited and rather short-lived success as a syntactic theory, no doubt because it never developed appealing accounts of any aspects of syntax other than grammatical-function-related phenomena, but the very extensive and cross-linguistic generalizations about the phenomena it did treat have not been realized in any other theory besides CG.

[26] I should point out that I am assuming that the grammatical direct object in *Mary gave John a book* is *John*, not *a book* (in accord with the (final stratum) Relational Grammar analysis). See Dowty (1982) for discussion.

[27] Admittedly, not all researchers in categorial and TLG have explicitly endorsed Wrap; the main reason for this, I believe, is that those researchers have not viewed this set of descriptive linguistic

2.5.3 *Tectogrammatics vs. Phenogrammatics*

As soon as the possibility of non-concatenative syntactic operations is raised, a useful way of viewing the relationship between syntax and semantics for the purposes of studying compositional interpretation is to draw H. B. Curry's distinction between TECTOGRAMMATICS and PHENOGRAMMATICS (Curry 1963), as advocated in Dowty ([1992] 1996). In Curry's words, "tectogrammatics bears the same relation to phenogrammatics as morphology bears to morphophonemics"; tectogrammatics refers to the hierarchical sequence of syntactic steps by which a phrase or sentence is constructed syntactically from its parts. Phenogrammatics refers to the way in which the tectogrammatical assembly of a sentence is *linguistically manifested*, which involves the order of words (and alternative word order possibilities), inflectional morphology (both agreement and government), prosodic indications of structure, and possibly (or possibly not) sensitivity to constituent groupings as traditionally understood: most linguistic motivations for constituent structure will fall out of the possibilities of tectogrammatical assembly that a grammar offers; Dowty (1996) argues that the hierarchical constituent structure that can be motivated at the phenogrammatical level is actually fairly limited in English.

Curry's distinction corresponds exactly to Montague's distinction between SYNTACTIC RULES and SYNTACTIC OPERATIONS (Montague 1970: 375): a syntactic rule specifies the category or categories of the input(s) for the rule and the category of the output: syntactic rules determine what category (or sequences of categories) of inputs can combine to produce what categories of output, and thus determine the tectogrammatical structure of a sentence. Each syntactic rule is indexed to a unique syntactic operation: the syntactic operations specify what actual linguistic form (morphosyntactic form and word order) the outputs of the syntactic rule take—the phenogrammatical structure of the output.

Note that compositional interpretation is determined by the steps and syntactic rules are used to build up a sentence from the words in it, but it does not depend in any way on exactly what these operations actually do.[28] In other words, the tectogrammatical structure (plus of course the word meanings) is all that is relevant to compositional semantics; phenogrammatical manifestation is not relevant.

problems in syntax as central to their theoretical goals, and/or have not yet examined linguistic data in these areas closely.

[28] Montague first defined interpretation as a homomorphism on the algebra of syntactic operations, but then the results of operations are filtered by syntactic rules (to select those operation results that are appropriately assigned to syntactic categories); nowhere does the linguistic realization of individual syntactic operations directly affect compositional interpretation.

The analytic strategy implicitly intended by Curry and Montague is then as follows: it is assumed at the onset that compositional semantics is based on the tectogrammatical derivation using a (more or less) context-free semantic interpretation, so our task as linguists is to compare the linguistic form of the language data we empirically observe, and the meanings we likewise observe that the sentences in our data have, then we infer (simultaneously) (i) what tectogrammatical steps can be hypothesized to compute these meanings from their various parts, and (ii) what phenogrammatical operations would be needed to produce the observed linguistic forms for each step of the tectogrammatical derivation.

It is probably unlikely that there will be any motivation for treating tectogrammatical rules as non-context-free. What expressions can combine with what other expressions (ignoring what fashion they might combine in) depends only on the syntactic categories that some syntactic rule or other takes as inputs, not on what categories these have been assembled from previously. Given that word order and constituent order must be specified in phenogrammatical operations in any event, there may not even be reason to include linear precedence in tectogrammatical structure (unless you think you really have to use a directional rather than a non-directional CG for your logic of syntax).

On this view, the proper construal of the "levels", or components, of language structure are (i) semantics, that is the semantic units and semantic operations that can be assembled compositionally (but not details of lexical semantics that are not compositionally relevant); (ii) tectogrammatical structure, which defines the "interface" between syntax and compositional semantics; and (iii) morphosyntax (phenogrammatics), including (linear or partial) word order, inflectional morphology, and prosody.

2.5.3.1 *Phenogrammatics and Compositional Transparency* The complication in Montague's and Curry's strategy is that we do not really want to take it for granted at the onset that natural language compositional semantics is entirely context-free. Yet just how context-free our compositional analysis can be will depend on (among other things) just how context-free our phenogrammatical syntactic analysis is, and *vice versa*. How to address the dilemma? Since we know that a substantial portion of phenogrammatical syntax (of English and similar languages) is context-free, but almost certainly not all of it, and that natural language semantics is mostly context-free, but perhaps not all of it, an obvious strategy for now is to proceed bilaterally with context-free analyses as far as possible and, where that fails, look for the best-motivated combination of (near-)context-free syntax and (near-)context-free semantics. But this strategy will break down when we venture beyond languages like English, which are rigid in word order but poor in inflection, to those that are relatively free in word order and instead make use of a rich system of inflectional morphology to signal much of what English does with word order. Surely that kind of language too is compositionally transparent for its speakers.

Ultimately, the question of the optimal ways that phenogrammatical syntax can encode tectogrammatical structure is one for psycholinguistics: what ways of manifesting tectogrammatical structure are efficient for the human cognitive parsing apparatus? (It may be interesting, however, to approach the study of parsing from the point of view of pheno- vs. tectogrammatical structure: note that from this perspective, all the human parser really needs to do is discern the correct tectogrammatical structure, and this may not necessarily require analyzing all the phenogrammatical details that linguists have traditionally assumed must be parsed. For example, when morphological agreement and word order carry "redundant" information, then detecting one but not the other may suffice to recover the tectogrammatical structure. Which reminds us, conversely, that redundancy is one way of increasing transparency that evidently makes the trade-off in decreased syntactic economy worthwhile in a natural language.) Understanding compositional transparency is thus a long-term goal, but hopefully one we can make headway on with the tools we have at hand.

2.6 CF-Compositionality in Local Cases: Argument Accessibility

A very interesting way to see the implications that context-free compositionality can have in "local" syntactic analyses (cases not involving unbounded phenomena) is in the problem of ARGUMENT ACCESSIBILITY: which arguments of a verb are semantically "accessible" to the meanings of various kinds of adverbial modifiers? In particular, it is valuable to examine these implications under the most conservative possible assumptions as to what structure meanings have and under the assumption that semantics is context-free.

Whatever structure propositions actually need to have for other reasons, suppose for now we restrict ourselves to compositional semantics operations that cannot access the internal structures of propositions. If individuals are the only other type we can construct meanings from, we will have these possibilities for properties, relations, and meanings of adjuncts:

1. Let p be the (primitive) type of propositions and e the type of individuals.
2. Properties (of individuals) will be functions from individuals to propositions. (type $\langle e,p \rangle$)

3. Two-place relations between individuals will be functions from individuals to properties ("Curried" binary relations). (type $\langle e,\langle e,p\rangle\rangle$)
4. Three-place relations will be functions from individuals to two-place relations. Etc.
5. Sentential adjuncts will denote functions from propositions to propositions. (type $\langle p,p\rangle$)
6. VP adjuncts (modifiers of properties) denote functions from properties to properties). (type $\langle\langle e,p\rangle, \langle e,p\rangle\rangle$)
7. Adjuncts to TVs would therefore be functions from two-place relations to two-place relations. (type $\langle\langle e,\langle e,p\rangle\rangle, \langle e,\langle e,p\rangle\rangle\rangle$) (Etc.)

2.6.1 *Sentential vs. Subject-Oriented Adjuncts*

Since the components of the proposition formed when subject and predicate have combined are not thereafter separately accessible to context-free compositional interpretation, it follows that an adverb classified as a sentential adjunct can generate no entailments specific to the subject or object arguments of the sentence (or anything else "inside" it for that matter). Thus if *possibly* is such an adverb, then in (7)

(7) Possibly, John is sitting on Mary's left.

possibly cannot tell us anything about John specifically, beyond what is already entailed by the proposition expressed in *John is sitting on Mary's left*. In fact this is appropriate: *possibly* tells us only about the kind of "truth" its proposition has (viz., that it is not definitely true but has some relationship to truth in the actual world). The same is true for adverbs *definitely*, *clearly*, *perhaps*, *obviously*, etc.

What does that rule out? A large class of adverbs, sometimes called *subject-oriented* or *passive-sensitive* adverbs, do have argument-specific entailments, as first noted by Jackendoff (see Ernst (2003) for references and discussion). These include *inadvertently*, *(un)willingly*, *consciously*, *maliciously*, *(un)knowingly*, *shyly*, *nervously*, etc. For example, (8) entails something about John's intention with respect to an action or state:

(8) John is willingly sitting on Mary's left.

This can be seen from the fact that (making the assumption that both Mary and John are seated and are facing the same direction), (9) is not equivalent to (8), even though (10*a*) is equivalent to (10*b*):

(9) Mary is willingly sitting on John's right.

(10) (*a*) John is sitting on Mary's left.

(*b*) Mary is sitting on John's right.

The contrast with the sentential adverb is that no such difference is found in the pair in (11):

(11) (*a*) John is possibly sitting on Mary's left.

(*b*) Mary is possibly sitting on John's right.

Parallel to this is the observation that (12*b*) has a prominent reading not found in (12*a*), despite the synonymy of their host sentences when the adverb is removed, cf. (13).[29] Here again, we find synonymy with sentence adverbs, (14*a*) and (14*b*).

(12) (*a*) The doctor willingly examined John.

(*b*) John was willingly examined by the doctor.

(13) (*a*) The doctor examined John.

(*b*) John was examined by the doctor.

(14) (*a*) Possibly, the doctor examined John. / The doctor possibly examined John.

(*b*) Possibly, John was examined by the doctor. / John was possibly examined by the doctor.

[29] In evaluating this claim, it is important to pay close attention to some differences in the lexical semantics of certain adverbs. Although the adverbs *deliberately* and *intentionally* are often used to illustrate the paradigm of (8)–(12), these two permit, for certain speakers, what is called FREE or PRAGMATIC control, others require true SYNTACTIC CONTROL. In the latter case, the "controller" (person to whom an intention and/or emotion is ascribed) must be denoted by an NP in a specific syntactic configuration, while in the former, this identity is actually inferred from the overall context of utterance, even though in many cases this may happen to be a person denoted by the NP in the same syntactic configuration. That *intentionally* is of the former type for some English speakers is demonstrated by this not infrequently attested sentence:

(i) This page is intentionally blank.

That is, it is understood to have been the intention of some unmentioned but relevant person that the page be blank, not the intention of the page itself. (Schmerling (1978) suggested other examples like this one.) But if that contextual source of interpretation is possible for (i), then doubt arises as to what we can really conclude from *John is intentionally sitting on Mary's left*, etc. (To be sure, some other English speakers find (i) a distinctly abnormal sentence.) Be that as it may, there are plenty of other adverbs that do not allow pragmatic control; while adverbs of intention (*intentionally, deliberately*) seem to be most susceptible to pragmatic control, adverbs attributing a cognitive or emotional state do not. Thus, there is a difference in the readings available for (ii) vs. (iii), yet pragmatic control seems impossible, even in a sentence where that kind of reading would be prima facie plausible, (iv):

(ii) The police cheerfully arrested the demonstrators. *(police are cheerful)*

(iii) The demonstrators were cheerfully arrested by the police. *(either police or demonstrators cheerful)*

(iv) #I'm in a great mood: the final version of my paper is now cheerfully in the hands of the editor.

Similar example sets can be constructed with adverbs entailing emotion or thought but which, NB, can sensibly be attributed to either the Patient or the Agent of certain types of actions: *shyly, guiltily, (un)willingly, nervously, self-consciously, sheepishly*.

If subject-oriented adverbs are treated as VP adjuncts, then their meanings are functions from properties to new properties, where the property is the one denoted by VP. That is, *willingly* is a function that maps a property (such as the property of performing an action) into the new property of willingly having that property (willingly performing that action). Because of the lexical semantics of *willingly*, this amounts to doing that action plus having a willing attitude toward doing that action. The important point is that this modification is done *before* the property is ascribed to a particular individual. Since the property of willingly sitting on Mary's left implies willingness on John's part but not Mary's, it follows that (8) should be different in meaning from (9).

Viewed a different way—and the way relevant to the point being made here—from the fact that (12*a*, 12*b*) have the meaning difference they do, it follows from context-free semantics that this adverb *must* be a VP adjunct, not a sentential adjunct.

Notice that this reasoning does not depend in any way on what properties and propositions actually are except for the assumption that properties are things that combine with individuals to form propositions (and the context-free assumption that once you have the proposition you cannot recover the individual and property).

(Sentential adverbs in English can also occur sentence finally, thus should also belong to *S\S* in a categorial analysis; if you are familiar with CG, you might notice that the so-called *Geach rule* (or *Division*) would make any adverb in category *S\S* also belong to category *VP\VP* (and by a second application of the same rule, it would belong to *TV\TV* as well).[30] This does not, however, alter the semantic facts just discussed. As you can confirm by working out the lambda-calculus derivations, an adverb like *possibly* (etc.) syntactically converted to *VP\VP* cannot yield any entailments about its subject argument specifically, any more than the corresponding original adverb in *S\S* can, but gives only meanings exactly equivalent to those possible with the *S\S* adverb. This is an instance of the principle that in the pure Lambek Calculus (or in a CCG which amplifies applicative CG only with Type-Lifting, Functional Composition, and Geach rules), use of such category-shift rules cannot lead to kinds of semantic interpretations that could not be produced without these rules. Semantically distinctive VP-adverbs like *willingly* differ as a consequence of their *lexical* semantics from anything expressible with an *S\S* adverb.

[30] This is a fortunate result, incidentally, in that it allows sentence adverbs to occur in *VP* complements (as in *Mary wanted to leave tomorrow*), even though we don't derive such complements syntactically from full sentences.

2.6.1.1 *Object-Oriented Adjuncts* There are also adjuncts that have entailments involving the direct object argument:

(15) (*a*) Mary ate the meat raw.

(*b*) John hired Mary to fix the sink.

(*c*) Mary bought a book to read ____ to the children.

(*d*) John threw the letter into the wastebasket.

(That is, on the readings relevant here, it's the meat that is raw, not Mary; it's Mary who is to fix the sink, not John personally; the book gets read to the children; and it's the letter that goes into the wastebasket.)

2.6.2 *Object Argument Accessibility and TV\TV Adjuncts*

Under the categorial account of argument structure and the assumption of context-free semantics, direct-object arguments are not completely "inaccessible" to adjuncts semantically but rather are accessible only to a particular kind of adjunct, to TRANSITIVE-VERB ADJUNCTS: in categorial terms, these have category *TV\TV*. Just as a VP meaning must differ from a sentence meaning, under the argument structure theory explained in §2.5.2.1, in that the VP meaning is a property (a function from individuals to propositions—recall that VP abbreviates *np\s*), so a TV meaning will be a function from individuals to properties (TV abbreviates *vp/np*, which is (*np\s*)/*np*). A ditransitive meaning will be a function from individuals to a transitive verb meaning, and so on (if there are verbs having more than three arguments).

From the point of view of semantics, this might seem equivalent to treating a TV meaning as a function from an ordered pair of individuals to a proposition (i.e. a two-place relation). This is not quite the case, however: a relevant important difference here is that CG and the Curried argument theory predicts the possibility of a syntactic distinction between *VP-modifiers*, which would have category *vp\vp*, and *TV-modifiers*, in category *TV\TV* (alternatively written, (*vp/np*)\(*vp/np*)). Note, though, that if Wrapping is the operation always used to combine any phrasal transitive verb with its object argument, then the word order of a VP containing a *TV\TV* adjunct would be the same as a VP containing a *VP\VP* adjunct: see examples (16*a*), (16*b*).

Under the assumptions of context-free semantics and Curried argument structure, adjuncts combining with a category *A* have more possibilities for semantic interaction with the head (more "argument accessibility") the more unsaturated arguments that category *A* has: just as a *VP* adjunct has accessibility to the subject *NP* that an *S* adjunct does not, so a *TV\TV* has accessibility to the object argument, but a *VP**VP* does not, etc. For example, if *raw* is a transitive modifier, it applies to the *eat* relation to produce the *eat raw* relation: given an appropriate semantics for the adjunct, to “eat raw” could mean to eat (a thing) when (that thing) is in a raw state, that is its meaning can ascribe some property to the direct object argument. But if *eat* were first combined with *the meat*, it would denote the property of eating the meat; then no adjunct combining with this VP could result in a property that entails anything about the meat, because to do that would require looking back to see what the earlier derivation of the meat-eater property had been. (It is important to realize that this pattern in argument accessibility holds not because categorial grammarians have decided that their theory of argument accessibility should be set up this way but rather follows *solely* from the CG argument-structure theory and from assuming context-free semantics.

To use for illustration VP-final adjectival adjuncts (which sometimes go under the confusing name *depictive adjuncts*)[31] the object-modifying derivation of *Mary ate the meat raw* proceeds as in (16*a*); here tv_W abbreviates $vp/_W np$, the slash labeled “$/_W$” indicates the wrapping mode of combination, so that the actual word order produced by this derivation is *Mary ate the meat raw* (this derivation does not show phenogrammatics explicitly). And for comparison, the subject-modifying *VP*-adjunct example *Mary left the room alone* is derived in (16*b*).

(16) (*a*)

$$\dfrac{\dfrac{\text{John}}{np} \qquad \dfrac{\dfrac{\dfrac{\text{ate}}{tv_W} \quad \dfrac{\text{raw}}{tv_W\backslash tv_W}}{tv_W} \qquad \dfrac{\text{the meat}}{np}}{vp}}{s}$$

(*b*)

$$\dfrac{\dfrac{\text{Mary}}{np} \qquad \dfrac{\dfrac{\dfrac{\text{left}}{tv_W} \quad \dfrac{\text{the room}}{np}}{vp} \qquad \dfrac{\text{alone}}{vp\backslash vp}}{vp}}{s}$$

Since the categories of the two adjuncts must be different, it is predicted that they could differ in syntactic properties in one way or another. In fact, one difference is that the subject-modifying (VP\VP) adjunct can be preposed while the object-modifying adjunct (TV\TV) cannot:

(17) (*a*) Alone, Mary ate the meat.

(*b*) *Raw, John ate the meat.

(i.e., * *on the reading where the meat is raw)*

[31] “Confusingly,” because why should *dissatisfied* “depict” dissatisfaction in *A customer left dissatisfied* but not depict dissatisfaction in *A customer was dissatisfied* or *A dissatisfied customer left*?

In this case, context-free argument accessibility does not, by itself, predict that preposability should be one of the syntactic properties that differentiates the two types. But in other cases, the nature of a syntactic difference is specifically predicted. One of these is a difference in the possibility of combining with VP ellipsis:

(18) (*a*) Usually, John eats lunch with a friend but Mary usually eats lunch alone.

(*b*) Usually, John eats lunch with a friend, but Mary usually does so alone.

(19) (*a*) John ate the meat raw and Mary ate the meat cooked.

(*b*) *John ate the meat raw and Mary did so cooked.

(20) (*a*) John spotted the swimmers nude, and Mary spotted them fully clothed. *(ambiguous: adjunct modifies subject or object)*

(*b*) John spotted the swimmers nude, and Mary did so fully clothed. *(unambiguous: adjunct modifies subject only)*

The reason for this prediction, which is obscured by the discontinuous word order, is this:

(21) **Argument Accessibility and Ellipsis/Anaphora:** A head of category *A/B* can combine with an adjunct of category (*A/B*)\(*A/B*) before combining with its argument *B*, and/or can combine with an adjunct of category *A**A* after it combines with its argument *B*.

But if the head and its argument are replaced by an anaphoric form of category *A*, then the (*A/B*)\(*A/B*) adjunct is no longer possible—there is no *A/B* to modify separately. An *A**A* adjunct is still possible, however.

If, as is generally assumed, English *do so* and post-auxiliary VP ellipsis are anaphoric substitutes for category *VP*[32] but not for category *TV*, then all the data in (18)–(20) follow immediately.

2.6.3 *Object-Modifying Purpose Infinitive Adjuncts*

Metcalf (2005) observes that an object-modifying adjunct cannot occur with *do so*, although a subject-modifying rationale clause can:

(22) (*a*) John took a day off from work to fix the sink, and Bill did so to paint the roof. *(similarly with "... in order to fix the sink")*

[32] Although there is some dispute whether this traditional claim holds uniformly (Miller 1992), it clearly holds for the majority of cases. See however note 33 below.

(*b*) *John hired Mary to fix the sink, and Bill did so to unstop the bathtub. *(i.e., * on reading where Mary herself is to fix the sink)*

2.6.4 *Object-Modifying Directional Adjuncts*

The familiar pattern below is predicted by the accessibility-and-ellipsis principle—because (23*a*) means that the water goes into the sink, not that George does:[33]

(23) (*a*) Haj poured water into the bathtub before George could pour water into the sink.

(*b*) *Haj poured water into the bathtub before George could do so into the sink.

By contrast, the directional PP adjunct in (24) has a subject entailment, not an object entailment: it is you that changes location from here to the airport or bus station, not the subway per se. Thus by the reasoning above, the PP should be a *VP\VP* (Bach 1980; Dowty 1982), hence (24) ought to be better than (23*b*):

(24) At rush hour, you can take the subway from here to the airport faster than you can from here to the bus station.

2.6.5 *A Different Ellipsis/Anaphor Contrast: Sentential* (Believe so) *vs. VP Ellipsis*

CF-semantics predicts the same kind of distinction with "ellipsis" anaphora as between transitive vs. intransitive adjuncts. If *so* is an anaphoric replacement for a sentence (as in *I believe so*), it should be able to co-occur with a sentential adverb but not a VP adverb, which does seem to be the case:[34]

(25) (*a*) Mary didn't commit a crime, though John believes that that was possibly so (was possibly the case).

(*b*) *Mary didn't commit a crime deliberately, though John believes that this was inadvertently so (was inadvertently the case).

[33] The situation with directionals is actually more complicated than this, since directional adjuncts to intransitives also do not occur with *do so* ellipsis: **John ran to the park before Mary could (do so) to the station*; this is NB an exception to the pattern of all other data in this section. Although space does not permit me to discuss it, there is evidence that directional PPs are syntactically complements, even though their semantics seems quite consistent with an adjunct analysis.

[34] This assumes that the word order *Inadvertently, Mary committed a crime* is in principle possible, although speakers vary in how natural they find this word order.

2.6.6 *Argument Reduction and Adjuncts*

Another prediction is made that is parallel to the one involving ellipsis:

(26) **Argument Reduction and Adjuncts:** If a verb of some category *A/B* can undergo a lexical rule of argument reduction (argument suppression) giving it category *A* (e.g. detransitivizing a transitive verb) then the complementless verb in *A* will no longer permit adjuncts of category (*A/B*)\(*A/B*) that it could have combined with in its original category *A/B*.

It can however combine with an adjunct of category *A**A*.

For example, when *eat* and *drink* are detransitivized (27*a*, 27*b*), then they can no longer occur with object-modifying adjuncts (27*c*, 27*d*) (although they still can with subject-modifying adjuncts (27*e*, 27*f*)), not even with null-complement anaphora (28). The same prediction is made about purpose infinitive adjuncts (29).

(27)	(*a*)	Mary has eaten lunch.	Mary has eaten
	(*b*)	John drinks beer a lot	John drinks a lot
	(*c*)	Mary ate it raw	*Mary ate raw
	(*d*)	John drinks beer cold	*John drinks cold.
	(*e*)	Mary ate lunch alone	Mary ate alone
	(*f*)	John drinks beer to forget his sorrows.	John drinks to forget his sorrows.

(28) (*a*) Mary came in without John, and no one noticed. (= "noticed Mary")

(*b*) Mary entered without John, and no one noticed her unaccompanied.

(*c*) * Mary entered without John, and no one noticed unaccompanied. *(*on reading where it was Mary who was unaccompanied)*

(29) (*a*) The waiter served the customers hors d'oeuvres.

(*b*) The waiter served the customers.

(*c*) The waiter served the customers hors d'oeuvres to munch on while waiting for dinner.

(*d*) * The waiter served the customers to munch on while waiting for dinner.

2.6.7 *Argument Access in Objects vs. Obliques*

A further consequence of the CG "curried" account of argument structure together with context-free semantics is that any adjuncts with entailments about an oblique object would have to be of a different category both from subject-modifying *and* object-modifying adjuncts. (For reasons noted above, a syntactic Geach type-raising from TV\TV to (TV/NP)\(TV/NP) would preserve the direct-object-modifying entailments, so only a lexical (TV/NP)\(TV/NP) would be able to access the oblique object semantically.) If English does have any adjuncts with entailments about oblique objects, it is predicted that some differences could exist between them and TV\TV adjuncts, parallel to those discussed above for other kinds of adjuncts. As this kind of prediction does not seem to be made in other syntactic and compositional theories, a contrast of this kind would be striking evidence supporting these assumptions. Unfortunately, few test cases seem to exist in English, and judgments about the data in these cases are cloudy. Although on the whole I believe they slightly support the predictions made, space precludes a discussion here. But my primary goal in this chapter is methodological; in this case, it is to point out what kind of potentially testable predictions are made by the Curried argument structure theory under context-free semantics, not to try to argue at this point that these predictions are correct in all cases.

2.6.8 *Semantic "Explanation" of Syntactic Facts*

By now, if not sooner, you can expect to hear the response "Oh, but there is independent evidence that subject-modifying VP adjectival adjuncts (rationale infinitives, etc.) are constituents of a (higher) *VP*, while object-modifying adjectival adjuncts, etc. are constituents of the same *VP* (or *V*-bar) as the head verb, and this structure difference would account for the differences in preposability (17), ellipsis possibilities (20), and possibly more of this data as well."

This may well be the case, but it misses the main point I want to make here, which is that not only these data but the existence of the structural difference itself (and therefore of any observed evidence for it) is already predicted to exist by the *semantic* difference between subject and object modification, under the two hypotheses under discussion. If we accept the relevance of compositional transparency and syntactic economy, that prediction is worth paying attention to. It might strike some syntacticians as odd or unprecedented to think of explanations of syntactic facts coming from this source, but this is an illustration of the view of language syntax and semantics I am suggesting: that we *should* expect the necessity of expressing certain compositional semantic relationships to influence the form syntax takes—at least as often as the possibility of some but not other syntactic structures influences the way compositional semantics must work. (You might want to reflect on the possibility that once a child learning English has understood that *Mary ate the meat raw* is about the meat being raw, rather than Mary, the child might, from that (rather noticeable) fact alone, analyze the adjunct as having a different syntactic structure from *Mary ate the meat alone*.)

However, a further reason not to dismiss the pattern of differences between subject-oriented and object-oriented adjuncts as merely a purely syntactic difference in structure is the possibility that the same pattern can be observed in a domain where no parallel constituent-structure differences (of the traditional kind) have been proposed on syntactic grounds (or perhaps, would even seem plausible): this is the topic of the next section.

2.6.9 *Accessibility Beyond Adjuncts: Subject-Controlled vs. Object-Controlled Infinitive Complements*

There is a categorial analysis of subject-controlled complements (*promise*) vs. object-controlled complements (*persuade*) which originated with Rich Thomason and Barbara Partee in the early 1970s and was first thoroughly explored by Bach (1979, 1980). According to this, *persuade* has category *(VP/NP)/INF* while *promise* has category *(VP/INF)/NP* (INF = infinitive VP complement). The assumption was made that Wrap combines a direct object NP with a phrasal TV: so for example TV *persuade to leave* is combined with NP *Mary* so as to produce the word order *persuade Mary to leave*. This is linearly parallel to *promise Mary to leave* but tectogrammatically different. Here, "$/_w$" indicates that wrapping rather than concatenation is the syntactic operation to be used.

(30) 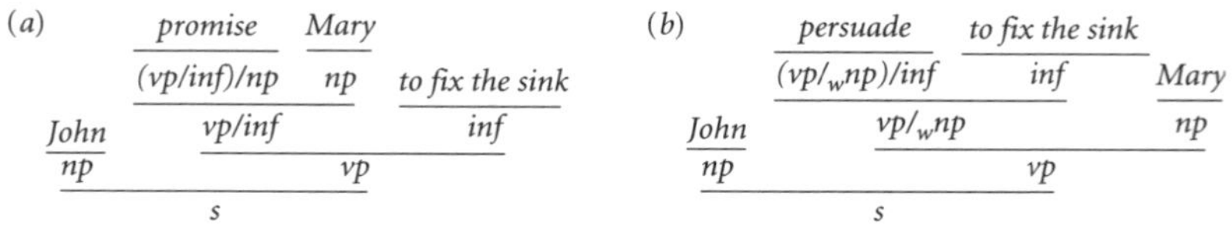

This structural difference was supposed to predict the facts that (i) the INF complement is controlled by the object NP in the case of *persuade*, but by the subject NP in the case of *promise*; (ii) passives are possible with the object-controlled case but not with the subject-controlled—*John was persuaded to leave by Mary* vs. * *John was promised to leave by Mary*, the observation known as VISSER'S GENERALIZATION; and (iii) differences in the results of traditional syntactic diagnostics for constituent structure such as pseudoclefts, right-node-raising, right-node-raising out of coordinations, and questions (Bach 1979: 523–4), not just with the infinitive-complement *persuade* vs. *promise* but also parallel differences in other complement types, such as *regard NP as Adj*, in *(VP/NP) AdjP*, vs. *strike NP as Adj*, in *(VP/AdjP)/NP*.

The absence of passives follows from the category difference under Bach's view of passive—passive is a syntactic (not lexical) rule which applies to the category TV to convert it to (intransitive) VP and adds passive morphology, even when the TV is phrasal rather than a single lexical verb. Thus *persuade to leave* in TVP becomes *be persuaded to leave*.

A further observed generalization is that (iv) subject-control verbs can sometimes be detransitivized while retaining the infinitive complement (*Mary promised John to leave* vs. *Mary promised to leave*), but object-control verbs never can (**Mary persuaded to leave*); this last principle has been called "Bach's generalization".

However, critics pointed out that under the lexical account of control of subjectless infinitive complements that Bach assumed, it is just as possible to associate subject control with the category *(VP/NP)/INF* as with *(VP/INF)/NP*, since complement "control" in that account is just a matter of specifying the lexical semantics of the controlling verbs appropriately. (Note infinitives are not derived from sentences with a PRO or other subject in his framework.) Thus, appealing to control to motivate the category difference (which in turn would block passives for *promise*) is ad hoc. Moreover, "Bach's generalization" does not follow from anything in Bach's analysis.

There is, however, a hypothesis under which *all* of these observations follow from the argument-accessibility constraints imposed by context-free semantics. It is well known that there are many cases where characteristics of adjuncts and characteristics of complements are both exhibited by the same constructions, confounding the attempt to categorize the constructions as definitely one or the other in a motivated way. Dowty (2003) argues that this is best explained by the hypothesis that a constituent can have a "dual analysis", as both adjunct and complement. A possible interpretation of "dual analysis" (not the only one) is that what starts out as an adjunct is in one or more senses "reanalyzed" as a complement. Space does not permit the hypothesis to be explained in full here, nor the kinds of motivations that can be given for it, so Dowty (2003) must be consulted for the justification of this view. The general pattern is that the basic and visible syntactic properties in such cases (word order, internal constituency, agreement, and government), as well as a loose approximation of the semantics, are those normally found in adjunct constructions, while limits on distribution dependent on choice of head verb (i.e. its exact subcategorization frame) and the "fine-grained" semantics are those of complements.

Infinitive complements such as those under discussion fit well into this account. While they do qualify as complements, without any doubt, they have conspicuous properties of adjuncts: in internal syntax and in word order, for example, they exactly parallel adjuncts such as purpose infinitives. Also, their semantics is actually rather similar to purpose infinitives: both kinds of infinitives report a possible future event, intended or desired by the agent, which might take place as a consequence of the action denoted by the main verb. But with the infinitive complements, each complement-taking verb entails a more specific semantic relation between action and potential result.

What would follow from the assumption that the infinitives with *promise* and *persuade* were adjuncts? The adjunct with *promise* need only be a *VP\VP*,[35] since it has entailments only about the subject argument (who is to carry out the action denoted in the adjunct), but argument accessibility requires the adjunct occurring with *persuade* to be a *TV\TV* adjunct because of its entailments about the object NP (the person to carry out the action in this case). The adjunct analyses would be these:

(31) (*a*)
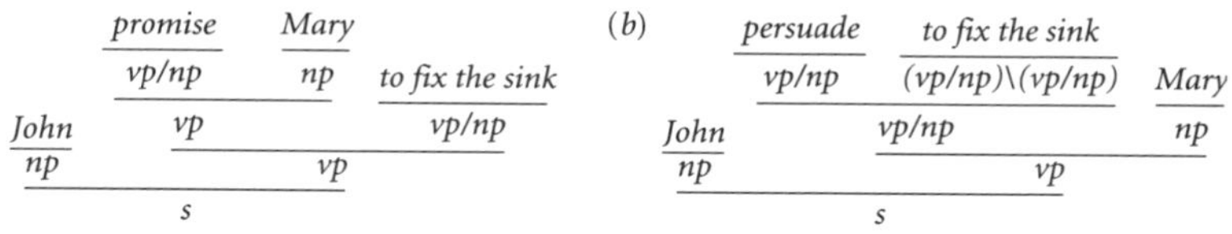
promise
vp/np
Mary
np
to fix the sink
John
np
vp
vp/np
vp
s
(b)
persuade
vp/np
to fix the sink
(vp/np)\(vp/np)
Mary
np
John
np
vp/np
vp
s

All the predictions discussed earlier for adjuncts will follow from (31*a*) vs. (31*b*). If *persuade* were basically a simple transitive verb, then if detransitivized it could no longer combine with a *TV\TV* adjunct. Thus anomaly or ungrammaticality would arise in a sentence such as (*)*Mary persuaded to leave.*[36] On the other hand, detransitivizing a transitive should not at all affect the possibility of combining it with a *VP\VP* adjunct; under the hypothetical adjunct analysis for *promise*, you would expect (32*b*) to be grammatical:

(32) (*a*) Mary promised John to fix the sink.
(*b*) Mary promised to fix the sink.

[35] I am making the assumption that this hypothetical *promise* is a TV, as it is in *John promised Mary a book*; cf. *John promised a book to Mary*, and *A book was promised to Mary by John*.

[36] Unless, of course, *to leave* could be interpreted as subject-modifying, but that is at odds with the core lexical meaning of *persuade*.

In other words, principle (26), Argument Reduction and Adjuncts, predicts "Bach's Generalization".

Similarly, VP ellipsis should be possible with *promise* but not *persuade*. And though (33*a*, 33*b*) do not sound completely natural (to me), they definitely seem better than (34*a*, 34*b*):

(33) (*a*) ? John promised Mary to take her to the movies before Bill did to invite her for dinner.

(*b*) ? John is more likely to promise Mary to take her to the movies than Bill is to invite her for dinner.

(34) (*a*) *John persuaded Mary to go to the movies with him before Bill did to have dinner with him.

(*b*) *John is more likely to persuade Mary to go to the movies with him than Bill is to have dinner with him.

(I am not aware of any "purely syntactic" evidence for any syntactic distinction between *promise* and *persuade* that would predict these differences in VP ellipsis and detransitivization possibilities, in the way that a V-bar vs. VP distinction would for the earlier cases.)

Under the view of Passive as a rule applying to possibly phrasal TVs, passives should be possible with TVs containing TV adjuncts, and it would follow that the adjunct meaning would then be associated semantically with the "surface" subject. Indeed this is the case with all kinds of TV\TV adjuncts, including the hypothetical *persuade* adjunct:

(35) (*a*) The meat was eaten raw (by Mary).

(*b*) The paper was thrown into the wastebasket (by John).

(*c*) Mary was hired (by John) to fix the sink.

(*d*) John was persuaded (by Mary) to go to the party.

But what should happen to a *VP\VP* in a passive? Such an adjunct cannot be added *before* passivizing (because passive takes TV as input). If applied after passive, then it should be associated compositionally with the "surface subject" argument: that was the kind of reading we found (as the primary reading) for *willingly* in *John was willingly examined by the doctor*). In the same way, a compositionally derived adjunct reading of the infinitive with a hypothetical TV *promise*,

(36) (*)John was promised (by Mary) to leave.

could only mean that John's leaving was the event that he intended to result from letting himself be promised (something or other) by Mary.[37]

It should be noted here that the adjunct-to-complement "reanalysis" view entails that when these constructions acquire a complement analysis from the underlying adjunct analysis, the subject-controlled case will necessarily have the category *(NP/INF)/NP*, and the object-controlled case will necessarily have *(VP/NP)/INF*: they could not end up with the same syntactic category, nor with the reverse category associations.[38] And once this category assignment is imposed, then passives would be impossible with the category *(NP/INF)/NP* on strictly syntactic grounds, in exactly the way Bach originally proposed.

2.6.10 *Other Local Effects of Context-Free Argument Accessibility*

It should be stressed that the argument-accessibility predictions of context-free semantics considered here are only a small sample of the predictions that will eventually be made when a greater variety of syntactic constructions is examined from this perspective, and the results may look quite different elsewhere. Among cases that may be particularly challenging to understand on this view are complex predicate constructions and deverbal noun constructions like those found in Japanese, such as those treated by Kubota (2005) (already mentioned) where a number of compositional semantic phenomena are seemingly at odds with the apparent syntactic structure and are instead characteristic of the compositional semantics of a (non-existent) clause.

2.7 Compositionality in Non-Local Cases

Long-distance *wh*-binding, wide-scope NP-quantification and anaphoric binding present the greatest challenge for strictly context-free semantics. In this section, I will (i) raise the questions whether and when the tacticof "encoding" long-distance dependencies into context-free analysis is

[37] In discussing TV vs. VP adjuncts in the previous sections, I bypassed the question of what happens with $VP\backslash VP$ adjuncts under passive in various constructions. The answer is complicated and cannot be pursued here; it is made more difficult by the possibility of "free control" or "pragmatic control" of adjuncts expressing intensionality (as already discussed for *This page is intentionally blank* in footnote 29, such as the control of the purpose infinitive in the frequently cited example *The ship was sunk to collect the insurance.*

[38] This can perhaps be most easily appreciated by comparing the adjunct analyses in (31) with the complement analyses in (30) and noting that as complements, the infinitives are introduced at the same step in the derivation as they were as adjuncts, while the NP arguments have the same relative position in the derivation in both adjunct and complement versions. Under the categorial analysis of the adjunct-complement "shift", it involves what would appear to be type-raising of the lexical head to make the adjunct into a complement (but as Dowty (2003) emphasizes, this is not the same as ordinary type-raising but rather a derivation by lexical rule).

motivated, and (ii) use the perspective of compositional transparency to make general comparisons between free-variable-binding and combinatory analyses of anaphoric binding, then (iii) try to shed some light on combinatory analyses by looking at alternative ways to implement them.

2.7.1 *The Local-Encoding Escape Hatch*

In principle, it is always possible to "encode" non-local syntactic dependencies as strictly local ones, by extending the set of syntactic categories (perhaps by invoking additional syntactic features on categories) and reformulating the existing local rules. Consider the very simple PS grammar having the rules (37*a*); this produces, for example, (37*b*):

(37) (*a*)

$$\begin{array}{llll} A & \rightarrow & B & C \\ A & \rightarrow & D & C \\ C & \rightarrow & E & F \\ E & \rightarrow & G & H \\ E & \rightarrow & J & H \end{array}$$

(*b*)

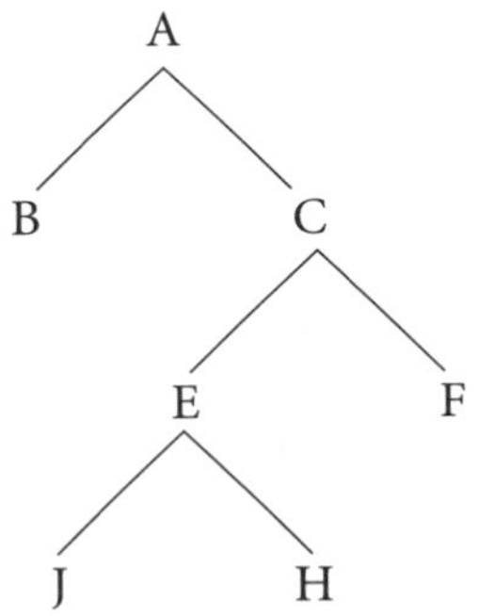

As the rules are context-free, whether E is expanded as G H or J H is independent of whether A is expanded as B C or D C. But suppose we decide we want G to be chosen at the lower node only if B is introduced at the higher, not when D is introduced there; doing this sounds like introducing a context-sensitive condition, say, by replacing the fourth rule with this one:

$$E \rightarrow G\ H/B\_\_\_$$

However, we could accomplish this dependency between *B* and *G* by introducing additional categories *C′* and *D′* and changing the rules to these:

(38)

$$\begin{array}{llll} A & \rightarrow & B & C' \\ A & \rightarrow & D & C \\ C & \rightarrow & E & F \\ C' & \rightarrow & E' & F \\ E' & \rightarrow & G & H \\ E & \rightarrow & J & H \end{array}$$

We can obviously extend this tactic to introduce dependences between nodes that are separated from each other at greater distances by duplicating each of the categories that can appear along the path between these two nodes; if that path includes an opportunity for recursion, unbounded dependencies are captured.

A well-known and precedent-setting use of this method in linguistic theory was the "slash-feature" of GPSG (Gazdar *et al.* 1985), in which the dependence between a *wh*-gap and a higher *wh*-trigger (e.g. a relative pronoun) was mediated by a path of "slash categories" through the intervening tree. The later HPSG theory (Pollard and Sag 1994) greatly extends this technique by taking syntactic categories to be elaborate feature structures, which can "percolate" multiple kinds of syntactic information through a path in a tree.

In compositional semantics, likewise, the possibility of locally "encoding" long-distance relationships presents itself—but again, note that it is meanings themselves we will be modifying to get variants of our original meanings, not merely *labels* or *categories* or other symbolic "markers" on meanings; we might instead speak of local *transmission* of long-distance dependencies. To impose upon Cooper Storage one more time as an example, it can be viewed as local encoding: we expand original meanings into complex objects that can include as a proper subpart a meaning that we want to "connect up" to something at some distance: each local semantic operation along the propagation path copies the stored sub-meanings into its output meaning.

It is not necessarily the case that local encoding is "cheating" in any way, or that context-free semantic compositionality is thereby violated. A local-encoding analysis can have observable independent linguistic motivation. To illustrate, you can view the famous "bagel sentence" example (39*a*) from the late 1960s as an abundantly clear instance of well-motivated "local encoding": a prima facie long-distance dependency can be said to exist between the highest subject NP *the bagel* and the most deeply embedded verb *eaten*, in light of the semantically parallel (39*b*):

(39) (*a*) The bagel was believed by Max to have been claimed by Sam to have been eaten by Seymour.

(*b*) Max believed Sam claimed Seymour ate the bagel.

As soon as you embrace the possibility of treating passivization not as an operation which moves around (or re-indexes) *NP*s but as an operation on verb meanings by themselves (affecting the way they interpret their arguments), the possibility exists of chaining together the effects of these verbal modifications and thereby accomplishing the long-distance "linkage" in (39*a*) semantically. Then, the obvious changes in verb morphology and syntax at each intermediate step in (39*a*) (as compared to the corresponding verbs in (39*b*)) are the best possible motivation for local encoding.

Possibly "local encoding" can be motivated in some way or other in less transparent cases. An example of such evidence in syntax is the Scandinavian extraction phenomenon discussed by Maling and Zaenen (1982), in which some words along the path between the *wh*-element and the extraction site have morphological marking specific to the *wh*-construction—that is, there is prima facie visible evidence that the syntactic categories along the extract path are in fact slightly distinct from the categories that would appear in the same kind of syntactic structure not on an extraction path. A long-distance movement analysis, or other analysis which linked the two sites in a way that did not involve any of the intervening structure, would not predict this kind of phenomenon, as Maling and Zaenen note. And, although they are not traditionally viewed that way, the phenomenon of extraction island constraints could also be seen as evidence that the nature of the syntactic structure that intervenes in a long-distance dependency affects its behavior, and thus that local encoding is motivated for it.

Therefore, our theoretical goal should perhaps be to try to characterize *when* local encoding is the right way to go, when it is wrong, and under what conditions a locally-encoded analysis and a direct long-distance analysis should be considered equivalent for all relevant theoretical purposes. What kind of argument should count for/against local encoding?

2.8 Non-Local Cases: Bound Anaphora

2.8.1 *Combinatory vs. Variable-Binding Theories*

There are two fundamentally different approaches to the semantics of bound anaphora: one is inherited from variable binding in first-order logic, which I will term the *promiscuous free variable binding* approach; the other is a *combinatory* approach, which comes in several variants, of which Jacobson's (1999) is one.[39]

In characterizing these approaches below, I take pains to try to isolate consequences that follow solely from the essential compositional *semantic* strategy of each method and to distinguish these from features that are traditionally associated with the analysis but not really entailed by the semantics. Observing

[39] Unfortunately, space does not permit me to include discussion of the continuations analysis of bound anaphora of Shan and Barker (2005). Also, it is not clear to me whether it is best viewed as intermediate between the two approaches or as a third type. At present, I think I can make a more meaningful comparison of the other two types of analysis, which are older and better understood.

this distinction is vital for assessing the semantic structural economy and the predictions made about compositional transparency (or lack thereof) by each of the two types of analysis.

2.8.1.1 *Promiscuous Free Variable Binding* Free-variable analyses all derive from the basic notions of variable, quantifier, and variable binding from first-order predicate logic, so they inherit these properties from them, unless and until specific additional features are added in the linguistic analysis in question which override these properties.

- Because individual variables have the same syntactic distribution as individual constants (names) and have the same logical type of denotations (individuals), they will belong to the same syntactic category as individual constants (i.e. putting them in a different category would be a complication not motivated by semantics or logical syntax).
- The syntactic step of combining a quantifier (of the first-order-logic variety) with a formula is completely independent, in logical syntax, of the syntactic introduction variables; no syntactic dependency at all exists between the two.[40] Consequently, a quantifier may turn out to bind one variable, many variables, or no variables. In this sense, logical free variable binding is "promiscuous".
- The binding of logical variables is a sentence-level operation in logical syntax, as required by the Tarski semantics (and/or by the proof theory) of first-order logic (but see also footnote 47 below).
- Because logical quantifiers work semantically like sentence operators, while natural languages (of the English type) manifest quantification in NPs, some syntactic or interpretive mechanism must be provided for resolving this syntactic/semantic discrepancy (such as Quantifying-In, Quantifier-Raising/Lowering, Storage, etc.).
- A frequently suggested way to incorporate the interpretation of discourse/deictic pronouns (and probably the simplest way) is to let variable assignments do double duty as context parameters (like time, place, etc. of utterance), i.e. free it_n or she_n etc. would denote the n-th salient thing (person) in the context or previous discourse. Thus variables which remain unbound would receive a context-dependent interpretation, but the interpretation of bound variables would be unaffected by this strategy.
- For multiple reasons, it is necessary to be able to determine whether one occurrence of a variable is the "same variable" as another occurrence of a

[40] You might be inclined to think of "in the scope of" as such a dependency, but that is not a syntactic connection, it is something that arises from the compositional interaction of the semantics of variables and that of quantifiers.

variable ("same" here referring to type-identity not token-identity) or is a different variable. Variable indexing then classifies any two constituents as "co-indexed" or "non-co-indexed".

2.8.1.2 *Combinatory Anaphoric Binding* What I will here call COMBINATORY ANAPHORIC BINDING originates with Quine's (1966) demonstration that variables in predicate logic can be "explained away" by using combinators (as in the COMBINATORY LOGIC of Curry (1963) and others). There are multiple, quite distinct ways to implement the combinatory approach (Hepple 1990; Szabolcsi 1992; Moortgat 1996; Jacobson 1999, and an alternative version introduced below);[41] note that by the term *combinatory anaphoric binding* I do not refer only to Jacobson's particular combinatory analysis (or to analyses specific to CCG—despite the similarity in terminology), but rather to any account of anaphoric binding characterized by the following features:

- At the heart of a combinatory analysis is the "doubling" combinator[42] $\lambda f \lambda x[f(x)(x)]$ (also symbolized simply as **W**): this is an operator which combines with a two-place predicate to form a one-place predicate, interpreting the sole argument of the derived one-place predicate as if it had occurred as both arguments of the original predicate. Alternatively, some other combinator can be used that accomplishes what **W** does, such as Jacobson's combinator $\lambda f \lambda G \lambda x[f(G(x))(x)]$, symbolized **Z**, a multi-place relative of **W**.
- A doubling combinator is essentially an operator on two-place (or multi-place) predicates, thus it does not have the same logical type as names and other nouns (nor, in its simplest use, would it have the same syntactic category).
- Because anaphoric relations in natural language can extend over arbitrary distances, anaphoric binding cannot be treated solely with a **W**-like combinator, which combines with a single verb: some means must be provided for "extending" the reach of the combinator to span more syntactic material (and scope over more semantic structure).
- The "extension" of the reach of the anaphoric binding combinator can be accomplished either by the iterated use of a local semantic operation

[41] Jäger (2001) is a treatment resembling in some ways combinatory binding as I describe it, but it is different in important ways too. Jäger, it should be noted, gives a very useful summary of the combinatory analyses listed here and a further one by Glyn Morrill.

[42] As Carpenter (1997) notes, a standard definition of a combinator is a *closed lambda term*, a lambda expression consisting only of bound variables and lambda-binders; $\lambda V \lambda v[V(v)(v)]$ is an example. Curry's combinatory logic (Curry 1963) uses single symbols as combinators instead (**S**, **W**, **B**, **I**, etc.), but that difference is not important in this context.

(cf. **G** in Jacobson (1999)) or by a "long-distance" semantic operation applying only once (cf. below).

- Combinatory anaphoric binding does not in itself involve "quantification" in the sense of first-order logic (or generalized quantifier theory), since binding is only an operation on predicates, not an operation on sentences, and not one that comes in various "flavors" (∃, ∀, etc.).
- A specific, unique link between each pronominal anaphor and its antecedent is defined syntactically, even in long-distance cases, and a particular compositional relationship is determined by this syntactic relationship. This has (at least) these four consequences:
  - *First*: indexing of variables is not needed to treat overlapping scopes of different anaphoric bindings (*Every man$_i$ told every woman$_j$ that he$_i$ admired her$_j$*) or for other reasons.
  - *Second*: combinatory binding is inherently asymmetric with respect to grammatical functions and syntactic embedding,[43] so a requirement that the "antecedent" NP must always F-command the argument slot that the combinator binds is imposed either (i) automatically, by interactions with other aspects of CG, or else (depending on the particular implementation) (ii) by the choice of which of two possible combinators you employ in the anaphora interpretation rule.[44]
  - *Third*: binding of multiple pronominal anaphors by the same antecedent (*No man$_i$ admitted that he$_i$ thought anyone disliked him$_i$*) cannot be produced by a single quantifier simultaneously binding two or more co-indexed variables, but can only result either from one combinatory binding step applying to the output of another (binding applies twice to the same VP before it combines with its argument), or in the right configurations, when one pronoun's argument "slot" binds another pronoun's.[45]

[43] Note that an account like Jäger's (2001), however, is asymmetric for linear precedence but not necessarily for F-command; the analyses discussed here are asymmetric for F-command but not necessarily for linear precedence.

[44] When **W** is used to reduce the adicity of a predicate, assuming a curried argument structure, reduction by one argument eliminates the most oblique one of them (assuming you don't go out of your way by introducing a new special category and syntactic operation that will mimic behavior of a grammatical function which is lower on the obliqueness hierarchy); adding a mechanism to extend the scope of **W** allows the bound argument position to be somewhere inside a more oblique argument or F-commanded adjunct. Because **Z** is a multi-place operator, a choice between it and Curry's **S** is theoretically available; that choice has the consequences discussed in Jacobson (2002).

[45] I know of no consequences of this fact for the choice between binding methods.

– *Fourth*: a difference with probably the most striking consequences of all (see below). Whereas free-variable binding makes the compositional connection between binder and anaphor a relationship overlaid "on top of", as it were, the rest of the syntactic/compositional structure of a sentence, combinatory binding is *embedded as an integral part of* that structure. Thus, potentially, interactions with other compositional processes could take place that would not arise with the free-variable-binding theory.

2.8.1.3 *Compositional Transparency in the Two Methods* From the point of view of transparent compositionality, the most noteworthy thing favoring a free-variable-binding analysis over a combinatory one is that it puts bound pronouns in the same syntactic category as individual constants, that is names: natural language pronouns do have the same kind of morphological properties and syntactic distributions as names and other nouns. Furthermore, if deictic/discourse pronouns are treated in the manner mentioned above, syntactic economics implies that they should be indistinguishable from bound anaphoric pronouns in appearance and distribution, which seems to be the case across natural languages.

And with respect to compositional transparency, the most notable weakness in the combinatory analysis is its category for bound pronouns. Because bound anaphors are, semantically, functors of some kind applying to the meanings of verbs (or applying to verbs plus other structures embedded under the verb heads), the most economical syntax should be one in which anaphoric binders resembled verbal affixes, auxiliary verbs, VP-adverbs, or the like. But this is not how bound anaphoric forms look in most languages.

However, this consequence of the combinatory approach is not an unmitigatedly negative one. In their cross-linguistic study of local/reflexive anaphora, Sells *et al.* (1987) observe that manifestations of such anaphora seem to fall into one of two types: either local reflexive anaphora is realized by a distinctive form of pronoun, or else it is signaled by an affix or clitic that attaches to the verb. The latter, of course, would be the ideally transparent form under the combinatory theory.[46]

To be sure, it is certainly quite possible to contrive a combinatory analysis involving some expression that appears where an *np* argument appears and looks and behaves like a name or other NP, and proponents of combinatory

[46] An important question, however, is what happens with non-local bound anaphora in these languages (assuming they do express it somehow): the simple affix on transitive verbs, with **W** as its meaning, could not handle those as it stands, so depending on just how the non-local binding is manifested in morphology and/or syntax, bound non-local anaphora in those languages could still present the same puzzle for the combinatory account as it does in English.

analyses have shown great ingenuity in finding ways to do this. The point here is that under any such analysis, natural language bound anaphora is still uneconomical syntactically and obscure compositionally.

Discourse/deictic pronouns are a dilemma under the combinatory analysis: if treated as combinators (which Jacobson's analysis can readily do), they will fail to have the same category as names and NPs. If treated like individual-denoting terms, the similarity to names is captured, but then discourse pronouns would fail to have the same category as bound pronouns, which of course they are always indistinguishable from in appearance.

The most traditional versions of variable-binding analyses posit a level of Logical Form (or abstract notion thereof) in which quantifiers are outside the clauses in which they appear in "surface" structure, just as they are in the syntax of first-order logic. Thus at the level of LF itself, transparency and semantic structural economy are perfect. But when viewed from the vantage point of surface structure, the free-variable-binding analysis makes English look bad on both these criteria. English surface syntax would have been more efficient and transparent, if free-variable binding is the right analysis, if quantifiers always took the form of sentence adjuncts, and most transparent of all if its syntax had looked just like predicate logic. But though the logician's quasi-English paraphrase "For all x, there is some y such that x loves y" does have this form, that is definitely *not* a normal way of expressing quantification in English.[47]

An exception, however, is so-called *adverbial quantification*, which as David Lewis observed, appears to a limited extent in English; an example is *Quadratic equations usually have two solutions*, where *usually* does not have a temporal meaning but an atemporal quantificational one, like "Most quadratic equations have ... " or "In most cases ... "; *usually* of course *is* a sentential adjunct! A number of natural languages have adverbial quantification as their only form of quantification.

[47] There is another possible kind of analysis: (i) rather than first-order-style quantifiers to bind variables, use lambda-abstraction for all free-variable binding (possibly with abstraction defined over all logical types), and (ii) let the denotations of NPs be generalized quantifiers. Then *Every man thinks he will win* would have the logical form $\mathbf{every}'(\mathbf{man}')(\lambda x_i[\mathbf{thinks}'([\mathbf{F}\,\mathbf{win}'(x_i)])(x_i)])$. This is in effect a mixture of the two analyses. Note that the step of constructing the VP-meaning $\lambda x_i[\mathbf{thinks}'([\mathbf{F}\,\mathbf{win}'(x_i)])(x_i)]$ from the VP meaning $\mathbf{thinks}'([\mathbf{F}\,\mathbf{win}'(x_i)])$ is semantically the same as combinatory binding in that it links two argument "slots" together, the argument of the VP itself (i.e. what will become its subject) with one (or more) argument positions embedded somewhere inside it (the free x_i): schematically it turns $\ldots x_i \ldots$ into $\lambda x_i[\ldots x_i \ldots (x_i)]$; this puts the position of the quantifier in Logical Form "closer" to its surface position, perhaps simplifying the c-command constraint on Quantifier-Raising/Lowering. But as free variable binding still plays a role *inside* the VP scope, (non-)co-indexing is still needed to distinguish overlapping scopes of different NPs, and crossover constraints are still necessary.

The usual means to resolve the discrepancy between Logical Form and natural language "surface structure" are the Quantifier-Raising, Quantifier-Lowering, and Quantifying-In analyses (although syntactic economy would of course have been improved if no Quantifier Raising (etc.) had been needed at all).

Interestingly, the c-command constraint on position of the binder vis-à-vis the variables bound does not literally serve any semantic purpose in the variable-binding analysis, because the actual scope of the binder at the level relevant for semantic interpretation is one wider than *all* occurrences of the bound variables, hence which one of these variables the quantifier is raised from (is lowered to, respectively) can have no consequences in the semantics.

Free-variable-binding analyses critically depend on indexing (to distinguish between co-indexed and non-co-indexed), but this is reflected only very weakly in natural language anaphora, by gender, number and/or other agreement. Combinatory analyses do not need indexing.

But the most interesting way that combinatory analyses are favored is connected with the fact that in the free-variable-binding approach itself, variables have no semantically motivated syntactic connection to their binders at all, whereas in the combinatory analyses, they crucially do. Hence the possibility of their interaction with other syntactic/compositional processes is predicted. In fact, such interactions do occur which have visible effects in linguistic data. This works as follows.

A distinctive feature of CG is that expressions which normally play the role of functors can, in certain contexts, also serve as arguments. For example, quantificational NPs, analyzed as generalized quantifiers (type $\langle\langle e, t\rangle, t\rangle$), typically act as functors applying to VPs as their arguments. But in NP coordinations (e.g. *A man or a woman was at every window, Neither most men nor most women preferred shampoo B over A.*), they need to be the arguments of coordinating conjunctions, to get the compositional semantics right.[48]

Likewise with the combinatory account of anaphora, it would be possible for the combinator itself to become an argument in some contexts—in other words, the process of "anaphoric binding" itself becomes a syntactic and semantic object that can be manipulated compositionally, like syntactic constituents and their meanings. This is the key ingredient that permits a combinatory analysis of the otherwise quite puzzling cases of "Double-Binding", functional questions, etc. for which Jacobson has provided combinatory analyses.

[48] In Montague's PTQ, the role of the conjunction is obscured because he treated all coordinations syncategorematically. If treated categorically, the category of *and* and *or* in these examples would be $(NP\backslash NP)/NP$, where NP abbreviates s/vp; spelled out, this category is $((s/vp)\backslash(s/vp))/(s/vp)$.

This role may be somewhat easier to grasp, I believe, in the alternative formulation of combinatory binding given below in §2.8.3 than it is in Jacobson's original formulation, because in the former it literally is the combinator meaning itself that is affected compositionally. In Jacobson's formulation, what crucially interacts compositionally is instead one part of the combinatory analysis, a function from individuals to individuals (type $\langle e, e \rangle$, always labeled f in her derivations), which because of the role of **G** in turn "piggy-backs" on top of another constituent (so the type manipulated compositionally may be $\langle\langle e, e\rangle, \langle e, t\rangle\rangle$, etc.). (In her treatment the interaction of the **Z** combinator itself is not so obvious.) But insofar as I can see, essentially the same observation applies to both, so I will use the former, simpler phrasing.

What happens in the combinatory analysis of (40) (in the reading in which *his* is somehow simultaneously bound by both *every man* and *no man*),

(40) Every man loves but no man marries his mother.

is that the combinator meaning signaled by *his mother* is, in effect, distributed across the two conjuncts by cross-categorial coordination, in the same way that the semantics of coordination would distribute the meaning of any other kind of constituent across two conjuncts. But examples like (40) are paradoxical for any first-order free-variable-binding analysis, as "the same variable bound by two different quantifiers" makes no sense in the standard semantics of variable binding. (The possibility of course exists of treating these by introducing additional abstractness between surface and LF levels, such as reconstruction or manipulating co-indexing in LF prior to semantic interpretation; see Jacobson (1999: 168–71) for discussion of some attempts and why they have not succeeded in accomplishing what her combinatory account does.)[49]

The combinatory analysis of functional questions (see Jacobson (1999: 148–54) and the alternative formulation in §2.8.3.2 below) also results from treating an anaphoric combinator's meaning, in effect, as a unit participating in compositional interpretation, as would the analysis of topicalizations such as (41*a*, 41*b*) (i.e. not via syntactic reconstruction but with the familiar way of treating a topic constituent in CG: as a constituent of the highest clause, compositionally interpreted in that position, but interpreted as a binder of an embedded gap); this requires topicalization to be generalized across syntactic

[49] A compositionally more direct and more transparent way to try to expand the variable-binding approach to handle cases like (40) would be the radical step of altering the Tarski semantics of free variable binding itself to make sense of "two distinct quantifiers binding the same variable". I have no idea whether that is possible at all, and such a proposal would of course have to be supported with completely explicit details of its model-theoretic interpretation. I am not aware of any proposals of this kind.

categories, a move which has independent motivation here as it does with functional questions.

(41) (*a*) Himself, most any man would consider best qualified for the job.

(*b*) Herself, every woman admired but no woman was complacent about.

Jacobson's papers (1999, 2000) deal with numerous further ramifications of her combinatory method and comparisons between it and a variety of variable-binding treatments of the same problems.

2.8.1.4 *Reconciling the Differences?* I cannot leave this topic without mentioning the one possible (if very speculative) hypothesis I know of that could potentially reconcile the conflict in the results of this comparison (that it might do this is the only motivation for the hypothesis I can provide here). The following observations were made, mainly in conversation, by various people during the 1980s (by Barbara Partee (p.c.), Robin Cooper (p.c.), and myself, although possibly by others as well): it is known that children acquire understanding of quantification fairly late in language acquisition; thus there would be no real justification for a generalized quantifier analysis of NPs in a grammar describing a child's language before this point. Nor does the syntactically marked definite/indefinite distinction motivate quantifiers, because this has been argued to mark a distinction between discourse referents that are familiar and those that are unfamiliar in the context. Thus there is no reason not to treat all NPs as having denotations of type *e*. Under that view, the generalized quantifier analysis of NPs is something superimposed on the child's grammar at a later stage, yielding a grammar for adult speech that is superficially *similar* to the child's in syntax but quite *different* in semantics. Of course, in a language with no way to express real quantification, there can be no motivation for bound anaphora either: it would suffice for all pronouns to be interpreted as definite discourse anaphors.

This two-stage hypothesis subsequently became one of the primary motivations cited for the DYNAMIC THEORY OF SYNTAX advocated in Dowty (1996), the other being the adjunct reanalysis hypothesis described (in part) in §2.6.9 (Dowty 2003). Under this hypothesis, it is likely that Compositional Transparency and Syntactic Economy play their most important roles at the early stages of language acquisition, when children are first trying to grasp the most basic features of the syntax and compositional interpretation of their native language. Compositional transparency would become less critical for the language as semantically "expanded" by adults (who have long since mastered its basic syntactic and compositional structure). In this way, an analysis of quantification and bound anaphora could plausibly arise which had much less economy and compositional transparency than a grammar ought to have had it needed to be able to express quantification and anaphoric binding "from the start". Then (i) the resemblance of pronouns to names and other nouns is expected, since they are semantically alike at the stage where transparency/economy are most important; but (ii) it is not really a strong objection to the combinatory account that it treats anaphoric binding as an operation on verbs, since that analysis only needs to be postulated when compositional transparency plays a less important role.

2.8.2 *"Local Encoding" and Combinatory Analyses*

To what extent do the noteworthy successes of Jacobson's combinatory analysis depend on the interaction of all the particular features it has in her formulation? In particular, is "local interpretation" really necessary? In fact, there are multiple ways to instantiate a combinatory analysis that appear to be able to capture crossover constraints, the Right-Node-Raising ("double binding") examples, Functional Questions, and related phenomena such as Paycheck Anaphora (but I don't claim at this point that all the other constructions Jacobson has analyzed will have alternative combinatory analyses—Antecedent Contained Ellipsis, for example, is unclear in this respect). "Local Interpretation" does not seem to be strictly necessary.

I will assume familiarity with Jacobson's treatment and not review more details of it, nor of Mark Hepple's similar analysis that proceeded it; see Hepple (1990), Jacobson (1999, 2002, and other references therein). (Readers who are more familiar with the program of TLG than with CCG might want to read the survey of this research described in type-logical terms in Jäger (2001) before going on to read Jacobson's original papers.)

We want to distinguish among four ingredients in Jacobson's approach: (i) the rejection of promiscuous indexed-free-variable binding in favor of a combinatory analysis of binding; (ii) iterated use of the **G** combinator to pass on long-distance anaphoric dependencies one constituent level at a time (as required by local interpretation); (iii) giving pronouns the identify function as their meaning and assigning them to a special syntactic category so that they will trigger introduction of the **G** combinator; and (iv) general features of the CCG framework.

2.8.2.1 *Local Encoding,* **G**, *and Type-Logical Rules* The "Geach" Rule can be implemented either as a type-local inference (or "type-raising") rule, (42), or with equivalent effects a G(EACH) COMBINATOR as defined in (43));[50] the two have parallel effects:

(42) $$\frac{A/B : \alpha}{(A/C)/(B/C) : \lambda V \lambda v[\alpha(V(v))]}\mathbf{G}$$

(43) (*a*) $\mathbf{G}(A/B) = (A/C)/(B/C)$

(*b*) If $\text{Type}(A) = \langle a,b\rangle$, $\text{Type}(C) = c$, then $\text{Type}(\mathbf{G}A) = \langle\langle c,b\rangle, \langle c,a\rangle\rangle$. (Semantically, $\mathbf{G} = \lambda V_1 \lambda V_2 \lambda v[V_1(V_2(v))]$)

"Geach" (either version) can be seen as a kind of local encoding of a long-distance dependency in the following sense. A typical CG derivation is:

(44) $$\frac{A/B \quad \dfrac{B/C \quad C}{B}}{A}$$

But suppose that you wanted to apply *A/B* to an argument immediately, temporarily ignoring fact that *B/C* should get a *C* argument first, yet you want to remember that dependency for later purposes. So instead of using A/B, you can use **G**(*A/B*), then by applying **G**(*A/B*) to *B/C* as argument, you get *A/C*; the fact that you still need the *C* argument is preserved. If *A* were itself a functoral type, you could postpone application to a *C* argument again (and again). This is (approximately) how Jacobson "locally encodes" the bound pronoun's dependency using **G**.

Jäger (2001) points out that instead of using **G** multiple times locally, you could take advantage of the fact that **G** (plus its various generalizations) is, in effect, derivable as a theorem in the Lambek Calculus, using the Slash-Introduction rule, and multiple versions of **G** combinators would not be needed. Also, a Lambek Calculus derivation could produce in one "long-distance" step the effect of iterated **G** combinators.[51]

How this might look is shown in the simple derivation in (45) (from Jäger (2001)): this employs Slash-Introduction rather than **G** but retains Jacobson's **Z** (recast here as an inference rule) and the pronoun category (and its

[50] Jacobson's notation is slightly different: she types **G** by its argument, e.g. $\mathbf{G}_C$, and in her semantics has a parallel operator $\mathbf{g}_c$; rather than $(A/C)/(B/C)$ she introduces a second mode of combination indicated with a superscript, so the type resulting from applying **G** to A/B is written A^C/B^C.

[51] Note that Jäger's own analysis does not employ the Lambek Slash "/" to treat anaphoric binding but rather a Contraction type-constructor (2001: 97–120), the Introduction rule for Contraction does in effect the work that **G** does for Jacobson, whereas its Elimination rule corresponds to **Z** (p. 120)—with the important exception that the logical rules for this combinator are sensitive to left–right order but *not* to c-command, making it an analysis that makes different empirical predictions about the situations where binding can occur.

meaning).[52] Following Jäger, I write "$A|B$" for Jacobson's notation "A^B", to emphasize its parallel to the other type constructor(s), "A/B" (etc.).

(45)

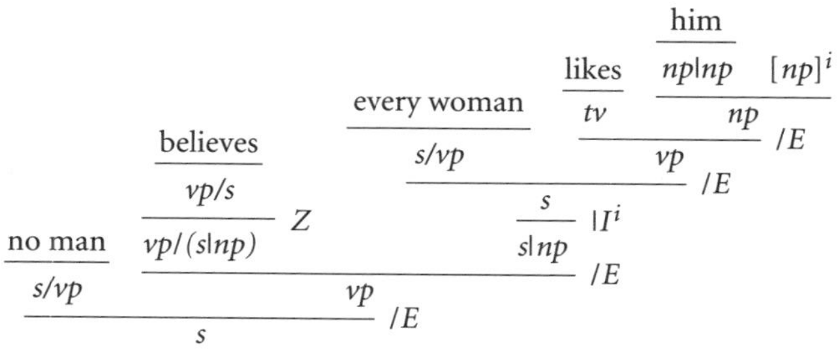

Possibly misleading is that (45) resembles "free variable binding", in that the hypothesized category is marked with an index, that is "$[np]^i$", and the "$|I^i$" step bears the same index. But this is not really variable binding. The Lambek Calculus, like type-logical grammar in general, quite literally treats syntax as logical deduction. "Slash-Introduction" is nothing more than the rule of Conditional Proof in statement logic (also called "Hypothetical Reasoning" or "$\rightarrow$-Introduction"): the "$[np]^i$" is the assumption (hypothesis) step of a Conditional Proof (often annotated as "ϕ: Assumption") and the "$\rightarrow$-Intro" step is the proof step (concluding "$(\phi \rightarrow \psi)$" after having just proved "ψ" by using "ϕ" in the proof). The index i here is thus analogous to the vertical line drawn in the left column that some logic textbooks prescribe as an aide to making it clear which assumption each conditional proof step is dependent on, so you can easily check whether each assumption and the proof dependent on it are in a permissible configuration.

Insofar as you view the connection between the assumption and conditional proof step in a logical proof as a "long distance dependency", the anaphoric dependency in (44) is being treated as a long-distance dependency too. Jäger's recasting of Jacobson thus shows that Local Encoding is not necessary in a combinatory binding analysis. (Below, more interesting examples than (44) are analyzed with Slash-Introduction.)

Jäger (2001: 93) maintains that the need for an infinite number of variations on the **G** combinator, each technically a different primitive combinator, is an undesirable artifact of the CCG as Jacobson employs it. However, since Jacobson derives her infinite supply of **G**s by a formal recursive definition, it is not clear whether specific problems arise from her method, or whether Jäger's

[52] Note that although I have combined $np|np$ with a "hypothesized" np argument here, which parallels Hepple's analysis but not Jacobson's, there would be various ways to prevent over-generations with $np|np$, e.g. Hepple's modal operator, or simply a syntactic feature.

objection amounts to a complaint that her analysis is much more untidy than it needed to be.

A final observation: it was pointed out earlier that morphological marking along the "extraction path" in a *wh*-dependency, such as is found in Icelandic, was one possible kind of evidence for local encoding as opposed to a direct long-distance analysis; the effect of island constraints on extraction paths could conceivably be viewed as another. It is relevant to point out, then, that such morphological marking and sensitivity to island constraints have been observed only for *wh*-binding (and possibly some wide scoping of NPs), but never for anaphoric binding as far as I know. Finding such a case for anaphoric binding would be a positive argument for local encoding; whether the absence of such evidence (in light of its existence elsewhere) should really count against local encoding is hard to say at this point.

2.8.3 *An Alternative Version of Combinatory Anaphoric Binding: The S–M–D Analysis*

Nor, it turns out, does the success of a combinatory binding analysis of the interesting problems of "Double-Binding" Right-Node-Raising examples, functional questions (which extends to paycheck pronoun analyses, etc.) necessarily depend on assigning pronouns to the $np|np$ category (and with the identify function as their meaning) and giving the task of argument doubling to an abstract **Z** combinator rather than some other way of performing argument doubling. One thing that a successful combinatory binding analysis of these constructions does require, as mentioned above, is a syntactic theory in which you always have at hand a ready means for generalizing interpretation to higher logical types (which you do in CCG and TLG) so that a combinator (or at least a part thereof) can become an argument of another meaning.

To demonstrate these claims, I will introduce at this point a sketch of an alternative treatment of anaphoric binding that (a) is combinatory, (b) takes advantage of generalization to higher types, but (c) is otherwise different from Jacobson's; then briefly show how this alternative handles two of the above phenomena (double-binding in R-N-R coordination and functional questions). The point of this is not to criticize or try to replace Jacobson's, only to try to gain a deeper understanding of how combinatory analyses in general work.

This alternative follows Szabolcsi (1992) in making the **W** combinator $\lambda f \lambda x[f(x)(x)]$ part of the meaning of the pronoun itself—indeed, the entire meaning of it—although in contrast to Szabolcsi, it does not attempt to build into the pronoun and its category membership a means for extending the scope of the combinator over unbounded distances.

Rather, it extends pronoun binding scope by using something needed independently in any theory of semantics: a means of producing the wide-scope readings of quantificational NPs. In fact, any of several mechanisms for NP scoping could be employed in this alternative—Quantifying In/Out, Cooper's NP-Storage, etc. The one I will choose here, however, is Moortgat's (1997) SCOPING TYPE-CONSTRUCTOR, symbolized as "$\Uparrow$". Since the analysis that results adopts something from Szabolcsi (making the pronoun itself denote the doubling combinator) and something from Moortgat, but incorporates them into a larger package, I will call it the "S(zabolcsi)–M(oortgat)–D(owty)" alternative for now.[53]

In summary: in the Jacobson analysis (i) the syntactically abstract **G** combinator, triggered by the category of the (semantically vacuous) pronoun, first passes the anaphoric dependency up to the main verb of the VP, (ii) then the **Z** combinator semantically links the pronominal argument slot (transmitted to it by **G**) with the subject argument slot of this VP; syntactically, it turns the "marked" category back into a normal category at that point. In the alternative, (i) the binding combinator is assigned as the meaning of the pronoun, but it does not enter compositional interpretation immediately; rather (ii) the generalized "storage" rule holds this meaning in reserve (for an indefinite time), then (iii) the "scoping out" step takes the combinator out of storage and uses it to bind the embedded argument slot (where it originated and had been put in storage) to the argument slot of the VP. Both analyses thus involve "long distance" transmission of a binding relation, followed by application of a "doubling" combinator to link the two argument slots.

Carpenter (1997) describes the combinator which is employed for both wide NP-scope and anaphoric binding this way: "The category $B \Uparrow A$ is assigned to expressions that act locally as Bs but take their semantic scope over an embedding expression of category A. For instance, a generalized quantifier noun phrase will be given category $np \Uparrow s$ because it acts like a noun phrase *in situ* but scopes semantically to an embedding sentence."

(46) Definition 1 *Scoping Constructor*

(*a*) $B \Uparrow A \in \text{Cat}$, *if* $A, B \in \text{Cat}$

(*b*) $Typ(B \Uparrow A) = \langle\langle Typ(B), Typ(A)\rangle, Typ(A)\rangle$

[53] Moortgat in fact employed this kind of analysis for locally bound anaphora (reflexives), but did not seem to notice or pursue (nor did Jäger in discussing this device) any of its various possibilities for dealing with the complexities in binding that Jacobson discovered combinatory treatments of.

Since the generalized quantifiers *everybody*, etc. have category $np\Uparrow s$, their translations are logical constants of type $Typ(np\Uparrow s) = \langle\langle Typ(np), Typ(s)\rangle, Typ(s)\rangle = \langle\langle e, t\rangle, t\rangle$.

The Elimination Rule for $B\Uparrow A$ (or *scoping scheme* as Carpenter (1997) calls it), has a more succinct formulation in the Gentzen Sequent format,

(47) Definition 2 *Scoping Sequent Scheme*

$$\frac{\Delta_1, B{:}x, \Delta_2 \Rightarrow A{:}\beta \qquad \Gamma_1, A{:}\alpha(\lambda x.\beta), \Gamma_2 \Rightarrow C{:}\gamma}{\Gamma_1, \Delta_1, A\Uparrow B{:}\alpha, \Delta_2, \Gamma_2 \Rightarrow C{:}\gamma}\Uparrow l \qquad [x\ fresh]$$

than its somewhat cumbersome formulation in Natural Deduction format, (48). But as natural deduction derivations themselves are always easier to read than Gentzen Sequent derivations, I'll use only the Natural Deduction in derivations.

(48) Definition 3 *Scope Elimination Scheme* (natural deduction format)

$$\cfrac{\cfrac{\begin{array}{ccc} \vdots & \vdots & \vdots \\ \vdots & \cfrac{B\Uparrow A{:}\ \alpha}{B{:}\ x}\Uparrow e^i & \vdots \\ & \overline{} & \\ \vdots & \vdots & \vdots \end{array}}{A{:}\ b}}{A{:}\,\alpha(\lambda x.b)}\Uparrow e^i$$

This schema involves two distinct deductive steps, which may be separated by any number of other kinds of steps. In Carpenter's notation (see (49) below) both steps are labeled "$\Uparrow e^i$"; a more common convention, which I subsequently follow, labels the second step with only the index i of the rule application. In (49), there are two instances of the generalized quantifier category $np\Uparrow s$. Each is converted into category np by the first step, from which point forward it "behaves like an np locally". In the second step of the deduction, the syntactic category, namely s, remains unchanged:

(49)

$$\cfrac{\cfrac{\cfrac{\cfrac{\cfrac{\textit{somebody}}{np\Uparrow s : \textbf{somebody}'}}{np : x}\Uparrow E^2 \qquad \cfrac{\cfrac{\textit{loves}}{tv : \textbf{loves}'} \qquad \cfrac{\cfrac{\textit{everybody}}{np\Uparrow s : \textbf{everybody}'}}{np : y}\Uparrow E^0}{vp : \textbf{loves}'(y)}}{s : \textbf{loves}'(y)(x)}}{s : \textbf{somebody}'(\lambda x[\textbf{loves}'(y)(x)])}2}{s : \textbf{everybody}'(\lambda y[\textbf{somebody}'(\lambda x[\textbf{loves}'(y)(x)])])}0$$

(Doing the two last ⇑E steps in the opposite order produces the other scope reading of (49).) You may immediately notice a parallel between such a derivation and Cooper's NP-storage (Cooper 1983) (both in the semantics and syntax): the first deductive step is like Cooper's *NP-storage*, the second is like his *NP-Scoping*, in which the generalized quantifier meaning that had been put aside at the first step is used at the level of some "higher" s, but without any observable syntactic effect—the actual quantificational NP remains "in situ". In fact, the formal nature of this type-logical analysis is entirely different from NP-storage: the question of the relationship between the two approaches is ultimately a very important one but is too complex to pursue here. For our immediate purposes, those differences may be ignored completely. With that important caveat made, I will use "storage" and "scoping" to refer to the steps in the ⇑-E inference rule.

Whereas Cooper Storage and other Quantifier Raising/Lowering analyses are, by their definitions, restricted to storing an NP and scoping it out at category S, the scoping type constructor $B \Uparrow A$ has been defined for any two categories A and B (just as TLG does with the ordinary slash A/B, other type constructors, and all logical rules), thus ⇑ permits any category B to be "stored" and then later "scoped out" at any category A it is embedded within. Consequently, the category we need for anaphoric binding already exists: it is $np \Uparrow vp$. A bound pronoun, if put in this category, will be "something that 'behaves locally' as an *np* but takes its scope over some *vp* in which it is embedded." What I am calling the "storage" mechanism that is involved is exactly the same one used for NP "storage". All that remains to do is to give (all) pronouns the lexical meaning $\lambda G \lambda v[G(v)(v)]$, which is the binding combinator. This combinator meaning is then "stored" until some *vp* is reached, then when "taken out of storage" and applied to this *vp* meaning, it will bind the original pronoun "slot" in the *vp*, with the result that the *np* argument the *vp* next combines with becomes anaphorically linked to the pronoun "slot".

The translation for the scoping-out step of the ⇑-E rule, from (48), is repeated in (50*a*), where α is the meaning that has been "stored", x marks the argument position that is abstracted over, and β is the translation of the expression that α will now have scope over. Examples (50*b*), (50*c*) show the parallel to NP-storage as produced by this same rule:

(50) (*a*) $\alpha(\lambda x[\beta])$

(*b*) $\mathbf{everyone}'(\lambda x[\beta])$ (*equivalently*, $\lambda P \forall x\, [\mathbf{person}' \rightarrow P(x)](\lambda x[\beta])$)

(*c*) $\mathbf{it}'(\lambda x[\beta])$ (*equivalently*, $\lambda G \lambda v[G(v)(v)](\lambda x[\beta])$)

The following example shows both "NP-storage" and "pronominal combinator storage". The step labeled 1 is the scope interpretation of the pronoun *it*, and that labeled 2 is that for the *np every dog*. For perspicuity I show the English syntax and the λ-calculus translation with separate parallel derivations, (51*a*) and (51*b*):

(51) (*a*)

$$\dfrac{\dfrac{\dfrac{np\Uparrow s : \textit{every dog}}{np : \textit{every dog}}\Uparrow E^{2} \qquad \dfrac{\dfrac{vp/s' : \textit{thinks} \qquad \dfrac{s'/s : \text{that} \qquad \dfrac{\dfrac{np\Uparrow vp : \textit{it}}{np : \textit{it}}\Uparrow E^{1} \qquad \dfrac{vp\backslash vp : \textit{loudest} \quad vp : \textit{barks}}{vp : \textit{barks loudest}}\backslash E}{s}\backslash E}{s'}/E}{vp : \textit{think that it barks loudest}}/E}{vp : \textit{thinks that it barks loudest}}1}{s : \textit{every dog thinks that it barks loudest}}\backslash E}{s : \textit{every dog thinks that it barks loudest}}2$$

(*b*)

$$\dfrac{\dfrac{\dfrac{np\Uparrow s : \lambda P\forall x[\mathbf{dog}'(x)\rightarrow P(x)]}{np : x_2}\Uparrow E^{2} \qquad \dfrac{\dfrac{vp/s' : \mathbf{think}' \qquad \dfrac{s'/s : \lambda p[p] \qquad \dfrac{\dfrac{np\Uparrow vp : \lambda G\lambda x[(G(x))(x)]}{np : x_1}\Uparrow E^{1} \qquad \dfrac{vp : \mathbf{bark}' \quad vp\backslash vp : \mathbf{loudest}'}{vp : \mathbf{ldst.}'(\mathbf{bark})'}}{s : \mathbf{ldst.}'(\mathbf{bark}')(x_1)}\backslash E}{s'}/E}{vp : \mathbf{think}'(\mathbf{ldst}'(\mathbf{bark}')(x_1))}/E}{vp :\ \lambda G\lambda x[(G(x))(x)](\lambda x_1[\mathbf{think}'(\mathbf{ldst}'(\mathbf{bark}')(x_1))])}1}{s : \lambda y[\mathbf{think}'(\mathbf{ldst}'(\mathbf{bark}')(y))(y)](x_2)}\backslash E}{s : \forall x[\mathbf{dog}'(x)\rightarrow\mathbf{think}'(\mathbf{loudest}'(\mathbf{bark}')(x))]}2$$

2.8.3.1 *Doubly Bound R-N-R Coordination Sentences in the S–M–D Analysis* When the "double binding" of one pronoun by two different quantificational antecedents in a coordination with "Right-Node-Raising" (cf. example (40), "Every man loves but no man marries his mother") was mentioned earlier, I said that the combinatory anaphoric binder works as ***argument*** of a higher-order function in the S–M–D analysis, yet still performs its role as an in-situ combinator scoping out to a higher verb.

Recall first how a non-anaphoric coordinated R-N-R sentence would be derived, for *John likes but Mary detests George W. Bush*: (a) Start by producing two sentences in which the right-most NP is only a *hypothesized* category, viz. *John likes [np]* and *Mary detests [np]*. Then (b) by *Slash-Introduction*, discharge the hypothesized *np* in each case, deriving *John likes* and *Mary detests*, each in *s/np*. (c) With generalized Boolean coordination, form *John likes and Mary detests*, also in *s/np*. Then (d) combine this with the *np George W. Bush* to produce the sentence.

In sentences such as (49)–(51), however, we want to begin with category *np*⇑*vp* as the hypothesized category (in each conjunct). The hypothesized

$np\Uparrow vp$ still can (indeed must) undergo $\Uparrow$-E to change to np, after which things proceed as expected until *every man loves [np]* is derived in category s; then Slash-Introduction withdraws the hypothesized category:

(52) Derivation of left conjunct, *Every man loves*:

$$\dfrac{\dfrac{s/vp : \textit{every man} : \mathbf{every\text{-}man'} \qquad \dfrac{\dfrac{vp/np : \textit{loves} : \mathbf{love'} \qquad \dfrac{[vp\Uparrow np : \Delta]^1 : U_1}{np : x_1}\,{\Uparrow}E}{vp : \textit{loves np} : \mathbf{love'}(x_1)}\,/E}{vp : \textit{loves } x_1 : U_1(\lambda x_1[\mathbf{love'}(x_1)])}\,1}{s : \textit{every man loves np} : \mathbf{everyman'}(U_1(\lambda x_1[\mathbf{love'}(x_1)]))}\,/E}{s/(vp\Uparrow np) : \textit{every man loves} : \lambda U_1[\mathbf{everyman'}(U_1(\lambda x_1[\mathbf{love'}(x_1)]))]}\,/I^i$$

Notice carefully: when we withdraw the hypothesis via /-Introduction, the category $s/(np\Uparrow vp)$ is produced, and *not* s/np: $np\Uparrow vp$ was the original hypothesis, np was not. This expression and the right-hand conjunct *no man marries* (produced in the same way) are combined with *but*; the relevant instance of its category schema $X\backslash(X/X)$ in this case is $((s/vp\Uparrow np)\backslash(s/vp\Uparrow np))/(s/vp\Uparrow np)$. Finally the argument *his mother* in $np\Uparrow vp$ is added (which is derived from the sequence $np\Uparrow vp\ cn$).

(53)

$$\dfrac{\dfrac{\dfrac{\text{Every man loves}}{s/(vp\Uparrow np)} \qquad \dfrac{\dfrac{\text{but}}{((s/vp\Uparrow np)\backslash(s/vp\Uparrow np))/(s/vp\Uparrow np)} \qquad \dfrac{\text{no man marries}}{s/np\Uparrow vp}}{(s/vp\Uparrow np)\backslash(s/vp\Uparrow np)}\,/E}{s/(vp\Uparrow np)}\,\backslash E \qquad \dfrac{\dfrac{\text{his}}{(s/vp\Uparrow np)/cn} \qquad \dfrac{\text{mother}}{cn}}{vp\Uparrow np}\,/E}{s}\,/E$$

I've assumed that *his* here takes a relational noun (*mother*) as argument and should have the translation (54*a*), where "ι" is the definite description operator. Then for *his mother* we have (54*b*):

(54) (*a*) $\textit{his} \Rightarrow \lambda R\lambda G\lambda x[[G(\iota y : R(y, x))](x)]$

(*b*) **his mother** $\Rightarrow \lambda G\lambda x[G(\iota y : \textit{mother}'(y, x))(x)]$

(R is a variable over relations, G is as before, and the resulting translation has the type $\langle e, \langle\langle e, t\rangle, \langle e, t\rangle\rangle\rangle$, the right type for expressions in the combinator category $np\Uparrow vp$.)

Reducing the translation of the left conjunct:

(55) $\text{everyman}'(U_1(\lambda x_1[\text{love}'(x_1)]))(\lambda G\lambda x[G(\iota y : \textit{mother}'(y, x))(x)]) =$
$\text{everyman}'(\lambda G\lambda x[G(\iota y : \textit{mother}'(y, x))(x)](\lambda x_1[\text{love}'(x_1)])) =$
$\text{everyman}'(\lambda x[\text{love}'(\iota y : \text{mother}'(y, x))(x)])$

With the right conjunct derived the same way, the whole sentence will have the form $[\Phi \sqcap \Psi](\mathit{his\text{-}mother}')$ (where $\sqcap$ is generalized conjunction); this is equivalent to $[\Phi(\mathit{his\text{-}mother}') \wedge \Psi(\mathit{his\text{-}mother})']$. So we have (56) for the whole sentence:

(56) $\mathbf{every\text{-}man}'(\lambda x[\mathbf{love}'(\iota y{:}\mathbf{mother\text{-}of}'(y, x))(x)]) \wedge$
$\mathbf{no\text{-}man}'(\lambda z[\mathbf{marry}'(\iota w{:}\mathbf{mother\text{-}of}'(w, z))(z)])$

(It should be emphasized that nothing has been added just to produce this kind of sentence; we can use $np \Uparrow vp$ as a hypothesis simply because we can use *any* category as a hypothesis.) So where, exactly, in this derivation, do the quantifiers *every man* and *no man* "bind" the *his*? This happens in the step where combinatory pronoun scoping takes place, the step labeled "1". The perhaps unexpected thing is that a "hypothesized" combinator can scope out and thus be in a position to do the semantic binding just as a "real" combinatory pronoun binder can. It is the final step that gives the binding combinators their actual denotations, that of *his mother*; because of the coordination, the same binding combinator distributes to each conjunct, and, in the semantics, each instance of it "binds a VP" separately.

2.8.3.2 *Functional Questions in the S–M–D Analysis* The *functional* reading of a question such as (57) is the one on which the answer is (58*b*), with *his* understood to be taking *every Englishman* as its "antecedent" (as contrasted with (58*a*) as an answer).

(57) Who does every Englishman$_i$ love above all other women?

(58) (*a*) *The Queen* (referential answer)

(*b*) His$_i$ mother (*functional answer*)

The strategy for functional questions in the alternative analysis is similar to that for the R-N-R case. But first, just as Jacobson begins by generalizing the category of the question word *who*, we must do the same thing here; rather than put *who* in category $Q/(s/np)$ only, we generalize its category to $Q/(s/X)$, for some set of categories X. (A generalization of the category of *wh*-gaps is needed in any event, and exactly how general X should be does not matter here as long as X includes $np \Uparrow vp$.) Using this, we can derive (60).

(59) (*a*) Original category of *who(m), what* (as question words) = $Q/(s/np)$

(*b*) Generalized category of *who(m), what,* (as question words) = $Q/(s/X)$

(60)

$$\dfrac{\dfrac{Q/(s/(np\Uparrow vp)) : who \quad \dfrac{\dfrac{s/vp : ev\text{-}Eng : \mathbf{ev\text{-}Engmn'} \quad \dfrac{\dfrac{vp/np : admires : \mathbf{admire'} \quad \dfrac{vp\Uparrow np : [U_1]^i}{np : x_1}\Uparrow E}{vp : admires\ x_1 : \mathbf{admire'}(x_1)}/E}{vp : admires\ x_1 : U_1(\lambda x_1[\mathbf{admire'}(x_1)])}1}{s : ev\text{-}Eng\ admires\ x_1 : \mathbf{ev\text{-}Eng'}(U_1(\lambda x_1[\mathbf{admires'}(x_1)]))}/E}{s/(vp\Uparrow np) : ev\text{-}Eng\ admires : \lambda U_1[\mathbf{ev\text{-}Eng'}(U_1(\lambda x_1[\mathbf{admires'}(x_1)]))]}/I^i}{Q : who(\lambda U_1[\mathbf{ev\text{-}Eng'}(U_1(\lambda x_1[\mathbf{admires'}(x_1)]))])}/E}{}$$

It may be hard to see that this interpretation is really what we want for a functional question, but we can understand it better by observing how answer and question fit together. To keep things simple, note that the question meaning is derived in the form **who** $(\lambda v[\alpha])$, in which $\lambda v[\alpha]$ is a property: in the first-order question one something like "is an x such that John loves x"—and in the functional question "is an f such that John loves $f(John)$". The constituent answer should, if it is a correct answer, denote something we can ascribe this property to and get a true proposition. So, if the question was "who does John love", the property is $\lambda x[\textbf{John loves } x]$, and if the answer is "Mary", then $\lambda x[\textbf{John loves } x](\textbf{Mary})$ should be true; this formula is of course equivalent to $[\textbf{John loves Mary}]$. We would also expect the same thing to hold if the variable x has some other logic type, as long as x's type is the same as the answer's type.

Suppose the functional answer to the above functional question was *His mother*, in category $np\Uparrow vp$; we produced (61) for this earlier:

(61) **his mother** $\Rightarrow \lambda G \lambda x[G(\iota y : \mathbf{mother}'(y, x))(x)]$

So we will try applying the property abstract from (59) to this as argument:

(62) $\lambda U_1[\textbf{every Englishman}'(U_1(\lambda x_1[\mathbf{admires}'(x_1)]))]$
$(\lambda G \lambda x[G(\iota y{:}\mathbf{mother}'(y, x))(x)])$

Working out the β-reductions:

(63) (*a*) $\textbf{every Englishman}'(\lambda G \lambda x[G(\iota y{:}\mathbf{mother}'(y, x))(x)])$
$(\lambda x_1[\mathbf{admires}'(x_1)])$

(*b*) $\textbf{every Englishman}'(\lambda x[\lambda x_1[\mathbf{admires}'(x_1)]$
$(\iota y{:}\mathbf{mother}'(y, x))(x)])$

(*c*) $\textbf{every Englishman}'(\lambda x[\mathbf{admires}'(\iota y{:}\mathbf{mother}'(y, x))(x)])$

Spelling out *every Englishman* in terms of a first-order quantifier with a restriction, (63*c*) becomes the more familiar-looking:

(64) $\forall x[\mathbf{Englishman}'(x) \rightarrow \mathbf{admires}'(x, \iota y{:}\mathbf{mother}'(y, x))]$

From this, you can see clearly why it is that the pronoun *his* does not need to be present in the functional question itself to account for the functional reading, even though we have made the pronoun the bearer of the duplicator combinator meaning. (The fact that functional questions do not themselves contain the "functional pronoun" has sometimes been thought to provide an argument that Szabolcsi's approach of letting the pronoun denote the binding combinator will founder on functional questions.) But notice the logical TYPE of a stored combinator appears in the meaning of the functional question in the above analysis: it is the type of the "gap" used in generating the question. A value for this gap (a VP-binding combinator) is what the question asks for, but only the answer to the question can supply the right duplicator combinator to provide that functional answer.

2.8.3.3 *Additional Categories for Pronominal Combinatory Binders* Use of a pronominal binder in category $np \Uparrow vp$ must inevitably make the subject NP of the sentence the antecedent for the bound pronoun, but not all bound pronouns' antecedents in English are subjects. For example, if the antecedent NP is to be a direct object (*Mary persuaded every man to shave himself*), the pronominal binder category needs to be $np \Uparrow tv$. English will need at least these pronominal combinator categories:

Pronoun's category:	**Antecedent:**	**Pronoun's scope:**
$np \Uparrow vp$	Subject	vp
$np \Uparrow (vp/_w np)$	Direct Object	$vp/_w np$
$np \Uparrow ((vp/_w np)/prdp)$	Direct Object	phrasal $vp/_w np$ with PredP complement
$np \Uparrow ((vp\backslash vp)/_w np)/prdp$	Object of Prep.	"phrasal preposition", $(vp\backslash vp)/_w np$

(An example showing the need for the fourth category is *With Mary so upset with herself about her mistake, we'll never be finished on time*, that is assuming (as some though not all syntacticians would) that *with __ upset about herself* is a phrasal preposition (analogous to a "complex predicate").

We can avoid assigning pronouns to four or more individual categories by assigning them to a schematic category (as we do with "cross-categorial" *and*, *or* and various other cases in CG). Following notational precedents, I use "*A\$*" for a schema that includes all categories having zero or more complements and *A* as a final result category (*A, A/B, (A/B)/C, ((A/B)/C)/D*, etc.) The schemata for categories and translations of all anaphorically "bound" pronouns will therefore be:

Pronoun Category schema:	**Translation schema:**
$np \Uparrow vp\$$	$\lambda G \lambda x[(G(x))(x)]$ (Where $Typ(x) = e$ and $Typ(G) = \langle e, \langle e, a\rangle\rangle$, for any type a)

Anaphors in adjuncts will also be accommodated, no matter which of the syntactic roles their antecedents have—for example *We will sell no wine before its time*, which, as noted by Chris Barker, has a direct object antecedent for a bound pronoun inside an adjunct. We would probably prefer to class *before np's time* as a sentential modifier ("Before my grandfather's time, there were no telephones"), but as noted earlier, the automatic availability of type-raising (of the Geach variety) will ensure that any adjunct produced in $s\backslash s$ will also be a member of $vp\backslash vp$, $tv\backslash tv$, etc., so this example is derived by combining the adjunct, type-shifted into this last category, with TV *sell*, giving *sell before its time*, also in TV, at which point the pronoun *its* (in its category instance $np \Uparrow vp/np$) scopes out over this TVP; thus when the TVP is combined with *no wine* as argument (via Wrapping), *no wine* becomes the antecedent for bound *its*.

References

Bach, E. 1979. 'Control in Montague grammar', *Linguistic Inquiry*, 10: 515–32.

—— 1980. 'In defense of passive', *Linguistics and Philosophy*, 3: 297–342.

—— 1984. 'Some generalizations of categorial grammars', in F. Landman and F. Veltman (eds), *Varieties of Formal Semantics*. Dordrecht: Foris Publications. 55–80.

Barker, C. 2002. 'Continuations and the nature of quantification', *Natural Language Semantics*, 10: 211–42.

Carpenter, B. 1997. *Type-Logical Semantics*. Cambridge, MA: MIT Press.

Cooper, R. 1983. *Quantification and Syntactic Theory*. Dordrecht: Reidel.

Curry, H. B. 1963. 'Some logical aspects of grammatical structure,' in R. Jakobson (ed.), *Structure of Language and its Mathematical Aspects: Proceedings of the Twelfth Symposium in Applied Mathematics*. American Mathematical Society. 56–68.

—— and Feys, R. 1958. *Combinatory Logic: vol. I.* Amsterdam: North Holland.

Dever, J. 1999. 'Compositionality as methodology', *Linguistics and Philosophy*, 22: 311–26.

Dowty, D. 1979. *Word Meaning and Montague Grammar*, volume 7 of *Studies in Linguistics and Philosophy*. Dordrecht: Reidel.

—— 1982. 'Grammatical relations and Montague grammar', in P. Jacobson and G. Pullum (eds), *The Nature of Syntactic Representation*. Dordrecht: Reidel. 79–130.

—— [1992] 1996. 'Toward a minimalist theory of syntactic structure', in H. Bunt and A. van Horck (eds), *Discontinuous Constituency*. (Paper originally presented at a 1992 conference.) Berlin: de Gruyter. 11–62.

—— 1996. 'Non-constituent coordination, wrapping, and multimodal categorial grammars', in M. L. Dalla Chiara, K. Doets, D. Mundici, and J. van Banthem (eds),

Structures and Norms in Science, Proceedings of the 1995 International Congress of Logic, Methodology, and Philosophy of Science, Florence. Dordrecht: Kluwer. 347–68.

—— 2003. 'The dual analysis of adjuncts/complements in categorial grammar', in E. Lang and C. Maienborn (eds), *Modifying Adjuncts*. Berlin: de Gruyter. 33–66.

Ernst, T. 2003. 'Semantic features and the distribution of adverbs', in E. Lang and C. Maienborn (eds), *Modifying Adjuncts*. Berlin: de Gruyter. 307–34.

Frege, G. 1892. 'Über Sinn und Bedeutung', *Zeitschrift für Philosophie und philosophische Kritik*, 100: 25–50.

Gallin, D. 1975. *Intensional and Higher-Order Modal Logic*. Amsterdam: North-Holland.

Gazdar, G., Klein, E., Pullum, G., and Sag, I. 1985. *Generalized Phrase Structure Grammar*. Oxford: Blackwell.

Hepple, M. 1990. The Grammar and Processing of Order and Dependency. Ph.D. thesis, University of Edinburgh.

Hinrichs, E. 1986. A Compositional Semantics for Aktionsarten and NP Reference in English. Ohio State University Dissertation.

Hoeksema, J. and Janda, R. 1988. 'Implications of process morphology for categorial grammar', in R. Oehrle, E. Bach, and D. Wheeler (eds), *Categorial Grammars and Natural Language Structures*. Dordrecht: Reidel. 199–248.

Jacobson, P. 1982. 'Visser revisited', in K. Tuite, R. Schneider, and R. Chametzky (eds), *Papers from the 18th Regional Meeting of the Chicago Linguistic Society*. Chicago: Chicago Linguistic Society. 218–43.

—— 1999. 'Towards a variable-free semantics', *Linguistics and Philosophy*, 22: 117–84.

—— 2000. 'Paycheck pronouns, Bach-Peters sentences, and variable-free semantics', *Natural Language Semantics*, 8: 77–155.

—— 2002. 'The (dis)organization of the grammar: 25 years', *Linguistics and Philosophy*, 25: 601–26.

Jäger, G. 2001. *Anaphora and Type-Logical Grammar*. Habilitationsschrift, to Humboldt University Berlin, published as UIL-OTS Working Papers 01004-CL/TL, Utrecht Institut of Linguistics (OTS), University of Utrecht dissertation.

Janssen, T. 1986. 'Foundations and applications of Montague Grammar, part i: Philosophy, framework, computer science.' CWI tract 19, Center of Mathematics and Computer Science, Amsterdam.

—— 1997. 'Compositionality', in J. van Benthem and A. ter Meulen (eds), *Handbook of Logic and Language*. Amasterdam: Elsevier. 417–73.

Kamp, J. A. W. 1968. Tense Logic and the Theory of Linear Order. Dissertation, University of California, Los Angeles.

Kaplan, R. M. and Bresnan, J. 1982. 'Lexical-functional grammar: A formal system for grammatical representation', in J. Bresnan (ed.), *The Mental Representation of Grammatical Relations*. Cambridge, MA: MIT Press. 173–281.

Keenan, E. L. and Faltz, L. M. 1985. *Boolean Semantics for Natural Language* (Synthese Language Library 23). Dordrecht: Reidel.

Klein, E. and Sag, I. 1985. 'Type-driven translation', *Linguistics and Philosophy*, 8: 163–201.

Kruijff, G.-J. M. 2001. *A Categorial-Modal Architecture of Informativity: Dependency Grammar Logic & Information Structure*. Prague, Czech Republic: Charles University dissertation.

Kubota, Y. 2005. 'Verbal nouns, complex predicates and scope interpretation in Japanese. Unpublished paper, Ohio State University Linguistics Department.

Levine, R. D. and Meurers, W. D. 2005. 'Introduction', in R. D. Levine and W. D. Meurers (eds), *Locality of Grammatical Relationships*, number 58 in OSU Working Papers in Linguistics. Ohio State University Department of Linguistics.

Lewis, D. 1974. ''Tensions', in M. Munitz and P. Unyer (eds), Semantics and Philosophy. New York: New York University Press. 49–61.

Maling, J. M. and Zaenen, A. 1982. 'A phrase structure account of Scandinavian extraction phenomena', in P. Jacobson and G. K. Pullum (eds), *The Nature of Syntactic Representation*. Dordrecht: Reidel. 229–82.

Metcalf, V. 2005. 'Argument structure in HPSG as a lexical property: Evidence from English purpose infinitives', in R. D. Levine and W. D. Meurers (eds), *Locality of Grammatical Relationships*, number 58 in OSU Working Papers in Linguistics. Ohio State University Department of Linguistics.

Miller, P. 1992. *Clitics and Constituents in Phrase Structure Grammar*. Outstanding Dissertations in Linguistics. New York: Garland.

Montague, R. 1970. 'Universal grammar', *Theoria*, 36: 373–98.

Moortgat, M. 1996. 'Generalized quantifiers and discontinuous type constructors', in H. Bunt and A. van Horck (eds), *Discontinuous Constituency*. Berlin: de Gruyter. 181–208.

—— 1997. 'Categorial type logics', in J. van Benthem and A. ter Meulen (eds), *Handbook of Logic and Language*. Amsterdam: Elsevier. 93–177.

Partee, B. 1984. 'Compositionality', in F. Landman and F. Veltman (eds), *Varieties of Formal Semantics*. Dordrecht: Foris. 281–312.

—— and Rooth, M. 1983. 'Generalized conjunction and type ambiguity', in R. Bäuerle, C. Schwarze, and A. von Stechow (eds), *Meaning, Use, and Interpretation of Language*. Berlin: de Gruyter. 361–83.

Pelletier, F. J. 1994. 'On an argument against semantic compositionality', in D. Prawitz and D. Westerståhl (eds.), *Logic and Philosophy of Science in Uppsala*. Dordrecht: Kluwer. 599–610.

Perlmutter, D. and Postal, P. M. 1984. 'The 1-advancement exclusiveness law', in D. Perlmutter and C. Rosen (eds), *Studies in Relational Grammar 2*. Chicago: University of Chicago Press. 81–125.

Pollard, C. and Sag, I. 1994. *Head-Driven Phrase-Structure Grammar*. Chicago: University of Chicago Press.

QUINE, W. V. 1966. 'Variables explained away', in W. V. Quine, *Selected Logic Papers*. New York: Random House. 227–35.

REICHENBACH, H. 1947. *Elements of Symbolic Logic*. New York: Macmillan.

SCHMERLING, S. 1978. 'Synonymy judgments as syntactic evidence', in P. Cole (ed.), *Syntax and Semantics 9: Pragmatics*. New York: Academic Press. 299–314.

SELLS, P., ZAENEN, A., and ZEC, D. 1987. 'Reflexivization variation: Relations between syntax, semantics and lexical structure', in M. Iida, S. Wechsler, and D. Zec (eds), *Working Papers in Grammatical Theory and Discourse Structure: Interactions of Morphology, Syntax and Discourse*. CA: Stanford, CSLI. 169–238.

SHAN, C.-C. and BARKER, C. 2006. 'Explaining crossover and superiority as left-to-right evaluation', *Linguistics and Philosophy*, 29: 91–134.

SZABÓ, Z. 2000. 'Compositionality as supervenience', *Linguistics and Philosophy*, 23: 475–505.

SZABOLCSI, A. 1992. 'Combinatory grammar and projection from the lexicon', in *Lexical Matters*, volume 24 of *CSLI Lecture Notes*. Stanford, CA: CSLI.

THOMASON, R. H. 1980. 'A model theory for propositional attitudes', *Linguistics and Philosophy*, 4: 47–70.

VAN BENTHEM, J. 1983. 'The semantics of variety in categorial grammar'. Report 83–29, Department of Mathematics, Simon Fraser University, Burnaby.

WESTERSTÅHL, D. 1998. 'On mathematical proofs of the vacuity of compositionality', *Linguistics and Philosophy*, 21: 635–43.

ZADROZNY, W. 1994. 'From compositional to systematic semantics', *Linguistics and Philosophy*, 17: 329–42.

ZIMMERMANN, E. 1993. 'On the proper treatment of opacity in certain verbs', *Natural Language Semantics*, 1: 149–79.

3

Direct Compositionality on Demand*

CHRIS BARKER

3.1 Two Equally Valid Views of the Syntax–Semantics Interface

The problem is that many natural language expression types lead a double life, simultaneously here and there, masquerading as a local lump but somehow interacting directly with distant elements. The two main examples discussed here are bound anaphora, in which an anaphor depends for its value on some distant binder; and quantification, in which some local element takes semantic scope over a properly containing constituent. Such action-at-a-distance confronts theories of the syntax–semantics interface with a dilemma: should we interpret these elements locally, where they enter into the syntactic structure, or globally, where they take semantic effect?

Both approaches have staunch defenders. One well-established approach (e.g. Heim and Kratzer 1998) emphasizes the global perspective, relegating the interpretation of anaphors to variable assignment functions, and postponing

* This chapter owes debts to three people: first and foremost, Pauline Jacobson, whose work inspired the workshop from which this chapter developed, and who discussed many of the ideas below with me during my sabbatical visit to Brown in the fall of 2003. Second, David Dowty, whose remarks on the formal nature of direct compositionality expressed at the workshop and in conversation planted the seed that grew into this chapter. Third, Gerhard Jäger, who first introduced me to the display property for type logics ("it is always possible to glue two adjacent constituents together before building the larger constituent. This requires a lot of cut applications ..." (in an email from fall 2003)), which approximates my on-demand property. (See §3.8 for a discussion of the display property in comparison with the DCOD property.) Finally, I would like to point out that the crucial technical innovation that gives the logic presented below the on-demand property, namely, the rule of disclosure for quantification, *q*LR, was directly inspired by Jäger's (2005) similar rule for his binding analysis. In some sense, then, this paper merely emphasizes the importance of a symmetry already present in Jäger's LLC, and extends the same symmetry to quantification. Substantial improvements over the first draft are due to discussions with Chung-chieh Shan and Anna Szabolcsi.

the interpretation of quantifiers until their scope has been revealed via Quantifier Raising at a level of Logical Form.

Another tradition, going back at least to Montague, and recently championed by many working within Categorial Grammar and its related frameworks, emphasizes local interpretation. Jacobson, in a series of papers (e.g. Jacobson 1999), names this approach "Direct Compositionality": roughly (to be made somewhat more precise below), expressions must deliver their entire semantic payload at the moment they enter into a syntactic relationship.

I claim that both views are indispensable, and that any grammar which ignores either mode of meaning is incomplete. Can we hope for a system that adheres to direct compositionality, but without giving up the clarity and simplicity of a global view?

Of course, there is an uninteresting, trivial answer, which involves simply combining a directly compositional grammar with an empirically equivalent, redundant grammar that allows non-local action.

I will propose what I believe is a more interesting answer, in the form of DCOD (for "Direct Compositionality On Demand"), a grammar in which the long-distance and local analyses arise from one and the same set of rules, none of which are redundant. The on-demand property allows us to have our cake and eat it too: we can connect an anaphor directly with its antecedent, and we can connect a quantifier to its scope in a single intuitive leap; or else, if we prefer, we can articulate each derivation into incremental steps that reveal the semantic contribution of each syntactic constituent.

To give a slightly more detailed preview, for every derivation in DCOD in which an expression is bound at a distance or takes wide scope, there will be a syntactically and semantically equivalent derivation on which the semantic contribution of each constituent is purely local. Furthermore, the interconvertibility of the two styles of derivation does not simply follow from grafting a direct-compositional grammar onto an action-at-a-distance grammar; rather, the duality in the syntax–semantics interface follows from a natural symmetry in the grammar itself. The symmetry concerns Gentzen's rules of use and rules of proof. Roughly, in the grammar below, rules of use connect expressions directly over long distances, and embody the global view. Rules of proof help characterize the contribution of individual expressions within a complex constituent. Crucially, I introduce rules of disclosure, which establish an explicit connection between the long-distance semantic effect of an element with its local denotation. As a consequence, we can use the global-style rules of use without the slightest hesitation, confident that we can produce a parallel, strictly directly compositional elaboration upon demand.

The on-demand property, at least as I envision it below, is by no means a general characteristic of type-logical grammars. In particular, Jäger's (2005) LLC+q (LLC supplemented with rules for quantification) does not have the DCOD property. Nor do Display Calculi (Goré 1998; Bernardi 2002) necessarily have the property, despite the fact that Display Calculi guarantee a similar constraint, the "display property": that any syntactic constituent can be given a self-contained denotation. (More technically, that any structural element can be isolated on the left-hand side of a sequent.) The problem with these grammars is that the value determined by exercising the display guarantee often incorporates information about the derivation of elements external to the constituent in question. This is a fairly subtle but important point, and is developed in §3.8.

3.2 Three Characteristics of Direct Compositionality

The essence of direct compositionality is that every syntactic operation that combines two smaller expressions into a larger expression comes along with a semantic operation that combines the meanings of the smaller expressions to arrive at the meaning of the larger expression. This is just an informal characterization of Montague's Universal Grammar (as instantiated in, e.g., Montague 1974).

The conceptual simplicity and straightforwardness of direct compositionality has tremendous appeal. On the other hand, direct compositionality requires a certain amount of book-keeping: as we shall see, every semantically relevant aspect of a constituent must be available at the point at which the constituent enters into a syntactic structure, whether that aspect is relevant at that point or not. Thus combination rules must be adjusted to make use of information when it is required, and ignore it (but without discarding it!) when it is not.

3.2.1 *No Postponement*

On the direct compositional view, the order of syntactic combination is identical to the order of semantic combination.

This view of the syntax–semantics interface contrasts with the standard Quantifier-Raising (QR) approach to quantifier scope:

(1)

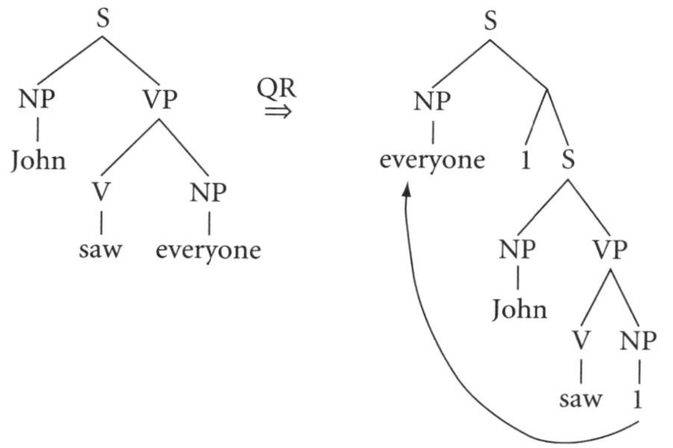

The reason that this approach fails to be directly compositional is that there is a point in the derivation at which *everyone* has already been combined syntactically with *saw* to form a verb phrase constituent (as evident in the left-most tree), but the verb phrase does not yet have a well-formed semantic denotation. In particular, there is no (relevant) way to directly combine a transitive verb such as *saw* of type ⟨e, ⟨e, t⟩⟩ with a generalized quantifier such as *everyone* of type ⟨⟨e, t⟩, t⟩. Nor is there any obvious way of assigning a suitable denotation to the constituent *saw everyone*. It is only after the complete nuclear scope has been constructed (as in the right-most tree) that Quantifier Raising resolves the type mismatch and a complete meaning emerges.

The QR approach is rather like building a car on an assembly-line: it may be convenient to install the steering wheel before attaching the doors, even if the control cables and electronic connections that allow the steering wheel to guide the wheels do not get attached until later in the assembly process. Just so, in the QR model, the generalized quantifier *everyone* is inserted in direct object position, but its semantic control cables are left dangling until the rest of its clause has been assembled. I will call this sort of delayed evaluation POSTPONEMENT.

Forbidding postponement entails that no denotation has access to material contributed by an expression that is not part of the immediate syntactic expression. For instance, a pronoun must make its semantic contribution as soon as it enters into the syntactic construction, and cannot wait to find out what its antecedent is going to be.

The direct compositional ideal is a kind of zen semantics, living entirely in the moment of combination, unaware of what has happened or what is to come.

3.2.2 *Full Disclosure*

It follows from forbidding postponement that all syntactically and semantically relevant aspects of elements within a constituent must be accessible when the constituent combines with other elements. In other words, if a constituent contains a bindable pronoun or a quantifier, then that fact must be evident by inspecting the syntactic and semantic features of the constituent.

Jacobson (1999) works out in detail what full disclosure could look like for a directly compositional theory of binding; Shan and Barker (2006) show what full disclosure could look like for a theory of quantification.

3.2.3 *Self-Reliance*

The flip side of full disclosure is that the analysis of constituents should be self-contained. This means that the syntactic category and the semantic value should depend only on the lexical items dominated by the constituent and on the structure internal to the constituent. The analysis should certainly not depend in any way on any element external to the constituent.

I will suggest below that although the display property possessed by most type-logical grammars is capable of providing analyses of any constituent, those analyses often violate self-reliance. (See especially §3.8 below.) If the analysis of a subconstituent incorporates details that anticipate the specific structures in which it will be embedded, that is just a way of sneaking postponement through the back door.

3.3 DCOD, a Logic with Direct Compositionality on Demand

This section presents DCOD, the grammar analyzed in later sections. DCOD is a type-logical grammar. There are several quite different but more or less equivalent ways to present TLG. The two main styles are Natural Deduction vs. the Sequent Calculus presentation. I will use the sequent presentation here, since that will best facilitate the discussion of cut elimination further below. I have done my best to keep in mind readers who are not already familiar with sequent systems, but it may be helpful to consult more leisurely presentations of sequent logics such as Moortgat (1997), Restall (2000), or Jäger (2005).

3.3.1 *General Strategy*

The cut rule plays a special role in providing direct compositionality on demand. As discussed below, the cut rule expresses a kind of transitivity governing inference. Most discussions of the cut rule concentrate on proving that all cuts can be eliminated without reducing the generative power of the system, and thus that the cut rule is logically redundant. Cut elimination is important in order to prove such properties as logical consistency, guaranteed termination for the proof search algorithm, or that there will be at most a finite number of distinct interpretations for any given sentence. When considering these results, it is easy to get the impression that getting rid of cuts is always a very good thing.

But in fact it is *being able to* get rid of cuts that is the good thing. Cuts themselves are often quite useful: they correspond to proving a lemma, which you can then use and reuse in different contexts without having to re-prove it each time. The connection with constituency is that it is possible to think of deriving, say, a noun phrase as a lemma. To say that a noun phrase is a constituent is to say that we could, if we chose, derive the noun phrase separately from the rest of the proof as a lemma, and then insert the lemma into the larger derivation in the position that the noun phrase occupies.

3.3.2 *DCOD*

Each rule in Example (2) relates either one or two antecedent sequents (appearing above the line) with exactly one consequent (below the line). Here, a sequent consists of a structure on the left-hand side of the sequent symbol ("$\Rightarrow$") and a single formula on the right-hand side. A structure is either a single formula or an ordered pair (Γ, Δ) in which Γ and Δ are both themselves structures. A formula is either a symbol such as np, n, or s, or else has the form $A\backslash B$, A/B, A^B, or $q(A, B, C)$, where A, B, and C are metavariables over formulas. For instance, the sequent $(np/n, n) \Rightarrow np$ says that a structure consisting of a determiner of category np/n followed by a noun of category n can form an NP of category np. From a linguistic point of view, formulas serve the role of syntactic categories, and structures indicate constituency. (You can think of a structure as a standard linguistic tree but without any syntactic category labels on the internal nodes.)

There are two kinds of information present in the rules given in Example (2): logical information, encoded by formulas expressing types; and semantic information, encoded by terms in the λ-calculus expressing how the meanings of the elements in the inference rule relate to one another. Thus x: B stands for an expression of category B whose semantic value is named by x. In the derivations below, I will often omit the semantic part of the derivation when it enhances clarity.

Two rules are special, the axiom rule and the cut rule. The axiom rule is a simple tautology: given A, conclude A ("if it's raining, then it's raining").

(2)

$$\frac{}{\texttt{x}: A \Rightarrow \texttt{x}: A}\ \text{Axiom}$$

$$\frac{\Delta \Rightarrow \texttt{m}: A \quad \Gamma[\,\texttt{x}: A] \Rightarrow \texttt{p}: B}{\Gamma[\Delta] \Rightarrow \texttt{p}\{\texttt{m}/\texttt{x}\}: B}\ \text{Cut}$$

Rules of use (left rules):

$$\frac{\Delta \Rightarrow \texttt{x}: A \quad \Gamma[\,\texttt{y}: B] \Rightarrow \texttt{m}: C}{\Gamma[(\,\texttt{f}: (B/A), \Delta)] \Rightarrow \texttt{m}\{(\texttt{fx})/\texttt{y}\}: C}\ /\text{L}$$

$$\frac{\Delta \Rightarrow \texttt{x}: A \quad \Gamma[\,\texttt{y}: B] \Rightarrow \texttt{m}: C}{\Gamma[(\Delta,\ \texttt{f}: (A\backslash B))] \Rightarrow \texttt{m}\{(\texttt{fx})/\texttt{y}\}: C}\ \backslash\text{L}$$

$$\frac{\Delta \Rightarrow \texttt{m}: A \quad \Gamma[\,\texttt{x}: A][\,\texttt{y}: B] \Rightarrow \texttt{n}: C}{\Gamma[\Delta][\,\texttt{f}: B^A] \Rightarrow \texttt{n}\{\texttt{m}/\texttt{x}; (\texttt{fm})/\texttt{y}\}: C}\ \uparrow\text{L}$$

$$\frac{\Delta[\,\texttt{x}: B] \Rightarrow \texttt{m}: C \quad \Gamma[\,\texttt{y}: D] \Rightarrow \texttt{n}: E}{\Gamma[\Delta[\,\texttt{g}: q(B, C, D)]] \Rightarrow \texttt{n}\{(\texttt{g}(\lambda\texttt{x}.\texttt{m}))/\texttt{y}\}: E}\ q\text{L}$$

Rules of proof (right rules):

$$\frac{(\Gamma,\ \texttt{x}: A) \Rightarrow \texttt{m}: B}{\Gamma \Rightarrow \lambda\texttt{x}.\texttt{m}: (B/A)}\ /\text{R}$$

$$\frac{(\,\texttt{x}: A, \Gamma) \Rightarrow \texttt{m}: B}{\Gamma \Rightarrow \lambda\texttt{x}.\texttt{m}: (A\backslash B)}\ \backslash\text{R}$$

Rules of disclosure (left–right rules):

$$\frac{\Delta[\,\texttt{x}: A] \Rightarrow \texttt{m}: B}{\Delta[\,\texttt{f}: A^C] \Rightarrow \lambda\texttt{y}.\texttt{m}\{(\texttt{fy})/\texttt{x}\}: B^C}\ \uparrow\text{LR}$$

$$\frac{\Pi[\,\texttt{x}: A] \Rightarrow \texttt{m}: B}{\Pi[\,\texttt{g}: q(A, C, D)] \Rightarrow \lambda\texttt{f}.\texttt{g}(\lambda\texttt{x}.(\texttt{fm})): q(B, C, D)}\ q\text{LR}$$

DCOD: a resource-sensitive logic with binding and quantification that guarantees Direct Compositionality On Demand. The only novel element compared with Jäger's (2005: 100) LLC is qLR.

The cut rule, which plays an important role in the discussion here and below, expresses a fundamental kind of logical transitivity: given $\Delta \Rightarrow A$, which says that Δ constitutes a proof of the formula A; and given $\Gamma[A] \Rightarrow B$, which says that Γ is a proof of B that depends on assuming A, it follows that $\Gamma[\Delta] \Rightarrow B$: substituting the reasoning that led to the conclusion A into the spot in the proof Γ where Γ depends on assuming A constitutes a valid complete proof of B. For instance, if you can prove that *the* plus *dog* forms a noun phrase (expressed in syntactic categories, $(np/n, n) \Rightarrow np$), and if you can prove that any noun phrase plus *barked* forms a complete sentence (i.e. $(np, np\backslash s) \Rightarrow s$), then the cut rule entitles you to conclude that ((*the dog*) *barked*) forms a complete sentence ($((np/n, n), np\backslash s) \Rightarrow s$).

In the cut rule, the notation $\Gamma[A]$ schematizes over structures Γ that contain at least one occurrence of the formula A somewhere within it. The notation $\Gamma[\Delta]$ in the consequent represents a structure similar to Γ except with Δ substituted in place of (the relevant occurrence of) A. (Examples immediately below will illustrate how this works.)

Apart from axiom and cut, most of the remaining rules introduce a single new logical connective (i.e. one not occurring in the antecedents) into the consequent, either on the left-hand side of the sequent symbol (the "left" rules) or else on the right-hand side (the "right" rules). As discussed below, the two crucial rules for the discussion here introduce a new connective on both sides of the sequent, and so are "left–right" rules. (Purely for the sake of expository simplicity, I have omitted logical rules for the • ("product") connective, which plays a prominent role in many type-logical discussions, but is not needed for any of the derivations below.)

A derivation is complete if all of its branches end (reading bottom up) using only instances of the Axiom as antecedents, and if each conclusion is derived from the antecedents above it via a legitimate instantiation of one of the logical rules. Here is a complete derivation proving that *the dog barked* is a sentence:

(3)
$$\dfrac{\dfrac{\dfrac{}{n \Rightarrow n}\,\text{Axiom} \quad \dfrac{}{np \Rightarrow np}\,\text{Axiom}}{(np/n, n) \Rightarrow \boxed{\text{np}}}\,/\text{L} \qquad \dfrac{\dfrac{}{np \Rightarrow np}\,\text{Axiom} \quad \dfrac{}{s \Rightarrow s}\,\text{Axiom}}{(\boxed{\text{np}}, np\backslash s) \Rightarrow s}\,\backslash\text{L}}{\left(\left(\begin{matrix} np/n \\ \texttt{the} \end{matrix}, \begin{matrix} n \\ \texttt{dog} \end{matrix}\right), \begin{matrix} np\backslash s \\ \texttt{barked} \end{matrix}\right) \Rightarrow \begin{matrix} s \\ \texttt{barked(the(dog))} \end{matrix}}\,\text{Cut}$$

I have placed boxes around the formulas that instantiate the As targeted by the cut rule. (From this point on, I will assume that applications of the axiom rule are obvious, and so do not need to be explicitly indicated.)

An expression is generated by a type-logical grammar just in case there are lexical items whose category labels match the formulas in the result (bottom-most) sequent and which appear in the same order as the formulas in the sequent. Thus if the word *the* has meaning `the` and category np/n, *dog* has meaning `dog` and category n, and *barked* has meaning `barked` and category $np\backslash s$, then the derivation here proves that *the dog barked* has category s, with semantic interpretation `barked(the(dog))`. Furthermore, in that derivation, *the dog* forms a constituent.

In this case, the structure of the derivation corresponds to the constituent structure of the conclusion sequent: the NP $(np/n, n)$ is a constituent in the conclusion sequent, and the main subderivation on the left (the first antecedent of the lowest inference) shows how to construct a subproof that $(np/n, n)$ forms an NP. Unfortunately, this graceful correspondence between the form of the derivation and constituency (as determined by the structure in the conclusion sequent) is not guaranteed. Indeed, arriving at such a guarantee is the main topic of this paper.

3.4 Rules of Use, Rules of Proof, and Rules of Disclosure

Following Lambek (1958) (in turn following Gentzen), the distinctive feature of TLG compared to plain categorial grammar is the ability to employ hypothetical reasoning. In terms of the sequent presentation used here, there are two types of logical rules, called left rules and right rules, or rules of use and rules of proof. Plain categorial grammar gets by with only (the equivalent of) the left rules, the rules of use. Because rules other than rules of use will be crucial for my main argument, this section briefly motivates the utility of rules of proof for linguistic analyses.

The usual motivating examples typically involve either function composition or relative clause formation. But these examples also require structural postulates that render function application associative, which would significantly complicate exposition at this point (structural postulates are discussed below in §3.9).

But even in the absence of associativity, rules of proof can perform useful linguistic work by deriving a certain class of lifted predicates. Dowty (2000) suggests that adjuncts may sometimes be re-analyzed as arguments. If *sing* has category v (where v abbreviates the category $(np\backslash s)/np$), then if *well* is a verbal adjunct of category $v\backslash v$, *sing well* is correctly predicted to be a complex v, as shown here:

(4)
$$\frac{v \Rightarrow v \qquad v \Rightarrow v}{\left(\begin{matrix} v \\ \mathtt{sing} \end{matrix}, \begin{matrix} v\backslash v \\ \mathtt{well} \end{matrix}\right) \Rightarrow \begin{matrix} v \\ \mathtt{well(sing)} \end{matrix}}\ \backslash L$$

It is also possible for a higher-order verb to take a verbal modifier as an argument:

(5)
$$\dfrac{v\backslash v \Rightarrow v\backslash v \quad v \Rightarrow v}{\left(\begin{array}{c} v/(v\backslash v) \\ \texttt{behave} \end{array}, \begin{array}{c} v\backslash v \\ \texttt{well} \end{array}\right) \Rightarrow \begin{array}{c} v \\ \texttt{behave(well)} \end{array}} /L$$

A language learner may not be able to tell whether to assign *sing* to the category v or the category $v/(v\backslash v)$. This is harmless, however, since as the following derivation shows, it is a theorem of DCOD (and any Lambek grammar) that anything in the category v can behave as if it were of category $v/(v\backslash v)$, the same category as *behave*:

(6)
$$\dfrac{\dfrac{v \Rightarrow v \quad v \Rightarrow v}{(v, v\backslash v) \Rightarrow v} \backslash L}{\begin{array}{c} v \\ \texttt{sing} \end{array} \Rightarrow \begin{array}{c} v/(v\backslash v) \\ \lambda\texttt{a.a(sing)} \end{array}} /R$$

Thus whether you think of *sing* in *sing well* as the argument of *well* or else as a lifted predicate that takes *well* as an argument is completely optional as far as the logic is concerned. We can assume, then, that the simplest lexicon will be one in which *sing* has category v, but verbs that require a modifier must be of category $v/(v\backslash v)$.

One prediction that this analysis makes is that it should be possible to conjoin a simple verb like *sing* with a verb of higher category like *behave*. This is a good prediction, since *sing and behave well* certainly is a legitimate coordination:

(7)
$$\dfrac{v/(v\backslash v) \Rightarrow v/(v\backslash v) \quad \dfrac{\dfrac{\dfrac{v \Rightarrow v \quad v \Rightarrow v}{(v, v\backslash v) \Rightarrow v} \backslash L}{v \Rightarrow v/(v\backslash v)} /R \quad v/(v\backslash v) \Rightarrow v/(v\backslash v)}{(v, (v/(v\backslash v))\backslash(v/(v\backslash v))) \Rightarrow v/(v\backslash v)} \backslash L}{\left(\begin{array}{c} v \\ \texttt{sing} \end{array}, \left(\begin{array}{c} X\backslash(X/X) \\ \texttt{and} \end{array}, \begin{array}{c} v/(v\backslash v) \\ \texttt{behave} \end{array}\right)\right) \Rightarrow \begin{array}{c} v/(v\backslash v) \\ \lambda\texttt{m.m(sing)} \wedge \texttt{behave(m)} \end{array}} /L$$

In this derivation, the phrase *and behave* is something that is looking for an expression of the same category as *behave* in order to form a coordinate structure. *Sing* is able to fill that role because of the /R rule, which is a crucial part of the deduction that *sing* is able to combine with an adverb. Note that in the semantic interpretation, the variable `m` (representing a manner) corresponding to the adverb *well* modifies *sing*, but serves as an argument to *behave*, as desired.

In any case, rules of proof can be motivated independently of the main issues of this paper.

The innovative rules in DCOD, however, are not straightforward rules of proof. True rules of proof such as \R or /R introduce a new connective only on the right side of the sequent. The rules of special interest here do introduce a new connective on the right side of the sequent, but they also introduce a new connective on the left side of the sequent at the same time. Following a suggestion of Chung-chieh Shan (p.c.), I will label such rules LR rules: simultaneously left rules and right rules. (Thus the rule Jäger (2005) refers to as ↑R I will call ↑LR.) These LR rules are not really rules of use, since they are not sufficient to license the use of, say, a pronoun or a quantifier; and they are not really rules of proof, since they do not discharge any hypotheses in the way that \R or /R do. (Section 3.7 will discuss other unusual properties of the LR rules with respect to cut elimination.) As we shall see, what these new rules do is transmit information about subconstituents to higher levels. Therefore I will call them **rules of disclosure**.

Thus DCOD leaves open the question of what a true rule of proof would be for binding or for quantification. This is an area of active research; for one detailed view of how to handle scope-taking in a type-logical grammar, see Barker and Shan (in press).

3.5 First Case Study: Binding

Here is the swooping (cut-free) derivation of *John$_i$ said he$_i$ left.*

(8)

$$\frac{np \Rightarrow np \qquad \dfrac{np \Rightarrow np \qquad \dfrac{s \Rightarrow s \qquad \dfrac{np \Rightarrow np \qquad s \Rightarrow s}{(np, np\backslash s) \Rightarrow s}\,\backslash\mathrm{L}}{(np, ((np\backslash s)/s, s)) \Rightarrow s}\,/\mathrm{L}}{(\boxed{\mathrm{np}}, ((np\backslash s)/s, (\boxed{\mathrm{np}}, np\backslash s))) \Rightarrow s}\,\backslash\mathrm{L}}{\left(\begin{matrix}np\\ \texttt{John}\end{matrix}, \left(\begin{matrix}(np\backslash s)/s\\ \texttt{said}\end{matrix}, \left(\begin{matrix}np^{np}\\ \texttt{he}\end{matrix}, \begin{matrix}np\backslash s\\ \texttt{left}\end{matrix}\right)\right)\right) \Rightarrow \begin{matrix}s\\ \texttt{said(left(he(j)))(j)}\end{matrix}}\,\uparrow\mathrm{L}$$

The form of the binding rule in Example (2) requires some comment. In the second antecedent, $\Gamma[A][B]$ matches a structure Γ that contains an occurrence α of the formula A and an occurrence β of formula B. (In addition, α must precede β, but linear precedence will not be an important factor below.) In the conclusion, $\Gamma[\Delta][A^B]$ indicates the structure constructed by starting with Γ, replacing α with Δ, and replacing β with the formula A^B. In the diagram immediately above, α is the left box, and β is the right box. In the conclusion, α is replaced with np (no net change), and β is replaced with np^{np}.

In this derivation, there is exactly one application of the binding rule $\uparrow$L, operating over a potentially unbounded distance. I have boxed the NP targets of the $\uparrow$L rule, that is the elements to be bound. Intuitively, the rule in effect coindexes the boxed elements, guaranteeing that their interpretations will be linked. Naturally, the pronoun denotes a function from NP meanings to NP meanings, in this case, the identity function (see, e.g. Jacobson 1999 for discussion on this point).

Crucially, this analysis does not provide self-contained interpretations for each constituent. That is, this derivation is not directly compositional. In particular, consider the constituent *he left*. If any substring of the larger sentence deserves to be a constituent, it is the embedded clause! The final sequent recognizes that *he left* is a syntactic constituent, since *he* and *left* are grouped together into a substructure (as indicated by the parentheses in the bottom-most sequent) yet there is no point at which the denotation of the constituent is treated as a semantic unit.

To see why, focus on the second (lower) instance of \L, repeated here with full Curry–Howard labeling:

$$(9) \quad \cfrac{\begin{array}{c}np \\ x\end{array} \Rightarrow \begin{array}{c}np \\ x\end{array} \quad \left(\begin{array}{c}np \\ y\end{array}, \left(\begin{array}{c}(np\backslash s)/s \\ \text{said}\end{array}, \begin{array}{c}s \\ p\end{array}\right)\right) \Rightarrow \begin{array}{c}s \\ \text{said(p)(y)}\end{array}}{\left(\begin{array}{c}np \\ y\end{array}, \left(\begin{array}{c}(np\backslash s)/s \\ \text{said}\end{array}, \left(\begin{array}{c}np \\ x\end{array}, \begin{array}{c}np\backslash s \\ \text{left}\end{array}\right)\right)\right) \Rightarrow \begin{array}{c}s \\ \text{said(left(x))(y)}\end{array}} \backslash L$$

This is the step that articulates the embedded clause into a subject and a verb phrase, so this is the step that justifies the claim that *he* and *left* are structural siblings. The contribution to the semantic value made by this step is the expression left(x), where x is a variable introduced by the instance of the axiom rule that justifies the left-most antecedent. This variable does not receive a value until the binding rule ($\uparrow$L) applies in the next derivational step, at which point the value of the embedded subject is bound to the value of the matrix subject. But the matrix subject is external to the constituent in question, so this labeling constitutes semantic postponement, and violates semantic self-reliance.

In other words, the cut-free derivation above clearly associates the position of the pronoun with its antecedent, so it accounts beautifully for the long-distance aspect of binding. However, quite sadly, it does not provide a full account of the sense in which *he left* is a constituent in its own right.

The main result of this paper guarantees the existence of a distinct derivation in DCOD that arrives at the same constituent structure and that has an identical semantic value, but in which each constituent can be associated with a self-contained semantic value. It is this second, related, derivation that provides the missing piece of the puzzle, and that characterizes *he left* as a constituent.

Arriving at such an alternative derivation involves use of the rule of proof ($\uparrow$LR) and several applications of the cut rule. Here's one way to do it:

(10)

$$\dfrac{\dfrac{\dfrac{np \Rightarrow np \qquad s \Rightarrow s}{(np, np\backslash s) \Rightarrow s}\,\backslash L}{\left(\begin{matrix} np^{np} \\ \texttt{he} \end{matrix}, \begin{matrix} np\backslash s \\ \texttt{left} \end{matrix}\right) \Rightarrow \begin{matrix} s^{np} \\ \lambda\texttt{x.left(he(x))} \end{matrix}}\,\uparrow LR \qquad \dfrac{\dfrac{s \Rightarrow s \qquad np\backslash s \Rightarrow np\backslash s}{((np\backslash s)/s, s) \Rightarrow np\backslash s}\,/L}{((np\backslash s)/s, s^{np}) \Rightarrow (np\backslash s)^{np}}\,\uparrow LR}{\left(\begin{matrix} (np\backslash s)/s \\ \texttt{said} \end{matrix}, \left(\begin{matrix} np^{np} \\ \texttt{he} \end{matrix}, \begin{matrix} np\backslash s \\ \texttt{left} \end{matrix}\right)\right) \Rightarrow \begin{matrix} (np\backslash s)^{np} \\ \lambda\texttt{y.said(left(he(y)))} \end{matrix}}\,\text{Cut}$$

This derivation for the verb phrase constituent *said he left* can participate in a complete derivation as follows:

$$\dfrac{(np\backslash s)/s, (np^{np}, np\backslash s) \Rightarrow (np\backslash s)^{np} \qquad \dfrac{np \Rightarrow np \qquad \dfrac{np \Rightarrow np \qquad s \Rightarrow s}{(np, np\backslash s) \Rightarrow s}\,\backslash L}{(np, (np\backslash s)^{np}) \Rightarrow s}\,\uparrow L}{\left(\begin{matrix} np \\ \texttt{John} \end{matrix}, \left(\begin{matrix} (np\backslash s)/s \\ \texttt{said} \end{matrix}, \left(\begin{matrix} np^{np} \\ \texttt{he} \end{matrix}, \begin{matrix} np\backslash s \\ \texttt{left} \end{matrix}\right)\right)\right) \Rightarrow \begin{matrix} s \\ \texttt{said(left(he(j)))(j)} \end{matrix}}\,\text{Cut}$$

The final sequents of the two completed derivations are identical, so both derivations provide the same constituency and the same final semantic interpretation. However, the second derivation provides a self-contained denotation for each constituent, where "self-contained" means that each element in the denotation either turns out to be the denotation of a word in the final sequent (e.g., `left`) or else is a variable that is bound within the denotation (e.g., `x` in λ`x.left(x)` but not in `left(x)`).

This cut-full derivation beautifully captures the intuition that *he left* is a constituent. However, now the link between the pronoun and its binder has been sadly obscured.

In order to emphasize the role of the cut rule in encapsulating the meaning of a subconstituent, the diagram above provides Curry–Howard semantic labels only for the final sequent in a derivation and for the first antecedent of each application of the cut rule, that is the antecedent that corresponds to an encapsulated constituent. (It should be clear how to complete the labelings of each of the derivations based on the labeling annotations in Example (2).) Here is what a complete labeling for the constituent *he left* would look like:

(11)
$$\dfrac{\dfrac{\texttt{x}\colon np \Rightarrow \texttt{x}\colon np \qquad \texttt{p}\colon s \Rightarrow \texttt{p}\colon s}{(\,\texttt{x}\colon np,\ \texttt{left}\colon (np\backslash s)) \Rightarrow \texttt{left(x)}\colon s}\,\backslash L}{\left(\begin{matrix} np^{np} \\ \texttt{he}\end{matrix}, \begin{matrix} np\backslash s \\ \texttt{left}\end{matrix}\right) \Rightarrow \begin{matrix} s^{np} \\ \lambda\texttt{x.left(he(x))}\end{matrix}}\,\uparrow LR$$

This complete labeling of the constituent shows how the ↑LR rule binds the argument of the pronoun, making the denotation self-contained. The troublesome element in the swooping derivation was the variable x, whose value was determined from outside the constituent. In the final labeling here, λx.left(x), x is bound by the lambda.[1] As Jäger points out, it is not a coincidence that the syntactic category and the denotation of *he left* coincides exactly with the analysis proposed in Jacobson's (1999) directly compositional theory; in other words, both analyses say the same thing about the directly compositional aspect of the binding relationship.

In the swooping derivation, there is no syntactic category labeling the structure corresponding to the constituent *he left*. In the directly compositional derivation, the syntactic category is revealed to be s^{np}, a sentence containing a bindable pronoun. Thus the DC derivation imposes full disclosure, annotating on the category the presence of bindable pronoun inside. Similarly, in the swooping derivation, there is no semantic denotation corresponding exactly to the constituent *he left*. There is a contribution to the Curry–Howard labeling, but one of the elements contributed (namely, the variable x) ultimately depends on material outside of the constituent for its final value, rather than on some function of the meanings of the words contained within the constituent. Thus in addition to a transparent constituent structure, the DC derivation also imposes semantic self-reliance.

On the other hand, only in the swooping derivation can we clearly see the net result of the series of incremental abstractions and substitutions that the DC derivation plods through. By linking the boxed *np*s directly in the swooping derivation, we get a satisfying account of what the pronoun takes as its antecedent. In addition, it is worth noting that the swooping derivation is considerably shorter and simpler.

Which derivation is superior? With DCOD, we do not need to decide: both are equally available. Furthermore, as we shall see below, it is possible

[1] The version of ↑LR given here is simplified from Jäger's (2005: 100) more general rule. Jäger's rule handles cases in which more than one pronominal element is bound by the same antecedent.

to prove that they are equivalent. Therefore they are equally valid analyses of the sentence in question, and neither one alone tells the full story.

3.5.1 *Deictic Pronouns*

One of the virtues of Jacobson's treatment is that there is no lexical distinction between bound pronouns and deictic pronouns: a deictic pronoun is simply a pronoun that never happens to get bound. Yet in the DCOD grammar, the only way of introducing a functional dependency (a category with shape B^A) is either by way of the ↑L rule, in which case there is an overt binder somewhere else in the derivation, or by way of the ↑LR rule, in which case the functional dependency is linked to the denotation of the result category, and in effect bound from above. Another way of saying this is that the denotations assigned by DCOD are all closed, that is, they are lambda terms containing no free variables. If DCOD pronouns are always bound by something, does this mean that we need to introduce a second strategy to handle deictic uses?

No. Since the ↑ rules in the DCOD grammar are (simplified) versions of Jäger's rules, they share the strengths and weaknesses of his analysis. Just like Jacobson's system, Jäger's grammar and the DCOD grammar automatically accommodate deictic uses. To see how this works, here is a derivation of the deictic reading of the same example that was given a bound reading above at the beginning of §3.5:

(12)

$$\dfrac{\dfrac{np \Rightarrow np \qquad \dfrac{s \Rightarrow s \qquad \dfrac{np \Rightarrow np \qquad s \Rightarrow s}{(np, np\backslash s) \Rightarrow s}\backslash L}{(np, ((np\backslash s)/s, s)) \Rightarrow s}/L}{(np, ((np\backslash s)/s, (np, np\backslash s))) \Rightarrow s}\backslash L}{\left(\begin{matrix}np\\ \texttt{John}\end{matrix}, \left(\begin{matrix}(np\backslash s)/s\\ \texttt{said}\end{matrix}, \left(\begin{matrix}np^{np}\\ \texttt{he}\end{matrix}, \begin{matrix}np\backslash s\\ \texttt{left}\end{matrix}\right)\right)\right) \Rightarrow \begin{matrix}s^{np}\\ \lambda\texttt{x.sd(lft(he(x)))(j)}\end{matrix}}\uparrow LR$$

The derivations are the same until the last step. Instead of applying the ↑L rule in order to bind the pronoun to the matrix subject, the ↑LR rule discloses the presence of the bindable pronoun at the top level of the derivation. (There is, of course, an equivalent directly compositional derivation as well.)

In fact, to the extent that Jäger's left and left–right rules are indeed two logical aspects of a single inference type, they arguably provide an analysis of bound vs. deictic pronouns that is more unified even than Jacobson's, since on her analysis, the analog of the binding rule (↑L, her **z** type-shifter) and the analog of the disclosure rule (↑LR, her Geach type-shifter, **g**) do not resemble each other in any obvious way.

3.6 Second Case Study: Quantification

The analysis of binding in DCOD is (intended to be) identical to Jäger's (2005) treatment. Therefore his LLC has direct compositionality on demand, at least with respect to binding. This section considers quantification, a different kind of action at a distance, and shows how the qLR rule in Example (2) guarantees the DCOD property for quantification as well.

Here is the swooping derivation of *John saw everyone*:

(13)

$$\dfrac{\dfrac{np \Rightarrow np \qquad \dfrac{np \Rightarrow np \qquad s \Rightarrow s}{(np, np\backslash s) \Rightarrow s}\backslash L}{(np, ((np\backslash s)/np, np)) \Rightarrow s}/L \qquad s \Rightarrow s}{\left(\begin{matrix} np \\ \texttt{John} \end{matrix}, \left(\begin{matrix} (np\backslash s)/np \\ \texttt{saw} \end{matrix}, \begin{matrix} q(np, s, s) \\ \texttt{everyone} \end{matrix}\right)\right) \Rightarrow \begin{matrix} s \\ \texttt{eo}(\lambda\texttt{x.saw(x)(j)}) \end{matrix}}qL$$

The qL rule applies only after the entire scope of the quantificational element is in view, linking the quantifier with its nuclear scope in one leap. Nevertheless, the final structure clearly indicates that *saw everyone* is a syntactic constituent.

Now for the corresponding direct compositional derivation.

(14)

$$\dfrac{\dfrac{np \Rightarrow np \qquad np\backslash s \Rightarrow np\backslash s}{((np\backslash s)/np, np) \Rightarrow np\backslash s}/L}{\left(\begin{matrix} (np\backslash s)/np \\ \texttt{saw} \end{matrix}, \begin{matrix} q(np, s, s) \\ \texttt{everyone} \end{matrix}\right) \Rightarrow \begin{matrix} q(np\backslash s, s, s) \\ \lambda\texttt{f.eo}(\lambda\texttt{x.f(saw(x))}) \end{matrix}}qLR$$

This derivation for the verb phrase constituent *saw everyone* can participate in a complete derivation as follows:

$$\dfrac{(np\backslash s)/np, q(np, s, s) \Rightarrow q(np\backslash s, s, s) \qquad \dfrac{\dfrac{np \Rightarrow np \qquad s \Rightarrow s}{(np, np\backslash s) \Rightarrow s}\backslash L \qquad s \Rightarrow s}{(np, q(np\backslash s, s, s)) \Rightarrow s}qL}{\left(\begin{matrix} np \\ \texttt{John} \end{matrix}, \left(\begin{matrix} (np\backslash s)/np \\ \texttt{saw} \end{matrix}, \begin{matrix} q(np, s, s) \\ \texttt{everyone} \end{matrix}\right)\right) \Rightarrow \begin{matrix} s \\ \texttt{eo}(\lambda\texttt{x.saw(x)(j)}) \end{matrix}}\text{Cut}$$

Once again, *saw everyone* is a constituent. It is not, however, a simple VP of category $np\backslash s$; rather, full disclosure requires that it be of category $q(np\backslash s, s, s)$, that is, a quantificational verb phrase: something that functions locally as a verb phrase, takes scope over a clause, and produces a clause as a result.

In other words, arriving at a directly compositional treatment has turned the verb phrase transparent, so that the category reveals the presence of a quantificational element somewhere within.

As in the previous case study, once again I will provide a full Curry–Howard labeling for the lemma analyzing the constituent under study, *saw everyone*:

(15)
$$\dfrac{\dfrac{\mathtt{x}\colon np \Rightarrow \mathtt{x}\colon np \qquad \mathtt{r}\colon (np\backslash s) \Rightarrow \mathtt{r}\colon (np\backslash s)}{(\ \mathtt{saw}\colon ((np\backslash s)/np),\ \mathtt{x}\colon np) \Rightarrow \mathtt{saw(x)}\colon (np\backslash s)}\ /\mathrm{L}}{\left(\begin{matrix}(np\backslash s)/np \\ \mathtt{saw}\end{matrix},\ \begin{matrix}q(np, s, s) \\ \mathtt{everyone}\end{matrix}\right) \Rightarrow \begin{matrix}q(np\backslash s, s, s) \\ \lambda\mathtt{f.everyone}(\lambda\mathtt{x.f(saw(x))})\end{matrix}}\ q\mathrm{LR}$$

Here $\mathtt{f}$ is a function from verb phrase denotations of category $np\backslash s$ to clause denotations of category s. As a result, the semantic type of this constituent is $\langle\langle\langle \mathtt{e}, \mathtt{t}\rangle, \mathtt{t}\rangle, \mathtt{t}\rangle$: a function from a function from verb phrase meanings to truth values to truth values. This is exactly the type for a continuized verb phrase in the (directly compositional) continuation-based approach to quantification described in Barker (2002).

Once again, the swooping derivation is simpler, both conceptually and practically, an advantage that increases dramatically as the quantifier takes wider and wider scope. And once again the DC version imposes the discipline of full disclosure and self-reliance, giving a full accounting of the syntactic and semantic nature of each syntactic constituent.

3.6.1 *The Locus of Scope Ambiguity*

When more than one quantificational expression is present, the order in which the quantifiers are introduced into the derivation can give rise to scope ambiguity. Because we have the DCOD property, we know that every distinct construal will have an equivalent derivation in which each constituent is given a self-contained denotation. We might ask, therefore, which constituents must or can participate in scope ambiguities.

In order to explore this question, I will consider a sentence that contains three quantificational expressions, such as *Most people gave something to every child.* Assume that this sentence has a construal on which it entails that for every child, most people gave that child something, and that the scope relations are *every* > *most* > *some*. For expository simplicity, I will ignore the preposition *to*.

Let Q abbreviate the category $q(np, s, s)$. Then on the swooping derivation, the scope construal depends in a straightforward manner on the order of the instantiations of the qL rule:

(16)

$$\dfrac{\dfrac{\dfrac{\dfrac{np \Rightarrow np \qquad \dfrac{np \Rightarrow np \qquad \dfrac{np \Rightarrow np \quad s \Rightarrow s}{(np, np\backslash s) \Rightarrow s}\,\backslash\mathrm{L}}{(np, ((np\backslash s)/np, np)) \Rightarrow s}\,\backslash\mathrm{L}}{(np, ((((np\backslash s)/np)/np, np), np)) \Rightarrow s}\,\backslash\mathrm{L} \qquad s \Rightarrow s}{(np, ((((np\backslash s)/np)/np, Q_3), np)) \Rightarrow s}\,q\mathrm{L} \qquad s \Rightarrow s}{(Q_2, ((((np\backslash s)/np)/np, Q_3), np)) \Rightarrow s}\,q\mathrm{L} \qquad s \Rightarrow s}{(Q_2, ((((np\backslash s)/np)/np, Q_3), Q_1)) \Rightarrow s}\,q\mathrm{L}$$

Reading the derivation from the bottom upwards (as usual with sequent proofs), quantifiers that are eliminated earlier take wider scope. Here, $Q_1 > Q_2 > Q_3$, as desired. Since the qL rule can target any NP on the left-hand side of the sequent arrow, we have complete control over the scope relations among the quantifiers.

In the equivalent directly compositional derivation, we must cut out two subconstituents: the verb phrase, of course (category $np\backslash s$); and within the verb phrase, the constituent formed when the ditransitive verb combines with its first argument (category $(np\backslash s)/np$)). Because the verb phrase contains two quantifiers, full disclosure requires that the presence of both quantifiers must be registered on the category of the verb phrase. As a second abbreviation, let $Q(A)$ abbreviate the category $q(A, s, s)$. Then the category of the verb phrase after disclosure will be the category $Q(Q(np\backslash s)) = q(q(np\backslash s, s, s), s, s)$. Here, then, is a directly compositional analysis of the relevant construal of the verb phrase *gave something to everyone*:

(17)

$$\dfrac{\dfrac{\dfrac{np \Rightarrow np \quad (np\backslash s)/np \Rightarrow (np\backslash s)/np}{(((np\backslash s)/np)/np, np) \Rightarrow (np\backslash s)/np}\,\backslash\mathrm{L}}{(((np\backslash s)/np)/np, Q_3) \Rightarrow Q_3((np\backslash s)/np)}\,q\mathrm{LR} \qquad \dfrac{\dfrac{\dfrac{np \Rightarrow np \quad np\backslash s \Rightarrow np\backslash s}{((np\backslash s)/np, np) \Rightarrow np\backslash s}\,\backslash\mathrm{L}}{(Q_3((np\backslash s)/np), np) \Rightarrow Q_3(np\backslash s)}\,q\mathrm{LR}}{(Q_3((np\backslash s)/np), Q_1) \Rightarrow Q_1(Q_3(np\backslash s))}\,q\mathrm{LR}}{((((np\backslash s)/np)/np, Q_3), Q_1) \Rightarrow Q_1(Q_3(np\backslash s))}\,\mathrm{Cut}$$

Because we could have instantiated the two right-most applications qLR rules in the opposite order, there are two distinct possible analyses of the verb phrase. These alternatives correspond to the two relative scope relations between Q_1 and Q_3. In general, in a directly compositional derivation, the derivation of each constituent fully determines the relative scope of all (and only!) those quantifiers contained within that constituent.

At this point, we need only show how to compose the subject quantifier with the verb phrase:

(18)
$$\dfrac{\dfrac{\dfrac{\dfrac{np \Rightarrow np \quad s \Rightarrow s}{(np, np\backslash s) \Rightarrow s}\,\backslash\mathrm{L} \qquad s \Rightarrow s}{(np, Q_3(np\backslash s)) \Rightarrow s}\,q\mathrm{L} \qquad s \Rightarrow s}{(Q_2, Q_3(np\backslash s)) \Rightarrow s}\,q\mathrm{L} \qquad s \Rightarrow s}{(Q_2, Q_1(Q_3(np\backslash s))) \Rightarrow s}\,q\mathrm{L}$$

To complete the derivation of the entire sentence, simply cut the derivation of the verb phrase given just above against this derivation of a complete clause.

The order of the qL rules here controls whether the subject outscopes both quantifiers in the verb phrase, or else takes intermediate scope (as shown here), or else takes narrow scope with respect to both verb phrase quantifiers. However, this part of the derivation has no power to affect the relative order of the quantifiers within the verb phrase, since that is fully determined by the derivation of the verb phrase, as described above.

Thus in a directly compositional derivation with full disclosure, the derivation of each constituent determines the relative scoping of all of the quantifiers it contains. In particular, even though the quantifiers involved take scope only over complete clauses (and not over verb phrases), the verb phrase nevertheless exhibits its own local scope ambiguity, and it is those local scope relations that determine the contribution of the verb phrase to the scope relations of the larger derivation in which it is embedded. In other words, semantic self-reliance requires that each constituent takes full responsibility for every aspect of the contribution of its contents within the larger derivation.

3.7 Direct Compositionality on Demand

Having provided two examples in detail, I now establish that it is always possible to provide both a swooping and a directly compositional analysis for any sentence generated by DCOD. Furthermore, the two analyses are guaranteed equivalent structurally and semantically, and interconvertible in both directions.

Converting from the DC analysis to the swooping analysis requires eliminating cuts, so I first show that the cut rule is admissible in DCOD (i.e. that cuts can always be eliminated). Then I show how to add cuts back in where desired in order to construct a fully DC analysis.

3.7.1 *Cut Elimination for DCOD*

Jäger (2005: 102) sketches cut elimination for LLC (see pages 43ff, 102ff, and 127), a logic similar to DCOD except in two respects: (i) DCOD leaves out the • connective (for purely expository reasons), which does not affect cut elimination; and (ii) DCOD adds qL and qLR. Therefore we need only show that adding qL and qLR does not interfere with cut elimination. The only potentially troublesome situations are ones in which some application of qLR is cut against an instance of either qL or qLR.

Consider first a derivation containing a cut of qLR against qL (for instance, as in the DC derivation of *John saw everyone* above in §3.6):

(19)
$$\dfrac{\dfrac{\Pi[A] \Rightarrow B}{\Pi[q(A,C,D)] \Rightarrow q(B,C,D)}\,q\mathrm{LR} \qquad \dfrac{\Delta[B] \Rightarrow C \qquad \Gamma[D] \Rightarrow E}{\Gamma[\Delta[q(B,C,D)]] \Rightarrow E}\,q\mathrm{L}}{\Gamma[\Delta[\Pi[q(A,C,D)]]] \Rightarrow E}\,\mathrm{Cut}$$

For each derivation of this form, there will necessarily be an equivalent derivation of the following form:

(20)
$$\dfrac{\dfrac{\Pi[A] \Rightarrow B \qquad \Delta[B] \Rightarrow C}{\Delta[\Pi[A]] \Rightarrow C}\,\mathrm{Cut} \qquad \Gamma[D] \Rightarrow E}{\Gamma[\Delta[\Pi[q(A,C,D)]]] \Rightarrow E}\,q\mathrm{L}$$

The replacement derivation still has a cut, but it is a cut of a lower degree (see, e.g., Jäger (2005) for a suitable definition of degree; the intuition is that the cut involves a lemma covering a smaller amount of material). As long as it is possible to replace any cut with one of strictly lower degree, cuts can be pushed upwards until they reach an axiom and can be entirely removed.

If qLR were a true rule of proof, there would be nothing more left to say concerning cut elimination. But because the qLR rule is two-sided—that is, it introduces the q connective on both the left and the right—then just as with Jäger's binding rules, we must also consider cutting an instance of qLR with another instance of qLR:

(21)
$$\dfrac{\dfrac{\Pi[A] \Rightarrow B}{\Pi[q(A,C,D)] \Rightarrow q(B,C,D)}\,q\mathrm{LR} \qquad \dfrac{\Gamma[B] \Rightarrow E}{\Gamma[q(B,C,D)] \Rightarrow q(E,C,D)}\,q\mathrm{LR}}{\Gamma[\Pi[q(A,C,D)]] \Rightarrow q(E,C,D)}\,\mathrm{Cut}$$

Once again, given the resources provided by the antecedents of the first derivation, we can reconfigure the proof with a cut of strictly lesser degree.

(22)
$$\dfrac{\dfrac{\Pi[A] \Rightarrow B \qquad \Gamma[B] \Rightarrow E}{\Gamma[\Pi[A]] \Rightarrow E}\text{Cut}}{\Gamma[\Pi[q(A, C, D)]] \Rightarrow q(E, C, D)}q\text{LR}$$

Thus the cut rule is admissible in DCOD, which is to say that any derivation in DCOD containing a cut can be replaced with an equivalent derivation that is cut-free.

3.7.2 *Adding Cuts Back in to Provide Direct Compositionality on Demand*

Now that we know that it is possible to eliminate cuts completely, we can consider adding back some cuts in order to provide direct compositionality.

Definition (*Directly composable*) Consider a specific derivation in DCOD with conclusion $\Gamma[(\Delta, \Pi)] \Rightarrow A$. That derivation is DIRECTLY COMPOSABLE just in case there exists a formula X and an equivalent derivation of the following form:

$$\dfrac{(\Delta, \Pi) \Rightarrow X \qquad \Gamma[X] \Rightarrow A}{\Gamma[(\Delta, \Pi)] \Rightarrow A}\text{Cut}$$

in which each of the antecedent derivations is also directly composable. (Two derivations count as equivalent if they have identical conclusion sequents with Curry–Howard labelings that are equivalent up to α and β equivalence.)

The first step in establishing that DCOD is directly compositional is the following simple but important observation:

Lemma (Categorization) Every structural constituent can be assigned a category.

Proof. Only two rules create complex constituents, that is structures of the form (Δ, Π), namely, $\backslash$L and /L. Consider $\backslash$L:

$$\dfrac{\Delta \Rightarrow A \quad \Gamma[B] \Rightarrow C}{\Gamma[(\Delta, A\backslash B)] \Rightarrow C}\backslash\text{L}$$

The rule itself provides us with a suitable choice for categorizing the constituent, namely, B, and we can replace the $\backslash$L step just given with the following reasoning:

$$\dfrac{\dfrac{\Delta \Rightarrow A \quad B \Rightarrow B}{(\Delta, A\backslash B) \Rightarrow B}\backslash\text{L} \qquad \Gamma[B] \Rightarrow C}{\Gamma[(\Delta, A\backslash B)] \Rightarrow C}\text{Cut}$$

In other words, using cut we can arrange for every application of $\backslash$L to have an axiom instance as its second antecedent.

The situation for /L is symmetric. □

The categorization lemma guarantees that each constituent can be associated with a syntactic category, but that is not enough to ensure full disclosure and semantic self-reliance. There are only two situations in DCOD in which self-reliance might be violated: when the binding rule $\uparrow$L links an anaphor inside the constituent in question with an antecedent outside the constituent; or when the quantification rule qL links a quantifier inside the constituent with a nuclear scope that properly contains the constituent in question. In each case, it will be necessary to adjust the syntactic category identified by the categorization lemma in order to align it with the principle of full disclosure.

3.7.2.1 *Full Disclosure for Binding* A violation of self-reliance due to binding has the following form:

(23)
$$\frac{\Sigma \Rightarrow A \quad \Pi[A][(\Delta[B],\Gamma)] \Rightarrow C}{\Pi[\Sigma][(\Delta[B^A],\Gamma)] \Rightarrow C}\uparrow\mathrm{L}$$

This is just an application of $\uparrow$L where the anaphor (but not the antecedent) is inside the constituent (Δ, Γ).

First, assume that the derivations of the antecedents above the line are directly composable. Then there is some formula X such that we can cut out the constituent under consideration, (Δ, Γ), as a separate subproof.

(24)
$$\frac{\Sigma \Rightarrow A \quad \dfrac{(\Delta[B],\Gamma) \Rightarrow X \quad \Pi[A][X] \Rightarrow C}{\Pi[A][(\Delta[B],\Gamma)] \Rightarrow C}\mathrm{Cut}}{\Pi[\Sigma][(\Delta[B^A],\Gamma)] \Rightarrow C}\uparrow\mathrm{L}$$

Next, we use $\uparrow$LR to disclose the fact that the constituent contains an anaphor, replacing the category X with X^A. We can also bind the anaphor at the stage at which we form X^A, as long as we interchange the order of $\uparrow$L with cut:

(25)
$$\frac{\dfrac{(\Delta[B],\Gamma) \Rightarrow X}{(\Delta[B^A],\Gamma) \Rightarrow X^A}\uparrow\mathrm{LR} \qquad \dfrac{\Sigma \Rightarrow A \quad \Pi[A][X] \Rightarrow C}{\Pi[\Sigma][X^A] \Rightarrow C}\uparrow\mathrm{L}}{\Pi[\Sigma][(\Delta[B^A],\Gamma)] \Rightarrow C}\mathrm{Cut}$$

Then the left-most antecedent of the cut inference constitutes a complete and self-contained proof that (Δ, Γ) is a constituent of category X^A, and the original derivation is directly composable.

The situation when the anaphor is inside Γ instead of Δ is closely analogous.

In constructing the DC derivation, an instance of $\uparrow$LR is cut against an instance of $\uparrow$L, exactly the sort of situation that the cut elimination theorem is at pains to eliminate. But this is exactly what we need in order to arrive at a self-contained analysis of the syntactic constituent under consideration.

3.7.2.2 *Full Disclosure for Quantification* A violation of self-reliance due to quantification has the following form:

(26)
$$\frac{\Pi[(\Delta[B], \Gamma)] \Rightarrow C \quad \Sigma[D] \Rightarrow E}{\Sigma[\Pi[(\Delta[q(B, C, D)], \Gamma]]] \Rightarrow E}\, q\text{L}$$

This is just an application of qL where the quantifier and its scope are on different sides of the targeted constituent boundary. The argument proceeds exactly as for the binding case.

Once again, assume that the antecedents are directly composable, so that we can cut out the constituent under consideration, (Δ, Γ), as a separate subproof.

(27)
$$\frac{\dfrac{(\Delta[B], \Gamma) \Rightarrow X \quad \Pi[X] \Rightarrow C}{\Pi[(\Delta[B], \Gamma)] \Rightarrow C}\,\text{Cut} \qquad \Sigma[D] \Rightarrow E}{\Sigma[\Pi[(\Delta[q(B, C, D)], \Gamma)]] \Rightarrow E}\, q\text{L}$$

Next, we use qLR to disclose the fact that the constituent contains a quantifier, replacing the category X with $q(X, C, D)$. At the same stage, we can fix the scope of quantificational X with an application of qL, as long as we interchange the order of qL with cut:

(28)
$$\frac{\dfrac{(\Delta[B], \Gamma) \Rightarrow X}{(\Delta[q(B, C, D)], \Gamma) \Rightarrow q(X, C, D)}\, q\text{LR} \qquad \dfrac{\Pi[X] \Rightarrow C \quad \Sigma[D] \Rightarrow E}{\Sigma[\Pi[q(X, C, D)]] \Rightarrow E}\, q\text{L}}{\Sigma[\Pi[(\Delta[q(B, C, D)], \Gamma)]] \Rightarrow E}\,\text{Cut}$$

Thus the original derivation is directly composable.

Once again, we have an instance of qLR cut against an instance of qL, which we now recognize as the way full disclosure delivers semantic self-reliance.

Proposition (Direct Compositionality On Demand) For any valid sequent generated by DCOD, there is an equivalent swooping (cut-free) proof in which anaphors and their antecedents are coindexed by a single application of $\uparrow$L, and in which quantificational elements and their scope are related by a single application of qL. For each such derivation, there is another, equivalent, directly composable proof in which each constituent receives a self-contained analysis that obeys full disclosure and semantic self-reliance.

Proof. (sketch) For each constituent in the final conclusion structure, working from smallest to largest, and beginning with the axioms and working downwards, apply the categorization lemma and impose full disclosure. Since there are a strictly finite number of constituents, anaphors, and quantifiers, and since none of these operations introduces new constituents, the process is guaranteed to terminate. □

One of the pleasant properties of cut-elimination is that it leads to an algorithm for deciding whether a sequent is derivable. Since each application of a rule (other than cut) adds at least one logical connective, the conclusion will always be strictly more complex than the antecedents. One can simply try all applicable rules, stopping when a valid proof is found.

Since the on-demand theorem introduces cuts, it is worth considering whether there is an algorithm for finding the DC proof. Since there is an algorithm for finding a cut-free proof, and since there is an algorithm for constructing the equivalent DC proof, there is an algorithm for constructing the DC proof.

In fact, there is an alternative parsing strategy for logics that satisfy the DC on-demand property. Given a set of lexical categories, since the DC analysis of each constituent has the subformula property, the complete set of usable proofs for each constituent can be constructed in finite time. For a string of length n, the number of possible constituents is at most n^2, and for each constituent the time cost for trying all relevant cuts is proportional to n, giving a time cost of order n^3 in the length of the string.

3.8 Why the Display Property Alone is not Sufficient

There is a class of substructural logics called Display Logics that are relevant for type-logical grammar. Display Logics have what is called the Display Property. As Bernardi (2002: 33) puts it, "any particular constituent of a sequent can be turned into the whole of the right or the left side by moving other constituents to the other side [of the sequent symbol]".

At first blush, the display property sounds like exactly what we want, since it guarantees that it is always possible to arrive at a syntactic category and a self-contained denotation for any syntactic constituent. Furthermore, there will be such an analysis for each distinct interpretation provided by the grammar.

Certainly no grammar can be directly compositional without having the display property. For instance, the standard QR story (e.g. as presented in Heim and Kratzer 1998) does not have the display property, and is not directly compositional, since there is no way to factor out a syntactic and semantic analysis of a verb phrase such as *saw everyone* (at least, not when the quantifier takes scope over an entire clause).

However, in this paper I am advocating the desirability of an even stronger property than the display property. I will first give two concrete examples of the sort of analyses the display property gives for constituency, then I will point out some shortcomings that motivate seeking a stronger property such as DCOD.

First, here is an analysis in which the display property provides a category and a denotation for the constituent *saw everyone* in *John saw everyone*:

(29)

$$\dfrac{\dfrac{\dfrac{\vdots}{\text{[as derived in §3.6]}}}{\boxed{(np, ((np\backslash s)/np, q(np, s, s))) \Rightarrow s}}}{((np\backslash s)/np, q(np, s, s)) \Rightarrow np\backslash s}\backslash R \quad \dfrac{np \Rightarrow np \quad s \Rightarrow s}{(np, np\backslash s) \Rightarrow s}\backslash L$$
$$\overline{\left(\begin{matrix} np \\ \texttt{John} \end{matrix}, \left(\begin{matrix} (np\backslash s)/np \\ \texttt{saw} \end{matrix}, \begin{matrix} q(np, s, s) \\ \texttt{everyone} \end{matrix}\right)\right) \Rightarrow \begin{matrix} s \\ \texttt{eo}(\lambda \texttt{x.saw(x)(j)}) \end{matrix}}\ \text{Cut}$$

The peculiar thing about this derivation is that it begins with a complete derivation of the entire sentence: the boxed sequent is identical to the final conclusion sequent. Having the final conclusion before us in this way allows us to work backwards to figure out what the contribution of the verb phrase must have been, using a technique familiar from basic algebra:

$$\dfrac{\dfrac{p * (r * (y * x)) = s}{(r * (y * x)) = s/p}}{(y * x) = (s/p)/r}$$

Thus the logic of basic algebra has the display property.[2] In this instance of the display property approach, the constituent *saw everyone* has category $np\backslash s$, and although that hides the fact that the verb phrase is quantificational, it certainly works out to the correct final result. The problem is that this analysis for the constituent only works in situations in which the quantifier does not need to take wider scope. That is, the analysis of the constituent is sensitive to the material that surrounds it, violating the spirit of self-reliance.

In order to demonstrate this sensitivity to factors external to the constituent, consider an analogous treatment of *Someone claimed John saw*

[2] I borrow this analogy from Rajeev Goré.

everyone (with the interpretation on which *everyone* takes wide scope over *someone* in mind[3]). This time, the results are not as appealing:

(30)

$$
\begin{array}{c}
\vdots \\
\hline
(np, ((np\backslash s)/s, (np, ((np\backslash s)/np, np)))) \Rightarrow s \quad s \Rightarrow s \\
\hline
(q(np, s, s), ((np\backslash s)/s, (np, ((np\backslash s)/np, np)))) \Rightarrow s \quad s \Rightarrow s \\
\hline
(q(np, s, s), ((np\backslash s)/s, (np, ((np\backslash s)/np, q(np, s, s))))) \Rightarrow s \\
\hline
((np\backslash s)/s, (np, ((np\backslash s)/np, q(np, s, s)))) \Rightarrow q(np, s, s)\backslash s \\
\hline
(np, ((np\backslash s)/np, q(np, s, s))) \Rightarrow ((np\backslash s)/s)\backslash((q(np, s, s)\backslash s)) \\
\hline
\begin{pmatrix} (np\backslash s)/np & q(np, s, s) \\ \texttt{saw} & \texttt{everyone} \end{pmatrix} \Rightarrow \begin{array}{c} np\backslash(((np\backslash s)/s)\backslash((q(np, s, s)\backslash s))) \\ \lambda x.\lambda R.\lambda\mathscr{P}.\texttt{eo}(\lambda y.\mathscr{P}(\lambda z.R(\texttt{saw}(y)(x))(z))) \end{array}
\end{array}
\begin{array}{l} \\ \\ qL \\ qL \\ \backslash R \\ \backslash R \\ \backslash R \end{array}
$$

Thus we have a category and a self-contained denotation for the constituent *saw everyone*. I have not filled in the details of how to cut this into a complete derivation of the original sentence, but that is easy (if tedious) to do.

Once again the starting point is a complete swooping derivation of the whole sentence. In general, the starting derivation must include the entire scope domain of every element within the target constituent. Then we exploit the rules of proof in order to pick off the elements in the structure until only the desired constituent remains.

And once again we have arrived at an analysis for the constituent that does not disclose the presence of a quantificational element within it (since the $q(np, s, s)$ present in the result category corresponds to the quantificational NP *someone* in matrix subject position, not to *everyone*, i.e. to a quantifier *external* to the constituent under study). This is certainly a possible approach; however, when comparing the two analyses of the same constituent (i.e. the two display-property factorizations of *saw everyone* in different sentences), some disturbing patterns emerge:

- *Complexity inversion.* Given a particular derivation, the analyses of smaller constituents tend to be more complex than the analyses of the larger constituents.
- *Unbounded complexity.* Given a particular constituent, but varying the larger expression in which it is embedded, there is no bound on the complexity of the syntactic and semantic analyses that the display property

[3] Many native speakers report that allowing a quantifier to take scope out of a tensed clause is difficult. Most people accept *Someone tried to see everyone*, which can be used to make the same point, although at the cost of spoiling the parallelism in the embedded clause.

associates with the constituent across the full range of its syntactic environments.

- *Spurious ambiguity.* Since any given constituent can have at most a finite number of distinct interpretations, it follows from unbounded complexity that there will be more distinct analyses than there are distinct interpretations.
- *Dependence on material outside of the constituent.* Since any given constituent will have at most finitely many parts, it follows from unbounded complexity that the analyses must incorporate some aspects of the expression that are external to the constituent in question.

In a nutshell, using the display property to assign analyses to embedded constituents in effect recapitulates the future derivation of the constituent. This means that it does not provide a completely satisfying characterization of the contribution of the constituent (at least, not of the contribution proper to the constituent itself). It is an indirect method at best, as if we tried to describe a hand exclusively by showing what it looks like inside a variety of gloves and mittens.

The analysis of quantification in Hendriks' (1993) Flexible types has similar properties, in that the category of a constituent containing a quantifier can be arbitrarily complex depending on how wide a scope the quantifier needs to take. See Barker (2005) for a discussion of Hendriks' system in the context of Jacobson's variable-free, directly compositional treatment of binding.

3.9 Structural Postulates

Unlike most type-logical grammars, the DCOD grammar as presented above does not contain any structural postulates. Most type-logical grammars contain structural postulates that at least make implication associative. There is strong linguistic motivation for making implication associative (at least under highly constrained circumstances), including analyses of so-called non-constituent coordination (Steedman 1985; Dowty 1988, 1997) and various applications of function composition (e.g. Jacobson 1999), as well as many multimodal analyses (see Moortgat 1997 for a survey).

Structural postulates complicate the discussion of direct compositionality considerably. The reason is that direct compositionality is all about constituency, and the express purpose of structural postulates is to scramble constituent structure. For instance, here is a structural postulate that provides associativity:

$$\frac{(A, (B, C)) \Rightarrow D}{((A, B), C) \Rightarrow D}\ \text{ASSOC}$$

The double line indicates that the inference is valid in both directions: given the top sequent, infer the bottom one, or given the bottom sequent, infer the top one.

Without using this postulate, we can easily prove that [*John* [*saw* [*Mary*]]] is a sentence, that is $(np, ((np\backslash s)/np, np)) \Rightarrow s$. As a result of adding this postulate to the grammar, we can also prove that [[*John saw*] *Mary*], with the opposite constituency, is a sentence. The display property allows us to calculate an appropriate self-contained denotation for the pseudo-constituent *John saw*:

(31)

$$\dfrac{\dfrac{\dfrac{\dfrac{np \Rightarrow np \qquad \dfrac{np \Rightarrow np \quad s \Rightarrow s}{(np, np\backslash s) \Rightarrow s}\,\backslash L}{(np, ((np\backslash s)/np, np)) \Rightarrow s}\,/L}{((np, (np\backslash s)/np), np) \Rightarrow s}\,\text{Assoc}}{\left(\begin{array}{c} np \\ \texttt{John} \end{array}, \begin{array}{c} (np\backslash s)/np \\ \texttt{saw} \end{array}\right) \Rightarrow \begin{array}{c} s/np \\ \lambda\texttt{x.saw(x)(John)} \end{array}}\,/R \qquad \dfrac{np \Rightarrow np \quad s \Rightarrow s}{(s/np, np) \Rightarrow s}\,/L}{\left(\left(\begin{array}{c} np \\ \texttt{John} \end{array}, \begin{array}{c} (np\backslash s)/np \\ \texttt{saw} \end{array}\right), \begin{array}{c} np \\ \texttt{Mary} \end{array}\right) \Rightarrow \begin{array}{c} s \\ \texttt{saw(Mary)(John)} \end{array}}\,\text{Cut}$$

As mentioned above, there is fairly compelling evidence motivating associativity as desirable from a linguistic point of view. For instance, adding associativity allows deriving Right Node Raising examples such as *John saw and Tom called Mary*, in which the alleged constituent *John saw* coordinates with *Tom called.*

At least for terminological purposes, it is convenient to discriminate between two notions of constituent: NATURAL constituency, as determined by the function/argument structure of the lexical predicates involved, vs. CALCULATED constituency, as derived from natural constituency via structural postulates. The display property will always provide an appropriate analysis for calculated constituents.

In contrast to my remarks in the previous section criticizing the result of using the display property to arrive at analyses of natural constituents, the display property technique seems to be exactly the right way to understand a calculated constituent such as *John saw*: it is the quotient of a complete sentence after factoring out the direct object.

Full disclosure of anaphors and quantifiers still applies to calculated constituents. For instance, in *John$_i$ saw, and his$_i$ mother called, Mary*, in a DC analysis the calculated constituent *his mother called* will have category $(s/np)^{np}$ with corresponding denotation.

3.10 Conclusions

Bernardi describes (a Natural Deduction version of) the qL rule given above, and remarks (2002: 103) that "in the multimodal setting . . . the q connective of course cannot be a primitive connective". Instead, Bernardi suggests synthesizing q via a collection of multimodal logical and structural rules (see Moortgat (1997) for one concrete implementation of this strategy), and defining the swooping q as a "derived inference". This is perfectly coherent and feasible, of course; but it relegates the long-distance mode of analysis to a rule that is entirely redundant and eliminable ("admissible" in the logical jargon).

This paper explores the possibility of finding a grammar in which both views of constituency are simultaneously present, but each one of whose rules is indispensable. For instance, unlike Bernardi's derived inference rule for q, none of the rules in the DCOD logic given above is admissible. That is, eliminating any rule other than cut would reduce the number of valid sequents. In particular, it is only possible to prove the sequent

(32) $$\left(\begin{matrix}(np\backslash s)/np \\ \texttt{saw}\end{matrix}, \begin{matrix}q(np,s,s) \\ \texttt{everyone}\end{matrix}\right) \Rightarrow \begin{matrix}q(np\backslash s,s,s) \\ \lambda\texttt{f.everyone}(\lambda\texttt{x.f(saw(x))})\end{matrix}$$

using qLR, so qLR is not admissible.

There are many pressures on the design of a grammar, and I do not expect that any system based on DCOD will serve all purposes. Rather, I offer DCOD here as an example showing that it is possible to reconcile the local and long-distance aspects of the syntax–semantics interface within a single unified grammar. With any luck, there will be other grammatical systems that can semantically link distant elements directly, yet still provide complete, self-contained constituent analyses with full disclosure: long-distance linking, but with direct compositionality on demand.

References

Barker, C. 2002. 'Continuations and the nature of quantification', *Natural Language Semantics*, 10: 211–42.

—— 2005. 'Remark on Jacobson 1999: Crossover as a local constraint', *Linguistics and Philosophy*, 28: 447–72.

——and SHAN, C.-C. In press. 'Types as graphs: Continuations in Type-Logical Grammar', *Journal of Logic, Language, and Information*.

BERNARDI, R. 2002. Reasoning with polarity in categorial type logic. Ph. D. dissertation, Utrecht Institute of Linguistics, Utrecht University.

DOWTY, D. 1988. 'Type raising, functional composition, and non-constituent coordination', in R. Oehrle, E. Bach, and D. Wheeler (eds), *Categorial Grammars and Natural Language structures*. Dordrecht: Reidel. 153–98.

——1997. 'Non-constituent coordination, wrapping, and multimodal categorial grammars', in M. L. Dalla Chiara, K. Doets, D. Mundici, and J. van Benthem (eds), *Structures and Norms in Science: Volume Two of the Tenth International Congress of Logic, Methodology and Philosophy of Science, Florence, August 1995*. Dordrecht: Kluwer. 347–68.

——2000. 'The dual analysis of adjuncts/complements in Categorial Grammar', ZAS Papers in Linguistics, 17.

GORÉ, R. 1998. 'Gaggles, Gentzen and Galois: How to display your favourite substructural logic', *Logic Journal of the IGPL*, 6: 669–94.

HEIM, I. and KRATZER, A. 1998. *Semantics in Generative Grammar*. Oxford: Blackwell.

HENDRIKS, H. 1993. *Studied Flexibility*. Amsterdam: ILLC Dissertation Series.

JACOBSON, P. 1999. 'Towards a variable-free semantics', *Linguistics and Philosophy*, 22: 117–84.

JÄGER, G. 2005. *Anaphora and Type Logical Grammar*. Dordrecht: Springer. [Page numbers refer to the 2001 manuscript version.]

LAMBEK, J. 1958. 'The mathematics of sentence structure', *American Mathematical Monthly*, 65: 154–70.

MONTAGUE, R. 1974. 'The proper treatment of quantification in ordinary English', in R. Thomason (ed), *Formal Philosophy: Selected Papers of Richard Montague*, New Haven, CT: Yale University Press, 247–70.

MOORTGAT, M. 1997. 'Categorial type logics', in J. van Benthem and A. ter Meulen (eds), *Handbook of Logic and Language*. Amsterdam: Elsevier Science. 93–177.

RESTALL, G. 2000. *An Introduction to Substructural Logics*. London: Routledge.

SHAN, C.-C. and BARKER, C. 2006. 'Explaining crossover and superiority as left-to-right evaluation', *Linguistics and Philosophy*, 29: 91–134.

STEEDMAN, M. 1985. 'Dependency and coordination in the grammar of Dutch and English', *Language*, 61: 523–68.

4

Linguistic Side Effects*

CHUNG-CHIEH SHAN

This paper relates cases of *apparent noncompositionality* in natural languages to those in programming languages. It is shaped like an hourglass: I begin in §4.1 with an approach to the syntax–semantics interface that helps us build compositional semantic theories. That approach is to draw an analogy between *computational side effects* in programming languages and what I term by analogy *linguistic side effects* in natural languages.

This connection can benefit computer scientists as well as linguists, but I focus here on the latter direction of technology transfer. *Continuations* have been useful for treating computational side effects. In §4.2, I introduce a new metalanguage for continuations in semantics.

The metalanguage I introduce is useful for analyzing both programming languages and natural languages. For intuition, I survey the first use in §4.3, then point out the virtues of this treatment in §4.4.

Turning to natural language in §4.5, I describe in detail how this perspective helped Chris Barker and me study binding and crossover, as well as *wh*-questions and superiority. I have also used continuations to study quantifier and *wh*-indefinite scope, particularly in Mandarin Chinese, but there is only room here to sketch these further developments, in §4.6.

As explicated below, a commitment to direct compositionality leads programming-language and natural-language semanticists together to a principled and fruitful study of three themes:

* Thanks to Stuart Shieber, Karlos Arregi, Chris Barker, Daniel Büring, Matthias Felleisen, Andrzej Filinski, Danny Fox, Barbara Grosz, Daniel Hardt, C.-T. James Huang, Sabine Iatridou, Pauline Jacobson, Aravind Joshi, Jo-wang Lin, Fernando Pereira, Avi Pfeffer, Chris Potts, Norman Ramsey, Dylan Thurston, Yoad Winter, and the audiences at Harvard AI Research Group, OGI Pacific Software Research Center, Boston University Church Research Group, 8th New England Programming Languages and Systems Symposium, 2003 Harvard Linguistics Practicum in Syntax and Phonology, University of Vermont, and University of Pennsylvania. This research is supported by the United States National Science Foundation Grants IRI-9712068 and BCS-0236592.

- *uniformity* across side effects,
- *interaction* among side effects, and
- an operational notion of *evaluation*.

I conclude in §4.7 by speculatively elevating this methodological preference into empirical claims.

4.1 Side Effects

Let me begin with Frege's painfully familiar example (Frege 1891, 1892; Quine 1960).

(1) (*a*) the morning star
    (*b*) the evening star

The semantic problem with these two phrases starts with the pretheoretic intuition that they "mean" the same thing, namely Venus. Furthermore, we have the intuition that the "meaning" of a sentence such as

(2) Alice saw the morning star

is (or at least includes) whether it is true or false. Perhaps we have all been brainwashed the same way in our introductory semantics courses. In any case, these pretheoretic intuitions we have about what phrases mean are at odds with compositionality, because there exist contexts, involving words like *think*, under which *the morning star* and *the evening star* are no longer interchangeable: maybe Alice thinks Bill saw the morning star, but Alice does not think Bill saw the evening star.

In this example, we have some pretheoretic notions of what certain phrases mean, which turn out to be incompatible with compositionality. In other cases, we are uncertain what certain phrases should mean at all, for example *the king of France (is bald)* or *most unicorns (are happy)*. That is when we are tempted to concoct technical devices like partial functions or syntactic movement, so that a larger phrase may have a meaning without each of its constituent parts also having a meaning.

The same challenge faces programming languages (Søndergaard and Sestoft 1990, 1992). For example, here are two program phrases (which happen to be in the Python programming language, but most of them look alike anyway).

(3) (*a*) $f(2) \times f(3)$
    (*b*) $f(3) \times f(2)$

The first program means to apply the function f to the numbers 2 and 3, then multiply the results. The second program means to apply the function f

to the numbers 3 and 2, then multiply the results. These two programs intuitively have the same meaning, but as it turns out, there too are contexts that distinguish between them. For example, suppose that we define the function f to print out its argument to the terminal before returning it.

(4)
```
def f(x):
    print x × 10
    return x
```

Then $f(2) \times f(3)$ would print out "20 30" before returning 6, while $f(3) \times f(2)$ would print out "30 20" before also returning 6. We can blame this discrepancy on the presence in our programming language of a command like "print". And this is only a mild case: what denotations, if any, can we assign to program phrases that request input from the user, or commands like "goto" that jump to a different point in the program to continue executing?

The commonality here between natural and programming language semantics is that we have some pretheoretic notion of what phrases mean—for example, the expression $f(2)$ "means" whatever you get when you feed the function f the number 2, and the noun phrase *the morning star* "means" Venus—yet two phrases that supposedly mean the same thing turn out to be distinguished by a troublemaking context involving verbs like *think* or commands like "print". This kind of situation—where, in short, equals cannot be substituted for equals—is what I take *referential opacity* to mean (as opposed to *referential transparency*, which is when equals can be substituted for equals). A vaguer way to define referential opacity is that it is when meaning "depends on context". Worse than referential opacity, sometimes we do not have any pretheoretic notion of meaning. For example, what does *the king of France* mean, and what does "goto" mean, anyway?

These issues, of referential opacity and downright lack of reference, are common to both programming and natural languages. Programming language researchers call instances of these issues *computational side effects*, such as

- output ("print"),
- input ("read"), and
- control ("goto").

By analogy, I call a natural language phenomenon a *linguistic side effect* when it involves either referential opacity or the lack of any pretheoretic notion of meaning to even challenge compositionality with. Some examples of linguistic side effects are:

- intensionality (*think*),
- binding (*she*),

- quantification (*most*),
- interrogatives (*who*),
- focus (*only*), and
- presuppositions (*the king of France*).

As I said, side effects are a common problem in both natural and programming language semantics. A way to treat side effects that is very popular in both linguistics and computer science is *type-lifting*—in other words, enriching denotations to encompass the additional aspect of "meaning" under discussion. For example, in order to distinguish denotationally between *the morning star* and *the evening star*, it is standard to intensionalize a natural language semantics, introducing functions from possible worlds. For another example, programming language semanticists deal with "print" by lifting denotations from numbers to number-string pairs, where the string is the terminal output.

Just to be complete, I should acknowledge that lifting denotation types is not the whole story. Whenever we lift denotations, we also have to lift the composition rules that combine them. Moreover, we need to specify how to get a truth value at the top level from a semantic value that is now richer, more complicated.

The type-lifting operations used in linguistics and in computer science are very similar. I mentioned above the standard possible-world semantics for intensionality. The same idea of turning denotations into functions from a fixed set is used to treat the computational side effect of input in programming languages. A second case where linguistics and computer science came up with the same type-lifting is Hamblin's (1973) alternative semantics for questions, which is how *nondeterminism* in programming languages—commands like "flip a coin" or "roll a die"—is often analyzed.

A third case of this convergence in type-lifting is quantification (Montague 1974). It is the focus of the rest of this paper. As linguists, we know how useful generalized quantifiers are, but I want to tell you how computer scientists use them to model programming languages, then come back after a few sections to apply their perspective to linguistics.

4.2 A New Metalanguage

To ground the discussion, I now introduce a toy programming language, where everything is a string. The + sign means to concatenate two strings, so the program

(5) "compositional" + " " + "semantics"

concatenates the strings "compositional", a space, and "semantics". When a computer executes this program, it first concatenates "compositional" and a space, and then concatenates the result with "semantics". The result is "compositional semantics". I write this computation as a sequence of reductions:

(6) $\underline{\text{“compositional”} + \text{“ ”}}$ + "semantics"
$\Rightarrow$ $\underline{\text{“compositional ”} + \text{“semantics”}}$
$\Rightarrow$ "compositional semantics"

Each $\Rightarrow$ indicates a step, and underlining indicates the subexpression next reduced. So far everything is pretty straightforward, and it is easy to write down a trivial denotational semantics for this language, where quotations denote strings, the + sign denotes the string concatenation function, and so on.

Now I add two features to this programming language, due to Danvy and Filinski (1989, 1990, 1992), with roots in work by Felleisen (1987, 1988) and others. These features may seem weird at first, but bear with me for the moment. The *shift* command is written $\xi f.\, e$, where f is a variable name and e is an expression. The symbol ξ in a shift-expression plays the same role as λ does in a function expression: it opens the scope of a variable-binding construct. When $\xi f.\, e$ is reduced, it first sets aside its context as f. For example, in the program

(7) "compositional " + ($\underline{\xi f.\,\text{“directly ”} + f(\text{“semantics”})}$),

the context of the shift-expression is

(8) "compositional " + __,

where the blank __ indicates the location of the shift-expression itself. This context is bound to the variable f within the body e. Furthermore, the body e (in this example, "directly " + f("semantics")) becomes the new current expression to be evaluated. Hence the following reduction sequence. (Ignore the square brackets for now; we shall come to them momentarily.)

(9) "compositional " + ($\underline{\xi f.\,\text{“directly ”} + f(\text{“semantics”})}$)
$\Rightarrow$ "directly " + $\underline{(\lambda x.\,[\text{“compositional ”} + x])(\text{“semantics”})}$
$\Rightarrow$ "directly " + $[\underline{\text{“compositional ”} + \text{“semantics”}}]$
$\Rightarrow$ "directly " + $\underline{[\text{“compositional semantics”}]}$
$\Rightarrow$ $\underline{\text{“directly ”} + \text{“compositional semantics”}}$
$\Rightarrow$ "directly compositional semantics"

The result of the very first reduction is the body of the shift-expression, with f replaced by $\lambda x.$ ["compositional " + x], which is a function that represents the context (8).

The second feature to add to this programming language is *reset*. A reset is notated by a pair of square brackets, such as those in (9). Resets delimit the extent to which an enclosed shift can grab its surrounding context. For example, in the program

(10) $\text{“really ”} + \big[\text{“compositional ”} + (\xi f.\, \text{“directly ”} + f(\text{“semantics”}))\big]$,

the shift can only grab its surrounding context as far as (and excluding) the closest enclosing square brackets, which shield “really ” from being captured. Hence “really ” stays at the beginning of the program throughout the reduction sequence.

(11)
$$
\begin{aligned}
&\text{“really ”} + \big[\text{“compositional ”} + (\underline{\xi f.\, \text{“directly ”} + f(\text{“semantics”})})\big]\\
&\Rightarrow \text{“really ”} + \big[\text{“directly ”} + \underline{(\lambda x.\, [\text{“compositional ”} + x])(\text{“semantics”})}\big]\\
&\Rightarrow \text{“really ”} + \big[\text{“directly ”} + \big[\underline{\text{“compositional ”} + \text{“semantics”}}\big]\big]\\
&\Rightarrow \text{“really ”} + \big[\text{“directly ”} + \underline{\big[\text{“compositional semantics”}\big]}\big]\\
&\Rightarrow \text{“really ”} + \big[\underline{\text{“directly ”} + \text{“compositional semantics”}}\big]\\
&\Rightarrow \text{“really ”} + \underline{\big[\text{“directly compositional semantics”}\big]}\\
&\Rightarrow \underline{\text{“really ”} + \text{“directly compositional semantics”}}\\
&\Rightarrow \text{“really directly compositional semantics”}
\end{aligned}
$$

We can imagine that every program is implicitly surrounded by a reset, so in the absence of any explicit bracketing, shift grabs all of its surrounding context.

As a technical detail (Shan 2004), when shift grabs a context and stores it in a bound variable, the stored context is bracketed by reset. That is why the context (8) corresponds to the function $\lambda x.\, [\text{“compositional ”} + x]$, not just $\lambda x.\, (\text{“compositional ”} + x)$.

Another technical detail: if you are used to working with the pure λ-calculus, you might have the habit of looking for whatever subexpression can be reduced by λ-conversion and reducing it right away. It used to be that different reduction orders always give the same final result, but that is no longer so in the presence of shift and reset. Instead, we need to replace that habit with a systematic recursive traversal that turns each subexpression (like concatenation) into a value (like a string) before moving on.[1] In particular, no reduction is allowed in the body of a λ-abstraction. Moreover, λ-conversion can take place only if the argument is an (irreducible) value. In computer

[1] Or better, use Kameyama and Hasegawa's (2003) axiomatization of shift and reset. Their equations are sound and complete with respect to observational equivalence under reductions by the systematic recursive traversal described here.

science parlance, this programming language *passes parameters by value*, or is *call-by-value*. Call-by-value is not the only parameter-passing convention, but it is the most popular one among programming languages, and the only one for which shift and reset have been defined and studied.

4.3 Encoding Computational Side Effects

Shift and reset, like "goto", are known as *control operators* in computer science. Unlike "goto", shift and reset are control operators that manipulate *delimited contexts*,[2] which means that the context grabbed by shift is made available to the program in the form of a function (Felleisen 1987, 1988). Shift and reset are interesting to computer scientists because many computational side effects can be encoded with them, in other words treated as syntactic sugar for them (Filinski 1994, 1996, 1999). I give four examples below.

4.3.1 *Abort*

A popular feature of programming languages is to be able to abort a computation in the middle of its execution (to "throw an exception"). To model such a feature, we might want an "abort" command, such that

(12) "directly " + abort("compositional") + " semantics"

evaluates to just "compositional". To achieve this, we can treat abort as simply a special case of shift, where the shifted context f is never used.

(13) abort $= \lambda x.\, \xi f.\, x$

Substituting (13) into (12) gives the following reduction sequence, as desired.

(14) "directly " + $\underline{(\lambda x.\, \xi f.\, x)(\text{"compositional"})}$ + " semantics"
$\Rightarrow$ "directly " + $\underline{(\xi f.\, \text{"compositional"})}$ + " semantics"
$\Rightarrow$ "compositional"

4.3.2 *Random*

Another popular feature, which I alluded to above, is nondeterminism. We want the program

(15) random("direct")("indirect") + "ly"

to evaluate to a set containing two strings, "directly" and "indirectly". We can treat random as another special case of shift, as long as we turn the overall

[2] Delimited contexts are also known as *composable, partial, functional,* or *truncated* contexts.

expression into a singleton set (hence the outermost pair of braces in (17)).

(16) random $= \lambda x.\, \lambda y.\, \xi f.\; f(x) \cup f(y)$

(17) $\{(\lambda x.\, \lambda y.\, \xi f.\; f(x) \cup f(y))(\text{“direct”})(\text{“indirect”}) + \text{“ly”}\}$
$\Rightarrow \{(\lambda y.\, \xi f.\; f(\text{“direct”}) \cup f(y))(\text{“indirect”}) + \text{“ly”}\}$
$\Rightarrow \{\xi f.\; f(\text{“direct”}) \cup f(\text{“indirect”}) + \text{“ly”}\}$
$\Rightarrow (\lambda x.\, [\{x + \text{“ly”}\}])(\text{“direct”}) \cup (\lambda x.\, [\{x + \text{“ly”}\}])(\text{“indirect”})$
$\Rightarrow [\{\text{“direct”} + \text{“ly”}\}] \cup (\lambda x.\, [\{x + \text{“ly”}\}])(\text{“indirect”})$
$\Rightarrow [\{\text{“directly”}\}] \cup (\lambda x.\, [\{x + \text{“ly”}\}])(\text{“indirect”})$
$\Rightarrow \{\text{“directly”}\} \cup (\lambda x.\, [\{x + \text{“ly”}\}])(\text{“indirect”})$
$\Rightarrow \{\text{“directly”}\} \cup [\{\text{“indirect”} + \text{“ly”}\}]$
$\Rightarrow \{\text{“directly”}\} \cup [\{\text{“indirectly”}\}]$
$\Rightarrow \{\text{“directly”}\} \cup \{\text{“indirectly”}\}$
$\Rightarrow \{\text{“directly”}, \text{“indirectly”}\}$

The two computational side effects discussed so far, abort and random, are encoded by shift expressions whose bodies use the captured context f either never (for abort) or twice (for random). By contrast, the computational and linguistic side effects considered below are encoded by shift expressions that use the captured context exactly once.

4.3.3 *Input*

A third important feature of programming languages, which I also mentioned above, is input. We want the program

(18) input + “ semantics”

to evaluate to the function that appends the word “semantics” to every string. We can write input in terms of shift as well. It is just $\xi f.\; f$.

(19) input $= \xi f.\; f$

(20) $(\xi f.\; f) + \text{“ semantics”} \;\Rightarrow\; \lambda x.\, [x + \text{“ semantics”}]$

4.3.4 *Output*

We can treat output in the same framework as input. We want the program

(21) output(“semantics”) + “ ” + input

to evaluate to “semantics semantics”, where the second word “semantics” is fed to the input-expression to the right by the output-expression to the left.

Once again, output can be written in terms of shift.[3]

(22) $\text{output} = \lambda x.\, \xi f.\, f(x)(x)$

(23)
$$
\begin{aligned}
&\underline{(\lambda x.\, \xi f.\, f(x)(x))(\text{``semantics''})} + \text{`` ''} + (\xi f.\, f) \\
\Rightarrow\ &\underline{(\xi f.\, f(\text{``semantics''})(\text{``semantics''}))} + \text{`` ''} + (\xi f.\, f) \\
\Rightarrow\ &\underline{(\lambda y.\, [y + \text{`` ''} + (\xi f.\, f)])(\text{``semantics''})}(\text{``semantics''}) \\
\Rightarrow\ &\big[\underline{\text{``semantics''} + \text{`` ''}} + (\xi f.\, f)\big]\, (\text{``semantics''}) \\
\Rightarrow\ &\big[\text{``semantics ''} + (\underline{\xi f.\, f})\big]\, (\text{``semantics''}) \\
\Rightarrow\ &\underline{\big[\lambda z.\, [\text{``semantics ''} + z]\big]}\, (\text{``semantics''}) \\
\Rightarrow\ &\underline{(\lambda z.\, [\text{``semantics ''} + z])(\text{``semantics''})} \\
\Rightarrow\ &\underline{\big[\text{``semantics ''} + \text{``semantics''}\big]} \\
\Rightarrow\ &\underline{[\text{``semantics semantics''}]} \\
\Rightarrow\ &\text{``semantics semantics''}
\end{aligned}
$$

You may be able to see where I am going: output is like the creation of a discourse referent, and input is like a pronoun to be bound. Indeed, that is what relates shift and reset to dynamic semantics, not to mention crossover in binding and superiority in *wh*-questions. However, before I move back to linguistics, let me point out three crucial virtues of shift and reset.

4.4 Three Virtues of Shift and Reset

The first virtue of shift and reset is that there is a perfectly compositional denotational semantics for them.

So far I have described shift and reset in terms of how they are evaluated, which gives them a very operational—or, in linguistic terms, derivational—feel. But thanks to this denotational semantics, we can treat this programming language with shift and reset as just another metalanguage for writing down model-theoretic denotations: good old functions and sets and so on in the simply typed λ-calculus. The only theoretical commitment that is required of us before we can use shift and reset in our semantic theories is that there are modes of semantic combination other than pure function application (like Montague's (1974) use of variables and Hamblin's (1973) of alternatives). Not even type-shifting is needed if you do not like that. I will not go into details about this denotational semantics here, but it is based on *continuations*, which generalize generalized quantifiers (Barker 2002; Shan 2002). Thus

[3] This encoding of input and output forces invocations of input and output to match one-to-one. For applications such as sloppy identity in verb-phrase ellipsis, this requirement may not be desirable. If so, we can instead define $\text{input} = \xi f.\, \lambda x.\, f(x)(x)$ and apply the function $\lambda v.\, \lambda x.\, v$ at the top level of all programs. This way, each output can feed zero or more inputs.

even computer scientists with nothing to do with natural language still care about generalized quantifiers, although many of them have never heard of the term.

The translation from a metalanguage with shift and reset to one without is called the *continuation-passing-style* (CPS) transform.[4] The type system of the CPS transform's target language serves as a refined type system for the source language with shift and reset. For example, the expressions for input and output in (19) and (22) above may look like they have the types e and $\langle e, e\rangle$, respectively, but they translate to λ-terms with the types

(24) $\langle\langle \boxed{e}, \alpha\rangle, \langle e, \alpha\rangle\rangle$

and

(25) $\langle\langle \boxed{\langle e,}\, \langle\langle \boxed{e}, \langle e, \gamma\rangle\rangle, \gamma\rangle \boxed{\rangle}, \beta\rangle, \beta\rangle$,

respectively. Here α, β, and γ are type variables that can be instantiated with any type. The boxed portions in the types above are vestiges of the pre-refinement types e and $\langle e, e\rangle$.

The second virtue of shift and reset is that they connect our desire for a denotational semantics that specifies what each phrase means to our intuitive understanding of what happens when a computer executes a program or when a person processes a sentence.

For example, in the Python example (3) at the beginning of this paper, it is intuitive that if $f(2)$ is evaluated before $f(3)$, then 2 is printed before 3, and vice versa. This notion of *evaluation order* is preserved in our treatment of output in terms of shift and reset. That is, we can take "print" to be shorthand for a shift expression, such that, if the shift expression for "print 2" is evaluated before that for "print 3", then 2 is printed before 3, and vice versa.

Similarly, recall from §4.3 that the program (21), repeated below, produces the result "semantics semantics".

(21) output("semantics") + " " + input

For the input above to successfully consume the output, the shift-expression for output must be reduced (evaluated) before that for input. In particular, if we stipulate that evaluation takes place from left to right, then the "flipped" program

(26) input + " " + output("semantics")

[4] As Danvy and Filinski (1990) point out, the translation for shift and reset should technically be called the continuation-*composing*-style transform instead.

will not work:

$$
\begin{aligned}
(27)\quad & \underline{(\xi f.\ f)} + \text{“ ”} + \big(\lambda x.\ \xi f.\ f(x)(x)\big)(\text{“semantics”}) \\
& \Rightarrow \lambda x.\big[x + \text{“ ”} + \big(\lambda x.\ \xi f.\ f(x)(x)\big)(\text{“semantics”})\big]
\end{aligned}
$$

Evaluation stops after one reduction, resulting in a function that waits for an input x—an input that the yet-to-be-evaluated output of "semantics" fails to provide. Even if we provide some input (say "syntax") "by hand", evaluation still halts at an attempt to apply a string as a function to another string:

$$
\begin{aligned}
(28)\quad & \big(\lambda x.\big[x + \text{“ ”} + \big(\lambda x.\ \xi f.\ f(x)(x)\big)(\text{“semantics”})\big]\big)(\text{“syntax”}) \\
& \Rightarrow \big[\underline{\text{“syntax”} + \text{“ ”}} + \big(\lambda x.\ \xi f.\ f(x)(x)\big)(\text{“semantics”})\big] \\
& \Rightarrow \big[\text{“syntax ”} + \underline{\big(\lambda x.\ \xi f.\ f(x)(x)\big)(\text{“semantics”})}\big] \\
& \Rightarrow \big[\text{“syntax ”} + \underline{(\xi f.\ f(\text{“semantics”})(\text{“semantics”}))}\big] \\
& \Rightarrow \big[\underline{\big(\lambda x.\big[\text{“syntax ”} + x\big]\big)(\text{“semantics”})}(\text{“semantics”})\big] \\
& \Rightarrow \big[\underline{\big[\text{“syntax ”} + \text{“semantics”}\big]}(\text{“semantics”})\big] \\
& \Rightarrow \big[\underline{\big[\text{“syntax semantics”}\big]}(\text{“semantics”})\big] \\
& \Rightarrow \big[\underline{\text{“syntax semantics”}(\text{“semantics”})}\big] \\
& \Rightarrow \text{type error!}
\end{aligned}
$$

The refined type system mentioned above flags this problem as a type error in (26).

The shift-reset metalanguage thus provides a link between our operational impulses and our denotational desires. Specifically, continuations provide a denotational foundation for the operational notion of evaluation order. There are other denotational foundations, such as Moggi's (1991) computational metalanguage, that are less concrete than continuations.

The third virtue of shift and reset is that we do not just know how to treat *many* computational side effects in terms of shift and reset, in other words how to translate abort, random, input, output, etc. into shift and reset. There turns out to be a systematic procedure for implementing *any* computational side effect in terms of shift and reset, under a certain technical definition of what a computational side effect is. The technical details are in Filinski's (1996) doctoral dissertation, but you do not need to read it to get the hang of the procedure. For instance, when treating nondeterminism in §4.3.2 above, the top-level expression in (17) needs to be a singleton set, which can be thought of as the trivial amount of nondeterminism. That is a step prescribed by Filinski's systematic procedure: at the top level, always put the trivial amount of whatever computational side effect you want to encode.

Because shift and reset are so broadly applicable, they allow computer scientists to treat multiple computational side effects in a uniform framework, and linguists to treat multiple linguistic side effects in a uniform framework. Instead of lifting our semantics once, and differently, for each of intensionality and variable binding and tense and questions and focus and quantification and indefinites and conventional implicature—just think of how complicated the denotation of *John* can get before all these are taken into account, with or without dynamic type-shifting—we need only specify a single lifting of types and denotations, to which everything can be reduced. Or so I hope.

4.5 Encoding Linguistic Side Effects

Having expressed the hope of treating all linguistic side effects in a uniform framework, I will now get to work.

4.5.1 *Quantification*

First on the agenda is in-situ quantification.

(29) Alice loves everyone's mother.

We want the program

(30) $\text{alice}\backslash(\text{love}/(\text{everyone}\backslash\text{mother}))$

(forward and backward slashes denote forward and backward function application) to evaluate to $\forall x.\, \text{love}(\text{mother}(x))(\text{alice})$. The standard denotation of *everyone*, as given by Montague (1974), can be translated into our λ-calculus enriched with shift and reset.

(31) $\text{everyone} = \xi f.\, \forall x.\ f(x).$

This definition enables the reduction sequence

(32)
$$
\begin{aligned}
&\text{alice}\backslash(\text{love}/((\underline{\xi f.\, \forall x.\ f(x)})\backslash\text{mother}))\\
&\Rightarrow \forall x.\, \underline{(\lambda y.\, [\text{alice}\backslash(\text{love}/(y\backslash\text{mother}))])(x)}\\
&\Rightarrow \forall x.\, \big[\text{alice}\underline{\backslash}(\text{love}\underline{/}(x\underline{\backslash}\text{mother}))\big]\\
&\Rightarrow \forall x.\, \underline{[\text{love}(\text{mother}(x))(\text{alice})]}\\
&\Rightarrow \forall x.\, \text{love}(\text{mother}(x))(\text{alice}),
\end{aligned}
$$

as desired.

If you think of shift from the reduction (or operational) point of view, you might be reminded of covert movement and predicate abstraction. For example, the reduction sequence above may be depicted as the following tree.

(33)

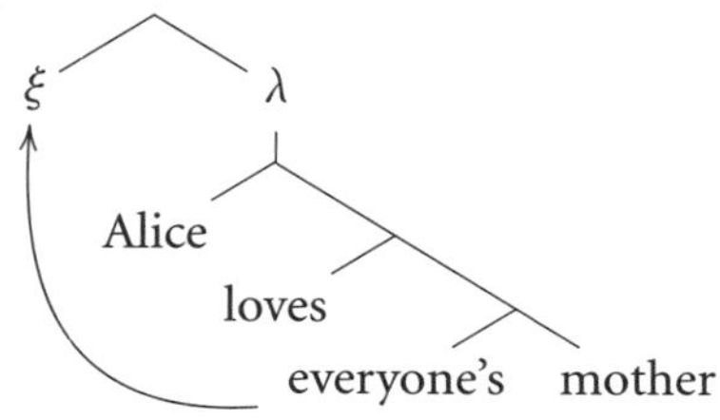

This is a fine intuition to have as a first approximation, but it is only an approximation. To reiterate, shift and reset are simply notation for denotations in a directly compositional semantics based on continuations. One difference that this compositional nature makes is that constituents containing *everyone*, like *everyone's mother* and *loves everyone's mother*, are every bit as quantificational as *everyone* is.[5] There is no reason other than tradition to draw (32) as (33) rather than either of the following pictures.

(34)

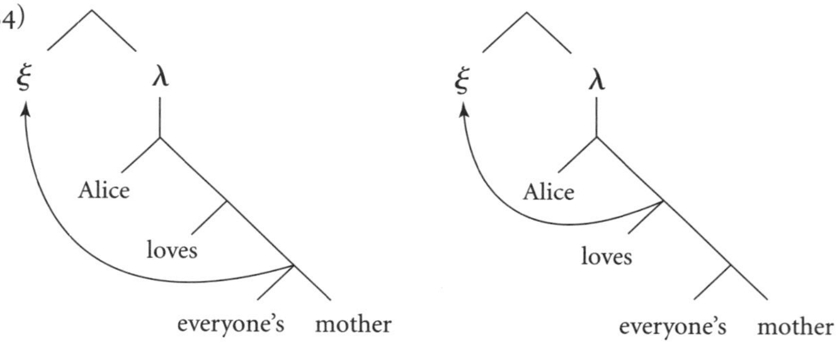

If X is a noun phrase that incurs side effects, then *X's mother* incurs side effects as well.[6] This fact will be useful when we treat pied-piping in §4.5.4 below.

4.5.2 *Binding*

As I alluded to above, binding in natural language can be decomposed into output (the creation of discourse referents) and input (the evaluation

[5] This property is shared by other compositional treatments of in-situ quantification, such as Cooper storage (1983), Keller storage (1988), and Moortgat's type constructor q (1988, 1995, 1996).

[6] A special case of this statement is that, if X contains a pronoun yet to be bound, then so does *X's mother*, as in Jacobson's variable-free semantics for binding (1999, 2000).

of a pronoun). This analogy to output and input in programming languages (§4.3.3–4) is the basic idea behind the continuation-based analysis of binding and crossover by Chris Barker and me (Shan and Barker 2006). To take one example, the sentence

(35) Everyone's$_i$ father loves her$_i$ mother

performs output at *everyone* and input at *her*. We would like the corresponding program

(36) $(\text{output}(\text{everyone})\backslash\text{father})\backslash(\text{love}/(\text{input}\backslash\text{mother}))$

to evaluate to $\forall x.\,\text{love}(\text{mother}(x))(\text{father}(x))$. Luckily, it already does, given the definitions in (19), (22), and (31):

(37)
$$
\begin{aligned}
&(\text{output}(\underline{\text{everyone}})\backslash\text{father})\backslash(\text{love}/(\text{input}\backslash\text{mother}))\\
&\Rightarrow \forall x.\,\underline{(\lambda y.\,[(\text{output}(y)\backslash\text{father})\backslash(\text{love}/(\text{input}\backslash\text{mother}))])(x)}\\
&\Rightarrow \forall x.\,\big[(\underline{\text{output}(x)}\backslash\text{father})\backslash(\text{love}/(\text{input}\backslash\text{mother}))\big]\\
&\Rightarrow \forall x.\,\big[(\underline{(\xi f.\,f(x)(x))}\backslash\text{father})\backslash(\text{love}/(\text{input}\backslash\text{mother}))\big]\\
&\Rightarrow \forall x.\,\big[\underline{(\lambda y.\,[(y\backslash\text{father})\backslash(\text{love}/(\text{input}\backslash\text{mother}))])(x)}(x)\big]\\
&\Rightarrow \forall x.\,\big[\,[(x\backslash\text{father})\backslash(\text{love}/(\underline{\text{input}}\backslash\text{mother}))]\,(x)\big]\\
&\Rightarrow \forall x.\,\big[\underline{[\lambda y.\,[(x\backslash\text{father})\backslash(\text{love}/(y\backslash\text{mother}))]]}(x)\big]\\
&\Rightarrow \forall x.\,\big[\underline{(\lambda y.\,[(x\backslash\text{father})\backslash(\text{love}/(y\backslash\text{mother}))])(x)}\big]\\
&\Rightarrow \forall x.\,\big[\,[(x\underline{\backslash}\text{father})\underline{\backslash}(\text{love}\underline{/}(x\underline{\backslash}\text{mother}))]\big]\\
&\Rightarrow \forall x.\,\big[\underline{[\text{love}(\text{mother}(x))(\text{father}(x))]}\big]\\
&\Rightarrow \forall x.\,\underline{[\text{love}(\text{mother}(x))(\text{father}(x))]}\\
&\Rightarrow \forall x.\,\text{love}(\text{mother}(x))(\text{father}(x))
\end{aligned}
$$

Just as our treatment of quantification accounts for quantifiers buried in noun phrases like any other quantifier, this treatment of binding deals with what Büring (2001) calls *binding out of DP* right away. In the sentence above, *everyone*, buried inside *everyone's father*, can still bind *her*.

The reduction sequence above involves three shifts, and so can be approximately depicted by a tree that invokes covert movement and predicate abstraction three times:

(38)

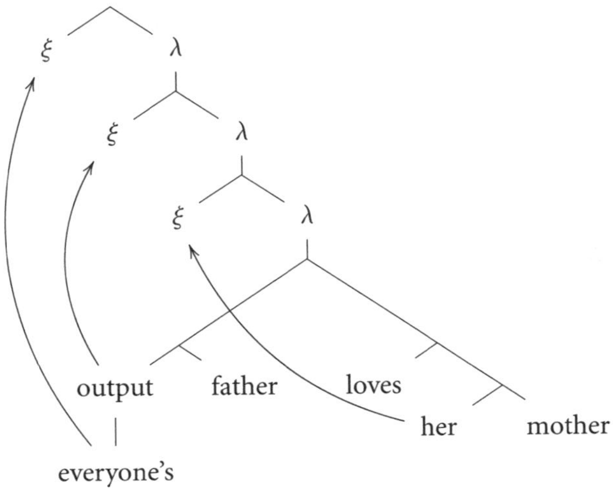

On this view, the binder and the pronoun both raise covertly, such that the landing site of the binder immediately c-commands the landing site of the pronoun. Among the three constituents moved, the linear order of base positions from left to right corresponds to the hierarchical order of landing sites from high to low. Such *tucking-in* (Richards 1997) approximates our stipulation in §4.4 that expressions be evaluated from left to right. Because *output(everyone)* contains *everyone*, there is no linear precedence to speak of between these two constituents. Rather, *everyone* is an argument to *output*, so the call-by-value evaluation discipline specified in §4.2 requires that *everyone* be raised first, followed by the remnant *output(__)*, in an instance of inverse linking (May 1977) and remnant movement (den Besten and Webelhuth 1990; among others).

Despite these similarities between shift and movement, I hope all these arrows do not obscure the fact that the shift-reset metalanguage is not just a technical implementation of movement and LF. For example, to the extent (**??**) below can be described in movement terms, it is crucial that reconstruction can take place both before and after Move and Merge, as dictated by the lexical items involved. More complex configurations are possible, especially in cases of ellipsis.

In any case, defaulting to left-to-right evaluation rules out crossover. The unacceptability of

(39) * Her$_i$ father loves everyone's$_i$ mother

is predicted, because the program

(40) (input\father)\(love/(output(everyone)\mother))

evaluates input before output, and so gets stuck as (27) on page 142 does. This correct prediction manifests as a type mismatch in the refined type system mentioned in §4.4. Or, roughly speaking in movement terms, to prohibit crossover is to require crossing rather than nested movement (Shan and Barker 2002).

4.5.3 *Evaluation Order and Thunks*

All this talk of left-to-right evaluation and linear order may leave you suspecting that Barker and I predict simply that the binder has to occur to the left of the pronoun. That better not be the case, because of fronted *wh*-phrases in sentences like the following.

(41) (*a*) Whose present for him$_i$ did every boy$_i$ see?
(*b*) *Which boy$_i$ does his$_i$ mother like?

In (41*a*) is an instance of acceptable cataphora; in (41*b*) is an instance of unacceptable anaphora.

Fortunately, left-to-right evaluation does not entail that every binder must be pronounced before any pronoun it binds. More generally, evaluation order only affects binary operators like "+" (string concatenation), "\" (backward function application), and "/" (forward function application). Left-to-right evaluation does not mean that one subexpression is evaluated before another whenever the former appears to the left of the latter. On the contrary, call-by-value parameter passing dictates, for instance, that function arguments be fully evaluated before λ-conversion.

For example, in the computer program (42), the command to print "sitional" appears before the command to print "compo". Yet, when the program runs, it prints "compositional", not "sitionalcompo".

(42)
```
def f(): print "sitional"
def g(): print "compo"
g()
f()
```

Merely defining f to be a function that prints "sitional" does not print "sitional". Merely that the program contains "sitional" before "compo" does not entail that it prints "sitional" before "compo".

In general, the side effect of a piece of code is incurred when it is executed (zero or more times), not where it appears literally in the program text (once). The time of execution can differ from the location of definition, because a program can pass around functions with side effects, like f and g, without invoking them. Hence left-to-right evaluation does not mean that side effects all happen in the order in which they are mentioned in the program. All it means is that, for an operator such as "+", where in principle either branch can be evaluated first, we break the symmetry and evaluate the left branch first.

At this point, it is convenient to introduce a new type into our λ-calculus. The new type is the *singleton* type—a set with only one element in it; it does not matter which. The singleton can be thought of as a 0-tuple, just as an ordered pair is a 2-tuple. I write this new type as "()". I also write the unique element of this type as "()". Thus the unique function from the singleton type to the singleton type is $\lambda().\,()$; in fact, there is a unique function from any type to the singleton type, namely $\lambda x.\,()$. The singleton type is also known as the *unit* or *terminal* type in computer science.

In the standard λ-calculus, the singleton type is not useful. For example, a function from () to e is equivalent to just an individual. More generally, the types $\langle (), \alpha \rangle$ and α are always equivalent: every time you see a function whose domain is the singleton type, you may as well strip off that function layer without losing any information.

In the presence of side effects, however, things get more interesting. A function from () to e is no longer necessarily just a function that always returns the same individual; it could be a function that first triggers some side effects (like producing some output or consuming some input), then returns an individual—maybe not even the same one each time! The singleton is just a dummy argument to build a function—an excuse to defer side effects for later, as in (42). Such a function, whose domain is the singleton type, is called a *thunk* (Hatcliff and Danvy 1997; Ingerman 1961).[7]

4.5.4 Wh-*questions; Topicalization*

Back to linguistics: how do thunks help us understand the following interactions of quantificational binding with *wh*-questions and topicalization?

(43) (*a*) [Whose present for him$_i$] did every boy$_i$ see?

(*b*) *[Which boy$_i$] does his$_i$ mother like?

(44) (*a*) [Alice's present for him$_i$], every boy$_i$ saw.

(*b*) *[Every boy$_i$], his$_i$ mother likes.

Fronted phrases, like the bracketed parts of (43–44), may be thought to obligatorily reconstruct to the gap location. The following tree for (43*a*) indicates

[7] Etymology: The word "thunk" is "the past tense of 'think' at two in the morning" (Raymond *et al.* 2003).

this approximate understanding by arrows on both ends of the outermost curve.

(45)

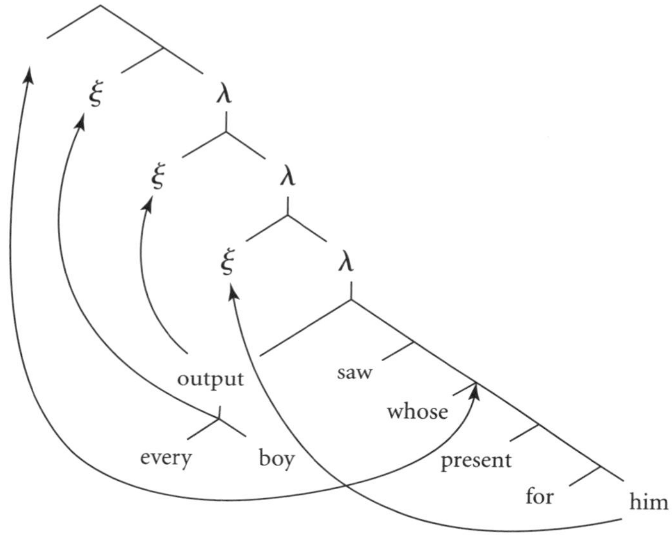

First, the quantifier *every boy* raises; second, the remnant *output* tucks in; third, the *wh*-phrase *whose present for him* reconstructs; finally, the pronoun *him* tucks in further.

As one might expect, the crucial piece of this puzzle is how to analyze filler-gap dependencies. We introduce into our grammar a silent element, which I follow tradition in notating as __ and pronouncing as "trace". The trace denotes the following. It should be reminiscent of input in (19).

(46) $\_\_ = \xi f.\, \lambda g.\, f(g())$

The best way to understand this denotation is to watch it in action. We can now generate a gapped clause like *Alice loves* __.

(47) $\text{alice}\backslash(\text{love}/\underline{\_\_})$
$\Rightarrow \lambda g.\, \big[\big(\lambda x.\, \text{alice}\backslash(\text{love}/x)\big)\big(g()\big)\big]$

The denotation comes out to be a λ-abstraction of type $\langle\langle(), e\rangle, t\rangle$, in that we need to feed it a thunked individual (in other words, a value of type $\langle(), e\rangle$) in order to recover a saturated proposition. For example, for a sentence like *Bob, Alice loves*, we feed it the thunked individual that simply returns Bob with no side effect.

(48) $\underline{(\lambda().\,\mathrm{bob})\backslash\big(\lambda g.\,\big[\big(\lambda x.\,\mathrm{alice}\backslash(\mathrm{love}/x)\big)\big(g()\big)\big]\big)}$
$$\begin{aligned}
&\Rightarrow \big[\big(\lambda x.\,\mathrm{alice}\backslash(\mathrm{love}/x)\big)\big(\underline{(\lambda().\,\mathrm{bob})()}\big)\big]\\
&\Rightarrow \big[\underline{\big(\lambda x.\,\mathrm{alice}\backslash(\mathrm{love}/x)\big)(\mathrm{bob})}\big]\\
&\Rightarrow \big[\mathrm{alice}\underline{\backslash}(\mathrm{love}\underline{/}\mathrm{bob})\big]\\
&\Rightarrow \underline{[\mathrm{love}(\mathrm{bob})(\mathrm{alice})]}\\
&\Rightarrow \mathrm{love}(\mathrm{bob})(\mathrm{alice})
\end{aligned}$$

One way to think of the trace, as defined here, is as follows. Shift and reset are a concrete implementation of covert movement, but our system has no direct correlate of overt movement. Roughly speaking, our trace encodes overt movement using covert movement: instead of overtly raising some phrase, we raise a silent phrase, the trace. The overt material is base-generated, so to speak, right next to the landing site of this movement. Because the trace is silent, it makes no empirical difference whether it raises covertly or overtly; our account of fronting claims the denotational equivalent of the trace's moving covertly. Cinque (1990) and Postal (1998) have made similar proposals for overt movement, at least for topicalization.

(49)

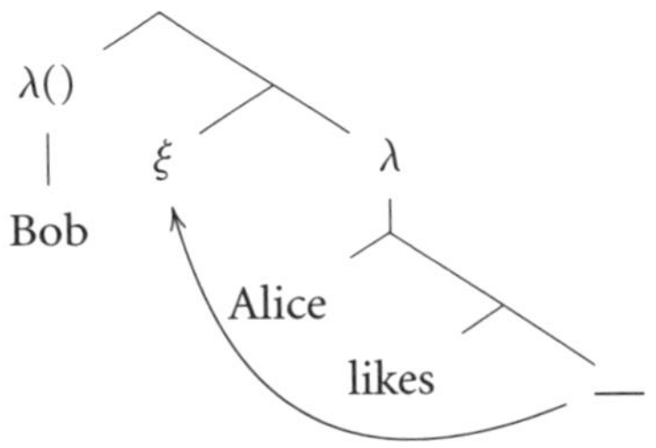

In the trivial example (49), the only side effect is the shift by the trace. There is no binding, no quantification, and no *wh*-question. There are a variety of ways in which life can become more exciting. First of all, note that we now have a unified analysis of raised and in-situ *wh*-phrases. Suppose that we analyze a *wh*-phrase like *who* as simply input.

(50) $\mathrm{who} = \xi f.\, f$

Then, we can treat not only in-situ *wh*-questions such as (51), as shown in (52)—

(51) Alice saw who?

(52) $\mathrm{alice}\backslash(\mathrm{see}/\underline{\mathrm{who}}) \Rightarrow \lambda x.\,[\mathrm{alice}\backslash(\mathrm{see}/x)]$

—but also raised *wh*-questions like (53), by thunking the *wh*-phrase and using it in conjunction with the trace:

(53) Who did Alice see?

(54) $(\lambda().\,\mathrm{who})\backslash\big[\mathrm{alice}\backslash(\mathrm{see}/\_\_)\big]$

$$\begin{aligned}
&\Rightarrow (\lambda().\,\mathrm{who})\backslash\underline{\big[\lambda g.\big[(\lambda x.\,\mathrm{alice}\backslash(\mathrm{see}/x))(g())\big]\big]}\\
&\Rightarrow \underline{(\lambda().\,\mathrm{who})\backslash\big(\lambda g.\big[(\lambda x.\,\mathrm{alice}\backslash(\mathrm{see}/x))(g())\big]\big)}\\
&\Rightarrow \big[(\lambda x.\,\mathrm{alice}\backslash(\mathrm{see}/x))\big(\underline{(\lambda().\,\mathrm{who})()}\big)\big]\\
&\Rightarrow \big[(\lambda x.\,\mathrm{alice}\backslash(\mathrm{see}/x))(\underline{\mathrm{who}})\big]\\
&\Rightarrow \underline{\big[\lambda y.\big[(\lambda x.\,\mathrm{alice}\backslash(\mathrm{see}/x))(y)\big]\big]}\\
&\Rightarrow \lambda y.\big[(\lambda x.\,\mathrm{alice}\backslash(\mathrm{see}/x))(y)\big]
\end{aligned}$$

The last line is equivalent to the desired question denotation $\lambda y.\,\mathrm{see}(y)(\mathrm{alice})$, as can be seen by applying it to bob and continuing reducing. Note that *who* is evaluated right after the trace is, and no earlier.

Recall from §4.5.1 that *everyone's mother* is as genuinely quantificational as *everyone* alone. Similarly, *whose mother* in this treatment of *wh*-questions is as genuinely interrogative as *who* alone. Therefore, raised *wh*-phrases can pied-pipe surrounding material: to generate the sentence

(55) Whose mother did Alice see?

we can place *whose mother* together in a fronted thunk:

(56) $(\lambda().\,\mathrm{who}\backslash\mathrm{mother})\backslash\big[\mathrm{alice}\backslash(\mathrm{see}/\_\_)\big]$

$$\begin{aligned}
&\Rightarrow (\lambda().\,\mathrm{who}\backslash\mathrm{mother})\backslash\underline{\big[\lambda g.\big[(\lambda x.\,\mathrm{alice}\backslash(\mathrm{see}/x))(g())\big]\big]}\\
&\Rightarrow \underline{(\lambda().\,\mathrm{who}\backslash\mathrm{mother})\backslash\big(\lambda g.\big[(\lambda x.\,\mathrm{alice}\backslash(\mathrm{see}/x))(g())\big]\big)}\\
&\Rightarrow \big[(\lambda x.\,\mathrm{alice}\backslash(\mathrm{see}/x))\big(\underline{(\lambda().\,\mathrm{who}\backslash\mathrm{mother})()}\big)\big]\\
&\Rightarrow \big[(\lambda x.\,\mathrm{alice}\backslash(\mathrm{see}/x))(\underline{\mathrm{who}}\backslash\mathrm{mother})\big]\\
&\Rightarrow \underline{\big[\lambda y.\big[(\lambda x.\,\mathrm{alice}\backslash(\mathrm{see}/x))(y\backslash\mathrm{mother})\big]\big]}\\
&\Rightarrow \lambda y.\big[(\lambda x.\,\mathrm{alice}\backslash(\mathrm{see}/x))(y\backslash\mathrm{mother})\big]
\end{aligned}$$

The last line is equivalent to the desired question denotation $\lambda y.\,\mathrm{see}(\mathrm{mother}(y))(\mathrm{alice})$, as can be seen by applying it to bob and continuing reducing. Note that *whose mother* is evaluated right after the trace is, and no earlier.

4.5.5 *Binding in* Wh-*Questions*

Another way to make life with the trace more exciting is to put output or input in the fronted phrase. In other words, let us consider when a raised *wh*-phrase can bind a pronoun or contain a pronoun to be bound. For simplicity, I assume that *who* in (57) is a raised *wh*-phrase.

(57) Who_i __ saw his_i mother?

(58) $$(\lambda().\,\text{output}(\text{who}))\backslash\big[\underline{\_\_}\backslash(\text{see}/(\text{input}\backslash\text{mother}))\big]$$
$$\Rightarrow (\lambda().\,\text{output}(\text{who}))\backslash\underline{\big[\lambda g.\,\big[(\lambda x.\,x\backslash(\text{see}/(\text{input}\backslash\text{mother})))(g())\big]\big]}$$
$$\Rightarrow \underline{(\lambda().\,\text{output}(\text{who}))\backslash\big(\lambda g.\,\big[(\lambda x.\,x\backslash(\text{see}/(\text{input}\backslash\text{mother})))(g())\big]\big)}$$
$$\Rightarrow \big[(\lambda x.\,x\backslash(\text{see}/(\text{input}\backslash\text{mother})))\big(\underline{(\lambda().\,\text{output}(\text{who}))()}\big)\big]$$
$$\Rightarrow \big[(\lambda x.\,x\backslash(\text{see}/(\text{input}\backslash\text{mother})))\big(\text{output}(\underline{\text{who}})\big)\big]$$
$$\Rightarrow \underline{\big[\lambda y.\,\big[(\lambda x.\,x\backslash(\text{see}/(\text{input}\backslash\text{mother})))\big(\text{output}(y)\big)\big]\big]}$$
$$\Rightarrow \lambda y.\,\big[(\lambda x.\,x\backslash(\text{see}/(\text{input}\backslash\text{mother})))\big(\text{output}(y)\big)\big]$$

The last line is equivalent to the desired question denotation $\lambda y.\,\text{see}\big(\text{mother}(y)\big)(y)$, as can be seen by applying it to bob and continuing reducing. Note that *output(who)* is evaluated when the trace is, which is before *input* is evaluated, because the trace occurs before *his*. Binding thus succeeds.

By contrast, binding fails if the trace occurs after the pronoun. This happens in (43b) above and (59) below.

(59) *Who_i did his_i mother see __?

(60) $$(\lambda().\,\text{output}(\text{who}))\backslash\big[(\underline{\text{input}}\backslash\text{mother})\backslash(\text{see}/\_\_)\big]$$
$$\Rightarrow (\lambda().\,\text{output}(\text{who}))\backslash\underline{\big[\lambda x.\,\big[(x\backslash\text{mother})\backslash(\text{see}/\_\_)\big]\big]}$$
$$\Rightarrow (\lambda().\,\text{output}(\text{who}))\backslash\big(\lambda x.\,\big[(x\backslash\text{mother})\backslash(\text{see}/\_\_)\big]\big)$$

After two reduction steps, we see a type mismatch: the variable x needs to be an individual (of type e) in order to be passed to mother, but $\lambda().\,\text{output}(\text{who})$ is a thunked individual (of type $\langle(), e\rangle$). Binding thus fails as desired, just as in (27).

Furthermore, combining left-to-right evaluation with thunking makes correct predictions not just when the *wh*-phrase itself tries to bind, but also when a subphrase of the *wh*-phrase tries to bind.

(61) (*a*) Whose_i friend's_j neighbor_k did Alice think __ saw $\text{his}_{i/j/k}$ mother?

(*b*) Whose_i friend's_j neighbor_k did Alice think $\text{his}_{*i/*j/*k}$ mother saw __?

Barker and I call these cases "pied-binding".

4.5.6 *Superiority*

We have just seen how raised *wh*-phrases interact with binding. Raised *wh*-phrases also interact with in-situ *wh*-phrases, under the rubric of superiority.

The basic pattern of superiority is shown by the contrast between (62) and (63).

(62) Who __ saw who?

(63) *Who did who see __?

Our theory turns out to already predict these judgments. The difference between these examples is again due to evaluation order.

In the acceptable question (62), the trace is evaluated before the in-situ *who*. The trace makes the gapped clause __ *saw who* call for a thunked individual that is the filler phrase, a need nicely fulfilled by the fronted *who*.

(64)
$$\begin{aligned}
&(\lambda().\,\mathrm{who})\backslash\big[\underline{__}\backslash(\mathrm{see}/\mathrm{who})\big]\\
&\Rightarrow (\lambda().\,\mathrm{who})\backslash\underline{\big[\lambda g.\,\big[(\lambda x.\,x\backslash(\mathrm{see}/\mathrm{who}))(g())\big]\big]}\\
&\Rightarrow \underline{(\lambda().\,\mathrm{who})\backslash\big(\lambda g.\,\big[(\lambda x.\,x\backslash(\mathrm{see}/\mathrm{who}))(g())\big]\big)}\\
&\Rightarrow \big[(\lambda x.\,x\backslash(\mathrm{see}/\mathrm{who}))\big(\underline{(\lambda().\,\mathrm{who})()}\big)\big]\\
&\Rightarrow \big[(\lambda x.\,x\backslash(\mathrm{see}/\mathrm{who}))(\underline{\mathrm{who}})\big]\\
&\Rightarrow \underline{\big[\lambda y.\,\big[(\lambda x.\,x\backslash(\mathrm{see}/\mathrm{who}))(y)\big]\big]}\\
&\Rightarrow \lambda y.\,\big[(\lambda x.\,x\backslash(\mathrm{see}/\mathrm{who}))(y)\big]
\end{aligned}$$

The last line is equivalent to the desired question denotation

(65) $\lambda y.\,\lambda z.\,\mathrm{see}(z)(y)$,

as can be seen by applying it to alice and bob and continuing reducing.

In the unacceptable question (63), an in-situ *who* is evaluated first. The in-situ *who* makes the gapped clause *did who see* __ call for an unthunked individual that is the answer to the *wh*-question, which the fronted *who* is not—so evaluation gets stuck, as desired.

(66)
$$\begin{aligned}
&(\lambda().\,\mathrm{who})\backslash\big[\underline{\mathrm{who}}\backslash(\mathrm{see}/__)\big]\\
&\Rightarrow (\lambda().\,\mathrm{who})\backslash\underline{\big[\lambda x.\,\big[x\backslash(\mathrm{see}__)\big]\big]}\\
&\Rightarrow (\lambda().\,\mathrm{who})\backslash\big(\lambda x.\,\big[x\backslash(\mathrm{see}__)\big]\big)
\end{aligned}$$

One way to understand the problem encountered after two reduction steps above is as a type mismatch: in-situ *who* requires an unthunked individual as input, but what the fronted filler provides is a thunked individual. But even were the raised *who* not thunked, the sentence (63) still does not mean (65). Rather, the expression

(67) $\mathrm{who}\backslash\big[\mathrm{who}\backslash(\mathrm{see}/\_\_)\big]$

denotes—reduces to—something incoherent that might be paraphrased "Which *x* answers the question 'who saw __?'?".

The two examples above show that evaluation order imposes an "intervention effect" (Beck 1996; Pesetsky 2000) or a "minimal link condition" (Chomsky 1995) between the filler and the gap in a multiple *wh*-question.

4.5.7 *Formalization*

In the presentation so far, I have mainly used example sentences to buttress the intuition that linguistic phenomena can be fruitfully treated as computational side effects. Barker and I have implemented these ideas in a combinatory categorial grammar that fits on a single page (Shan and Barker 2006), and tested them using a parser he wrote. We are unaware of any other implemented parser that deals with quantification, binding, and *wh*-questions at the same time, while ruling out crossover and superiority.

One particularly nice thing about having a machine-executable implementation of our theory is that you can flip a switch—simply enable the right-to-left evaluation rule and disable the left-to-right evaluation rule—and watch the grammar reverse its predictions regarding crossover and superiority. This reversal convinced us that left-to-right evaluation is a viable, unifying explanation for crossover and superiority, and I think an intuitively appealing one as well.

4.6 Levels of Scope-Taking

Throughout the discussion above, I have completely neglected the issue of scope ambiguity. As it stands, our grammar generates only one reading for the ambiguous sentence

(68) Someone loves everyone.

The reading that we do predict is surface scope, where *someone* scopes over *everyone*. This prediction is because we stipulate left-to-right evaluation, and quantifiers evaluated earlier scope wider.

(69) $(\underline{\xi f. \exists x. f(x)})\backslash\big(\text{love}/(\xi f. \forall y.\ f(y))\big)$
$\Rightarrow \exists x.\ \underline{\big(\lambda z.\ \big[z\backslash\big(\text{love}/(\xi f. \forall y.\ f(y))\big)\big]\big)(x)}$
$\Rightarrow \exists x.\ \big[x\backslash\big(\text{love}/(\underline{\xi f. \forall y.\ f(y)})\big)\big]$
$\Rightarrow \exists x.\ \big[\forall y.\ \underline{\big(\lambda z.\ [x\backslash(\text{love}/z)]\big)(y)}\big]$
$\Rightarrow \exists x.\ \big[\forall y.\ \big[x\underline{\backslash}(\text{love}\underline{/y})\big]\big]$
$\Rightarrow \exists x.\ \big[\forall y.\ \underline{[\text{love}(y)(x)]}\big]$
$\Rightarrow \exists x.\ \underline{[\forall y.\ \text{love}(y)(x)]}$
$\Rightarrow \exists x.\ \forall y.\ \text{love}(y)(x)$

The shift for *someone* is evaluated before the shift for *everyone*, so the former quantifier dictates the outermost shape of the final result. No matter what evaluation order we specify, as long as our semantic rules remain deterministic, they will only generate one reading for the sentence, never both.

To better account for the data, we need to introduce some sort of nondeterminism into our theory. There are two natural ways to proceed. First, we can allow arbitrary evaluation order, not just left-to-right. This route has been pursued with some success by Barker (2002) and de Groote (2001), but it contradicts the unified account of crossover and superiority in §4.5 above. A second way to introduce nondeterminism is to maintain the hypothesis that natural language expressions are evaluated from left to right, but allow multiple *context levels* (Barker 2000; Danvy and Filinski 1990) to keep multiple side effects out of each other's way. I now explain this second way.

As introduced in §4.2, a shift in our metalanguage only affects up to the closest enclosing reset. Multiple context levels relax this restriction by placing a subscript on each shift and reset operator. The effect of an nth-level shift, written $\xi_n f.\, e$ where f is a variable name and e is an expression, is restricted to the closest enclosing mth-level reset, written $[_m \cdots]$, such that $m \leq n$. The following reductions illustrate.

(70) $\text{“real ”} + \big[_1 \text{“compositional ”} + (\xi_1 f.\, \text{“directly ”} + f(\text{“semantics”}))\big]$
$\Rightarrow \cdots \Rightarrow \text{“real directly compositional semantics”}$

(71) $\text{“real ”} + \big[_1 \text{“compositional ”} + (\xi_0 f.\, \text{“directly ”} + f(\text{“semantics”}))\big]$
$\Rightarrow \cdots \Rightarrow \text{“directly real compositional semantics”}$

(72) $\text{“real ”} + \big[_0 \text{“compositional ”} + (\xi_1 f.\, \text{“directly ”} + f(\text{“semantics”}))\big]$
$\Rightarrow \cdots \Rightarrow \text{“real directly compositional semantics”}$

(73) $\text{“real ”} + \big[_0 \text{“compositional ”} + (\xi_0 f.\, \text{“directly ”} + f(\text{“semantics”}))\big]$
$\Rightarrow \cdots \Rightarrow \text{“real directly compositional semantics”}$

Danvy and Filinski (1990) give a denotational semantics for shift and reset at multiple context levels, using multiple levels of continuations. Taking advantage of their work, we let quantifiers manipulate the context at any level, say the nth level.

(74) $\text{everyone}_n = \xi_n f.\, \forall x. f(x)$

(75) $\text{someone}_n = \xi_n f.\, \exists x. f(x)$

In other words, we posit that each occurrence of *everyone* and *someone* is ambiguous as to the level n at which it shifts.

The ambiguity of (68) is now predicted as follows. Suppose that *someone* shifts at the mth level and *everyone* shifts at the nth level.

(76) Someone$_m$ loves everyone$_n$.

If $m \leq n$, the surface scope reading results. If $m > n$, the inverse scope reading results. For example, when $m = 1$ and $n = 0$, the inverse scope is computed by the following reductions.

(77) $\underline{\text{someone}_1}\backslash(\text{love}/\text{everyone}_0)$

$$\begin{aligned}
&\Rightarrow \exists x.\, \underline{\big(\lambda z.\, \big[_1 z\backslash(\text{love}/\text{everyone}_0)\big]\big)(x)} \\
&\Rightarrow \exists x.\, \big[_1 x\backslash(\text{love}/\underline{\text{everyone}_0})\big] \\
&\Rightarrow \forall y.\, \underline{\big(\lambda z.\, [_0 \exists x.\, [_1 x\backslash(\text{love}/z)]]\big)(y)} \\
&\Rightarrow \forall y.\, \big[_0 \exists x.\, \big[_1 x\underline{\backslash}(\text{love}\underline{/y})\big]\big] \\
&\Rightarrow \forall y.\, \big[_0 \exists x.\, \underline{[_1 \text{love}(y)(x)]}\big] \\
&\Rightarrow \forall y.\, \underline{[_0 \exists x.\, \text{love}(y)(x)]} \\
&\Rightarrow \forall y.\, \exists x.\, \text{love}(y)(x)
\end{aligned}$$

This analysis of inverse scope may be reminiscent of accounts that posit a hierarchy of functional projections at the clausal boundary. We can think of each context level as a functional projection, which attracts quantifiers destined for that level or any inner level.

(78)

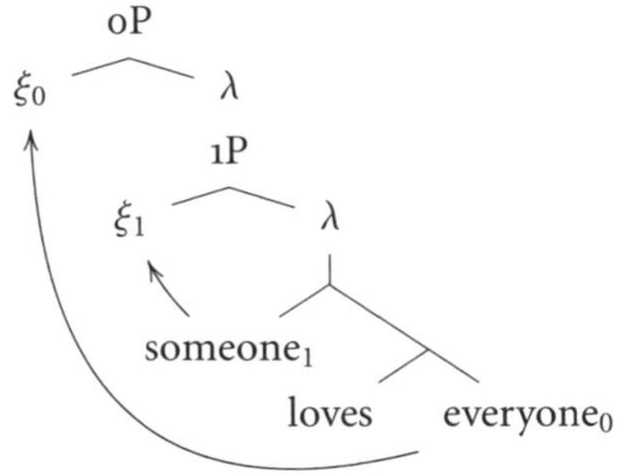

The same hierarchy of context levels allows in-situ *wh*-phrases to take scope ambiguously (Baker 1968).

(79) Who remembers where we bought what?

(*a*) Alice remembers where we bought the vase.

(*b*) Alice remembers where we bought what.

The same treatment applies to more complicated cases of multiple quantification. For example, we predict correctly that the following sentence, with three quantifiers, is five-way (not six-way) ambiguous.

(80) Every representative of some company saw most samples.

Moreover, it is natural to express generalizations about quantifier scope as constraints on which quantifiers can shift at which context levels. For example, perhaps quantifiers but not *wh*-indefinites take linear scope in Mandarin Chinese because quantifiers are constrained to shift at a fixed level whereas *wh*-indefinites shift more freely (Shan 2003). Multiple context levels thus provide a denotational understanding of quantifier raising that accords with our theoretical intuitions and empirical observations.

4.7 Conclusion

To sum up, let me use the linguistic analyses in this paper as a poster child for the broader agenda that I set out at the beginning: to relate computational and linguistic side effects. As may be suggested by the fact that the topic of this paper, linguistic side effects, is defined in terms of (challenges to) compositionality, I am a fan of direct compositionality as a research strategy. That is, it is fruitful to take up instances of apparent noncompositionality in natural language as not just a collection of disconnected puzzles but a coherent body of challenges to meet in a principled way. I certainly do not think that Chris Barker and I have now completely uncovered the mysteries of crossover and superiority, but to the extent that our approach is successful, it epitomizes three goals on my agenda, namely *uniformity*, *interaction*, and *evaluation*.

4.7.1 *Uniformity*

All linguistic side effects can be treated under the same framework. In this paper, that framework is the metalanguage of shift and reset. When we added to our grammar lexical items for quantification, binding, *wh*-questions, and so on, all we did was that—adding lexical items. We did not have to revise our composition rules or re-lift our semantic types. From the analogy between linguistic and computational side effects, we can derive intuition for how to treat all of the settings in natural language where referential transparency seems to be at stake.

Of course, even though I just used the word “can”, there is always the possibility that the pieces may not all fall into place by themselves as we work on our grand uniform theory of linguistic side effects. They probably will not—at least not so easily. For now, I can only make a methodological observation: isn’t it curious how we developed this nice semantic theory by working with not just the pure λ-calculus but also shift and reset? You can also further speculate that this curiosity tells us about how human language works, especially how apparent noncompositionality in human language works.

Some readers may complain that shift and reset can treat so many linguistic side effects only because they are so powerful—too powerful to yield any insight or constraint on natural language. But as I emphasized in §4.4, shift and reset are just metalinguistic shorthand for continuations, which are a generalization of good old generalized quantifiers. Shift and reset, and their link to computational side effects, tell us how to fully exploit the power that already comes with generalized quantifiers, without further complicating the basic machinery of syntax and semantics with possible worlds for intensionality, variables for binding, alternatives for focus, undefinedness for presupposition, and so on.

4.7.2 *Interaction*

Because all our analyses are phrased in terms of the same framework, there is at least a shred of hope that, if we just bang some lexical items that deal with quantification against some other items that deal with binding, we would get an harmonious analysis of quantification and binding. In the cases surveyed in this paper, this shred of hope did work out, although there were technical details that needed to be dealt with, which for me was made easier by the connection to computational side effects.

By the way, the picture is not entirely rosy on the programming-language side either. The engineering ideal would be for the issues of multiple, interacting computational side effects to be solved to the extent where you can just throw together any number of arbitrary side effects and get a working programming language by stirring the mix. That would make it much easier for people to design new programming languages as well as understand existing ones, but there are unresolved technical difficulties. Who knows—perhaps these technical difficulties in programming language engineering correspond to empirical generalizations or constraints in natural languages, however skilled speakers of natural languages and users of programming language may be at getting around them.

4.7.3 *Evaluation*

One thing that I found helpful as I studied programming-language semantics is how it relates denotational and operational models of meaning, as I mentioned earlier in §4.4. When a computer scientist says that some program expression denotes some value, there is no philosophical commitment being made as to what the "true meanings" of programs are. A lot of insight and understanding can often be gained by spelling out *two* semantics for the same language and proving them equivalent. For example, one semantics might be denotational in that it assigns a semantic value to each expression, and another might be operational in that it specifies reductions on terms that correspond to how the program might be executed by a computer. These are both valid viewpoints.

In the linguistics I just presented, there are three places where a link between denotational and operational semantics helps us formulate a theory that gives insight and makes correct predictions.

1. The shift-reset metalanguage. It is often easier for me to understand what is going on by looking at a shift-reset expression instead of a huge number of λs in the pure λ-calculus.
2. Left-to-right evaluation. Once we take a naïve processing explanation and couch it in terms of denotations (with the help of continuation semantics), we can explain cases (such as those in §4.5.5) where the empirical data are the exact opposite of what would be predicted by the naïve left-to-right account.
3. Thunking. We used thunking to analyze overt *wh*-fronting in §4.5.4: it corresponds to delayed evaluation, which postpones the side effects incurred by a program expression.

Of course, the insight that linguistic expressions are like program instructions is already present in dynamic semantics (Groenendijk and Stokhof 1991; Heim 1982; Kamp 1981; see also Moschovakis 1993). Dynamic semantics has been applied to a variety of natural-language phenomena, such as basic crossover and verb-phrase ellipsis (van Eijck and Francez 1995; Gardent 1991; Hardt 1999). However, dynamic semantics alone does not account for interactions among binding, quantification, and *wh*-questions. The work described here enables dynamic semantics to compose meanings at the intrasentential level, and generalizes it to side effects other than binding, existential quantification, and presupposition.

It might be strange for me to speak of semantics that are not denotational, especially since the topic of this workshop, "direct compositionality", pretty much presupposes that a semantic theory is one that assigns denotations to phrases. But denotations do not have to be sets, and composition does not have to be function application. For example, I find it promising that *game semantics* is taking hold in both programming language semantics and natural language semantics (Abramsky and McCusker 1997; among others). In linguistics, a lot of questions are being asked about the proper line, if any, to draw between semantics and pragmatics, or between semantics and syntax. In computer science, as it turned out, even something as innocent-looking as the pure λ-calculus is useful to analyze as a model of computation by interaction.

These are bona fide semantics, even though they are not model-theoretic in the original Montagovian sense, but closer to a proof-theoretic ideal that models language use, in context, more directly.

4.7.4 *Farewell*

So, there you have it: uniformity, interaction, and evaluation. These are what I think we can achieve and clarify in our theory of linguistic side effects in natural languages, by drawing an analogy with computational side effects in programming languages. I hope that I have given you some concrete examples of this approach, in the form of proposed theories that are, I think, improvements over their predecessors (and I mean "predecessors" in terms of both time and intellectual heritage).

References

ABRAMSKY, S. and MCCUSKER, G. 1997. 'Game semantics', presented at the 1997 Marktoberdorf Summer School. 26 Sep. 2000, http://web.comlab.ox.ac.uk/oucl/work/samson.abramsky/mdorf97.ps.gz.

BAKER, C. L. 1968. Indirect questions in English. Ph.D. thesis, University of Illinois.

BARKER, C. 2000. 'Notes on higher-order continuations', MS, University of California, San Diego.

—— 2002. 'Continuations and the nature of quantification', *Natural Language Semantics*, 10: 211–42.

BECK, S. 1996. 'Quantified structures as barriers for LF movement', *Natural Language Semantics*, 4: 1–56.

DEN BESTEN, H. and WEBELHUTH, G. 1990. 'Stranding', in (eds), *Scrambling and Barriers*. G. Grewendorf and W. Sternefeld, Amsterdam: John Benjamins. 77–92.

BÜRING, D. 2001. 'A situation semantics for binding out of DP', in R. Hastings, B. Jackson, and Z. Zvolensky (eds), *Proceedings from Semantics and Linguistic Theory XI*. Ithaca, NY: Cornell University Press. 56–75.

CHOMSKY, N. 1995. *The Minimalist Program*, chap. 4 (Categories and transformations), 219–394. Cambridge, MA: MIT Press.

CINQUE, G. 1990. *Types of Ā-dependencies*. Cambridge, MA: MIT Press.

COOPER, R. 1983. *Quantification and Syntactic Theory*. Dordrecht: Reidel.

DANVY, O. and FILINSKI, A. 1989. 'A functional abstraction of typed contexts', Tech. Rep. 89/12, DIKU, University of Copenhagen, Denmark. http://www.daimi.au.dk/~danvy/Papers/fatc.ps.gz.

—— and —— 1990. 'Abstracting control', in *Proceedings of the 1990 ACM conference on Lisp and functional programming*. New York: ACM Press. 151–60.

—— and —— 1992. 'Representing control: A study of the CPS transformation', *Mathematical Structures in Computer Science*, 2: 361–91.

VAN EIJCK, J. and FRANCEZ, N. 1995. 'Verb-phrase ellipsis in dynamic semantics', in L. Pólos and M. Masuch (eds), *Applied logic: How, what, and why: Logical approaches to natural language*. Dordrecht: Kluwer. 29–60.

FELLEISEN, M. 1987. The calculi of λ_v-CS conversion: A syntactic theory of control and state in imperative higher-order programming languages. Ph.D. thesis, Computer Science Department, Indiana University. Also as Tech. Rep. 226.

—— 1988. 'The theory and practice of first-class prompts', in *POPL '88: Conference record of the annual ACM symposium on principles of programming languages*. New York: ACM Press. 180–90.

FILINSKI, A. 1994. 'Representing monads', in *POPL '94: Conference record of the annual ACM symposium on principles of programming languages*. New York: ACM Press. 446–57.

—— 1996. Controlling effects. Ph.D. thesis, School of Computer Science, Carnegie Mellon University. Also as Tech. Rep. CMU-CS-96-119.

—— 1999. 'Representing layered monads', in *POPL '99: Conference record of the annual ACM symposium on principles of programming languages*. New York: ACM Press. 175–88.

FREGE, G. 1891. 'Funktion und Begriff'. Vortrag, gehalten in der Sitzung vom 9. Januar 1891 der Jenaischen Gesellschaft für Medizin und Naturwissenschaft, Jena: Hermann Pohle. English translation Frege (1980*a*).

—— 1892. 'Über Sinn und Bedeutung', *Zeitschrift für Philosophie und philosophische Kritik*, 100: 25–50. English translation Frege (1980*b*).

—— 1980*a*. 'Function and concept', in Frege (1980*c*), 21–41. Reprinted as Frege (1997*b*).

—— 1980*b*. 'On sense and reference', in Frege (1980*c*), 56–78. Reprinted as Frege (1997*c*).

—— 1980*c*. *Translations from the philosophical writings of Gottlob Frege*, ed. Peter Geach and Max Black. 3rd ed. Oxford: Blackwell.

—— 1997*a*. *The Frege reader*, ed. Michael Beaney. Oxford: Blackwell.

—— 1997*b*. 'Function and concept', in Frege (1997*a*), 130–48.

—— 1997*c*. 'On Sinn and Bedeutung', in Frege (1997*a*), 151–71.

GARDENT, C. 1991. 'Dynamic semantics and VP-ellipsis', in J. van Eijck (ed.), *Logics in AI: European workshop JELIA '90*, Lecture Notes in Artificial Intelligence 478, Berlin: Springer. 251–66.

GROENENDIJK, J. and STOKHOF, M. 1991. 'Dynamic predicate logic', *Linguistics and Philosophy*, 14: 39–100.

DE GROOTE, P. 2001. 'Type raising, continuations, and classical logic', in R. van Rooy and M. Stokhof (eds), *Proceedings of the 13th Amsterdam Colloquium*. Institute for Logic, Language and Computation, University of Amsterdam. 97–101.

HAMBLIN, C. L. 1973. 'Questions in Montague English', *Foundations of Language*, 10: 41–53.

HARDT, D. 1999. 'Dynamic interpretation of verb phrase ellipsis', *Linguistics and Philosophy*, 22: 185–219.

Hatcliff, J. and Danvy, O. 1997. 'Thunks and the λ-calculus', *Journal of Functional Programming*, 7: 303–19.

Heim, I. 1982. The semantics of definite and indefinite noun phrases. Ph.D. thesis, University of Massachusetts, Amherst.

Ingerman, P. Z. 1961. 'Thunks: A way of compiling procedure statements with some comments on procedure declarations', *Communications of the ACM*, 4: 55–8.

Jacobson, P. 1999. 'Towards a variable-free semantics', *Linguistics and Philosophy*, 22: 117–84.

—— 2000. 'Paycheck pronouns, Bach-Peters sentences, and variable-free semantics', *Natural Language Semantics*, 8: 77–155.

Kameyama, Y. and Hasegawa, M. 2003. 'A sound and complete axiomatization of delimited continuations', in *ICFP '03: Proceedings of the ACM international conference on functional programming*. New York: ACM Press. 177–88.

Kamp, H. 1981. 'A theory of truth and semantic representation', in J. A. G. Groenendijk, T. M. V. Janssen, and M. B. J. Stokhof. *Formal methods in the study of language: Proceedings of the 3rd Amsterdam Colloquium*. Amsterdam: Mathematisch Centrum. 277–322.

Keller, W. R. 1988. 'Nested Cooper storage: The proper treatment of quantification in ordinary noun phrases', in U. Reyle and C. Rohrer, (eds), *Natural language parsing and linguistic theories*. Dordrecht: Reidel. 432–47.

May, R. C. 1977. The grammar of quantification. Ph.D. thesis, *MIT*. Reprinted by New York: Garland, 1991.

Moggi, E. 1991. 'Notions of computation and monads', *Information and Computation*, 93: 55–92.

Montague, R. 1974. 'The proper treatment of quantification in ordinary English', in R. Thomason (ed.), *Formal philosophy: Selected papers of Richard Montague*, New Haven, CT: Yale University Press. 247–70.

Moortgat, M. 1988. *Categorial investigations: Logical and linguistic aspects of the Lambek calculus*. Dordrecht: Foris.

—— 1995. 'In situ binding: A modal analysis', in P. Dekker and M. Stokhof (eds), *Proceedings of the 10th Amsterdam Colloquium*. Institute for Logic, Language and Computation, University of Amsterdam. 539–49.

—— 1996. 'Generalized quantifiers and discontinuous type constructors', in H. C. Bunt and A. van Horck (eds), *Discontinuous Constituency*. Berlin: Mouton de Gruyter. 181–207.

Moschovakis, Y. N. 1993. 'Sense and denotation as algorithm and value', in J. Oikkonen and J. Vaananen (eds), *Logic Colloquium '90: Association of Symbolic Logic summer meeting*. Lecture Notes in Logic 2. Poughkeepsie, NY: Association for Symbolic Logic. Reprinted by Natick, MA: A K Peters. 210–49.

Pesetsky, D. 2000. *Phrasal Movement and its Kin*. Cambridge, MA: MIT Press.

Postal, P. M. 1998. *Three Investigations of Extraction*. Cambridge, MA: MIT Press.

Quine, W. V. O. 1960. *Word and Object*. Cambridge, MA: MIT Press.

RAYMOND, E. S., *et al.* (eds). 2003. *The Jargon File.* http://www.catb.org/~esr/jargon/. Version 4.4.7. Version 4.0.0 was published by MIT Press as *The New Hacker's Dictionary.*

RICHARDS, N. W., III. 1997. What moves where when in which language? Ph.D. thesis, MIT. Published as *Movement in Language: Interactions and Architectures* by Oxford University Press, 2001.

SHAN, C.-C. 2002. 'A continuation semantics of interrogatives that accounts for Baker's ambiguity', in B. Jackson (ed.), *Proceedings from Semantics and Linguistic Theory XII.* Ithaca, NY: Cornell University Press. 246–65.

—— 2003. 'Quantifier strengths predict scopal possibilities of Mandarin Chinese *wh*-indefinites', Draft MS, Harvard University; http://www.eecs.harvard.edu/~ccshan/mandarin/.

—— 2004. 'Shift to control', in O. Shivers and O. Waddell (eds), *Proceedings of the 5th workshop on Scheme and functional programming.* Tech. Rep. 600, Computer Science Department, Indiana University. 99–107.

—— and BARKER, C. 2002. 'A unified explanation for crossover and superiority in a theory of binding by predicate abstraction', poster presented at the North East Linguistic Society conference (NELS 33).

—— and —— 2006. 'Explaining crossover and superiority as left-to-right evaluation', *Linguistics and Philosophy*, 29: 91–134.

SØNDERGAARD, H. and SESTOFT, P. 1990. 'Referential transparency, definiteness and unfoldability', *Acta Informatica*, 27: 505–17.

—— and —— 1992. 'Non-determinism in functional languages', *The Computer Journal*, 35: 514–23.

5

Type-Shifting with Semantic Features: A Unified Perspective*

YOAD WINTER

5.1 Introduction

Since their introduction by Partee and Rooth (1983) into linguistic theory, type-shifting principles have been extensively employed in various linguistic domains, including nominal predicates (Partee 1987), kind-denoting NPs (Chierchia 1998), interrogatives (Groenendijk and Stokhof 1989), scrambled definites (van der Does and De Hoop 1998), and plurals (Winter 2001, 2002). Most of the accounts that use type-shifting principles employ them as "last resort" mechanisms that apply only when other compositional mechanisms fail. This failure is often sloppily referred to as *type mismatch*. The motivation for introducing type mismatch into the compositional mechanism is twofold: on the one hand, it allows lexical items to be assigned the minimal types that are needed for describing their denotation; on the other hand, it has been argued that the "last resort" strategy of type-shifting prevents derivation of undesired meanings.

From the perspective of direct compositionality, type-shifting principles have a special role. Although it is possible to use such principles also within non-compositional theories, their introduction is often motivated by considerations of compositionality. A classical example is the Montagovian lexical type-shifting of proper names from the type of entities (e.g. e) to the type of quantifiers (e.g. $(et)t$). Introducing this shifting allows the interpretation of coordinations such as *Mary and every other teacher*, *John or some other student*, etc. without any transformational non-compositional rule such as "conjunction reduction". It is therefore safe to say that at least

* I wish to thank the participants of the workshop on Direct Compositionality, and especially Pauline Jacobson and Chung-chieh Shan. I am grateful to Nissim Francez for his thorough remarks on an earlier draft.

part of the motivation for the type-shifting of proper names comes from the assumption of direct compositionality. Similar points can be made with respect to many other type-shifting principles that have been proposed in the literature.

The first goal of this paper is to define a simple notion of type mismatch, which will rather closely follow Partee and Rooth's original proposal but will be expressed within more familiar terms of categorial semantics. After introducing this implementation of traditional type mismatch, it will be argued that in fact it covers only one possible kind of trigger for type-shifting principles. Partee and Rooth's notion of mismatch is "external" in that the type of an expression is changed only when it combines with another type to which it cannot compose using the "normal" compositional mechanism. It will be argued that, within an appropriate type system, another notion of mismatch is also useful. This is the kind of mismatch in which the semantic type of an expression does not match its syntactic category. Two such cases will be explored: mismatch between morphosyntactic number (singular or plural) and semantic number (a denotation ranging over atoms or sets), and mismatch between syntactic category (noun, DP, adjective etc.) and semantic role (predicate, quantifier, predicate modifier, etc.). Both "external" and "internal" mismatch, which were proposed as triggers for type-shifting in Winter (2001), will be formalized in one system where the definition of types more closely matches natural linguistic notions of semantic roles and semantic number.

5.2 Partee and Rooth's Type-Fitting—Twenty Years Later

The type-shifting approach of Partee and Rooth (1983) assumes a traditional Montague Grammar, where expressions have syntactic categories (indicating their semantic types) and meaning composition is achieved using translation rules corresponding to syntactic rules. In later versions of Categorial Semantics (Van Benthem 1986, 1991; Hendriks 1993), where a semantic *type calculus* is responsible for the composition of denotations and their types, translation rules are no longer necessary. Type-shifting principles in Partee and Rooth's conception only apply when the grammar (or calculus) fails to compose types, or in Partee and Rooth's terms: when there is a *type mismatch*. To emphasize this "last resort" strategy for the application of type-shifting principles, I will henceforth refer by *type-fitting* to type-shifting with the "last resort" resolution strategy. Under this conception, type mismatch is only a matter of *semantic* types, with no regard to the syntactic categories they originate from.

Partee and Rooth argue for type-shifting as a last resort operation on the basis of the following examples.

(1) John caught and ate a fish.
$\not\Leftrightarrow$ John caught a fish and ate a fish.

(2) John hugged and kissed three women.
$\not\Leftrightarrow$ John hugged three women and kissed three women.

(3) John needed and bought a new coat.
$\Leftrightarrow$ John needed a new coat and bought a new coat.

(4) John wants and needs two secretaries.
$\Leftrightarrow$ John wants two secretaries and needs two secretaries.

In sentences (1) and (2), where two verbs that are extensional on their object argument are conjoined, the interpretation is not equivalent to "conjunction reduction" of the object argument. By contrast, when one of the verbs is intensional (as in (3)) or when both of them are (as in (4)), conjunction reduction leads to the correct paraphrase. Partee and Rooth propose to account for this phenomenon using the following three principles:

- Intensional verbs such as *need*, *want* etc. have a "high" lexical type, as in Montague (1973).
- Extensional verbs such as *catch*, *eat*, *hug*, kiss, and *buy* have the "high" type of intensional verbs, as well as a lower type $e(et)$.
- A general "last resort" strategy rules out a high type when a derivation using a lower type is available.

A conjunction of extensional verbs can be handled in type $e(et)$, and the resulting interpretation gives the object wide scope over the conjunction, as intuitively required in sentences (1) and (2). By contrast, when an intensional verb appears in a conjunction, the types of all the verbs in it must be of the higher type, and this leads to the "conjunction reduction" readings in (3) and (4). Hendriks (1993), following Groenendijk and Stokhof (1989), implements Partee and Rooth's proposal without their "last resort" principle, and consequently type-shifting in his system is free to occur whenever the resulting type sequence is derivable in the type calculus. Hendriks' system does not share with Partee and Rooth's the motivation to account for contrasts like the ones between (1)–(2) and (3)–(4), and Hendriks explicitly argues against the judgments of Partee and Rooth in relation to these sentences. Ignoring the empirical debate, I will illustrate in this section how Partee and Rooth's "last resort" mechanism can be implemented using a simple fragment, which in §5.4 will be extended to deal with other phenomena.

The simple fragment that will be introduced below consists of two calculi: a *syntactic calculus* $\mathcal{C}_{\mathbf{syn}}$ that manages categories, and a *semantic calculus* $\mathcal{C}_{\mathbf{sem}}$ that manages types and respective denotations. Let $\mathsf{C}_1, \mathsf{C}_2, \ldots$ be the categories of a sequence of expressions, and let $\tau_1 : \varphi_1, \tau_2 : \varphi_2, \ldots$ be their respective types and denotations. Assume that a category C is derived in one derivation step of $\mathcal{C}_{\mathbf{syn}}$ from $\mathsf{C}_1, \mathsf{C}_2, \ldots$. Assume further that the type and denotation $\tau : \varphi$ are derived in $\mathcal{C}_{\mathbf{sem}}$ from $\tau_1 : \varphi_1, \tau_2 : \varphi_2, \ldots$. Then the following is a *derivation step* in the syntactic–semantic calculus $\mathcal{C}_{\mathbf{syn,sem}}$.

$$\frac{\mathsf{C}_1 : \tau_1 : \varphi_1 \quad \mathsf{C}_2 : \tau_2 : \varphi_2 \quad \ldots}{\mathsf{C} : \tau : \varphi}$$

This is a fairly standard view of the interactions between a syntactic and a semantic calculus (see e.g. Hendriks 1993). However, our definition of $\mathcal{C}_{\mathbf{syn,sem}}$ will also allow the application of type-fitting principles when the syntactic calculus derives a category C from $\mathsf{C}_1, \mathsf{C}_2, \ldots$ but the semantic calculus fails to derive any type (and denotation) from the types $\tau_1, \tau_2, \ldots$ and the respective denotations. In such situations a sequence $\Pi = \pi_1, \pi_2, \ldots$ of type-shifting operators is allowed to apply to the respective types and denotations in $\tau_1 : \varphi_1, \tau_2 : \varphi_2, \ldots$. If this derives the type and denotation $\tau : \varphi$ by $\mathcal{C}_{\mathbf{sem}}$, the following derivation step in $\mathcal{C}_{\mathbf{syn,sem}}$ is licensed:

$$\frac{\mathsf{C}_1 : \tau_1 : \varphi_1 \quad \mathsf{C}_2 : \tau_2 : \varphi_2 \quad \ldots}{\mathsf{C} : \tau : \varphi}\ \Pi$$

For simplicity, the fragment will employ only extensional types, using Definition 1 below. This definition is the standard definition of extensional types, with an additional type for coordinators. This special type is used here in order not to employ richer type systems with polymorphic coordination (see e.g. Emms 1991).

Definition 1 (extensional types) *Let* TYPE_1 *be the smallest set containing* e *(for* entities*) and* t *(for* truth values*), such that for every* $\tau, \sigma \in \mathrm{TYPE}_1$*:* $(\tau\sigma) \in \mathrm{TYPE}_1$*. The set of* extensional types *is* $\mathrm{TYPE}_1 \cup \{\mathsf{coor}\}$*, where* coor *is a special type for coordinators.*

Outermost parentheses of types are omitted. Each type in TYPE_1 classifies a domain according to the following standard definition.

Definition 2 (typed domains) D_e *is an arbitrary non-empty set.* $D_t = \{0, 1\}$*. If* τ *and* σ *are types then* $D_{\tau\sigma} = {D_\sigma}^{D_\tau}$*, the set of functions from* D_τ *to* D_σ*.*

The type coor for coordinators like *and* and *or* has no domain, but expressions of this type are interpreted in all *Boolean* domains according to the following definitions of Partee and Rooth.

Definition 3 (Boolean type) *An extensional type* τ *is* Boolean *iff* $\tau = t$ *or* $\tau = \sigma_1\sigma_2$, *where* σ_2 *is a boolean type.*

Thus, Boolean types are those types that are of the form $\sigma_1(\sigma_2(\ldots(\sigma_n t)\ldots))$, for some natural $n \geq 0$. For the corresponding domains conjunction is defined as follows, and similarly the other Boolean operators.

Definition 4 (polymorphic conjunction) *Let* τ *be a Boolean type. Let* $\wedge_{t(tt)}$ *be standard propositional conjunction. We denote:*

$$\mathbf{and}'_{\tau^c} = \begin{cases} \wedge_{t(tt)} & \text{if } \tau = t \\ \lambda X_\tau.\lambda Y_\tau.\lambda Z_{\sigma_1}.X(Z)\ \mathbf{and}'_{\sigma_2{}^c}\ Y(Z) & \text{if } \tau = \sigma_1\sigma_2 \end{cases}$$

The notation τ^c *is an abbreviation for type* $\tau(\tau\tau)$, *and the notation* A **and**$'$ B *is of course a "sugaring" for* $(\mathbf{and}'(A))(B)$.

The set of categories is standardly defined as a closure of a set of *primitive* categories under the slash ('/') and backslash ('\') constructors. Formally:

Definition 5 (categories) *Let* CAT_0, *the set of* primitive categories, *be a finite non-empty set. The set* CAT_1 *is the smallest set containing* CAT_0 *that satisfies for every* X *and* Y $\in$ CAT_1: (X/Y) $\in \mathrm{CAT}_1$ *and* (X\Y) $\in \mathrm{CAT}_1$. *The set of* categories *is* $\mathrm{CAT}_1 \cup \{\&\}$, *where '&' is a special category for coordinators.*

In the grammar architecture that is used here, unlike traditional Montague Grammar, the semantic type of an expression is not predictable from its syntactic category. This allows type-shifting not to affect the syntactic category and to introduce complex semantic operations (e.g. the composition of a transitive verb with its object) without complicating the syntactic categories that are assumed for expressions.

As a *syntactic calculus* for this toy grammar we need nothing more than the simple **AB** (Ajdukiewicz/Bar-Hillel) calculus, with its '/' and '\' elimination rules, augmented by a coordination rule. The resulting calculus, called '**AB**$^+$ calculus', is defined as follows.

Definition 6 (AB$^+$calculus) *For any categories* X, Y $\in \mathrm{CAT}_1$:

$$\frac{\mathsf{X/Y}\quad \mathsf{Y}}{\mathsf{X}}\ /E \qquad \frac{\mathsf{Y}\quad \mathsf{Y\backslash X}}{\mathsf{X}}\ \backslash E \qquad \frac{\mathsf{X}\quad \&\quad \mathsf{X}}{\mathsf{X}}\ C$$

For a *semantic calculus* in Partee and Rooth's framework we simply use the parallel of the **AB**$^+$ calculus for undirected types with the appropriate semantics. We call this the '**A**$^+$ calculus' (*Ajdukiewicz*$^+$ *calculus*):

TABLE 5.1 A toy P&R lexicon

	Category	Type	Denotation
John	NP	$(et)t$	**john′**
a fish	NP	$(et)t$	**a_fish′**
catch	(NP\S)/NP	$e(et)$	**catch′**
eat	(NP\S)/NP	$e(et)$	**eat′**
need	(NP\S)/NP	$((et)t)(et)$	**need′**
and	&	coor	**and′**

Definition 7 (A⁺ calculus) *For any types τ, $\sigma \in$ TYPE$_1$ and A, B, C denotations of the appropriate types:*

Function Application (APP): $\dfrac{\tau\sigma : A \quad \tau : B}{\sigma : A(B)}$

Permutation (PERM): $\dfrac{\tau : B \quad \sigma : A}{\sigma : A \quad \tau : B}$

Coordination (COOR): $\dfrac{\tau : A \quad \text{coor} : C \quad \tau : B}{\tau : (C_{\tau^c}(A))(B)}$ (for any Boolean type τ)

The toy lexicon we use for this grammar is given in Table 5.1. In this lexicon CAT$_0$, the set of primitive categories, is simply the set {NP, S}. The lexicon uses the following abbreviations, in addition to the non-logical constants **catch′**, **eat′**, and **need′**.

$$\mathbf{john}' = \lambda P_{et}.P(\mathbf{j}')$$
$$\mathbf{a\_fish}' = \lambda P_{et}.\exists x[P(x) \wedge \mathbf{fish}'_{et}(x)]$$

The main insight of Partee and Rooth's proposal is in the application of "type correction" rules when "type mismatch" occurs. Formally, type mismatch is a situation where a string is syntactically well-formed according to the syntactic calculus, but semantically ill-formed according to the semantic type calculus. In such cases (only) type-fitting operators are allowed to apply. In Partee and Rooth's original proposal, the only available type-fitting rule is the following rule of *argument raising* (AR, cf. Hendriks 1993). The AR operator lifts the $e(et)$ type of transitive verbs to type $((et)t)(et)$, which composes with the quantifier type $(et)t$ as a first argument. Formally:

Argument Raising: $\text{AR}_{(e(et))(((et)t)(et))} \stackrel{def}{=} \lambda R_{e(et)}.\lambda Q_{(et)t}.\lambda y.Q(\lambda x.R(x)(y))$

Since the AR operator is the only type-fitting principle in the toy grammar we define, we use a singleton set Σ of type-shifting principles: $\Sigma = \{\text{AR}\}$.

The notions of type mismatch and its resolution are made explicit in the following definition of the syntactic–semantic calculus $\mathcal{C}_{\mathbf{syn,sem}}$.

Definition 8 (**$\mathcal{C}_{\mathbf{syn,sem}}$ and type mismatch resolution**) *Let $\mathcal{C}_{\mathbf{syn}}$ and $\mathcal{C}_{\mathbf{sem}}$ be syntactic and semantic calculi over given sets of categories and types. Let Σ, the set of* type-shifting operations, *be a finite set of typed denotations. Let* $\text{exp}_1, \text{exp}_2, \ldots$ *be expressions of categories* $\mathsf{C}_1, \mathsf{C}_2, \ldots$, *types* $\tau_1, \tau_2, \ldots$ *and denotations* $\varphi_1, \varphi_2, \ldots$, *respectively. Let* Π *be a sequence of operators* $op_1, op_2, \ldots$ *where each operator* op_i *is of type* $\tau_i\sigma_i$ *s.t. either* $op_i \in \Sigma$ *or* op_i *is the identity function of type* $\tau_i\tau_i$ $(\sigma_i = \tau_i)$. *A* derivation step *in* $\mathcal{C}_{\mathbf{syn,sem}}$, *the syntactic–semantic calculus over* $\mathcal{C}_{\mathbf{syn}}$, $\mathcal{C}_{\mathbf{sem}}$ *and* Σ, *ensues whenever the following hold:*

1. *Category* C *is derived from* $\mathsf{C}_1, \mathsf{C}_2, \ldots$ *by one derivation step of* $\mathcal{C}_{\mathbf{syn}}$.
2. *One of the following holds:*
   a. $\tau_1, \tau_2, \ldots \overset{\mathcal{C}_{\mathbf{sem}}}{\vdash} \tau$ *(type* τ *is derivable in* $\mathcal{C}_{\mathbf{sem}}$ *from* $\tau_1, \tau_2, \ldots$*); or*
   b. *There is no type* $\tau \in \text{TYPE}$ *s.t.* $\tau_1, \tau_2, \ldots \overset{\mathcal{C}_{\mathbf{sem}}}{\vdash} \tau$ *(type mismatch), and* $\sigma_1 : op_1(\varphi_1), \sigma_2 : op_2(\varphi_2), \ldots \overset{\mathcal{C}_{\mathbf{sem}}}{\vdash} \tau : \varphi$ *(resolution).*

In the second case we say that $\mathsf{C} : \tau : \varphi$ is resolved *by* Π *from* $\mathsf{C}_1 : \tau_1 : \varphi_1, \mathsf{C}_2 : \tau_2 : \varphi_2, \ldots$. *The derivation step is denoted:*

$$\frac{\mathsf{C}_1 : \tau_1 : \varphi_1 \quad \mathsf{C}_2 : \tau_2 : \varphi_2 \quad \ldots}{\mathsf{C} : \tau : \varphi} \ (\Pi)$$

Appearance of the sequence Π *indicates type mismatch resolution using the operators in* Π *(case 2b above).*

In the **AB**$^+$ and **A**$^+$ calculi there are at most two items in a derivation step to which fitting operators can apply. Thus, instead of talking about resolution using a *sequence* of operators we talk about *left-* and/or *right-resolution* and use the following simpler notation.

$$\frac{\mathsf{C}_1 : \tau_1 : \varphi_1 \quad (\& : \mathsf{coor} : \varphi_c) \quad \mathsf{C}_2 : \tau_2 : \varphi_2}{\mathsf{C} : \tau : \varphi} \ op_1(l)\ op_2(r)$$

When this derivation step in $\mathcal{C}_{\mathbf{syn,sem}}$ involves a coordination, we of course have $\mathsf{C}_1 = \mathsf{C}_2 = \mathsf{C}$, $\tau_1 = \tau_2 = \tau$ (a Boolean type) and $\varphi = (\varphi_c(\varphi_1))(\varphi_2)$. We omit the notation $op_1(l)$ (or $op_2(r)$) when op_1 (or op_2, respectively) is an identity function. This derivation characterizes the following scenario: a sequence of expressions forms an expression that is well-formed according to the syntactic calculus, but whose meaning is not derivable using the semantic calculus. This is referred to as a situation of *type mismatch*. A (pair of)

$$\dfrac{\dfrac{\text{John}}{\mathsf{NP}:(et)t:\mathbf{john'}} \quad \dfrac{\dfrac{\dfrac{\text{caught}}{(\mathsf{NP\backslash S})/\mathsf{NP}:e(et):\mathbf{catch'}} \quad \dfrac{\text{and}}{\&:\mathsf{coor}:\mathbf{and'}} \quad \dfrac{\text{ate}}{(\mathsf{NP\backslash S})/\mathsf{NP}:e(et):\mathbf{eat'}}}{(\mathsf{NP\backslash S})/\mathsf{NP}:e(et):\mathbf{catch'}\ \mathbf{and'}_{e(et)^c}\ \mathbf{eat'}} \quad \dfrac{\text{a fish}}{\mathsf{NP}:(et)t:\mathbf{a\_fish'}}}{\mathsf{NP\backslash S}:et:(\mathrm{AR}(\mathbf{catch'}\ \mathbf{and'}_{e(et)^c}\ \mathbf{eat'}))(\mathbf{a\_fish'})}\ \mathrm{AR}(l)}{\mathsf{S}:\ t:\ \mathbf{john'}((\mathrm{AR}(\mathbf{catch'}\ \mathbf{and'}_{e(et)^c}\ \mathbf{eat'}))(\mathbf{a\_fish'}))}$$

$$\Updownarrow$$

$$\exists x[\mathbf{fish'}(x) \wedge \mathbf{catch'}\ (x)(\mathbf{j'}) \wedge \mathbf{eat'}(x)(\mathbf{j'})]$$

$$\dfrac{\dfrac{\text{John}}{\mathsf{NP}:(et)t:\mathbf{john'}} \quad \dfrac{\dfrac{\dfrac{\text{needed}}{(\mathsf{NP\backslash S})/\mathsf{NP}:((et)t)(et):\mathbf{need'}} \quad \dfrac{\text{and}}{\&:\mathsf{coor}:\mathbf{and'}} \quad \dfrac{\text{caught}}{(\mathsf{NP\backslash S})/\mathsf{NP}:e(et):\mathbf{catch'}}\ \mathrm{AR}(r)}{(\mathsf{NP\backslash S})/\mathsf{NP}:e(et):\mathbf{need'}\ \mathbf{and'}_{((et)t)(et)^c}\ \mathrm{AR}(\mathbf{catch'})} \quad \dfrac{\text{a fish}}{\mathsf{NP}:(et)t:\mathbf{a\_fish'}}}{\mathsf{NP\backslash S}:et:(\mathbf{need'}\ \mathbf{and'}_{((et)t)(et)^c}\ \mathrm{AR}(\mathbf{catch'}))(\mathbf{a\_fish'})}}{\mathsf{S}:\ t:\ \mathbf{john'}((\mathbf{need'}\ \mathbf{and'}_{((et)t)(et)^c}\ \mathrm{AR}(\mathbf{catch'}))(\mathbf{a\_fish'}))}$$

$$\Updownarrow$$

$$\mathbf{need'}(\mathbf{a\_fish'})(\mathbf{j'}) \wedge \exists x[\mathbf{fish'}(x) \wedge \mathbf{catch'}(x)(\mathbf{j'})]$$

FIGURE 5.1 *caught and ate* vs. *needed and caught*

type-fitting operator(s) in Σ is said to (left/right) *resolve* the mismatch in case it can apply to the (leftward/rightward) type(s) in the given sequence and lead to a new sequence of types that can be composed using the semantic calculus. Note that in principle, we could have allowed recursive applications of type-fitting principles until type resolution is achieved. However, for the sake of the analysis of the examples in this paper such a complication would not have any empirical advantages, and I am not aware of examples where it would. Moreover, the kind of type mismatch that is exemplified in Partee and Rooth's paper can always be resolved by applying AR to one of the types in the sequence (the predicate's type), and no other type-shifting principle is available in the system. The situation will be different in §5.4.

In Figure 5.1 we see an illustration of the above system for Partee and Rooth's examples. In the case of *caught and ate a fish*, type mismatch appears only when the conjunction *caught and ate* composes with the object *a fish*. The AR operator is therefore allowed to apply (only) at this stage, which leads to the only attestable reading, entailing that there was a fish that was both caught and eaten. By contrast, in *needed and caught a fish*, type mismatch must apply already when the semantic calculus composes the denotations of *needed* and *caught*. The resolution of this type mismatch, by applying AR to the second conjunct, leads to the reading where a fish was needed, and some actual fish was caught.[1]

[1] Typically, this is the kind of reading where a fish was needed *de dicto* (any fish, not a particular one). The other reading of the sentence, stating that there was a particular fish that was needed and caught, would be derived by any standard scope-shifting principle (quantifying-in, quantifier raising, etc.). Interestingly, the statement according to which one particular fish was needed (*de re*) and another one was caught, does not seem to be among the readings of the sentence, in agreement with what a system with scope shifting would expect.

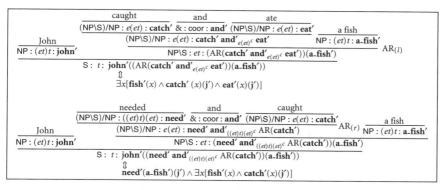

The general architecture of a grammar with type fitting à la Partee and Rooth creates situations where syntactically well-formed expressions are semantically "marked" since their meaning cannot be derived by the semantic calculus alone. There are two possible ways to view this mismatch between syntax and semantics. One way is to consider it a failure of the compositional system, which should always be resolved by some type-shifting operator. Another way to look at the syntax–semantics mismatch is to consider it as a potential source of semantic anomaly. For instance, if a type system is developed in order to describe violations of selectional restrictions, type mismatch in syntactically well-formed expressions may be allowed, and the type violation might be used to reflect the anomaly of expressions like *colorful green ideas*. In a standard type system such as the present one, which deals only with denotational issues, the first option is more attractive, and puts a strong restriction on the grammar as a whole (lexicon, syntax, and semantics). Let me state this restriction as the following general hypothesis.

No type-anomalous expressions: *Whenever a given lexicon and given syntactic and semantic calculi lead to a type mismatch, there should be type-shifting principles in* Σ *that resolve it.*

Cases that would go against this hypothesis would be examples in natural language where the semantic type system would more naturally rule out a deviant expression than the syntactic system. In this paper I will not try to see whether such cases exist.

5.3 Type-Fitting, Category-Shifting, and Plurals

Should type-fitting be the only strategy of meaning shift? In other words: are there situations that require a change of meanings using covert operators, but in which Partee and Rooth's "last resort" strategy cannot apply? In Winter (2001) I argue that there are reasons to assume a "non-fitting" shifting strategy, which is, however, not based on shifting the type of expressions but on shifting their *semantic category* (e.g. from predicates to arguments or *vice versa*). In this section I will briefly review the reasons, mainly coming from the semantics of plurals, for assuming such a *category-shifting* mechanism, which in the following section will be couched within a revision of Partee and Rooth's type-fitting strategy.

In Bennett (1974), Scha (1981), and subsequent work, "plural individuals" are treated as elements of type *et*—standard one-place predicates, isomorphic to *sets* of atomic entities of type *e*. In Bennett's proposal, types no longer represent "semantic roles" in the sentence. For instance, type *et* is for both plural individuals (arguments of predicates) and predicates over singularities; type $(et)t$ is both for predicates over pluralities and for quantifiers over singularities, etc. This stands in opposition to the Link (1983) tradition, where "plural individuals" are of type e and the D_e domain is some algebraic structure (e.g. a lattice) over the set of atomic entities. Although the Link tradition is by far more popular in the literature than the Bennett/Scha tradition, both strategies have their advantages and disadvantages. The Bennett/Scha tradition complicates the types that are associated with natural language expressions, whereas the Link tradition complicates the ontology. In Winter (2001) I argue that under the Bennett/Scha typing, some of the main operators for the semantics of plurals can be implemented as type-fitting operators using Partee and Rooth's strategy. The three type-fitting principles that are employed are defined below, in set theoretical notation:

Predicates	type:	$et \rightarrow (et)t$
	definition:	$pdist(A) \stackrel{def}{=} \wp(A) \setminus \{\emptyset\}$
	role:	a distributivity operator mapping predicates over singularities to "distributive" predicates over pluralities
Quantifiers	type	$(et)t \rightarrow ((et)t)t$
	definition:	$qfit(Q) \stackrel{def}{=} \{\mathcal{A} \subseteq \wp(E) : \{x \in E : \{x\} \in \mathcal{A}\} \in Q\}$
	role:	mapping quantifiers over singularities to "distributive" quantifiers over pluralities
Determiners	type:	$(et)((et)t) \rightarrow ((et)t)(((et)t)t)$
	definition:	$dfit(D) \stackrel{def}{=} \{\langle \mathcal{A}, \mathcal{B} \rangle \in \wp(\wp(E)) \times \wp(\wp(E)) : \langle \cup\mathcal{A}, \cup(\mathcal{A} \cap \mathcal{B}) \rangle \in D\}$
	role:	mapping determiners over singularities to "collective" determiners over pluralities

A typical example for the use of the *pdist* operator is when a collective predicate of type $(et)t$ and a "distributive" predicate of type et are conjoined, as in the following familiar kind of examples due to Dowty (1986) and Roberts (1987).

(5) The girls met in the bar and had a beer.

The *pdist* type-fitting operator resolves the type mismatch in this case in a similar way to the type mismatch resolution by the AR operator in examples such as (3). Formally, this generates the following conjunction of type $(et)t$.

$\mathbf{meet}'_{(et)t}\ \mathbf{and}'_{((et)t)^c}\ pdist(\mathbf{had\_beer}'_{et})$

Another use that Winter (2001) makes in the above principles is in accounting for the difference between the determiners *every* and *all*. It is assumed that there is no denotational difference between these two determiners, which like all determiners are assumed to be of the "distributive" type $(et)((et)t)$. Both *every* and *all* denote the standard universal determiner, which is denoted '**every**′'. However, the different plurality features of *every* and *all* affect the types of expressions in sentences that they appear in. For instance, in sentence (6) below, the singular predicates for *student* and *met* (the set of students and the set of "meeting entities", respectively) are both of type et, and no type mismatch with the determiner *every* occurs. The result is the unacceptable reading of sentence (6) in (6a), claiming that each student is a "meeting entity".

(6) #Every student has met.

(*a*) $\mathbf{every'}_{(et)((et)t)}(\mathbf{student\_sg'}_{et})(\mathbf{meet\_sg'}_{et})$

(*b*) $*\ (dfit(\mathbf{every'}))(pdist(\mathbf{student\_sg'}))(pdist(\mathbf{meet\_sg'}))$

A statement using type-shifting as in (6*b*) is ruled out since no type mismatch is present. By contrast, when plurals are involved, I assumed in Winter (2001) that the type of plural nominals (e.g. *students*) and verb phrases (e.g. *have met*) is $(et)t$. In sentence (7) below, the type mismatch that ensues with the determiner can only be resolved using the *dfit* operator, leading to the collective reading of (7) in (7*b*).

(7) All the students have met.

(*a*) $\mathbf{every'}_{(et)((et)t)}\ \mathbf{students\_pl'}_{(et)t}\ \mathbf{meet\_pl'}_{(et)t}$ – type mismatch

(*b*) $(dfit(\mathbf{every'}))(\mathbf{students\_pl'})(\mathbf{meet\_pl'})$

A similar contrast to the one between (6) and (7) exists between the following sentences.

(8) Every committee has met.

(9) All the committees have met.

While (8) is unambiguous and means that each of the committees had a separate meeting, sentence (9) is ambiguous between a "collective" reading (a joint meeting of the committees) and a "distributive" reading equivalent to (8). One complication that arises in the system of Winter (2001) is that in order to capture this ambiguity of (9), plural nominals like *students* or *committees* have to be treated as type ambiguous: the $(et)t$ type leads to the collective reading, whereas the et type leads to the distributive reading. The system proposed in the present paper avoids this type ambiguity.

In addition to type-fitting principles à la Partee and Rooth, Winter (2001) proposes using a different kind of covert semantic operators that are not triggered by type mismatch. These are called *category-shifting* principles, and their triggers are purely syntactic. In the most straightforward implementation, category-shifting principles are denotations of empty syntactic elements. These operators change *semantic features* of expressions but not necessarily their semantic type. Two kinds of semantic features are discussed in Winter (2001). One is the traditional distinction between predicates and quantifiers. Another semantic feature of denotations is whether they range over atoms (e type individuals) or over sets (et type "plural individuals"). The two category-shifting principles proposed in Winter (2001) change these two features:

1. A *Minimum operator* maps $(et)t$ quantifiers over atoms to $(et)t$ predicates over sets as follows:

   For each quantifier Q: $\mathrm{MIN}(Q) \stackrel{def}{=} \{A \in Q : \forall B \subseteq A[B \in Q \rightarrow B = A]\}$
   – the minimal sets in Q.

2. An *existential operator* maps τt predicates over atoms ($\tau = e$) or over sets ($\tau = et$) to a $(\tau t)t$ quantifier:

   For each predicate P: $\mathrm{E}(P) \stackrel{def}{=} \{A \subseteq D_\tau : A \cap P \neq \emptyset\}$
   – the existential quantifier over P.

   (In fact, the proposed mechanism is a more complicated existential operation, involving *choice functions*, but this is immaterial for the present purposes.)

Let us consider some examples for the application of these two principles in Winter (2001). Sentence (10) below is analyzed as in (10*a*), where the atomic quantifier denotation of the predicate nominal *John and Mary* is mapped to the predicate over sets $\{\{\mathbf{j}', \mathbf{m}'\}\}$. The statement in (10*a*) claims that this predicate is among the sets in the quantifier over sets for *these people.*

(10) These people are John and Mary.

(*a*) $\mathbf{these\_people}'_{((et)t)t}(\mathrm{MIN}((I_j \cap I_m)_{(et)t}))$,
where $I_x = \{A \subseteq E : x \in A\}$.

Sentence (11) is a simple example for the use of the E operator, which in (11*a*) maps the set of students to an existential quantifier.[2]

(11) A student arrived.

(*a*) $(\mathrm{E}(\mathbf{student}'_{et}))_{(et)t}(\mathbf{arrived}'_{et})$

Combining the two category shifts is the basis for the account in Winter (2001) of the collective reading of NP coordination. Thus, for instance, sentence

[2] In English, the same effect can be achieved by letting the indefinite article *denote* an existential determiner, but in languages that lack an indefinite article this is not a viable option.

(12) below is treated as in (12*a*), where the quantifier over atoms for *John and Mary* is first mapped to a predicate over sets as in (10*a*). The existential operator then maps this predicate over sets to a quantifier over sets, which captures the collective reading of *John and Mary*.

(12) John and Mary met.

(*a*) $(\mathrm{E}(\mathrm{MIN}((I_j \cap I_m)_{(et)t})))_{((et)t)t}(\mathbf{meet'}_{(et)t})$,

In this treatment, category-shifting principles cannot be activated by the "last resort" principle of Partee and Rooth. To see why this is so, reconsider sentence (10). In this case the type of the predicate nominal does not change: it remains $(et)t$. Hence, type-fitting is not necessary to begin with. Similarly, in (12), there is no need to apply the MIN operator, since the E operator itself could have resolved the type mismatch between the $(et)t$ subject and the $(et)t$ predicate (although this would lead to an undesired interpretation). In general, since MIN does not change the type of its argument, it cannot be triggered by type mismatch.

A different example for the impossibility of using type mismatch as a trigger for category shifting in a compositional system comes from the following example, due to Hoeksema (1988).

(13) Dylan and Simon and Garfunkel wrote many hits in the 1960s.

(*a*) $(\mathrm{E}(\mathrm{MIN}((I_d)_{(et)t})) \cap \mathrm{E}(\mathrm{MIN}((I_s \cap I_g)_{(et)t})))_{((et)t)t}$
$(\mathbf{wrote\_many\_hits'}_{(et)t})$

To get the prominent reading (13*a*) of (13), where only *Simon and Garfunkel* are collectivized and not the whole subject,[3] category-shifting has to apply *within* the subject, at a level lower than the one where type mismatch between the subject and predicate is detected. Applying category-shifting at the level of the subject leads to an existing reading, although less prominent than (13*a*). According to this reading the three artists together wrote many hits in the 1960s.

A similar problem appears in the following example.

(14) A student and a teacher arrived.

(*a*) $(\mathrm{E}(\mathbf{student'}_{et}) \cap \mathrm{E}(\mathbf{teacher'}_{et}))_{(et)t}(\mathbf{arrived'}_{et})$

For each of the indefinites in (14) to be existentially quantified separately, the E operator must apply twice within the subject, before the mismatch between

[3] Of course, syntactic ambiguity in (13) leads to other readings as well, but due to obvious factors of world knowledge, they are not as prominent as the "collective Simon and Garfunkel" reading.

the subject and predicate ensues. Applying E only at the level of the subject would lead to the existing but insufficient reading, according to which one person arrived, who is both a student and a teacher.

The conclusion in Winter (2001), as opposed to Partee (1987), is that although category-shifting principles like E and MIN are useful for the derivation of meanings, they cannot be activated by type mismatch considerations à la Partee and Rooth (1983). However, as we shall see in the next section, revising the type system and the principles of "type mismatch" allows a unified mechanism that generalizes category-shifting and type-fitting.

5.4 Internal and External Type Fitting

This section introduces a unified perspective on type-fitting and category-shifting mechanisms. These two different modules that change different semantic resources—types as opposed to semantic categories—are replaced by one module for type change. To achieve that, the notion of type is redefined in a way that represents both function–argument relations (as in standard types) and the semantic categories (predicate/quantifier, atom/set) of natural language expressions. Type change arises in this system as a result of two kinds of mismatch:

1. *External mismatch*—as in Partee and Rooth (1983)—a mismatch between typed denotations that cannot be composed by the type calculus.
2. *Internal mismatch*—between the semantic type and the corresponding syntactic feature of one and the same expression.

The underlying intuition of this distinction is that external mismatch is a *failure* of the compositional mechanism, whereas internal mismatch is only an *unsteady state* of the syntax–semantics interface, which does not prevent interpretation but nevertheless sanctions application of type-change operations. There are two correspondences that are assumed between syntactic features and semantic types, and their violation will be assumed to lead to internal mismatch. The assumed correspondences are the following:

- Syntactic number (singular/plural)—Semantic number (atom/set);
- Syntactic category (DP/NP)—Semantic role (quantifier/predicate).

As a result of this system, type change no longer involves empty syntactic categories as in Winter (2001); the notion of internal mismatch is justified by the natural correspondence assumed between the syntax and the semantics, and the lexical ambiguity of plural predicates in Winter (2001) is avoided.

The type system is first modified as follows. Instead of standardly having e and t as the primitive types of the system, we now have primitive types for quantifiers and predicates of all arities, with a semantic *number feature* (1 or 2) to denote semantic number. In addition to types, whose semantic number is unique in this definition, we add so-called *hyper-types*, which denote the type of operators that may change semantic number.

Definition 9 (types and hyper-types)
For any $n \in \{1, 2\}$, let TYPE_1 be the smallest set s.t.:

1. $\langle \mathsf{q}, n\rangle \in \text{TYPE}_1$ (quantifiers)
2. $\langle \mathsf{p}m, n\rangle \in \text{TYPE}_1$ for any natural number $m \geq 0$ (m-ary predicates)
3. If $\langle A, n\rangle$ and $\langle B, n\rangle$ are in TYPE_1 then $\langle (A \rightarrow B), n\rangle$ is in TYPE_1 (functions)

The set of *types* is $\text{TYPE}_1 \cup \{\mathsf{coor}\}$, and the set of *hyper-types* is $\{(\tau \rightarrow \sigma) : \tau, \sigma \in \text{TYPE}_1\}$.

Conventions: Types $\langle \mathsf{p}0, 1\rangle$ and $\langle \mathsf{p}0, 2\rangle$ (truth values) are both abbreviated 't'. In addition, for any type $\tau = \langle C, n\rangle$:

1. C is called the *semantic role* of τ: $C = \text{SROL}(\tau)$;
2. n is called the *semantic number* of τ: $n = \text{NUM}(\tau)$

The corresponding definition of set-theoretical domains (unlike the type-theoretical domains of Definition 2), employs two "basic domains": E_1 for atoms, and $\wp(E_1) \setminus \{\emptyset\}$ for non-empty sets of atoms. Officially:

Definition 10 (domains) Let $E_1 \neq \emptyset$ be an arbitrary set, and $E_2 = \wp(E_1) \setminus \{\emptyset\}$. The *domains of types* over $n \in \{1, 2\}$ are defined by:

1. $D_{\langle \mathsf{q},n\rangle} = \wp(\wp(E_n))$.
2. $D_{\langle \mathsf{p}m,n\rangle} = \wp((E_n)^m)$, where $(E_n)^0 = \{\emptyset\}$.
3. $D_{\langle A \rightarrow B,n\rangle} = D_{\langle A,n\rangle}{}^{D_{\langle B,n\rangle}}$.

The *domains of hyper-types* are defined by:

$$D_{\tau \rightarrow \sigma} = D_{\sigma}{}^{D_{\tau}}.$$

Some examples for types under Definition 9 and for their standard parallels are given in Table 5.2. In this type system, semantic number is a feature of a type. Hence, there are no types that mix semantic number. For instance: there is no type for functions like the *pdist* operator, from one-place predicates over atoms to one-place predicates over sets. Consequently, such functions that mix

TABLE 5.2 Examples for some useful types

Type	Standardly	Denoting
$\langle q, 1\rangle$	$(et)t$	quantifiers over atoms
$\langle q, 2\rangle$	$((et)t)t$	quantifiers over sets
$\langle p1, 1\rangle$	et	one-place predicates over atoms
$\langle p1, 2\rangle$	$(et)t$	one-place predicates over sets
$\langle p2, 1\rangle$	$e(et)$	two-place predicates over atoms
$\langle p2, 2\rangle$	$(et)((et)t)$	two-place predicates over sets
$\langle p1 \rightarrow q, 1\rangle$	$(et)((et)t)$	determiners over atoms
$\langle p1 \rightarrow q, 2\rangle$	$((et)t)(((et)t)t)$	determiners over sets
$\langle p1 \rightarrow p1, 1\rangle$	$(et)(et)$	modifiers of one-place predicates over atoms
$\langle p1 \rightarrow p1, 2\rangle$	$((et)t)((et)t)$	modifiers of one-place predicates over sets

TABLE 5.3 Type-shifting operators and their hyper-types

Type-shifting operator	Hyper-type	
AR	$\langle pm, n\rangle \rightarrow \langle q \rightarrow p(m-1), n\rangle$	$(m \geq 1)$
pdist	$\langle p1, 1\rangle \rightarrow \langle p1, 2\rangle$	
qfit	$\langle q, 1\rangle \rightarrow \langle q, 2\rangle$	
dfit	$\langle p1 \rightarrow q, 1\rangle \rightarrow \langle p1 \rightarrow q, 2\rangle$	
MIN	$\langle q, 1\rangle \rightarrow \langle p1, 2\rangle$	
E	$\langle p1, n\rangle \rightarrow \langle q, n\rangle$	$(n = 1, 2)$

semantic number are described only using hyper-types. For instance: *pdist* is of hyper-type $\langle p1, 1\rangle \rightarrow \langle p1, 2\rangle$. This leads to the following hypothesis:

Hypothesis: *Types are sufficient for describing denotations of lexical entries. Hyper-types are needed only for type-shifting operators.*

The set Σ of type-shifting operators is given in Table 5.3. Note that the hyper-types for the AR and the E operators do not change semantic number and hence can also be represented using types.[4]

Note that all the primitive types in TYPE_1 have set theoretical domains, so conjunction can be defined for all types in TYPE_1 as follows (and similarly for the other Boolean operators).

[4] Winter (2001) also argues for an E operator composed with distribution. This operator must be of a hyper-type $\langle p1, 2\rangle \rightarrow \langle q, 1\rangle$, which is not reducible to a type. For the sake of the discussion in this paper we will ignore this point.

Definition 11 (polymorphic conjunction) *Let τ be a type in* TYPE_1. *We denote:*

$$\textbf{and}'_{\tau^c} \quad = \quad \begin{cases} \sqcap & \text{if } \tau \text{ primitive (a quantifier or } m\text{-ary predicate)} \\ \lambda X_\tau.\lambda Y_\tau.\lambda Z_{\langle C_1,n\rangle}.X(Z)\ \textbf{and}'_{\langle C_2,n\rangle^c}\ Y(Z) & \text{if } \tau{=}\langle C_1{\rightarrow}\, C_2,\, n\rangle \end{cases}$$

The notation $\langle C, n\rangle^c$ is an abbreviation for type $\langle C{\rightarrow} (C{\rightarrow} C), n\rangle$.

The Application rule of the $\mathbf{A}^+$ calculus in Definition 7 is redefined as follows, according to the new type system.

$$\frac{\langle A \rightarrow\ B, n\rangle : f \quad \langle A, n\rangle : x}{\langle B, n\rangle\ :\ f(x)}\ n = 1, 2$$

For sake of completeness, we also add a rule that identifies the types $\langle \mathsf{p0}, 1\rangle$ and $\langle \mathsf{p0}, 2\rangle$ for truth values, which justifies the notation t for both of them.

$$\frac{\langle \mathsf{p0}, m\rangle : \varphi}{\langle \mathsf{p0}, n\rangle : \varphi}\ n, m = 1, 2$$

The set of categories is defined below using a slight revision of Definition 5, to allow number features on categories.

Definition 12 (categories) *Let* CAT_0, *the set of* primitive categories, *be a finite non-empty set. The set* CAT_1 *is the smallest set containing* $\text{CAT}_0 \cup \{\mathsf{X}_n : \mathsf{X} \in \text{CAT}_0, n \in \{1, 2\}\}$ *that satisfies for every* X *and* $\mathsf{Y} \in \text{CAT}_1$*:* $\mathsf{X/Y} \in \text{CAT}_1$ *and* $\mathsf{Y\backslash X} \in \text{CAT}_1$. *The set of* categories *is* $\text{CAT}_1 \cup \{\&\}$.

For the lexicon that will be introduced in the sequel we assume:

$$\text{CAT}_0 \;=\; \{\mathsf{NP}, \mathsf{D'}, \mathsf{DP}, \mathsf{S}\}.$$

We use the following notation for semantic *features* of categories.

1. $\text{NUM}(\mathsf{X}_n) = \text{NUM}(\mathsf{X}_n/\mathsf{Y}_n) = \text{NUM}(\mathsf{Y}_n\backslash\mathsf{X}_n) = n$
2. $\text{SROL}(\mathsf{D'}_n) = \mathsf{q}$

The rationale behind these definitions is that for a category C and a feature FEAT, FEAT(C) is specified to be a value *val* if *val* is a preferred semantic feature of C, but not its only possible semantic feature. Hence, the preferred denotation of a singular (plural) expression is assumed to be based on atoms (sets), but this is not obligatory. The preferred denotation of $\mathsf{D'}$ is a quantifier, but it can also be a predicate. For DP (NP), the quantifier (predicate) denotation is obligatory, hence SROL(DP) and SROL(NP) are not defined.

As a syntactic calculus we still use the $\mathbf{AB}^+$ calculus of Definition 6, but in order to take care of number features within *and* conjunctions, the coordination rule is defined as follows when the conjoined categories include number features.

$$\frac{\mathsf{X}_l \quad \& \quad \mathsf{X}_m}{\mathsf{X}_k}\ C$$

where $l, m, k \in \{1, 2\}$ s.t. either $k = 2$ and ($\mathsf{X} = \mathsf{D}'$ or $\mathsf{X} = \mathsf{DP}$), or $l = m = k$

This condition on syntactic number reflects the general requirement of *and* conjunctions. With the exception of nominals, conjunction requires identity of the number feature on the conjuncts. See for instance, in English, the (un)acceptability of predicate conjunctions such as *smiles and dances/*dance* or *smile and dance/*dances*. However, with certain nominals, which here are classified as D′, conjunctions are uniformly in the plural, independently of the number of the conjunct (cf. *John and Mary*, *some teacher and some author*). For more complex implications of this rule see example (15) below.

A toy lexicon that is used for illustration purposes is given in Table 5.4. The lexicon includes two empty elements (ϵ) that map a category N to D′, and a D′ to DP, without any change in type or denotation.

The definition of type mismatch and its resolution remain as in Definition 8. However, to model the triggers for the category-shifting mechanisms

TABLE 5.4 Another toy lexicon

	Category	Type	Denotation
every	$\mathsf{DP}_1/\mathsf{NP}_1$	$\langle \mathsf{pl} \to \mathsf{q}, 1\rangle$	$\mathbf{every}' = \{\langle A, B\rangle \in \wp(E) \times \wp(E) : A \subseteq B\}$
all (the)	$\mathsf{DP}_2/\mathsf{NP}_2$	$\langle \mathsf{pl} \to \mathsf{q}, 1\rangle$	$\mathbf{every}'$
some	$\mathsf{D}'_n/\mathsf{NP}_n$	$\langle \mathsf{pl} \to \mathsf{q}, n\rangle,\ n = 1, 2$	$\mathrm{E} = \{\langle A, B\rangle \in \wp(E) \times \wp(E) : A \cap B \neq \emptyset\}$
a	$\mathsf{NP}_1/\mathsf{NP}_1$	$\langle \mathsf{pl} \to \mathsf{pl}, 1\rangle$	id
student	NP_1	$\langle \mathsf{pl}, 1\rangle$	$\mathbf{student}'$
students	NP_2	$\langle \mathsf{pl}, 1\rangle$	$\mathbf{student}'$
teacher	NP_1	$\langle \mathsf{pl}, 1\rangle$	$\mathbf{teacher}'$
teachers	NP_2	$\langle \mathsf{pl}, 1\rangle$	$\mathbf{teacher}'$
committee	NP_1	$\langle \mathsf{pl}, 1\rangle$	$\mathbf{committee}'$
committees	NP_2	$\langle \mathsf{pl}, 1\rangle$	$\mathbf{committee}'$
John	D'_1	$\langle \mathsf{q}, 1\rangle$	$I_{\mathbf{j}'} = \{A \subseteq E : \mathbf{j}' \in A\}$
Mary	D'_1	$\langle \mathsf{q}, 1\rangle$	$I_{\mathbf{m}'} = \{A \subseteq E : \mathbf{m}' \in A\}$
smiles	$\mathsf{DP}_1\backslash\mathsf{S}$	$\langle \mathsf{pl}, 1\rangle$	$\mathbf{smile}'$
smile	$\mathsf{DP}_2\backslash\mathsf{S}$	$\langle \mathsf{pl}, 1\rangle$	$\mathbf{smile}'$
meets	$\mathsf{DP}_1\backslash\mathsf{S}$	$\langle \mathsf{pl}, 2\rangle$	$\mathbf{meet}'$
meet	$\mathsf{DP}_2\backslash\mathsf{S}$	$\langle \mathsf{pl}, 2\rangle$	$\mathbf{meet}'$
and	&	coor	$\mathbf{and}'$
ϵ	$\mathsf{D}'_n/\mathsf{NP}_n,\ n = 1, 2$	$\langle \mathsf{pl} \to \mathsf{pl}, m\rangle,\ m = 1, 2$	id
ϵ	$\mathsf{DP}_n/\mathsf{D}'_n,\ n = 1, 2$	$\langle \mathsf{q} \to \mathsf{q}, m\rangle,\ m = 1, 2$	id

of Winter (2001), we now also adopt the following definition of "internal" mismatch between type and category.

Definition 13 (internal mismatch resolution) *Let* exp *be an expression of category* C, *type* τ, *and denotation* φ. *Let op be a type-shifting operator of hyper-type* $\tau \rightarrow \tau'$. *Assume that the following hold for a feature* FEAT=NUM *(*FEAT=SROL*):*

1. $\mathrm{FEAT}(\mathsf{C}) \neq \mathrm{FEAT}(\tau)$
2. $\mathrm{FEAT}(\mathsf{C}) = \mathrm{FEAT}(\tau')$

Then we say that $\mathsf{C} : \tau' : op(\varphi)$ *is derived by op from* $\mathsf{C} : \tau : \varphi$ *due to N-mismatch (S-mismatch), and denote:*

$$\frac{\mathsf{C} : \tau : \varphi}{\mathsf{C} : \tau' : op(\varphi)} \; op(N/S)$$

This definition captures the situation where an expression has a category and a type with features that do not match. This can be a singular (plural) expression whose denotation ranges over atoms (sets, respectively), or an expression of a quantificational (predicative) category whose type is predicative (quantificational, respectively). When such a mismatch occurs and one of the type-shifting principles in Σ can resolve it, then it is allowed to apply.

Consider for example Figure 5.2. In the first derivation, of the sentence *every committee meets*, the only internal mismatch is within the verb *meet*, between its singular number and set-based denotation. However, this internal mismatch cannot be resolved in the present system since no type-shifting operator in Σ maps a denotation over sets to a denotation over atoms. The only mismatch that is resolved is an external mismatch, between the type of the predicate *meets* and the type of the subject. Two type-shifting operators are needed to resolve this mismatch: the *qfit* operator changes the semantic number of the subject from atom to set; the AR operator allows the predicate to combine with a quantifier. The result is the derivation of the only reading

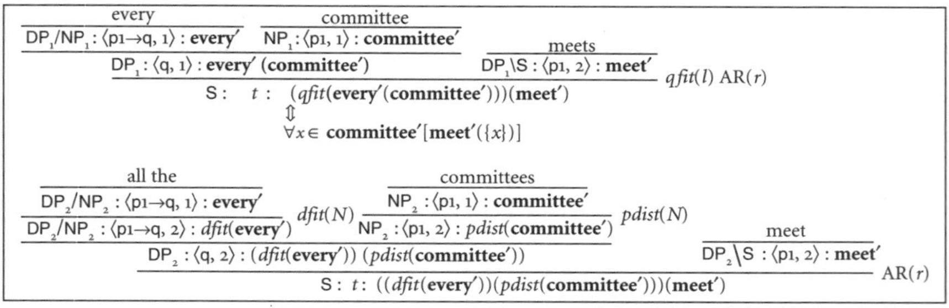

FIGURE 5.2 *every* vs. *all*

$$
\begin{array}{c}
\cfrac{
  \cfrac{
    \cfrac{
      \cfrac{
        \cfrac{
          \cfrac{\text{John}}{\mathrm{D'_1} : \langle q, 1 \rangle : I_{j'}} \quad \cfrac{\text{and}}{\& : \text{coor} : \mathbf{and'}} \quad \cfrac{\text{Mary}}{\mathrm{D'_1} : \langle q, 1 \rangle : I_{m'}}
        }{\mathrm{D'_2} : \langle q, 1 \rangle : I_{j'} \cap I_{m'}}
      }{\mathrm{D'_2} : \langle p1, 2 \rangle : \mathrm{MIN}(I_{j'} \cap I_{m'})} \; \mathrm{MIN}(N)
    }{\mathrm{D'_2} : \langle q, 2 \rangle : \mathrm{E(MIN)}(I_{j'} \cap I_{m'}))} \; \mathrm{E}(S)
  }{\mathrm{DP_2} : \langle q, 2 \rangle : \mathrm{E(MIN)}(I_{j'} \cap I_{m'}))}
}{S : t : \begin{array}{c} (\mathrm{E(MIN)}(I_{j'} \cap I_{m'})))(\mathbf{meet'}) \\ \Updownarrow \\ \mathbf{meet'}(\{j', m\}) \end{array}}
\qquad
\cfrac{\text{meet}}{\mathrm{DP_2 \backslash S} : \langle p1, 2 \rangle : \mathbf{meet'}} \; \mathrm{AR}(r)
$$

$$\cfrac{\epsilon}{\mathrm{DP_2/D'_2} : \langle q \rightarrow q, 2 \rangle : id}$$

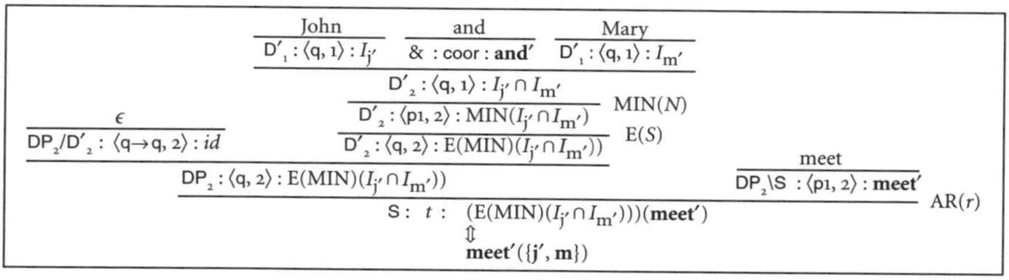

FIGURE 5.3 *John and Mary met*

of the sentence, talking about separate committee meetings. The situation is different in the sentence *all the committees meet*. In this case there are internal mismatches in both the determiner and the noun, which are resolved by the *dfit* and *pdist* operators, respectively. This leads to the collective reading. Note however that these resolutions are not obligatory in the derivation, and an additional derivation where they are not performed leads to another meaning, parallel to the "separate meeting" reading of the sentence *every committee meets*. This eliminates the need for lexical ambiguity of plurals in Winter (2001).

Consider now the derivation in Figure 5.3 of the sentence *John and Mary met*. Due to the *and* rule, the conjunction *John and Mary* is of syntactic number 2 even though its denotation ranges over atoms. This creates an internal mismatch, which the MIN operator resolves. However, the MIN operator itself creates an internal mismatch between the semantic role of the subject category (quantifier) and its semantic type (predicate). This is resolved by the E operator.[5]

Finally, let us consider the following sentences, and the present restatement of Winter's (2001) account of the effects they exemplify.

(15) (*a*) A great author and a famous mathematician has passed away. (Hoeksema 1988)

(*b*) A great author and a famous mathematician have passed away.

Sentence (15*a*) entails that one person has passed away who was both an author and a mathematician. By contrast, sentence (15*b*) does not have this entailment and moreover implies that two different people have passed away. In Figure 5.4 the phenomena that these two cases exemplify are analyzed in the given fragment. The singular reading of the conjunction *a student and*

---

[5] An additional analysis of the sentence is when the *qfit* operator applies to the subject without resolving the internal mismatch in it. This analysis, however, leads to the implausible statement "Mary met and John met".

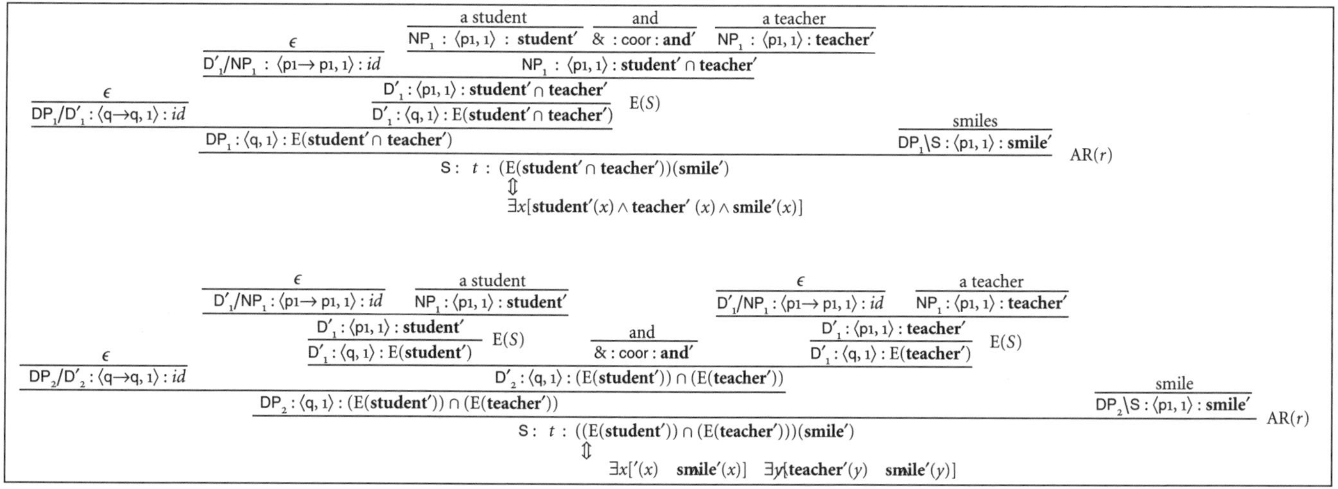

a student
and
a teacher
ϵ
NP₁ : ⟨p1, 1⟩ : student′
& : coor : and′
NP₁ : ⟨p1, 1⟩ : teacher′
D′₁/NP₁ : ⟨p1→ p1, 1⟩ : id
NP₁ : ⟨p1, 1⟩ : student′ ∩ teacher′
ϵ
D′₁ : ⟨p1, 1⟩ : student′ ∩ teacher′
E(S)
DP₁/D′₁ : ⟨q→q, 1⟩ : id
D′₁ : ⟨q, 1⟩ : E(student′ ∩ teacher′)
smiles
DP₁ : ⟨q, 1⟩ : E(student′ ∩ teacher′)
DP₁\S : ⟨p1, 1⟩ : smile′
AR(r)
S : t : (E(student′ ∩ teacher′))(smile′)
⇕
∃x[student′(x) ∧ teacher′ (x) ∧ smile′(x)]
ϵ
a student
ϵ
a teacher
D′₁/NP₁ : ⟨p1→ p1, 1⟩ : id
NP₁ : ⟨p1, 1⟩ : student′
D′₁/NP₁ : ⟨p1→ p1, 1⟩ : id
NP₁ : ⟨p1, 1⟩ : teacher′
D′₁ : ⟨p1, 1⟩ : student′
E(S)
and
D′₁ : ⟨p1, 1⟩ : teacher′
E(S)
ϵ
D′₁ : ⟨q, 1⟩ : E(student′)
& : coor : and′
D′₁ : ⟨q, 1⟩ : E(teacher′)
DP₂/D′₂ : ⟨q→q, 1⟩ : id
D′₂ : ⟨q, 1⟩ : (E(student′)) ∩ (E(teacher′))
smile
DP₂ : ⟨q, 1⟩ : (E(student′)) ∩ (E(teacher′))
DP₂\S : ⟨p1, 1⟩ : smile′
AR(r)
S : t : ((E(student′)) ∩ (E(teacher′)))(smile′)
⇕
∃x[′(x) smile′(x)] ∃y[teacher′(y) smile′(y)]

FIGURE 5.4 *a student and a teacher*—singular vs. plural

a teacher must be derived as an NP conjunction since the conjunction rule derives singularity of conjunctions within the DP only when singular NPs are conjoined. Therefore, the conjunction must denote an intersection of the sets for *student* and *teacher*, as intuitively required. By contrast, when the conjunction bears plural agreement it cannot be analyzed as an NP conjunction and must be analyzed as a D′ (or DP) conjunction, in which case internal mismatch occurs between the derived pl semantic role and the q semantic role of the D′ category. This allows application of the existential operator E and leads to the desired intersection of two existential quantifiers.

Consider now the following sentences, in contrast to the examples in (15).

(16) (*a*) *Some great author and some famous mathematician has passed away.

(*b*) Some great author and some famous mathematician have passed away.

Since *some* is analyzed as generating a D′, these conjunctions must be plural, hence (16*a*) is syntactically ruled out and (16*b*) is analyzed parallel to the analysis of (15*b*) in Figure 5.4.

5.5 Conclusions

This paper started by reviewing Partee and Rooth's (1983) conception of type-shifting as a strategy for type mismatch resolution. A formalization of Partee and Rooth's principle was given within categorial semantics. Winter's (2001) additional mechanism of category-shifting was reviewed and was shown to be irreducible to Partee and Rooth's type-fitting strategy with standard types. A non-standard typing system was developed, which describes not only function–argument relations but also other features that are semantically relevant, like "semantic number" (atom/set) and "semantic role" (predicate/quantifier). It was shown that with this richer typing system it is possible to unify the principles of type-fitting and category-shifting. In the proposed system, type-shifting is the only flexibility operation, and the only trigger for type-shifting is mismatch. However, mismatch can be either between types of two expressions in a construction (Partee and Rooth's external type mismatch) or between a type and a category of the same expression (internal mismatch). It is important to note that both notions are in a sense independently motivated. External mismatch arises when using categorial semantic systems which are weaker than what the syntax requires for meaning composition. For instance, Partee and Rooth use the AR operator for composing a binary relation with a quantifier, which the syntax requires but simple categorial semantics cannot derive. On the other hand, internal mismatch can only occur when there are natural correspondences between syntactic and semantic features. Thus, it is natural to assume that morpho-syntactic singularity (plurality) corresponds to quantification over atoms (sets), and that different layers within the DP correspond to different semantic roles (predicate, argument, quantifier, etc.). Unlike previous works, the present paper suggests an optional, rather than obligatory, correspondence between such syntactic and semantic features, which leads to "unsteady states" in the syntax–semantics interface. Whether there are more features that allow this kind of optional correspondence between syntax and semantics is currently under investigation.

References

Bennett, M. 1974. 'Some extensions of a Montague fragment of English', Ph.D. thesis, University of California, Los Angeles.

Chierchia, G. 1998. 'Reference to kinds across languages', *Natural Language Semantics*, 6: 339–405.

Dowty, D. 1986. 'Collective predicates, distributive predicates and *all*', in *Proceedings of the Eastern States Conference on Linguistics, ESCOL3*. Cascadilla Press.

Emms, M. 1991. 'Polymorphic quantifiers', in G. Barry and G. Morrill (eds), *Studies in Categorial Grammar*. Edinburgh: Centre for Cognitive Science. 65–111.

Groenendijk, J. and Stokhof, M. 1989. 'Type shifting rules and the semantics of interrogatives', in G. Chierchia, B. Partee, and R. Turner (eds), *Properties, Types and Meaning*, ii. Dordrecht: Kluwer. 21–68.

Hendriks, H. 1993. Studied Flexibility: Categories and Types in Syntax and Semantics. Ph.D. thesis, University of Amsterdam.

Hoeksema, J. 1988. 'The semantics of non-Boolean *and*', *Journal of Semantics*, 6: 19–40.

Link, G. 1983. 'The logical analysis of plurals and mass terms: A lattice-theoretical approach', in R. Bäuerle, C. Schwarze, and A. von Stechow (eds), *Meaning, Use, and Interpretation of Language*. Berlin: de Gruyter. 302–23.

Montague, R. 1973. 'The proper treatment of quantification in ordinary English', in J. Hintikka, J Moravcsik, and P. Suppes, (eds), *Approaches to Natural Languages: Proceedings of the 1970 Stanford workshop on grammar and semantics*. Dordrecht: Reidel. 221–42. Reprinted in R. Thomason, (ed) 1974. *Formal Philosophy: Selected papers of Richard Montague*. New Haven, CT: Yale University Press. 222–46.

Partee, B. 1987. 'Noun phrase interpretation and type-shifting principles', in J. Groenendijk, D. de Jongh, and M. Stokhof (eds), *Studies in Discourse Representation Theory and the Theory of Generalized Quantifiers*. Dordrecht: Foris. 115–43.

Partee, B. and Rooth, M. 1983. 'Generalized conjunction and type ambiguity', in R. Bäuerle, C. Schwarze, and A. von Stechow (eds), *Meaning, Use, and Interpretation of Language*. Berlin: de Gruyter. 361–83.

Roberts, C. 1987. Modal Subordination, Anaphora, and Distributivity. Ph.D. thesis, University of Massachusetts, Amherst.

Scha, R. 1981. 'Distributive, collective and cumulative quantification', in J. Groenendijk, T. M. V. Janssen, and M. Stokhof (eds), *Formal Methods in the Study of Language*. Amsterdam: Mathematisch Centrum. 483–512.

van Benthem, J. 1986. *Essays in Logical Semantics*. Dordrecht: Reidel.

—— 1991. *Language in Action: Categories, lambdas and dynamic logic*. Amsterdam: North-Holland.

van der Does, J. and de Hoop, H. 1998. 'Type-shifting and scrambled definites', *Journal of Semantics*, 15: 393–416.

Winter, Y. 2001. *Flexibility Principles in Boolean Semantics: Coordination, plurality, and scope in natural language*. Cambridge, MA: MIT Press.

—— 2002. 'Atoms and sets: a characterization of semantic number', *Linguistic Inquiry*, 33: 493–505.

Part II

Case Studies

6

Direct Compositionality and Variable-Free Semantics: The Case of "Principle B" Effects*

PAULINE JACOBSON

6.1 Goals

This study starts from the premise that the hypothesis of direct compositionality (DC) is the simplest among current competing hypotheses as to the organization of the grammar, and so should be rejected only in the face of strong evidence to the contrary. The plot of this paper, therefore, is as follows. First I discuss the fact that under at least a reasonably strong version of direct compositionality, we would not expect to find constraints on non (strictly) local chunks of representations[1] (especially constraints which ultimately affect the possible range of interpretations of some sentences). For under a strong version of direct compositionality, the grammar has no way to state such constraints. And yet, there is a large body of lore which takes it as axiomatic that the grammar does indeed contain such constraints and

* The basic idea for Principle B which I pursue here came as the result of a conversation with Daniel Büring and Chris Barker on a lovely afternoon walk on a lovely beach in San Diego. When I got home and tried to reconstruct an idea Daniel had floated, it came out as roughly this proposal. But Daniel claims this isn't quite what he had in mind, so I've been presenting this as my work. Nonetheless, Daniel deserves far more than the usual thanks, as also does Chris. In addition I'd like to thank audiences at the Direct Compositionality Workshop, at UConn, NYU, Harvard, and ZAS for helpful comments, especially Anna Szabolcsi. Finally, special thanks to Danny Fox whose discussant comments at the workshop raised a number of potential problems and areas that need further work—only some of which I have space to discuss here.

[1] By "non strictly local" I mean a constraint whose domain is more than just a mother and its daughters. It should be noted that even a strictly local constraint *on representations* is not compatible with the direct compositional program (at least not with a strong version of it), for under this view one would not expect to find any constraints on representations at all. However, any strictly local constraint could be recast as a constraint on the syntactic combinatory rules which sanction the local bit of representation (e.g. phrase structure rules or their analog), and so it is only the non-local constraints that should worry a direct compositionalist.

this lore thus provides an obvious challenge to the (strong) direct compositional program. After all, we all learn in our introductory textbooks about "binding theory" principles such as A, B, C, and Weak Crossover; principles which are almost always stated in configurational terms and which make reference to the position of co-indexed material in global chunks of representation. There is also a second way in which "binding" phenomena provide a challenge to direct compositionality: we often find effects that look roughly like binding theory effects but where the appropriate representation on which to state the constraint is not found on the (audible) surface. Enter the notions of abstract levels of representation (e.g. LF) and/or silent or deleted material—which allow us to posit that the relevant representation is indeed found if one looks hard enough. But again these tools are generally incompatible with at least a reasonably strong version of direct compositionality, and so once again the apparent necessity for configurational constraints would seem to doom the direct compositional hypothesis. In view of all of this, it has become essentially a non-negotiable premise among a large number of linguists that DC is wrong (indeed, the way many textbook discussions proceed, the hypothesis of DC is not even on the radar scope).

But I propose to take a different strategy. Let us start with the observation that DC should be abandoned only in the face of strong evidence to the contrary. Is it really so obvious that the effects attributed to binding theory require statements about co-indexation which hold for non-strictly local syntactic chunks of representation? My claim is: no—quite the contrary. In fact, the usual strategy of casting these in this way is at best stipulative and unilluminating. At worst, the machinery that this strategy requires in order to really work is so baroque as to make this strategy completely implausible. This paper will be a case study intended to back up these claims: the case study centers on "Principle B" effects. After elaborating on these remarks in §§6.2–6.3 (and developing the tools of variable-free semantics which are crucial here to the direct compositional account that I will propose) the paper divides into two parts. Section 6.4 will document just how complicated it is to try to attribute these effects to a representational constraint on indices. Section 6.5 proposes an alternative account of these effects—one stated in the terms of a direct compositional (and variable-free) theory.[2]

[2] A different non-syntactic and non-representational account is explored in recent work by Schlenker (2005). Space precludes a comparison here with his account, although note that his analysis is not implemented in a direct compositional architecture.

6.2 The Hypothesis of Direct Compositionality and the Role of Structured Representations

In the broadest sense, the hypothesis of direct compositionality is compatible with a number of different theories of just how the syntax works and, in particular, a number of different possibilities as to how rich are the representations which are available to syntactic rules. (For some early discussion of this point showing that direct compositionality could be embedded within a full transformational framework, see Partee 1976; for more recent discussion of this general issue see Jacobson 2002.) That said, let me begin with a very strong version of direct compositionality—one which couples this hypothesis with a very constrained view of the syntax.

We can see any linguistic expression as a triple of ⟨sound, syntactic category, meaning⟩. Assume that a linguistic expression is nothing else: in particular it is not also associated with some kind of structured representation. Assume further that the grammar is simply a set of rules/principles (whichever label one prefers) which map one or more such triple(s) into another triple. (Note that the question of whether or not this is correct is quite independent of the question of whether or not the grammar contains just a few highly general statements.[3]) Under this view, there is no room to state constraints on structured representations. For "structure" is not something that the grammar ever gets to see—indeed it is just a representation for the convenience of the linguist. A tree is merely a representation of the proof of the well-formedness of some string, and a very partial representation of how the semantics worked to put meanings together. And—a point well stressed within Generalized Phrase Structure Grammar (GPSG, see, e.g., Gazdar *et al.* 1985)—all constraints and phenomena must be encoded into the rules themselves (which again might be stated in highly schematic form) rather than being constraints on representations. An important point to keep in mind is that *any* theory needs combinatory rules (or "principles") which "build" larger expressions from smaller ones—and so a theory which puts all of the work into these is adding no new machinery. The view that the grammar itself also keeps track of

[3] Thus much of the work within GPSG and Categorial Grammar maintains a direct compositional architecture of the type laid out above, and at the same time uses only a few very general statements concerning the syntactic and the semantic combinatorics. Note, moreover, that both of these theories contain principles to predict the semantic combinatorics in terms of the syntax. I point this out here because the notion of "type-driven" interpretation originated within these theories (see especially Klein and Sag 1985) and yet has come more recently to be associated with the non-direct compositional architecture of a theory in which the syntax first produces representations (surface structures which are then mapped to LFs) which are subsequently interpreted by the semantics.

representations and uses these in the statements of other constraints requires extra machinery—and so the burden of proof should be on that position.

Of course it has been known since at least the mid 1980s—when there was vigorous discussion on the feasibility of the theory of GPSG—that natural languages require more than a context-free grammar (see, e.g. Culy 1985; Shieber 1985). I will therefore back off from the strongest version of direct compositionality given above, and will assume that grammars also contain Wrap operations (see, e.g. Bach 1979, 1980; Dowty 1982; Pollard 1984; Jacobson 1987 and others) which allow one string to be infixed within another. This means that it is not true that linguistic expressions have *no* associated structural information. For if there are operations which infix one expression into another, then there must at least be enough information to define the infixation point. Hence assume that the input to the rules are not pure phonological strings, but rather strings with a defined infixation point. (For some different ways to formalize Wrap operations, see Pollard 1984; Vijay-Shanker *et al.* 1986; Hoeksema and Janda 1988; Jacobson 1992). But we will tentatively adopt the view that this is the only amount of structure that the grammar gets to "see": full-blown representations like trees are not part of grammar but again are just convenient representations for the linguist. Note, incidentally, that the class of languages which can be described by grammars with Wrap operations is—at least under some formalizations of Wrap—quite well understood (see, e.g. Vijay-Shanker *et al.* 1986). The known deficiencies with context-free grammars disappear, while there remain constraints on the class of possible languages allowed by this apparatus.

6.3 Relevance of "Binding" Phenomena

6.3.1 *The Standard View*

One of the most visible challenges to the DC view comes from so-called "binding theory" principles: that is, principles governing the distribution and interpretation of pronouns, reflexives, etc. In many textbooks and in many circles, there is an unquestioned assumption that in order to capture the distribution and interpretation of these items, the grammar must contain principles which constrain co-indexation and which are stated across non-local chunks of representation. Note that co-indexation is a purely syntactic notion and so such constraints in and of themselves would tell us nothing about the interpretation (which is ultimately what is at issue), but it is also assumed that these indices have an effect on the interpretation. Of course this program is also generally implemented within a theory with a level of LF (which inputs the compositional, model-theoretic semantics), and so when I use the term "standard view" in this paper I generally refer to this conception of things.

Although this paper is primarily about Principle B, here I will illustrate the basic point with reference to another representationally stated constraint on "binding": the purported constraint that a "binder" must c-command a bindee. As point of departure for the discussion, then, consider (1) which is one possible way to state such a constraint:

(1) If α "binds" β (a notion to be defined below but which is assumed to hold at LF) and α is co-indexed with β, then α must c-command β.

Before continuing, let me clarify that the claim that a "binder" must c-command its bindee has been used in two different senses. In one sense, this is often claimed to be something which must hold at LF. But, as we will see below, this is a somewhat uninteresting principle, since once we give a sensible definition of "binding" this becomes true by definition (given a few completely standard assumptions). Thus (1) would amount simply to an observation (and a fairly trivial one) rather than a principle in the grammar. The second way in which this constraint is thought of is as a constraint on some non-LF level of syntactic representation—for the purposes of this discussion let us say surface structure. Under this view, the idea is that such a constraint is motivated by the existence of Weak Crossover effects, as in (2):

(2) (*a*) Every man_i loves his_i mother.

(*b*) *His_i mother loves every man_i.

(Here and throughout this paper I reserve subscripts like i and j as a way to notate the reading of a sentence without any commitment to these standing for indices used in the grammar. For indices themselves, I will use arbitrarily chosen integers or, when more convenient, I will use variables like m and n as variables over grammatical indices. I will of course ultimately be arguing that there are no such things as indices in the grammar.) I realize that there are any number of proposals as to how to account for WCO effects using all sorts of different theories and theoretical apparatus, so my discussion below of the defects in the formulation in (1) should not be taken in and of itself to constitute an argument *against* configurational constraints and/or against LF. Nonetheless, I think that exposing the problems in a statement like (1) is instructive of the types of problems which emerge with constraints of this nature.

Note that (1) involves three crucial ingredients: c-command, co-indexation, and, quite crucially, the notion that *every man* is in some special "binding" relationship with *his*. What I would like to argue here is that there really is no simple notion of "binding" which takes care of the relevant cases. I will illustrate the point via a modified version of the account in Heim and Kratzer (1998). (The modifications here are almost all terminological; there is one content modification made for expository convenience (and which will be pointed out where relevant), but this actually has no effect on the central point here.) My reason for taking the HK account as a point of departure is simply because it is one of the few accounts which is fully explicit and which actually gives a definition of the semantic notion of "binding" and ties this definition into its use in the statement of "binding constraints".

First, let us consider one way to view the LF for (2*a*), which is to assume that a surface sentence such as (2*a*) pairs with an LF of the form in (3).[4]

(3)

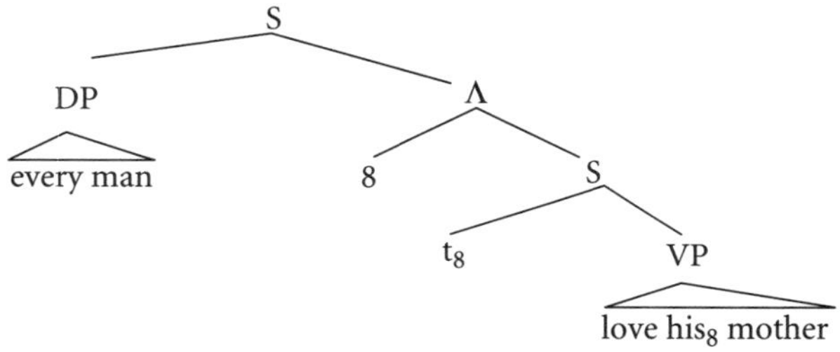

I am using the HK notation here (with my own addition of Λ as a node label), but a comment is in order about HK's use of an index like 8 as a terminal symbol in the tree. The rationale for this is its role in the semantic composition. The system is such that the sister to this node will have as its meaning a function from assignment functions to propositions, and since it contains at least one "open variable *n*", that means that the [[S]] in question will (in general) have a different value according to assignment functions which differ on the value that they assign to *n*. (More precisely: [[S]] is a function from assignment functions to propositions. The value of this function will (in general) be different for different assignment functions which disagree on the value assigned to *n*.) The role of an index sister to S in this system is to trigger "λ-abstraction" and "close off" the variable *n*. Thus the interpretation of the expression I have labeled Λ is a function from assignment functions to properties, such that for any assignment function g, [[Λ]](g) is a function

[4] When I discuss the HK system—and other systems within the basic framework making use of LF—I will use the term DP; when I switch to a discussion of this within CG I use the term "NP" for the same creature. It is hoped that this will cause no confusion; my rationale for this is to use the vocabulary which is standard in each theory.

which maps each individual x into the value of S on the assignment function just like g except that 8 is assigned to x.

A point which will become important below is that the use of the index as a terminal symbol in the tree is just one particular way to make sure that the meaning of S (a non-constant function from assignment functions to propositions) "shifts" into a function from assignment functions to meanings of type <e,t> by what we can think of as the semantics of λ-abstraction. One could have removed this label from the tree and posited a more complex combinatory rule for combining S directly with the meaning of the DP. This is essentially the route taken in Montague (1973) (although his was framed in a direct compositional architecture where LF played no role in the grammar). Under this account a sentence roughly like that shown above combined directly in the syntax with the DP (which was substituted on to a pronoun in subject position), and the semantics involved two steps: shifting the meaning of S by λ-abstracting over the relevant variable, and taking the resultant property as an argument of the DP. A third alternative would be to dispense with the "silent" operator 8 here in the tree and leave the rest as shown there, with the node Λ exhaustively dominating S_8 (hence note that the index is instead made a subscript on S); the rule interpreting Λ on the basis of $[[S_n]]$ is the obvious one. I belabor these points here because my claim below is that once one considers the semantics, there really is no obvious sense in which *every man* "binds" *his*. I will develop this point using the HK details, but it is important to note that the point is independent of those particular details.

As noted above, this account of binding—and indeed any account which makes use of variables—posits that each constituent (at the level at which meaning is assigned) has as its semantic value a function from the set of assignment functions to something else. Assume further that each assignment function is a total function from the set of variables to model-theoretic objects (i.e. individuals in the cases relevant here). This is relatively standard but is actually different from the treatment in HK: they take assignment functions to be partial and I will comment on one reason for this below. However, since the exposition is eased by using total functions, we will do so here. Notice then, that if a constituent C contains no unbound variables within it, it will denote a constant function from the set of assignment functions.

Let G be the set of assignment functions, and let G/n be any subset of G such that each member of G/n agrees on the value of all of the variables except that assigned to *n*. Then we can define the notion of a "free variable" as follows: *n* is *free* within C if there is a G/n with two members g_1 and g_2 such that $[[C]](g_1) \neq [[C]](g_2)$. (A notational point: I use $[[C]](g)$ rather than the more familiar $[[C]]^g$ to highlight the fact that $[[C]]$ is actually a function from the set of assignment functions and g is an argument of that function.) Informally, the idea is that a variable *n* is free within some expression if [[C]] gives different values according to different ways to assign individuals to the variable *n*. Otherwise, *n* is *bound.* Once *n* is "bound", then [[C]] will assign the same value to all assignment functions which differ only on the value that they assign to *n*. A caveat here: strictly speaking, this is probably not the definition of "free" that corresponds to our syntactic intuitions about what is free. The reason is that there might be variables we would want to define as free within C but where [[C]] is a constant function for irrelevant reasons, as for example the case of tautologies like *8 walks or 8 doesn't walk.* This is avoided under the partial function approach. Hence HK's definition of "free within C" is actually slightly different than that given here. But this modification will not affect the main point below as the interested reader can verify.

So far, this gives a semantic basis for the notion of "free" vs. "bound", but what does it mean to say that one thing "binds" another? HK's definition proceeds in two steps, the first of which is to define "sem-binding":

Definition of Sem-Binding: α sem-binds X (for X a pronoun or a trace) iff the sister to α is the smallest subtree in which X is free.

Notice that this definition requires simultaneous reference to a *representation* (since it uses the notion "sister", "subtree", etc.) and to the *interpretation* of that representation. It is, then, a definition which can be checked by the grammar only at the stage of a compositional interpretation of LF. If it is part of a constraint (such as WCO) used in the grammar, the constraint itself must simultaneously check *the level at which c-command is required to hold* (say, surface structure), an *LF representation*, and the *interpretation of that LF.*

This already should make us suspicious that something is amiss: it requires a very complex view of the architecture of the grammar. But there is another problem: the above definition does not actually give us the notion of "binding" that we need in order to account for WCO effects (or for other kinds of effects which are often stated in terms of co-indexation and "binding"). For according to this definition, the sem-binder for *his* in (3) is not *every man* but rather is the node whose label is the index 8. Quite importantly, this is not just some accidental property of this particular system or some accidental quirky oversight on the part of HK. As long as *every man* is treated as a generalized quantifier, then in all well-understood ways to do the compositional semantics using variables there really is no privileged relationship between the semantic contribution of the pronoun he_n and *every man.* The only sensible way to think about a he_n as going from "free" to "bound" is to point to the step in the semantic composition when the meaning changes from a non-constant function on any G/n to a constant function on G/n. But this has nothing to do with the semantic contribution of *every man*.[5] It can be done by a silent operator given as an integer (as in HK), by one of the steps in Montague's "Quantifying In" treatment, or by a type-shift rule. In first order logic (or in other systems where quantification is over assignment functions)[6] it makes some sense to think of the contribution of the quantifier as "binding" the pronoun, but not in any system where *every man* is of type <<e,t>,t>.

Therefore, in order to establish any relationship between the DP and the pronoun, HK define a second notion of binding based on the first. They call this a "derivative notion of semantically bound"; I will refer to it as "LF binding":

Definition of LF binding: α LF binds β iff β and the trace of α are sem-bound by the same thing. (Note: HK refer to this as a "derivative notion of semantically bound")

I can now cash in a promissory note given earlier: the claim that a "binder" must c-command its "bindee" at LF now follows by definition (as long as we also assume that a DP must c-command its trace at LF). The interested reader can verify for themselves that this follows from the definitions here; it will follow equally well in most other systems making use of this type of apparatus.

Of course in standard accounts this definition of "binding" is supposed to interact with constraints on indices in the syntax (this is the whole point, after all—this is used to get typical "binding theory" constraints). Hence in order to tie this definition into something of use to the syntax, HK first give a further definition:

Definition of syn(tactic) binding: α syn-binds β iff
α is co-indexed with β
α c-commands β (at some level—assume here surface structure)
... (other conditions here would be to capture other aspects of "binding")

Finally, WCO—and other bits of the "binding theory"—will now follow from the constraint in (4) (notice that this replaces (1)):

(4) If α LF binds β then α must syn-bind β and *vice versa*.

It seems to me that this account leaves plenty of room for suspicion. As pointed out above, the relationship between co-indexation and true semantic

[5] In the HK system—in which assignment functions are partial functions—the "binding" of a variable is not a matter of going from non-constant to constant function, but is instead a change in the set of assignment functions for which the value of the expression is defined. But the remark above holds here too: this semantic shift again has nothing to do with the semantic contribution of the generalized quantifier.

[6] As, for example, is argued for in Heim (1997); there it does make some sense to talk about the quantifier as "binding" the pronoun.

"binding" is both complex and indirect, and it took considerable work to come up with a definition of "binding" according to which *every man* "binds" the pronoun. And, as already discussed above, a constraint such as (4) requires reference to multiple levels simultaneously: surface structure (or whatever is the level at which "syn-binds" is intended to hold), LF representation, and the interpretation of LF. Of course this is only one version of WCO—a defender of this basic program might hope that the fault lies not with the general strategy but with this kind of account of WCO. I suspect, though, that many different accounts—both of WCO and of other kinds of constraints on "binding"—will suffer from similar problems. Perhaps we are on the wrong track trying to reduce the empirical effects to constraints which make use of configurational properties. The effects are, after all, semantic effects—can they be built directly into the semantic (and possibly also syntactic) combinatorics as opposed to building them into representations? I will argue below that they can.

But before going there, let me point to another reason to be suspicious of configurational accounts. The fact is that we very often find cases which show "binding" types of effects but where the relevant configuration is *not* found in the audible (or visible) surface structure. Typical cases which have been discussed over and over in the literature involve a host of "connectivity" effects in, for example, copular sentences. Of relevance to the point here would be "bound variable connectivity" as in (5):

(5) The woman who every Englishman$_i$ loves (the most) is his$_i$ mother.

Since it is so often assumed that a "binder" must c-command a pronoun that it "binds", it is assumed that the post-copular constituent here must (at some level) be a full sentence *every Englishman loves his mother.* Of course, unless one posits silent material surrounding *his mother* at *surface* structure, the level at which the c-command condition is met is not surface structure, so one would need to define the WCO requirement as holding for some other level. Incidentally, some of the literature which invokes a "c-command" constraint on binding as evidence for additional material surrounding *his mother* seems to be concerned not with the fact that there would otherwise be a WCO violation, but rather seems to assume that a "binder" must c-command a "bindee" at LF (hence, this literature posits that at least at LF we have material surrounding *his mother*). But as we have seen above, there is no empirical content to the claim that a "binder" must c-command its "bindee" at LF—it is true by definition. Thus I assume that what people really mean when they say that there is a c-command constraint at LF and that hence *every Englishman* must c-command *his* at LF is that there is no other way to give a semantics for this sentence. But first, simply positing a representation with c-command is not the same as actually showing that this *does* provide a semantics for this sentence.[7] Second, as shown in Jacobson (1994) (see also Sharvit 1999), the claim that there is no way to give a semantics for (5) without having *his* be c-commanded by a "binder" is incorrect: the correct meaning can easily be compositionally composed (without c-command) by a perfectly natural extension of the analysis of functional questions (Groenendijk and Stokhof 1983; Engdahl 1986). Jacobson (1994) further shows that this comes for free under the variable-free program, and nothing extra is needed to get a meaning for this sentence without positing silent, deleted, and/or reconstructed material in the post-copular position. (We return to this briefly in §6.5.3.) The moral: the belief that there are configurational constraints on indices (which play an indirect role in getting the semantics right) forces the positing of extra material in (5) and hence extra machinery to make sure that it is silent. All of this is simply to satisfy configurational constraints which are quite complicated to state in the first place. Thus I hope to have convinced the reader that perhaps it is best to move on to an entirely different strategy.

6.3.2 *The Variable-Free Alternative*

To elucidate a non-configurational alternative, I will first briefly review the variable-free approach to pronoun "binding" discussed in detail in Jacobson (1999, 2000). By way of comparison, consider the following properties of the standard view. Take sentences such as:

(6) (*a*) Every man_i believes that he_i lost.

(*b*) Every man_i loves his_i mother.

Under the standard view, any expression which is or contains within it an "unbound" pronoun is (by definition of "unbound" as discussed above) a non-constant function from assignment functions to propositions. Hence $[[\text{he}_n \text{ lost}]]$ is a (non-constant) function from assignment functions to propositions, $[[\text{his}_n \text{ mother}]]$ is a (non-constant) function from assignment functions to individuals, and $[[\text{he}_n]]$ is a (non-constant) function from assignment functions to individuals, where $[[\text{he}_n]](g) = g(n)$. (Note again that I use i in

[7] To be fair, there is one proposal which actually *does* give a semantics for the associated representation: this is the "question/answer" proposal in Ross (1972), recently revived in den Dikken *et al.* (2000) and Schlenker (2003) (see also Romero (this volume)). A discussion of the feasibility of this proposal is obviously beyond the scope of this paper; for some relevant discussion see Romero (this volume) and Caponigro and Heller (this volume).

the above sentences to simply illustrate the relevant meaning, whereas *n* is a variable over an actual index.)

Under the variable-free view put forth in Jacobson (1999, 2000), an expression with a pronoun which we intuitively would want to call "unbound" within that expression denotes a function from individuals to something else. Hence *he lost* denotes a function from individuals to propositions; *his mother* is a function from individuals to individuals, and so is *he* (where the particular function denoted by *he* is the identity function—modulo gender information which I will ignore here). There are no indices here, and so we see right away one interesting difference between this and the standard view. Under the standard view there are actually an infinite number of (homophonous) pronouns, each with a different index: under the variable-free view there is but one (ignoring case, number, and gender).

Thus *he lost* is the function which maps each individual x into the proposition that x lost. I will continue to ignore the contribution of gender, and with this simplification, *he lost* thus has the same semantic value as *lost*. How do we get this result? Phrasing this more generally: pronouns occur wherever NPs can occur. If an NP is of type e, the function which takes it as argument has as its domain things of type e. But then how can a pronoun—or material which contains a pronoun unbound within it—occur in the same places, since these have meanings of type <e,e>?

The answer is via a unary rule; that is, a rule taking a single expression (a triple) as input and returning a single expression (a triple) as output. "Type-shift" rules are a subspecies of these rules but are not the only logically possible ones. In fact, most of the work on "type-shift" operations is framed in a non Categorial Grammar framework and is often seen as a rule which shifts *only* the meaning (and the semantic type) and not also the syntactic category. But since I am embedding the general program within a Categorial Grammar syntax, any unary rule which shifts the semantic type of something will also have to shift its syntactic category. I assume basic familiarity with the Categorial Grammar notation; one addition to the usual CG apparatus is the existence of categories of the form A^B (for any two categories A and B). Any expression whose category is A^B denotes a function from B type meanings to A type meanings. Semantically, then, these would be the same as a category of the form A/B but the syntax is different: an A^B is something that generally distributes like an A but contains within it (or is) an (unbound) proform of category B. A pronoun is thus listed in the lexicon as having category NP^{NP} and its meaning is the identity function on individuals. We can now formulate a rule which allows an ordinary expression such as *lost*—which wants an NP in subject position and is a function of type <e,t>—to map into a new homophonous expression wanting an NP^{NP} in subject position and wanting an argument of type <e,e>. I call this the "Geach" rule (Geach 1972) and notate this as **g**:

(7) Semantics of the **g** rule: let f be a function of type <a,b>, then **g**(f) is a function of type <<c,a>,<c,b>>, where $\mathbf{g}\,(f) = \lambda V_{\text{of type}<c,a>} [\lambda x_{\text{of type c}} [f(v(c))]]$

(Note that this is a unary version of the function composition operator: it takes a function f and maps it into a new function which takes as argument a function h, such that $\mathbf{g}(f)(h) = f \circ h$.) The full **g** rule, then, is formulated as in (8); I will hereafter use the prime-notation (α') interchangeably with the double bracket notation ($[[\alpha]]$) to notate the meaning of α:

(8) Let α be an expression of the form $<[\alpha]; A/B; \alpha'>$. Then there is an expression β of the form: $<[\alpha]; A^C/B^C; \mathbf{g}(\alpha')]>$

Example (9) illustrates the syntactic and semantic composition of *he lost;*

(9) lost; S_L/NP; lost; $\rightarrow$ $_{\mathbf{g}}$lost; $S^{NP}/_R NP^{NP}$; $\lambda f_{<e,e>} [\lambda x[\ lost'(f(x))]]$
he; NP^{NP}; $\lambda y[y]$
he lost; S^{NP}; $\lambda f_{<e,e>} [\lambda x[\ lost'(f(x))]](\lambda y[y]) = lost'$

To complete the analysis of (6), we need one further unary rule which accomplishes the effect of "binding". Of course I should point out that there is no real notion of "binding" in the sense of some notion which plays a role in the grammar, and so I use this term informally to mean the operation which is necessary to give a particular reading. Thus "binding" is accomplished by what I call the **z** rule. I first define its semantics in (10), and the unary rule is given in (11):

(10) Let h be a function of type <a,<e,b>>. Then **z**(h) is a function of type <<e,a>,<e,b>> where $\mathbf{z}(h) = \lambda f_{\text{of type }<e,a>} [\lambda x[h(f(x))(x)]]$

(11) Let α be an expression of the form $<[\alpha]; (A/NP)/B; \alpha'>$. Then there is an expression β of the form $<[\alpha]; (A/NP)/B^{NP}; \mathbf{z}(\alpha')>$

For a generalization of this to the case of three-place verbs see Jacobson (1999). (The fact that (11) is formulated to apply only to items of category (A/NP)/B (rather than more generally to (A/C)/B) and the corresponding fact that **z** is defined only for functions which contain an e-argument slot is purely for exposition; there is as far as I know no reason not to give (11) in fully general form.) Hence the semantic composition of *Every man$_i$ believes that he$_i$ lost* involves **z** on *believes* as follows:

(12) believe; (S/NP)/S; [[believe]] $\rightarrow_{\mathbf{z}}$ believe; $(S/NP)/S^{NP}$;
$\lambda P_{<e,t>}\ [\lambda x[\text{believe}'(P(x))(x)]]$
believe he lost: (S/NP); **z**(believe′)(lost′)
$= \lambda P_{<e,t>}\ [\lambda x[\text{believe}'(P(x))(x)]](\text{lost}') = \lambda x[\text{believe}'(\text{lost}'(x))(x)]]$
this then occurs as argument of the generalized quantifier *every man*

A case like *every man*$_i$ *loves his*$_i$ *mother* is similar. *his mother* denotes the function mapping each individual into that person's mother (again, ignoring gender information); call this the-mother-of function. *loves* undergoes **z** to expect as object an expression containing a pronoun, and its new meaning is $\lambda f_{<e,e>}[\lambda x[\text{loves}'(f(x))(x)]]$. When this combines with the object we get the syntactic expression *loves his mother* whose meaning is **z**(love′) applied to the-mother-of function. That boils down to the set of self-mother's-lovers, and that occurs as argument of the subject. For full details, see Jacobson (1999) in which it is shown that the system (with modest generalizations on the rules above) can handle cases with any number of pronouns, any number of binders, and bindings in any order.

Readers unfamiliar with direct compositionality and with Categorial Grammar style analyses are often uncomfortable with the fact that this approach to binding makes use of two unary rules. There are some observations which should set such readers at ease. First, one can always trade in a unary rule for a silent operator, if the latter gives greater comfort. So instead of having a rule shifting the meaning (and syntactic category), one could recast **z** and **g** as silent little lexical items which combine in the syntax with *believe* and *love.* (Any unary rule can be repackaged as an "empty operator", and *vice versa.*) Second, note that every analysis (that I know of) involves a unary (i.e. type-shift) rule and/or an empty operator to perform binding. In the standard view it is the rule (or operator) which accomplishes λ-abstraction. The difference, then, is not between the existence of a type-shift rule (or operator) to do binding, but simply the domain to which this rule applies. In the standard view, the "binding" of the pronoun involves a shift which takes place on a big domain: the meaning of a sentential expression like t_8 *loves his*$_8$ *mother* shifts (from open proposition to closed property).[8] Here the shift is a very local one, and applies instead to *loves* in (6*b*) (and *believes* in (6*a*)). But both systems make use of a unary (type-shift) rule (or empty operator). In fact, then, there is just one additional unary rule here: the **g** rule. But this is a rather simple and natural rule; it is just a unary (Curry'ed) version of function composition.

[8] Under the "Derived VP" approach to binding (Partee and Bach 1981), the domain is somewhat smaller; the meaning of the VP shifts.

Let me forestall one potential misunderstanding. I am certainly not claiming that there is no syntactic side to "binding" and to the distribution of pronouns, and I am not claiming that everything is "done in the semantics". In fact, such a claim would be somewhat at odds with the general Categorial Grammar program, in which the two systems are tightly linked. Indeed it is quite crucial that the system does make use of syntactic information: the syntactic categories play a role in the statement of the rules above and so the grammar most certainly does get to "see" syntactic category. (As would be the case in any system.) What it does not get to see, though, is configurational information.

Can we thus get the effects of supposed configurational constraints such as, for example, WCO? Indeed we can—and in fact it is built into the system above. "Binding" is the result of the **z** rule: this rule maps a function of type <a,<e,b>> into one which wants an <e,a> as its first argument, and it "merges" the newly created e-argument slot with one of its later argument slots. Syntactically, it allows for its first argument to contain a pronoun. Thus the open argument slot which is ultimately contributed by the meaning of the pronoun is "merged" with a higher argument slot, and this is what gives the right semantics. If we assume that **z** is the only rule that accomplishes "binding", then the WCO effects automatically follow. In order to get WCO violations such as that shown in (2*b*), we would need a backwards version of this rule (call it **s**) which mapped a function of type <e,<a,b>> into one of type <e,<<e,a>,b>> and "merged" the newly created e-argument slot (which will ultimately be contributed a pronoun) to the earlier (or, lower) argument position. (For details of how this could indeed give a WCO violation, see Jacobson 1999.) The bottom line, then, is that the effect is built into the combinatory system rather than being stated on a configuration which is the *result* of the combinatory system. Since any theory does need the combinatory rules (including unary rules) the hope is that all such effects can follow from the rules and no use of representations is needed. This is what DC would lead us to expect.

Two final points before concluding this section; one concerns the analysis of free pronouns, as in:

(13) He lost.

In the account here, this actually does not denote a proposition, but rather a function from individuals to propositions. I assume that in order to extract propositional information, a listener supplies this to some contextually salient individual. Note that the standard account making use of variables has no real advantage here. For here too (13) is not a proposition—but a function from assignment functions to propositions. In fact, all sentences are functions from assignment functions to propositions. Yet listeners do compute propositional information. In the case of a closed sentence (with no unbound pronouns) there is no mystery as to how this is done: since these denote constant functions from assignment functions, it does not matter which assignment function is picked. But in (13), it does. Presumably, then, a listener computes propositional information by applying this to some contextually salient assignment function (as opposed to the tack taken here, where the function is applied to a contextually salient individual).

A second point of interest concerns the analysis of (5), which shows "bound variable connectivity" without apparent c-command. But this is quite unproblematic in this account—the notion that a "binder" c-commands a "bindee" is all an illusion. (In fact, there is no real notion of binding, binders, etc.—we merely have the semantic composition doing its job, and the **z** rule "merges" an argument slot contributed by a pronoun to a higher argument slot.) More concretely, the semantic composition of (5) can be shown informally as follows (see Jacobson 1994 for more thorough discussion):

(14) the unique function f with range woman such that every Englishman z(loves) f is the-mother-of function.

As discussed also in von Stechow (1990) and Sharvit (1999), this involves just a generalization of the analysis of functional questions given in Groenendijk and Stokhof (1983) and Engdahl (1986). But what is of interest here is that functional questions in general and extensions to these cases follow immediately from the mechanisms discussed above. Since *loves* can undergo **z**, it follows that there can be a "functional" gap here. These phenomena are not some special creatures requiring new sorts of traces or other devices—they are just part and parcel of the machinery needed for "binding" in general. Moreover, the fact that the post-copular constituent can denote the-mother-of function is an automatic consequence of the system here too (since it contains a pronoun, it is a function from individuals to individuals). I should note that this analysis of the compositional semantics of (5) is sometimes reported in the following terms: the functional analysis of (5) allows one to construct a semantics in which *his* is not c-commanded by *every Englishman* and is therefore not actually "bound" by *every Englishman*. This kind of phrasing misses the point. Under the variable-free view, "binding" (in the sense of some privileged semantic connection between *every man* and the pronoun) and "c-command" are *always* an illusion—and no new analysis of "binding" is needed for the case here.

The remarks above illustrated the direct compositional and variable-free hypotheses. But the ultimate success of these two related hypotheses depends on their ability to meet three challenges: (i) *The challenge for direct compositionality*: can all phenomena which have appeared to necessitate non-local constraints on representation be handled (in a simple and natural way) without such constraints? (ii) *The challenge for variable-free semantics*: can all phenomena which have appeared to necessitate constraints on co-indexation (and hence indices) be accounted for in some other way (and in a simple and natural way)? (iii) *The challenge for the purely semantic view of connectivity*: can all connectivity effects be accounted for without abstract levels and/or silent material? Obviously I am not about to try to answer all of these questions here, but my strategy will be to investigate one persistent "thorn" for direct compositionality and variable-free semantics: Principle B effects. The remainder of this paper attempts to demonstrate two things. First, the account of Principle B effects using representationally stated constraints on co-indexing requires so much unmotivated complexity as to be extremely dubious. Second, these effects can indeed be handled (much more simply) under direct compositionality and variable-free semantics.

6.4 Principle B Effects: The "Standard" Account

Principle B is supposed for the contrasts shown below. I am surrounding these with some discourse context, since judgments about coreference possibilities are often highly context-dependent and some of the claims in the literature about the lack of possible coreference might well hold only because it is difficult to imagine appropriate contexts. I have therefore tried to give the (*b*) cases every possible chance to be good, and the contrast between (*a*) and (*b*) seems to show that the Principle B effect is quite real (note that all of the (*b*) cases become perfect when a reflexive replaces the pronoun):

(15) What happened at the press conference yesterday?

 (*a*) Bush_i defended his_i decision to go to war.

 (*b*) *Bush_i defended him_i (in the face of severe criticism).

(16) How does Bush manage to fool so many people?

 (*a*) Well, he_i praises his_i policies whenever he gets a chance.

 (*b*) *Well, he_i praises him_i whenever he gets a chance.

(17) What happens on campaign trails?

 (*a*) Oh, every candidate_i goes around praising his_i mother (for raising him so right).

 (*b*) *Oh, every candidate_i goes around praising him_i.

And so, conventional wisdom tells us that there is a constraint such as the following:

(18) A pronoun cannot be co-indexed with a c-commanding NP within the same local domain.

The definition of "local domain" varies from account to account—for our purposes let us take the local domain of some node to be the lowest S or NP node dominating it—but the particular definition will have no effect on the points in this section.

Before continuing, let me note that there are a number of well-known complexities as to just where we find these effects. They are, for example, mitigated with focus on either the subject or on the object pronoun. Moreover, the strength of the Principle B effect varies with the verb in question. *praise*—which I use throughout—is perhaps not the strongest verb to illustrate the point (*introduce* displays extremely strong Principle B effects, as will be discussed later). I nonetheless continue to use *praise* because the effect here seems strong enough to demonstrate the point (*introduce* would involve the additional irrelevant complication of dealing with a three-place verb). I will return to some of the issues in the final section (see especially §6.6.2); for now I will flatten the domain in a way which, hopefully, does no significant damage to the theoretical points.

Thus the existence of a principle such as (18) creates obvious challenges to the claims here. First, of course, it is not stated as a strictly local constraint (on sisters and/or mothers) and so could not be directly recast as a constraint on the combinatorics. Second, its statement requires the use of indices. And third, Principle B displays the typical connectivity effects, as shown in (19):

(19) (*a*) *What Bush_i always does (on the campaign trail) is praise him_i.

(*b*) *What every candidate_i does (on the campaign trail) is praise him_i.

If one were to take the position that the post-copular constituent contains no deleted, reconstructed, or silent material, then (18) cannot account for the deviance here, for *him* is not co-indexed with a c-commanding NP in the relevant local domain.

6.4.1 *The Inadequacies of a Constraint on Co-Indexation*

6.4.1.1 *Problem 1: Coreference with Free Pronouns* Yet there are at least two well-known problems with the co-indexation account. First, it has been known since at least as early as Reinhart (1983) that a constraint on *co-indexation* is not good enough for cases such as (15*b*) and (16*b*). Given the usual assumptions about how "binding" works, it will block the relevant reading of (17*b*)—where we have a bound pronoun—but it will not suffice to block the readings shown in (15*b*) and (16*b*). This is because in (15*b*), nothing would stop the pronoun from being a free pronoun, which happens to pick up the individual Bush who is, after all, quite contextually salient. And yet this reading is still impossible. Similarly for (16*b*): why can both pronouns not be free, not co-indexed, and yet both happen to pick up the same individual?

Interlude: Are we sure that this is a problem? Obviously my answer to the question raised above in the subsection title is going to be "yes"—but I think it is worth pausing to consider a possible "way out" for the Principle B account. Could we posit a constraint on assignment functions which would rule out the possibility of differently indexed pronouns (or an NP and a pronoun with different indices) picking out the same thing? The idea is that if the pronoun were free, the only way it could pick out the same individual as the subject is to have a different index on it. Hence a constraint on co-indexation (classic Principle B, as stated in (18)) will suffice: (18) rules out the co-indexed representation, and the constraint on assignment functions rules out the other possible way to get the "wrong" interpretation of this sentence. In fact I suspect that this is essentially what was assumed in the early literature on indices: the assumption there seems to have been that there is a one-to-one correspondence between individuals and indices, which made the idea of a constraint against co-indexing look like a reasonable way to account for constraints on coreferential interpretations. While standard views of assignment functions do not contain such a constraint, it is worth revisiting the issue to see if this can work.

First, however, we should be a bit more explicit about the LF representations for, for example, (15*b*); this will also come in useful later. We will assume that *Bush* can be in the raised position at LF and can bind a trace in subject position (this assumption is fairly standard in order to allow for the possibility of sloppy readings with VP Ellipsis; I come back to this below). Take any "QRed" DP. It will be the sister to some index n and there will be a t_n in the position from which it raised. We can ask about the index on the DP itself in LF. Must it have the same index? Can it have a different index? Or will it have no index? (See, e.g., Büring 2005 for extensive discussion.) This point will become important in the section "Interlude again" below; for now we will simply not notate any index on it (as already shown in §6.3.1, the index does no work in any case). Thus (15*b*) can have two different LFs:

(20) (*a*) Bush $[_{\Lambda} 8$ [t_8 defended him_8]]

(*b*) Bush $[_{\Lambda} 8$ [t_8 defended him_7]]

So the question at issue here is the following: can the representation in (20*b*) give rise to the "reading" (or "understanding") shown in (15*b*)? The proposal under consideration here is that it cannot, if we constrain assignment functions as follows:

(21) For any assignment function g, if $m \neq n$, then $g(m) \neq g(n)$

The interpretation of free pronouns presumably proceeds as follows: a sentence with a "free" pronoun within it has as its value a non-constant function from assignment functions to propositions. Its interpretation involves the listener applying this to some contextually salient assignment function. But on any assignment function g, $[[\Lambda]](g)$ is the function that maps an individual x to the proposition that x defended g(7), where g(7) cannot be x. So pick any g such that $[[\Lambda]](g)$ is a function which is defined for Bush. It follows that under that assignment function g(7) cannot be Bush, and so there is no way to get the bad reading indicated in (15*b*). (Incidentally, my own account will bear some resemblance to this, although this will not be achieved through the use of assignment functions.)

One might be tempted to immediately dismiss the constraint in (21) on the grounds that it would not allow for the strict reading of (22):

(22) $George_i$ loves his_i mother, and Dick does too.

The usual way to think about this is that the sloppy reading comes about by having the first clause have an LF representation analogous to (20*a*) (where the pronoun and the subject trace are co-indexed), while the strict reading is the result of the representation analogous to (20*b*) (the pronoun is free and happens to pick up George). And so the constraint in (21) would seem to incorrectly rule out the strict reading. But, in fact, to dismiss (21) on these grounds would be premature, for there is another story that we could tell about the strict reading. The details depend on just how to treat VP ellipsis: to pick one approach, assume that VP ellipsis involves "supplying" a meaning of type <e,t> at the position of the ellipsis site, where that meaning must be the meaning of some other expression at LF. Then the sloppy reading can come about in just the way noted above, but for the strict reading we can simply be picking up the meaning of an LF VP—whose meaning is just the value of the expression *loves 8's mother*. (Thus for the sloppy reading the missing meaning—on any assignment function g—is the set of self-mother lovers—which is the meaning for the entire constituent labeled Λ—and for the strict reading the meaning—on any assignment function g—is the set of individuals who love g(8)'s mother. In both cases consider only assignment functions in which g(8) = George, and we get both readings.)

Nonetheless, the constraint on assignment functions proposed in (21) is untenable: it gives rise to a class of problems which can be exemplified by the following:

(23) Bill$_i$ thinks that no one at the moment is living in his$_i$ house.

If we were to adopt (21), then we incorrectly predict that (23) means that Bill thinks that no one other than himself is living in his house. To demonstrate: assume for the moment that *no one* has to undergo QR here. Suppose that *Bill* (or, the trace of *Bill*) and *no one* have the same index. Then in that case we do not get the reading in (23) because *no one* will "bind" the pronoun. The LF will be:

(24) Bill [8 [t$_8$ thinks that no one [8 [t$_8$ is living in his$_8$ house]]]]

So suppose instead that *Bill* (or its trace) and *no one* (or its trace) have different indices; for example let *no one* (or its trace) have the index 6. The relevant LF is then:

(25) Bill [8 [t$_8$ thinks that no one [6 [t$_6$ is living in his$_8$ house]]]]

This means that on an assignment function g, the argument of [[no one]](g) is the function which maps each individual x into the proposition g′(6) lives in Bill's house where g′ is the assignment function just like g except that x is assigned to 6. However, there is no g′ just like g except where Bill is assigned to 6 (because Bill has already been assigned to 8). Hence the argument of *no one* has to be a partial function, undefined for Bill. Thus Bill must believe that there is no one in the set characterized by the (partial) function which maps an individual to true in case they live in Bill's house and are not Bill—and so we get the reading where Bill believes that no one but himself is living in his house. It is quite clear that this is not the right reading for this sentence.

There is one last trick we might try to save this constraint on assignment functions. We began the discussion of (23) by assuming that *no one* had to undergo QR. But suppose that that is wrong: let it stay in the subject position where the meaning of the VP directly is taken as its argument in the semantic composition. The point of this "trick" is that in this case its index will not matter for anything (there is never a stage in the semantic composition at which we λ-abstract over the index of a variable in subject position). And so *no one* could be co-indexed with *Bill* but without the bad consequence seen earlier: it will not mistakenly "bind" the pronoun *his*. This final attempt is easy to sabotage, simply add in another pronoun which must be "bound" by *no one*, as in:

(26) Bill$_i$ thinks that no man$_j$ could possibly live in his$_i$ house unless he$_j$ can stand cockroaches.

The interested reader can verify that—given the general way of doing the semantic composition under discussion here—*no man* would have to undergo QR and hence the bottom line will be that this should have an "except Bill" reading, which it does not.

Interestingly, my own proposed solution also results in a somewhat specialized version of the problem discussed here. But in the case of my proposal the "problem" (if it is one) appears only in a special set of cases (cases which exemplify the Principle B environment). As it turns out, in just those cases, in fact, it is not clear that the prediction that there is a "no one but self" reading is incorrect. The facts are a bit complex and so I return to this in §6.6.

6.4.1.2 *Problem 2: Co-Bound Material* A related problem with Principle B has been discussed (e.g. Heim 1993; Fox 2000; Büring 2005): the co-indexing constraint given in (18) does not rule out the indicated reading for a case such as (27). The reason is that other facts (to be discussed momentarily) force us to allow for an LF such as (28), where this would correspond to a surface structure in which the subject and object of *praise* are not co-indexed.

(27) *Every candidate$_i$ thinks that he$_i$ should say that he$_i$ will praise him$_i$.

(28)

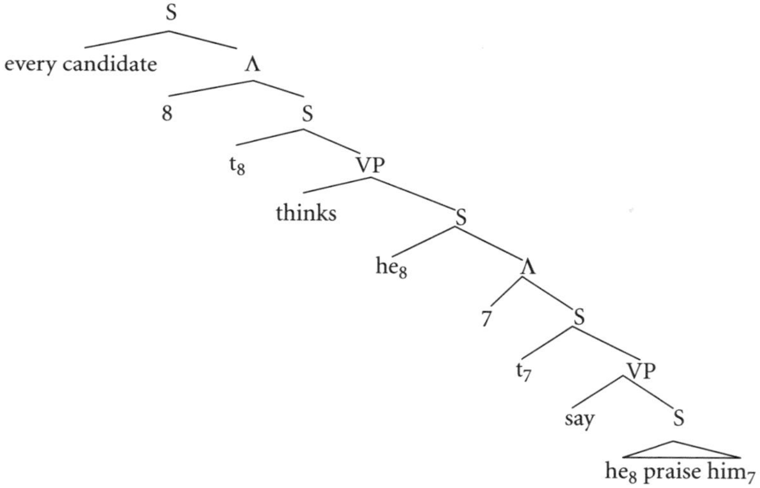

Interlude Again: Are we sure that LFs such as (28) are possible? Once again, I am going to answer the question posed immediately above in the affirmative (of course this answer is relative to the hopefully counterfactual world in which there are indices and LFs). This question is actually addressed in past literature (see especially Fox 2000); I will take Fox's discussion as a point of departure but will fine-tune his argument slightly. The question at issue, then, is whether the index on the binder must always match the index which performs the semantics of λ-abstraction. In other words, is the following tree bit well-formed?[9]

(29) he_8[7 S]

If this were ill-formed, then Principle B (as stated in (18)) would be enough to block the indicated reading in (27); Principle B blocks the representation in which the subject (or subject trace) is co-indexed with the object pronoun, and (28)—which seems to be another way to let in the bad reading—would be ill-formed.

Fox (2000) claims that the well-formedness of (28) can be demonstrated by considering the range of possible interpretations for (30):

(30) Every man_i only thinks that HE_i should give a present to his_i mother.

The reading of interest here is:

(31) every man only thinks that HE (bound) should give a present to his (bound, but non-sloppy) mother

(That is, each man wants to be the sole present-giver to his own mother.) Hence this reading can be associated with the LF in (32) which, note, allows for a case where the "LF binder" (by the HK definition earlier) of a trace has a different index than the trace itself:

(32) every man_8 [8 [t_8 thinks HE_8 [7 [t_7 should give a present to his_8 mother]]]]

This makes the alternatives within the focused domain be things like:

(33) he_6 [7 [t_7 should give a present to his_8 mother]]

7 is bound all the way through. Hence the alternatives within the thoughts of each man are alternative present-givers (as we want), but the mother stays constant (as we want).

But we are not quite home free if we wish to show that (32) (and hence more generally the configuration in (29)) should be allowed. For we do not really need to resort to the representation in (32) to get the relevant meaning. Suppose we simply do not apply QR to HE, so that the relevant LF is:

[9] One answer to this put forth in Fox (2000) is that such representations come "for free" and thus something extra would be needed to block them. But this is not really true. Suppose that we assume that all DPs (proper names, quantified DPs, etc.) have an index and that this index is preserved under QR. Then representations such as *he_8[7 $t_z$say he_8 praise him_7]* would simply never come about (I've underlined the offending portion). It is true that the indices on full NPs and quantified NPs do no work, but it's easy enough to ensure that they match the index on the "binder". (For relevant discussion, see Büring 2005)

(34) every man_8 [8 [t_8 thinks HE_8 should give a present to his_8 mother]]

since HE_8 is what is focused, the relevant alternatives are he_7, he_9, etc. and so we get alternatives such as:

(35) he_9 should give a present to his_8 mother

which is what we want. (The alternatives within each man's thoughts are exactly the same in (32) as in (34) since the two are semantically equivalent.)

Nonetheless, the basic argument is correct and just needs a bit more work to get it to go through. We can construct more involved versions of this case where the way out in (34) is unavailable. The strategy is to make sure that HE must be QR′ed by having it bind a different pronoun, one which is interpreted sloppily. Consider, then, the scenario in (36), followed by the sentence in (37):

(36) **Scenario:** There was a bad accident involving a bus full of elderly women from a nursing home. Several were injured, and brought to the hospital. Of those, many had sons who came to the hospital to see them—and each woman had several other relatives who also came. As is typical in hospitals, all the sons and the relatives were waiting around for hours—not being able to see their mother/relative and not even being told when they would be able to see them. This of course was very frustrating.

(37) Each man_i hoped that at least HE_i would soon be told when $he'd_i$ be allowed to see his_i mother.

The relevant (and very salient) reading is notated in (38):

(38) Each man hoped that at least HE (bound) would soon be told when he'd (bound, sloppy) be allowed to see his (bound, strict) mother

In other words, the alternatives within each man's hopes are about alternative relevant people (hence, the other relatives of that man's mother) who might be told something about when each of these alternative people might get to see someone, but the mother remains constant in each person's thoughts. If *HE* were not raised here then the representation would be as in (39), and the alternatives (within each man's hopes) would be about other people being told when he (the man himself) could see that man's mother:

(39) every man_8 [8 [t_8 hoped HE_8 be told when he_8 could see his_8 mother]]

To get the relevant reading we need the representation in (40):

(40) every man_8 [8 [t_8 hoped HE_8[7 [t_7 told when he_7 could see his_8 mother]]]]

But in that case, we must allow the configuration in (29) which in turn means that Principle B (as stated in (18)) cannot block the "co-bound" reading for (27), since the LF in (28) cannot be ruled out.

There is still one further tack that one might take to allow LFs like (40) while still blocking the LF in (28). Note that HE_8 is focused. Suppose we assume that only focused pronouns can raise and thus have a different index from the index on the trace that they bind. This might be a tenable position—but we can show that one can construct cases analogous to (37) which still exhibit Principle B effects. Consider, then, the following scenario. In the year 2525 the US finally has a multi-party system. Unfortunately, all the candidates for president and vice-president are males that year. (I invoke the multi-party system simply to make *each presidential candidate* felicitous; and I invoke the male-only candidate scenario so that the presence of *he* is not odd.) Enter the moderator of a debate involving each presidential candidate and his running mate:

(41) **Moderator of the debate:**
This – our second debate in our series – is the attack debate. The rules of this debate are very strict. You are allowed to attack your opponents all you want. But you're not allowed to do any praising—neither of yourself, nor of your running mate, until you're told that you're allowed to. Moreover I—and only I—know when each of you will be told that you're now allowed to go into praising mode.

Needless to say, this puts quite a stress on the candidates but

(42) ?*Each presidential candidate hoped that at least HE would soon be told that he could now praise him.
(That is, he_i is not sufficiently optimistic as to hope that his running mate will be informed of when he (the running mate) will be allowed to praise him_i.)

The impossible (or at least quite difficult) reading—but which should be quite salient—is exactly parallel to the bus accident scenario. The first HE is bound, the second *he* is bound and "sloppy" (the contrast set is another relevant individual—and in the reading at issue this is the candidate's running mate), but the last *him* is strict. Yet here this reading is at best quite difficult. I think it might be slightly better than the Principle B violating reading in (15)—and this is not surprising given the mitigating influence of focus—but it still remains degraded (as other informants have confirmed).

So the bottom line is that a configurational constraint on co-indexing—like (18)—fails not only to account for the coreference-without-binding cases but also fails to account for cases in which the subject and object are not co-indexed, but the binding pattern is such that they are in what I call the "co-bound" configuration. Here too the relevant reading is blocked.

6.4.2 *Some Proposed Solutions*

6.4.2.1 *Proposed Solution 1: Grice* What we see above is that a simple constraint against co-indexation really does not do the trick: it rules out certain structures but it does not rule out the actual meanings (or interpretations) that we want. There has, however, been a very seductive alternative in the literature since at least as early as Dowty (1980) (see also Reinhart 1983; Sadock 1983, and many since). This is to posit that the grammar contains nothing analogous to Principle B: the effect is purely Gricean. The offending configurations are, after all, just those in which a reflexive could have been used. Since a pronoun is ambiguous and a reflexive is not, the use of the reflexive is more informative. Hence by Gricean principles, if a speaker did not use a reflexive the listener will assume that non-coreference (or non-binding) was intended. This, a single account, covers all of the above cases, and removes the entire domain from that of grammar.

This kind of solution is certainly appealing. It covers *all* of the above cases, and it explains why, for example, Principle B violations such as (43) are not as bad as those in (15)–(17) (this was pointed out to me by Jerry Sadock):

(43) How do you manage to get everyone to vote for you?
?*Oh, I just praise me every chance I get.

(The logic here is that using *myself* is no more informative than using *me.*) Notice that if a Gricean account could work, then direct compositionality and variable-free semantics would be perfectly happy. The Gricean account makes no use of a configurational constraint, there is no use of indices, and the account would also extend to explain the badness of (19) without having to posit additional structure around the post-copular constituent. Thus if a Gricean account could be made to work, this paper could end here.

Unfortunately, a purely pragmatic account does not seem feasible, for the effect resists any kind of cancellation and simply does not behave like other known phenomena with pragmatic explanations. Note first that the Gricean story is somewhat odd to begin with. It is not quite true that the *meaning* of *Bush saw him* is less informative than the meaning of *Bush saw himself.* Under the standard story, the meaning of the first is a non-constant function from assignment functions to propositions while the latter is a constant function and so they do not form a scale in the usual way found for the case of scalar implicatures. (Similar remarks hold with respect to their meanings under the variable-free view; there they do not even have the same type of meaning.) The correct way to think of this is that the proposition denoted by *Bush saw him* is not fully specified, whereas *Bush saw himself* is. But other analogous cases—in which a sentence is either ambiguous or unspecified in some way—simply do not give rise to corresponding implicatures. Thus (44*a*) obviously does not implicate (44*b*) (even though (44*c*) is "more informative"):

(44) (*a*) Bush's mother likes him.

(*b*) Bush's mother likes someone (and that someone is someone other than Bush).

(*c*) Bush's mother likes Bush.

Moreover, analogous cases where we have an ambiguity or underspecification are perfectly happy when followed by extra clarificatory material:

(45) (*a*) Barbara praised him . . . that is to say, George.

(*b*) Barbara praised him—that is to say, she praised George.

(46) (*a*) I went to the bank—that is to say, the river bank.

(*b*) I went to the bank—that is to say, I went to the river bank.

Yet such clarification does nothing to remove a Principle B violation:

(47) (*a*) *Bush praised him—that is to say, himself.

(*b*) *Bush praised him—that is to say, he praised himself.

Sentences (47*a*, 47*b*) do not even remotely smack of an improvement, and indeed I can think of no way at all to cancel the "implicature" or remove the ambiguity. If this is a Gricean phenomenon, it behaves unlike others that we know of, and unless and until we have an explanation for this it appears that we probably have to live with the conclusion that the effect is located in the grammar. (Again, however, if it is not, then DC will be perfectly happy.)

6.4.2.2 *Proposed Solution 2: Principle B Plus a Transderivational Principle* We now arrive at the solution most commonly accepted in at least the modern formal semantics (LF-based, non-DC-based) literature. This is to posit that there really are two principles at work here. One is what we can call "core Principle B" and is the principle given in (18): it is a principle regulating the distribution of indices. It will block the relevant reading for (17*b*) (in which the pronoun has to be bound), and it will block the representation of (15*b*) shown in (20*a*). As to the fact that this is not enough to block the relevant understanding of (20*b*) (where the pronoun can remain free) and (28) (where there is co-binding), the idea is that there is a second "transderivational" principle—which blocks these readings in virtue of the fact that—were it not for Principle

B—the bound reading would have resulted in the same interpretation. This has been stated in a couple of different ways; let me take the formulation in Büring (2005) which is closely based on the formulations in Fox (2000) which in turn is based on Heim (1993) which in turn is based on Grodzinsky and Reinhart (1993):

(48) For any two NPs α and β, if α could bind (i.e. if it c-commands β and β is not bound in α's c-command domain already), α must bind β, **unless that changes the interpretation** (use of boldfaced mine, PJ)

This is intended to account for both of the cases discussed above in §6.4.1. Consider first the LF in (28)—where neither pronoun binds the other. Example (48) will block this LF, because the interpretation of this LF is identical to one in which the subject pronoun binds the other. Consider the LF in (20*b*)—where the pronoun is "free"—but where there is an "interpretation" where it happens to pick up *Bush.* (Technically this is not quite the right way to put it: the sentence is a non-constant function from assignment functions, and we apply it to one where 7 is assigned to Bush. But I will continue to use the more informal terminology here.) The idea of (48) is that that LF cannot have that interpretation. The reason is that there is another LF (i.e. (20*a*)) in which the pronoun is bound and which results in the same interpretation. Note that "interpretation" here does not mean just the output of the compositional semantics—in order for this to block the reading where the free pronoun in (20*b*) "picks up" Bush, "interpretation" has to mean the output of the processing system.

It seems to me that the claim that there is a principle like (48) cannot survive serious scrutiny; it has problems which seem insurmountable.[10] Perhaps the most important of these derives from the fact that "could bind" in this case *has to overlook "Core Principle B" violations!* That is, Principle B (as given in (18)) says that in (15*b*), the subject *cannot* "bind" *him.* (It rules out co-indexation and therefore binding.) But the non-co-indexation reading will have to be ruled out in virtue of the fact that the co-indexation (binding) structure would have been possible and would have yielded the same interpretation. And yet co-indexation would *not* have been possible. Thus we need to rule out one case in virtue of another "bad" case. This fact alone, it seems to me, should be enough to make us reject this right away. Note that competition effects—where one representation/interpretation pair is blocked

[10] To be fair, (48) is designed not only to account for the full range of Principle B effects, but also for a puzzle surrounding ellipsis due originally to Dahl (1974). The reader should consult Fox (2000) for a full discussion. I have no speculation to offer here as to how to account for Dahl's puzzle, but I hope the remarks below convince the reader that (48) is quite implausible, despite this apparent side benefit.

in virtue of a competing representation/interpretation pair—may well exist as constraints on processing. For example, Gricean principles themselves rely on speaker/hearer awareness of competition effects. But this is a case where one pair is blocked on the basis of a competing *bad* representation/interpretation pair—a situation which, as far as I know, is unprecedented.

In fact, it is worth taking very seriously what kinds of competition effects are known to exist in processing. One kind are competition effects based on *form*—these include typical Gricean effects. A listener hears form F_1 which is vague (or perhaps ambiguous) and can be literally true in a certain set of situations X as well as in a broader or different set of situations Y. However, there is another (generally equally easy to say) form F_2 which can only be true in X, and hence F_2 makes a stronger (or less ambiguous) statement than F_1. The listener infers that had the speaker intended to convey that the set of situations X holds, s/he would have said F_2, so it must be the case that we are not in situation X (i.e. that the proposition expressed by F_2 is false). So, here is a case where one form blocks a particular interpretation for another form. The other kind of competition effects that are well-known concern the case of competing meanings. Here there is a single form with more than one possible interpretation, but because one meaning M_1 is (for whatever reason) more accessible than another meaning M_2, M_1 blocks M_2. (Garden-path effects are examples of this phenomenon.)

But the kind of competition here is neither of these (and we have already seen that trying to reinterpret this as a Gricean effect unfortunately does not seem viable). For here the two forms are the same, and the two meanings (or, interpretations) are the same! The claim here is that one way to *derive* a certain interpretation for a given form is blocked in view of the fact that there was another way to derive the same interpretation from the same form. (And of course, as has already been pointed out, the "other way" is itself actually bad.) I know of no processing principles which would motivate this kind of competition, and know of no plausible story which has ever been proposed to explain this. Note too that this cannot be a direction or strategy to the processor specifically for how to assign meanings to "free" pronouns since it must also block the cobound cases. But neither can it be a constraint on LF representations (which do not have a pronoun bound less locally if it can be bound more locally without changing the interpretation) since this will not constrain the computation of free pronouns (which is not given by the compositional semantics).[11]

[11] At first glance it also appears that the existence of a constraint such as (i) would undermine the standard story regarding the possibility of both strict and sloppy readings in:

(i) $John_i$ loves his_i mother and Bill does too.

6.5 A Direct Compositional, Variable-Free Analysis

6.5.1 *The Analysis*

What we have seen is that configurationally based accounts of Principle B effects (based also on co-indexing) seem extremely unlikely to be correct; the complexities involved should make us very suspicious that such accounts are really missing the point. Can we do better with a direct compositional approach—one which skips the representational steps and tries to capture the effect in terms of the syntactic and semantic combinatorics? I will propose that we can.

My proposal is embedded within a Categorial Grammar syntax and makes crucial use of one fundamental property of CG: each syntactic category is an encoding of distributional properties (it also encodes semantic types). With respect to verbs (and other "function" or "complement-taking" categories), the category label itself encodes exactly what complement an item can take. Thus an expression of category $A/_RB$ takes a B-category expression to its right to give a resulting expression of category A, and an $A/_LB$ takes a B to its left to give an A. (As noted in §6.2, I assume that there are also expressions which take their arguments as infixes and expressions which themselves infix into their arguments. For details, see Jacobson (1992).)

As noted earlier, an expression with the general distribution of A-type expressions but which contains within it an "unbound" pronoun of category C is an expression of category A^C. This means that material with a pronoun within it is not quite the same category as corresponding material without the pronoun in it: and so if we have a verb with, for example, the category (S/NP)/NP (an ordinary transitive verb) it cannot combine with an NP that contains an unbound pronoun within it. But there are two unary rules which shift it into something which can. One is the **g** rule (which shifts it to $(S/NP)^{NP}/NP^{NP}$—the semantic effect here is to allow the verb to take a function of type <e,e> as argument—and it passes up the argument slot of that function for later binding. (In other words, the result after the verb combines with its object is a function of type <e,<e,t>> rather than an <e,t>. The second rule is the **z** rule, which shifts an ordinary transitive verb into one of category $(S/NP)/NP^{NP}$. Here the semantic effect is again that a function of type <e,e> is expected as object argument, but here the argument

The apparent problem is that—in the way it is usually put—the strict reading arises when the first *his* is a free pronoun not co-indexed with *John*. But (i) would then disallow such a representation to be paired with an interpretation where *his* is free and happens to pick out *John*. This has, in fact, worried past researchers (see Reinhart 2000 and Büring 2005 for discussion). Actually, though, this is not really a problem, for one could allow only the "bound" representation for *his* while still allowing the strict reading, by using the strategy outlined on p. 210 above.

slot of that function is "merged" with the subject slot. Thus after the verb takes its object the result is of type <e,t>; we can say that in this case the pronoun within the object is "merged with" or "bound to" the subject slot.

In my previous work, I treated pronouns themselves and material containing (unbound) pronouns as having exactly the same syntactic category (and semantic type). Both were of category NP^{NP} (and both denote functions of type <e,e>). But what we learn from a close look at Principle B effects is that bare pronouns actually do not seem to have the same distribution as pronouns sunk within further material. (I return below to the case of pronouns within argument-type PPs as in *He_i gave a book to him_i.*) Let us suppose, then, that bare pronouns are listed in the lexicon not as just NP^{NP} but actually they contain a special feature [p], where NP^{NP} and $NP[p]^{NP}$ are not the same thing. All of this is just to say: pronouns cannot occur except where they are specifically sanctioned. (I return below to the fact that they always seem happy in subject position.)

The informal idea, then, is as follows. Take an ordinary transitive verb like *praise*, and assume that it is listed in the lexicon with syntactic category (S/NP)/NP and with meaning of type <e,<e,t>>. Moreover, its meaning is just as we have always thought: it characterizes the set of all ordered pairs of praisers–praisees, including the reflexive pairs. But because of its syntax, this verb cannot directly take a pronoun in object position. A pronoun has a special category and it cannot occupy ordinary NP argument slots. Note of course that the lexical item *praise* could in any case not take a pronoun in object position—it would have to be mapped first into **z**(praise) or into **g**(praise). But the new point here is that even after *praise* undergoes one of the other rules it is still unable to take an ordinary pronoun in object position. **g**(praise) is of category $(S/NP)^{NP}/NP^{NP}$ and **z**(praise) is of category $(S/NP)/NP^{NP}$. So neither would be happy with a bare pronoun.

We thus posit one more unary rule—a rule that allows the lexical item *praise* to map into a new verb which (once it undergoes one of the two rules above) will be able to take a bare pronoun in object position. Syntactically this rule maps the NP argument slot in object position into an NP[p] argument slot. The interesting part is the semantics: the new verb becomes undefined for the reflexive pairs in the original denotation. Thus the rule is as follows (it would need to be generalized for the case of three-place verbs, but this is straightforward and is left as an exercise for the reader):

(49) Let α be an expression of the form <[α]; (S/NP)/NP; α'>. Then there is an expression β of the form: <[α]; (S/NP)/NP[p]; **irr**(α') >
where for any function f of type <e,<e,t>>, **irr**(f) is the function

mapping any x and y as follows:

irr (f) (x) (y) = 1 if f(x)(y) = 1 and x ≠ y
irr(f) (x)(y) = 0 if f(x)(y) = 0 and x ≠ y
irr (f)(x)(y) is undefined if x = y

The happy part of this is that Principle B effects derive from the syntactic and semantic combinatorics—the account directly regulates a correspondence between what syntactic categories can occur where (in this case, it regulates the distribution of pronouns) and meaning. The even happier part is that this—with no further ado—accounts for all three of the cases that we have seen above. Let us take them each in turn.

6.5.2 *Accounting for all Three Principle B Cases*

6.5.2.1 *The Bound Case*

As noted above, the mapping of ordinary *praise* to **irr** (praise) is still not enough to allow a bare pronoun in object position: this becomes possible only with the additional application of **z** or **g**. Consider the badness of the "bound" case in (50):

(50) *Every candidate$_i$ praised him$_i$.

Here the pronoun is "trying" to be bound by the subject slot, and so a sequence of steps which produced this reading would involve the application of **z** to **irr**(praise), whose category and meaning are as follows:

(51) **z**(praise$_{irr}$); (S/NP)/NP[p]^{NP}; $\lambda f[\lambda z[\lambda x[\lambda y_{y \neq x}\ [praise'(x)(y)]](f(z))(z)]]$
$= \lambda f[\lambda z_{z \neq f(z)}\ [praise'(f(z))(z)]$

There is nothing wrong with this meaning (indeed we will see momentarily that it is useful), but nonsense ensues when this takes as argument the ordinary meaning of a pronoun: that is the identity function. This is what happens in (50). Thus the meaning of the VP in (50) is the function characterizing the set of self-praisers, but defined only for those individuals who are not equal to themselves (hence of course undefined for everyone).

As noted directly above, there is nothing incoherent about the meaning of **z**(**irr**(praise)) (syntactically, this verb will require a bare pronoun in object position[12]); the incoherence ensues only when (51) is applied to the identity function over individuals. This means that if a bare pronoun could have some other meaning—in addition to the identity function on individuals—then it could combine with this verb. And in fact, in Jacobson (2000) I argued that paycheck pronouns are derived from ordinary pronouns via the Geach rule; a

12 This assumes that non-pronouns cannot appear in slots marked NP[p], just as items of category NP[p] cannot appear in ordinary NP slots.

paycheck pronoun is thus the identity function over functions of type <e,e>. What this means is that we should be able to combine **z**(**irr**(praise)) with the paycheck meaning of a pronoun, thereby binding "into" the argument slot of the paycheck. This prediction is correct: there is no problem with the reading of (52) notated above, which involves this verb:

(52) Every Democratic candidate$_i$ tried to distance himself from his$_i$ father$_f$, while every Republican candidate$_j$ continually praised him$_{f(j)}$

Again I use indices in the obvious way merely to indicate the intended reading.

6.5.2.2 *The Free Case* Next consider the case of a "free" pronoun, as in (53).

(53) *Bush$_i$ praises him$_i$.

The difficulty with the standard account is that there was no non-tortured way to rule out an understanding of this sentence in which *him* remains free and just happens to pick up Bush. But here this is ruled out. A "free" pronoun in the account here is one which was introduced via the application of **g** (or, really, applications of **g** all the way through the semantic combinatorics)—which has the effect of allowing a function of type <e,e> to occur in some normal e-slot, and "passes up" the binding. But in a free case, we never get an application of **z**—and so the final result is a function from individuals to propositions. This, then, is one possible meaning for a sentence such as *Bush praises him*. It is, however, a function which is defined only for individuals other than Bush.

To explicitly show the details, I need to point out that the free reading of the derivation will involve treating the subject as a generalized quantifier (i.e. the "lifted" meaning of *Bush*). With that, we can spell out the full derivation of *Bush praises him*:

(54) praise; (S/NP)/NP; praise′
$\rightarrow_{\mathbf{irr}}$ praise; (S/NP)/NP[p]; $\lambda x[\lambda y_{y \neq x}[\text{praise}'(x)(y)]] \rightarrow_{\mathbf{g}}$ praise;
$(S/NP)^{NP}/NP[p]^{NP}$; $\lambda f[\lambda z[\lambda x[\lambda y_{y \neq x}[\text{praise}'(x)(y)]](f(z))]]$
$= \lambda f[\lambda z[\lambda y_{y \neq f(z)}[\text{praise}'(f(z))(y)]]]$
praise him; $(S/NP)^{NP}$; $\lambda f[\lambda z[\lambda y_{y \neq f(z)}[\text{praise}'(f(z))(y)]]]\ (\lambda x[x])$
$= \lambda z[\lambda y_{y \neq z}[\text{praise}'(z)(y)]]$
(thus note that $\mathbf{g}(\mathbf{irr}(\text{praise}'))(\text{him}') = \mathbf{g}(\mathbf{irr}(\text{praise}'))$)
Bush; S/(S/NP); $\lambda P[P(b)] \rightarrow_{\mathbf{g}} S^{NP}/(S/NP)^{NP}$;
$\lambda R_{<e,<et>>}[\lambda x[\lambda P[P(b)](R(x))]] = \lambda R[\lambda x[R(x)(b)]]$
Bush praises him; S^{NP}; $\lambda R[\lambda x[R(x)(b)]](\lambda z[\lambda y_{y \neq z}[\text{praise}'(z)(y)]])$
$= \lambda x[\lambda z[\lambda y_{y \neq z}[\text{praise}'(z)(y)]]\ (x)(b)] =$
$\lambda x[\lambda y_{y \neq x}\ [\text{praise}'(x)(y)](b)] = \lambda x_{x \neq b}[\text{praise}'(x)(b)]$

(The last line in the steps which are notational simplifications of the meaning is not an ordinary λ-conversion, but the reader can verify that it is the correct equivalence.) In the end, then, the sentence denotes a function from individuals to propositions, but one defined only for those individuals distinct from Bush. Hence the reading indicated in (53) amounts to a presupposition violation.

6.5.2.3 *The Co-Bound Case* Now let us consider how this accounts for the impossibility of (55):

(55) *Every candidate$_i$ thinks that he$_i$ said that he$_i$ praised him$_i$.

Recall that the problem for the traditional account is that this cannot be blocked by a simple constraint on co-indexing since the two most deeply embedded pronouns could have different indices, but where the subject of *say* "binds" the subject of *praise* and *every candidate* "binds" the subject of *say* and the object of *praise*. (I of course use this terminology loosely since we have already seen that there is no obvious sense in which one NP "binds" another, but I use this as loose terminology for the LF shown in (28).) It will be useful at this point to give an informal rendering of this LF by means of the diagram shown in (56):

(56)

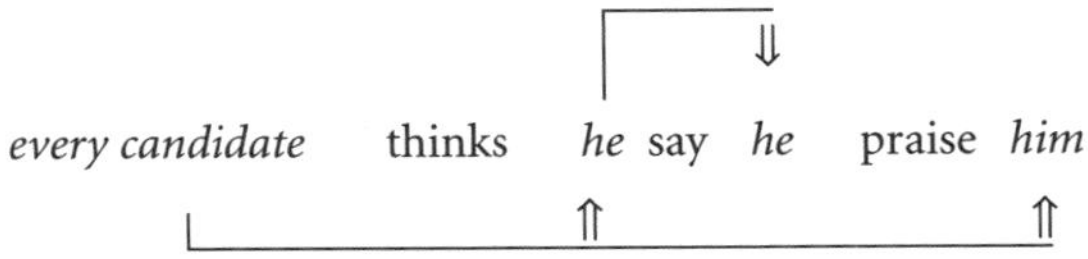

The question for the variable-free view, then, is to determine whether or not there is any kind of analogous problem. Before answering this, we first need to consider what happens in general when there are two pronouns which are "bound" by the same thing. Consider, for example, (57):

(57) Every man$_i$ in our dog park thinks that the woman he$_i$'s engaged to should walk his$_i$ dog.

As discussed in Jacobson (1999), the two pronouns in (57) necessarily are *not* semantically "linked" in terms of the meaning of the embedded S. In the normal view, they can correspond to the same variable—but there is nothing analogous to this here. Rather, the meaning of the S embedded under *think* is the two-place relation

(58) λx[λy[the woman that x is engaged to should walk y's dog]]

How then do we get the reading in (57)? In this case this comes about by two applications of **z** on *thinks*—which has the effect of "merging" these two slots (each is "merged" with the subject slot). The details are space-consuming and so the interested reader can consult the full details in Jacobson (1999).

Let us consider the LF (28) as a way in the standard theory to get the meaning for (56) indicated above. There is nothing exactly analogous to this in the variable-free view, but the closest analog would be a derivation in which *say* undergoes both **z** and **g** in such a way that **z** "merges" its subject slot with the argument slot created by the object pronoun, and **g** "passes" up the other pronoun (the subject of *praise*) for higher binding. *Thinks* then undergoes two applications of **z**—one "binds" the subject position of *say* to the subject position of *thinks*; and the other "binds" the passed-up pronoun slot (the object of *praise*) to the subject position of *thinks* which then merges these two. It is hoped that the diagram in (59) will help illustrate this, and will clarify the parallel between this derivation and the LF in (28) (I omit a number of applications of **g** from this picture):

(59)

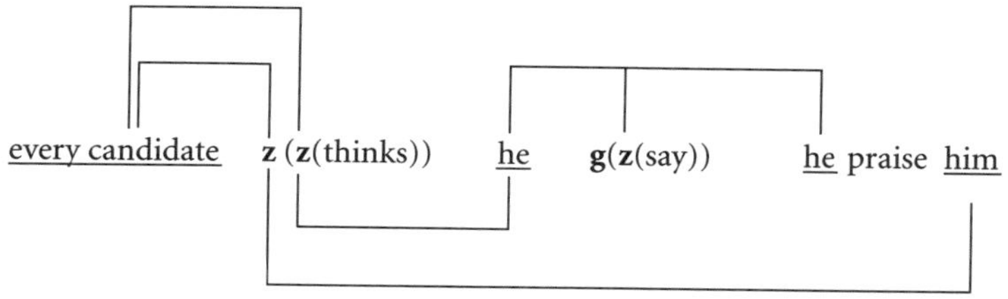

But note that *praise* is the irreflexive version of [[praise]]—as it must be in order to have a pronoun in the object position. It follows from this that *he praise him* is itself [[praise_{irr}]]. And given this, the derivation sketched above gives nonsense at the end of the day, as we would expect. To show this out formally we need to point out that undefinedness (like other presuppositions) projects upwards as, for example, the case of the gender presupposition in (60):

(60) *John said that every man_i loves her_i mother.

Given this, consider the full details of the derivation sketched above.

(61) $\mathbf{z}(\mathbf{g}(\text{say})) = \lambda R[\lambda w[\lambda z\ [z \text{ say } R(w)(z)]]]$

said he praised him:

$= \lambda R[\lambda w[\lambda z\ [z \text{ say } R(w)(z)]]]\ (\lambda x[\lambda y_{\ y \neq x}[\text{praise}'\ (x)(y)]])$

$= \lambda w[\lambda z\ [z \text{ say } \lambda x[\lambda y_{\ y \neq x}[\text{praise}'\ (x)(y)]]\ (w)(z)]]$

$= \lambda w[\lambda z\ [z \text{ say } \lambda y_{\ y \neq w}[\ \text{praise}'\ (w)(y)]]\ (z)]$

$= \lambda w[\lambda z_{\ z \neq w}[z \text{ say } [\text{praise}'\ (w)(z)]]]$

$z(z(\text{think})) = \underline{\lambda R[\lambda x[x \text{ thinks } R(x)(x)]]}$:
apply to above: *thinks he said he praised him* = $\lambda x_{x \neq x}$ [x thinks x said x praised x]

Thus, exactly as in the case of (50), the VP here is nonsense and is not defined for any individual.

Of course it should be pointed out that there are other ways one could attempt to get the relevant reading; in order to show that this is "nonsense" under all such derivations one would need to show out every possible derivation. Space precludes doing this here; hopefully the above gives a flavor of why, once we are dealing with the irreflexive version of *praise*, we will have no way to get this kind of a Principle B violation.

6.5.3 *Principle B Connectivity Effects*

To complete the discussion, note now that the appearance of Principle B effects in a copular case such as (62*b*) is completely expected without positing any complex analysis regarding the representation of the post-copular constituent:

(62) (*a*) What every candidate$_i$ does (every chance he gets) is praise his$_i$ mother.

(*b*) *What every candidate$_i$ does (every chance he gets) is praise him$_i$.

The "null hypothesis" is that the post-copular constituent has no deleted or silent material surrounding it, and the appearance of Principle B effects does not require us to abandon this hypothesis, since the effect is encoded purely locally within the post-copular VP, and so there is no need to surround it by additional material in order to satisfy a representational, non-strictly local constraint such as the one in (18). Roughly, then, the compositional semantics for (62*a*) is as represented in (63*a*), and the compositional semantics for (62*b*) is shown in (63*b*):

(63) (*a*) the property P such that P is true for every candidate is
the property of z-praising the mother function

(*b*) the property P such that P is true for every candidate is
the property of z-praising (irr) the identity function
(i.e., the property of being a self-praiser, defined only for those individuals not equal to themselves)

For a case like (19*a*) there are two ways one might try to get the impossible reading:

(19) (*a*) *What Bush$_i$ always does (on the campaign trail) is praise him$_i$.

One would involve application of **z** to irreflexive *praise* in the post-copular constituent, and this will yield nonsense exactly as in the case of (63*b*). The other is to let *him* be "free"—by which is meant that **g** will apply to irreflexive *praise.* In the end, then, the entire sentence will denote a function from individuals x to the proposition that "what Bush does is praise x", but where this function is defined only for individuals not equal to the subject of *praise.* Thus the function is undefined for Bush, in much the same way as in the ordinary case of (15*b*). (The full details have to do with the entailments of a copular sentence; but it is clear that under any way to think of the semantics of the copula here it will follow that *him* cannot be Bush. We will leave the full details for the interested reader to supply.)

6.6 Open Questions

There are many well-known complexities surrounding Principle B effects, and some of these raise questions for this analysis as well as for more "standard" analyses. There are also some questions raised by this analysis in particular. While there is no way I can cover all of the questions that arise, this section will conclude with a look at some of these.

6.6.1 *Some Mechanical Issues*

First, the analysis is not complete and some of the details have not been fully spelled out above. The analysis needs to be extended to the case of three-place verbs (as in (64)); it needs to be extended to cover the case of a pronoun within an argument PP (as in both (64) and (65)) and it needs to be refined to account for the fact that pronouns are always happy in subject position:

(64) (*a*) *I introduced every man_i/$Bush_i$ to him.

(*b*) *$Bush_i$/every man_i introduced me to him.

(65) *$Bush_i$/Every man_i talked about him.

Without giving the full details here, I believe that most of the requisite machinery is fairly straightforward. For the case of three-place verbs, we simply assume that there is a generalization of the **irr** operation (such extensions are needed in general for three-place verbs), which allows the feature [p] to occur on non-subject argument slot, and removes from the denotation of the verb all triplets which are such that the same individual occurs in the relevant argument slot and in one of the higher slots. (Recall that I am assuming a Wrap analysis for (64) in which *every man/Bush* is introduced later than the PP and is "wrapped" in (infixed) during the syntactic composition.)

The fact that a pronoun cannot be embedded in an argument PP is hopefully easy to capture with judicious use of "feature passing". More precisely, prepositions like *to* or *about* which yield argument are of category PP/NP and can map into PP[p]/NP[p]. Hopefully the fact that the [p] feature is passed from argument to result in this case follows from something more general, but I will not pursue this here. I assume that the meaning of such prepositions is the identity function, so the meaning of *to him* will be the same as the meaning of *him* (it is the identity function on individuals). (We further assume that the convention that NP[p] can occur only where specifically asked for holds equally well for PP[p].) As to the fact that pronouns are always happy in subject position, we might assume that the feature [p] which we are concerned with here occurs only on accusative pronouns. None of these suggestions are terribly insightful, but they would seem to be straightforward mechanical extensions of the type needed for other phenomena.

6.6.2 *Lexical Variation in the Strength of Principle B Effects*

A more interesting wrinkle concerning Principle B effects which, I believe, has not been sufficiently appreciated in past literature is that the strength of the effect is very lexically specific. Some verbs allow Principle B violations (with a bit of work) relatively easily; others resist these. This observation, by the way, will account for a glaring contradiction in the literature. Fiengo and May (1994) claim that Principle B effects survive ellipsis, and use an example along the lines of the following:

(66) (*a*) *John introduced her_i to everyone before she_i did.

(*b*) *John introduced her_i to Bill, but she_i already had.

(All of these improve somewhat if the subject is *she herself* rather than just *she*, and this improvement holds throughout all of the sentences cited below. I will not speculate here on why this is so; I will however keep the data consistent by never using this form.) But on the other side of the coin it is well-known that focus ameliorates Principle B effects, and cases such as (67) are typical of the cases cited in the literature to show this:[13]

(67) (*a*) Mary pities him_i, Sue pities him_i, and ??I even think that HE_i pities him_i.

(*b*) ??I only think that HE_i pities him_i.

[13] The literature varies on whether or not these are perfect or whether they are just improved with focus on the subject but still not perfect. My very unsystematic check with (a very small sample of) informants would seem to indicate the latter—I have consulted with three speakers (obviously not statistically significant)—and they find these to be still somewhat off. Obviously this needs to be checked further, but I will assume here and below that focus merely improves but does not completely remove the Principle B effect.

The fact that the effect is ameliorated by focus but not by ellipsis should come as a complete surprise (it is odd that this has not, to my knowledge, been commented on in the literature). The two often behave alike in matters of this type (in fact, ellipsis actually requires focus, so it is hard to understand why a difference occurs); and from what we know about the two we would expect that—if anything—ellipsis would be "less fussy" here.

But there really is no contradiction: the difference stems from the fact that *pity* is what we might call a relatively weak Principle B verb while *introduce* shows very strong Principle B effects which resist amelioration in any context. Thus note that (68) remains awful despite the fact that the subject is focused, and (69) shows that VP ellipsis ameliorates the violation with *pity*:

(68) (*a*) *John introduced her_i to Bill, Sam introduced her_i to Bill, and I even think that SHE_i introduced her_i to Bill.

(*b*) *I only think that SHE_i introduced her_i to Bill.

(69) (*a*) ??John pities her even more than she does.

(*b*) ??John pities her, and she does too.

In fact, the effects are so strong with *introduce* that one might be tempted by a suggestion of Tamina Stephenson (p.c.) that there are really just two separate verbs *introduce.* The first (call it *introduce*$_1$ —which occurs in all of the examples above—is lexically irreflexive: one simply cannot introduce$_1$ oneself to another. The other is *introduce*$_2$ which is *only* reflexive and is therefore the verb that occurs with a reflexive as in *Mary introduced herself to Bill.* This seems tempting, but unfortunately it would make it quite a mystery as to why (70) is perfect:

(70) (*a*) Mary introduced herself to Bill before Sam had a chance to.

(*b*) Mary introduced herself to Bill because Sam wouldn't.

I should point out that the asymmetry between "Principle A" effects with *introduce* in (70) and Principle B effects is actually a bit of a mystery given certain plausible views of the semantic contribution of a reflexive, but it seems to me that any reasonable story about why (70) is good would make it quite difficult to maintain the two verbs *introduce* theory. I will assume, then, that some other explanation is needed for the different Principle B strengths with different verbs.

It seems quite likely that the explanation will ultimately lie in a suggestion by Heim (1993) that pronouns are of individual concepts (of type <s,e>) and that Principle B requires that the subject and object be distinct individual concepts. To use Heim's informal terminology, apparent Principle B violations are possible when the subject and object are extensionally equivalent, but characterize the same individual "in different guises". The extent to which a verb allows apparent violations will depend on the extent to which its meaning is such that it makes salient the possibility of the subject and object having the same extension while being distinct individual concepts.

6.6.3 *Raising to Object Cases*

Whenever I present this analysis, someone inevitably asks about "Raising to Object" (or "ECM") verbs, as in:

(71) *John$_i$ expects him$_i$ to win.

These, of course, present a problem for the analysis only if one believes that *him* is a subject in the lower clause and hence not an argument of *expect*. But in the general tradition assumed here, there is plenty of independent reason to believe that *him to win* is not a clausal complement of *expect*. (For example, this form of the verb *expect* has—as noted in Rosenbaum (1967)—a passive counterpart. If Passive is a rule rearranging the argument structure (the syntactic and semantic argument *slots*) of a verb, then of course *him* in (71) must be an argument of *expect*.

Within the Categorial Grammar and related literature, there are two distinct ways which have been proposed to treat Raising to Object verbs, and either one will be compatible with the proposal here. In one (see especially Dowty 1985) *expect* and *persuade* have the same argument structure in the lexicon: they both take an infinitive VP and then an NP to give a VP. The familiar "raising" vs. "control" are simply a matter of fine-grained facts about the meanings of these verbs (and control itself is a consequence of entailments associated with the verbs). A somewhat different analysis is developed in Jacobson (1990) which more closely mimics the traditional "raising to object" analysis (Rosenbaum 1967). Here *expect* is—as in the standard view—listed in the lexicon as taking an S complement, and it denotes a relation between individuals and propositions. However, it (obligatorily) function composes with its complement, and so *expect to win* results, is an (S/NP)/NP, and the object "wraps" in. Note that this analysis is also perfectly compatible with the present account of Principle B effects: *expect to win* is a complex-transitive verb; it cannot take a pronoun in the (wrapped-in) object position until it undergoes the reflexive rule. The difference between the two accounts lies simply in just how it is that the phrase *expect to win* is composed, but the end result is the same. In other words, as long as *him* is an argument of *expect to win* we have no problem here.[14]

14 In comments on this paper at the Direct Compositionality Workshop, Danny Fox claimed that there seems to be a difference between "ECM" verbs and others in their Principle B effects, in that in the

6.6.4 *Amelioration under Focus*

There remains the question as to *why* focus ameliorates the effect. An answer to this question is of particular urgency for the account here since the amelioration has often been taken to support the existence of something like the transderivational constraint in (48). For in certain cases when the subject is focused, the representation in which the object is "bound" by the subject actually has different truth conditions from the non-coindexed structure (interpreted with "coreference"), and so (48) will not apply. There are, however, reasons to doubt this explanation. First, the truth conditions are indeed changed if the focused subject falls within the scope of *only*, but they are not changed with simple focus (or when the subject falls within the scope of *even*) yet still there is an amelioration (see, e.g., (67a)). Second, the amelioration does not seem in general to be complete. The facts seem quite fuzzy (as a few other informants have confirmed) whereas we would expect a complete disappearance of the effect (with *only*) if the above story were correct.

One hypothesis is that the sentences with focus on the subject continue to exhibit a presupposition violation, but since focus makes salient the alternatives (in which there is no such violation), we are able to accommodate this violation. The fact that focus ameliorates the situation but does not make it perfect is consistent with the hypothesis that accommodation is at work here. This explanation, however, cannot be the whole story—since it gives no insight into why the violation persists so strongly in the case of *introduce*. (Notice that the more standard explanation given above suffers from the same problem.) I thus leave this as an unsolved problem.

case of the former, there is no survival of this effect under ellipsis; thus Fox contrasts cases like (i) with cases like (ii) (Fox's actual sentences involve a proper name in object position in the first clause which introduces an irrelevant complication into the discussion so I have changed these; the distribution of *s here is essentially that reported by Fox (modulo the fact that his sentences are slightly different as noted above)):

(i) Mary likes him. *He does too. <like himself>

(ii) I expected him to win the race. He did, too. <expect himself to win the race>

But we have already seen that Principle B effects in general can be ameliorated by ellipsis and I think that the contrast between (i) and (ii) is anything but sharp. We see above, moreover, that the strength of Principle B effects is subject to a lot of lexical variation, and *expect* might just be one of the weaker Principle B verbs. Other Raising to Object verbs seem to me to show the effect somewhat more strongly:

(iii) I consider him to be competent. ??He does too.

I thus do not think this is a systematic difference between Raising to Object verbs and other verbs.

6.6.5 *Conjoined Objects*

Anna Szabolcsi (p.c.) has raised the following objection to this analysis. Consider (72) (note that the pronoun here is *not* intended to be understood as "coreferential" with the subject of *likes*):

(72) John$_i$ thinks that Bill$_j$ likes (both) himself$_j$ and him$_i$.

Szabolcsi's worry goes as follows. Since we have the pronoun *him* in object position, then we must be dealing with *likes$_{irr}$*—the verb which characterizes the set of pairs (x,y) such that x likes y and x $\neq$ y. Actually this is a slightly oversimplified way of stating the problem, for here we have a plural object. The worry, however, is that the meaning of *likes* which takes this plural object would have to be such that it takes a group X and distributes such that for each atomic part x of X, the subject stands in the *likes*$_{irr}$ to x. But then how could we possibly have the reflexive here? (Note that the problem is independent of one's formal account of reflexives.)

But there is actually no problem, once we note that the NP *himself and him* is itself not a pronoun—and hence presumably does not carry the feature [p]. Hence *likes* is not the irreflexive variant (or, more precisely, is not the variant which would distribute to the irreflexive *likes*). In other words, the [p] feature is not "passed" from one conjunct to the entire coordinated constituent (there is no reason to think it would be; it is passed only in the case of NPs within PPs). This hypothesis is easily tested: we need merely to see whether Principle B effects in general survive coordination. It seems to me (and the three other informants whom I have consulted) that they do not:

(73) (*a*) Bush$_i$/every man$_i$ praised (both) Barbara and him$_i$.

(*b*) Bush$_i$/every man$_i$ praised (both) him$_i$ and Barbara.

This is not the end of the story, for Szabolcsi (p.c.) informs me that the Hungarian situation is much like the English situation in all other respects, but that Principle B effects do survive in cases analogous to (73). (Yet cases analogous to (72) are fine.) Obviously, then, the Hungarian case needs to be looked at in greater detail.

6.6.6 *The "Except Bill" Case*

Recall the discussion on pp. 211–12 concerning sentences like (23):

(23) Bill$_i$ thinks that no one at the moment is living in his$_i$ house.

The question raised in that section was whether or not one could adopt a constraint on assignment functions such that for any two distinct variables, their value on any assignment function g must be distinct individuals. As discussed there, this would mean that (23) says that Bill thinks that no one except himself is living in his house, which is clearly the wrong meaning.

Interestingly, the proposal here suffers from a version of this same problem—but in this case the "problem" arises only in the contexts where we find Principle B effects. Thus (23) is unproblematic (Bill himself is not exempted), but we do get the "except for Bill" reading in local cases like (74); I leave it to the interested reader to verify why we get this prediction:

(74) (*a*) Bill_i thinks that no one voted for him_i.

(*b*) Bill_i thinks that no one likes him_i.

In this case, though, it is not clear to me that there is anything pernicious about this prediction. The literature seems to assume that here *no one* literally should not exclude *Bill*. Yet I think our intuitions are not at all clear on this. The prevailing wisdom is to the extent that it "feels like" *no one* does not include Bill. This is for pragmatic reasons—literally the subject is interpreted to be no one including Bill. This is a perfectly reasonable conclusion, but it seems to me to be equally reasonable to assume that the actual literal meaning here does exclude Bill. It is certainly clear that the "no one except Bill" understanding is much more robust in (74) than in (23) (it seems entirely absent in (23)).

6.6.7 *Full NPs in Object Position?*

So far, I have taken the Principle B effect to be relevant only to pronouns in object position, as in (75*a*). But we see (roughly) similar "non-coreference" effects when proper names and other full NPs are in object position, as in (75*b*) or (75*c*)

(75) (*a*) *Bush_i praises him_i.

(*b*) *Bush_i praises Bush_i.

(*c*) *He_i praises Bush_i.

The account developed above says nothing about cases such as (75*b*), and I think that this is probably a good thing. The situations under which names (or full NPs in general) can be coreferential to other names (or pronouns) are very poorly understood. But in any case whatever accounts in general for the appearance of "Principle C" effects will automatically extend to account for (75*b*) and (75*c*) and so I have deliberately confined my account of Principle B effects to be relevant only to the appearance of pronouns in object position.

Suppose, however, that we do find evidence that (75*b*) and (75*c*) go beyond the routine "Principle C" effect and violate some additional principle. Should that turn out to be the case, the analysis here can be extended: we merely say that a verb like *praise* maps into an irreflexive verb if it takes anything but an NP with a reflexive feature on it in object position. For now, however, I will assume that irreflexive *praise* requires only a non-pronominal object.

In the remarks above I appealed to "Principle C" effects to account for (75*a*) and (75*b*). Of course it remains to spell out just what these are. Note that the relevant principle is another apparent counterexample to the hypothesis of direct compositionality since it—like the standard account of Principle B—is stated both non-locally and makes use of indices. But the standard account will turn out to have many of the same problems as were discussed above with respect to Principle B; co-indexation will not rule out the coreferential interpretation in many cases and so a transderivational principle such as (48) will be required. Thus regardless of one's feelings about direct compositionality, one should be suspicious of this kind of account. My hunch is that Principle C effects will derive from constraints on the packaging of information in discourse, as has been argued by, among others, Kuno (1987). If this is the case, these have nothing at all to do with the compositional syntax and semantics (unlike Principle B effects which—if the account above is correct—are located in the semantic/syntactic composition). But this is left for another day.

References

BACH, E. 1979. 'Control in Montague grammar', *Linguistic Inquiry*, 10: 515–32.

—— 1980. 'In defense of passive', *Linguistics and Philosophy*, 3: 297–342.

BÜRING, D. 2005. *Binding Theory*. Cambridge: Cambridge University Press.

CULY, C. 1985. 'The complexity of the vocabulary of Bambara', *Linguistics and Philosophy*, 8: 345–51.

DAHL, Ö. 1974. 'How to open a sentence: abstraction in natural language', in *Logical Grammar Reports*, 12, University of Gothenburg.

DEN DIKKEN, M., MEINUNGER, A., and WILDER, C. 2000. 'Pseudoclefts and ellipsis', *Studia Linguistica*, 54: 41–89.

DOWTY, D. 1980. 'Comments on the paper by Bach and Partee', in J. Kreiman and A. Ojeda (eds), *Papers from the Parasession on Pronouns and Anaphora*. Chicago: Chicago Linguistic Society. 29–40.

—— 1982. 'Grammatical relations and Montague grammar', in P. Jacobson and G. K. Pullum (eds), *The Nature of Syntactic Representation*. Dordrecht: Reidel. 79–130. (Reprinted by Springer, *Classic Titles in Linguistics*, 2006.)

—— 1985. 'On recent analyses of the semantics of control', *Linguistics and Philosophy*, 8: 291–331.

ENGDAHL, E. 1986. *Constituent Questions*. Dordrecht: Reidel.

FIENGO, R. and MAY, R. 1994. *Indices and Identity*. Cambridge, MA: MIT Press.

Fox, D. 2000. *Economy and Semantic Interpretation.* Cambridge, MA: MIT Press.

Gazdar, G., Klein, E., Pullum, G., and Sag, I. 1985. *Generalized Phrase Structure Grammar.* Oxford: Blackwell.

Geach, P. 1972. 'A program for syntax', in D. Davidson and G. Harman (eds), *Semantics of Natural Language.* Dordrecht: Reidel. 483–97.

Grodzinsky, Y. and Reinhart, T. 1993. 'The innateness of binding and coreference', *Linguistic Inquiry*, 24: 69–101.

Groenendijk, J. and Stokhof, M. 1983. 'Interrogative quantifiers and Skolem functions', in K. Ehlich and H. van Riemsdijk (eds), *Connectedness in Sentence, Discourse and Text, Tilburg Studies in Language and Literature* 4. Tilburg: Tilburg University.

Heim, I. 1993. 'Anaphora and semantic interpretation: A reinterpretation of Reinhart's approach', SfS-Report-07-93, University of Tübingen.

—— 1997. 'Predicates or formulas? Evidence from ellipsis', in A. Lawson and E. Cho (eds), *Proceedings of the Seventh Conference on Semantics and Linguistic Theory.* Cornell: CLC Publications. 197–221.

—— and Kratzer, A. 1998. *Semantics in Generative Grammar.* Oxford: Blackwell.

Hoeksema, J. and Janda, R. 1988. 'Implications of process-morphology for Categorial Grammar', in R. Oehrle, E. Bach, and D. Wheeler (eds), *Categorial Grammars and Natural Language Structures.* Dordrecht: Reidel. 199–248.

Jacobson, P. 1987. 'Phrase structure, grammatical relations, and discontinuous constituents', in G. Huck and A. Ojeda (eds), *Syntax and Semantics 20: Discontinuous Constituency.* New York: Academic Press. 27–69.

—— 1990. 'Raising as function composition', *Linguistics and Philosophy*, 13: 423–75.

—— 1992. 'Flexible categorial grammars: Questions and prospects', in R. Levine (ed.), *Formal Grammar: Theory and Implementation.* Oxford: Oxford University Press. 129–167.

—— 1994. 'Binding connectivity in copular sentences', in M. Harvey and L. Santelmann (eds), *Proceedings of the Fourth Conference on Semantics and Linguistic Theory.* Cornell: CLC Publications. 161–78.

—— 1999. 'Towards a variable-free semantics', *Linguistics and Philosophy*, 22: 117–84.

—— 2000. 'Paycheck pronouns, Bach-Peters sentences, and variable-free semantics', *Natural Language Semantics*, 8: 77–155.

—— 2002. 'The (dis)organization of the grammar: 25 years', *Linguistics and Philosophy*, 25: 601–26.

Klein, E. and Sag, I. 1985. 'Type-driven translation', *Linguistics and Philosophy*, 8: 163–201.

Kuno, S. 1987. *Functional Syntax: Anaphora, Discourse, and Empathy.* Chicago: University of Chicago Press.

Montague, R. 1973. 'The proper treatment of quantification in ordinary English', in K. J. J. Hintikka, J. M. E. Moravcsik and P. Suppes (eds), *Approaches to Natural Language.* Dordrecht: Reidel. 221–42.

Partee, B. 1976. 'Some transformational extensions of Montague Grammar', in B. Partee (ed.), *Montague Grammar.* New York: Academic Press. 51–76.

PARTEE, B. and BACH, E. 1981. 'Quantification, pronouns, and VP anaphora', in J. Groenendijk, T. Janssen, and M. Stokhof (eds), *Formal Methods in the Study of Language: Proceedings of the Third Amsterdam Colloquium.* Amsterdam: Mathematisch Centrum. 445–81.

POLLARD, C. 1984. Generalized Phrase Structure Grammars, Head Grammars, and Natural Language. Ph.D. dissertation, Stanford University.

REINHART, T. 1983. *Anaphora and Semantic Interpretation.* London: Croom Helm.

—— 2000. 'Strategies of anaphora resolution', in H. Bennis, M. Everaert, and E. Reuland (eds), *Interface Strategies.* Amsterdam: Royal Netherlands Academy of Arts and Sciences. 295–324.

ROSENBAUM, P. 1967. The Grammar of English Predicate Complement Constructions. Ph.D. dissertation, MIT. Cambridge, MA: MIT Press.

ROSS, J. R. 1972. 'Act', in D. Davidson and G. Harman (eds), *Semantics of Natural Language.* Dordrecht: Reidel. 70–126.

SADOCK, J. 1983. 'The necessary overlapping of grammatical components', in J. F. Richardson, M. Marks, and A. Chukerman (eds), *Papers from the Parasession on the Interplay of Phonology, Morphology, and Syntax.* Chicago: CLS. 198–221.

SCHLENKER, P. 2003. 'Clausal equations (a note on the connectivity problem)', *Natural Language and Linguistic Theory*, 21: 157–214.

—— 2005. 'Non-redundancy: Towards a semantic reinterpretation of binding theory', *Natural Language Semantics*, 13: 1–92.

SHARVIT, Y. 1999. 'Connectivity in specificational sentences', *Natural Language Semantics*, 7: 229–339.

SHIEBER, S. 1985. 'Evidence against the context-freeness of natural language', *Linguistics and Philosophy*, 8: 333–43.

VON STECHOW, A. 1990. 'Layered traces', paper presented at the Conference on Logic and Language, Revfülöp, Hungary.

VIJAY-SHANKER, K., WEIR, D., and JOSHI, A. 1986. 'Adjoining, wrapping, and headed strings', in *Proceedings of the 24th Meeting of the Association for Computational Linguistics.* New York: ACL.

7

The Non-Concealed Nature of Free Relatives: Implications for Connectivity in Specificational Sentences*

IVANO CAPONIGRO AND DAPHNA HELLER

7.1 Introduction

Connectivity is the name for the effect that elements within the pre- and the post-copular phrases in specificational sentences behave as if they were in a c-command configuration, although they are not. This effect is found with a range of syntactic and semantic phenomena, which are therefore referred to as *connectivity effects*. Examples of connectivity effects are the distribution of anaphors and negative polarity items, the availability of opaque readings and binding relations, and Case and agreement markings. The existence of these effects poses a real challenge to direct compositionality, because a direct-compositional analysis of connectivity requires abandoning well-established analyses of these phenomena that are all based on c-command and instead developing new analyses that do not rely on such a notion.

An apparently simpler option is to assume a grammatical operation that posits the desired c-command configuration at an abstract level of representation; this would allow one to maintain the current c-command-based analyses of the different phenomena. This option, which we will generally refer to as the *reconstruction strategy*, has received a number of implementations in the generative literature in the last forty years. One of the main problems with these implementations is the lack of independent motivation for the abstract

* We would like to thank our language consultants without whom this work would not have been possible: Slavica Kochovska, Aniko Liptak, Orr Ravitz, Heather Robinson, Maryame Sy, Anna Szabolcsi, Harold Torrence, and the native speakers of English at the UCLA linguistics department. A slightly different version of this paper appeared as Chapter 2 in Heller (2005).

level of representation. A promising implementation of the reconstruction strategy is the so-called "question–answer" approach, originally due to Ross (1972), which takes specificational sentences to be question–answer pairs. Under this approach, the desired c-command configuration is restored in the post-copular full answer. The "question–answer" approach is particularly attractive because positing the desired c-command configuration is independently motivated by the status of the post-copular phrase as a full answer.

Two versions of the question–answer approach have been proposed recently. Den Dikken *et al.* (2000) analyze the pre-copular phrase as a question syntactically and semantically, while Schlenker (2003) and Romero (2005, this volume) propose that the pre-copular phrase is syntactically a nominal and is only interpreted as a question, that is, it is a "concealed question".

This paper argues against the question–answer approach to specificational sentences by presenting cross-linguistic data showing that the pre-copular phrase in a specificational sentence is not a question, neither syntactically nor semantically. We focus on the status of the pre-copular phrase as a question because it stands at the core of the question–answer approach. If the pre-copular phrase in a specificational sentence is not a question, there is no motivation to posit a post-copular full answer that has the desired c-command configuration.

The paper is organized as follows. We begin by presenting the range of connectivity effects in §7.2 and then briefly review the direct compositionality strategy and the reconstruction strategy in §7.3. Section 7.4 presents cross-linguistic data showing that the *wh*-clause in the pre-copular position of a specificational sentence is not an embedded *wh*-interrogative, contra den Dikken *et al.*; instead, we argue that it is a free relative. Section 7.5 argues against the concealed question version of the question–answer approach, namely, against Schlenker's (2003) and Romero's (2005, this volume) implementations, in which the pre-copular nominal in a specificational sentence, whether a free relative or a headed nominal, is a syntactic nominal that is interpreted as a question. We conclude that this attractive version of the reconstruction strategy to connectivity, that is, the question–answer approach, suffers from the same weakness as the others: the lack of independent motivation for positing the desired c-command relation at an abstract level.

7.2 Connectivity Effects

This section presents the full range of connectivity effects: our goal is to illustrate the diversity of this group of syntactic and semantic phenomena which is important for understanding the conceptual difference between the direct compositionality strategy and the reconstruction strategy. What these phenomena have in common is that they are usually found only under a c-command configuration, but in specificational sentences they occur even though this configuration is absent.

7.2.1 *"Binding Theory" Connectivity*

This group of connectivity effects deals with the distribution of anaphoric elements—the terminology of Binding Theory (Chomsky 1981) is borrowed only in order to label the generalizations regarding different anaphors. The examples in (1) illustrate Principle A connectivity: the anaphor *himself* is licensed in the post-copular phrase, even though it is not c-commanded by its antecedent *John* which is embedded inside the pre-copular phrase. In the examples in (2), the pronoun *him* cannot take the nominal *John* as its antecedent, even though the desired antecedent does not c-command the pronoun. Finally, in the examples in (3), the pronoun *he* and the nominal *John* cannot corefer, even though they are not in a c-command relation.

(1) *Principle A connectivity*

(*a*) [What John is _] is proud of himself.

(*b*) [The person John likes most _] is himself.

(2) *Principle B connectivity*

(*a*) *[What John_i is _] is proud of him_i.

(*b*) *[The person John_i likes most _] is him_i.

(3) *Principle C connectivity (from Sharvit 1999)*

(*a*) *[What he_i is _] is a nuisance to John_i.

(*b*) *[The people he_i saw _] were John_i and some of Mary's friends.

Notice that in each pair example (*a*) has a pre-copular *wh*-clause, that is, it is a pseudocleft, and example (*b*) has a headed nominal in the same position. As pointed out as early as Higgins (1973), connectivity effects are not special to pseudoclefts, but are found in all specificational sentences. We will show the same below for the other connectivity effects.

7.2.2 *Opacity Connectivity*

De dicto readings are usually available only in opaque contexts, that is, under the scope of an intensional operator, where scope is defined in terms of c-command. In (4), the nominal *a pink giraffe* in the post-copular phrase has a *de dicto* reading, that is, the existence of pink giraffes is not entailed, even though the nominal is not in the scope of the intensional predicate *look for*, which is embedded inside the pre-copular phrase. A *de re* reading, where the existence of pink giraffes is entailed, is also available.

(4) (*a*) [What John is looking for _] is a pink giraffe.

(*b*) [The only thing that John is looking for _] is a good job.

7.2.3 *NPI Connectivity*

It is standardly assumed that Negative Polarity Items (NPIs) like *any* can only occur in restricted environments, one of which is under the scope of negation, where scope is usually defined in terms of c-command. In the specificational sentences in (5), *any* is licensed despite the fact that it is not c-commanded by the negation. That negation is indeed the licensor is illustrated by the contrast with the sentences in (6): the lack of negation leads to ungrammaticality.

(5) (*a*) [What John didn't buy _] was any books. (Sharvit 1999)

(*b*) [The one thing he didn't do _] was buy any wine. (den Dikken *et al.* 2000)

(6) (*a*) *[What John bought _] was any books.

(*b*) *[The one thing he did _] was buy any wine.

7.2.4 *Bound Variable Connectivity*

The usual configuration of a quantified expression binding a pronoun is c-command.[1] Nonetheless, both *no man* and *no student* can bind *his* in (7), although in both cases such configuration is absent (both examples are from Sharvit 1999).

(7) (*a*) [The women [no man]$_i$ listens to _] are his$_i$ wife and his$_i$ mother-in-law.

(*b*) [What [no student]$_i$ enjoys _] is his$_i$ finals.

7.2.5 *Case Connectivity*

Case is usually assigned locally under a c-command configuration, but in specificational sentences the post-copular phrase is marked for the same Case assigned to the gap position in the pre-copular phrase. The examples in (8) illustrate this connectivity effect in Hebrew, where definite direct objects must be marked by *et*. The post-copular constituent in the specificational

[1] We only discuss specificational sentences here, but bound variable connectivity is also found in predicational sentences—see Sharvit (1997, 1999).

pseudoclefts in (8) is neither a subject nor a direct object,[2] nevertheless it exhibits the same restrictions on the distribution of *et* as the gap in the pre-copular *wh*-clause: when the gap is in direct object position, *et* must precede the post-copular phrase (8*a*), and when the gap is in subject position, *et* cannot mark the post-copular phrase (8*b*).

(8) (*a*) *Object gap*

[ma še-kaninu ba-šuk _] ze *(et) ha- sveder ha-kaxol
what that-we-bought in-the-market is Acc the-sweater the-blue
'What we bought at the market was the blue sweater.'

(*b*) *Subject gap*

[ma še _ nafal alay] ze (*et) ha-sveder ha-kaxol
what that fell on-me is Acc the-sweater the-blue
'What fell on me was the blue sweater.'

7.2.6 *Agreement Connectivity*

Like Case assignment, agreement is usually local, but in specificational sentences the post-copular phrase exhibits agreement with the subject inside the pre-copular *wh*-clause even though there is no c-command relation between the agreeing elements. The examples in (9) illustrate agreement connectivity in Hebrew, where a predicate obligatorily agrees with the subject in number and gender. In (9*a*), the post-copular predicate must be feminine in accordance with the gender of the subject inside the free relative, whereas in (9*b*) the post-copular predicate must be masculine in accordance with the masculine subject inside the free relative (examples are from Heller 2002).

(9) (*a*) [ma še-**rut** hayta _] ze {*mo'il / **mo'ila**} la-xevra
what that-Ruth was(f) is *helpful(m) / helpful(f) to-the-society
'What Ruth was was helpful to society.'

(*b*) [ma še-**dan** haya _] ze {**mo'il** /*mo'ila} la-xevra
what that-Dan was(m) is helpful(m)/*helpful(f) to-the-society
'What Dan was was helpful to society.'

All the examples above show the two main properties of connectivity effects: their extremely heterogeneous nature and the lack of the c-command relation, which is otherwise assumed to license these effects.

2 Unless the copula is analyzed as a standard transitive verb. But then we would expect the post-copular phrase to be marked Accusative in all cases and not just when the position of the gap in the pre-copular phrase is in object position—(8*b*) shows that this is not the case.

7.3 Direct Compositionality and Connectivity

As we mentioned earlier, there are two main strategies to approach connectivity: the direct compositionality strategy and the reconstruction strategy. The two crucially differ in their perspective on the implications of the existence of connectivity effects. The reconstruction strategy takes the fact that all these phenomena are otherwise licensed under c-command to indicate that c-command is available in specificational sentences as well. Since no c-command is found on the surface, it must be available at an abstract level. Positing c-command at an abstract level derives all connectivity effects at once.[3] Direct compositionality, on the other hand, takes the heterogeneous syntactic and semantic nature of connectivity effects as evidence that they do not constitute a single phenomenon and, therefore, call for a revision of the analyses that rely on c-command.

A non-structural analysis of various connectivity effects has been developed by Jacobson (1994), Sharvit (1999), Cecchetto (2000), and Heller (2002). In this strategy, specificational sentences are an equation between the pre- and post-copular phrases as they appear on the surface, and connectivity effects arise as a by-product of semantic equation. For instance, following Jacobson (1994), Principle A connectivity in (1*a*) (repeated below as (10*a*)) is the result of equating a free relative denoting a maximal predicate with the post-copular reflexive predicate (10*b*).

(10) (*a*) [What John is _] is proud of himself.

(*b*) $\iota P[P(j)] = \lambda x.\text{proud-of}'(x,x)$ (Jacobson 1994)

Analyses of other phenomena that show up as connectivity effects have been developed for bound variable connectivity (Jacobson 1994), opacity connectivity (Sharvit 1999), effects pertaining to quantifier scope (Cecchetto 2000), and Case and agreement connectivity (Heller 2002). At this point, the main challenge for direct compositionality is to account for NPI connectivity (which has been shown by den Dikken *et al.* (2000) to be non-reversible—see §7.4) and for the distribution of pronouns and proper names, that is for Principle B and Principle C connectivity, which requires a non-structural analysis of the distribution of anaphors.

A reconstruction analysis of connectivity has been proposed as early as Peters and Bach (1968). They posit a level of representation at which the post-copular phrase is surrounded by a copy of the free relative, as in (11*b*). In a different analysis, Hornstein (1984) proposes that the c-command relation is

[3] This may not always be a desirable result, because of the existence of anti-connectivity effects (see Sharvit 1999) and also because of the existence of connectivity patterns like the Hebrew one, where different kinds of pseudoclefts exhibit a different subset of connectivity effects—see Heller (2002).

achieved by having the post-copular phrase in the position of the gap inside the free relative, as in (11*c*).

(11) (*a*) [What John$_i$ is _] is proud of himself$_i$.

(*b*) [What John$_i$ is _] is John$_i$ is proud of himself$_i$.

(*c*) [What John$_i$ is proud of himself$_i$] is proud of himself$_i$.

These analyses face a number of problems—see Higgins (1973, Ch. 2) for the earliest discussion. But the main objection to deriving connectivity in this way is that the level of representation at which the c-command relation is posited makes little semantic sense and is also not independently motivated—it is specifically tailored to account for connectivity.

A more recent mechanism for deriving connectivity effects is Heycock and Kroch's (1999) "iota-reduction", which manipulates the logical representation of a specificational pseudocleft post LF, turning it into the corresponding simple sentence. This is illustrated in (12*b*) for the pseudocleft in (12*a*).

(12) (*a*) [What John$_i$ is _] is proud of himself$_i$.

(*b*) (ιP: John is P) = proud-of-himself $\rightarrow$ John is proud of himself

As pointed out in Schlenker (2003), this account of connectivity also faces the problem that it is not independently motivated. That is, Heycock and Kroch do not present independent evidence for positing the additional level of representation beyond LF.[4]

The advantage of the question–answer approach over other reconstruction analyses is that it derives connectivity effects using mechanisms that already exist in the grammar. In particular, the reason for reconstruction is not particular to specificational sentences, but rather it is based on similarities with question–answer pairs. The resemblance of the *wh*-clause in specificational pseudoclefts in English to an embedded *wh*-interrogative has led Ross (1972, 1997) to propose that specificational pseudoclefts like the one in (13*a*) are analyzed as in (13*b*), that is, as an equation between a *wh*-question Q (14*a*) and an elided (or short) answer ANS (14*c*), which is assumed to be derived from the full answer (14*b*) by a process of phonological deletion.

(13) (*a*) What John is is proud of himself.

(*b*) [$_{\text{Q}}$ What John is] is [$_{\text{ANS}}$ ~~John$_i$ is~~ proud of himself$_i$].

(14) (*a*) [$_{\text{Q}}$ What is John$_i$]? *Question*

(*b*) John$_i$ is proud of himself$_i$. *Full answer*

(*c*) [$_{\text{ANS}}$ ~~John$_i$ is~~ proud of himself$_i$]. *Short answer according to Ross*

[4] In addition, not all specificational sentences have a "corresponding" simple sentence.

According to this analysis, we hear the short answer, but we compute the full answer as far as grammatical principles are concerned. This is crucial, since it is in the full answer that the relevant c-command configuration is found.

A similar account can be given to other connectivity effects we have seen here, as schematically shown in (15)–(19).

(15) *Principle B*

(*a*) What is John$_i$? *~~John~~$_i$ ~~is~~ proud of him$_i$.

(*b*) *[$_Q$ What John$_i$ is] is [$_{ANS}$ ~~John~~$_i$ ~~is~~ proud of him$_i$].

(16) *Principle C*

(*a*) What is he$_i$? *~~He is~~ proud of John$_i$.

(*b*) *[$_Q$ What he$_i$ is] is [$_{ANS}$ ~~he~~$_i$ ~~is~~ proud of John$_i$].

(17) *Opacity*

(*a*) What is John looking for? ~~John is looking for~~ a pink giraffe.

(*b*) [$_Q$What John is looking for] is [$_{ANS}$ ~~John is looking for~~ a pink giraffe].

(18) *NPI*

(*a*) What didn't John buy? ~~John didn't buy~~ any books.

(*b*) [$_Q$ What John didn't buy] was [$_{ANS}$ ~~John didn't buy~~ any books].

(19) *Bound variable*

(*a*) What does [no student]$_i$ enjoy? ~~[No student]~~$_i$ ~~enjoys~~ his$_i$ finals.

(*b*) [$_Q$ What [no student]$_i$ enjoys] is [$_{ANS}$ ~~[No student]~~$_i$ ~~enjoys~~ his$_i$ finals].

To support the existence of question–answer equations, Ross presents examples in which the post-copular answer is not elided:

(20) (*a*) What I did then was [call the grocer]. (Ross 1972)

(*b*) What I did then was [I called the grocer].

(21) (*a*) What John did was [buy some wine]. (den Dikken *et al.* 2000)

(*b*) What John did was [he bought some wine].

The logic is that in order to account for the existence of (20*b*) and (21*b*), one has to assume that the grammar allows for question–answer pairs in copular sentences. Having a pair of a question and an elided answer, as in (20*a*) and (21*a*), comes "for free" due to the independent existence of ellipsis in answers. That is, these examples show that analyzing specificational sentences as question–answer pairs does not involve postulating new mechanisms in the grammar.

Two versions of the question–answer analysis have been proposed recently. Den Dikken *et al.* (2000) analyze the pre-copular phrase as a question syntactically and semantically, while Schlenker (2003) and Romero (2005, this volume) propose that the pre-copular phrase is syntactically a nominal and is only interpreted as a question, that is, it is a "concealed question". In what follows, we examine the status of the pre-copular phrase in specificational sentences and conclude that there is no evidence that it is a question syntactically, contra den Dikken *et al.*, or semantically, contra Schlenker and Romero.

The reason for focusing on the status of the pre-copular phrase as a question is that it constitutes the motivation for the question–answer approach. If the pre-copular phrase in a specificational sentence is not a question, then the post-copular phrase cannot be an answer and we cannot explain connectivity by relating it to parallel effects found in question–answer pairs. In addition, since being an answer concerns the discourse status of an indicative sentence but is not marked syntactically or semantically, it is easier to examine whether the pre-copular phrase is a question, since questions are expected to have certain syntactic and/or semantic properties.

It should be pointed out that our goal is not to determine whether there exist question–answer pairs in copular sentences. That such sentences exist has already been demonstrated by Ross—see again (20) and (21) above. In fact, the existence of question–answer pairs in copular sentences is predicted by any theory that assumes a cross-categorial "*be* of identity". Rather, our goal is to assess the claim that question–answer pairs are responsible for connectivity.

The next section shows that the *wh*-clause in a specificational pseudocleft is syntactically a free relative and not a *wh*-interrogative, contra what has originally been proposed by Ross (1972) and argued for by den Dikken *et al.* (2000). Then, in §7.5, we show that the pre-copular phrase in a specificational sentence is also not interpreted like a question, contra Schlenker's and Romero's versions of the question–answer approach.

7.4 The *Wh*-Clause in Specificational Pseudoclefts is Syntactically not a Question

Den Dikken *et al.* (2000) adopt Ross's (1972) original idea and analyze specificational pseudoclefts as "self-answering questions". In their analysis, the pre-copular *wh*-clause is an embedded *wh*-interrogative and the post-copular phrase is an (obligatorily) elided full IP that answers the question in the pre-copular *wh*-interrogative. Their primary motivation comes from Ross's examples in which the post-copular IP is not elided—see again examples (20)–(21). Note, crucially that the existence of question–full answer pairs as we saw in (20*a*) and (21*a*) only shows that such copular sentences are allowed by the grammar. It does not show that specificational sentences are such question–answer pairs.

Den Dikken *et al.* distinguish this type of pseudocleft (which they call "Type A") from reversed pseudoclefts ("Type B"), which they analyze as predicational sentences in which the predicate is a free relative. This distinction is motivated by the irreversibility of NPI connectivity. In particular, they notice that NPIs are licensed in the post-copular phrase by the negation inside the pre-copular *wh*-clause, as in (22*a*) and (23*a*), but reversing the order of the elements around the copula renders the sentences ungrammatical, as in (22*b*) and (23*b*), that is, the NPI in the pre-copular phrase is not licensed by the negation inside the post-copular *wh*-clause.

(22) (*a*) What John didn't buy was any books. **Type A**

(a′) [What John didn't buy] was [$_{\text{IP}}$ ~~he didn't buy~~ any books]

(*b*) *[$_{\text{DP}}$ Any book] is/was [what John didn't buy]. **Type B**

(23) (*a*) What wasn't available was a doctor who knew anything about babies.

(a′) [What wasn't available] was [$_{\text{IP}}$ ~~there wasn't available~~ a doctor who knew anything about babies].

(*b*) *[$_{\text{DP}}$ A doctor who knew anything about babies] was [what wasn't available].

Taking as their starting point the standard assumption that NPIs are licensed by a c-commanding negation, den Dikken *et al.* assume that the licensing of an NPI in (22*a*) and (23*a*) indicates that negation is present in a c-commanding position, and hence conclude that the post-copular phrase is an elided full IP. Den Dikken *et al.* claim that the ungrammaticality of (22*b*) and (23*b*) suggests that the pre-copular phrase in Type B pseudoclefts is not an elided IP but rather an XP—a DP in the examples here.

This section is not intended to review den Dikken *et al.*'s arguments. Instead, it presents cross-linguistic data arguing that the *wh*-clause in a specificational pseudocleft is not an embedded interrogative, but rather a free relative. Our logic is that if the pre-copular phrase is not a question, then the post-copular phrase cannot be an answer, so we lose the motivation for reconstructing a full IP in the post-copular position.

7.4.1 *Morphological Differences Between* wh-*interrogatives and Specificational Pseudoclefts*

The resemblance of the *wh*-clause in a specificational pseudocleft in English to an embedded *wh*-interrogative has led den Dikken *et al.* (2000) to analyze it as syntactically a *wh*-interrogative. In English, embedded *wh*-interrogatives and free relatives look identical, but other languages distinguish the two constructions overtly. We present data from Macedonian, Hungarian, Wolof, and Hebrew showing that in those languages the *wh*-clause in the pre-copular position of a specificational pseudocleft is a free relative.

In Macedonian, free relatives differ from embedded interrogatives in that they are introduced by *ona* "that". When the *wh*-clause occurs in the complement of *kazhi* "tell", as in (24*a*), *ona* cannot occur, and when the same *wh*-clause occurs in the complement of *sakam* "love", as in (24*b*), *ona* must occur. Crucially, *ona* is also obligatory in the specificational pseudocleft in (24*c*): this pseudocleft is made sure to be specificational as it exhibits Principle A connectivity.

(24) MACEDONIAN

(*a*) *Embedded interrogative*

Kazhi mi [(*ona) shto navistina Petar saka].
tell me that what really Petar love
'Tell me what Petar really loves.'

(*b*) *Free relative*

(Jas) sakam [*(ona) shto Petar saka].
I love that what Petar loves
'I love what Petar loves.'

(*c*) *Specificational pseudocleft*

[*(Ona) shto Petar saka] e samiot sebe si.
that what Petar loves is alone himself
'What Petar loves is himself.'

In Hungarian, the words that introduce free relatives are characterized by a prefix *a*- that make them distinguishable from the *wh*-words that introduce interrogatives. In (25*a*) the *wh*-clause occurs as the complement of *mondd* 'tell', that is it is an interrogative (INT), and in (25*b*) the *wh*-clause occurs as the complement of *megettem* "ate", that is, it is a free relative (FR). While in the former environment only *mit* "what" is possible, the opposite pattern is observed in the latter environment, that is, only *amit* "what" can occur. Crucially, only *amit* can occur in the specificational pseudocleft in (25*c*). It is important to point out that (25*c*) is ambiguous between a *de dicto* and a *de re* reading, that is, it exhibits opacity connectivity.

(25) HUNGARIAN

(*a*) *Embedded interrogative*

Mondd meg [***amit/mit** fo"zött]
tell me what$_{FR}$/what$_{INT}$ cooked
'Tell me what he cooked.'

(*b*) *Free relative*

Megettem [**amit/*****mit** fo"zött]
I-ate what$_{FR}$/what$_{INT}$ cooked
'I ate what he cooked.'

(*c*) *Specificational pseudocleft*

[**Amit/*****mit** keres _] az Chomsky legújabb könyve
What$_{FR}$/What$_{INT}$ is-looking-for that C.'s latest book
'What he is looking for is Chomsky's latest book.'

In Wolof, a Niger-Congo West Atlantic language spoken mainly in Senegal and Gambia, the (contracted) *wh*-words result from combining the many classifiers of the language with the suffix *-u*, while the words that introduce free relatives are formed by adding the suffix *-i* to the same classifiers. Again, we compare the clause that occurs as the complement of an interrogative-taking verb like *yëg* "found out" in (26*a*) with that of an individual-taking verb like *bañ* "hate" in (26*b*). The former predicate only allows for a clause introduced by *l-u*, which is an interrogative, while the latter requires a clause introduced by *l-i*, which is a free relative. Crucially, the specificational pseudocleft in (26*c*), which exhibits Principle A connectivity, allows only for the free-relative version with *l-i*.[5]

(26) WOLOF

(*a*) *Embedded interrogative*

yëg -na [***l-i /l-u** móódu gën-ë bëgg].
find out-neutral cl-FR/cl-INT[6] Moodu surpass-inf like
'She found out what Moodu likes most.'

(*b*) *Free relative*

bañ-na [**l-i /*****l-u** móódu gën-ë bëgg].
hate-neutral cl-FR/cl-INT Moodu surpass-inf like
'She hates what Moodu likes most.'

[5] Many thanks to Harold Torrence for collecting and analyzing the Wolof data.

[6] *cl-FR*: classifier + free relative morpheme; *cl-INT*: classifier + interrogative morpheme.

(*c*) *Specificational pseudocleft*

[**l-i** /***l-u** móódu gën-ë bëgg _] bopp-am la.
cl-FR/cl-INT Moodu surpass-inf like head-3sgposs be
'What Moodu likes most is himself.'

In Hebrew, free relatives are distinguished morphologically from *wh*-interrogatives in that they require the occurrence of the complementizer *še*. In the complement position of the verb *berer* "inquired" in (27*a*), the *wh*-clause cannot contain the complementizer. In the complement position of the verb *kara* "read" in (27*b*), the complementizer *še* must occur. The specificational pseudocleft in (27*c*) patterns with (27*b*) in that it requires the occurrence of the complementizer—this sentence is ensured to be a specificational pseudocleft as it exhibits both Principle A connectivity and Case connectivity.

(27) HEBREW

(*a*) *Embedded interrogative* (from Sharvit 1999)

dan berer [ma (***še**)-karati]
Dan inquired what $\text{that}_{\text{COMP}}$-(I)-read
'Dan inquired what I read.'

(*b*) *Free relative* (from Sharvit 1999)

dan kara [ma *(**še**)-karati]
Dan read what $\text{that}_{\text{COMP}}$-(I)-read
'Dan read what I read.'

(*c*) *Specificational pseudocleft*

[ma *(**še**)-dan ohev _] ze et acmo
what $\text{that}_{\text{COMP}}$-Dan loves is Acc himself
'What Dan loves is himself.'

The data presented here show that when a language overtly distinguishes *wh*-interrogatives from free relatives, the *wh*-clause in a specificational pseudocleft takes the form of the free relative and not that of the interrogative.

Den Dikken *et al.* (2000) also mention languages that show a similar pattern to that presented here for Hebrew, Wolof, Hungarian, and Macedonian (their footnote 23). In particular, they cite Bulgarian (following Izvorski 1997) and Greek (following Alexiadou and Giannakidou 1998) as languages that distinguish interrogatives and free relatives overtly and employ only the latter in specificational pseudoclefts. Den Dikken *et al.* propose analyzing these cases as their "Type B" pseudoclefts, that is, as simple copular sentences that do not involve questions and answers. The same analysis can be applied to the languages discussed here. But this would leave us with six languages (mostly genetically unrelated) in which den Dikken *et al.*'s analysis does not apply. Even if there are languages in which the *wh*-clause in a specificational sentence is an embedded interrogative, as proposed by den Dikken *et al.*, this is not true of specificational pseudoclefts cross-linguistically and therefore cannot be used as a general account of connectivity.

7.4.2 *The Range of* Wh-*Words in Free Relatives and Interrogatives*

But even in a language such as English where free relatives and *wh*-interrogatives are not distinguished overtly, it is possible to observe differences between the two constructions. In particular, the range of *wh*-words that occur in free relatives is a *subset* of those found in embedded *wh*-interrogatives. Crucially, this is the same subset of *wh*-words that occur in the pre-copular *wh*-clause of specificational pseudoclefts.

The examples in (28) present the range of *wh*-words in embedded interrogatives. In the examples in (29), the same *wh*-words are used in *wh*-clauses in the complement position of non-interrogative predicates, that is, free relatives. What we see is that free relatives introduced by *what* (29*a*) and *where* (29*b*) are judged fully acceptable, while free relatives introduced by *who* are marginal (29*c*) and free relatives introduced by complex *wh*-expressions such as *which*+NP or *how much* are completely unacceptable (29*d*, 29*e*). The specificational pseudoclefts in (30) exhibit exactly the same restriction on *wh*-words as free relatives (for more on the range of *wh*-words in free relatives see Caponigro 2003).

(28) *Embedded interrogatives*

- (*a*) I wonder [**where** she has lunch].
- (*b*) I wonder [**what** John is reading].
- (*c*) I wonder [**who** gave you the flowers].
- (*d*) I wonder [**which** book John is reading].
- (*e*) I wonder [**how much** Sue weighs].

(29) *Free relatives*

- (*a*) I have lunch [**where** she has lunch].
- (*b*) I read [**what** John is reading].
- (*c*) ?? I met [**who** gave you the flowers].

(*d*) * I read [**which** book John is reading].

(*e*) * I weigh [**how much** Sue weighs].

(30) *Specificational pseudoclefts*

(*a*) [**Where** she has lunch] is at the cafeteria.

(*b*) [**What** John is reading] is "Ulysses".

(*c*) ?? [**Who** gave you the flowers] was your advisor.

(*d*) * [**Which** book John is reading] is "Ulysses".

(*e*) * [**How much** Sue weighs] is 130 pounds.

These data show that although in English the *wh*-clause in specificational pseudoclefts seems to be morphologically identical to embedded interrogatives, a closer examination of this *wh*-clause shows that it patterns with free relatives and not with interrogatives.

It should be pointed out that den Dikken *et al.* (2000) do mention in a footnote the difference between the range of *wh*-words in embedded interrogatives and in specificational pseudoclefts. However, they attribute this fact to a restriction on the kinds of interrogatives that can appear in specificational pseudoclefts. Unfortunately, they do not offer any insight as to what this restriction may be, so at this point it is merely a stipulation.

7.4.3 *Headed Nominals as Embedded* Wh-*Interrogatives?*

Recall from §7.2 that connectivity effects are also available in specificational sentences in which the pre-copular phrase is a headed nominal rather than a *wh*-clause. In these cases, it is not clear that the pre-copular phrase is an interrogative in any syntactic sense. Den Dikken *et al.* propose that these nominals are in fact elided embedded interrogatives. For example, they propose that the non-pseudoclefted specificational sentence in (31*a*) is derived from (31*b*).

(31) (*a*) The one thing he didn't do was buy any wine.

(*b*) [$_{CP}$ ~~What~~ [the one thing he didn't do] ~~was~~ *t*] was [~~he didn't~~ buy any wine].

As noted by the authors, pursuing this analysis requires an explanation "for why ellipsis of this sort . . . is restricted to the 'topic' questions of specificational pseudoclefts" (den Dikken *et al.* 2000: 83). In other words, the authors acknowledge that the suggested ellipsis is highly specialized: it only applies to *wh*-interrogatives and only occurs in the pre-copular position of specificational sentences. While this may turn out to be a necessary kind of ellipsis, den Dikken *et al.* do not present any independent evidence that this is indeed the case. At this point, then, their suggestion is just a stipulation.

7.4.4 *Conclusions*

Den Dikken *et al.*'s version of the question–answer approach where the pre-copular phrase in a specificational sentence is analyzed as an embedded interrogative is only applicable to a very limited number of cases and requires several stipulations. First, it does not apply to languages where the *wh*-clause is clearly distinguishable from an embedded interrogative. We have mentioned six such languages: Macedonian, Hungarian, Wolof, Hebrew, Bulgarian, and Greek. Second, even in the languages like English in which the *wh*-clause in specificational sentences has the same form as an embedded interrogative, it is necessary to stipulate that certain *wh*-words cannot occur in specificational sentences, although they can in interrogatives. Third, the analysis can apply to specificational sentences with a headed nominal in the pre-copular position, rather than a *wh*-clause, only if an *ad hoc* ellipsis process is stipulated. The number of stipulations required in applying this analysis to specificational sentences is a strong indication that it is not on the right track.

The next section turns to consider a version of the question–answer analysis that avoids the problems raised here by analyzing the pre-copular phrase in a specificational sentence as a syntactic nominal and assuming that this nominal is interpreted as a question.

7.5 The Subject of a Specificational Sentence is not Interpreted as a Question

Schlenker (2003) acknowledges that the *wh*-clause in a specificational pseudocleft is syntactically not an interrogative, but rather a free relative. To maintain the question–answer analysis, Schlenker proposes that these free relatives, as well as all the headed nominals that occur in the pre-copular position of specificational sentences, are interpreted as questions. Interpreting the pre-copular phrase as a question motivates positing a post-copular answer. In Schlenker's analysis, this answer is an (obligatorily elided) full IP in which the desired c-command configuration is available.

How can the subject of a specificational pseudocleft be interpreted as a question if syntactically it is not an interrogative, but rather a nominal, whether a free relative or a headed nominal? It is known since the work of Baker (1968) that some English headed nominals can function as "concealed questions", that is be interpreted like questions, in a certain environment (see the Appendix for more on which headed nominals can be interpreted as concealed questions). The canonical environment for concealed question nominals is the complement position of (certain) interrogative-taking predicates. This is illustrated in (32)–(35) where the (a) examples are embedded *wh*-interrogatives and the (b) examples are the corresponding concealed question nominals (Baker 1968: 81).

(32) (*a*) Jane figured out [$_{CP}$what the plane's arrival time is].

(*b*) Jane figured out [$_{DP}$ the plane's arrival time].

(33) (*a*) John refused to tell the police [$_{CP}$who the fellows who have been involved were].

(*b*) John refused to tell the police [$_{DP}$ the fellows who have been involved].

(34) (*a*) Susan found out [$_{CP}$what the place where the meeting was to be held is].

(*b*) Susan found out [$_{DP}$ the place where the meeting was to be held].

(35) (*a*) Fred tried to guess [$_{CP}$what the amount of the stolen money was].

(*b*) Fred tried to guess [$_{DP}$ the amount of the stolen money].

While the complements in both the (a) and the (b) examples are interpreted as questions, they take different syntactic forms. Schlenker's proposal is that (i) the pre-copular position of a specificational sentence is another concealed question environment and (ii) both headed nominals and free relatives can be interpreted as concealed questions in this environment. Support for this analysis comes from Romero (2005, this volume), who presents interpretive similarities between headed nominals that can occur in both the canonical concealed question environment and the pre-copular position of specificational sentences. However, we will see that many nominals that occur in pre-copular position of specificational sentences are banned from the canonical concealed question environment and thus Romero's arguments are relevant only for a small subset of specificational sentences.

We present three arguments against the concealed question versions of the question–answer approach. First, we show that the availability of connectivity effects is not always associated with concealed question interpretations cross-linguistically, since there is at least one language—Macedonian—that exhibits connectivity and yet does not allow for concealed questions (§7.5.1). Then, we point out distributional differences between the pre-copular position of specificational sentences and the canonical concealed question environment (§7.5.2). In particular, we show that free relatives can occur in the pre-copular position of specificational sentences, but they are banned from the canonical concealed question environment (§7.5.2.1). Similarly, we show that some headed nominals that can occur in the pre-copular position of specificational sentences are unacceptable in the canonical concealed question environment (§7.5.2.2). Then, we discuss interpretive differences between *wh*-clauses that can occur in both environments and conclude that free relatives do not receive a concealed question interpretation in the pre-copular position of specificational sentences (§7.5.3).

7.5.1 *Argument I: Connectivity Without Concealed Questions*

If connectivity effects depended on the concealed question interpretation of nominals, we would expect any language that exhibits connectivity to have nominals that are interpreted as concealed questions in the canonical concealed question environment. The Macedonian data below show that this prediction is not borne out. Example (36) shows that Macedonian has specificational sentences. This is illustrated by the availability of two kinds of connectivity effects: Principle A connectivity and Opacity connectivity.

(36) (*a*) *Principle A connectivity*

[Ona shto Petar saka _] e samiot sebe si.
that what Petar loves is alone himself
'What Petar loves is himself.'

(*b*) *Opacity connectivity*

[Ona shto Petar bara _] e najnovata kniga od Chomsky.
that what Petar look-for is latest-the book by Chomksy
'What Petar is looking for is Chomsky's latest book.'

However, no nominals in Macedonian can be interpreted as concealed questions. Example (37) shows that even nominals that are easily interpreted as concealed questions in English and other languages do not receive a concealed question interpretation in Macedonian. When these nominals occur in the canonical concealed question environment, for example the complement position of the predicate *kazhi* 'tell', the resulting sentences are totally unacceptable.

(37) (*a*) * Kazhi mi go {saatot / chasot / vremeto}.
tell me it hour-the / hour-the / time-the
('Tell me the time.')

(*b*) * Kazhi mi ja {tezhinata / tvojata tezhina}.
tell me it weight-the / your-the weight
('Tell me your weight.')

(*c*) * Kazhi mi ja {goleminata / tvojata golemina} na chevlite.
tell me it size-the / your-the size-the of shoes-the
('Tell me your shoe size.')

The predicate *kazhi* "tell" was chosen because the correlates of *tell* cross-linguistically seem to be the most permissive in allowing concealed question nominals. In addition, we also checked a number of other predicates that can take interrogative complements—*prashuva* "wonder", *otkrie* "discover" and *doznava* "found out"—but none of them allowed for concealed question nominals.

This pattern suggests that the concealed question version of the question–answer analysis cannot account for connectivity cross-linguistically, as connectivity is found in languages that do not allow for concealed question nominals. It is still logically possible that Macedonian has a concealed question interpretation that is specific to the pre-copular position of specificational sentences. We examine this possibility, albeit for English, in §7.5.2.2.

7.5.2 *Argument II: Distributional Difference between the Canonical Concealed Question Environment and the Pre-Copular Position in Specificational Sentences*

If the pre-copular position of specificational sentences is a concealed question environment, we expect parallelisms with the canonical concealed question environment in the kinds of expressions they host. Contra this prediction, this section shows that not all nominals that occur in the pre-copular position of specificational sentences can also occur in the canonical concealed question environment, that is, as complements of interrogative-taking verbs. This is shown for free relatives in §7.5.2.1. and for headed nominals in §7.5.2.2.

7.5.2.1 *Free Relatives* As pointed out by Sharvit (1999), parallelisms between the pre-copular position of specificational pseudoclefts and the canonical concealed question environment can only be tested in languages that (i) distinguish free relatives and *wh*-interrogatives morphologically and (ii) allow for concealed question nominals. Sharvit tests this prediction for Hebrew, which allows concealed question nominals, as in (38*a*). Not surprisingly, embedded *wh*-interrogatives can freely occur in this position (38*b*), but, crucially, free relatives cannot. Recall from example (27) in §7.4.1 that free relatives in Hebrew differ from *wh*-interrogatives in the presence of the complementizer *še*.

(38) Hebrew

(*a*) *Concealed question*

dan berer et [$_{DP}$ ha-sha'a].
Dan inquired Acc the-hour
'Dan inquired about the time.'

(*b*) *Embedded interrogative*

dan berer [[ma karati].
Dan inquired what (I)-read
'Dan inquired what I read.'

(*c*) *Free relative*

* dan berer [ma še-karati].
Dan inquired what that$_{\text{COMP}}$-(I)-read
'Dan inquired what I read.'

In §7.4.1 we saw three other languages that distinguish embedded interrogatives and free relatives overtly: Macedonian, Wolof, and Hungarian. In the previous section (§7.5.1), we saw that Macedonian does not allow for any concealed question nominals, so examining free relatives is irrelevant here. In the rest of this section we apply Sharvit's argument to Wolof and Hungarian. These languages show the same pattern as Hebrew.

In Wolof, the verb *birëlé* "find out" can take as its complement a concealed question nominal in (39*a*) and an embedded interrogative in (39*b*), but not a free relative in (39*c*): the two clausal arguments differ in the word that introduces them: *l-u* for interrogatives and *l-i* for free relatives.

(39) WOLOF

(*a*) *Concealed question*

móódu birëlé-na [$_{\text{DP}}$ waxtu-wu ñëw-u avioη bi].
Moodu find.out-NEUTRAL time-u arrive-u airplane the
'Moodu found out the airplane's arrival time.'

(*b*) *Embedded interrogative*

birëlé-na [**l-u** móódu gën-ë bëgg].
find out-NEUTRAL cl-INT Moodu surpass-INF like
'She found out what Moodu likes most.'

(*c*) *Free relative*

* birëlé-na [**l-i** móódu gën-ë bëgg].
find out-NEUTRAL cl-FR Moodu surpass-INF like
'She found out what Moodu likes most.'

Turning to Hungarian, we also find concealed question nominals in the complement of an interrogative-taking verb, as in (40*a*). The same environment of course allows for *wh*-interrogatives, as in (40*b*), but not for free relatives, as in (40*c*): the two are distinguished morphologically in the form of the *wh*-word.

(40) HUNGARIAN

(*a*) *Concealed question*

Mondd meg [$_{DP}$ az eredményt].
tell me the score
'Tell me the score.'

(*b*) *Embedded interrogative*

Mondd meg [**mit** fo"zött].
tell me what$_{INT}$ cooked
'Tell me what he cooked.'

(*c*) *Free relative*

* Mondd meg [**amit** fo"zött].
tell me what$_{FR}$ cooked
'Tell me what he cooked.'

The data presented here show that free relatives cannot occur in the canonical position of concealed questions. If free relatives freely received a concealed question interpretation as proposed by Schlenker, this would be an unexpected result. These data show that free relatives do not receive a concealed question interpretation via a context-insensitive mechanism. It is still possible, however, that free relatives receive such an interpretation *only* in the pre-copular position of specificational sentences, that is via a context-sensitive mechanism. We argue against this option in §7.5.3. But, first, we turn to distributional facts concerning headed nominals.

7.5.2.2 *Headed Nominals* The previous section compared the availability of free relatives in the canonical concealed question environment and in the pre-copular position in specificational sentences. This section does the same for headed nominals. We find that some nominals that occur in the pre-copular position of specificational sentences and thus, according to Schlenker, receive a concealed question interpretation cannot occur in the canonical concealed question environment.

Example (41*a*) is a specificational sentence with the lexical nominal *the president of the United States* in the pre-copular position, which can also occur in the complement position of an interrogative predicate (41*a*′). By contrast, an apparently similar individual-denoting nominal like *the boy who ran over my pet snake* can occur in the specificational sentence in (41*b*), but not in the canonical concealed question environment in (41*b*′). Examples (42) and (43) show the same contrast for different lexical items.

(41) (*a*) [The president of the United States] is G.W. Bush.
(*a′*) Tell me [the president of the United States].
(*b*) [The boy who ran over my pet snake] was John.
(*b′*) */??Tell me [the boy who ran over my pet snake].

(42) (*a*) [The capital of France] is Paris.
(*a′*) Tell me [the capital of France].
(*b*) [The city I live in] is Paris.
(*b′*) ??Tell me [the city you live in].

(43) (*a*) [The candy Jill wants to buy] is jelly beans.
(*a′*) Tell me [the candy Jill wants to buy].
(*b*) [The money that was stolen] was Swiss Franks.
(*b′*) *Tell me [the money that was stolen].

As with free relatives, these data show that the expected parallelism between the pre-copular position of specificational sentences and the canonical concealed question environment is not found. As with free relatives, it is possible that the nominals in the (b) examples in (41)–(43) are not interpreted as concealed questions via a context-insensitive mechanism, but can receive such interpretation in special contexts, such as the pre-copular position of specificational sentences. Unfortunately, we did not find a way to test this claim. Without independent evidence, assuming that nominals can be freely interpreted as concealed questions only in the pre-copular position of specificational sentences is stipulative.

7.5.3 *Argument III: Interpretative Difference Between the Canonical Concealed Question Environment and the Pre-Copular Position in Specificational Sentences*

We saw in §7.5.2.1 that free relatives do not receive a concealed question interpretation in the canonical concealed question environment. In this section, we examine the possibility that the pre-copular position of a specificational sentence is special in that it allows for a concealed question interpretation of free relatives and other nominals that occur in this position. We will see that the interpretation that free relatives are expected to receive in this position is different from the interpretation that would be expected for free relatives as concealed questions.

If free relatives *do* receive a concealed question interpretation in specificational sentences, the question arises as to what this interpretation would be. In order to answer this question, we examine the interpretation of the relevant string in the canonical concealed question environment—we expect the free relative to denote a concealed question that is parallel to the embedded question. Consider, for example, the interpretation of the *wh*-clause in (44*a*)—we expect it to be similar to the interpretation of the nominal in (44*b*).

(44) (*a*) Tell me [what the capital of France is _].

(*b*) Tell me [the capital of France].

But what does the *wh*-clause mean in (44*a*)? This sentence is asking to identify Paris. That is, it would be fine to reply to (44*a*) by saying *Paris*, but it would be totally infelicitous to reply with *beautiful*.

Our next step looks at the interpretation of this string in a specificational pseudocleft. Interestingly, in this context we find the opposite pattern. In particular, if the same *wh*-clause occurs in the pre-copular position of a specificational pseudocleft, the post-copular phrase must be a property like *beautiful* (45*b*) and not an individual like *Paris* (45*a*).

(45) (*a*) *[What the capital of France is _] is Paris.

(*b*) [What the capital of France is _] is beautiful.

If we compare the two environments, we see that the free relative in (45) gets a different interpretation from what is expected from (44): while the concealed question asks for an individual, the specificational sentence requires a post-copular property. That is, even when we examine the expected interpretation of a free relative in the pre-copular position of a specificational, we do not find the concealed question interpretation. This pattern allows us to conclude that the pre-copular position of a specificational sentence is not a concealed question environment.

7.5.4 *Conclusions*

In this section, we have shown that the concealed question versions of the question–answer approach cannot account for cross-linguistic patterns of connectivity. First, not all languages that exhibit connectivity allow for concealed question nominals. The fact that connectivity is found in a language such as Macedonian that does not allow for concealed question nominals in the canonical concealed question environment suggests that the two phenomena are unrelated. Second, free relatives and some headed nominals that occur in specificational sentences cannot occur in the canonical concealed question environment. Both these arguments indicate that the pre-copular position of specificational sentences is different from the canonical concealed question position. Under the concealed question analysis, however, these positions are predicted to be parallel. One could still argue that while both are concealed question environments, the canonical environment is somehow more restricted. To address this option, we targeted the interpretation of nominals directly in the pre-copular position of a specificational sentence and showed that free relatives do not receive the interpretation that is expected if they were interpreted as questions.

As we mentioned earlier, Romero (2005, this volume) discusses headed nominals in the pre-copular position of specificational sentences that exhibit similarities to when they occur in the canonical concealed question environment. Based on these similarities, she concludes that these nominals also receive a concealed question interpretation when they occur in specificational sentences, and analyzes connectivity as arising from (concealed) question–answer pairs. This may be the right analysis for some copular sentences—the existence of such sentences is expected in any theory that allows for a cross-categorial *be* of identity. However, it is unclear that this analysis can be extended to the large set of nominals that we have discussed in this section that do not exhibit such similarities, and hence it cannot be adopted as a general account of connectivity.

7.6 Conclusions

In this paper, we have argued against the question–answer approach to connectivity in specificational sentences. Prima facie this analysis seems to have the best motivation for positing the desired c-command configuration, namely, positing a post-copular full answer. However, we have shown that, cross-linguistically, the pre-copular phrase of a specificational sentence is not a question, neither syntactically, contra den Dikken *et al.* (2000), nor semantically, contra Schlenker (2003) and Romero (2005, this volume). If the pre-copular phrase in a specificational sentence is not a question, then the post-copular phrase is not an answer, in which case we lose the motivation to reconstruct a full clause in this position. Without such reconstruction, we will not have the desired c-command configuration that could account for connectivity effects using the current analyses of these phenomena.

More generally, since all the mechanisms by which the desired c-command configuration is posited at an abstract level lack independent evidence, the apparent simplicity of the reconstruction strategy over direct compositionality disappears. Indeed, direct compositionality faces great challenges—Principle B and Principle C connectivity requires a non-structural theory of anaphora, and a direct-compositional analysis of NPI connectivity looks non-trivial—but it seems to be a more promising option if we aim for a general account of connectivity across languages.

Appendix: Which Nominals Can Be Interpreted as Concealed Questions?

The data presented in §7.5.2 and §7.5.3, which was used to argue that the pre-copular position in specificational sentences is not a concealed question environment, are also relevant to the study of concealed question nominals. The kinds of nominals that can occur in the canonical concealed question environment have not been discussed in the concealed question literature—this literature is mostly concerned with characterizing the predicates that allow for concealed question nominals (Grimshaw 1979; Heim 1979; Dor 1992). In this appendix, we would like to use our findings from examining the (concealed) question–answer approach to specificational sentences to shed light on which nouns are possible in the canonical concealed question environment. Our hope is that this will contribute to future research on concealed question nominals.

The examples we saw in §7.5.2.2 contrasted nominals such as *president*, *capital*, and *candy*, which can form concealed questions, with nominals such as *boy*, *city*, and *money*, which cannot. (46)–(49) present examples of other nouns that can occur in the canonical concealed question environment (as marked, some of the examples are cited from previous work).

(46) (*a*) John found out the **murderer** of Smith. (Heim 1979)
(*b*) Tell me the **president** of the United States.
(*c*) Tell me the **chair** of your department.
(*d*) Tell me the **winner** of last year's Pulitzer Prize.
(*e*) Tell me the **writer** who won the last Pulitzer Prize.

(47) (*a*) John discovered the **location** of the meeting. (Dor 1992)
(*b*) Tell me the **capital** of France.

(48) (*a*) John knows Bill's **telephone number**. (Heim 1979)
(*b*) Harold guessed the **time** of the meeting. (Dor 1992)
(*c*) Tell me your shoe **size**.
(*d*) Tell me your **height**.
(*e*) I couldn't figure out her **age**.
(*f*) Guess the **temperature** of the water.
(*g*) Tell me the **amount** of money that was stolen.
(*h*) Please tell me the **grade** you got in that class.

(49) (*a*) Harold knew the **kind** of candy that Jill liked. (Dor 1992)

(*b*) Harold learned the **outcome** of the trial. (Dor 1992)

(*c*) Guess the **color** of my eyes.

We propose that it is functional nouns (in the sense of Vikner and Jensen 2002) that allow for concealed question interpretation, that is, nouns whose interpretation depend on an additional argument. The nouns in (46) are functional nouns denoting people: a person is not a murderer by virtue of some properties inherent to the person himself; rather, that person must be a murderer of someone. The nouns in (47) are functional nouns denoting locations. In (48) the output of the function is a certain number and the nouns in (49) are other functional nouns.

In (50), the nouns themselves are not functional, but the whole phrase is. For example, while the noun *person* is not functional, the nominal *the person who won the last Pulitzer Prize* in (50*b*) is.

(50) (*a*) Tell me your **favorite movie.**

(*b*) Tell me **the person who won the last Pulitzer Prize.**

(*c*) Tell me **the candy Jill wants to buy**.

(*d*) John can't remember **the wine she likes.**

(*e*) Tell me **the largest city in Italy**.

However, this cannot be the whole story. In particular, the nominal we saw above in (42*b*) *the city you live in* is also functional—it is a function from you to the place you live in. While we believe that the generalization that only functional nominals are possible concealed questions is on the right track, a more fine-grained notion of functional is clearly needed. We leave this issue here—see Nathan (2006) for further development of this idea.

References

Alexiadou, A. and Giannakidou, A. 1998. 'Specificational pseudoclefts and the semantics of lists', *ZAS Papers in Linguistics*, 10: 1–21.

Baker, C. L. 1968. Indirect questions in English. Ph.D. dissertation, University of Illinois.

Caponigro, I. 2003. Free Not to Ask: On the Semantics of Free Relatives and Wh-words Cross-linguistically. Ph.D. dissertation, University of California, Los Angeles.

Cecchetto, C. 2000. 'Connectivity and anti-connectivity in pseudoclefts', in M. Hirotani (ed.), *Proceedings of the Thirtieth Annual Meeting of the North East Linguistics Society (NELS 30)*. pp. 137–151. Amherst, MA: Graduate Linguistics Student Association (GLSA), University of Massachusetts 137–51.

Chomsky, N. 1981. *Lectures on Government and Binding*. Dordrecht: Foris.

den Dikken, M., Meinunger, A., and Wilder, C. 2000. 'Pseudoclefts and ellipsis', *Studia Linguistica*, 54: 41–89.

Dor, D. 1992. 'Towards a semantic account of concealed questions', in M. Bernstein (ed.), *Proceedings of the Ninth Eastern States Conference on Linguistics (ESCOL '92)*. Ithaca, NY: Cornell University, 56–67.

Grimshaw, J. 1979. 'Complement selection and the lexicon', *Linguistic Inquiry*, 10: 279–326.

Heim, I. 1979. 'Concealed questions', in R. Bäuerle, U. Egli, and A. von Stechow (eds), *Semantics from Different Points of View*. Berlin: Springer. 51–60.

Heller, D. 2002. 'On the relation of connectivity and specificational pseudoclefts', *Natural Language Semantics*, 10: 243–84.

—— 2005. Identity and Information: Semantic and Pragmatic Aspects of Specificational Sentences. Ph.D. dissertation, Rutgers University.

Heycock, C. and Kroch, A. 1999. 'Pseudocleft connectedness: Implications for the LF interface level', *Linguistic Inquiry*, 30: 365–97.

Higgins, R. 1973. The Pseudocleft Construction in English. Ph.D. dissertation, MIT.

Hornstein, N. 1984. *Logic as Grammar*, Cambridge, MA: MIT Press.

Izvorski, R. 1997. 'On the type of *be* and the nature of the *wh*-clause in specificational pseudoclefts', paper given at the Workshop on the Syntax and Semantics of (Pseudo-)clefts, ZAS, Berlin, November.

Jacobson, P. 1994. 'Binding connectivity in copular sentences', in M. Harvey and L. Santelmann (eds), *Proceedings of Fourth Annual Semantics and Linguistic Theory Conference (SALT IV)*. Ithaca, NY: Cornell University. 161–78.

Nathan, L. 2006. On the Interpretation of Concealed Questions. Ph.D. dissertation, MIT.

Peters, S. and Bach, E. 1968. 'Pseudo-cleft sentences', unpublished MS, University of Texas, Austin.

Romero, M. 2005, 'Concealed questions and specificational subjects', *Linguistics and Philosophy*, 28: 687–737.

—— this volume, 'Connectivity in a unified analysis of specificational subjects and concealed questions'.

Ross, J. R. 1972. 'Act', in D. Davidson and G. Harman (eds), *Semantics of Natural Language*. Dordrecht: Reidel, 70–126.

—— 1997. 'That is the Question', paper presented at the University of Pennsylvania.

Schlenker, P. 2003. 'Clausal equations (A note on the connectivity problem)', *Natural Language and Linguistic Theory*, 21: 157–214.

Sharvit, Y. 1997. The Syntax and Semantics of Functional Relative Clauses. Ph.D. dissertation, Rutgers University.

—— 1999. 'Connectivity in specificational sentences', *Natural Language Semantics*, 7: 299–339.

Vikner, C. and Jensen, P. A. 2002. 'A semantic analysis of the English genitive. Interaction of lexical and formal semantics', *Studia Linguistica*, 56: 191–226.

8

Connectivity in a Unified Analysis of Specificational Subjects and Concealed Questions*

MARIBEL ROMERO

8.1 Introduction

Connectivity, found in a number of constructions involving typically a trace of movement or gap, is the effect by which a constituent behaves grammatically as if it occupied not its surface position but the position of the gap. The phenomenon is central to the debate between defendants of Direct Compositionality—where the semantics is read off the "visible", surface syntax—and the defendants of the so-called Logical Form (LF)—according to which semantics is computed on an abstract syntactic representation, LF, obtained after applying some transformations to the surface syntax.

The present paper is concerned with connectivity in specificational copular sentences. A simple specificational copular sentence is given in (1), where the post-copular constituent *Smith* identifies the actual value of the subject N(oun) P(hrase) *the murderer*. More complex examples reveal connectivity effects, as shown in (2)–(4) (Akmajian 1970; Higgins 1973; Halvorsen 1978; among others):

(1) The murderer is Smith.

(2) *Variable binding connectivity:*
The woman no man$_1$ likes *e* is his$_1$ mother-in-law.

* I am indebted to the participants of the Workshop on Direct Compositionality (Brown University, June 2003) for their helpful comments and criticisms. Thanks to Tonia Bleam, Lucas Champollion, Amy Forsyth, Elsi Kaiser, Martin Kappus, Sophia Malamud, Tatjana Scheffler and Vicki Tredinnick for their judgments and comments. Special thanks to the editors of this volume, Pauline Jacobson and Chris Barker, for making this volume possible. Remaining errors are mine.

(3) *Opacity connectivity*:
What Mary is looking for *e* is a unicorn.

(4) *Binding Theory connectivity* (under the specificational reading):

(*a*) Principle A: What John_1 is *e* is a nuisance to himself_1.

(*b*) Principle B: *What John_1 is *e* is a nuisance to him_1.

(*c*) Principle C: *What he_1 is *e* is a nuisance to John_1.

Example (2) illustrates variable binding connectivity. Under fairly standard assumptions (see, e.g., Heim and Kratzer 1998), a binder must c-command its bindee at LF. *No man* cannot move outside the complex NP-island in order to c-command *his* at LF. Nevertheless, a bound variable reading of *his* is possible in the specificational (2), as if the post-copular NP *his mother-in-law* occupied not its surface position but the position of the gap *e*. Opacity connectivity is illustrated in (3). Here the post-copular NP *a unicorn* has a de dicto reading with respect to *look for*, as if this NP, and not the gap, occupied the object position of the verb. Finally, the sentences in (4) exemplify the three types of Binding Theory connectivity. The anaphor in (4*a*) is not locally bound by *John*. It is, however, licensed under the specificational reading of the sentence, paraphrasable as "The property John has is this: to be a nuisance to himself" (Principle A connectivity). The pronoun *him* in (4*b*) is not locally c-commanded by *John*. Nevertheless, in the specificational reading "The property John has is this: to be a nuisance to him", *him* cannot corefer with *John* (Principle B connectivity). The name *John* in (4*c*) is not c-commanded by *he*. However, coreference between *John* and *he* is prohibited in the specificational reading "The property he has is this: to be a nuisance to John" (Principle C connectivity). In all three cases, the Binding Theory effect would straightforwardly follow if the post-copular NP directly occupied the gap position rather than its position after the copula.

Connectivity effects do not arise in predicational copular sentences. Sentence (5) is a simple predicational sentence, where the post-copular phrase *tall* predicates a property of the denotation of the subject NP *the murderer*. The predicational sentence (6) does not allow for a bound variable reading of *him*.[1] The most prominent reading of (7) is predicational, according to which the object John is looking for has the two properties predicated by the post-verbal NPs. *A unicorn* cannot be understood de dicto under this reading.

[1] I exclude from consideration variable binding without LF c-command by universal quantifiers, which is due to a special mechanism and has a different distribution than the standard connectivity effects. See Chierchia (1993) for an analysis of this phenomenon in questions and Sharvit (1999*b*) for an extension to Relative Clauses.

Finally, the structure *What NP is is a nuisance to NP* has a predicational reading paraphrasable as "Being what NP is (e.g., being a perfectionist) is a nuisance to NP". Under this reading, Binding Theory judgments are opposite from what we saw in (4). *Himself* is not licensed in (8*a*), *John* and *him* can corefer in (8*b*), and *he* and *John* can corefer in (8*c*). In (6)–(8), the observed judgments are directly predicted from the surface position of the post-verbal items. No connectivity is involved.

(5) The murderer is tall.

(6) *No variable binding connectivity*:
The woman no man_1 likes is interested in $him_{*1/2}$.

(7) *No opacity connectivity*:
What John is looking for is a unicorn and a nuisance to all of us. (* de dicto)

(8) *No Binding Theory connectivity*:

(*a*) Principle A: *What $John_1$ is *e* is a nuisance to $himself_1$.

(*b*) Principle B: What $John_1$ is *e* is a nuisance to him_1.

(*c*) Principle C: What he_1 is *e* is a nuisance to $John_1$.

Connectivity has been the main topic in the literature on specificational sentences since Higgins (1973). A recent exception is Romero (2005), who is concerned with the semantics of specificational sentences and makes no argument about connectivity. Romero observes that specificational subject NPs—that is, subjects of specificational sentences—display an interesting ambiguity shared by another type of NPs, the so-called "concealed question" NPs. This construction is illustrated in (9). The object NPs in (9) are called "concealed question" NPs because their sentences have the same truth conditions as the corresponding variants in (10) with embedded interrogatives. Romero proposes a unified account of specificational subjects and concealed questions to capture the common ambiguity.

(9) (*a*) Pete knows the temperature of the lake.

(*b*) John announced the winner of the contest.

(*c*) Mary guessed Joe's telephone number.

(10) (*a*) Pete knows how warm the lake is.

(*b*) John announced who won the contest.

(*c*) Mary guessed what Bill's telephone number is.

The goal of the present paper is to explore the consequences that this unified semantic analysis of specificational subjects (SSs) and concealed questions (CQs) has for connectivity. To this end, I will present three semantic characteristics that the two constructions share and that distinguish them from (some or all) ordinary uses of NPs; (i) ambiguity between reading A and reading B (from Romero 2005); (ii) flexible degree of exhaustivity; and (iii) pronominalization and coordination (building on Romero 2004). The unified semantic analysis from Romero (2005) will be further developed to account for these data. After each set, we will evaluate what repercussions the relevant aspects of the semantic analysis have for connectivity. Some arguments will pose serious challenges to some approaches to connectivity; others will only provide suggestive evidence on the matter. Overall, the data presented in this paper favor the "question plus deletion" approach to connectivity, which crucially uses non-surface LF syntax, over its competitors: over the movement account (based on LF or similar syntax), over the inverse predication account (based on Direct Compositionality), and over the "as is" account (based on Direct Compositionality).

The paper is organized as follows. Section 8.2 presents the ambiguity between reading A and reading B and summarizes the analysis of the phenomenon proposed in Romero (2005). These data and analysis present a challenge for movement approaches to connectivity (Akmajian 1970; Grosu 1973; Culicover 1977; Bošković 1997) and for inverse predication analysis (Williams 1983, 1994). Section 8.3 is concerned with degrees of exhaustivity in SSs and CQs. These data can be captured by implementing the core semantic analysis of §8.2 in two ways. The first implementation, implementation (i), is compatible with the "as is" approach to connectivity (Jacobson 1994; Sharvit 1999*a*; Cecchetto 2000; Heller 2002). The second implementation, implementation (ii), leads to the "question plus deletion" approach to connectivity (Ross 1972; den Dikken *et al.* 2000; Ross 2000; Schlenker 2003). Section 8.4 presents pronominalization and coordination data both on reading A and reading B, favoring implementation (ii) and thus the "question plus deletion" account. Section 8.5 shows how connectivity is derived in the "question plus deletion" account for reading A and for reading B. Section 8.6 summarizes the conclusions.

8.2 Ambiguity between Reading A and Reading B

In this section, I first present the data displaying the ambiguity between reading A and reading B (§8.2.1). The analysis proposed in Romero (2005) is summarized next (§8.2.2). Finally, consequences of this ambiguity and analysis are drawn for connectivity (§8.2.3).

8.2.1 *Reading A and Reading B for CQs and SSs*

An interrogative clause expresses a function from worlds to the set of true answers to that interrogative in that world (Karttunen 1977). This is illustrated in (11). This function combines with the denotation of (strongly exhaustive) *know* given in (12) (Heim 1994), to yield the truth conditions of sentence (13) spelled out in (14). Roughly, (14) states that John knows in w who arrived if and only if, for all his belief worlds w′, the set of true answers to this question in the belief world w′ is exactly the same as the set of true answers in the actual world w.

(11) $[\![\textit{who arrived}]\!] = \lambda w.\ \{p: p(w)\ \&\ \exists x\ [p=\lambda w''.\text{arrive}(x,w'')]\}$
(Karttunen 1977)

(12) $[\![\textit{know}_{\text{qu}}]\!] = \lambda q_{<s,<<s,t>,t>>} \lambda x_e \lambda w.\ \forall w' \in \text{Dox}_x(w)\ [\ q(w') = q(w)\ ]$
(Heim 1994: 9)

(13) John knows who arrived.

(14) $[\![\textit{John knows who arrived}]\!] = \lambda w.\ \forall w' \in \text{Dox}_j(w)$
$[\ \{p: p(w')\ \&\ \exists x\ [p=\lambda w''.\text{arrive}(x,w'')]\}$
$= \{p: p(w)\ \&\ \exists x\ [p=\lambda w''.\text{arrive}(x,w'')]\}\ ]$

This analysis can easily be extended to simple concealed question NPs. The NP *the capital of Italy*, when functioning as a CQ, contributes an individual concept, that is a function of type <s,e> from worlds to (possibly plural sums of) individuals. The semantic contribution of the CQ *the capital of Italy* is in (15). The concealed question counterpart of interrogative *know* is given in (16). When these combine in sentence (17), we obtain the truth conditions in (18). The λ-expressions in (18) state that John knows in w the capital of Italy if and only if, for all of John's doxastic alternatives w′, the value of this individual concept in w′ is exactly what it is in the actual world w.

(15) Semantic contribution of the CQ *[the capital of Italy]*:
$\lambda w''.\ \iota x_e\ [\text{capital-of-Italy}(x,w'')]$

(16) $[\![\textit{know}_{\text{CQ}}]\!] = \lambda \underline{y}_{<s,e>} \lambda x_e \lambda w.\ \forall w' \in \text{Dox}_x(w)\ [\ \underline{y}(w') = \underline{y}(w)\ ]$

(17) John knows the capital of Italy.

(18) $[\![\textit{John knows the capital of Italy}]\!]$
$= \lambda w. \forall w' \in \text{Dox}_j(w)$
$[\lambda w''.\iota x_e[\text{capital-of-Italy}(x,w'')]\ (w')$
$= \lambda w''.\iota x_e[\text{capital-of-Italy}(x,w'')]\ (w)]$
$= \lambda w. \forall w' \in \text{Dox}_j(w)\ [\iota x_e[\text{capital-of-Italy}(x,w')]$
$= \iota x_e[\text{capital-of-Italy}(x,w)]\ ]$

With this background, Heim (1979) presents an interesting ambiguity for nested CQs. A sentence like (19) has two readings, which Romero (2005) calls reading A and reading B.[2] Reading A, described in (20), can be unambiguously paraphrased as "John knows the same price that Fred knows".

(19) John knows the price that Fred knows. (Heim 1979)

(20) Reading A: "John knows the same price that Fred knows."

There are several relevant questions about prices:
'How much does the milk cost?'
'How much does the oil cost?'
'How much does the ham cost?'
Fred knows the answer to exactly one of these questions, e.g., to the first one.

John knows the answer to this question too.

Reading B, described in (21), can be unambiguously paraphrased as "John knows what price Fred knows."

(21) Reading B: "John knows what price Fred knows."

There are several relevant questions about prices:
'How much does the milk cost?'
'How much does the oil cost?'
'How much does the ham cost?'
Fred knows the answer to one of these questions, e.g., to "How much does the milk cost?."

Then, there is the "meta-question" asking which of these questions is the one whose answer Fred knows.

John knows the answer to the meta-question. That is, John knows that the question about prices whose answer Fred knows is "How much does the milk cost?."

Interestingly, as noted in Romero (2005), SSs with specificational *be* display readings parallel to reading A and reading B of CQs with *know*. In the same way that a given concealed question NP can contribute a question

[2] English CQs are not fully productive and are often restricted to nouns such as *price, time, capital-of, temperature*, etc. For example, as mentioned by a reviewer, sentence (i) is somewhat deviant (under any reading), even though it is completely parallel to (19). I will not seek to explain the partial productivity of CQs in the present paper. See Caponigro and Heller, this volume, for cross-linguistic data on the issue and Nathan (2005) for some properties of the distribution of CQs.

(i) Context: Talking about the red shift of stars.
? John knows the speed that Fred knows.

or a meta-question, so can a given specificational subject NP—for example *[$_{NP}$ the price that Fred thought was $1.29]*—ambiguously contribute a question or a meta-question. After the copula, the answer to that question or meta-question is enunciated, and this naturally disambiguates the reading. Reading A is illustrated in (22)–(23) and reading B in (24)–(25):

(22) The price that Fred thought was $1.29 was (actually) $1.79.

(23) Reading A: "The question whose answer Fred thought was '$1.29' has as its real answer '$1.79'."

There are several relevant questions about prices:
'How much is the milk?'
'How much is the oil?'
'How much is the ham?'
For one of these questions—e.g., the first one—Fred thought the answer was "$1.29".

But the actual answer to this question is "$1.79".

(24) The price that Fred thought was $1.29 was the price of milk.

(25) Reading B: "The question whose answer Fred thought was '$1.29' is 'How much is the milk?'."

There are several relevant questions about prices:
'How much is the milk?'
'How much is the oil?'
'How much is the ham?'
For one of these questions, Fred thought the answer was "$1.29".

Then, there is the "meta-question" asking which of these questions is the one whose answer Fred thought was $1.29.

The answer to the meta-question is 'How much is the milk?'.

That is, Fred thought that the price of milk is $1.29.

8.2.2 *Romero's (2005) Analysis of the Ambiguity of CQs and SSs*

Romero (2005) shows that using exclusively the extension of the NPs *the price that Fred knows* and *The price that Fred thought was $1.29* cannot capture the desired ambiguity. She compares *know* and *be* with intensional verbs such as *look for*, which take an intensional object as their argument (e.g. Zimmermann 1993; Moltmann 1997). This intensional object is often provided by the *intension* of its complement NP, as exemplified in (26). But this intensional object can also arise from the *extension* of a higher type NP. This second possibility is illustrated in (27), which has a de dicto reading on the extension of the NP that makes the sentence true in scenario (28):

(26) ⟦*look for*⟧ + INTENSION of the NP:

John is looking for the unicorn with the longest horn.

"In all of John's bouletic alternatives w′ in w: John finds in w′ the individual that is the unicorn with the longest horn in w′ (whichever that may be)."

(27) ⟦*look for*⟧ + EXTENSION of the NP:

John is looking for the unicorn Fred is looking for (: the one with the longest horn.)

"Each x out of John and Fred is such that, in all of x's bouletic alternatives w′ in w: x finds in w′ the individual that is the unicorn with the longest horn in w′ (whichever that may be)."

(28) *Scenario*:

John does not have any beliefs as to which unicorn has the longest horn. He wants to catch the unicorn with the longest horn, whichever that may be. Exactly the same holds for Fred.

Romero argues that the reading A/reading B ambiguity is nothing more than the possibility of drawing an intensional object from the extension or from the intension of the NP. Reading A results when this intensional object corresponds to the *extension* of the NP. Reading B arises when the intensional object is obtained from the *intension* of the NP:

(29) *Core analysis of the A/B ambiguity*

(*a*) Reading A: ⟦*know*⟧ or ⟦*be*⟧ + EXTENSION of the NP.

(*b*) Reading B: ⟦*know*⟧ or ⟦*be*⟧ + INTENSION of the NP.

Here I will exemplify the core analysis only for example (19), repeated here as (30). The tree in (31) shows the semantic computation of the concealed question NP:[3]

(30) John knows the price that Fred knows.

[3] In (31), the logical predicate *price* is a predicate of individual concept–world pairs, which applies truly to a pair $<\underline{x}_{<s,e>}, w^*>$ iff there is a (type of) object z_e (e.g. milk) in w^* such that, for all the $w'' \in W$, $\underline{x}(w'')$ has the property of being the price of (the counterpart of) z at w″. This formal translation is parallel to the formal translation of *know* in (32), which also takes an individual concept (an individual from the NP subject) and a world. Throughout the chapter, underlined variables range over intensional objects (e.g. $\underline{x}_{<s,e>}$) and non-underlined variables over extensional objects (e.g. x_e).

(31) $[\![\textit{the price that Fred knows}]\!]^g =$

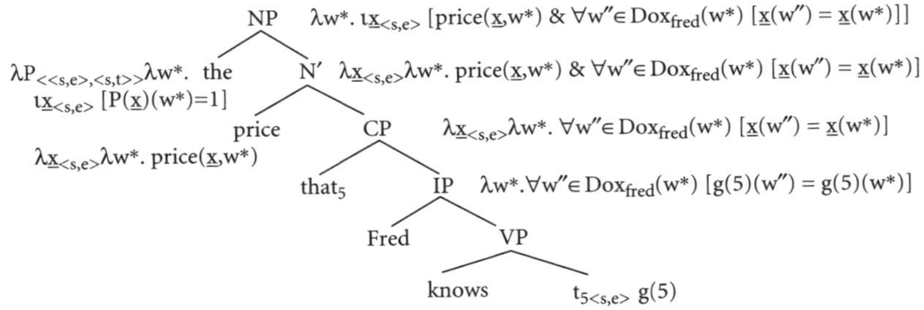

We then combine the semantic contribution of the NP with the cross-categorial lexical entry of $know_{CQ}$ in (32). Example (32) is like (16) except that $\underline{y}$ can now have type <s,e> or <s,<s,e>>.

(32) $[\![know_{CQ}]\!] = \lambda \underline{y} \lambda x_e \lambda w.\ \forall w'' \in Dox_x(w)\ [\ \underline{y}(w'') = \underline{y}(w)\ ]$

The two readings are derived as follows.

To obtain reading A, the extension of the NP at the evaluation world w_0—$[\![NP]\!](w_0)$, an intensional object itself, of type <s,e>—is entered as the argument of *know*. This is shown in (33).[4] The resulting truth conditions in (33*b*) roughly state the following: we are in a world w_0 such that the unique price $\underline{x}_{<s,e>}$ that Fred knows the value of in w_0 is such that John too knows the value of $\underline{x}_{<s,e>}$ in w_0. Reading A is correctly rendered by these truth conditions.

(33) *Reading A:*

(*a*) Extension of the NP in w_0:

$\iota \underline{x}_{<s,e>}\ [\ price(\underline{x},w_0)\ \&\ \forall w'' \in Dox_{fred}(w_0)\ [\underline{x}(w'') = \underline{x}(w_0)]]$

(*b*) *Know* + extension of the NP:

$\lambda w_0.\ \forall w' \in Dox_j(w_0)$
$[\iota \underline{x}_{<s,e>} [price(\underline{x},w_0)\ \&\ \forall w'' \in Dox_{fred}(w_0)\ [\underline{x}(w'') = \underline{x}(w_0)]](w') =$
$\iota \underline{x}_{<s,e>} [price(\underline{x},w_0)\ \&\ \forall w'' \in Dox_{fred}(w_0)\ [\underline{x}(w'') = \underline{x}(w_0)]]\ (w)]$

To obtain reading B, *know* takes the intension of the NP—$[\![NP]\!]$, of type <s,<s,e>>—as shown in (34). The resulting truth conditions in (34*c*) roughly state the following: we are in a world w_0 such that, in all of John's

[4] I assume that extensional NPs—here, in particular, the NP *the price that Fred knows*—come with a free world index that is later bound by some higher operator (see Farkas 1993; Percus 2000). Since here we use the NP's extension in the actual world, formal expressions corresponding to the predicates within the NP—$price(\underline{x},w_0)$ and $Dox_{fred}(w_0)$—get the same (actual) world variable w_0 as formal expressions corresponding to the matrix *know*—$Dox_j(w_0)$.

doxastic alternatives w′ in w_0, the price $\underline{x}_{<s,e>}$ that Fred knows in w′ is exactly the price $\underline{x}_{<s,e>}$ that Fred knows in the actual world w_0. This correctly captures reading B.

(34) *Reading B:*

(*a*) Intension of the NP:

$$\lambda w^*.\ \iota\underline{x}_{<s,e>}\ [\text{price}(\underline{x},w^*)\ \&\ \forall w''\in Dox_{fred}(w^*)\ [\underline{x}(w'') = \underline{x}(w^*)]]$$

(*b*) *Know* + intension of the NP:

$$\lambda w_0.\ \forall w'\in Dox_j(w_0)\ [\lambda w^*.\ \iota\underline{x}_{<s,e>}\ [\text{price}(\underline{x},w^*)\ \&\ \forall w''\in Dox_{fred}(w^*)\ [\underline{x}(w'') = \underline{x}(w^*)]]\ (w') = \lambda w^*.\ \iota\underline{x}_{<s,e>}\ [\text{price}(\underline{x},w^*)\ \&\ \forall w''\in Dox_{fred}(w^*)\ [\underline{x}(w'') = \underline{x}(w^*)]]\ (w_0)]$$

(*c*) Simplification:

$$\lambda w_0.\forall w'\in Dox_j(w_0)\ [\iota\underline{x}_{<s,e>}\ [\text{price}(\underline{x},w')\ \&\ \forall w''\in Dox_{fred}(w')\ [\underline{x}(w'') = \underline{x}(w')]] = \iota\underline{x}_{<s,e>}\ [\text{price}(\underline{x},w_0)\ \&\ \forall w''\in Dox_{fred}(w_0)\ [\underline{x}(w'') = \underline{x}(w_0)]]]$$

8.2.3 *Consequences for Connectivity*

Let us go back to the copular sentences exemplifying readings A and B:

(35) *Reading A:*
The price that Fred thought was $1.29 was (actually) $1.79.

(36) *Reading B:*
The price that Fred thought was $1.29 was the price of milk.

Are the sentences (35) and (36) specificational or predicational? That (35) is a specificational sentence seems straightforward: it is like the sentence *The price of milk is $1.79* except for the choice of definite description. As for (36), the intended meaning involves a de dicto reading of the post-copular phrase *the price of milk* under *thought*. That is, Fred thought: "The price of milk is $1.29". This is an instance of opacity connectivity, a trait of specificational but not of predicational sentences, as we saw in §8.1.

Romero (2005) also uses variable binding connectivity as a test. Romero gives scenario (37) and the examples (38), with reading A, and (39), with reading B. In both cases, variable binding of *no girl* into the post-copular phrase succeeds. As bound variable connectivity is a property of specificational but not of predicational sentences, the sentences must be specificational:

(37) *Scenario:*
A group of 2-year-old girls from the Ukraine were given in adoption

to several families in Barcelona. The director of the adoption program encouraged the biological relatives of each girl to keep in touch with her by writing letters, telling them though that they should not identify themselves using their name, family relationship, or address. After a couple of years, the girls have developed some hypotheses about who every secret writer may or may not be. For example, no girl thinks that the one who writes to her the least can possibly be her mother. In fact, they are all right about that, since, for every girl, the one who writes to her the least is her uncle.

(38) *Reading A:*
The anonymous writer that no $girl_1$ thinks can possibly be her_1 mother is (in fact) her_1 uncle.

(39) *Reading B:*
The anonymous writer that no $girl_1$ thinks can possibly be her_1 mother is the one who writes to her_1 the least.

What can the ambiguity between reading A and reading B tell us about connectivity? The ambiguity data and Romero's analysis of it argues against two of the main avenues to connectivity in the literature, namely the movement approach and the inverse predication approach.

Let us start with the movement approach (Akmajian 1970; Culicover 1977; Grosu 1973; Bošković 1997; among others). Early versions (e.g. Akmajian 1970) propose that the post-copular sentence is base-generated in the position of the gap at D-Str. Connectivity tests and semantic interpretation apply at D-Str. At S-Str the post-copular phrase moves and lands in its surface position. This is illustrated in (40). In a more recent version of this line, Bošković (1997) proposes that the post-verbal phrase is base-generated after the copula and that it replaces the *wh*...*e* chain at LF, as in (41).[5] At LF, connectivity is evaluated and the semantic computation is carried out.

(40) Akmajian (1970):

(*a*) D-Str: [It [John admires <u>himself</u> the most]] is ▲. ⇒ Connectivity, semantics

(*b*) S-Str: Who John admires *e* the most is himself.

(41) Bošković (1997):

(*a*) Up to Spell-Out: Who John admires *e* the most is himself.

(*b*) LF: ~~Who~~ John admires <u>himself</u> the most. ⇒ Connectivity, semantics

[5] For Bošković (1997), *who* in (41) is a surface anaphor and it—or, rather, the chain *who*...*e*—must be replaced by its antecedent *himself* at LF.

What the proposals in this line have in common is that, at the syntactic level at which connectivity and semantic interpretation apply, the SS has been modified and contains the surface post-verbal phrase inside. Note that connectivity tests and semantic interpretation must operate on the *same* syntactic representation of the SS, since some connectivity effects (e.g. opacity and variable binding) are in fact truth-conditional. This procedure may give us the correct result for our reading B examples (if we overlook some important details),[6] since the propositions expressed by the structures in (42*b*) and (43*b*) roughly match this reading:

(42) (*a*) S-Str: The price that Fred thought *e* was \$1.29 was the price of milk.

(*b*) D-Str or LF: Fred thought *the price of milk* was \$1.29.

(43) (*a*) S-Str: The anonymous writer that no girl_1 thinks *e* can possibly be her_1 mother is the one who writes to her_1 the least.

(*b*) D-Str or LF: No girl_1 thinks *the one who writes to* $\textit{her}_1$ *the least* can possibly be her_1 mother.

But the replacement strategy absolutely yields the wrong result for reading A. The structures (44*b*) and (45*b*) derived by the movement account express the propositions "that Fred thought \$1.79 equals \$1.29" and "that no girl x thinks x's uncle can possibly be x's mother", which do not match reading A.

(44) (*a*) S-Str: The price that Fred thought *e* was \$1.29 was (actually) \$1.79.

(*b*) D-Str or LF: Fred thought *\$1.79* was \$1.29.

(45) (*a*) S-Str: The anonymous writer that no girl_1 thinks *e* can possibly be her_1 mother is (in fact) her_1 uncle.

(*b*) D-Str or LF: No girl_1 thinks $\textit{her}_1$ *uncle* can possibly be her_1 mother.

To correctly generate reading A, the SS must remain untouched—it must remain in its surface shape, as a referential NP—at the syntactic level of representation at which semantics applies. This is at odds with the derivation of connectivity in the movement approach, which crucially relies on reconfiguring the SS before semantic interpretation.[7]

[6] Problems with the movement derivation of examples parallel to reading B have been extensively discussed in Higgins (1973: ch. 2). See also Sharvit (1999*a*: 326–7) and Heller (2002: 279–80).

[7] Heycock and Kroch's (1999) ι-reduction mechanism, although not based on movement, builds a structure similar to the ones proposed in the movement approaches above. However, they crucially argue that, while connectivity is evaluated after ι-reduction, the semantic computation is performed along the syntactic derivation. This might allow for a way to elude the problem created by reading A. I leave this issue to future research.

Inverse predication analyses (Williams 1983, 1994; Moro 1997; Partee 1986; among others) argue that specificational sentences are predicational sentences where the predicate precedes the subject. Williams develops an account of connectivity based on this assumption. He observes that a non-c-commanding antecedent within a predicate is sometimes able to bind into its subject, as in (46). The specificational sentence in (47) would then reflect this possibility of binding from the predicate into the subject without c-command.

(46) $[_{\text{Subject}}$ A picture of himself$_1]$ $[_{\text{Predicate}}$ displeased John$_1]$

(47) Williams (1983, 1994):
$[_{\text{Predicate}}$ Who John$_1$ admires the most$]$ is $[_{\text{Subject}}$ himself$_1]$.

One of the main appeals of the inverse predication approach is that it gives a principled explanation of the intuitive referential asymmetry between the pre- and post-copular phrase. As noted early on (see Higgins 1973 for discussion), the post-copular phrase feels more referential than the pre-copular phrase. This, it is argued, follows if the pre-copular phrase is the main predicate of the sentence and the post-verbal phrase is the argument. However, this special semantic status of SSs—including the reading A/reading B ambiguity—is shared by CQs. CQs function as arguments of verbs like *know*, *guess*, *announce*, etc. There is no derivation according to which CQs are the main predicate of their clause. Thus, the semantic analogy between SSs and CQs not only weakens one of the motivations for the inverse predication approach, but it also refutes the analysis on the grounds that it does not provide a unified explanation of CQs and SSs.[8]

To summarize §8.2, we have reviewed the reading A/reading B ambiguity that SSs share with CQs. Reading B is derived by maintaining the SS intact throughout the derivation and using its intension. Reading A is generated by maintaining the SS intact and using its extension. Movement approaches that syntactically reconfigure the SS before interpretation fail to capture reading A. Inverse predication approaches that attribute the special semantic status of SSs to their function as main predicates fail to explain the parallel semantic behavior between SSs and CQs.

8.3 Flexible Degrees of Exhaustivity

This section presents novel data showing that definite SSs and CQs have readings with different degrees of exhaustivity, and that these readings are

[8] See Heycock and Kroch (1999: 373) for an earlier version of this counterargument based exclusively on reading B type examples.

unavailable for regular NPs (§8.3.1). There are two possible avenues to formalize the exhaustivity of *know* with an interrogative clause (§8.3.2). The first avenue, implementation (i), when extended to CQs and SSs, yields the syntax corresponding to the "as is" approach to connectivity (§8.3.3). The second avenue, implementation (ii), yields the syntax corresponding to the "question plus deletion" account (§8.3.4).

8.3.1 *Data on Degrees of Exhaustivity in SSs and CQs*

Definite CQs and SSs in Spanish—no matter whether they appear as free relatives or as full-fledged NPs'—[9]allow for existential-like readings in contexts where ordinary NPs do not.[10] Consider, first, the italicized free relative in the predicational sentence uttered by speaker B in the dialog (48):

(48) *Subject of a predicational sentence:*

A: He oído que Carlos ayer llevaba un sombrero de
Have-1s heard that Carlos yesterday was-wearing a hat of
ala ancha
brim wide

que causó la admiración de todos los presentes.
that caused the admiration of all the those-present

'I heard Carlos was wearing a wide-brimmed hat yesterday that everybody admired.'

B: (??) *Lo que también llevaba* estaba pasado de moda.
The that also was-wearing-3s was passed of style
Y, además, no le sentaba nada bien.
And, on-top-of-that, not to-him suited-3s at-all well

'*What he was also wearing* was out of style. And, on top of that, it didn't suit him at all.'

A: De eso no había oído nada...
About that not have-1s heard nothing...
'I hadn't heard anything about that...'

The free relative *lo que también llevaba* "what he was also wearing" in (48) refers to the sum of (roughly) all the garments that Carlos was wearing other than the hat. Of this sum, it is predicated that it was out of style. That is, if

[9] I assume that free relatives are semantically definite, as extensively argued in Jacobson (1995), Rullmann (1995), Grosu (1996), Dayal (1997), and Grosu and Landman (1998), among others.

[10] For simplicity, throughout §8.3 we will illustrate existential-like uses of CQs and SSs only with reading B.

besides the hat Carlos was wearing pants, a shirt, a vest, and shoes, (roughly) all these garments were out of style.[11]

Consider now the free relative *lo que también llevaba* "what he was also wearing" used as a CQ under *saber* "know" in (49). Now the free relative has a much weaker reading. For speaker B to have the property ⟦*saber lo que también llevaba*⟧ "to know what he was also wearing" in (49), it suffices that B knows *something* that Carlos was wearing besides the hat. That is, if Carlos was wearing pants, a shirt, a vest, and shoes besides the hat, for it to be true that B knows what Carlos was (also) wearing in (49) it suffices that B knows that Carlos was wearing tight orange pants. In fact, the existential-like reading at issue is exactly the same as in the interrogative counterpart in (50). This reading is commonly referred to as the "mention-some" reading (Groenendijk and Stokhof 1984; Beck and Rullmann 1999).

(49) *Concealed question:*

B: Sabes *lo que también llevaba?* Unos pantalones
Know-2s the that also was-wearing-3s? Some pants
naranjas estrechos
orange tight

que estaban pasados de moda. Y, además, no le
that were passed of style. And, on-top-of-that, not to-him
sentaban nada bien.
suited at-all well

'Do you know *what he was also wearing*? A pair of tight orange pants that were out of style. And, on top of that, they didn't suit him at all.'

[11] Three comments about definiteness and exhaustivity in predicational sentences are in order. First, the sum reading in (48B) including *roughly all* the remaining garments—i.e., allowing for possible exceptions—can be derived using ill-fitting covers (Brisson 1998) or the impure atom strategy (Landman 2000; Winter 2002). Still, this reading is a near-universal reading of the NP, in contrast to the much weaker, existential-like reading to be discussed for (49)–(51) in the text below. Second, truly existential-like truth conditions for definites in predicational sentences can be obtained in team credit scenarios. For example, (i) is true even if just three out of twenty reporters asked questions. But (49)–(51) do not have a sensible team credit interpretation and still the existential-like reading is available. Finally, existential readings of free relatives in predicational sentences have been observed in configurations like the locative adjunct in (ii) (Caponigro 2004). The examples (48), (49), and (51) in the text are construed as a minimal triple to factor out these configurations. See also footnote 12.

(i) The press/the reporters asked the candidate about his campain.

(ii) John has been where no one has been before.

(*a*) Existential reading: 'John has been in *some* place where no one has been before.'

(50) *Interrogative clause:*

B: Sabes qué llevaba también? Unos pantalones
Know-2s what was-wearing-3s also? Some pants
naranjas estrechos
orange tight

que estaban pasados de moda. Y, además, no le
that were passed of style. And, on-top-of-that, not to-him

sentaban nada bien.
suited at-all well

'Do you know what he was also wearing? A pair of tight orange pants that were out of style. And, on top of that, they didn't suit him at all.'

Interestingly, SSs pattern like CQs and unlike ordinary NPs in allowing this type of mention-some reading. This is shown in (51). Sentence (51) is true if Carlos was wearing tight orange pants besides the hat regardless of whether he was wearing any other garments or not. That is, the truth conditions of (51) are parallel to those of the existential paraphrase "*Something* he was wearing besides the hat was a pair of tight orange pants".

(51) *Specificational Subject:*

B: *Lo que también llevaba* eran unos pantalones naranjas
The that also was-wearing-3s were some pants orange
estrechos
tight

que estaban pasados de moda. Y, además, no le
that were passed of style. And, on-top-of-that, not to-him

sentaban nada bien.
suited at-all well

'*What he was also wearing* was a pair of tight orange pants that were out of style. And, on top of that, they didn't suit him at all.'

The following are two naturally occurring examples of free relative SSs with non-exhaustive readings. In (52), the SS *lo que también puede notar un usuario de Windows* "what a Windows user may also note" does not require an exhaustive listing of the remaining differences between Windows Internet Explorer and Firefox after the copula:

(52) http://www.tonyworld.net/?p=188
Mozilla Firefox es un potentísimo navegador, el cual está en su versión 1 recien estrenada. A simple vista de un usuario final, lo que más se

distingue en este, es la navegación por pestañas, muy útil para no tener varios navegadores consumiendo recursos o para *ahorrar espacio* en tu escritorio. A la larga *lo que también puede notar un usuario de Windows* es que Firefox es más seguro. Bien es cierto que hay muchas webs que solamente funcionan en un Explorer, pero todo eso debe ir cambiando.

'Mozilla Firefox is a very powerful navigator, now in its first version, recently released. For a final user, at first sight what is most distinctive in it is the navigation with tabs, very useful in order not to have several navigators using up resources or in order to save space on your desktop. In the long run, *what a Windows user may also notice* is that Firefox is safer. It's true that many web pages only work with the Explorer, but all that should change.'

In (53), *Lo que también puede suceder* "what may also happen" is equated with just one (other) thing that may happen in the cases at issue, without conveying exhaustivity. In fact, a few sentences later—in the sentence starting with *tambien* "also"—the speaker provides another example of what else may happen in these cases, clearly showing that the preceding specificational sentence was not meant exhaustively.

(53) http://notas.gemidos.com.ar/home.php?id=209
Los especialistas afirman que a sus consultorios llegan personas que sostienen tener sexo con sus parejas hasta incluso después de tres años de separados. En estos casos, ambos miembros de la pareja suelen mantener relaciones con terceros, pero no por ello dejan de tenerlas con sus ex. No es lo más común, por cierto, pero sucede. *Lo que también puede suceder*, señalan algunos de estos especialistas, es que exista un temor por parte de ambos de quedar solos, o bien de ver que su pareja rehizo su vida. Así, antes que quedarse solos, estas personas prefieren seguir manteniendo relaciones con su ex. [...] *También*, podría darse el caso de que mucho del enojo y la angustia que provocan los divorcios, pueda ser por lo menos aliviado mediante la seguridad de mantener un constante y seguro sexo, que además está prontamente disponible.

'The specialists claim that people come to their practices who have sex with their couples even three years after they separated. In these cases, both members of the couple usually have relations with third parties, but they don't stop having them with their ex. It isn't the most common thing, by the way, but it happens. *What also may happen*, as some specialists note, is that there is fear on both sides to end up alone or to see that their partner started a new life. Thus, rather than ending up alone, these people prefer to maintain their relation with their ex. [...] *Also*, it might happen that a lot of the anger and anguish caused by divorce might be palliated with the sense of security coming from regular and safe sex that is furthermore readily available.'

Definite NPs with overt *the* exhibit the same type of contrast between their use in predicational sentences on the one hand and their use as CQs and SSs on the other. I will illustrate the point with singular NPs linked to singular individuals rather than to plural sums. Here (non)-exhaustivity is recast as (non)-uniqueness.[12] The predicational sentence (54) presupposes that there is a unique album by Shakira that Luisa likes in addition to a particular one previously mentioned. In contrast, the CQ version in (55) is compatible with there being several other albums by Shakira that Luisa likes, as long as the speaker knows (/tells the hearer) the correct identity of one of them. The same holds for (56) with an embedded interrogative clause. Interestingly, non-uniqueness is allowed in the SS version in (57) as well. The specificational sentence in (57B), meant as a suggestion, does not commit the speaker to there being only one other album by Shakira that Luisa likes. It has an existential-like reading whose truth conditions can be paraphrased as "*There is an* album by Shakira that Luisa likes in addition to the salient one and that album equals *Dónde están los ladrones*."

(54) (?) Juan le ha regalado a Luisa_1 *el álbum de Shakira que*
Juan to-her has given to Luisa the album by Shakira that
también le_1 *gusta.*
also to-her pleases
'Juan gave Luisa_1 *the album by Shakira that* $\textit{she}_1$ *also likes*.'

(55) Si no sabes qué regalarle_1 a Luisa_1, sé /te diré
If not you-know what to-give+her_1 to Luisa_1, I-know /to-you I-will-tell
el álbum de Shakira que también le_1 *gusta.*
the album by Shakira that also to-her_1 pleases
'If you don't know what to give to Luisa_1, I know / I'll tell you *the album by Shakira that* $\textit{she}_1$ *also likes*.'

(56) Si no sabes qué regalarle_1 a Luisa_1, sé /te diré
If not you-know what to-give+her_1 to Luisa_1, I-know /to-you I-will-tell
qué álbum de Shakira también le_1 *gusta.*
what album by Shakira also to-her_1 pleases
'If you don't know what to give to Luisa_1, I know / I'll tell you *what album by Shakira* $\textit{she}_1$ *also likes*.'

[12] The uniqueness effect with singular definites in predicational sentences is exempt from the caveats and exceptions noted in footnote 11 for plurality-denoting definites.

(57) A: Luisa$_1$ ya tiene todos los álbumes de cantantes hispanos que me dijo que le$_1$ gustaban. Tiene *Un día normal*, *Servicio de lavandería*, *La flaca*, ... No se qué regarle.

'Luisa$_1$ already has all the albums by Hispanic singers that she$_1$ told me she$_1$ liked. She$_1$ has *A normal day*, *Laundry Service*, *The Thin One*, ... I don't know what to give her$_1$.'[13]

B: *El álbum de Shakira que también le$_1$ gusta* es *Dónde*
The album by S. that also to-her pleases is Where
están los ladrones.
are the thieves

Podrías regalarle ése. Creo que no lo tiene.
You-could give+her that. I-think that not it she-has

'*The album by Shakira that she$_1$ also likes* is *Where are the thieves*. You could give her$_1$ that one. I think she$_1$ doesn't have it.'

Example (58) is a naturally occurring example of a full-fledged definite NP functioning as SS without uniqueness. The sentence does not commit the speaker to there being only one other person (or one other *famous* person) staying at the relevant hotel. In fact, the speaker could continue enumerating other (famous) people staying at the hotel, as in (59).

(58) www.arcadi.espasa.com/000491.html
Context: Mr. Espada is staying at a certain hotel in Madrid.

Pues señor Espada, *la persona que también se aloja en ese hotel de*
So Mr. Espada, the person that also SE stays in that hotel in

Madrid es Viggo Mortensen.[14] Que ¿Por qué lo sé?
Madrid is Viggo Mortensen. COMPL how-come it I-know?
Sigo siendo periodista.
I-continue being journalist
'So, Mr. Espada, *the person that is also staying at that hotel in Madrid* is Viggo Mortensen. How come I know? I'm still a journalist.'

(59) ... Y también se hospeda allí la hermosa Natalie Portman, que realiza una actuación memorable en *La Guerra de las Galaxias—Episodio III*.

'And the beautiful Natalie Portman is also staying there, who gives a memorable performance in *Star Wars—Episode III*.'

[13] These three albums are by Juanés, Shakira and Jarabe de Palo respectively.
[14] V. Mortensen is best known for his role as Aragorn in the film trilogy *The Lord of the Rings*.

In sum, CQs and SSs pattern together in that they allow for mention-some readings with existential-like truth conditions, parallel to those found in interrogative clauses. They differ in this respect from their ordinary NP counterparts in predicational sentences. The latter require exhaustivity (or at least near-universality) and uniqueness in parallel contexts.[15]

8.3.2 *Degrees of Exhaustivity with Embedded Interrogatives*

Interrogative clauses can have a strongly exhaustive reading and a weakly exhaustive reading (Groenendijk and Stokhof 1984; Heim 1994), as illustrated in (60)–(61). Furthermore, as we saw above, they can also have a mention-some interpretation, witness (62) (Beck and Rullmann 1999):

(60) John knows who came.

⇒ Strongly exhaustive reading: 'For every x that came, John knows x came, and he knows that nobody other than those came.'

(61) John was surprised at who came (... but not at who didn't come).

⇒ Weakly exhaustive reading: 'For every x that came, John was surprised that x came.'

(62) John knows where you can buy Spanish ham.

⇒ Mention-some reading: 'For some x such that you can buy Spanish ham at x, John knows that you can buy Spanish ham at x.'

To capture this flexibility in degrees of exhaustivity, Heim (1994) and Beck and Rullmann (1999) use different answer operators, which we will call ANS_{STR} (for the strongly exhaustive answer reading), ANS_{WK} (for the weakly exhaustive answer interpretation), and ANS_{SOME} (for the mention-some answer).[16] Two implementations are in principle possible: (i) those operators are placed upon the meaning of the embedding verb, for example *know*, or (ii) those operators apply to the question meaning. In both of the

[15] Mention-some readings of CQs and SSs are more easily—though not exclusively—constructed using the particle *also* within the relative clause. In fact, the semantic contrast presented in the text is related to a judgment reported in Higgins (1973), suggesting that free relatives with embedded *también* "also" (associated with the trace) cannot be used in predicational sentences: "[i] has the specificational reading, [ii] the predicational reading" (Higgins 1973: 10). This grammaticality pattern is shared by many Spanish speakers: *también* "also" makes the predicational sentence (48B) somewhat deviant (signaled as ??) and the predicational (54) slightly marked (signaled as (?)), whereas it is perfectly fine in the corresponding CQs and SSs.

(i) What he is also pointing at is a kangaroo.

(ii) What he is pointing at is also a kangaroo.

[16] See van Rooy (2003) for an alternative approach to degrees of exhaustivity using Decision Theory.

implementations, the interrogative clause *[who came]* will be assumed to have a Karttunen-style question meaning, and, for the sake of illustration, it will be presumed to map the actual world w_0 to the set $\{\lambda w''.came(pat,w''), \lambda w''.came(sue,w'')\}$. This is sketched in (63):

(63) $[\![\textit{who came}]\!] = \lambda w.\ \{p: p(w)=1\ \&\ \exists x\ [p=\lambda w''.came(x,w'')]\}$
$= \text{e.g. } w_0 \text{ is mapped to } \{\lambda w''.came(pat,w''), \lambda w''.came(sue,w'')\}$

First, the exhaustivity operators are defined to apply to the verb *know*.[17] The resulting verbal complexes are given in (64)–(66). These verbal denotations combine with a question meaning (type <s,<<s,t>,t>>) and with the denotation of their subject to yield a proposition.

(64) $[\![\textit{know}\ \text{ANS}_{STR}]\!] = \lambda Q_{<s,<<s,t>,t>>}\lambda x_e\lambda w.\ \forall w' \in Dox_x(w)\ [Q(w') = Q(w)]$ STRONGLY EXH.

(65) $[\![\textit{know}\ \text{ANS}_{WK}]\!] = \lambda Q_{<s,<<s,t>,t>>}\lambda x_e\lambda w.\ \forall w' \in Dox_x(w)\ [Q(w') \supseteq Q(w)]$ WEAKLY EXH.

(66) $[\![\textit{know}\ \text{ANS}_{SOME}]\!] = \lambda Q_{<s,<<s,t>,t>>}\lambda x_e\lambda w.\ \exists q_{<s,t>}\ [q \in Q(w)\ \&\ \forall w' \in Dox_x(w)\ [q \in Q(w')]]$ MENTION-SOME

Alternatively, the answer operators may be designed to apply to a question meaning Q to yield a propositional concept. These operators are defined in (67)–(69). In this case, the denotation of the verb *know*—spelled out in (70)—will combine with the propositional concept ANS(Q) (type <s,<s,t>>) (or with a generalized quantifier over propositional concepts) and with the denotation of its subject to yield the final propositional meaning:[18]

(67) $\text{ANS}_{STR}(Q_{<s,<<s,t>,t>>}) = \lambda w\lambda w'.\ Q(w') = Q(w)$ STRONGLY EXH.

(68) $\text{ANS}_{WK}(Q_{<s,<<s,t>,t>>}) = \lambda w\lambda w'.\ Q(w') \supseteq Q(w)$ WEAKLY EXH.

(69) $\text{ANS}_{SOME}(Q_{<s,<<s,t>,t>>}) = \lambda P_{<<s,<s,t>>,<s,t>>}\lambda w.\ \exists p_{<s,t>}\ [p \in Q(w)\ \&\ P(\lambda w'\lambda w''.p(w'')=1)(w)]$ MENTION-SOME

(70) $[\![\textit{know}]\!] = \lambda p_{<s,<s,t>>}\lambda x_e\lambda w.\ \forall w' \in Dox_x(w)\ [p(w)(w')=1]$

17 For the purposes of this paper, it is immaterial whether there are operators in the lexicon that combine with the lexical entry *know* or whether *know* is simply lexically ambiguous.

18 Heim's (1994) actual ANS_{STR} and ANS_{WK} operators and Beck and Rullmann's (1999) ANS_{SOME} operator are the following:

(i) $\text{ANS2}(Q_{<s,<<s,t>,t>>},w) = \lambda w'.\ [\text{ANS1}(Q,w') = \text{ANS1}(Q,w)]$ STRONGLY EXHAUSTIVE

(ii) $\text{ANS1}(Q_{<s,<<s,t>,t>>},w) = \cap [\![Q]\!](w)$ WEAKLY EXHAUSTIVE

(iii) $\text{ANS3}(Q_{<s,<<s,t>,t>>},w) = \lambda P_{<s,<<s,t>,t>>}.\ \exists p_{<s,t>}\ [P(w)(p)\ \&\ p \in Q(w)]$ MENTION-SOME

Under either implementation, the combination of *know* with the answer operators and the question meaning yields the three interpretations in (71)–(73), varying in the strength of exhaustivity, as desired:

(71) $[\![$*John knows* ANS_{STR} *who came*$]\!]$

$= \lambda w.\ \forall w' \in Dox_{john}(w)\ [\ \{p: p(w')=1\ \&\ \exists x\ [p=\lambda w''.came(x,w'')]\} = \{p: p(w)=1\ \&\ \exists x\ [p=\lambda w''.came(x,w'')]\}\ ]$

$= 1$ e.g. in w_0 iff $\forall w' \in Dox_{john}(w_0)\ [\{p: p(w')=1\ \&\ \exists x\ [p=\lambda w''.came(x,w'')]\} = \{\lambda w''.came(pat,w''),\ \lambda w''.came(sue,w'')\}\ ]$

$= 1$ e.g. in w_0 iff $\forall w' \in Dox_{john}(w_0)\ [\ came(pat,w')\ \&\ came(sue,w')\ \&\ \neg\exists x\ [x \neq pat\ \&\ x \neq sue\ \&\ came(x,w')\ ]\ ]$

(72) $[\![$*John knows* ANS_{WK} *who came*$]\!]$

$= \lambda w.\ \forall w' \in Dox_{john}(w)\ [\ \{p: p(w')=1\ \&\ \exists x\ [p=\lambda w''.came(x,w'')]\} \supseteq \{p: p(w)=1\ \&\ \exists x\ [p=\lambda w''.came(x,w'')]\}\ ]$

$= 1$ e.g. in w_0 iff $\forall w' \in Dox_{john}(w_0)\ [\ \{p: p(w')=1\ \&\ \exists x\ [p=\lambda w''.came(x,w'')]\} \supseteq \{\lambda w''.came(pat,w''),\ \lambda w''.came(sue,w'')\}\ ]$

$= 1$ e.g. in w_0 iff $\forall w' \in Dox_{john}(w_0)\ [\ came(pat,w')\ \&\ came(sue,w')\ ]$

(73) $[\![$*John knows* ANS_{SOME} *who came*$]\!]$

$= \lambda w.\ \exists q_{<s,t>}\ [\ q \in \{p: p(w)=1\ \&\ \exists x\ [p=\lambda w''.came(x,w'')]\}\ \&\ \forall w' \in Dox_{john}(w)\ [q(w')=1]\ ]$

$= 1$ e.g. in w_0 iff $\exists q_{<s,t>}\ [\ q \in \{\lambda w''.came(pat,w''),\ \lambda w''.came(sue,w'')\}\ \&\ \forall w' \in Dox_{john}(w_0)\ [q(w')=1]\ ]$

8.3.3 *Implementation (i) for CQs and SSs and the "as is" Approach to Connectivity*

Implementation (i) combines the three answer operators with the verb. For *know* taking a CQ, this yields the verbal meanings (74)–(76). The only difference between these meanings and the ones in the previous section resides in the use of sums (of individuals) instead of sets (of worlds) and, consequently, on the use of the "part-of" relation $\leq$ instead of the membership relation $\in$ and subset relation $\subseteq$ (Link 1983).

(74) $[\![know_{CQ}\text{ANS}_{STR}]\!] = \lambda \underline{y}_{<se>} \lambda x_e \lambda w.\ \forall w' \in Dox_x(w)\ [\ \underline{y}(w') = \underline{y}(w)]$

STRONGLY EXHAUSTIVE

(75) $[\![know_{CQ}\text{ANS}_{WK}]\!] = \lambda \underline{y}_{<se>} \lambda x_e \lambda w.\ \forall w' \in Dox_x(w)\ [\ \underline{y}(w') \geq \underline{y}(w)\ ]$

WEAKLY EXHAUSTIVE

(76) $[\![know_{CQ}\text{ANS}_{SOME}]\!] = \lambda \underline{y}_{<se>} \lambda x_e \lambda w.\ \exists z_e[\ \underline{y}(w) \geq z\ \&\ \forall w' \in Dox_x(w)\ [\underline{y}(w') \geq z]]$

MENTION-SOME

This generates the three degrees of exhaustivity for the Spanish sentence (77) spelled out in (79)–(81). The semantic contribution of the CQ is given in (78). For the sake of illustration, I will assume that Pat and Sue are the persons that came in w_1 and that Pat, Sue, and Jane are the persons that came in w_2, as indicated in (78):[19]

(77) Juan sabe las personas que (también) vinieron.
Juan knows the persons that (also) came
'Juan knows what persons (also) came.'

(78) $[\![[\textit{the persons that came}]_{NP}]\!] = \lambda w''.\ \sigma x{:}came(x,w'')$
$= \text{e.g. } w_1 \text{ is mapped to pat+sue}$
$= \text{e.g. } w_2 \text{ is mapped to pat+sue+jane}$

(79) $[\![\textit{John know}_{CQ}\text{ANS}_{STR}\ \textit{the persons that came}]\!]$
$= \lambda w.\ \forall w' \in Dox_{john}(w)\ [\sigma x{:}came(x,w') = \sigma x{:}came(x,w)\ ]$
$= 1 \text{ e.g. in } w_1 \text{ iff } \forall w' \in Dox_{john}(w_1)\ [\sigma x{:}came(x,w') = pat+sue\ ]$

(80) $[\![\textit{John know}_{CQ}\text{ANS}_{WK}\ \textit{the persons that came}]\!]$
$= \lambda w.\ \forall w' \in Dox_{john}(w)\ [\sigma x{:}came(x,w') \geq \sigma x{:}came(x,w)\ ]$
$= 1 \text{ e.g. in } w_1 \text{ iff } \forall w' \in Dox_{john}(w_1)\ [\sigma x{:}came(x,w') \geq pat+sue\ ]$

(81) $[\![\textit{John know}_{CQ}\text{ANS}_{SOME}\ \textit{the persons that (also) came}]\!]$
$= \lambda w.\ \exists z_e[\ \sigma x{:}came(x,w) \geq z\ \&\ \forall w' \in Dox_j(w)\ [\sigma x{:}came(x,w') \geq z]]$
$= 1 \text{ e.g. in } w_2 \text{ iff } \exists z_e[\ pat+sue+jane \geq z\ \&\ \forall w' \in Dox_j(w_2)$
$[\sigma x{:}came(x,w') \geq z]]$

Parallel verbal meanings can be provided for specificational *be*:

(82) $[\![\text{ANS}_{STR}\ be_{SS}]\!] = \lambda x_e \lambda \underline{y}_{<s,e>} \lambda w.\ [\ \underline{y}(w) = x]$ STRONGLY EXHAUSTIVE

(83) $[\![\text{ANS}_{WK}\ be_{SS}]\!] = \lambda x_e \lambda \underline{y}_{<s,e>} \lambda w.\ [\ \underline{y}(w) \geq x\ ]$ WEAKLY EXHAUSTIVE

(84) $[\![\text{ANS}_{SOME}\ be_{SS}]\!] = \lambda x_e \lambda \underline{y}_{<s,e>} \lambda w.\ \exists z_e[\ \underline{y}(w) \geq z\ \&\ z = x\ ]$
MENTION-SOME

These verbal meanings yield the following degrees of exhaustivity for the Spanish sentence (85):[20]

[19] As with interrogative clauses, weakly exhaustive readings of CQs easily arise with verbs like Spanish *sorprender* 'surprise'. E.g., (i) is true in a scenario where the hearer will be surprised that the invited students were indeed invited without being surprised that the non-invited students were not (see Beck and Rullmann 1999).

(i) Ven a la fiesta y verás. Te sorprenderás de los estudiantes a los que
Come to the party and you'll-see. REFL be-surprised-Fut-2nd-sing of the students A the that
he invitado.
I-have invited
'Come to the party and you'll see. You'll be surprised at what students I have invited.'

[20] I was not able to find a context that would make a weakly exhaustive reading of *be* discernibly available. I return to this issue, and to the truth conditions in (87), at the end of §8.3.

(85) Las personas que (también) vinieron fueron Patricia y Susana.
The persons that (also) came were Patricia and Susana
'The persons that (also) came were Patricia and Susana.'

(86) ⟦*The persons that came* ANS_{STR} *were Pat and Sue*⟧
= $\lambda w.\ [\sigma x{:}came(x,w) = pat{+}sue\ ]$

(87) ⟦*The persons that came* ANS_{WK} *were Pat and Sue*⟧
= $\lambda w.\ [\sigma x{:}came(x,w) \geq pat{+}sue\ ]$

(88) ⟦*The persons that (also) came* ANS_{SOME} *were Pat and Sue*⟧
= $\lambda w.\ \exists z_e[\sigma x{:}came(x,w) \geq z\ \&\ z = pat{+}sue\ ]$

Under this implementation of exhaustivity with specificational *be*, the post-copular phrase in (85) is simply the NP $[_{NP}$ *Pat and Sue*$]$.[21] This is exactly the syntax that the "as is" approach to connectivity defends. According to the "as is" approach, the pre- and post-copular constituents are exactly as we see them in the surface string. Semantic interpretation and connectivity are read off from this surface syntax. Semantically, *be* is taken as the cross-categorial expression of identity ('='), asserting that the pre- and post-copular sentences have the same denotation. This is exemplified in (89)–(90). Connectivity follows from the resulting semantics (opacity connectivity) once we add Skolem functions (for variable binding connectivity) and some version of Reinhart's (1983) rule I (for Binding Theory connectivity).[22]

(89) What Mary read was *Huck Finn.*

(90) *"As is" account:*

(*a*)S-Str / LF: $[_{NP}$ What Mary read$]$ was $[_{NP}$ *Huck Finn*$]$

(*b*)Semantics: $Max\ (\lambda x.read(m,x)) = hf$

(*b′*) Semantics: $\lambda w.\ [\ Max\ (\lambda x.read(m,x,w)) = hf\ ]$

8.3.4 *Implementation (ii) for CQs and SSs and the "Question Plus Deletion" Account*

In implementation (ii) the answer operators combine with the argument NP. In a parallel way to (67)–(69), the answer operators defined below apply to the individual concept contributed by the CQ or SS to yield a propositional concept (or a generalized quantifier over propositional concepts):

[21] One could of course define *be*+ANS in a way that would require a propositional argument after the copula. The point, though, is that it is possible to define *be*+ANS as taking a simple NP after the copula.

[22] See Sharvit (1999*a*) for details on the semantic derivation of connectivity. (90*b*) reproduces Sharvit's formulation, and (90*b′*) makes the world variables explicit.

(91) $\text{ANS}_{STR}(\underline{y}_{<s,e>}) \quad = \quad \lambda w \lambda w'.\ \underline{y}(w') = \underline{y}(w)$ STRONGLY EXH.

(92) $\text{ANS}_{WK}(\underline{y}_{<s,e>}) \quad = \quad \lambda w \lambda w'.\ \underline{y}(w') \geq \underline{y}(w)$ WEAKLY EXH.

(93) $\text{ANS}_{SOME}(\underline{y}_{<s,e>}) \quad = \quad \lambda P_{<<s,<s,t>>,<s,t>>} \lambda w. \exists z_e [\ \underline{y}(w) \geq z\ \&\ P(\lambda w' \lambda w''. \underline{y}(w'') \geq z)(w)]$ MENTION-SOME

When applied to the CQ or SS in (94), the results in (95)–(97) obtain:

(94) $[\![[\textit{the persons that came}]_{NP}]\!] = \lambda w''.\ \sigma x\text{: came}(x,w'')$
= e.g. w_1 is mapped to pat+sue
= e.g. w_2 is mapped to pat+sue+jane

(95) $\text{ANS}_{STR}([\![\textit{the persons that came}]\!]) = \lambda w \lambda w'.[\sigma x\text{:came}(x,w') = \sigma x\text{:came}(x,w)]$

(96) $\text{ANS}_{WK}([\![\textit{the persons that came}]\!]) = \lambda w \lambda w'.[\sigma x\text{:came}(x,w') \geq \sigma x\text{:came}(x,w)]$

(97) $\text{ANS}_{SOME}([\![\textit{the persons that came}]\!]) = \lambda P_{<<s,<s,t>>,<s,t>>} \lambda w. \exists z_e [\ \sigma x\text{:came}(x,w) \geq z\ \&\ P(\lambda w' \lambda w''. \sigma x\text{:came}(x,w'') \geq z)(w)]$

In the case of CQs, the complex ANS([[NP]]) then combines with *know*. The definition of *know* is the same as in (70), repeated below in (98). The Spanish example (77) *Juan sabe las personas que (también) vinieron* "Juan knows the people that (also) came" is then mapped to the following three sets of truth conditions:[23]

(98) $[\![\textit{know}]\!] = \lambda p_{<s,<s,t>>} \lambda x_e \lambda w.\ \forall w' \in Dox_x(w)\ [p(w)(w') = 1]$

(99) [[*John knows* ANS_{STR} *the persons that came*]]
$= \lambda w.\ \forall w' \in Dox_j(w)\ [\sigma x\text{:came}(x,w') = \sigma x\text{:came}(x,w)\ ]$
$= 1$ e.g. in w_1 iff $\forall w' \in Dox_j(w_1)\ [\sigma x\text{:came}(x,w') = \text{pat+sue}\ ]$

(100) [[*John knows* ANS_{WK} *the persons that came*]]
$= \lambda w.\ \forall w' \in Dox_j(w)\ [\sigma x\text{:came}(x,w') \geq \sigma x\text{:came}(x,w)\ ]$
$= 1$ e.g. in w_1 iff $\forall w' \in Dox_j(w_1)\ [\sigma x\text{:came}(x,w') \geq \text{pat+sue}\ ]$

(101) [[*John knows* ANS_{SOME} *the persons that (also) came*]]
$= \lambda w. \exists z_e [\ \sigma x\text{:came}(x,w) \geq z\ \&\ \forall w' \in Dox_j(w)\ [\sigma x\text{:came}(x,w') \geq z]\ ]$
$= 1$ e.g. in w_2 iff $\exists z_e [\ \text{pat+sue+jane} \geq z\ \&\ \forall w' \in Dox_j(w_2)\ [\sigma x\text{:came}(x,w') \geq z]\ ]$

In the case of SSs, a propositional version of *be* is needed that takes the propositional concept ANS([[SS]]) as its external argument. Note that

[23] (99)–(101) are identical to the formal translations (79)–(81) obtained in implementation (i).

ANS(⟦SS⟧) has to have a proposition-like type, since exhaustivity, built here into ANS(⟦CQ⟧) and ANS(⟦SS⟧), is encoded as part of the informativeness of a proposition (a more exhaustive proposition is a subset of the corresponding less exhaustive proposition). Once the complex ANS(⟦SS⟧) is assigned a proposition-like type, the post-copular argument must be propositional too. That is, the post-copular constituent in (102) must be taken as the partially elided sentence $[_{IP}$*Pat and Sue ~~came~~*$]$ rather than just as the NP $[_{NP}$ *Pat and Sue*$]$. This is because, if we take the post-copular phrase to be simply the NP $[_{NP}$ *Pat and Sue*$]$, there is no way to define a meaning of *be* that will derive the adequate equality accessing only the meanings of its proper arguments ANS(⟦SS⟧) and ⟦$[_{NP}$ *Pat and Sue*$]$⟧. In other words, if the post-copular constituent $[_{XP}$ *Pat and Sue*$]$ is of type e, *be* would need to access not the propositional concept ANS(⟦SS⟧), but the individual concept ⟦SS⟧ itself (which is in fact implementation (i)).

(102) Las personas que (también) vinieron fueron Patricia y Susana ~~vinieron~~.
The persons that (also) came were Patricia and Susana ~~came~~
'The persons that (also) came were Patricia and Susana ~~came~~.'

These compositionality considerations lead to the lexical entry for *be* in (103). When combined with the three ANS(⟦NP⟧) complexes in (95)–(97), the following truth conditions result:[24]

(103) $[\![be]\!] = \lambda q_{<s,t>} \lambda p_{<s,<s,t>>} \lambda w.\ p(w) = q$

(104) ⟦*The persons that came* ANS_{STR} *were Pat and Sue ~~came~~*⟧
$= \quad \lambda w\ [\ \lambda w'[\sigma x{:}came(x,w') = \sigma x{:}came(x,w)] =$
$\lambda w'[came(pat{+}sue,w')\ \&\ \text{nobody else came in } w']\ ]$
$= 1$ e.g. in w_1 iff $\lambda w'[\sigma x{:}came(x,w') = pat{+}sue] =$
$\lambda w'[came(pat{+}sue,w')\ \&\ \text{nobody else came in } w']$

(105) ⟦*The persons that came* ANS_{WK} *were Pat and Sue ~~came~~*⟧
$= \quad \lambda w\ [\ \lambda w'[\sigma x{:}came(x,w') \geq \sigma x{:}came(x,w)] =$
$\lambda w'[came(pat{+}sue,w')]\ ]$
$= 1$ e.g. in w_1 iff $\lambda w'[\sigma x{:}came(x,w') \geq pat{+}sue] =$
$\lambda w'[came(pat{+}sue,w')]$

(106) ⟦*The persons that (also) came* ANS_{SOME} *were Pat and Sue ~~came~~*⟧
$= \lambda w.\ \exists z_e[\sigma x{:}came(x,w) \geq z\ \&\ [\ \lambda w'.\sigma x{:}came(x,w') \geq z$

[24] (104) and (106) capture the same truth conditions—although with different λ-expressions—as (86) and (88) respectively under implementation (i). For the addition of *& nobody else came in w′* in (104), see text below. See also text below for (105).

$$= \lambda w'.\text{came}(\text{pat+sue},w')]]$$
$$= 1 \text{ e.g. in } w_2 \text{ iff}$$
$$\exists z_e[\text{pat+sue+jane} \geq z \ \&\ [\lambda w'.\sigma x{:}\text{came}(x,w') \geq z = \lambda w'.\text{came}(\text{pat+sue},w')]]$$

Let us turn now to connectivity. Under implementation (ii), we have seen that the post-copular phrase must be a full clause underlyingly. This is exactly the syntax that the "question plus deletion" approach proposes in order to account for connectivity (Ross 1972; den Dikken *et al.* 2000; Ross 2000; Schlenker 2003). The pre-copular constituent is considered to be either syntactically an interrogative clause (Ross 1972; den Dikken *et al.* 2000; Ross 2000) or syntactically an NP and semantically a question (Schlenker 2003). The post-copular constituent is a partially elided clause. Connectivity follows from the internal syntactic configuration of the post-verbal clause. This is illustrated in (107) for variable binding, in (108) for opacity, and in (109) for Binding Theory connectivity.

(107) *Variable binding connectivity:*
[$_{CP/NP}$ The woman no man$_1$ likes *e*] is [$_{IP}$ ~~no man likes~~ his$_1$ mother-in-law].

(108) *Opacity connectivity:*
[$_{CP/NP}$ What Mary is looking for *e*] is [$_{IP}$ ~~Mary is looking for~~ a unicorn]

(109) *Binding Theory connectivity:*

(*a*) Principle A: [$_{CP/NP}$ What John$_1$ is *e*] is [$_{IP}$ ~~John$_1$ is~~ a nuisance to himself$_1$]

(*b*) Principle B: *[$_{CP/NP}$ What John$_1$ is *e*] is [$_{IP}$ ~~John$_1$ is~~ a nuisance to him$_1$]

(*c*) Principle C: *[$_{CP/NP}$ What he$_1$ is *e*] is [$_{IP}$ ~~he$_1$ is~~ a nuisance to John$_1$]

Before concluding §8.3, some comments about the lexical entries for weak exhaustivity in implementation (i) and (ii) are in order. In implementation (i), the denotation of the complex [*ANS*$_{WK}$ *be*$_{SS}$] in (83) is modeled after the denotation of *[know*$_{CQ}$*ANS*$_{WK}$*]* in (75). The latter produces truth conditions distinctively corresponding to a weakly exhaustive reading of *know*. But, interestingly, [*ANS*$_{WK}$ *be*$_{SS}$] produces truth conditions, given in (87), that are equivalent to the mention-some reading in (88). This means that no distinctive weakly exhaustive reading of specificational *be* is generated. As for implementation (ii), Schlenker (2003) proposes that, in specificational sentences, the proposition asserted by the post-copular clause *[Pat and Sue ~~came~~]* can be intersected with the implicature arising from focal stress on *Pat* *and Sue*, that is, with the implicature that nobody else (other than them) came. This gives us the proposition "that Pat, Sue and nobody else came". Using ANS_{STR} and Schlenker's idea, (104) derives the strongly exhaustive reading of the sentence. Interestingly, when the weakly exhaustive operator ANS_{WK} is used, we obtain the strongly exhaustive reading again and not a weakly exhaustive reading. In other words, (105) with ANS_{WK} describes exactly the same set of worlds that (104) with ANS_{STR} does. An interesting consequence follows from these logical equivalences: no weakly exhaustive reading of *be* can be generated under implementation (i) nor under implementation (ii). This is a welcome result, since, in fact, I could not find a context that would bring up a distinctive weakly exhaustive reading of specificational *be*. The two implementations, thus, derive in a principled manner a full paradigm for *know* and a partial paradigm for *be* in terms of degrees of exhaustivity.[25]

To summarize §8.3, we have seen that definite CQs and SSs have, unlike ordinary NPs in predicational sentences, a flexibility in degrees of exhaustivity comparable to that previously observed in the literature for interrogative clauses. The exhaustivity data are compatible with the "as is" approach to connectivity and with the "question plus deletion" account, each under one possible implementation of flexible exhaustivity. In implementation (i), ANS combines with the verb and the post-copular constituent is fully overt, as in the "as is" account of connectivity. In implementation (ii), ANS combines with the CQ or SS and the post-copular constituent is a partially elided clause, as in the "question plus deletion" approach to connectivity.

The question, then, is: is there any empirical evidence to prefer one implementation of exhaustivity over the other, thus indirectly supporting one approach to connectivity over its contender? This question is addressed in the next section.

8.4 Pronominalization and Coordination

Building on Romero (2004), in this section I present two other properties that SSs and CQs share and that distinguish them from ordinary uses of NPs: pronominalization in languages with a referentially based gender system, and verbal coordination in languages without subject pro-drop. These data favor implementation (ii) and the "question plus deletion" account over implementation (i) and the "as is" account.

[25] I leave open whether the intersection of asserted and implicated content in embedded contexts is, in fact, generally allowed by the grammar or not. If it is, then ANS_{STR} will simply duplicate the result of ANS_{WK} in implementation (ii). If it isn't, then ANS_{STR} will yield the empty set of worlds and the reading will be discarded as a contradiction. Either way, a weakly exhaustive reading will not be generated for sentence (102).

8.4.1 *Pronominalization*

In English, when the NP *the actress that caused the trouble* is used as an ordinary NP argument of an extensional verb, a pronoun referring back to the semantic contribution of this NP must be in the feminine, as in (110). The same is true if a similar NP functions as argument of an ordinary intensional verb such as *look for*, witness (111):

(110) The actress that caused the trouble was very sorry. **She / *It** apologized.

(111) Every 4-year-old girl is looking for her fairy godmother because she's scared, and every 6-year-old girl is looking for **her / *it** because she's curious.

It has been noted that NPs used as SSs differ in this sense. When a singular NP is the subject of a specificational sentence, the neuter pronoun *it* must be used (Higgins 1973; Heycock and Kroch 1999 for English; see also Büring 1998 for German, Mikkelsen 2004 for Danish):[26]

(112) The actress that caused the trouble wasn't Jolie. **It / #She** was Kidman.

As noted in Romero (2004), CQs in English must pronominalize in the neuter form as well:[27]

(113) John guessed the winner of the Oscar for best actress before I guessed **it/ *her**.

Sentences (112) and (113) are examples of reading B, since the NP contributes its intension—here, an individual concept of type <s,e>—in both cases. Note that the requirement to pronominalize with *it* holds for SSs and CQs regardless of whether they involve reading B or reading A. Consider the examples (114) and (115) with reading A. There is an individual concept $\underline{x}_{<s,e>}$ or "question" about Oscar winners that we couldn't guess the value of. This $\underline{x}_{<s,e>}$ is referred to by the NP *The winner of the Oscar for best actress they couldn't (guess)*. Let us say $\underline{x}_{<s,e>}$ equals the individual concept "The winner of the Oscar for best actress in 2003". In (114), speaker A asserts that the value of $\underline{x}_{<s,e>}$ at the actual world w_0 is Jolie, and speaker B asserts that the correct value of $\underline{x}_{<s,e>}$ at w_0 is Kidman. In (115) it is asserted that Amy guessed what the correct value of $\underline{x}_{<s,e>}$ is at w_0. In both sentences, the pronoun anaphoric to the SS and to the CQ must appear in the neuter form.

26 If *She* is used in (112), the sentence is understood as identificational. This would be the case in a scenario where we see an actress cause some trouble from afar and we are trying to identify who she is from her looks. In this paper we are concerned only with specificational copular sentences.

27 *Her* is out in (113) for all the speakers I consulted. As for the neuter form *it*, some speakers found it slightly marked (with one question mark ?), preferring the VP-ellipsis version *[... before I did]*. Other speakers, though, did not hesitate to use *it*.

(114) (*a*) The winner of the Oscar for best actress they couldn't guess was Jolie.

(*b*) No! **It** / ***She** was Kidman.

(115) People were trying to guess the winner of the Oscar for best actress we couldn't, and Amy guessed **it** / ***her**.

The pattern described in (110)–(115) is not an accident of English. Finnish yields the same judgments. The inflected form of pronoun *hän* "she/he" for human referents must be used in the Finnish translation of (110)–(111). The pronoun *se* "it" for non-human referents must be used in the other four sentences.

What can the pronominalization pattern tell us about implementations (i) and (ii) and, thus, indirectly, about connectivity? According to implementation (i), CQs and SSs provide an individual concept of type <s,e> or an individual concept concept of type <s,<s,e>> that combines directly with the verbs *know* and *be*, as in (116).

(116) *Implementation (i)*:

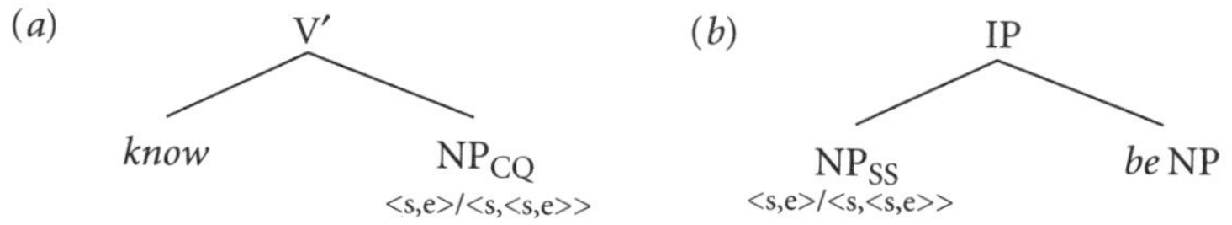

In contrast, in implementation (ii), CQs and SSs form a new constituent with ANS, and the semantic value of this new constituent is a propositional concept (type <s,<s,t>>). This is sketched in (117). Under this account, the syntax–semantics of the verbs *know* and *be* is more complicated than that of extensional or intensional verbs taking ordinary NPs. An extra propositional layer, provided by ANS, intervenes between *know* and *be* and their NPs.

(117) *Implementation (ii)*:

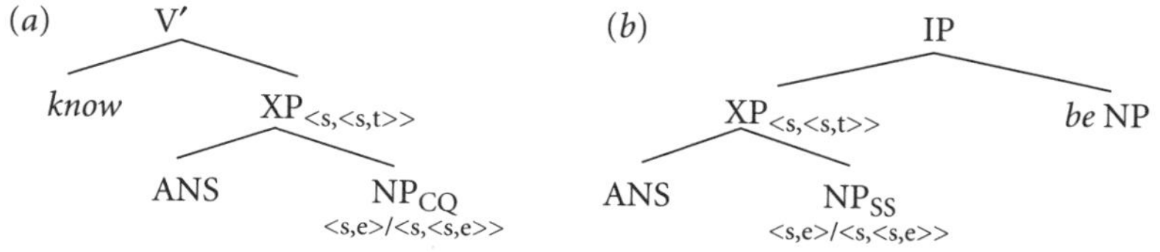

The contrast between CQs and SSs on the one hand and ordinary extensional and intensional NPs on the other is left unexplained under implementation (i). It is certainly expected that an individual of type e should be referred to by a pronoun in the appropriate gender in (110). But all the remaining examples—(111) with *look for*, (112) and (114) with *be*, and (113) and (115) with *guess* (or *know*)—involve a pronoun standing for an individual concept (concept) directly in argument position, and thus all these cases are expected to pattern alike. It is not clear why a given individual concept should be referred to by *she(/he)* in ordinary intensional contexts and by *it* in CQ and SS environments.

In implementation (ii), instead, the contrast between CQs/SSs and ordinary extensional/intensional NPs can be easily accounted for. Referents that are individual-like are pronominalized with different gender markings. In the same way that an individual of type e must be referred to with the appropriate gender pronoun, as in (110), so must an individual concept pronominalize with the appropriate gender, as in (111). Referents that are proposition-like are pronominalized invariably in the neuter form. The argument of *know* and *be* is propositional in nature. In the same way that a proposition is referred to by a neuter pronoun, as in (118), the propositional concepts ANS(⟦CQ⟧) and ANS(⟦SS⟧) must be referred to by neuter *it* in (112)–(115).

(118) Lucasz heard [that Barça won the league] on TV. Martin read **it** in the Kicker.

8.4.2 *Coordination*

As observed in Romero (2004), coordination of a verb taking a CQ—for example *know* or *guess*—with an extensional verb is deviant. This is shown in (119), which sounds like a play on words (in fact, like a zeugma). Similarly, specificational *be* cannot be coordinated with an extensional predicate like *have too much self-confidence*. Example (120) is judged ungrammatical:

(119) * John guessed and kissed the winner of the Oscar for best actress.

(120) * The person (/Who) $John_1$ admires the most is $himself_1$ and has too much self-confidence.

The examples above have reading B. The same ill-formedness in coordination obtains with reading A:

(121) * John guessed and kissed the Oscar winner Fred (only) guessed.

(122) * The anonymous writer that no $girl_1$ thought could possibly be her_1 mother was in fact her_1 oldest uncle and doesn't like family ties.[28]

28 See scenario (37) and compare the acceptable (38)—without coordination—with the ungrammatical (122)—with coordination.

What can these data tell us about implementations (i) and (ii), and thus indirectly about connectivity? Compare the unacceptable examples (119)–(122) involving *know* (or *guess*) and *be* with the grammatical example (123) involving *look for*. In (123), an ordinary intensional verb like *look for* is coordinated with an extensional verb. The resulting sentence is perfectly grammatical under the de dicto reading of the shared NP under *look for*. This means that, although *look for* requires an intensional argument and *find* expects an extensional individual, the two verbs can share their argument in a coordinated structure. Presumably, some type-shifting operation is able to relate the intensionalized individual of *look for* (a property in Zimmermann (1993), an intensional generalized quantifier in Moltmann (1997), or an individual concept) to the extensional individual of *find*.

(123) John is looking for but will not find a (/the best) secretary that speaks seven languages.

But, then, why is coordination between CQs/SSs and extensional verbs impossible?

In implementation (i), the pattern in (119)–(123) is hard to explain. If the difference between the individual concept <s,e> (or property <s,<e,t>>) required by *look for* and the extensional individual of type e required by *find* can be salvaged in (123), it is not clear why the same difference cannot be overlooked in (119)–(122).

Implementation (ii) offers a line of explanation: the semantic argument of *know* and *be* is not an intensionalized individual, but a propositional concept. The difference between an intensionalized individual and an extensional individual can be overcome. But the difference between a proposition-like object and an extensional individual cannot. The argument of an extensional verb and the argument of *know/be* are simply too different in nature: the former is individual-like, the latter is propositional. Thus, one NP cannot provide the right type of argument at the same time for an extensional verb and for *know/be* in the coordinated structures (119)–(122).

This coordination pattern is not an accident of English, but is supported by cross-linguistic data from German, Finnish, and Russian. In these languages, coordination between an ordinary intensional verb and an extensional verb is acceptable. Coordination between *know* or specificational *be* and an extensional predicate is disallowed, both in reading A and in reading B.[29]

To sum up §8.4, SSs and CQs—both in reading A and in reading B—exhibit special pronominalization and coordination patterns that distinguish

[29] One caveat needs to be made: I was unable to determine the status of the German example corresponding to (122), as my German informants did not agree with each other.

them from NPs in ordinary extensional and intensional contexts. SSs and CQs, unlike ordinary NPs, must pronominalize in the neuter form in languages with a referentially based gender system. This suggests that the semantic argument of *be* and *know* is not individual-like, but proposition-like. *Be* and *know*, unlike ordinary verbs, cannot share their argument with purely extensional verbs in a coordination structure. This suggests that the semantic argument of *be/know* and that of an ordinary verb are too different in nature. These observations follow straightforwardly from implementation (ii) and remain unaccounted for under implementation (ii). Thus, by supporting implementation (ii), the data in this section indirectly favor the "question plus deletion" approach to connectivity over the "as is" account.

8.5 Connectivity and the Post-Verbal Constituent in the "Question Plus Deletion" Account

All the arguments so far in this paper about specificational sentences have been concerned with the pre-copular phrase. In this section I turn to the post-copular constituent. I apply and extend the "question plus deletion" account from Schlenker (2003). The post-copular constituent is an (often) partially elided clause, and connectivity follows from the syntax–semantics of this clause. We will need the lexical entry for specificational *be* in (124*a*), repeated from (103), and I will illustrate the readings with the ANS$_{STR}$ operator in (124*b*), repeated from (91):[30]

(124) (*a*) $[\![be]\!] = \lambda q_{<s,t>} \lambda p_{<s,<s,t>>} \lambda w.\ p(w) = q$

(*b*) $\text{ANS}_{STR}(\underline{y}_{<s,e>}) = \lambda w \lambda w'.\ \underline{y}(w') = \underline{y}(w)$ STRONGLY EXH.

I start with examples of reading B. A simple example is (125*a*), with the underlying syntax in (125*b*). Example (126) contains the most important steps of the semantic computation:

(125) *Reading B:*

(*a*) The price that Fred thought *e* was \$1.29 was the price of milk.

(*b*) The price that Fred thought *e* was \$1.29 was [$_{IP}$ ~~Fred thought~~ the price of milk ~~was \$1.29~~]

30 In all the semantic computations below, for the ease of readability, I use ANS$_{STR}$ and add Schlenker's exhaustivity implicature in plain English when needed. [Note that, in (126*d*) and (129*e*), the uniqueness conveyed by Schlenker's implicature should be considered a presupposition, rather than part of the assertion, of the post-copular clause.] Also, the computations below are simplified in that I do not spell out how the meaning of the copular sentence embedded under *thought* is achieved. I only spell out the computation of the matrix copular sentences.

(126) *Semantic computation of reading B in (125):*

(*a*) Intension of the pre-copular NP:
$\lambda w''.\ \iota \underline{x}_{<s,e>}$ [price($\underline{x}$,w'') & $\forall w''' \in Dox_{fred}(w'')$ [$\underline{x}$(w''') = \$1.29]]

(*b*) ANS + NP's intension:
$\lambda w \lambda w'.$ [$\iota \underline{x}_{<s,e>}$ [price($\underline{x}$,w') & $\forall w''' \in Dox_{fred}(w')$ [$\underline{x}$(w''') = \$1.29]] = $\iota \underline{x}_{<s,e>}$ [price($\underline{x}$,w) & $\forall w''' \in Dox_{fred}(w)$ [$\underline{x}$(w''') = \$1.29]]]

(*c*) Post-verbal clause:
$\lambda w'.\ \forall w''' \in Dox_{fred}(w')$ [ιx_e [price-of-milk(x,w''')] = \$1.29]

(*d*) Entire sentence:
λw_0 [$\lambda w'.$ [$\iota \underline{x}_{<s,e>}$ [price($\underline{x}$,w') & $\forall w''' \in Dox_{fred}(w')$ [$\underline{x}$(w''') = \$1.29]] = $\iota \underline{x}_{<s,e>}$ [price($\underline{x}$,w_0) & $\forall w''' \in Dox_{fred}(w_0)$ [$\underline{x}$(w''') = \$1.29]]] =
$\lambda w'.\ \forall w''' \in Dox_{fred}(w')$ [ιx_e[price-of-milk(x,w''')] = \$1.29]
(and Fred thinks so of no other price)]

To paraphrase it informally, (126*d*) states that we are in a world w_0 such that correctly saying in w_0 what price Fred thought was \$1.29 is the same as saying that Fred thought the price of milk was \$1.29. Thus, the syntax–semantics of the post-copular clause derives the de dicto reading of *the price of milk* under *thought* (opacity connectivity), as desired.

An example of variable binding connectivity is (127*a*), with the underlying syntax in (127*b*). The pre-copular NP has a functional reading, just like the interrogative clause in (128). Functional readings in interrogative clauses have been derived using Skolem functions of type <e,e> (Engdahl 1986, among others), as in (128*a*), or choice functions of type <<e,t>,e> (Reinhart 1992, among others), as in (128*b*). I will use the former here for simplicity. In the same way that *what* in (128) does not range over individuals but over <e,e> functions, the value of $\iota \underline{x}$[...] in the SS in (127) at a given world will not be an individual but an <e,e> function. Other than that, the computation in (129) is parallel to the one for the previous example.

(127) *Reading B:*

(*a*) The anonymous writer that no $girl_1$ thinks *e* can possibly be her_1 mother is the one who writes to her_1 the least.

(*b*) The anonymous writer that no $girl_1$ thinks *e* can possibly be her_1 mother is [$_{IP}$ ~~no $girl_1$ thinks~~ the one who writes to her_1 the least ~~can possibly be her_1 mother~~]

(128) Q: Which relative of his_1 does everybody_1 like (best)? (A: His_1 oldest sibling.)

(*a*) $\lambda w \lambda p_{<s,t>}.\exists f_{<e,e>} [\forall x \in Dom(f)\ [\text{relative-of}(f(x),x,w] \ \&\ p = \lambda w'.\forall x\ [\text{like}(x,f(x),w')]\ ]$ (Skolem function)

(*b*) $\lambda w \lambda p_{<s,t>}.\exists f_{<<e,t>,e>} [p = \lambda w'.\ \forall x\ [\text{like}\ (x,\ f(\{y: \text{relative-of}(y,x,w')\}),\ w')]]$ (Choice function)

(129) *Semantic computation for reading B of (127):*

(*a*) Intension of the pre-copular NP:
$\lambda w''.\iota \underline{x}_{<s,<e,e>>} [\text{anon-writer}(\underline{x},w'') \ \&\ \neg\exists x_e[\text{girl}(x,w'') \wedge \forall w''' \in Dox_x(w'')\ [\underline{x}(w''')(x) = \iota u(\text{mother-of}(u,x,w'''))]]]$

(*b*) ANS + NP's intension:
$\lambda w \lambda w'.\ [\iota \underline{x}_{<s,<e,e>>} [\text{anon-writer}(\underline{x},w') \ \&\ \neg\exists x_e[\text{girl}(x,w') \wedge \forall w''' \in Dox_x\ (w')\ [\underline{x}(w''')(x) = \iota u(\text{mother-of}(u,x,w'''))]]]] =$
$\iota \underline{x}_{<s,<e,e>>} [\text{anon-writer}(\underline{x},w) \ \&\ \neg\exists x_e[\text{girl}(x,w) \wedge \forall w''' \in Dox_x(w)\ [\underline{x}(w''')(x) = \iota u(\text{mother-of}(u,x,w'''))]\ ]\ ]\ ]$

(*c*) Post-verbal clause:
$\lambda w'.\ \neg\exists x_e[\text{girl}(x,w') \wedge \forall w''' \in Dox_x(w')\ [\iota v(\text{write-least}(v,x,w''')) = \iota u(\text{mother-of}(u,x,w'''))]\ ]$

(*d*) Entire sentence:
$\lambda w_0\ [\lambda w'.\ \iota \underline{x}_{<s,<e,e>>} [\text{anon-writer}(\underline{x},w') \ \&\ \neg\exists x_e[\text{girl}(x,w') \wedge \forall w''' \in Dox_x\ (w')\ [\underline{x}(w''')(x) = \iota u(\text{mother-of}(u,x,w'''))]\ ]\ ]$
$= \iota \underline{x}_{<s,<e,e>>} [\text{anon-writer}(\underline{x},w_0) \ \&\ \neg\exists x_e[\text{girl}(x,w_0) \wedge \forall w''' \in Dox_x(w_0)\ [\underline{x}(w''')(x) = \iota u(\text{mother-of}(u,x,w'''))]\ ]\ ]$
$= \lambda w'.\neg\exists x_e[\text{girl}(x,w') \wedge \forall w''' \in Dox_x(w')\ [\iota v(\text{write-least}(v,x,w''')) = \iota u(\text{mother-of}(u,x,w'''))]\ ]$ (and there is no other anonymous writer-of <e,e> function with that characteristic)]

Informally paraphrased, (129*d*) states that we are in a world w_0 such that correctly saying in w_0 what (type of) anonymous writer no girl thinks can possibly be her mother is the same as saying that no girl thinks the anonymous writer that writes to her the least can possibly be her mother. This accounts for variable binding and opacity connectivity on the overt segment *the one who writes to* $\textit{her}_1$ *the least.*

I turn now to examples of reading A. According to Schlenker, even in very simple specificational sentences such as (130), the underlying syntax of the post-verbal constituent is clausal. The post-verbal clause here consists of a dyadic predicate *worry* of type <e,<e,<s,t>>> and the arguments *his* and *himself*, as in (131):

(130) His_1 worry is himself_1.

(131) Post-copular clause:

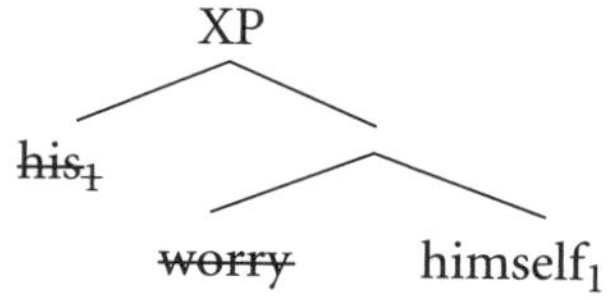

I will follow Schlenker in this respect. Furthermore, for reading A examples, we will need to take the extra step of creating a (dyadic or monadic) predicate that contains, as part of the defining property, the extension of the preceding SS.

Let us see this for sentence (132*a*). The monadic predicate we need in the post-verbal clause is *that price*, of type $<e,<s,t>>$, where *that* is anaphoric to the SS. This predicate describes the property "to be the value of that price", namely of the price $\iota \underline{x}_{<s,e>}[\ldots]$ referred to by the SS. This property is formally spelled out in (133*c*). Other than that, the semantic computation proceeds as usual.

(132) *Reading A:*

(*a*) The price that Fred thought *e* was \$1.29 was (in fact) \$1.79.

(*b*) The price that Fred thought *e* was \$1.29 was [$_{\text{Clause}}$ ~~that price~~ \$1.79]

(133) *Semantic computation of reading A in (131):*

(*a*) Extension at w_0 of the pre-copular NP:
$\iota \underline{x}_{<s,e>}$ [price($\underline{x}$,w_0) & $\forall w''' \in Dox_{fred}(w_0)$ [$\underline{x}(w''') = \$1.29$]]

(*b*) ANS + NP's extension:
$\lambda w \lambda w'.[\iota \underline{x}_{<s,e>}$ [price($\underline{x}$,w_0) & $\forall w''' \in Dox_{fred}(w_0)$ [$\underline{x}(w''') = \$1.29$]] $(w') = \iota \underline{x}_{<s,e>}$ [price($\underline{x}$,w_0) & $\forall w''' \in Dox_{fred}(w_0)$ [$\underline{x}(w''')$ $= \$1.29$]] (w)]

(*c*) The property "to be the value of that price":
$\lambda y_e \lambda w'.\ \iota \underline{x}_{<s,e>}$ [price($\underline{x}$,w_0) & $\forall w''' \in Dox_{fred}(w_0)$ [$\underline{x}(w''') = \$1.29$]] $(w') = y$

(*d*) Post-verbal clause:
$\lambda w'.\ \iota \underline{x}_{<s,e>}$ [price($\underline{x}$,w_0) & $\forall w''' \in Dox_{fred}(w_0)$ [$\underline{x}(w''') = \$1.29$]] $(w') = \$1.79$

(*e*) Entire sentence:
$\lambda w_0\ [\lambda w'.[\iota \underline{x}_{<s,e>}$ [price($\underline{x}$,w_0) & $\forall w''' \in Dox_{fred}(w_0)$ [$\underline{x}(w''')$] $= \$1.29$]] $(w') = \iota \underline{x}_{<s,e>}$ [price($\underline{x}$,w_0) & $\forall w''' \in Dox_{fred}(w_0)$ [$\underline{x}(w''') = \$1.29$]] (w_0)]
$= \lambda w'.\ \iota \underline{x}_{<s,e>}$ [price($\underline{x}$,w_0) & $\forall w''' \in Dox_{fred}(w_0)$ [$\underline{x}(w''') = \$1.29$]] $(w') = \$1.79$]

The λ-expression in (133*e*) states that we are in a world w_0 where the following is true. Consider the price $\underline{x}_{<s,e>}$ that Fred thought in w_0 had \$1.29 as its value. No matter what $\underline{x}_{<s,e>}$ actually stands for (e.g., for "the price of milk", "the price of oil", etc.), correctly saying at w_0 what value $\underline{x}_{<s,e>}$ has when applied to the actual world is the same as saying that $\underline{x}_{<s,e>}$ yields value \$1.79 when applied to the actual world. Notice that no opacity connectivity arises here: the value \$1.79 is never in the scope of the quantifier $\forall w'''$ over Fred's doxastic alternatives. This is a welcome result, as the sentence makes no claims about Fred's thoughts about the value \$1.79.[31]

Finally, (134) illustrates the creation of a dyadic predicate based on the SS's extension. We need the dyadic predicate *writer-of with those characteristics* (or something like it), of type <e,<e,<s,t>>>, where *those* is anaphoric to the SS. Furthermore, we need to assume that the Genitive position of that predicate is occupied by the elided quantified NP *every girl*, as in (134*b*):

(134) *Reading A:*

(*a*) The anonymous writer that no $girl_1$ thinks *e* can possibly be her_1 mother is (in fact) her_1 oldest uncle.

(*b*) The anonymous writer that no $girl_1$ thinks *e* can possibly be her_1 mother is

$[_{Clause}$ ~~every girl's$_1$ writer with those characteristics~~ her_1 oldest uncle]

This predicate describes the property formalized in (135*c*). Consider the $\underline{x}_{<s,<e,e>>}$ referred to by the preceding SS, namely the $\underline{x}_{<s,<e,e>>}$ such that no girl x thinks in the actual world w_0 that $\underline{x}_{<s,<e,e>>}(w_0)(x)$ equals x's mother. Never mind what $\underline{x}_{<s,<e,e>>}$ stands for (e.g., for "the anonymous writer that writes to her the least", "the anonymous writer that only writes to her on Sundays", etc.). Whatever it is that $\underline{x}_{<s,<e,e>>}$ stands for, the dyadic property ⟦*writer-of with those characteristics*⟧ applied to (an anonymous writer) y, to (a girl) z and to a world w′ yields TRUE iff $\underline{x}_{<s,<e,e>>}(w')$ is a function that maps (the girl) z to (the anonymous writer) y, that is, iff y anonymously writes to the girl z at w′ in the way required by $\underline{x}_{<s,<e,e>>}$. The rest of the computation proceeds as usual:

(135) *Semantic computation for reading A of (134):*

(*a*) Extension at w_0 of the pre-copular NP:

$$\iota\underline{x}_{<s,<e,e>>}\ [\text{anon-writer}(\underline{x},w_0)\ \&\ \neg\exists x_e[\text{girl}(x,w_0) \wedge \forall w''' \in \text{Dox}_x(w_0)\ [\underline{x}(w''')(x) = \iota u(\text{mother-of}(u,x,w'''))]\ ]\ ]$$

[31] Thus, the problem faced by the movement approach to connectivity described in §8.2.3 does not arise here: \$1.79 is not equated to \$1.29 in Fred's doxastic alternatives.

(*b*) ANS + NP's extension:
$\lambda w \lambda w'. [\iota \underline{x}_{<s,<e,e>>} [\text{anon-writer}(\underline{x},w_0) \ \&\ \neg\exists x_e[\text{girl}(x,w_0) \wedge \forall w''' \in Dox_x(w_0)\ [\underline{x}(w''')(x) = \iota u(\text{mother-of}(u,x,w'''))]]]]\ (w')$
$= \iota \underline{x}_{<s,<e,e>>} [\text{anon-writer}(\underline{x},w_0) \ \&\ \neg\exists x_e[\text{girl}(x,w_0) \wedge \forall w''' \in Dox_x(w_0)\ [\underline{x}(w''')(x) = \iota u(\text{mother-of}(u,x,w'''))]]]]\ (w)\ ]$

(*c*) The function <e,<e,<s,t>>> 'anonymous writer-of with those characteristics':
$\lambda y_e \lambda z_e \lambda w'. \iota \underline{x}_{<s,<e,e>>} [\text{anon-writer}(\underline{x},w_0) \ \&\ \neg\exists x_e[\text{girl}(x,w_0) \wedge \forall w''' \in Dox_x(w_0)\ [\underline{x}(w''')(x) = \iota u(\text{mother-of}(u,x,w'''))]]]]\ (w')\ (z) = y$

(*d*) Post-verbal clause:
$\lambda w'. \forall z\ [\text{girl}(z,w') \rightarrow \iota \underline{x}_{<s,<e,e>>} [\text{anon-writer}(\underline{x},w_0) \ \&\ \neg\exists x_e[\text{girl}(x,w_0) \wedge \forall w''' \in Dox_x(w_0)\ [\underline{x}(w''')(x) = \iota u(\text{mother-of}(u,x,w'''))]]]]\ (w')\ (z) = \iota v(\text{oldest-uncle-of}(v,z,w'))\ ]$

(*e*) Entire sentence:
$\lambda w_0\ [\ \lambda w'. [\ \iota \underline{x}_{<s,<e,e>>} [\text{anon-writer}(\underline{x},w_0) \ \&\ \neg\exists x_e[\text{girl}(x,w_0) \wedge \forall w''' \in Dox_x(w_0)\ [\underline{x}(w''')(x) = \iota u(\text{mother-of}(u,x,w'''))]]]]\ (w')$
$= \iota \underline{x}_{<s,<e,e>>} [\text{anon-writer}(\underline{x},w_0) \ \&\ \neg\exists x_e[\text{girl}(x,w_0) \wedge \forall w''' \in Dox_x(w_0)\ [\underline{x}(w''')(x) = \iota u(\text{mother-of}(u,x,w'''))]]]]\ (w_0)]$
$= \lambda w'. \forall z\ [\text{girl}(z,w') \rightarrow \iota \underline{x}_{<s,<e,e>>} [\text{anon-writer}(\underline{x},w_0) \ \&\ \neg\exists x_e[\text{girl}(x,w_0) \wedge \forall w''' \in Dox_x(w_0)\ [\underline{x}(w''')(x)$
$= \iota u(\text{mother-of}(u,x,w'''))]]]]\ (w')\ (z)$
$= \iota v(\text{oldest-uncle-of}(v,z,w'))\ ]\ ]$

The resulting λ-expression in (135*e*) states that we are in a world w_0 such that correctly saying at w_0 what value $\underline{x}_{<s,<e,e>>}$ has when applied to the actual world is the same as saying that $\underline{x}_{<s,<e,e>>}$ applied to the actual world yields a function of type <e,e> that maps every girl to her oldest uncle. Note that this derives variable binding connectivity but no opacity connectivity for the post-verbal segment *her oldest uncle.* Binding of ⟦*her*⟧—that is of the variable z in $\iota v(\text{oldest-uncle-of}(v,z,w'))$—by *every girl* produces the effect of variable binding connectivity. But ⟦*her oldest uncle*⟧ never gets evaluated, not even indirectly, under Fred's doxastic worlds w''', and hence opacity does not ensue. This is the correct empirical result. As the reader can check, sentence (134*a*) makes no claims about any girl's beliefs about her oldest uncle.[32]

In sum, the original "question plus deletion" account uniformly derives all types of connectivity—opacity, variable binding, etc.—for specificational

[32] Thus, (135*e*) avoids the problem discussed for the movement approach in §8.2.3: her oldest uncle is not equated to her mother under any girl's doxastic alternatives.

sentences with reading B. Once we consider properties that are built using the extension of the preceding SS, the "question plus deletion" account derives the correct *partial* connectivity pattern for specificational sentences with reading A. This partial connectivity pattern includes variable binding but not opacity.[33]

8.6 Conclusions

The present paper has been concerned with the semantic characterization of the pre-copular phrase—called Specificational Subject (SS)—in specificational copular sentences and with the consequences of this characterization for connectivity. Three sets of data have been presented concerning the interpretation of SSs. In all three cases, SSs with *be* pattern like concealed question NPs (CQs) with *know* and differ from (some or all) ordinary NPs, arguing for a unified analysis of SSs and CQs. After each set of data, the consequences of the empirical data and the corresponding analysis for connectivity have been evaluated, reaching the following conclusions.

The first set of data introduced Romero's (2005) ambiguity between reading A and reading B in SSs and CQs. The same ambiguity, it was argued, is found in ordinary NPs functioning as arguments of intensional verbs. To generate reading A, the SS must maintain its surface form at the syntactic level of representation at which semantics applies. This conflicts with the replacement mechanism in the movement approach to connectivity. As for the inverse predication analysis of specificational sentences and connectivity, it cannot explain the parallel semantic behavior of SSs and CQs.

The second set of data showed that definite SSs and CQs in Spanish allow for flexible degrees of exhaustivity, much like interrogative clauses and unlike ordinary NPs in extensional contexts. This flexibility is compatible with the "as is" approach to connectivity—under implementation (i) of exhaustivity—and with the "question plus deletion" approach—under implementation (ii).

The third set contained data on pronominalization and coordination. The patterns found suggest that the semantic argument of *be* and *know*

[33] Heller (2002) discusses a certain type of copula in Hebrew—agreeing pronZ—that also exhibits partial connectivity. Among other characteristics (see her summary on page p. 277), Heller claims that agreeing pronZ displays variable binding connectivity but not opacity. However, note that her examples of variable binding connectivity involve the quantifier *every* (her (32)), which is known to allow binding outside a Relative Clause even in predicational sentences (see footnote 1 in the present paper). Hence, it is not clear whether agreeing pronZ displays the type of variable binding connectivity that characterizes specificational sentences. The example (134) of reading A above, with the quantifier *no*, illustrates the relevant variable binding connectivity and, thus, it is a clear example of partial connectivity. I regret having to leave other connectivity effects in reading A—e.g. Binding Theory connectivity—for future research.

is proposition-like, whereas the semantic argument of ordinary extensional and intensional verbs is individual-like. This supports implementation (ii) of exhaustivity, where the ANS operator creates an extra propositional layer between *be/know* and the NP itself. This, in turn, favors the "question plus deletion" approach to connectivity over the "as is" account.

Finally, we have illustrated how connectivity is derived from the syntax–semantics of the post-copular constituent in the "question plus deletion" account. This account correctly derives the full connectivity paradigm for reading B examples and a partial connectivity paradigm for examples with reading A.

References

AKMAJIAN, A. 1970. 'On deriving cleft sentences from pseudocleft sentences', *Linguistic Inquiry*, 1: 140–68.

BECK, S. and RULLMANN, H. 1999. 'A flexible approach to exhaustivity in questions', *Natural Language Semantics*, 7: 249–98.

BOŠKOVIĆ, Z. 1997. 'Pseudoclefts', *Studia Linguistica*, 51: 235–77.

BRISSON, C. 1998. Distributivity, Maximality, and Floating Quantifiers, Ph.D. dissertation, Rutgers University.

BÜRING, D. 1998. 'Identity, Modality, and the Candidate Behind the Wall', in D. Strolovitch and A. Lawson (eds), *Proceedings of Semantics and Linguistic Theory VIII*, CLC. Ithaca, NY: Cornell University. 36–54.

CAPONIGRO, I. 2004. 'The semantic contribution of *wh*-words and type-shifts: Evidence from free relatives crosslinguistically', in R. Young (ed.), *Proceedings of Semantics and Linguistic Theory XIV*. CLC, Ithaca, NY: Cornell University. 38–55.

—— and HELLER, D. This volume. 'The non-concealed nature of free relatives: Implications for connectivity in specificational sentences', in C. Barker and P. Jacobson (eds), *Direct Compositionality*. Oxford: Oxford University Press. 237–63.

CECCHETTO, C. 2000. 'Connectivity and anti-connectivity in pseudoclefts', in M. Hirotani, A. Coetzee, N. Hall, and J.-Y. Kim (eds), *Proceedings of the North East Linguistic Society 30*. GLSA, Amherst, MA: University of Massachusetts. 137–51.

CHIERCHIA, G. 1993. 'Questions with Quantifiers', *Natural Language Semantics*, 1: 181–234.

CULICOVER, P. 1977. 'Some observations concerning pseudo-clefts', *Linguistic Analysis* 3: 347–75.

DAYAL, V. 1997. 'Free relatives and *ever*: Identity and free choice readings', in A. Lawson (ed.), *Proceedings of Semantics and Linguistic Theory VII*. CLC, Ithaca, NY: Cornell University. 99–116.

DEN DIKKEN, M., MEINUNGER, A., and WILDER, C. 2000. 'Pseudoclefts and ellipsis', *Studia Linguistica*, 54: 41–89.

ENGDAHL, E. 1986. *Constituent Questions*. Dordrecht: Reidel.

Farkas, D. 1993. 'Modal anchoring and NP scope', Linguistics Research Center working paper LRC-93-08, University of California, Santa Cruz.

Groenendijk, J. and Stokhof, M. 1984. Studies on the Semantics of Questions and the Pragmatics of Answers. Ph.D. dissertation, University of Amsterdam.

Grosu, A. 1973. 'On the status of the so-called right roof constraint', *Language*, 49: 294–311.

—— 1996. 'The proper analysis of "missing-P" free relative constructions', *Linguistic Inquiry*, 27: 257–93.

—— and Landman, F. 1998. 'Strange relatives of the third kind', *Natural Language Semantics*, 6: 125–70.

Halvorsen, P. K. 1978. The Syntax and Semantics of Cleft Constructions. Ph.D. dissertation, University of Texas, Austin.

Heller, D. 2002. 'On the relation of connectivity and specificational pseudoclefts', *Natural Language Semantics*, 10: 243–84.

Heim, I. 1979. 'Concealed questions', in R. Bäuerle, U. Egli, and A. von Stechow (eds), *Semantics from Different Points of View*. Berlin: Springer. 51–60.

—— 1994. 'Interrogative semantics and Karttunen's semantics for *know*', in R. Buchalla and A. Mittwoch (eds), *Proceedings of the Israeli Association for Theoretical Linguistics I*. Jerusalem: Akademon.

—— and Kratzer, A. 1998. *Semantics in Generative Grammar*. Oxford: Blackwell.

Heycock, C. and Kroch, A. 1999. 'Pseudocleft connectedness: Implications for the LF interface level', *Linguistic Inquiry*, 30: 365–97.

Higgins, R. 1973. *The Pseudocleft Construction in English*. Ph.D. Dissertation, MIT [revised version published by Garland, New York, 1979; page references are to this version].

Jacobson, P. 1994. 'Binding connectivity in copular sentences', in M. Harvey and L. Santelmann (eds), *Proceedings of Semantics and Linguistic Theory IV*. CLC, Ithaca, NY: Cornell University. 161–78.

—— 1995. 'On the quantificational force of English free relatives', in E. Bach, E. Jelinek, A. Kratzer, and B. Partee (eds), *Quantification in Natural Languages*, ii, Dordrecht: Kluwer. 451–86.

Karttunen, L. 1977. 'Syntax and semantics of questions', *Linguistics and Philosophy*, 1: 3–44.

Landman, F. 2000. *Events and Plurality*. Dordrecht: Kluwer.

Link, G. 1983. 'The logical analysis of plurals and mass terms', in R. Bäuerle, C. Schwarze, and A. von Stechow (eds), *Meaning, Use and Interpretation of Language*, Berlin: de Gruyter. 302–23.

Mikkelsen, L. 2004. Specifying who: On the structure, meaning, and use of specificational copular clauses. Ph.D. dissertation, University of California, Santa Cruz.

Moltmann, F. 1997. 'Intensional verbs and quantifiers', *Natural Language Semantics*, 5: 1–52.

Moro, A. 1997. *The Raising of Predicates: Predicative Noun Phrases and the Theory of Clause Structure*. Cambridge: Cambridge University Press.

NATHAN, L. 2005. 'The interpretation of concealed questions', talk presented at the West Coast Conference in Formal Linguistics 24.

PARTEE, B. 1986. 'Ambiguous pseudoclefts with unambiguous *be*', in S. Berman, J. Choe, and J. McDonough (eds), *Proceedings of the North East Linguistic Society 16*. GLSA, Amherst, MA: University of Massachusetts. 354–66.

PERCUS, O. 2000. 'Constraints on some other variables in syntax', *Natural Language Semantics*, 8: 173–229.

REINHART, T. 1983. 'Coreference and bound anaphora', *Linguistics and Philosophy*, 6: 47–88.

—— 1992. 'Wh-in-situ: An apparent paradox', in P. Dekker and M. Stokhof (eds), *Proceedings of the 8th Amsterdam Colloquium*, ILLC / Department of Philosophy, University of Amsterdam. 483–91.

ROMERO, M. 2004. 'Intensional noun phrases with *know* and *be*', *Catalan Journal of Linguistics*, 3: 147–78.

—— 2005. 'Concealed questions and specificational subjects', *Linguistics and Philosophy*, 28: 687–737.

VAN ROOY, R. 2003. 'Questioning to resolve decision problems', *Linguistics and Philosophy*, 26: 727–63.

ROSS, J. R. 1972. 'Act', in D. Davidson and G. Harman (eds), *Semantics of Natural Language*. Dordrecht: Reidel. 70–126.

—— 2000. 'The frozenness of pseudoclefts—towards an inequality-based syntax', MS, University of North Texas.

RULLMANN, H. 1995. Maximality in the Semantics of WH-Constructions. Ph.D. dissertation, University of Massachusetts, Amherst.

SCHLENKER, P. 2003. 'Clausal equations (a note on the connectivity problem)', *Natural Language and Linguistic Theory*, 21: 157–214.

SHARVIT, Y. 1999*a*. 'Connectivity in specificational sentences', *Natural Language Semantics*, 7: 299–339.

—— 1999*b*. 'Functional relative clauses', *Linguistics and Philosophy*, 22: 447–78.

WILLIAMS, E. 1983. 'Semantic vs. syntactic categories', *Linguistics and Philosophy*, 6: 423–46.

—— 1994. *Thematic Structure in Syntax*. Cambridge, MA: MIT Press.

WINTER, Y. 2002. 'Atoms and sets: A characterization of semantic number', *Linguistic Inquiry*, 33: 493–505.

ZIMMERMANN, E. 1993. 'On the proper treatment of opacity in certain verbs', *Natural Language Semantics*, 1: 149–79.

9

Degree Quantifiers, Position of Merger Effects with their Restrictors, and Conservativity

RAJESH BHATT AND ROUMYANA PANCHEVA

9.1 Outline

Degree clauses are arguments of the degree quantifiers *-er* and *as,* yet the dependency is discontinuous. The surface position of the degree clause is not arbitrary, however, but marks the scope of the comparison. In earlier work (Bhatt and Pancheva 2004), we accounted for these facts by proposing that degree quantifiers are composed with their first argument—the degree clause (marked as A in (1))—in a post-quantifier raising (QR) scope position.

(1) 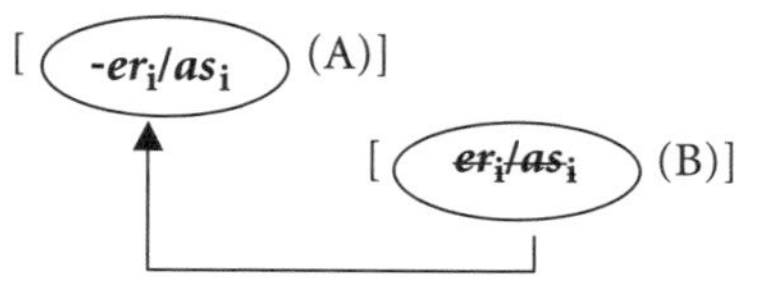

late merger to the QRed *-er/as*

We argued that late merger for comparative clauses is motivated by two factors, namely the non-conservative semantics of *-er* and Fox's (2001, 2002) mechanism of interpreting copies of moved expressions. We showed that an early merger of the comparative clause to an in-situ *-er* leads to a contradiction. Thus, late merger is the only option. However, this explanation is not available for equatives. The meaning of *as*, according to the standard definition (cf. (2*a*)) is conservative. Thus, early merger of the equative clause does not lead to a contradiction. We explore the consequences of positing an alternative meaning for *as* in (2*b*). We also consider the contribution of the factor argument of *as*, as in (3).

(2) (*a*) *as* (A)(B) = 1 iff $A \subseteq B$

(*b*) *as* (A)(B) = 1 iff $A = B$

(3) John is *twice* as tall as Tim is.

Finally, we discuss the connection between the conservativity of quantifiers and the position of merger of their restrictors, arriving at the generalization in (4).

(4) Restrictors of non-conservative quantifiers are merged late at the quantifier's scope position.

In exploring the question of why (4) holds, we conclude that conservativity is not a lexical property of quantifiers. Instead it arises as the result of early merger of the quantifier's restrictor and its subsequent interpretation in both the base and scope positions.

9.2 Background: Constituency in Degree Constructions

This section is a brief overview of the arguments in favor of the architecture of degree constructions that we assume. Much of the discussion can be found in Bhatt and Pancheva (2004).

We take the degree clause to be a syntactic argument of the degree quantifier head, and its semantic restrictor. An important motivation for the syntactic analysis comes from the fact that there are selectional restrictions between the degree head and the degree clause, despite the discontinuous dependency. As illustrated in (5), *-er* selects *than*, while *as* selects *as.*

(5) (*a*) *-er* (+ many/much = *more*)/ (+ little = *less*)/ (+ few = *fewer*) . . . *than*

(*b*) *as* (+ many/much/little/few) . . . *as*

Selectional restrictions are the hallmark of head–complement relationships. It is thus reasonable to conclude that the degree clause is the syntactic argument of the degree head, as in the classical analysis in (6) (cf. Chomsky 1965; Selkirk 1970; Bresnan 1973, 1975; Carlson 1977; Heim 2000, among others).

(6)

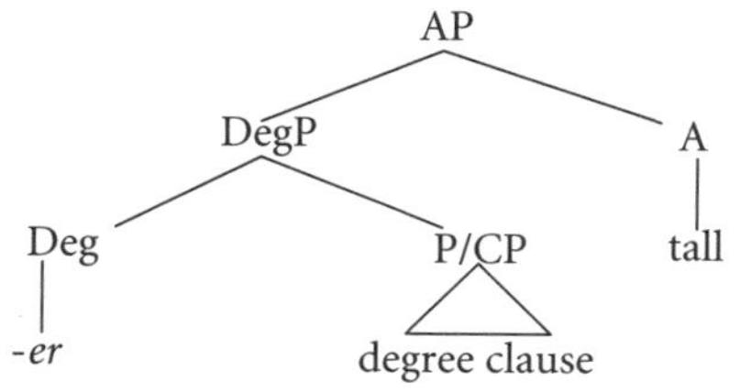

Another argument for (6) comes from a consideration of semantic constituency, and is as follows: if degrees can be explicitly referred to (cf.(7)), it is also to be expected that they can be quantified over (cf.(8)), just like it happens with individuals. The degree head and the degree clause in (8) form a semantic constituent, a degree quantifier (DegP) argument of the matrix gradable predicate (cf. Cresswell 1976; von Stechow 1984; Heim 1985, 2000, among others). And in fact, Heim (2000) shows that this degree quantifier can take scope independent of the matrix gradable predicate (see her paper for examples and discussion).

(7) John is 6 feet / that (much) tall.

(8) (*a*) John is taller than 6 feet.

(*b*) John is $[_{AP}$ $[_{DegP}$ *-er* than 6 ft] tall]

(*c*) $[_{DegP}$ *-er* than 6 ft$]_1$ John is $[_{AP}$ t_1 tall]

Finally, antecedent-contained deletion (ACD) resolution in degree clauses is best explained by a constituency as in (6) (cf. Wold 1995; Heim 2000). In sentences such as (9), QR of the DegP will allow for ACD resolution. QR of the DP *more trees* is not expected, because this is a weak noun phrase. Extraposition of the degree clause alone will also not account for ACD (see also Larson and May 1990; Fox and Nissenbaum 1999; Fox 2002, for a critique of extraposition as a way of ACD resolution).

(9) John was climbing more trees than Bill was.

Thus, there are good reasons, syntactic and semantic, to analyze degree constructions as involving the constituency in (6). But even though the degree clause is a complement of the degree head, the degree head and the degree clause cannot appear as a constituent.

(10) (*a*) *Ralph is more *than Flora is* tall. vs. Ralph is taller *than Flora is.*

(*b*) *Ralph is as *as Flora is* tall. vs. Ralph is as tall *as* Flora is.

In other words, if the degree clause is a complement of the degree head, and we assume it is, it must be obligatorily extraposed.

The surface position of the degree clause is not arbitrary, however. Rather, it marks the scope of the comparison (Williams 1974; Gueron and May 1984). In Bhatt and Pancheva (2004), we show that the surface position of the comparative clause is *exactly* as high as the scope of the comparison. This is illustrated in (11). In (11*a*) the degree clause is in the embedded clause, as indicated by the fact that it precedes the rationale clause *to get tenure* and an adjunct to the embedded verb *publish*. Correspondingly, the DegP is in the scope of the matrix verb *require*. When the degree clause is extraposed to the matrix clause (cf. (11*b*)), as indicated by the fact that it follows the rationale clause, the DegP has scope over *require*.

(11) (*a*) John is required [to publish fewer papers this year [than that number] in a major journal] [to get tenure].
≈ If John publishes more than a certain number of papers, he will not get tenure. (His university has an unusual tenure policy.)
degree clause is in the embedded clause
simplified LF: *required* [*er* [than n] λd [PRO publish d-few papers]]

(*b*) John is required [to publish fewer papers this year in a major journal] [to get tenure] [than that number].
≈ The number of papers that John has to publish to get tenure is upper-bounded. He can publish more than that number but he doesn't have to.
degree clause is outside the matrix clause
simplified LF: [*er*[than n]] λd [*required* [PRO publish d-few papers]]

The following example shows that the same facts hold for equatives. The surface position of the *as*-clause determines the scope of the equation.

(12) (*a*) John is required [to publish exactly *as* many papers this year [as that number] in a major journal] [to get tenure].
≈ If John publishes more than a certain number of papers, he will not get tenure. (His university has an unusual tenure policy.)
degree clause is in the embedded clause
simplified LF: *required* [[exactly *as*] [as n] λd [PRO publish d-many papers]]

(*b*) John is required [to publish exactly *as* many papers this year in a major journal] [to get tenure] [as that number].
≈ The number of papers that John has to publish to get tenure is upper-bounded. He can publish more than that number but he doesn't have to.
degree clause is outside the embedded clause
simplified LF: [exactly *as*] [as n] λd [*required* [PRO publish d-many papers]]

The availability of the *-er/as* > *required* reading in (11*b*) and (12*b*) shows that the structure involving a degree abstraction that crosses *required* is semantically well-formed. The absence of this reading in (11*a*) and (12*a*) shows that the scope of *-er/as* is marked exactly by the surface position of the degree clause, that is that the degree quantifier [$_{\text{DegP}}$ *-er than n*]/[$_{\text{DegP}}$ *exactly as as n*] cannot move further. The implication for the classical view of degree constructions is that the extraposition of the degree clause is not an independent syntactic fact, unrelated to the interpretation of the construction. Rather, the relation between the degree clause and the degree head has to be re-established, somehow, at LF, with the degree head "seeking" to establish scope at the position where the degree clause is attached. In other words, the derivation must proceed as follows: first the degree clause is extraposed to some position on the right edge of the tree, and then the degree quantifier is QRed to the exact same position.

(13)

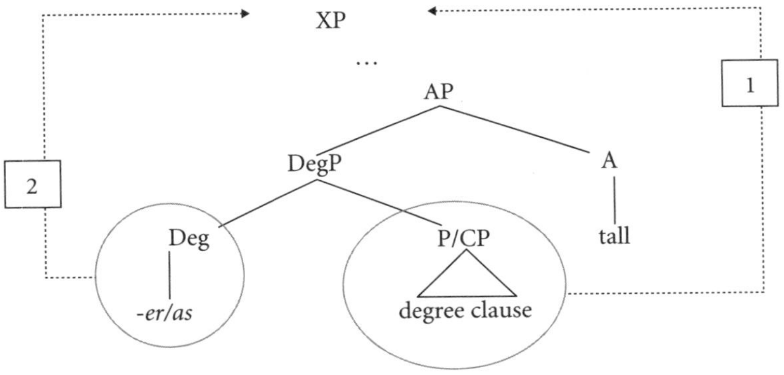

These facts and their interpretation raise several questions. We need to explain why degree clause extraposition is obligatory. Further, why does the surface position of the degree clause completely determine the scope of the degree head? What mechanisms are involved in the derivation of extraposition? More generally, how do syntax and semantics interact in degree-quantificational structures?

9.3 Late Merger

In Bhatt and Pancheva (2004) we proposed that the way to resolve the above issues is to posit that extraposition in degree constructions involves "covert" movement of the degree head to a scope position, followed by late merger of the degree clause to the QRed degree head. The steps of the derivation are illustrated in (14). First, the DegP composed of only the degree head, without a complement, undergoes QR (cf. (14*a*). The QRed DegP adjoins to the right to a suitable XP and is targeted by the degree clause (cf. (14*b*). The degree clause is merged as a complement to the degree head at the scope position and the degree head is pronounced at the base position (cf. (14*c*).

(14) (*a*)

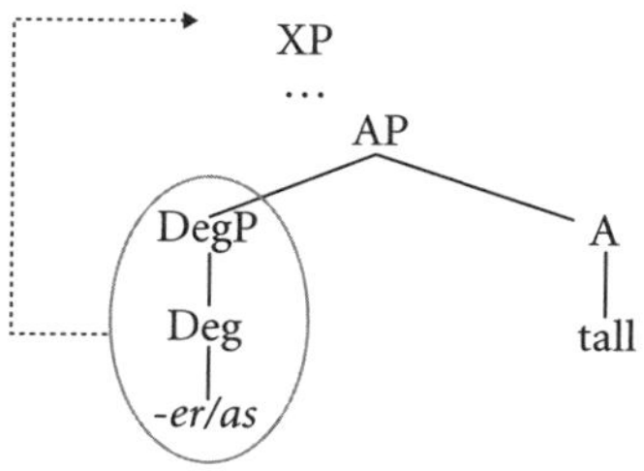

(*b*)

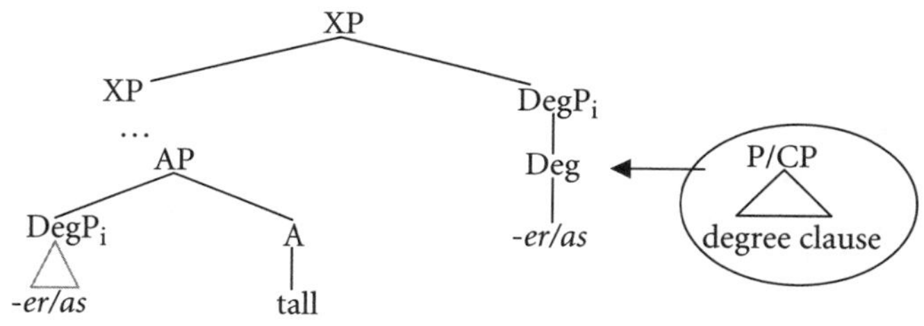

(*c*)

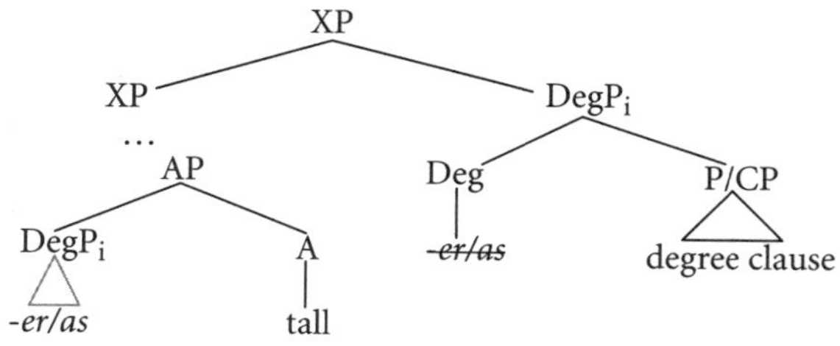

Evidence that the surface position of the degree clause is the position of its first merge comes from correlations between extraposition and obviation of Condition C effects, extraposition and the scope of the degree head with respect to intensional predicates, ellipsis size and the scope of the degree head, ellipsis size and Condition C effects, and ellipsis resolution and the movability of syntactic material following the degree clause. Here we need not illustrate the details as they can be found in Bhatt and Pancheva (2004).

As for the intellectual debt, the mechanism of late merger to a QRed QP is found in Fox and Nissenbaum's (1999) and Fox's (2002) analysis of relative clause extraposition. The idea of late merger goes back to Lebeaux (1990), who proposed it as a solution to the argument/adjunct distinction with respect to A′-movement reconstruction. A more distantly related idea of quantifiers and their restrictors being introduced separately is found in Sportiche (1997, 1999).

Regarding the mechanism of extraposition, our proposal does not involve any actual movement of the degree clause itself. It is not merged with the degree head and then moved to the right, to its surface position. Instead, the only moving piece is the degree head. Thus we use "extraposition" only as a descriptive term. We do not assume any specialized operation of extraposition.

Regarding the question of why the degree clause may not appear adjacent to the degree head, the answer is twofold. The degree clause does not appear in the base position of the degree head because it is merged late. (Why it has to be merged late, we still need to explain.) The degree head does not appear adjacent to the degree clause, at the edge of the tree, because it is pronounced at the base. In this respect, our analysis relates to what has come to be known as the Phonological Theory of QR (cf. Bobaljik 1995, 2002; Pesetsky 2000, among others). On that approach to QR, QR is covert not in a timing sense but in the sense that it itself does not affect PF. This is because the lower copy of the QR-chain is pronounced, rather than the head of the chain. It still remains to be explained why the degree head needs to be pronounced in the base position. (In the case of other quantifier phrases, overt scrambling of the QP could be thought of as the option where the head of the chain is pronounced.) A suggestion is made in Bhatt and Pancheva (2004) that this is so because the degree head is an adjectival affix and needs to be adjacent to an adjective (thus, in cases of nominal comparison, the adjectival *many/much* is necessary).

Finally, the question of why there is a correlation between the scope of the degree head and the surface position of the degree clause is also partially answered—the degree clause is first merged in the scope position of the degree head. Given that the surface position of the degree clause is the position of its first merge, a prediction is made that the scope of the degree quantifier has to be *at least as high* as the level at which the degree clause is attached. One question that remains to be answered is why the scope of the degree has to be *exactly* as high. That is, why is further covert movement of the DegP, now composed of the degree head and the degree clause, not possible? Such a movement would result in a semantic scope for the DegP that is higher than the overt position of the degree clause. In addition, while the proposal allows for late merger of degree complements, it does not force it. This allows for extraposition but does not derive the fact that degree clause extraposition is obligatory. Therefore, we need a way to force late merger of degree clauses.

9.4 Motivation for Late Merger

9.4.1 *Three Questions and One Answer*

The discussion in the previous section has raised the following three questions. First of all, why is late merger of degree clauses obligatory, that is why are degree clauses obligatorily extraposed? The behavior of degree clauses, in that respect, is quite different from that of relative clauses. A line of work (Lebeaux 1990; Chomsky 1993; Fox 2000; Fox and Nissenbaum 1999) has noted that relative clauses can be merged late. But unlike degree clauses, they do not have to be. Second, why does the surface position of the degree clause *exactly* indicate the LF scope of the degree quantifier? And finally, why is it possible to merge the degree clause late, when it is a complement of the degree head? We know from the literature on late merger that late merger is restricted to adjuncts. The answer to all of these questions arises from an interaction between the semantics of degree heads and the way copies left by movement are interpreted. The generalization in (15) emerges from our discussion.

(15) Restrictors of non-conservative quantifiers are merged late at the quantifier's scope position.

9.4.2 *The Interpretation of Copies and Conservativity*

We make an assumption along the lines of Fox (2001, 2002), that copies of moved quantificational phrases have to be taken into consideration during the calculation of meaning at LF, rather than being converted to simple variables. This results in the interpretation of the restrictor of the quantifier inside the quantifier's scope. The copy of a quantificational expression is modified by two LF operations, Variable Insertion and Determiner Replacement. Variable Insertion adds a free variable into the restriction, which can then be bound by the next link in the movement chain. Determiner Replacement replaces the determiner in question with a uniqueness operator with semantics similar to *the*. The precise operations involved are shown in (16).

(16) *Trace Conversion* (from Fox 2001, 2002)
~~Det Predicate~~ → Det [Predicate $\lambda y\ (y = x)$] → *the* [Pred $\lambda y\ (y = x)$]

In two steps, we go from, for example, an uninterpretable copy of the QRed *every boy* to the interpretable *the boy x*, where *x* is the free variable which is bound by the next link in the movement chain involving *every boy* (cf. 17*b*)).

(17) [every boy]$_i$ [[~~every boy~~]$_i$ danced]

(*a*) not: [every boy] λx [x danced]

(*b*) rather: [every boy] λx [*the* [boy λy (y = x)] danced]
[every boy] λx [*the* λy [boy (y) and y = x)] danced]
[every boy] λx [*the* boy x danced]

If copies are interpreted as simple traces, we get (17*a*), while if copies are interpreted using Trace Conversion we get (17*b*). However, (17*a*) and (17*b*) are only trivially different. Fox (2001) notes that this is so because *every* is conservative, as seemingly all natural language determiners are (cf. Keenan 1981; Keenan and Stavi 1986). Conservativity is defined as in (18): informally, a quantifier is conservative if its second argument can be substituted by the intersection of its first and second arguments. As long as we are dealing with conservative quantifiers, interpreting structures involving QR will yield the same output, whether this is done by treating the copy of the quantifier phrase as a simple trace, or by Trace Conversion. The equivalence is shown in (19) (from Fox 2001).

(18) Q (A) (B) iff Q (A) (A∩B) conservativity

(19) Q(A,B) = Q(A)(A∩B) (by conservativity)
= Q(A)(A∩ [λx : A(x).B(x)]) (by assumptions about Presupposition Projection)
= Q(A)(λx : A(x).B(x)) (by conservativity)
= Q(A)(λx B(the[Ax]))

Fox (2001) further points out that, given this mechanism of trace interpretation, non-conservative quantifiers would only have trivial meanings. A case in point is *only*, which, if it were a determiner, would be non-conservative (cf. (20)). To see that (20*a*) is the case, consider the meaning of, for example, *Only Norwegians danced*, which can be true if and only if the set of dancers is a subset of the set of Norwegians. Correspondingly, *Only Norwegians were Norwegians who danced* is true if and only if the dancing Norwegians are a subset of the Norwegians (cf. (20*b*)). But now, it may be the case that the first statement is false, for example, both Norwegians and Bulgarians danced. It is still the case that the second statement is true, since no other nationality but the Norwegians were Norwegians who danced.

(20) *only* (A) (B) $\not\Leftrightarrow$ *only* (A) (A$\cap$B)

(*a*) *only* (A) (B) = 1 iff B $\subseteq$ A

(*b*) *only* (A) (A$\cap$B) = 1 iff A$\cap$B $\subseteq$ A

When we consider the result of interpreting with Trace Conversion a structure with the putative determiner *only*, we see that the result is a tautology (cf. (21*b*)). On the other hand, a copy interpreted as a simple variable yields a contingency (cf. (21*a*)).

(21) [only Norwegians]$_i$ [[~~only Norwegians~~]$_i$ danced]

(*a*) [only Norwegians] λx [x danced] contingent statement

(*b*) [only Norwegians] λx [the Norwegians x danced] tautology

If we assume that the interpretation of chains involves an operation like Trace Conversion, then it follows that an element with the semantics of *only* cannot be a determiner. This is an important argument in favor of Trace Conversion.

Conservativity is standardly taken to be a lexical property of natural language determiners. Fox's observation opens the door to a line of inquiry which allows us to provide a structural explanation for the conservativity generalization. We explore the extent to which it is possible to tease out the property of conservativity from the lexical meanings of particular determiners and have it follow from the way movement chains are interpreted using Trace Conversion. Our particular extension of Fox's observation involves noting that early merger of the degree clause to non-conservative *-er* leads to a contradiction and that given certain assumptions about the semantics of *as*, it "overrides" a non-conservative meaning of *as*. Thus, in both cases, early merger of the restrictor is incompatible with a non-conservative meaning for the degree quantifier. The exact nature of the incompatibility will be explicated in the course of the discussion.

9.4.3 *The Semantics of* -er *and Position of Merger Effects*

9.4.3.1 *The Meaning of* -er We have noted that the degree clause is best analyzed as the complement of the degree head. The degree head semantically combines first with the degree clause and then with the main clause.

(22) (*a*) [*-er* [degree clause]] [main clause]

(*b*) Bill is taller than Ann is.

(*c*) *-er* [λd [Ann is d-tall]] [λd [Bill is d-tall]]

With the syntax in (22), we need to assign the semantics in (23) to *-er*. This is so, because sets of degrees have the monotonicity property: if the set contains a certain degree, it also contains all the degrees lesser than that degree (cf. (24)).

(23) *-er* (A)(B) = 1 iff $A \subset B$
where, e.g., $[\![A]\!] = \lambda d$ [Ann is d-tall]
$[\![B]\!] = \lambda d$ [Bill is d-tall]

(24) $\forall d \in D_d\ [d \in A \Rightarrow \forall d' \in D_d\ [d' \leq d \Rightarrow d' \in A]]$
where D_d, the domain of degrees, is the set of positive real numbers together with 0.

The meaning assigned to *-er* in (23) makes it non-conservative. *-er* (A) (B) and *-er* (A) ($A \cap B$) are not equivalent. The former is a contingent statement while the latter is a contradiction. To see that this is the case, consider (25). *-er* (A) (B) is true when $A \subset B$ and false otherwise (cf. (25*a*)), as per the definition of *-er*. *-er* (A) ($A \cap B$) is true when its first argument is a proper subset of the second and false otherwise (cf. (25*b*)), again according to the definition of *-er*. However, $A \subset A \cap B$ can never be true. Given that both A and B are sets of degrees, they can have three possible relations—A can be a proper superset of B, A and B can be equal, or A can be a proper subset of B. If the first of these is the case, $A \cap B = B$, but $A \subset B$ is false. If the second is the case, that is $A = B$, their intersection will be equal to both, and $A \subset A \cap B$ will be false since A cannot be a proper set of itself. Finally, if the third relation obtains, and $A \subset B$, the intersection of A and B will be A. But as we just said, $A \subset A$ is false. In sum, *-er* (A) ($A \cap B$) is a contradiction.

(25) *-er* (A) (B) $\not\Leftrightarrow$ *-er* (A) ($A \cap B$)

(*a*) *-er* (A) (B) = 1 iff $A \subset B$ contingent

(*b*) *-er* (A) ($A \cap B$) = 1 iff $A \subset A \cap B$ contradiction

It is worth noting that we need to assign *-er* non-conservative semantics because of our syntactic assumptions, that is that *-er* first combines with the degree clause and then with the main clause. If the order of composition were to be reversed, then the degree head would in fact come out as conservative. Thus, an alternative degree quantifier *-ER* with the syntax in (26*a*) will have the semantics in (26*b*), requiring its second argument to be a subset of the first. According to (26*b*), *-ER* is conservative (cf. (27)).

(26) (*a*) [*-ER* [main clause]] [degree clause]

(*b*) *-ER* (B) (A) = 1 iff $A \subset B$ where $[\![A]\!] = \lambda d$ [Ann is d-tall]
$[\![B]\!] = \lambda d$ [Bill is d-tall]

(27) *-ER* (B) (A) $\Leftrightarrow$ *-ER* (B) ($A \cap B$)

(*a*) *-ER* (B) (A) = 1 iff $A \subset B$ contingent

(*b*) *-ER* (B) ($A \cap B$) = 1 iff $A \cap B \subset B$ contingent

To see that the equivalence in (27) holds, first let us assume that *-ER* (B) (A) is true, that is $A \subset B$, following the definition of *-ER*. But if $A \subset B$, then $A \cap B = A$. This means that *-ER* (B) ($A \cap B$) is also true: according to the meaning of *-ER*, its second argument has to be a proper subset of its first argument and this is the case since $A \cap B = A$ and $A \subset B$. Thus, when *-ER* (B) (A) is true, so is *-ER* (B) ($A \cap B$). Now let us assume that *-ER* (B) ($A \cap B$) is true, that is following the definition of *-ER*, $A \cap B \subset B$. Given the properties of degree sets we know that either $A \subseteq B$ or $B \subseteq A$. This means that $A \subset B$, which then means that *-ER* (B) (A) is true. In other words, we have shown that the equivalence in (27) holds, that is that *-ER* is conservative.

The conclusion of this discussion is that whether a particular relationship between two sets yields a conservative quantifier or not depends upon the syntax of the quantifier, that is which set counts as the restrictor and which as the nuclear scope. We will return to this point later, when we propose that conservativity is not a lexical property of quantifiers, but is derived on the basis of the interaction between their lexical meaning and syntax. For now, we just note that we take the arguments in §9.2 above to be sufficient to justify a conclusion that the comparative quantifier is *-er* rather than *-ER*.

9.4.3.2 *The Consequences of Early and Late Merger* If the *than*-clause is merged to the degree head *-er* in situ, QR would create a structure where the *than*-clause has to be interpreted twice—once as a restrictor of *-er* (in the head of the A′-chain created by QR) and for a second time inside the second argument of *-er* (see (28)).

(28) *Early merger* (to the in-situ *-er*)

(*a*) [*-er* [than Ann is tall]]$_i$ [Bill is [~~-er [than Ann is tall]~~]$_i$ tall]

(*b*) *-er* [λd [Ann is *d*-tall]] [λd [Bill is [*the* [[λd [Ann is d-tall]] λd_1 (d_1 = d)] tall]]]

(*c*) *-er* (A) [λd [Bill is [*the* [A λd_1 (d_1 = d)] tall]]]

(*d*) *-er* (A) ($A \cap B$)

If, on the other hand, the *-er*-clause is merged late, after the degree head *-er* has already undergone QR, there will be no copy of the restrictor of *-er* to interpret inside the second argument of *-er* (see (29)).

(29) *Late merger* (to the QRed *-er*)

(*a*) [*-er*$_i$ [than Ann is tall]] [Bill is ~~*-er*~~$_i$ tall]

(*b*) *-er* [λd [Ann is d-tall]] [λd [Bill is *the* [λd_1 (d_1 = d)] tall]]

(*c*) *-er* (A) [λd [Bill is d-tall]]

(*d*) ***-er* (A) (B)**

Clearly, given the meaning of *-er* in (23), the result of early merger (28*d*) (= (30*a*)) is a contradiction. We discussed this above in connection with (25*b*). Thus, only late merger, as in (29*d*) (=(30*b*)), can yield a contingent meaning for comparatives.

(30) (*a*) *-er* (A) (A ∩ B) = 1 iff A ⊂ A ∩ B contradiction

(*b*) *-er* (A) (B) = 1 iff A ⊂ B contingent

We thus have an answer to the first question posited in §9.4.1—why do comparative clauses have to be merged late. We have shown that, given the non-conservative semantics of *-er*, early merger of the degree clause would lead to a contradictory meaning. We next discuss the second question—can the DegP move, after the comparative clause has been merged to the comparative head in a scope position?

9.4.3.3 *Can* -er *and the Degree Clause Move Together, After Late Merger* Above we saw that the semantics forces obligatory late merger of the comparative clause, or in other terms "obligatory extraposition". But the question of whether the *-er* and the degree clause can move covertly further from the point of late merger remains unanswered. If such further movement were allowed, the scope of the comparison would not correspond to the surface position of the comparative clause.

It turns out that exactly the same logic that forces late merger of the degree clause also blocks any movement of *-er* with the degree clause. Such a movement would re-create the problem with early merger because it would leave a copy of the degree clause behind. That is, we would need to interpret the degree complement of *-er* in two locations, one of them a copy, leading to the contradiction in (31*c*).

(31) (*a*) [$_{DegP}$ *-er*$_i$ (A)] [~~*-er*~~$_i$ (B)] late merger

(*b*) [$_{DegP}$ *-er*$_i$ (A)]$_j$ [~~[$_{DegP}$ *-er*$_i$ (A)]~~$_j$ [~~*-er*~~$_i$ (B)]] QR of *-er* and its restrictor

(*c*) ***-er* (A) (A ∩ B)**

In sum, the same interpretive reasons are behind both the obligatory late merger of the comparative clause and its subsequent "freezing" in place, resulting in an *exactly as high as* correlation between scope of *-er* and the surface position of the comparative clause.

9.5 The Semantics of *as* and Position-of-Merger Effects

9.5.1 *The Standard Meaning of* as

The non-conservative meaning of *-er*, coupled with the mechanism of interpreting copies of moved QPs that requires the copy of the restrictor to the Q to be interpreted intersectively with the second argument of Q, yields the desired results regarding comparative clause "extraposition". However, the analysis would not carry over to equative *as*. According to the standard meaning, *as* means "*at least as*" (as in (32)). The semantics for *as* is posited to be as in (32), because a sentence such as (33) can mean that Bill is at least as tall as Ann is, that is that the set of degrees to which Ann is tall is a subset of the set of degrees to which Bill is tall.

(32) *as* (A) (B) = 1 iff $A \subseteq B$

(33) (*a*) Bill is as tall as Ann is.

(*b*) *-as* [λd [Ann is d-tall]] [λd [Bill is d-tall]]

Now, the meaning in (32) makes *as* conservative. Examples (34*a*, 34*b*) hold according to the definition of *as*. But $A \subseteq A \cap B$ is true if and only if $A \subseteq B$.

(34) *as* (A) (B) $\Leftrightarrow$ *as* (A) ($A \cap B$)

(*a*)	*as* (A) (B) = 1	iff $A \subseteq B$	contingent
(*b*)	*as* (A) ($A \cap B$) = 1	iff $A \subseteq A \cap B$	contingent

Because the equivalence in (34) holds, both an early and late merger of the equatives clause would yield equivalent contingent statements.

(35) *Early merger* (to the in-situ *as*)

(*a*) [*as* [as Ann is tall]]$_i$ [Bill is [~~*as* [as Ann is tall]~~]$_i$ tall]

(*b*) *as* [λd [Ann is d-tall]] [λd [Bill is [*the* [[λd [Ann is d-tall]] λd_1 (d_1 = d)] tall]]]

(*c*) *as* (A) [λd [Bill is [*the* [A λd_1 (d_1 = d)] tall]]]

(*d*) **as (A) ($A \cap B$)**

(36) *Late merger* (to the QRed *as*)

(*a*) [*as*$_i$ [as Ann is tall]] [Bill is ~~*as*~~$_i$ tall]

(*b*) *as* [λd [Ann is d-tall]] [λd [Bill is *the* [λd_1 (d_1 = d)] tall]] (*c*) *as* (A) [λd [Bill is d-tall]]

(*d*) *as* (A) (B)

The degree complement of *as* obligatorily appears discontinuous from *as* just as the degree complement of *-er* obligatorily appears discontinuous from *-er*. Our explanation for this obligatory extraposition in the case of *-er* appealed to the non-conservative semantics of *-er*. If *as* has conservative semantics, we cannot extend this conservativity-based explanation to account for the similar obligatory extraposition found with the degree complement of *as*.

9.5.2 *Factorizing* as

So far we have considered equatives without a factor argument. By factor argument, we refer to the multiplier that can optionally appear in equatives. The factor argument is analogous to the differential argument of a comparative.

(37) (*a*) Ann is *twice* as tall as Sue is.

(*b*) Ann is *two cm* taller than Sue is.

Adding a factor argument makes an interesting difference. For any value of the factor argument that is greater than one, the augmented degree quantifier comes out as non-conservative. We take (38) to represent the general case of an equative with a factor argument. Example (32), where a factor argument is not present, falls out as a special case of (38), with the factor argument set to 1, and the assumption that degree sets have the monotonicity property (cf. (24)).[1]

(38) $n \times as\ (A)\ (B) = 1$ iff $n \times Max\ (A) \leq Max\ (B)$,
where $Max\ (A) = \iota d\ [d \in A \wedge \forall d' [d' \in A \Rightarrow d' \leq d]]$

We know that *Max* (A) is always greater than or equal to *Max* (A $\cap$ B). As long as *Max* (A) is not equal to zero, it follows that for any $n > 1$, $n \times Max$ (A) must be greater than *Max* (A$\cap$B). In other words, (39*b*) is a contradiction. The augmented equative quantifier $n \times as$ is not conservative.

1 The definition in (38) has been formulated with the plausible assumption that degree sets are closed intervals. It does not work for open intervals. If we also want to consider open intervals, we need the more complex definition of *Max* in (i):

(i) $Max\,(A) = \iota d\ \forall d'\ [d' < d \Rightarrow d' \in A] \wedge \forall d''\ [d'' \in A \Rightarrow d \geq d'']$

One consequence of this definition is that (32) does not fall out as a special case of (38) with the factor argument set to 1. The two definitions diverge when the two degree arguments of *as* are degree sets that differ at a single point. This is because *Max* returns the value *n* both when applied to the open interval A = 0 . . .) n and when applied to the closed interval B = 0 . . . n). As a result *as* (1)(A)(B) = *as* (1)(B)(A) = 1. But according to the earlier definition of *as*, *as* (B)(A) = 0, while *as* (A)(B) = 1. This special case aside, the two definitions return identical results.

(39) $n \times as$ (A) (B) $\not\Leftrightarrow$ $n \times as$ (A) (A $\cap$ B) for $n > 1$

(*a*) $n \times as$ (A) (B) = 1 iff $n \times Max$ (A) $\leq$ Max (B) contingent

(*b*) $n \times as$ (A) (A$\cap$B) = 1 iff $n \times Max$ (A) $\leq$ Max (A$\cap$B) contradiction

Therefore, only late merger of the equatives clause would yield a contingent statement. Early merger would result in a contradiction.

(40) (*a*) [$_{\text{DegP}}$ *twice as* [as Ann is tall]]$_i$ [Bill is ~~[$_{\text{DegP}}$ *twice as* [as Ann is tall]]~~$_i$ tall] early merger

(*b*) ***twice as*** **(A) (A $\cap$ B)**

(41) (*a*) [$_{\text{DegP}}$ *twice as*$_i$ [as Ann is tall]] [Bill is ~~*twice as*~~$_i$ tall] late merger

(*b*) ***twice as*** **(A) (B)**

For equatives with the factor argument > 1, just as for comparatives, we have an explanation for why the degree clause is obligatorily discontinuous from the degree quantifier—it is obligatorily merged late, given that an early merger will yield a contradictory LF.

It remains to be explained why late merger is obligatory for equatives without a factor argument (i.e. $n = 1$) or with factor arguments less than one. Let us therefore examine the conservativity properties of such equatives. Consider (42).

(42) Bill is (*half*) as tall as Ann is.

When the factor argument of the equative is less than or equal to 1, the resulting augmented degree quantifier is conservative.

(43) $n \times as$ (A) (B) $\Leftrightarrow$ $n \times as$ (A) (A $\cap$ B) for $n \leq 1$

(*a*) $n \times as$ (A) (B) = 1 iff $n \times Max$ (A) $\leq$ Max (B)

(*b*) $n \times as$ (A) (A $\cap$ B) = 1 iff $n \times Max$ (A) $\leq$ Max (A $\cap$ B)

(*c*) $n \times Max$ (A) $\leq$ Max (A $\cap$ B) iff $n \times Max$ (A) $\leq$ Max (B)

To see this, let us first assume that the left-hand side of (43*c*) is true, namely, that $n \times Max$ (A) $\leq$ Max (A $\cap$ B). A and B are sets of degrees, with the property in (24). Therefore one of the following two situations holds: (i) A $\subseteq$ B or (ii) B $\subset$ A. If A $\subseteq$ B, then Max (A) $\leq$ Max (B). It follows for any $n \leq 1$ that $n \times Max$ (A) $\leq$ Max (B). If B $\subset$ A, then A $\cap$ B = B and it follows directly from $n \times Max$ (A) $\leq$ Max (A $\cap$ B) (the left-hand side in (43*c*)) that $n \times Max$ (A) $\leq$ Max (B). Now let us assume that the right-hand side in (43*c*) is true. Once again, one of the following two situations holds: (i) A $\subseteq$ B or (ii) B $\subset$ A. If A $\subseteq$ B, then

$A \cap B = A$. For any $n \leq 1$, $n \times Max\,(A) \leq Max\,(A)$, and hence $n \times Max\,(A) \leq Max\,(A \cap B)$, that is the left-hand side follows. If $B \subset A$, then $A \cap B = B$. The left-hand side now follows directly from the right-handside.

To sum up, the result of taking the factor argument into consideration is that for factors greater than 1, the augmented degree quantifier is not conservative, whereas for factors less than or equal to 1, the resulting augmented quantifier is conservative.

The conservativity of the equative degree quantifier for values of the factor argument less than or equal to 1 means that we cannot straightforwardly extend to these equatives the conservativity-based argument developed to force obligatory extraposition. But as has been noted earlier, these equatives do not differ from other equatives and comparatives in the relevant aspects—obligatory extraposition and the surface position of the degree clause marking the scope of the comparison/equation. We therefore consider two strategies, which are not mutually exclusive, to account for obligatory extraposition of degree complement of *as*.

The first approach is based on the intuition that the syntactic system is not dependent upon the meanings of particular numerals involved in a particular derivation.[2] Under this approach, the fact that certain values of the factor argument block early merger of the degree complement of *as* is enough to block early merger of the degree complement in the general case. The degree quantifier itself consists of *as* together with its factor argument—this is the syntactic object that moves covertly. Depending upon the actual value of the factor argument, the resulting degree quantifier may or may not be conservative. But this information is not accessible to the syntactic system and early merger is ruled out. An unresolved puzzle here is why the syntactic system picks the late merge option in the case of indeterminacy. One plausible explanation, but one which requires some "intelligence" on the part of the syntactic system, is that late merger is the safe option in case of indeterminacy. If the quantifier in question turns out to have inherently conservative semantics, late merger will do no harm, but if the quantifier turns out to have non-conservative semantics, late merger is the only option. Early merger would lead to a contradiction. In our discussion of late merger of the complement of *-er*, we had noted that since early merge of the complement led

2 A similar insight is explored by Fox (2000: 66–74) in the context of Scope Economy. He notes that certain cases of scopally commutative quantifiers are treated by the syntactic system as scopally non-commutative. In these cases, proving scopal commutativity requires making reference to the arithmetic properties of the expressions involved, such as the meaning of expressions like *even/odd*, as well as the meanings of particular numerical expressions. He hypothesizes that such information is unavailable to the syntactic system.

to a contradiction, late merger was forced. But this left open the possibility of a derivation where the degree complement is merged early but the derivation is ruled out because after QR, it has contradictory semantics. The discussion from equatives suggests a more constrained picture. Early merger of degree complements is just not syntactically available. If it was available in principle and was constrained only by semantic convergence, we would expect equatives with factor argument less than or equal to one to allow for early merger. We will return to the architectural commitments that this way of thinking imposes in §§9.6 and 9.7.

The second approach we consider entertains a different meaning for *as*—an "*exactly as*" meaning as opposed to the more commonly assumed "*at least as*" meaning. The "*exactly as*" meaning is non-conservative and we observe that such a meaning is incompatible with early merger. If the degree complement of an *as* with an "*exactly as*" meaning is merged early, then the "*exactly as*" meaning does not survive. What we end up with is an "*at least as*" meaning.

9.5.3 *Another Meaning for* as

We have worked so far with the standard weak ("*at least as*") meaning as the basic meaning of *as*. This meaning yields a conservative quantifier (unless the factor argument is greater than 1). Alternatively we could consider another meaning as the basic meaning of *as*. Note that we do not know, a priori, what the semantic content of *as* is. We only know what equatives sentences mean, and based on that, we can extrapolate the lexical meaning of *as*.

Equative sentences have a strong ("*exactly as*") and a weak ("*at least as*") interpretation exemplified in (44) and (45*a*, 45*b*). An utterance such as (44) can be countered by (45*a*), or confirmed by (45*b*), illustrating the two readings of the equative (e.g. Horn 1972, 2001; Klein 1980).

(44) (I think that) Bill is *as* tall as Ann is.

(45) (*a*) No, he is not, he is taller. ("*exactly as*")

(*b*) Yes, in fact I know he is taller. ("*at least as*")

Traditional and more recent scalar implicature accounts (e.g. Horn 1972, 2001; Klein 1980; Chierchia 2004; Kratzer 2003) assign *as* a weak ("*at least as*") semantic content and derive the strong reading as a pragmatic effect, given that the two readings are scalarly ordered, and based on the (neo-) Gricean assumption that speakers make the most informative contribution possible (cf. (46)).

(46) *Grice (1968)'s Category of Quantity and its two maxims:*

1. Make your contribution as informative as is required (for the current purposes of the exchange).
2. Do not make your contribution more informative than is required.

The calculation of the meaning of an equative, according to this type of approach, is done as follows. The equative sentence is less informative than the corresponding comparative (cf. (47)). The equative is true in case Bill is of the same height as Ann or is taller than her; the comparative is true only in the latter case.

(47) Bill is *as* tall as Ann is. $\ll_{\text{informative}}$ Bill is tall*er* than Ann is.

The semantics of the equative is as in (48*a*). Example (48*b*) is a pragmatic inference, as if the stronger assertion in (47) were true, the speaker would have made it. Example (48*c*) follows from (48*a*) and (48*b*).

(48) Bill is *as* tall as Ann is.

(*a*) Bill is *at least as* tall as Ann is. semantic content

(*b*) Bill is not taller than Ann is. pragmatic inference

(*c*) Bill is *exactly as* tall as Ann is. pragmatic inference

As we noted above, the lexical meaning of *as* is not directly observable. The strategy in the above approach is to posit the weak meaning as basic and derive the strong one as a scalar implicature. The other alternative is to posit the strong meaning as basic and derive the weak one through some independently needed mechanism. We explore this other alternative, where *as* has strong lexical meaning, as in (49) and where the weak reading is derived from the strong reading.

(49) *as* (A) (B) = 1 iff A = B

In fact, something other than scalar implicature seems to be needed to account for scalar readings, on independent grounds. Fox (2003) notes a problem with the scalar implicature accounts. Given the pattern of reasoning that generates the strong reading of *as* as a scalar implicature from the weak reading of *as*, what blocks the reasoning in (51)? As indicated in (50), an "*as*" equative is less informative than an "*exactly as*" equative. Because of this, on Gricean principles, (51) would assert the weak "*at least as*" reading and also trigger the pragmatic inference that the more informative "*exactly as*" reading is not available. But then, as follows from (51*a*) and (51*b*), the inference is drawn that the corresponding comparative is true. The logic is exactly as in (47)–(48), but the result here is undesirable.

(50) Bill is *as* tall as Ann is. $\ll_{\text{informative}}$ Bill is *exactly as* tall as Ann is.

(51) Bill is *as* tall as Ann is.

(*a*) Bill is *at least as* tall as Ann is. semantic content

(*b*) Bill is not exactly as tall as Ann is. pragmatic inference

(*c*) Bill is tall*er* than Ann is. pragmatic inference

Adopting a strong meaning for *as* eliminates the problem raised by (51). Importantly for our purposes, the new meaning of *as* also makes it non-conservative (cf. (52)). It is easy to see that this is the case:

(52) $as\ (\mathrm{A})\ (\mathrm{B}) \not\Leftrightarrow as\ (\mathrm{A})\ (\mathrm{A} \cap \mathrm{B})$

(*a*) $as\ (\mathrm{A})\ (\mathrm{B}) = 1$ iff $\mathrm{A} = \mathrm{B}$

(*b*) $as\ (\mathrm{A})\ (\mathrm{A} \cap \mathrm{B}) = 1$ iff $\mathrm{A} = \mathrm{A} \cap \mathrm{B}$

(*c*) $\mathrm{A} = \mathrm{A} \cap \mathrm{B}$ iff $\mathrm{A} \subseteq \mathrm{B}$

Now, at least we have a common way of characterizing all cases of late merger: they all involve restrictors of (atomic) non-conservative quantifiers, that is *-er* and *as*.

At this point let us also consider the case of equatives with a factor argument. Their reformulated semantics is shown in (53).

(53) $n \times as\ (\mathrm{A})\ (\mathrm{B}) = 1$ iff $n \times Max\ (\mathrm{A}) = Max\ (\mathrm{B})$

The conservativity/non-conservativity of the resulting degree quantifier depends upon the value of the factor argument. In case the factor argument is ≥ 1, the derived quantifier is non-conservative. If the factor argument is < 1, the derived quantifier is conservative.

(54) $n \times as\ (\mathrm{A})\ (\mathrm{B}) \not\Leftrightarrow n \times as\ (\mathrm{A})\ (\mathrm{A} \cap \mathrm{B})$ for $n \geq 1$
$n \times as\ (\mathrm{A})\ (\mathrm{B}) \Leftrightarrow n \times as\ (\mathrm{A})\ (\mathrm{A} \cap \mathrm{B})$ for $n < 1$

(*a*) $n \times as\ (\mathrm{A})\ (\mathrm{B}) = 1$ iff $n \times Max\ (\mathrm{A}) = Max\ (\mathrm{B})$

(*b*) $n \times as\ (\mathrm{A})\ (\mathrm{A} \cap \mathrm{B}) = 1$ iff $n \times Max\ (\mathrm{A}) = Max\ (\mathrm{A} \cap \mathrm{B})$

(*c*) $n \times Max\ (\mathrm{A}) = Max\ (\mathrm{A} \cap \mathrm{B})$ iff $n = 1$ and $\mathrm{A} \subseteq \mathrm{B}$, or
$n < 1$ and $n \times Max\ (\mathrm{A}) = Max\ (\mathrm{B})$

We consider the $n < 1$ case first. Assuming a non-empty A, and the fact that A and B have the monotonicity property $n \times Max\ (\mathrm{A}) = Max\ (\mathrm{B})$ can only be true if $\mathrm{B} \subset \mathrm{A}$. If $\mathrm{B} \subset \mathrm{A}$, then $\mathrm{A} \cap \mathrm{B} = \mathrm{B}$, and it follows that $n \times Max\ (\mathrm{A}) = Max$

(A∩B). Similarly, $n \times Max$ (A) = *Max* (A ∩ B) can only be true if A ∩ B ⊂ A. If A ∩ B ⊂ A, then B ⊂ A, then $n \times Max$ (A) = *Max* (B). Hence for $n < 1$, *as* with strong semantics is conservative.

Next, let us consider the $n > 1$ case. Here we find that for non-empty A, $n \times$ *as* (A) (B) is a contingent statement while $n \times$ *as* (A) (A ∩ B) is a contradiction. The latter is a contradiction, because $n \times Max$ (A) = *Max* (A ∩ B) can be true if and only if *Max* (A) < *Max* (A ∩ B). However, since A ⊇ A ∩ B, *Max* (A) ≥ *Max* (A ∩ B). In other words, for $n > 1$, *as* with strong semantics is not conservative.

Before we go on to the $n = 1$ case, it is worth noting that so far the switch from a weak semantics for *as* to a strong semantics for *as* has not had any impact on the conservativity properties of the degree quantifiers in question. Irrespective of the semantics we adopt, when the factor argument is less than 1, the resulting degree quantifier is conservative and when the factor argument is greater than 1, the resulting degree quantifier is not conservative.

The distinctions between the weak semantics and the strong semantics for *as* become visible when we consider the case where the factor argument is equal to 1. In this case, $n \times$ *as* (A) (B) reduces to A = B, and $n \times$ *as* (A) (A ∩ B) reduces to A = A ∩ B, which in turn is equivalent to A ⊆ B. These statements are both contingent and they are not equivalent. Thus, with the strong semantics and the factor argument set to 1, *as* is not conservative, whereas with weak semantics and a factor of 1, *as* comes out as conservative.

Interestingly, the non-conservativity of *as* with a strong meaning and a factor of 1 has different effects than the non-conservativity of *as* with the factor argument greater than 1. When n is greater than 1, $n \times$ *as* (A) (A ∩ B)—which corresponds to the early merge structure—is a contradiction. This rules out early merger, that is it forces obligatory "extraposition". In contrast, when n is equal to 1, $n \times$ *as* (A) (A ∩ B), the output of the early merge structure, is not a contradiction—instead it is a contingent statement equivalent to A ⊆ B, the weak semantics for *as*. As a result, we cannot directly appeal to interpretation in this particular case to block early merger. Early merger yields a contingent statement, but one where the strong lexical meaning of *as* is "lost".

To sum up, adopting a strong semantics for *as* does not help to derive the prohibition against early merge in the $n \leq 1$ cases. Nothing at all changes for the $n < 1$ case, which remains conservative, while with $n = 1$, we get non-conservativity but it does not by itself block early merger. Nevertheless, if we allow for early merger of the degree complement of an *as* with strong semantics and degree argument set to one, we get the curious result that after

QR, we end up with a conservative quantifier with the semantics associated with the weak reading of *as*. In other words, early merger would override the non-conservative meaning. We speculate that late merger is motivated by the need to express non-conservative meanings which could not be expressed if early merge was obligatory.

Of course, the above motivation from non-conservative semantics for late merger does not extend to the cases of *as* with factor argument less than one which have been shown to have conservative semantics even if we assume a strong semantics for *as*. Setting aside temporarily the question of what blocks early merger in the $n < 1$ cases, let us consider one potential consequence of adopting a strong semantics for *as* in the context of our overall proposal for degree constructions.

9.5.4 *The Syntactic Account of the Scalar Interpretation of Equatives*

One consequence of adopting a strong semantics for *as* together with our overall proposal is that it suggests a way to derive the scalar interpretations of equatives in the syntax. Late merger of the equatives clause straightforwardly yields the strong "*exactly as*" reading of equatives, and early merger would yield the weak "*at least as*" reading, under the new definition of *as* as "*exactly as*".

(55) (*a*) *as* (A) $(A \cap B) = 1$ iff $A = A \cap B$ iff $A \subseteq B$ "*at least as*" reading

(*b*) *as* (A) $(B) = 1$ iff $A = B$ "*exactly as*" reading

However, early merger of the degree complement of *as* seems to not be actually available as shown by the obligatory "extraposition" of the equative clause. An alternative is to explore the idea that the weak readings of equatives arise through late merger of the degree clause, followed by short QR of the degree quantifier [$_{\text{DegP}}$ *as* (A)] (see (56*a*, 56*b*)). This movement creates a structure analogous to the early merger structure, and hence yields a weak reading (see (56*c*)).

(56) (*a*) [$_{\text{DegP}}$ *as*$_i$ (A)] [~~*as*~~$_i$ (B)] late merger

(*b*) [$_{\text{DegP}}$ *as*$_i$ (A)]$_j$ [~~[$_{\text{DegP}}$ *as*$_i$ (A)]~~$_j$ [~~*as*~~$_i$ (B)]] QR of *as* and its restrictor

(*c*) ***as*** **(A)** $\mathbf{(A \cap B)}$ "*at least as*" reading

A possible argument in support of the syntactic account for the scalar interpretations of equatives could come from ellipsis. It has been noted that the ellipsis site and its antecedent need to satisfy a Parallelism condition. Thus the following example is only two ways (and not four ways) ambiguous (from Fox 2000).

(57) A boy admires every teacher. A girl does, too <admire every teacher>.

(*a*) a boy > every teacher, a girl > every teacher

(*b*) *a boy > every teacher, every teacher > a girl

(*c*) *every teacher > a boy, a girl > every teacher

(*d*) every teacher > a boy, every teacher > a girl

The explanation for the absence of the readings in (57*b*, 57*c*) is based on the idea that ellipsis is only possible when the scopal relations in the ellipsis site and the antecedent are isomorphic. If isomorphism does not extend to the domain of implicature, we could use the disambiguation found in elliptical contexts as a probe into whether we are dealing with two independent structures/meanings or an instance of implicature. If there are two independent structures/meanings, we would expect to find disambiguation along the lines of (57). Otherwise if we have implicature, we might expect four-way ambiguity. So if the two readings of *John has three daughters* involve two distinct structures, we expect (58) to be two ways ambiguous, while if one of the readings is an implicature of the other, we would expect, in principle, that (58) could be four ways ambiguous.

(58) John has three daughters. Bill does, too.

(*a*) Reading 1: (exactly three, exactly three)
Background: one needs to have exactly three children to get a tax break.
John has exactly three daughters. Bill has exactly three daughters, too.

(*b*) *Reading 2: (exactly three, at least three)
Background: one needs to have exactly three children to get a tax break.
(58) cannot be true if John has three daughters and Bill has four daughters.

(*c*) *Reading 3: (at least three, exactly three)
Background: one needs to have at least three children to get a tax break.
If Reading 3 was available, we could take (58) to be false when John has three daughters but Bill has four.

(*d*) Reading 4: (at least three, at least three)
Background: one needs to have at least three children to get a tax break.
John has four children and Bill has five children.

The judgments in (58) are subtle because it is not easy to separate out the "*exactly n*" reading from the "*at least n*" reading without the additional contextual support indicated in (58). With the additional contextual support indicated, it seems that we do get disambiguation. The experiment in (58) can be replicated with equatives in (59) and once we set up similar contextual assumptions, with similar results. For example, in (59) to get Ian's role in a play, one might need to be exactly as tall as Ian. This would favor the *exactly as* reading. On the other hand, Ian might be a window-cleaner and to get his job, one might need to be at least as tall as him. This would favor the *at least* reading.

(59) Bill is as tall as Ian is and Chris is too.

(*a*) Bill is exactly as tall as Ian is and Chris is exactly as tall as Ian is.

(*b*) Bill is at least as tall as Ian is and Chris is at least as tall as Ian is.

(*c*) Bill is at least as tall as Ian is and Chris is exactly as tall as Ian is.

(*d*) Bill is exactly as tall as Ian is and Chris is at least as tall as Ian is.

(60) (*a*) Bill is [*as*$_i$ [as Ian is tall]][~~Bill~~ ~~*as*~~$_i$ tall] and Chris is Δ

(*b*) Bill λx [*as*$_i$ [as Ian is tall]][x ~~*as*~~$_i$ tall] and
Chris λx [*as*$_i$ [as Ian is tall]] [x ~~*as*~~$_i$ tall]

(61) (*a*) Bill is [*as*$_i$ [as Ian is tall]]$_j$[~~[*as*$_i$ [as Ian is tall]]$_j$~~ [~~Bill~~ ~~*as*~~$_i$ tall]] and Chris is Δ

(*b*) Bill λx [*as*$_i$ [as Ian is tall]]$_j$ [~~[*as*$_i$ [as Ian is tall]]$_j$~~ [~~x~~ ~~*as*~~$_i$ tall]] and
Chris λx [*as*$_i$ [as Ian is tall]]$_j$ [~~[*as*$_i$ [as Ian is tall]]$_j$~~ [~~x~~ ~~*as*~~$_i$ tall]]

As in (58), the judgments are subtle but we do seem to get disambiguation. This would seem to support the ambiguity hypothesis. But we think that the facts from disambiguation do not by themselves lend unequivocal support to the ambiguity hypothesis. They would do so if we could keep the background assumptions in the two conjuncts independent. In the examples at hand, the contextual assumptions in both conjuncts are the same. When they favor an *exactly* reading (as in the *a*/*b* examples), we get an *exactly* reading, and when they favor an *at least* reading (as in the *c*/*d* examples), we get an *at least* reading. Since there is a plausible implicature-based explanation of the disambiguation pattern, the disambiguation facts are ultimately compatible with either account.

Independently of the evidence from ellipsis, we note that if the strong and the weak readings of equatives are represented by two syntactic structures which differ along the lines we are suggesting, that is late merger vs. late merger followed by short QR, it will be in general (the problematic case of ellipsis discussed above aside) difficult to isolate empirically these two structures, as the weak reading is always only a step or short QR of the quantifier $[_{\text{DegP}}$ *as* (A)] away. Short QR of $[_{\text{DegP}}$ *as* (A)] is expected to have no effect on scopal interpretation, as the $[_{\text{DegP}}$ *as*] is already in its scope position when the degree clause is merged.

Deriving weak readings from short QR of *as* with the degree clause faces a potential challenge. To derive the weak reading from the strong reading, we assume short QR of the degree quantifier that consists of the degree head *as* and its degree complement. But because of the correlation between the surface position of the degree clause and the scope of the degree head (cf. 10), we need to block long QR of the degree quantifier that consists of the degree head *as* and its degree complement. It is potentially problematic to block long QR of the degree quantifier but still allow for short QR. In our basic proposal, early merger and further QR of the degree quantifier are both blocked by the non-conservative semantics of *-er*. We wish to appeal to the non-conservative semantics to block early merger of the degree complement of *as*. But then, further QR of the degree quantifier is also blocked. One way out of this quandary is to note that short QR and long QR have distinct formal properties. For example, while long QR is subject to the Principle of Scope Economy formulated in Fox (2000), short QR is not. In general, short QR seems to be an option that is always freely available. This distinction between short and long QR helps sustain the viability of the approach that derives the weak reading from the strong reading via short QR while still disallowing long QR. In what follows, the choice between weak and strong semantics is not directly relevant and so, having explored the implications of a strong semantics for *as*, we will stay agnostic for the rest of this paper on the question of what the right semantics for *as* is.

To sum up, we have considered two motivations for late merger of the degree complements of *as*: indeterminacy with respect to conservativity induced by the factor argument and a strong semantics for *as*. These two motivations are not mutually exclusive. The strong semantics motivation only applies to the case where the factor argument is equal to one. When the factor argument *n* is less than one, the [*n as*] quantifier has conservative semantics irrespective of what semantics for *as* we choose. Since the facts remain the same irrespective of the value of the factor argument, we need to appeal to the motivation from indeterminacy no matter what semantics we adopt for *as*.

9.6 Early Merger, Late Merger, and (Non-)Conservativity

Comparative *-er* has non-conservative semantics, and the conservativity of the combination of *as* and its factor argument depends upon the value of the factor argument. Both have their restrictors merged late. Early merger of the degree clause to *-er* yields a contradiction. Early merger of the degree clause to *as*, assuming strong semantics and factor argument equal to 1, would "override" the non-conservative lexical meaning of *as*, and would yield a conservative interpretation for *as* ("*at least as*").

(62) (*a*) *as* (A) $(A \cap B) = 1$ iff $A = A \cap B$ strong "*exactly as*" lexical meaning
(*b*) $A = A \cap B$ iff $A \subseteq B$ "*at least as*" derived reading

In other words, if its restrictor were merged early, the putative non-conservative meaning of *as* would never emerge, and speakers would never have evidence for it. Late merger of its restrictor would allow an *as* with strong semantics to "show" its lexical meaning. Thus, it turns out, an early merger of the restrictor is incompatible with non-conservative meanings for quantifiers. We can formulate the generalization in (63).

(63) Restrictors of non-conservative quantifiers are merged late, at the quantifier's scope position.

In fact, the generalization is even stronger:

(64) Early merger of restrictor $\Rightarrow$ conservative derived meaning (when allowed by the quantifier's lexical meaning)

(65) Q (A) (B) when A is early merged $\Leftrightarrow$ $[Q\ (A)]_i\ [\sout{\{Q\ (A)\}}_i\ (B)]$ $\Leftrightarrow$ Q (A) $(A \cap B)$

We are a step closer to deriving the conservativity property of natural language quantifiers from the mechanism of interpreting the copies of their restrictors. What is left is to show that restrictors of conservative quantifiers are always merged early. Then, we can derive conservativity as not a lexical property, but a property derived from the syntax of merger and the mechanism for copy interpretation. As we shall see in the next section, this turns out to be more involved than one might hope.

9.7 Late Merger of Complements

Why can the complement of *-er/as* be merged late but not the complement of, for example, *rumor*? If such late merger for complements of lexical predicates were allowed, (66) would be acceptable, rather than a condition C violation.

(66) ??Which rumor that $John_i$ liked Mary did he_i later deny?

The mechanism of interpreting copies suggests a possible answer for complements of lexical predicates (cf. Fox 2002). Higher and lower *rumor* are of different types, resulting in an illegitimate LF.

(67) *LF with late merger*:
[Which rumor that John liked Mary] λx [he denied [the rumor x]]

In the case of *as*, the Determiner Replacement part of Trace Conversion replaces the lower *as*. As a result, there is no offending copy in the base position that could cause a type mismatch. In (67), Determiner Replacement targets the copy of *which*, leaving behind the lower copy of *rumor*, which is responsible for the ensuing type mismatch.

Sauerland (p.c.), in Fox (2002), noted that the above line of explanation incorrectly predicted that it should be possible to late merge NP complements of determiners. Thus in (68), it should in principle be possible to merge *every* in the theta-position and late merge its restrictor.

(68) *I gave him [$_{D}$ every] yesterday [$_{NP}$ book that John wanted to read].

Two possible answers suggest themselves to us. The first is that degree clauses do not receive a theta-role, nor does *-er/as*. Determiners cannot receive a theta-role by themselves, thus their restrictors have to be merged early. The second answer, which follows from the preceding discussion, is that restrictors of conservative quantifiers have to be merged early. This answer links with the generalization that we reached earlier, regarding late merger and non-conservativity, but it relies on conservativity as a lexical property, and is a stipulation.

The most attractive answer would be that restrictors of quantifiers are merged early *whenever possible*. Non-conservative quantifiers do not "survive" early merger (cf. (64)), and, as a last resort, are merged late. This answer would allow us to not directly make reference to the conservativity of quantifiers. Rather early merger would filter out quantifiers with non-conservative semantics, yielding either contradictions, tautologies, or contingent conservative meanings. The only way to express non-conservative meanings would be by late merger. The fact that natural language quantifiers are conservative would follow from the syntax.

Given the above "merge early whenever possible" model, we would expect those *as* plus factor argument combinations which have conservative semantics to allow for early merger. We have seen that this is not the case. One option would be to say that this is because the syntactic system was unable to determine the conservativity of these combinations and so went for the safe late merger option. Only those quantifiers whose conservativity could be determined allowed for early merger. But once we do this, we lose our explanation from the interpretation of traces for the generalization that natural language quantifiers are conservative. Another option is to say that a syntactic uniformity consideration requires [*n as*] augmented quantifiers to have the same syntax, regardless of the value of *n*. Because for some values of *n* early merger leads to failure of interpretability, late merger is the only option for [*n as*]. This way of thinking allows us to not make reference to conservativity. Rather, the property of conservativity would fall out as the result of the syntactic derivation.

9.8 Concluding Remarks

We started with the observation of a puzzling need for extraposition of degree clauses, correlated with the fact that the surface position of the extraposition marks the scope of the degree quantifier. The mechanism of late merger was posited as the way the degree clause is syntactically integrated into the degree construction. This proposal gives us an answer to the puzzling facts. Regarding the motivation for late merger, we suggested that of relevance are the semantics of degree quantifiers and the mechanism for interpreting copies of moved expressions. With *-er* being non-conservative, late merger of the comparative clause is enforced as the only option, as both early merger and a further movement of *-er* and the degree clause together yield a contradiction. Given the standard meaning of *as*, *as* is conservative and early merger is not precluded. We observed that once we take into account the role of the factor argument of *as*, the conservativity properties of *as* plus the factor argument are dependent upon the exact value of the factor argument. This indeterminacy results in late merger due to considerations of syntactic uniformity. We also explored the consequences of redefining *as*, giving it a non-conservative meaning, as a way to account for the obligatory late merger. An additional consequence of this redefinition was that the scalar readings of equatives could be derived syntactically: late merger yielded the strong "exactly as" reading; late merger followed by short QR of *as* and the equative clause yielded the weak "at least as" reading.

We put forth the generalization that restrictors of non-conservative quantifiers and quantifiers whose conservativity cannot be determined by the syntactic system are necessarily merged late while restrictors of conservative quantifiers are merged early. Quantifiers whose lexical meaning does not clash with the interpretive requirement imposed by early merger are what we call conservative quantifiers. Late merger allows for expression of potential non-conservative meanings. We conclude with the following question. Why is it that quantifiers that range over individuals have inherently conservative semantics, while quantifiers that range over degrees can have non-conservative semantics? Why do we not find quantifiers over individuals with semantics that forces late merger of their restrictors?

References

Bhatt, R. and Pancheva, R. 2004. 'Late merger of degree clauses', *Linguistic Inquiry*, 35: 1–45.

Bobaljik, J. D. 1995. Morphosyntax: The Syntax of Verbal Inflection. Doctoral dissertation, MIT.

—— 2002. 'A-chains at the PF-interface: copies and "Covert" movement', *Natural Language and Linguistic Theory*, 20: 197–267.

Bresnan, J. 1973. 'Syntax of the comparative clause construction in English', *Linguistic Inquiry*, 4: 275–343.

—— 1975. 'Comparative deletion and constraints on transformations', *Linguistic Analysis*, 1: 25–74.

Carlson, G. 1977. 'Amount relatives', *Language*, 53: 520–42.

Chierchia, G. 2004. 'Scalar implicatures, polarity phenomena, and the syntax/pragmatics interface', in A. Belletti (ed.), *Structures and Beyond*. Oxford: Oxford University Press. 39–103.

Chomsky, N. 1965. *Aspects of the Theory of Syntax*. Cambridge, MA: MIT Press.

—— 1993. 'A minimalist program for linguistic theory', in K. Hale and S. Keyser (eds), *The View from Building 20: Essays in Linguistics in Honor of Sylvain Bromberger*. Cambridge, MA: MIT Press. 1–52.

Cresswell, M. 1976. 'The semantics of degree', in B. Partee (ed.), *Montague Grammar*. New York: Academic Press. 261–92.

Fox, D. 2000. *Economy and Semantic Interpretation*, Linguistic Inquiry Monographs 35. Cambridge, MA: MIT Press.

—— 2001. 'The syntax and semantics of traces', handout of November 2001 talk at the University of Connecticut.

—— 2002. 'Antecedent-contained deletion and the copy theory of movement', *Linguistic Inquiry*, 33: 63–96.

—— 2003. 'The interpretation of scalar items: Semantics or pragmatics, or both?', talk given at the University of Texas, Austin.

—— and Nissenbaum, J. 1999. 'Extraposition and scope: A case for overt QR', in *Proceedings of the WCCFL 18*, Palo Alto, CA: CSLI. 132–44.

Grice, P. 1968. 'Logic and conversation', in P. Grice, *Studies in the Way of Words*. Cambridge, MA: Harvard University Press.

Gueron, J. and May, R. (1984). 'Extraposition and logical form', *Linguistic Inquiry*, 15: 1–32.

Heim, I. 1985. 'Notes on comparatives and related matters', unpublished MS, University of Texas, Austin.

—— 2000. 'Degree operators and scope', in *Proceedings of SALT X*, Cornell University, Ithaca, NY, Cornell Linguistics Club. 40–64.

Horn, L. 1972. On the Semantic Properties of Logical Operators in English. Ph.D. thesis, UCLA.

——2001. *A Natural History of Negation.* Standford, CA: CSLI Publications.

KEENAN, E. 1981. 'A Boolean approach to semantics', in J. Groenendijk, T. Janssen, and M. Stokhof (eds), *Formal Methods in the Study of Language.* Amsterdam: Mathematisch Centrum. 343–79.

——and STAVI, J. 1986. 'A semantic characterization of natural language quantifiers', *Linguistics and Philosophy*, 9: 253–326.

KLEIN, E. 1980. 'A semantics for positive and comparative adjectives', *Linguistics and Philosophy*, 4: 1–45.

KRATZER, A. 2003. 'Scalar implicatures: Are there any?', talk given at the Workshop on Polarity, Scalar Phenomena, and Implicatures, University of Milan-Bicocca.

LARSON, R. and MAY, R. 1990. 'Antecedent containment or vacuous movement: Reply to Baltin', *Linguistic Inquiry*, 21: 103–22.

LEBEAUX, D. 1990. 'Relative clauses, licensing, and the nature of the derivation', *NELS 20*: 318–32.

PESETSKY, D. 2000. *Phrasal Movement and Its Kin.* Cambridge, MA: MIT Press.

SAG, I. 1976. Deletion and Logical Form. Doctoral dissertation, MIT.

SELKIRK, E. 1970. 'On the determiner systems of noun phrases and adjective phrases', MS, MIT.

SPORTICHE, D. 1997. 'Reconstruction and constituent structure', handout of a talk presented at MIT.

——1999. 'Reconstruction, constituency, and morphology', paper presented at GLOW, Berlin.

STECHOW, A. VON 1984. 'Comparing semantic theories of comparison', *Journal of Semantics*, 3: 1–77.

WILLIAMS, E. 1974. Rule Ordering in Syntax. Doctoral dissertation, MIT.

WOLD, D. 1995. 'Antecedent-contained deletion in comparative constructions', unpublished MS, MIT.

10

Two Reconstruction Puzzles*

YAEL SHARVIT

10.1 Introduction

This paper is concerned with the "low" reading of (1) (which has a superlative relative clause) and the "low" reading of (2) (a *which*-interrogative).

(1) The longest book John said Tolstoy had written was *Anna Karenina.* (Bhatt 2002)

"Low" reading: "*Anna Karenina* is the unique x such that John said that x is the longest book Tolstoy wrote".

This reading is called "low" because *longest book* is interpreted in the scope of *say*. The sentence has another reading, a "high" reading, where *longest book* is interpreted outside the scope of *say*.

(2) John knows which book(s) Tolstoy wrote.
(based on similar examples from Groenendijk and Stokhof 1982, 1984)

"Low" reading: "For every x that is actually a book by Tolstoy, John knows that x is a book and Tolstoy wrote x".

I call this reading "low" because *book* is interpreted in the scope of *know*. The sentence has another reading, a "high" reading, where *book* is not interpreted in the scope of *know*.

If we construct a *which*-interrogative on the basis of (1), we get (3*a*), which does not have the "low" reading in (3*b*), but may (at least for some speakers) have the reading in (3*c*).

* I thank the audiences at the Workshop on Direct Compositionality (Brown University), the 14th Amsterdam Colloquium, Penn Linguistics Speaker Series 2005, Rutgers Linguistics Colloquium 2005, and the MIT Question Reading Group 2006 for very helpful comments. Much of the discussion in §10.2 is based on joint work with Elena Guerzoni, which has appeared as Sharvit and Guerzoni (2003).

(3) (*a*) Which longest book did John say Tolstoy had written?

(*b*) "Which x is such that John said that x is the longest book Tolstoy wrote?"

(*c*) "Out of the set of entities such that each of them is the longest member in some set of books (e.g., {Book a (= longest member of set A), Book b (= longest member of set B), Book c (= longest member of set C)}), which entity is such that John said that Tolstoy wrote it?"

The generalization seems to be that (3*b*) is predicted to be a possible reading of (3*a*) if the generation of the "low" reading of (1) and the generation of the "low" reading of (2) involve the same "degree" of reconstruction. In other words, our theory will predict (3*b*) to be a possible interpretation of (3*a*) in one of three cases:[1] (i) if we assume that both the "low" reading of (1) and the "low" reading of (2) are obtained by "reconstructing" the relevant items (*-est* and *long book* in the case of (1); *book* in the case of (2)) in their base positions or in intermediate positions; (ii) if we assume that the "low" reading of (1) is obtained without "reconstruction" of the superlative morpheme *-est*, but with "reconstruction" of *long book*, and the "low" reading of (2) is obtained with "reconstruction" of *book*; (iii) if we assume that neither one of the "low" readings in (1) and (2) is obtained via "reconstruction". The first option is illustrated by (1′), (2′) and (3′), the second by (1″), (2′) and (3″), and the third by (1‴), (2″) and (3‴). The "reconstruction" method used here is the one that makes use of "copies", as this term is used in the Copy Theory of Movement (especially Fox 2002, according to which a copy contains a variable bound by the phrase whose movement created the copy).

(1′) **[the [1 John said-w_0 [2 [est-e_1 [5 [[long-w_2-d_5][6 Tolstoy wrote-w_2 the book-w_2 e_6]]]]]]]** ***is Anna Karenina***

(1″) **[the 1 est-e_1 [5 6 John said Tolstoy wrote a d_5-long book e_6]] is** ***Anna Karenina***

(1‴) **[the [1 est-e_1 [5 [long-d_5 book] [6 John said Tolstoy wrote e_6]]]] is** ***Anna Karenina***

(2′) **John knows-w_0 [which [1 C_{wh} Tolstoy wrote the book e_1]]**

(2″) **John knows-w_0 [which book [1 C_{wh} Tolstoy wrote e_1]]**

(3′) **which [1 [C_{wh} John said-w_0 [2 est-e_1 [5 [[long-w_2-d_5] [6 Tolstoy wrote-w_2 the book-$w_2 e_6$]]]]]]**

[1] There are probably more logical possibilities, but those that are considered here suffice to make the point.

(3″) **which 1 [C_{wh} [est-e_1 [5 6 John said Tolstoy wrote a d_5-long book e_6]]]**

(3‴) **which longest book 1 [C_{wh} John said Tolstoy wrote e_1]**

If the generation of the "low" reading of (1) and the generation of the "low" reading of (2) involve the same "degree" of reconstruction, it is hard to see what would block (3*b*) as a possible reading of (3*a*). But if they do not involve the same "degree" of reconstruction, it is plausible to assume that the grammar never generates an LF that yields (3*b*) as a possible reading of (3*a*). Therefore, to prevent (3*b*) from being a reading of (3*a*), the theory has to be such that the "low" readings of (1) and (2) are not generated in a similar way.

I argue that the "low" reading of (2) is obtained from (2″), and that there are fairly good reasons to believe that the "low" reading of (1) is obtained from (1′). This means that the "low" reading of (1) (i.e. of superlative relative clauses) is a reconstruction effect, but the "low" reading of (2) (i.e. of *which*-interrogatives) is not. The grammar generates (1‴), which yields the "high" reading of (1), but it does not generate (1″). The grammar also does not generate (2′), which means that both the "high" and the "low" readings of (2) are "read off" (2″). In addition, neither (3′) nor (3″) are generated, although (3‴) (which yields only the interpretation in (3*c*)) is.

Given that our theory has to allow "reconstruction" in principle (in order to generate (1′)), the theoretical problem that emerges from this is that the grammar has to have a mechanism that blocks "reconstruction" in *which*-interrogatives. I do not offer a solution to this problem. The goal of this paper, rather, is to point out that any theory of reconstruction has to be formulated in such a way as to block the undesired readings. This is as much a problem for semantic approaches to reconstruction as it is for syntactic approaches. For presentational purposes, I use the mechanism of the Copy Theory of Movement as my "reconstruction" mechanism, but it should be clear that everything I say holds also of a more semantic mechanism (i.e. one that either does not assume a level of LF at all—or assumes a level of LF that is not very different from surface structure—and according to which the relevant predicates can be interpreted in "low" positions by λ-conversion).

I begin by showing in §10.2 that *which*-interrogatives do not involve "reconstruction" (i.e. that (2′) is never generated, although (2″) is). I then show in §10.3 that superlative relative clauses probably do (i.e. that the grammar does generate (1′) and (1‴), but not (1″)). From this I conclude that neither (3′) nor (3″) are generated. In §10.4 I briefly discuss the implications of these conclusions for the theory of reconstruction.

10.2 "Low" Readings of *which*-interrogatives

An analysis of the *which*-interrogative *Which students left the room* along the lines of Karttunen (1977) says that it denotes the set of true propositions of the form 'that x left the room' in (4*b*, 4*c*), where possible values for x are actual students ('that x left the room' is shorthand for {w:x left the room in w}, and "p is true in w" is shorthand for w∈p; where x is an individual, p a proposition—a set of worlds, and w a world). This interpretation is obtained from an LF such as (4*a*), which does not have any "low" copies of the restrictor of *which*. *Which students* is an indefinite binding a variable inside the sister of the complementizer, and the complementizer introduces an equation of the proposition denoted by its sister and p (p itself is bound by a set-forming operator).

(4) (*a*) **which students 1 C_{wh} [$e_1$left the room]**

(*b*) {p:p is true in the actual world and there is a student x in the actual world such that p = 'that x left the room'}

(*c*) {'that Sally left the room', 'that Mary left the room', 'that Norma left the room', . . . }

Such an analysis correctly predicts that one cannot know which students left the room without believing the true answers to *Which students left the room*. But as Groenendijk and Stokhof (1982, 1984) show, although this analysis accounts for the "high" (or "de re") inference of (5), it fails to account for its "low" inference (which according to them comes from its "de dicto" reading).

(5) John knows which students left the room.
"High" inference
"For every student x who left the room, John knows that x left the room."
"Low" inference
"For every x, John knows whether it's true that x is a student and x left the room."

The problem is that according to (4), the propositions one believes when one knows which students left the room contain no information regarding the student status of the student leavers. Groenendijk and Stokhof further argue that (4) is too weak in one more respect: their intuition is that (5) is true only if John believes that the set of student leavers is the actual set of student leavers (as implied by the "low" inference in (5)), and not if he merely believes about every actual student x who left the room that x left the room (as implied by Karttunen's analysis).

To address these concerns, Heim (1994) suggests an analysis that combines ideas from both Groenendijk and Stokhof and from Karttunen. Accordingly, an interrogative denotes a set of propositions (as in Karttunen's analysis), but to know a question, in the "strong" sense, means to believe that the set of true answers to it equals the set of actual true answers to it. In other words, to know, in the "strong" sense, which students left the room means to believe the proposition in (6) (which we refer to as the "strong" "low" answer to *Which students left the room*).

(6) {w:{p:p is true in w and there is a student x in w such that p = 'that x left the room'} = {p:p is true in the actual world and there is a student x in the actual world such that p = 'that x left the room'}}

This "strong" analysis predicts that if you know which students left the room you have to know which individuals are student leavers and which individuals are not. Because the proposition in (6) has to be true in all the worlds compatible with the subject's beliefs, it guarantees that the relevant leavers are students in those worlds, thus capturing the "low" inference.[2] Heim suggests that this "strong" reading is generated in addition to the "weak", Karttunen-style, reading, according to which to know which students left the room is to believe the conjunction of the true propositions that comprise the question, which we refer to as the "weak" answer to *Which students left the room* (cf. Beck and Rullmann 1999; Sharvit 2002).

But according to Rullmann and Beck (1998), although Heim's solution addresses Groenendijk and Stokhof's objections to Karttunen's analysis, it fails to make the right connection between (5) and examples such as (7).

(7) John mistakenly believes that the cats in the backyard are unicorns, and he wants to play with some of them. Which unicorns does John want to play with?

The interrogative in (7) has a "low" reading, because the individuals we are asking about are cats in the actual world, not unicorns. Accordingly, the set {p:p is true in the actual world and there is a unicorn x in the actual world such that p = 'that John wants to play with x'} comes out empty, and the "low" reading is not captured. For Rullmann and Beck, the "low" reading of (5) and "low" reading of (7) have the same source. They propose to account for them by assuming a "low" copy of the restrictor of *which* at LF, which, they suggest, has the form of a definite description ('that the student x left the

[2] Example (5) also has a "strong" "high" reading, where *students* is interpreted outside the scope of *know*. We ignore this reading here; what is crucial for our purposes is that according to the Heim/Groenendijk and Stokhof view, the "low" inference comes from a "strong" interpretation.

room' is shorthand for {w∈{w′: there is a unique y such that y is a student in w′ and y = x}:the unique y such that y is a student in w and y = x left the room in w}).

(8) (*a*) **which 1 C_{wh} [the student e_1 left the room]**

(*b*) {p:p is true in the actual world and there is an x such that p = 'that the student x left the room'}

(*c*) {'that the student Sally left the room', 'that the student Mary left the room', ...}

(9) (*a*) **which 1 C_{wh} [John wants to play with the unicorn e_1]**

(*b*) {'that John wants to play with the unicorn Sam', 'that John wants to play with the unicorn Fred', ...}

Beck and Rullmann relate these examples to similar non-interrogative examples discussed in Karttunen (1974) and Heim (1992) (e.g. *John mistakenly believes that there was a murder, and he wants the murderer to be caught*). The treatment of the copy of the restrictor of *which* as a definite description is consistent with the fact that the question in (7) presupposes that John believes the relevant individuals to be unicorns. These "presuppositional" copies have been adopted by some proponents of the Copy Theory of Movement (e.g. Fox 2002).

But it seems to me that it is misleading to say that (5) and (7) are instances of one and the same phenomenon (as indeed predicted by the assumption that both their LFs have a presuppositional "low" copy of the restrictor of *which*), because (5) and (7) do not behave in the same way. For convenience, I call the "low" reading of (5), triggered by the question-embedding verb *know*, an "external" "low" reading; and the "low" reading of the interrogative in (7), triggered by the propositional attitude verb *want*, which is part of the question itself, an "internal" "low" reading. It seems to me that neither the "external" nor the "internal" "low" reading is a reconstruction effect. The former is best captured by the Heim/Groenendijk and Stokhof semantics, while the latter requires a completely different analysis. Let us elaborate on this point.

The problem with the presuppositional copies that Rullmann and Beck posit, at least for "external" "low" readings, is that they do not make the right predictions regarding some data involving quantificational variability effects (QVE; see Berman 1991 and Lahiri 1991, 2002). A basic example of QVE is given in (10*a*), where the main clause is preceded by an adverb of quantification. The sentence receives the interpretation in (10*b*).

(10) (*a*) For the most part, Mary knows who cried.

(*b*) There are more individuals who cried such that Mary knows that they cried than there are individuals who cried such that Mary doesn't know that they cried.

Notice that (10*b*) is a "weak" reading (i.e. it talks only about Mary's knowledge regarding those who cried, not her knowledge regarding those who did not cry). We will temporarily treat this as the only reading, but later we will consider the possibility that a "strong" reading is available too.

Regarding the "weak" reading of (10*a*) (that is to say, (10*b*)), the most influential analysis is due to Lahiri. According to that analysis, (10*a*) has the LF in (11*a*), where the embedded question is raised and becomes an argument of *for the most part*, and the trace left behind is interpreted as a variable over propositions (with the result that *know* is interpreted as a proposition-taking predicate, not a question-taking predicate). *For the most part* quantifies over the propositions that comprise the "raised" question.

(11) (*a*) [**for the most part** [**who cried**]] [1 **Mary** $\textbf{knows}^{\textbf{p}}$ $\textbf{e}_1$]

(*b*) MOST p∈{q:q is true in the actual world and there is an x such that q = 'that x cried'}, Mary knows p in the actual world

The fact that *for the most part* quantifies over true propositions only is consistent with the factivity of *know*: Mary cannot know a proposition unless it is true.

Notice that when the embedded interrogative is a *which*-interrogative (as in (12*a*), where the adverb is *with no exceptions*), Rullmann and Beck's analysis ((12*b*), with a presuppositional "low" copy) makes a different prediction compared to an analysis that does not involve copies (as in (12*c*)). Since Mary cannot know (or even merely believe) a proposition unless she believes its presuppositions, we have to accommodate any such presuppositions into the restriction of *with no exceptions*.

(12) (*a*) With no exceptions, Mary knows which children cried.

(*b*) For all p∈{q:q is true in the actual world and there is an x such that q = 'that the child x cried'} such that *Mary believes in the actual world the presuppositions of p* (namely, that x is a child), Mary knows p in the actual world.

(*c*) For all p∈{q:q is true in the actual world and there is a child x in the actual world such that q = 'that x cried'}, Mary knows p in the actual world.

The different predictions are illustrated by the scenario described in (13), in which (12*a*) is intuitively false. The analysis in (12*b*), where the propositions quantified over by *with no exceptions* contain a presuppositional copy, predicts (12*a*) to have a true reading in this state of affairs; (12*c*) does not.

(13) Dan and Sam are the children who cried. Mary believes that Dan is a child, but that Sam is not. She knows that Dan cried, but not that Sam did.

These predictions clearly favor (12*c*) over (12*b*).

Is it possible that LFs of *which*-interrogatives have copies but not presuppositional ones (as suggested in Hamblin 1973 and Beck and Rullmann 1999)? This proposal would yield (14) as the truth conditions of (12*a*), correctly predicting it to be false in scenario (13).

(14) For all p∈{q:q is true in the actual world and there is an x such that q = 'that x is a child and x cried'}, Mary knows p in the actual world.

The answer is that such an analysis is notoriously problematic. As Reinhart (1992) shows, a problem (sometimes referred to as the Donald Duck problem) arises when the question contains a downward entailing operator, as in (15). The non-presuppositional copies and the presuppositional copies yield interpretations that are illustrated in (16) and (17) respectively.

(15) Which philosophers didn't come to the party?

(16) Non-presuppositional copies yield (true) propositions of the form: 'NOT [x is a philosopher and x came to the party]'

(17) Presuppositional copies yield (true) propositions of the form: 'NOT [the philosopher x came to the party]'

(16) predicts that any non-philosopher (e.g. Donald Duck) qualifies as a suitable value for x. (17) does not have this problem, because the only possible values for x are "real" philosophers.

In addition, a non-presuppositional rendition of copies runs into problems when we consider data with *surprise*, such as (18).

(18) #Although Mary had expected Sam and Dan—the students who left—to leave, it still surprised her which students left because she had expected them not to be students.

The oddity of (18) comes, presumably, from the fact that in order for *It surprised Mary which students left* to be true, Mary has to have had wrong expectations about the "leaver" status of the student leavers, not wrong expectations about their student status. This is predicted by both Rullmann and

Beck's analysis, (19), and by Heim's, (20), but not by the assumption that the restrictor of *which* has a non-presuppositional copy, (21), which predicts (18) to be perfect.[3,4]

(19) Mary actually expected NOT $\cap$\{p:p is true in the actual world and there is an x such that p = 'that the student x left'\}

$\Rightarrow$ For all worlds w compatible with Mary's actual expectations, at least one actual student x who actually left is a student in w but didn't leave in w.

(20) Mary actually expected NOT $\cap$\{p:p is true in the actual world and there is a student x in the actual world such that p ='that x left'\}

$\Rightarrow$ For all worlds w compatible with Mary's actual expectations, at least one actual student x who actually left didn't leave in w.

(21) Mary actually expected NOT $\cap$\{p:p is true in the actual world and p = 'that x is a student and x left'\}

$\Rightarrow$ For all worlds w compatible with Mary's actual expectations, at least one actual student x who actually left is such that either x is not a student in w or x didn't leave in w.

The conclusion is that if moved <e,t>-type predicates such as *book*, *student*, *philosopher*, etc. have copies at all, these copies are presuppositional.

Nevertheless, we still have to ask ourselves whether (12*a*) has the reading in (14), which should come out false in a situation where Mary is misinformed about the child status of the children who cried (although she may be fully informed about their crying). This reading should be compared

[3] I'm assuming Lahiri's (1991) semantics for *surprise*, according to which to be surprised by a question (in the weak sense) is to expect the negation of the conjunction of its true answers, and I'm considering only the weak reading of (18), because there is evidence that suggests that *surprise*, unlike *know*, is inherently weak (Heim 1994; Sharvit 2002; Sharvit and Guerzoni 2003). This is illustrated by the following contrast.

(i) Although Mary knows that Dan and Sam—the students who left the room—left the room, she still doesn't know which students left (at least not completely), because she doesn't know that Ann didn't leave.

(ii) #Although Mary expected Dan and Sam—the students who left—to leave, it still surprised her which students left because she also expected Ann, who didn't leave, to leave.

Notice that because both (19) and (20) predict (18) to be unacceptable, we cannot use (18) to argue against presuppositional copies. QVE data with *surprise* would be relevant here, but the judgments are further complicated by the non-distributive nature of *surprise*.

[4] Some of the speakers I consulted accept (18). Although I do not have an explanation for this variation among speakers, notice that it is as problematic for the presuppositional-copy account as it is for the "copy"-less account (i.e. for both (19) and (20)), which predict (18) to be unacceptable. (21) would still be problematic, given the Donald Duck problem, as shown by (15)–(17).

to the "low" reading of *Mary knows which children cried* (without an adverb of quantification), which comes out false in such a situation (as predicted by Heim's semantics, cf. the "strong" answer to *Which students left* in (6) above: knowing this answer requires being fully informed about the student status of the students who left). It is not so clear whether this reading is as robust for (12*a*) (with *with no exceptions*) as it is for its "adverb-less" counterpart, but it certainly seems to exist (at least for some speakers). How can we account for it, then, given that we cannot use non-presuppositional copies?[5]

As mentioned above, Lahiri's analysis of QVE captures only the "weak" reading of (12*a*). It is argued in Beck and Sharvit (2002) that sentences involving QVE have "strong" readings as well. A possible strong reading of (12*a*) is the one paraphrased in (22), which entails (14).

(22) For all p of the form 'that x is a child and x cried', Mary knows in the actual world whether p is true.

This reading is not captured by Lahiri's account. One reason for this is that in that account, *know* is proposition-taking rather than question-taking. An analysis that can quite easily capture such readings is the one advocated in Beck and Sharvit, according to which QV effects are not the result of quantification over answers (or answer-parts) to the "raised" question (as in Lahiri's system), but rather over parts of that "raised" question that together comprise either a "weak" or a "strong" answer to the question. To illustrate, those question-parts whose (true) answers together comprise the "weak" answer to *Which children cried* (which is the following Karttunen-style proposition: $\cap${p:p is true in the actual world and there is a child x in the actual world such that p = 'that x cried'}; cf. (4)) are yes–no questions that have the form 'did x cry?' (where x ranges over actual children). Those question-parts whose (true) answers together comprise the "strong" "low" answer to *Which children cried* (which is the following Heim-style proposition: {w:{p:p is true in w and there is a child x in w such that p = 'that x cried'} = {p:p is true in the actual world and there is a child x in the actual world such that p = 'that x cried'}}; cf. (6)), are yes–no questions that have the form 'is it true that x is a child and x cried?' (where x ranges over all the individuals). Accordingly, one possible reading of (12*a*) would be (23).

[5] One possibility which can be easily discarded is that we do have presuppositional copies after all, but the presupposition of the copy is locally accommodated into the nuclear scope of the adverb. It would be hard to see how we could restrict the accommodation options to this one only, without allowing accommodation into the restriction as an alternative option given that we have to accommodate "p is true" into the restriction.

(23) For every question-part Q of *Which children cried* such that the actual answer to Q is entailed by the "strong" "low" answer of *Which children cried* (i.e. for all Q of the form 'is it true that x is a child and x cried?'), Mary knows in the actual world the actual answer to Q.

This reading does not make use of any copies, presuppositional or not. Because it does not rely on presuppositional copies, it does not run into the problem of accommodating undesirable presuppositions into the restriction of the adverb. Because it does not rely on non-presuppositional copies either, it does not run into the Donald Duck problem (crucially, question-parts whose answers together comprise the "weak" answer to *Which philosophers didn't come to the party* have the form "did x not come to the party?", and question-parts whose answers together comprise the "strong" "low" answer have the form "is it true that x is a philosopher and x didn't come to the party?" where "philosopher" is outside the scope of negation, cf. (16)). The "low" inference, according to this view of QVE, is a semantic effect, just like the "low" inference of "adverb-less" sentences with embedded questions in Heim's system is a semantic effect (and not a copy effect). What this analysis requires is a definition of "question-part" according to which "is it true that x is a child and that x cried" qualifies as a question-part of *Which children cried*, as discussed above. The reader is referred to Beck and Sharvit (2002) for a formal definition that has this consequence, and for a detailed discussion of the notion of "question-part" that is required independently to account for a wide variety of QVE. To sum up, even if a reading such as (14) (or one that entails (14)) exists, we can, and should, account for it without assuming copies at LF.

Interestingly, Beck and Sharvit's analysis offers a simple account of QVE with *agree*. Suppose no one is a student, and John and Bill believe that Fred and Sam are the only students who left. As for Mary, John believes she is a student who didn't leave, and Bill believes she is a non-student who left. The analysis correctly predicts (24) to be true.

(24) With no exceptions, John and Bill agree on which students left.

With no exceptions quantifies over questions of the form 'is it true that x is a student and x left?' (which John and Bill would answer with a No when x is Mary, and with a Yes when x is Fred or Sam). The view that says that *which students* has a presuppositional copy derives a true reading only if 'John and Bill believe that x is a student' is accommodated into the adverb's restriction (because Bill cannot agree or disagree with anyone on 'that the student Mary left' or 'did the student Mary leave?'). This conflicts with a suggestion due to Danny Fox (p.c.) to attribute the badness of (12*a*) in the scenario in (13) to a presupposition failure. Fox's solution requires that there be no possibility of accommodating presuppositions about the subject's beliefs into the adverb's restriction.

All this is true of "external" "low" readings of *which*-interrogatives. As for "internal" "low" readings (that is to say, those that are triggered by a propositional attitude verb which is part of the question itself), notice that (7) seems to require a "scare quote" intonation. This, in turn, suggests that the analysis of (7) is more complex, and that the "low" effect is a scare quote effect rather than a reconstruction effect. In addition, notice that the presuppositional copy analysis does not work in the following case (where the second question is uttered with a scare quote intonation on the *which*-phrase and) where the "internal" verb is the factive *know*.

(25) John mistakenly believes that the cats in the backyard are unicorns, and he knows that some of them have stripes. Which unicorns does John know have stripes?

In this scenario, asking *Which unicorns does John know have stripes*, with a scare quote intonation on the *which*-phrase, is tantamount to asking *Which cats does John know have stripes* (with a "normal" intonation) on its "high" (or "de re") reading. If we analyze the former along the lines of Rullmann and Beck's analysis, we will not predict this, because the true answers to *Which unicorns does John know have stripes* are of the form 'John knows that the unicorn x has stripes', and since *know* is factive, the propositions John knows have to be true. But there are no unicorns in the actual world, so there are no true propositions for John to know. In addition, the first sentence in (25) could be continued with *and he knows which unicorns have stripes* (again, with a "scare quote" intonation on *unicorns*). Once again, the presuppositional copy analysis will not predict the right reading, because John has to believe true propositions of the form 'the unicorn x has stripes'. This reinforces the claim that what is involved in (25) (and in (7)) is some form of quotation, and a theory of quotation is needed to handle such cases. My conclusion is that "low" copies are not involved in the generation of "external" "low" readings of *which*-interrogatives, and probably also not in their "internal" "low" readings.

We have just concluded that the "low" reading of (2) is indeed not a reconstruction effect (i.e. the grammar generates (2″), but not (2′)). This conclusion is compatible with "functional" approaches to questions with quantifiers (e.g. *Which relative of his does every man hate*?) advocated by Groenendijk and Stokhof (1984), Engdahl (1986), and others. We now have to investigate the origin of the "low" reading of (1). We will conclude in §10.3 that this reading is probably read off the LF in (1′), not (1″) or (1‴). Therefore, the grammar never generates (3′) or (3″). These conclusions jointly rule out “which x is such that John said that x is the longest book Tolstoy wrote” as a possible interpretation of *Which longest book did John say Tolstoy wrote?*.

10.3 “Low” Readings of Superlative Relative Clauses

Bhatt (2002) observes that (1), repeated below as (26), is ambiguous in the way indicated below.

(26) The longest book John said Tolstoy had written was *Anna Karenina.*

  (*a*) “High” reading (longest book >> say):
  John said about a bunch of books that they were written by Tolstoy. Of these books, *Anna Karenina* is the longest.

  (*b*) “Low” reading (say >> longest book):
  John said that *Anna Karenina* is the longest book written by Tolstoy.

A scenario where the “high” reading comes out true is this. John said: “Tolstoy wrote *Huckleberry Finn*, *Anna Karenina*, and *Tom Sawyer*. *Tom Sawyer* is the longest.” In this scenario, the “low” reading is obviously false because according to John, *Tom Sawyer*, not *Anna Karenina*, is the longest in {*Anna Karenina*, *Tom Sawyer*, *Huckleberry Finn*}, but in actual fact *Anna Karenina* is longest in that bunch. A scenario where the “low” reading comes out true is this. John said: “*Anna Karenina* is the longest book Tolstoy wrote. He also wrote *War and Peace* and some other shorter books”. The “high” reading is obviously false here because according to John, *War and Peace* is shorter than *Anna Karenina*, contrary to fact.

One way to account for this ambiguity is by adopting Heim’s (1999) semantics for the superlative operator, and the assumption that *-est*, *long*, and *book* may have “low” copies along the lines suggested by Hulsey and Sauerland (2006). The assumption underlying Heim’s semantics in (27) is that the <d,<e,t>>-argument of the superlative is downward monotonic (i.e. that gradable adjectives such as *long* denote downward monotonic relations between degrees and individuals so that, for example, *John is four feet tall* entails *John is three feet tall*).

(27) For any (downward monotonic) <d,<e,t>>-function R and any individual y, ⟦**est**⟧(y)(R) is defined only if for all relevant x there is a degree d such that R(d)(x) = True. Whenever defined, ⟦**est**⟧(y)(R) = True iff there is a degree d such that {z:R(d)(z) = True} = {y}.

This semantics derives the truth conditions of (the absolute reading of) *Tolstoy wrote the longest book* from the following LF.[6]

(28) **Tolstoy wrote [the 1 est-e_1 [long book]]** (where ⟦**long book**⟧= [λd . λx . x is a book and x's length is at least d]), and ⟦**the 1 est-e_1 [long book]**⟧ is the unique book that is longest in the set of books (if there is such a book).

Accordingly, *Tolstoy wrote the longest book*, on its absolute reading, presupposes that there is one book that is longer than any other book, and Tolstoy wrote it.

Assuming indeed that *-est*, *long*, and *book* can have "low" (base or intermediate) copies, we obtain the following as the "high" and "low" readings of *The longest book John said Tolstoy wrote was Anna Karenina.*

(29) "High": **the 1 est-e_1 [long-w_0 book-w_0 that John said-w_0 Tolstoy wrote]** ***is AK***

"*Anna Karenina* is the unique x such that x is longest in the actual world among {y: y is a book in the actual world and in all worlds w compatible with what John said in the actual world, Tolstoy wrote y in w}."

(30) "Low": **[the [1 John said-w_0 [2 [est-e_1 [5 [[long-w_2-d_5] [6 Tolstoy wrote-w_2 the book-w_2e_6]]]]]]] is *Anna Karenina***

"*Anna Karenina* is the unique x such that in all worlds w compatible with what John said in the actual world, x is longest in w among {y:y is a book in w and Tolstoy wrote y in w}."

The two readings seem to be captured correctly, and the "low" reading, in this analysis, is a reconstruction effect.[7]

However, Heycock (2005) observes that not all verbs support "low" readings. This observation suggests that we should reconsider the claim that "low" readings are the result of reconstruction. One verb that does not support "low" readings is *know*, as shown by (31) when judged against the scenario in (32) (cf. Bhatt and Sharvit, 2005).

(31) The longest book John knows Tolstoy had written was *War and Peace.*

[6] The absolute reading is the one according to which Tolstoy wrote the unique book which is longer than any of the other books. The sentence might have another reading, the comparative reading (to which we come back later).

[7] Notice that the copy of *long* is not part of a definite description, only the copy of *book* is. It is not so clear to me what rules out a representation where the copy of *long* is within a definite description, giving rise to some undesirable presuppositions (though see Hulsey and Sauerland 2006 for discussion). However, this point is not directly relevant to our discussion.

(32) Scenario: John believes that *War and Peace* is the longest book Tolstoy wrote. He also believes Tolstoy wrote other books, but he can't mention them or point at them.

Speakers reject (31) in this state of affairs. Since a "high" reading is pragmatically odd in such a scenario (given that the set of books that John said Tolstoy wrote is a singleton and given that superlatives usually require comparison sets that have more than one member), the reason speakers reject (31) must be due to the unavailability of a "low" reading.

Can we account for "low" readings without reconstruction? The first possibility to consider is that *-est*, *long*, and *book* do not have "low" copies. This is probably impossible, since under the "low" reading John may say false things about the lengths of the relevant books, but the sentence as a whole can still be true.[8] The only reading we can derive from such a structure is the one captured in (29). What we can still try to do, to derive the "low" reading from a structure different from (30), is interpret *-est* above *say* (without a "low" copy), but *long* and *book* below *say*.

(33) **the 1 est-e_1 [2 3 John said Tolstoy wrote a d_2-long book e_3] is *Anna Karenina***

"*Anna Karenina* is the unique x such that there is a degree d such that for all worlds w compatible with what John said in the actual world Tolstoy wrote x in w, x is a book in w, and x's length in w is at least d, and for all y distinct from x, all worlds w compatible with what John said are such that Tolstoy wrote y in w and y is a book in w, but not all of these worlds w are such that y's length in w is at least d."

This analysis is problematic for the following reason. One of the assumptions underlying Heim's proposal is that the <d,<e,t>>-argument of *-est* is downward monotonic. Heim adopts this assumption in order to account for the comparative reading of *Tolstoy wrote the longest book* ((34*a*); cf. Ross 1964 and Szabolcsi 1986), and the (comparative) split-scope reading of *Tolstoy needs to write the longest book* ((34*b*). Heim proposes that *-est* can scope out of the noun phrase in which it originates, and occupy a position above the main verb.

(34) (*a*) Out of the set of relevant writers, Tolstoy is the one who wrote at least one book that is longer than any of the books written by the others.

[8] See Bhatt (2002) and Hulsey and Sauerland (2006) for discussion of the "scare quote" interpretation/intonation of *book* in case John doesn't know which things are books.

This reading is obtained from: **Tolstoy 1 est-e_1 [2 3 e_3 wrote a d_2-long book]**, where *-est* has moved above *write* (leaving behind a degree-denoting trace), the definite article has been replaced by an indefinite, yielding $[\![$**2 3 e_3 wrote a d_2-long book**$]\!]$= [λd . λx . x wrote a book whose length is at least d]. Because of the Monotonicity assumption, *Tolstoy wrote the longest book* comes out true if and only if Tolstoy wrote at least one book that is longer than any book written by anyone else (but he could have written two equally long books that are longer than the books written by the other writers).

(*b*) Out of the set of relevant writers who have book-writing needs, John is the neediest (e.g. he won't make it in the literary scene unless he writes at least one book of 1,000 pages or more, but the others have to write at least one book of 900 or more).

This reading is obtained from: [**Tolstoy 1 est-e_1 [2 3 e_3 needs PRO write a d_2-long book]**], where *-est* has moved above *need*, and where the definite determiner has been replaced by an indefinite to yield $[\![$**2 3 e_3 need PRO write a d_2-long book**$]\!]$= [λd . λx . x needs to write a book whose length is at least d]. Because of the Monotonicity assumption, *Tolstoy needs to write the longest book* comes out true if and only if in all the worlds where Tolstoy's needs are satisfied, he writes at least one book whose length is at least 1,000, but for the other writers this isn't true (i.e., their needs are less demanding).

Indeed, the truth conditions of both the comparative reading of *Tolstoy wrote the longest book* and the (comparative) split-scope reading of *Tolstoy needs to write the longest book* are captured, but the analysis will not work for the "low" reading of (26), which according to (33) (an LF that mimics the one in (34*b*)) is predicted to be true in a situation where John says: "Tolstoy wrote *Anna Karenina* and *War and Peace*. *Anna Karenina* is 1,500 pages long or longer, and *War and Peace* is 1,000 pages long or longer". This goes against the intuitions people report about (26): it is judged unacceptable in such circumstances. Another problem is that (33) is too "extensional": it predicts that John has to have made a commitment about a particular length. This is not a requirement of (26), which is good even if John just says: "Anna Karenina is the longest book Tolstoy wrote, but I have no idea how long it is".

On the other hand, as pointed out by Hulsey and Sauerland (2006), sometimes (33) does make the right predictions, namely, when the embedding verb is a NEG-raising verb (and provided we adopt a particular analysis of

NEG-raising verbs). To see this, consider (35), the LF of *The longest book John believed Tolstoy wrote was* Anna Karenina, with the NEG-raising *believe*, and assume an analysis of *believe* along the lines of (36) (first suggested by Bartsch 1973).

(35) **[the 1 est-e_1 [2 3 John believed Tolstoy wrote a d_2-long book e_3]] is** ***Anna Karenina***

(36) 'x believes p' has a truth value (i.e. it is either true or false) only if x believes p or x believes NOT p.

Because of the Monotonicity assumption and the special presupposition of *believe*, the sentence comes out true only when there is a degree d such that *Anna Karenina* is d-long in all the worlds compatible with John's beliefs, and the other relevant books are not d-long (i.e. their lengths are smaller than d) in those worlds. This is exactly the interpretation we are after.

As it turns out, Heycock argues that the verbs that support "low" readings of superlative relative clauses are NEG-raising verbs. Even if this were the case, we would still have to ask why the non-NEG-raisers (e.g. *know*) do not give rise to what would be a perfectly plausible interpretation.

(37) **[the 1 est-e_1 [2 3 John knew Tolstoy wrote a d_2-long book e_3]] is** ***War and Peace***

"*War and Peace* is the only x such that there is a degree d such that John knows that x is a book whose length is at least d, and for all the z's distinct for x, John doesn't know that z is a book whose length is at least d"

According to (37), *The longest book John knew Tolstoy had written is War and Peace* should be acceptable if, for example, there are three books of the same length as *War and Peace*, but John only knows the length of *War and Peace*, he is wrong about the others. But it is not acceptable in such circumstances.

In addition, as observed by Bhatt and Sharvit (2005), it is not the case that only NEG-raising verbs support "low" readings of superlative relative clauses. In addition to *say*, there is *agree* (see Bhatt and Sharvit for discussion of other predicates that are problematic for Heycock's account).

(38) The longest book John and Mary agree Tolstoy wrote is *Anna Karenina.*

For (38) to be true it has to be the case that John and Mary independently think that *Anna Karenina* is Tolstoy's longest book. But *John and Mary do not agree that Mary left* does not imply that they agree Mary did not leave (any more than *John did not say that Mary left* implies that John said that Mary did not leave).[9] Therefore, I disagree with Hulsey and Sauerland that (33) is a possible LF of (26).

Notice that the undesirable predictions we made concerning NEG-raising verbs come from the particular semantics assumed for *-est*. We should now ask whether a non-reconstruction analysis of (26) is still possible, but with a different semantics for *-est* (one that would predict NEG-raising verbs and non-NEG-raising verbs to behave in the same way in superlative relative clauses). I think it is, but only if we abandon Heim's assumption that the <d,<e,t>>-argument of the superlative morpheme is monotonic (i.e. if we assume that, for example, *x is d-long* means 'x's length is exactly d'), and adopt a "non-monotonic" analysis of *-est*. Here is a suggestion.[10]

(39) $[\![\text{EST}]\!](x)(R)$ is defined only if for all relevant y there is a unique degree d such that $R(d)(y) = \text{True}$. Let d_y be the unique degree d such that $R(d)(y) = \text{True}$, for every relevant y. Then, whenever defined, $[\![\text{EST}]\!](x)(R) = \text{True}$ iff for all relevant $x' \neq x$, $d_{x'} < d_x$.

This semantics will work well if we replace (33) with (40).

(40) **[the 1 EST-e_1 [2 3 John said 4 Tolstoy wrote-w_4 a d_2-long book e_3]] is** ***Anna Karenina***

"*Anna Karenina* is the unique x such that for all relevant $x' \neq x$, $d_{x'} < d_x$ (where for all x′, $d_{x'}$ is the unique degree d such that for all worlds w compatible with what John said in the actual world Tolstoy wrote x′ in w and x′ is a book in w and the length of x′ is exactly d in w)."

The analysis guarantees that *Anna Karenina* is longer than the other books throughout the worlds compatible with what John said.

But the analysis in (40) also raises some difficult questions. First, if we adopt it, we lose Heim's account of (comparative) split-scope readings (see (34)). Without going into any deep debate over the advantages and disadvantages of the "monotonic" and the "non-monotonic" approach to gradable adjectives, it is important to note that the advantage of Heim's "monotonic" semantics of the superlative is precisely the fact that it accounts very nicely for split-scope readings.[11] Another problem is related to Bhatt's (2002) observation that (26)

[9] See Bhatt and Sharvit (2005) for a suggestion regarding why the "low" reading is sometimes unavailable (e.g. when the main verb is *know*).

[10] This suggestion still doesn't solve the extensionality problem alluded to above. We would have to adopt an intensionalized version of (39) in order to address that problem.

[11] See Sharvit and Stateva (2002) for arguments against Heim's movement analysis of split-scope readings of superlative constructions. But Stateva (2002) has argued that split-scope readings of comparative constructions (e.g. *John needs to climb a higher mountain than Bill*) do require a movement analysis (and therefore the Monotonicity assumption cannot be abandoned).

can be disambiguated by NPI placement, as shown in (41). Example (41*a*), where *ever* appears above *say*, has only a "high" reading, and (41*b*), where *ever* appears below *say*, has only a "low" reading.

(41) (*a*) The longest book John ever said Tolstoy had written was *Anna Karenina*.

(*b*) The longest book John said Tolstoy had ever written was *Anna Karenina*.

If we assume that the "low" reading requires a "low" copy of *-est*, we have an explanation for why this reading is missing from (41*a*): the NPI is not c-commanded by its licensor—the superlative—at LF (see Bhatt and Sharvit 2005 for an explanation of why the "high" reading is missing from (41*b*)). If we assume that *-est* is never reconstructed, we lose this explanation. In short, even if there is no conclusive evidence that the "low" reading of (26) is a reconstruction effect, there does not seem to be sufficient evidence in favor of the view that it is not (see the Appendix for the reason why the reconstruction analysis must assume a copy of *-est* in an intermediate position as in (1′), and not in any other position).

Therefore, I take the position that the explanation for the fact that *Which longest book did John say Tolstoy had written* does not mean "which x is such that John said that x is the longest book Tolstoy wrote" is that the "low" reading of a superlative relative clause is a reconstruction effect, but *which*-interrogatives are never generated from an LF that has a "low" copy of the restrictor of *which*. It is then plausible to assume that the only possible LF of *Which longest book did John say Tolstoy had written* is (3‴) (repeated below as (42)), where [**longest book**] denotes the <e,t>-function [λx . there is a set X such that x is longest in X][12] (and not the <d,<e,t>> function [λd . λx . x is a d-long book]).

(42) **which longest book 1 C_{wh} [John said Tolstoy wrote e_1]**

"Which x that is the longest member in some set of books, is such that John said that Tolstoy wrote x".

Our theory, then, has to do the following: (i) in superlative relative clauses, it has to allow the interpretation of *-est* above the main verb only when *long* and *book* are interpreted there as well (with a resulting "high" reading); and (ii) in constructions where the superlative appears in a "low" surface position, it has to allow movement of *-est* above the main verb (as in Heim's analysis of

[12] See Herdan and Sharvit (2006) for an analysis of indefinite superlatives which permits such an interpretation.

Tolstoy needs to write the longest book, assuming we indeed adopt this analysis for split-scope readings). These are somewhat conflicting demands, which the theory has to reconcile.

10.4 Summary and Discussion

Can current theories of reconstruction predict this difference between *which*-interrogatives and superlative relative clauses? It seems to me that the answer is No. The Copy Theory of Movement assumes that *wh*-movement leaves behind copies, without predicting this not to be possible in some cases. Semantic approaches to "reconstruction" have a similar problem. In §10.2 I argued that *which*-interrogatives do not involve reconstruction of the restrictor of *which*, but I do not think this holds for all *wh*-interrogatives. *How many*-questions, for example, seem to support "genuine" "low" readings (i.e. "low" readings that are reconstruction effects; see Kroch 1989, Heycock 1995).

(43) How many books that will sell well does Tolstoy want to read?

(*a*) "High" reading: "Which number n is such that there is a set of books x that will sell well, whose cardinality is n, such that Tolstoy wants to read x?"

(*b*) "Low" reading: "Which number n is such that Tolstoy wants it to be the case that there is a set of books x that will sell well, whose cardinality is n, such that he reads x"

The "low" reading is, presumably, obtained from the following LF:

(44) **how 1 C_{wh} Tolstoy wants to read d_1-many books that will sell well**

So the ban on reconstruction seems to be specific to *which*-questions. If this is indeed the case, this ban does not seem to follow independently from anything we know about such interrogatives.

Much of the debate surrounding reconstruction effects (Jacobson 1994; von Stechow 1995; Heycock 1995; Sharvit 1997, 1998; Romero 1998; Fox 1999; and others), including the discussion in this volume (Romero; Caponigro and Heller), focuses on whether syntactic reconstruction approaches (those involving copies at LF) have any advantage over semantic approaches (those that do not assume a level of LF at all, or do not assume that copies are present at LF). My goal here is different: I think that before we try to decide (hopefully, based on empirical grounds) whether "reconstruction" is done in the semantics or in the syntax, we should first have a clearer understanding of what reconstruction is, and why it does not always happen. I suspect that the semantic approach to reconstruction has a better chance of answering this question, because clearly, it is the semantics of the construction (*which*-interrogative vs. *how many*-interrogative) which seems to determine whether reconstruction is possible at all. However, I leave this question open for the time being.

Appendix

We concluded above that the "low" reading of *The longest book John said Tolstoy had written is Anna Karenina* is a reconstruction effect. We now briefly discuss (and discard) alternative reconstruction analyses of this "low" reading.

Hulsey and Sauerland (2006) explain why this reading is not derived from the following LF, where [**the longest book e_1**] is interpreted as "the unique y such that y = x and y is longest among the relevant books".

(45) **the [1 John said-w_0 [2 Tolstoy wrote-w_2 the longest book-$w_2 e_1$]]**

The implication is that John said that Tolstoy wrote the longest of all the books. This is not the "low" reading, and furthermore, the sentence does not have this reading at all. Hulsey and Sauerland invoke a pragmatic constraint to rule (45) out.

Another analysis to consider is the following (from Bhatt 2002), based on the following "monotonic" semantics for the superlative operator (from Heim 1999).

(46) For any (downward monotonic) <d,t>-function P and any set of <d,t> functions C, $[\![\textbf{Est}]\!](C)(P)$ is defined only if $P \in C$ and for all $P' \in C$, there is a degree d such that $P'(d) = \text{True}$.

Whenever defined, $[\![\textbf{Est}]\!](C)(P) = \text{True}$ iff there is a degree d such that $\{P' \in C : P'(d) = \text{True}\} = \{P\}$.

This analysis is designed primarily to account for comparative readings of sentences with a superlative expression in object position, where the subject is focused, as in the following example:

(47) TOLSTOY wrote the longest book ($\rightarrow$ all the other authors wrote shorter books).

The proposed LF for this sentence is this.

(48) **Est-C [[1[Tolstoy$_F$ wrote a d_1-long book]]$\sim$C]**

According to Rooth's (1992) theory of Association with Focus, the squiggle operator ($\sim$) imposes the following restriction on the value of the focus anaphor **C** (which is coreferential with the pronominal restrictor of the superlative morpheme): $[\![C]\!]^g \subseteq \{[\lambda d'.$ Tolstoy wrote a book whose length is at least d'], [λd'. Dostoevsky wrote a book whose length is at least d'], [λd'. Shakespeare wrote a book whose length is at least d'],...}. As a result, (48) receives the following interpretation: "there is a degree d such that Tolstoy wrote a d-long book, and for every other relevant author y, y didn't write a d-long book." Bhatt suggests that the "low" reading of *The longest book John said Tolstoy had written was Anna Karenina* is a comparative reading, obtained by having a copy of *longest book* below *say*, and moving the superlative morpheme to a position above *Tolstoy* but below *say*. Here, *-est* has a copy in an intermediate position, but it is not the same intermediate position as it has in (1'). The variable embedded inside the "low" copy is focused.

(49) **the 2 John said Est-C [[1 [Tolstoy wrote a d_1-long book [2]$_F$]]~C] was** ***Anna Karenina***

"*Anna Karenina* is the unique x such that John said that there is a degree d such that Tolstoy wrote a/the d-long book x, and such that no member P of $[\![C]\!]^g$ distinct from [λd'. Tolstoy wrote a/the book x whose length is d'-long book] is such that P(d) = True (where $[\![C]\!]^g \subseteq$ {[λd'. Tolstoy wrote a/the book *War and Peace* whose length is d'], [λd'. Tolstoy wrote a/the book *Anna Karenina* whose length is d'], ...}).

This interpretation is indeed the one we are after, but the following problem comes to mind. We expect the same surface string to have another "low" reading, resulting from an LF where *Tolstoy* is focused too. But that surface string does not have such a reading.

(50) The longest book John said TOLSTOY wrote was *Anna Karenina.*

the 2 John said Est-C [[1 [Tolstoy$_F$ wrote a d_1-long book [2]$_F$]]~C] was ***Anna Karenina***

"*Anna Karenina* is the unique x such that John said that there is a degree d such that Tolstoy wrote a/the d-long book x, and such that no member P of $[\![C]\!]^g$ distinct from [λd'. Tolstoy wrote a/the book x whose length is d'] is such that P(d) = True (where $[\![C]\!]^g \subseteq$ {[λd'. Tolstoy wrote a/the book *Anna Karenina* whose length is d'], [λd'. Dostoevsky wrote a/the book *Crime and Punishment* whose length is d'], [λd'. Mark Twain wrote a/the book *Tom Sawyer* whose length is d'], ...})".

The surface string in (50) does have the following reading: "*Anna Karenina* is the longest book John said Tolstoy wrote, and not the longest book John said some other author wrote." But this reading is obtained by attaching ~C to a higher position, not to the "low" position it is occupying in the LF in (50).

Reference

Bartsch, R. 1973. ' "Negative transportation" gibt es nicht', *Linguistische Berichte*, 27: 1–7.

Beck, S. and Rullmann, H. 1999. 'A flexible approach to exhaustivity in questions', *Natural Language Semantics*, 7: 249–98.

Beck, S. and Sharvit, Y. 2002. 'Pluralities of questions', *Journal of Semantics*, 19: 105–57.

Berman, S. 1991. On the Semantics and Logical Form of Wh-Clauses. Ph.D. dissertation, University of Massachusetts, Amherst.

Bhatt, R. 2002. 'The raising analysis of relative clauses: Evidence from adjectival modification', *Natural Language Semantics*, 10: 43–90.

____ and Sharvit, Y. 2005. 'A note on intensional superlatives,' in E. Georgala and J. Howell (eds), *Proceedings of SALT15*, CLC Publications, Cornell University. 62–79.

Engdahl, E. 1986. *Constituent Questions: The Syntax and Semantics of Questions with Special Reference to Swedish*. Dordrecht: Reidel.

Fox, D. 1999. 'Reconstruction, binding theory, and the interpretation of chains', *Linguistic Inquiry*, 30: 157–96.

____ 2002. 'Antecedent-contained deletion and the copy theory of movement', *Linguistic Inquiry*, 33: 63–96.

Groenendijk, J. and Stokhof, M. 1982. 'Semantic analysis of wh-complements', *Linguistics and Philosophy*, 5: 175–233.

____ and ____ 1984. Studies in the Semantics of Questions and the Pragmatics of Answers. Ph.D. dissertation, University of Amsterdam.

Hamblin, C. L. 1973. 'Questions in Montague English', *Foundations of Language*, 10: 41–53.

Heim, I. 1992. 'Presupposition projection and the semantics of attitude verbs', *Journal of Semantics*, 9: 183–221.

____ 1994. 'Interrogative complements of "know"', in R. Buchalla and A. Mittwoch (eds), *Proceedings of the 9th Annual Conference and of the 1993 IATL Workshop on Discourse*, Jerusalem: Akademon. 128–144.

____ 1999. 'Notes on superlatives', MS, MIT.

Herdan, S. and Sharvit, Y. 2006. 'Definite and non-definite superlatives and NPI licensing', *Syntax*, 9: 1–31.

Heycock, C. 1995. 'Asymmetries in reconstruction', *Linguistic Inquiry*, 26: 547–70.

____ 2005. 'On the interaction of adjectival modifiers and relative clauses', *Natural Language Semantics*, 13: 359–82.

Hulsey, S. and Sauerland, U. 2006 .'Sorting out relative clauses', *Natural Language Semantics*, 14: 111–37.

Jacobson, P. 1994. 'Binding connectivity in copular sentences', in M. Harvey and L. Santelmann (eds), *Proceedings of SALT IV*, CLC Publications, Cornell University. 161–78.

Karttunen, L. 1974. 'Presupposition and linguistic context', *Theoretical Linguistics*, 1: 181–94.

—— 1977. 'Syntax and semantics of questions', *Linguistics and Philosophy*, 1: 3–44.

Kroch, A. 1989. 'Amount quantification, referentiality, and long *wh*-movement', MS, University of Pennsylvania.

Lahiri, U. 1991. Embedded Interrogatives and Predicates that Embed Them. Ph.D. dissertation, MIT, distributed by MITWPL, Cambridge, MA.

—— 2002. *Questions and Answers in Embedded Contexts*. Oxford: Oxford University Press.

Reinhart, T. 1992. 'Wh-in-situ: An apparent paradox', in P. Dekker and M. Stokhof (eds), *Proceedings of the 8th Amsterdam Colloquium*. University of Amsterdam.

Romero, M. 1998. 'Problems for a semantic account of scope reconstruction', in G. Katz, S.-S. Kim, and H. Winhart (eds), *Reconstruction: Proceedings of the 1997 Tuebingen Workshop*, pp. 127–53. University of Tübingen. 127–53.

Rooth, M. 1992. 'A theory of focus interpretation', *Natural Language Semantics*, 1: 75–116.

Ross, J. R. 1964. A Partial Grammar of English Superlatives. MA thesis, University of Pennsylvania.

Rullmann, H. and Beck, S. 1998. 'Presupposition projection and the interpretation of *which*-questions', in D. Strolovitch and A. Lawson (eds), *Proceedings of SALT 8*. CLC Publications Cornell University. 215–32.

Sharvit, Y. 1997. Functional Relative Clauses. Ph.D. dissertation, Rutgers University.

—— 1998. 'Possessive *wh*-expressions and reconstruction', *Proceedings of the 28th meeting of the North Eastern Linguistic Society (NELS)*, University of Massachusetts, Amherst: GLSA Publications.

—— 2002. 'Embedded questions and "de dicto" readings', *Natural Language Semantics*, 10: 97–123.

—— and Stateva, P. 2002. 'Superlative expressions, context, and focus', *Linguistics and Philosophy*, 25: 453–505.

—— and Guerzoni, E. 2003. 'Reconstruction and its problems', in P. Dekker and R. van Rooy (eds), *Proceedings of the 14th Amsterdam Colloquium*, University of Amsterdam. 205–10.

Stateva, P. 2002. How Different are Different Degree Constructions. Ph.D. dissertation, University of Connecticut.

von Stechow, A. 1995. 'Against LF pied-piping', *Natural Language Semantics*, 4: 57–110.

Szabolcsi, A. 1986. 'Comparative superlatives', in N. Fukui, T. Rapoport, and E. Sagey (eds), *MIT Working Papers in Linguistics*, Vol. 8. Cambridge: MIT Press. 245–65.

Part III

New Horizons

11

Online Update: Temporal, Modal, and *de se* Anaphora in Polysynthetic Discourse*

MARIA BITTNER

11.1 Introduction

Temporality, modality, *de se* reports as well as incorporation all present difficult challenges for semantic composition. In LF-based theories (e.g. Bittner 1994; Muskens 1995; Stone and Hardt 1999; Schlenker 2003, among others) the input to semantic composition are not the surface forms that present these challenges. Instead, a more tractable *logical form* (LF) is first derived by means of operations that may involve movement, rebracketing, insertion of covert elements, or deletion of overt material. It might therefore seem that any problem that compounds all four of the above-mentioned challenges would be out of reach of any surface compositional theory, committed to interpreting the surface form directly, as is. In this paper I argue for the contrary: even very challenging surface forms can be interpreted directly by *online update*. Moreover, surface-based online update correctly predicts anaphoric dependencies of various types, both within and across sentence boundaries. It thus offers a simpler and more general account of such dependencies than indirect LF-based theories.

The problem to be considered is the interaction of temporal and modal quantifiers with *de se* attitudes in Kalaallisut (Eskimo-Aleut: Greenland). This

* I thank my Kalaallisut consultants for help with the data. Thanks are also due to Daniel Altshuler, Chris Barker, Judy Bauer, Sam Cumming, Polly Jacobson, Michael Johnson, Hans Kamp, Bill Ladusaw, and Sarah Murray, for helpful feedback. Parts of this material were presented in the 2003 workshop on Direct Compositionality at Brown, and in my Rutgers seminars on Modal Anaphora (2003), Temporal Anaphora in Tenseless Languages (2005), Bare Nouns in Discourse (2005), and (In)direct Reports in Discourse (2006). I thank the participants in all of these events for helpful feedback. This work was supported in part by the NSF grant BCS-9905600 to Rutgers.

massively polysynthetic[1] language builds words compositionally—like English, sentences—and has productive suffixes for quantifiers as well as *de se* attitudes (exemplified in (2*b*), (3*b*), (4)). The inflectional system of Kalaallisut distinguishes three classes of words: *verbs*, which inflect for mood and agreement; *nouns*, which inflect for agreement and case; and *particles*, which do not inflect.[2] A grammaticized centering system contrasts two forms of dependent inflections: *topical* vs. *backgrounded* (e.g. *-mi* "3s$_\top$" vs. *-at* "3s$_\bot$"). The centering status is explicitly marked on dependent nouns and verbs, but not on the matrix verb, where it is predictable: the subject of the matrix verb is always topical and any direct object, backgrounded.

The problem for semantic composition is semantic convergence across radically different surface forms. For instance, in the context of (1), (2*a*) is semantically equivalent to (2*b*), and (3*a*), to (3*b*):

(1) *Ataata-ga skakkir-tar-pu-q.*
dad-1s.sg play.chess-habit-IND.IV-3S
My dad$_\top$ plays chess.

(2) *Siurna arna-mi uqaluqatigii-mm-ani*
last.year mother-3s$_\top$.sg.ERG talk.with-FCT$_\bot$-3s$_\bot$.3s$_\top$
Last year when his$_\top$ mother talked with him$_\top$, ...

(*a*) uqar-*pu-q:* "*Amirlanir-tigut ajugaa-sar-pu-nga.*"
say-IND.IV-3S most-VIA win-habit-IND.IV-1S
...he$_\top$ said: "I mostly win."

(*b*) *amirlanir-tigut ajugaa-sar-*nirar*-pu-q.*
most-VIA win-habit-*say*-IND.IV-3S
...he$_\top$ said that he (= *se*) mostly won.

(3) *Ilaanni skakkir-a-mi,*
once play.chess-FCT$_\top$-3s$_\top$
Once when he$_\top$ was playing, ...

(*a*) isuma-qa-*lir-pu-q:* "*Immaqa ajugaa-ssa-u-nga.*"
belief-have-begin-IND.IV-3S maybe win-prospect-IND.IV-1S
...he$_\top$ began to think: "I might win."

[1] Sapir (1922) classifies languages based on the average number of morphemes per word, as *analytic* (e.g. English), *synthetic* (French), or *polysynthetic* (Eskimo).

[2] I use standard Kalaallisut orthography minus the allophones (*e*, *o*, *f*) of *i*, *u*, *v*. Glosses for (i) *centering status*: $\top$ = topic, $\bot$ = background; (ii)*dependent moods*: FCT$_\top$ = $\top$-factive (old fact about $\top$-subject), FCT$_\bot$ = $\bot$-factive, HAB$_\top$ = $\top$-habit, HAB$_\bot$ = $\bot$-habit; (iii) *matrix mood*: IND = indicative (new fact); (iv) *transitivity*: IV = intransitive, TV = transitive; (v) *case*: MOD = modalis (modifier), VIA = vialis (path).

(*b*) *immaqa ajugaa-ssa*-suri-*lir-pu-q*.
maybe win-prospect-*believe*-begin-IND.IV-3S
...he$_{\top}$ began to think that he (= *se*) might win.

Examples (2*a*) and (2*b*) report *de se* speech, whereas (3*a*) and (3*b*) report *de se* beliefs. Both speech and belief reports can be temporally quantified (as in (2*a*, 2*b*)) or modally quantified (see (3*a*, 3*b*)). In addition, *de se* reports with direct quotes (e.g. (2*a*), (3*a*)) have polysynthetic paraphrases (see (2*b*), (3*b*)). All of these reports are temporally and individually *de se* in the sense of Lewis (1979). That is, they are about the person that the agent or experiencer thinks of as *I* and the time he thinks of as *now*. The compositional problem is to derive the equivalence of type (*a*)-reports, with quotes, and their polysynthetic paraphrases of type (*b*), in spite of their radically different surface form.

At first blush, it might seem that this problem requires an LF-based solution. To begin with, in each of these four reports the matrix eventuality—a speech event or belief state—must be located at the time evoked by the initial factive clause. If this is to be accomplished by binding a temporal variable, then the binder must take scope over the initial factive clause as well as the matrix verb. None of the surface forms contains a likely binder. An LF theory can enrich the surface with a covert binder. But a surface compositional theory is committed to interpreting the surface form as is, so it cannot pursue this option.

What it can pursue, though, is dynamic binding. On this view, what matters is linear precedence, not c-command. The initial factive clause can set up a temporal *discourse referent* (*dref*) which can be anaphorically linked to the matrix verb. To represent anaphoric links most dynamic theories enrich the surface form with covert indices (e.g. Kamp and Reyle 1993; Muskens 1995; Stone and Hardt 1999). But adding covert elements has no place in strictly direct composition. So any theory with index-based anaphora is still not truly direct.

To achieve true direct composition, I implement the idea of Grosz *et al.* (1995) that anaphora is based, not on covert indices, but on grammatically marked centering status. To make this precise I develop a dynamic system like Muskens (1995) except that anaphora is based on compositionally built stacks (as in Dekker 1994; Bittner 2001) instead of arbitrary indices. A state of information-and-attention is a triple of a world and two stacks of prominence-ranked semantic dref objects. Topical drefs go on the top stack, which models the center of attention; backgrounded drefs, on the bottom stack, which models the periphery. Based on the current stacks, dref objects can then be retrieved by anaphoric demonstratives. The actual morphemes, which stack and retrieve dref objects, thus take over the role of covert indices. The two-stack architecture also permits a simple analysis of the dichotomy found in grammatical centering systems (e.g. obviation: "$3s_{\top}$" vs. "$3s_{\bot}$").

Quantification presents additional challenges. Since Lewis (1975) temporal quantification has been analyzed in terms of tripartite structures consisting of a quantifier and its two arguments—the restriction and the matrix. Heim (1982) extended the tripartite analysis to modal quantifiers, and Kamp and Reyle (1993) integrated it with a dynamic theory of tense and aspect. But to derive the requisite tripartite structures from polysynthetic reports such as (2*b*) or (3*b*), these theories would require rebracketing. That is, they would require a level of LF. Instead, I propose to maintain direct surface composition by encapsulating quantification along the lines of Stone (1997). The idea is that quantifiers relate drefs for functions that characterize distributed patterns. Specifically, I propose that temporal quantifiers relate drefs for *habits*—for example (2*b*) reports a habitual pattern of victories instantiated at the end of most of the chess games that instantiate the antecedent chess-playing habit, evoked in (1). Similarly, modal quantifiers relate drefs for *modal concepts* of eventualities—for example in the belief state of (3*b*) the expected end of the current chess game is realized, in some of the belief worlds, as a victory by the experiencer of this state.

Finally, what about individual and temporal *de se* dependencies? These, too, have been analyzed as variable-binding at LF (see, e.g. Chierchia 1989; Schlenker 2003). To derive the requisite LFs from polysynthetic *de se* reports such as (2*b*) or (3*b*) these theories would also require rebracketing, as well as assorted covert elements. Instead, I propose to maintain direct surface composition by developing an idea from the original proposal by Lewis (1979). One of Lewis's examples is an insomniac who lies awake at night wondering what time it is. Lewis concludes:

> To understand how he wonders, we must recognize that it is time-slices of him that do the wondering. [...] The slice at 3:49 A.M. may self-ascribe the property of being one slice of an insomniac who lies awake all night on such-and-such date at such-and-such place in such-and-such kind of world, and yet may fail to self-ascribe the property of being at 3:49 A.M. That is how this slice may be ignorant, and wonder what time it is, without failing in any relevant way to locate the continuant to which it belongs. It is the slice, not the continuant, that fails to self-ascribe a property. (Lewis 1979: section VII)

Unlike Lewis, I do not think that we ever talk about time-slices of people. But we do talk about speech acts that people perform and belief states they experience. I suggest that (2*a*, 2*b*) and (3*a*, 3*b*) exemplify such talk. A pair of a person and an eventuality—be it a speech act or a belief state—is as good as a time-slice for analyzing *de se* speech or *de se* belief. Better, in fact, since it also provides a location in space. And we get such pairs for free if we assume that report verbs—like all other verbs—have a Davidsonian argument: for example "say" refers to a speech event, and "believe", to a belief state. This must be assumed anyway in order to apply current theories of temporal anaphora to report verbs (see e.g. Kamp and Reyle 1993; Stone and Hardt 1999).

For Lewis, *de se* speech (or *de se* belief) was self-ascription of a property by a time-slice of the speaker (or the believer). Instead, I propose that the speaker (or the believer) is conscious of performing a certain speech act (experiencing a certain mental state) and identifies himself as the agent of that event (experiencer of that state). When an insomniac says *I am awake*, what he means is that the agent of this speech event is awake at the time of this event. This the insomniac can know even if he does not know that the time happens to be 3:49 a.m. Or if he is too sleepy to remember that he—the agent—is Mr Brown. Likewise for *de se* belief, *de se* desire, *de se* fear, etc. The *se* of a *de se* attitude state is the experiencer of that mental state.

This adaptation of Lewis's proposal is compatible with surface-based online update, if we assume an ontology of dref objects that includes events and states (following Partee 1984 and related work). As we will see, the proposed account will then also generalize to habitual reports—for example (4*a*) and (4*b*), which illustrate one more pair of quantified *de se* reports that can coherently follow the habitual sentence (1). In (4*a*) as well as (4*b*), the temporal description *aqagu-a-ni* "the next day" can be either outside or inside the scope of the temporal quantifier *-(g)ajut* "often" (as in the similarly ambiguous English translation). For standard tripartite quantification this too would require rebracketing at LF. But if we instead posit drefs for habits, then we can maintain surface-based online update simply by associating *-(g)ajut* "often" with an ambiguous anaphoric presupposition.

(4) Aqagu-*a-ni*
next.day-3s$_{\perp}$.sg-LOC
The next day...

(*a*) *uqar*-ajut-*tar-pu-q:* "*Ajugaa-sima-vu-nga.*"
say-*often*-habit-IND.IV-3S win-prf-IND.IV-1S
...he$_{\top}$ often says: "I won."

(*b*) *ajugaa-sima-nirar*-ajut-*tar-pu-q*.
win-prf-say-*often*-habit-IND.IV-3S
...he$_{\top}$ often says that he (= *se*) won.

In general, by replacing tripartite LFs and index-based LF-anaphora with drefs for patterns and stack-based surface-anaphora we can maintain direct surface interpretation even in a massively polysynthetic language. The rest of this paper develops this basic idea as follows. In §11.2 I introduce a framework for online update and illustrate it with a simple English example. Further lexical meanings are then added as needed for online interpretation of increasingly more complex Kalaallisut discourses: episodics in §11.3, habituals in §11.4, reported habits and attitudes in §§11.5 and 11.6, respectively, and habitual reports in §11.7. Section 11.8 returns to the comparison with LF-based theories. Finally, §11.9 is the conclusion.

11.2 Framework for Online Update

The basic idea of *online update* is that the surface string is interpreted as is, with each morpheme in turn updating the current state of information and attention. To implement this idea, I first define *Logic of Centering* (LC), a variant of the Logic of Change of Muskens (1995) with stack-based anaphora à la Bittner (2001). As usual, updating an input state yields a set of possible outputs. But in LC a state of information and attention is a triple of a world (information) and two stacks of prominence-ranked dref objects. Topical dref objects go on the *top stack* ($\top$, focal attention), while backgrounded dref objects go on the *bottom stack* ($\bot$, peripheral attention). As in the stack-based system of Dekker (1994), LC drefs are semantic objects, not variables. Two sets of variables, $Var^{\top}$ and $Var^{\bot}$, serve to add semantic dref objects to the top and bottom stack, respectively. Table 11.1 lays out the ontology of LC and the notation for the two sets of variables.

The ontology is crucial for stack-based anaphora: adding a dref object of type R to a stack demotes any other R-objects one notch, but has no effect on objects of types other than R. Stacked dref objects of type R can be referred to by *anaphoric demonstratives*, of the form $\mathbf{d}\textsc{r}_n$ or $d\textsc{r}_n$ (type $s\textsc{r}$). The demonstrative $\mathbf{d}\textsc{r}_n$ refers to the $(n + 1)$-st dref object of type R on the current top stack. Similarly, the demonstrative $d\textsc{r}_n$ refers to the $(n + 1)$-st dref object of type R on the current bottom stack. Unlike the covert indices of index-based theories, stack positions cannot be assigned at will, for they must accord with grammatically marked prominence status (e.g. subject vs. object, '$3\textsc{s}_{\top}$' vs. '$3\textsc{s}_{\bot}$', etc.).

The ontology in Table 11.1 is empirically motivated by grammatical marking in Kalaallisut, Yukatek, Mohawk, and English (see text studies at http://www.rci.rutgers.edu/~mbittner). Their grammars are very different, but they all motivate seven basic types of drefs: *worlds* (ω), *times* (τ), *places* (π),

TABLE 11.1 LC ontology and two sets of variables

Type	Abr.	Name of objects	$^{\top}Var$	$^{\perp}Var$
t		truth values		
ω		worlds	$\mathbf{w}$	w
τ		times	$\mathbf{t}$	t
π		places	$\mathbf{l}$	l
α		animate entities	$\mathbf{a}$	a
β		inanimate entities	$\mathbf{b}$	b
ε		events	$\mathbf{e}$	e
σ		states of entities	$\mathbf{s}$	s
$\varepsilon \vee \sigma$	$\varepsilon^{\bullet}$	atomic episodes	$\mathbf{e}^{\bullet}$	$e^{\bullet}$
$\varepsilon\varepsilon$		ε-chains	$\mathbf{ee}$	ee
$\omega\tau\mathrm{V}$	η^{V}	V-habits (V $\in \{\varepsilon, \sigma, \varepsilon\varepsilon\}$)	$\mathbf{h}^{\mathrm{V}}$	h^{V}
$\omega\varepsilon^{\bullet}\mathrm{N}$	κ^{N}	N-kinds (N $\in \{\alpha, \beta, \tau, \pi, \omega t\}$)	$\mathbf{k}^{\mathrm{N}}$	k^{N}
ωt	Ω	ω-domains	$\mathbf{p}$	p
$\omega\omega$	$\underline{\omega}$	ω-concepts	$\underline{\mathbf{w}}$	$\underline{w}$
$\omega\sigma$	$\underline{\sigma}$	σ-concepts	$\underline{\mathbf{s}}$	$\underline{s}$
$\omega\varepsilon$	$\underline{\varepsilon}$	ε-concepts	$\underline{\mathbf{e}}$	$\underline{e}$
$\underline{\varepsilon}(\underline{\varepsilon})$	$\underline{\varepsilon\varepsilon}$	ε-concept chains	$\underline{\mathbf{ee}}$	$\underline{e}$
$\varepsilon\underline{\sigma}$		ε-dependent σ-concepts	$\underline{\mathbf{s}}_{\varepsilon}$	$\underline{s}_{\varepsilon}$
$\varepsilon\underline{\varepsilon}$		ε-dependent ε-concepts	$\underline{\mathbf{e}}_{\varepsilon}$	$\underline{e}_{\varepsilon}$
$\alpha\kappa^{a}$		α-dependent α-kinds	$\mathbf{k}^{a}{}_{\alpha}$	$k^{a}{}_{\alpha}$
ζ		stacks (of dref objects)		z
$\omega \times \zeta \times \zeta$	s	states of information-&-attention		i, j
sst		update		

entities sorted into *animates* (α) and *inanimates* (β), and atomic episodes sorted into *events* (ε) and *states* (σ).

For online update we also need drefs of functional types. In all languages nouns evoke drefs of *nominal types*. Basic nominal types are animates, inanimates, times, places, and propositions (N $\in \{\alpha, \beta, \tau, \pi, \omega t\}$); nominal functions return values of nominal types. In Kalaallisut there are two classes of nouns, common (cn) and relational (rn), which take different inflections. Translated into LC, cn-roots evoke *kinds* (κ^{N}), while rn-roots evoke dependent kinds (e.g. type $\alpha\kappa^{\mathrm{N}}$; see Appendix).

Cross-linguistically, verbs evoke drefs of *verbal types*—that is, basic episodes (type ε or σ) or episode-valued functions. The latter include *processes*, represented in this ontology as chains of eventive stages (type $\varepsilon\varepsilon$); and *habits*, represented as modal patterns of recurrent episodes (type $\eta^{\mathrm{V}} := \omega\tau\mathrm{V}$, with V $\in \{\sigma, \varepsilon, \varepsilon\varepsilon\}$). Finally, the remaining functions in Table 11.1 will serve to

TABLE 11.2 LC constants

Type	Name of objects	Con
$\omega\alpha\sigma t$	stative α-property	*sleep*, *busy*,...
$\omega\alpha\varepsilon t$	eventive α-property	*wake.up*, *play.chess*, ...
$\omega\Omega\alpha\sigma t$	stative (α, Ω)-relation	*believe*, *doubt*, ...
$\omega\Omega\alpha\varepsilon t$	eventive (α, Ω)-relation	*say*, *think*, ...
⋮	⋮	⋮
$\omega\sigma\varepsilon$	state onset (beginning)	BEG
$\omega\varepsilon\sigma$	result state	RES
$\omega\varepsilon\alpha$	agent	AGT
$\omega\varepsilon^{\bullet}\alpha$	experiencer	EXP
$\omega\varepsilon^{\bullet}\tau$	time	ϑ
$\omega\varepsilon^{\bullet}\pi$	place	Π

encapsulate other forms of modal and temporal quantification (e.g. "maybe" in (3), "often" in (4)) as well as *de se* dependencies. All of these and other functions may be partial. This is important, for the domain of a functional dref may encode information that is necessary for online update (e.g. see (8) below).

Turning now to constants, a representative sample is laid out in Table 11.2. Note that a Kalaallisut process-verb (e.g. *skakkir-* "play chess") can be translated into LC by means of an event-predicate distributed down to the eventive stages of the process. Therefore, Table 11.2 only includes LC-predicates of basic aspectual types: events and states. Events, states, and other semantic domains are connected by a network of world-dependent mappings: *state onset* (BEG), *result state* (RES), *agent* (AGT), *experiencer* (EXP), *time* (ϑ), and *place* (Π). These functions, too, are partial. For instance, only actions have agents. Formally: $\forall w \in$ Dom AGT: Dom $\text{AGT}_w = (D_{\varepsilon,w}$—Ran $\text{BEG}_w)$, where $D_{\varepsilon,w}$ is the domain of atomic *events* in w.

Following the usual practice, I use DRT-style abbreviations for type-logical terms. I also freely mix type-logical terms with set-theoretic counterparts. For type uniformity, stacks are formalized as primitive semantic objects of type ζ. But they are constrained by a set of axioms, Ax1–5, to behave as sequences of stacked objects of *dref types* $\text{R} \in \Theta$, where Θ is the set of types based on $\{t, \omega, \tau, \pi, \alpha, \beta, \varepsilon, \sigma\}$ (cf. Dekker 1994 and Muskens 1995):

Ax1 $\exists z_\zeta: \forall n({}^{n}(z) = \dagger) \wedge \forall_{\text{R}}({}^{\text{R}}(z) = z)$

Ax2 $\forall z_\zeta \forall \text{R} \forall x_{\text{R}}: {}^{1}(x \cdot z) = x \wedge \forall n(n > 1 \rightarrow {}^{n}(x \cdot z) = {}^{n-1}(z))$

Ax3 $\forall z_\zeta \forall \text{R} \forall x_\text{R}: {}^{\text{R}}(x \cdot z) = (x \cdot {}^{\text{R}}(z)) \wedge \forall \text{R}'(\text{R}' \neq \text{R} \rightarrow {}^{\text{R}'}(x \cdot z) = {}^{\text{R}'}(z))$
Ax4 $\forall z_\zeta \forall \text{R} \forall x_\text{R} \exists z'_\zeta: (x \cdot z) = z'$
Ax5 $\forall z_\zeta \forall z'_\zeta: \forall n({}^{n}(z) = {}^{n}(z')) \rightarrow z = z'$

A sequence can be characterized by two projection functions: ${}^{n}(\ )$, which returns the nth coordinate, if it exists, or error †, otherwise; and ${}^{\text{R}}(\ )$, which returns the sub-sequence of type R coordinates. Ax1 defines ${}^{n}(\ )$ and ${}^{\text{R}}(\ )$ for the empty ζ-stack, and Ax2–3, for other ζ-stacks. Ax2–3 also define an operation which adds an R-object to a ζ-stack. On the resulting recentered stack, the newly added object is the most prominent R-object and any other R-objects are demoted one notch. The prominence ranking of other types of drefs is not affected. Ax4 ensures that any object of any dref type R can be added to any ζ-stack. Finally, Ax5 guarantees that a ζ-stack is fully identified by its coordinates.

This conception of stacks informs definition A1. This is the distinctive core of LC, which all of the other definitions will build on:

A1 For any information-and-attention state $i_s = \langle w_i, \top_i, \bot_i \rangle$, we write:

(i) $\mathbf{v}_\text{R} \cdot i_s$ for $\langle w_i, (\mathbf{v} \cdot \top_i), \bot_i \rangle$ if $\mathbf{v}_\text{R} \in {}^{\top}\text{Var}_\text{R}$
$v_\text{R} \cdot i_s$ for $\langle w_i, \top_i, (v \cdot \bot_i) \rangle$ if $v_\text{R} \in {}^{\bot}\text{Var}_\text{R}$

(ii) $(\mathbf{d}\text{R}_n)_i$ for ${}^{n+1}({}^{\text{R}}(\top_i))$
$(d\text{R}_n)_i$ for ${}^{n+1}({}^{\text{R}}(\bot_i))$
$\mathbf{d}\text{R}_i$ for $(\mathbf{d}\text{R}_0)_i$
$d\text{R}_i$ for $(d\text{R}_0)_i$

Information-and-attention update:

(iii) $[\text{v}_1 \ldots \text{v}_n | C]$ for $\lambda ij\, \exists \text{v}_1 \ldots \text{v}_n (j = (\text{v}_1 \cdot \ldots (\text{v}_n \cdot i)) \wedge Ci)$
$[|C]$ for $\lambda ij\, (j = i \wedge Ci)$
$(D_1; D_2)$ for $\lambda ij\, \exists i'(D_1 ii' \wedge D_2 i'j)$

Recall that an LC-state of information and attention, i_s, is a triple of a world and two stacks. These three coordinates are designated as follows: w_i for the *i-world* (or *i-reality*); $\top_i$, for the *i-top stack* of topical objects; and $\bot_i$ for the *i-bottom stack* of backgrounded objects.

By A1(i), we can add a semantic R-object to the top (or bottom) stack by means of a $\top$- (or $\bot$-) R-variable. This is a stack-building operation in the sense of the axioms: the value of the variable becomes the new most prominent R-object on the output stack.

A stacked R-object is a discourse referent (Karttunen 1976), for it can be referred to by an *anaphoric demonstrative*, $\mathbf{d}\text{R}_n$ or $d\text{R}_n$ (of type $s\text{R}$). By A1(ii), in any information-and-attention state i_s the $\top$-demonstrative $\mathbf{d}\text{R}_n$ (or

$\perp$-demonstrative d_{R_n}) refers to the $(n+1)$st R-object on the top (or bottom) stack. That is, we apply to $\top_i$ (or $\perp_i$) two projection functions: first $^{R}(\,)$, which only the R-coordinates survive; and then $^{n+1}(\,)$, which returns the $(n+1)$st of these surviving R-objects. Since anaphora usually targets the most prominent drefs, A1(ii) allows the default rank, $n = 0$, to be omitted—e.g. $\mathbf{d}\varepsilon_i$ abbreviates $(\mathbf{d}\varepsilon_0)_i$.

Clause (iii) of A1 is similar to Muskens (1995). However, in an LC box the order of the variables in the universe is important: it reflects the ranking of the new dref objects on the output stack(s). Also, LC conditions apply to the input state, not the output (see e.g. (7); compare Muskens 1995). Tests and sequencing are interpreted in the usual way.

Following Stalnaker (1978), I assume that the very fact that somebody speaks up has a "commonplace effect" on the context, which is crucial for the "essential effect"—that is, interpreting the content of what is said. In Stalnaker's own words:

> When I speak I presuppose that others know I am speaking.... This fact, too, can be exploited in the conversation, as when Daniels says *I am bald*, taking it for granted that his audience can figure out who is being said to be bald. I mention this commonplace way that assertions change the context in order to make it clear that the context on which assertion has its ESSENTIAL effect is not defined by what is presupposed before the speaker begins to speak, but will include any information which the speaker assumes his audience can infer from the performance of the speech act. (Stalnaker 1978: 323)

Formally, I implement Stalnaker's "commonplace effect" as a *start-up update*. As soon as somebody begins to speak, this very fact is noted, focusing the attention on three default topics. The speech reality becomes the default *modal topic*; the speech event, the default *perspective point*; and the speech time, the default *topic time*.

A2 Speech start-up conditions:

- $\mathbf{w} = r$ for $\lambda i.\ \mathbf{w} = w_i$
- (e: AGT $speak.up_{\mathbf{d}\omega}$) for $\lambda i.\ speak.up_{\mathbf{d}\omega i}(\mathbf{e}, \text{AGT}_{\mathbf{d}\omega i}\,\mathbf{e})$
- $\mathbf{t} = {}_{\mathbf{d}\omega}\vartheta\mathbf{d}\varepsilon$ for $\lambda i.\ \mathbf{t} = \vartheta_{\mathbf{d}\omega i}\ \mathbf{d}\varepsilon_i$

Indexicals—*I* ("1s"), *you* ("2s"), *he* ("3sm"), *was, is, here, there, today*, etc.—have anaphoric presuppositions concerned with the relation to the current perspective point. For example, "1s" refers to the agent of the speech act (default perspective $\mathbf{d}\varepsilon_i$) in the topical modality; "1p" refers to the agent's group; "2s", to the (singular) experiencer; and "3s", to a singular non-participant (cf. Kaplan 1978; Schlenker 2003).

A3 Indexical persons:

- $1s_{\mathbf{d}\omega,\mathbf{d}\varepsilon}$ **d**α for $\lambda i(sg\ \mathbf{d}\alpha_i \wedge \text{AGT}_{\mathbf{d}\omega i}\ \mathbf{d}\varepsilon_i = \mathbf{d}\alpha_i)$
  $1p_{\mathbf{d}\omega,\mathbf{d}\varepsilon}$ **d**α for $\lambda i(\neg\ sg\ \mathbf{d}\alpha_i \wedge \text{AGT}_{\mathbf{d}\omega i}\ \mathbf{d}\varepsilon_i \in \mathbf{d}\alpha_i)$
- $2s_{\mathbf{d}\omega,\mathbf{d}\varepsilon}$ **d**α for $\lambda i(sg\ \mathbf{d}\alpha_i \wedge \text{EXP}_{\mathbf{d}\omega i}\ \mathbf{d}\varepsilon_i = \mathbf{d}\alpha_i)$
- $3s_{\mathbf{d}\omega,\mathbf{d}\varepsilon}$ **d**α for $\lambda i(sg\ \mathbf{d}\alpha_i \wedge \neg(\mathbf{d}\alpha_i \bigcirc (\text{AGT}_{\mathbf{d}\omega i}\ \mathbf{d}\varepsilon_i + \text{EXP}_{\mathbf{d}\omega i}\ \mathbf{d}\varepsilon_i)))$

To see how this works, consider a simple example. Suppose you enter the office of a stranger, who says (5):

(5) I am busy.

Just before he speaks, the input context—initial "common ground"—is a set of information-and-attention states such as (6), where w_o is a candidate reality.[3]

(6) $i_o = \langle w_o, \langle\ \ \rangle, \langle\ \ \rangle\rangle$

As soon as the speech act begins, the input state (6) is updated by the *start-up update* (7), which sets up three default topics:

(7) $[\mathbf{w}|\ \mathbf{w} = r];\ [\mathbf{e}|\ \mathbf{e}\text{: AGT } speak.up_{\mathbf{d}\omega}];\ [\mathbf{t}|\ \mathbf{t} =_{\mathbf{d}\omega} \vartheta \mathbf{d}\varepsilon]$

First of all, the reality of the input state of information and attention is set up as the default modal topic. Applied to i_o, this update yields i_1, by the definitions on the right:

(7) (*a*) $i_o[\mathbf{w}|\ \mathbf{w} = r]i_1$

$\equiv \exists \mathbf{w}(i_1 = \langle w_{io}, \mathbf{w} \cdot \top_{io}, \bot_{io}\rangle \wedge \mathbf{w} = w_{io})$	A1, A2
$\equiv (i_1 = \langle w_o, (w_o \cdot \langle\ \ \rangle), \langle\ \ \rangle\rangle)$	(6)
$\equiv (i_1 = \langle w_o, \langle w_o\rangle, \langle\ \ \rangle\rangle)$	footnote 3

Next, the real speech act that has just begun is set up as the default perspective point. (Note that $\mathbf{d}\omega_{i1} = {}^{0+1}({}^{\omega}\langle w_o\rangle) = {}^{1}\langle w_o\rangle = w_o$.)

(7) (*b*) $i_1[\mathbf{e}|\ \mathbf{e}\text{: AGT } speak.up_{\mathbf{d}\omega}]i_2$

$\equiv\ \exists \mathbf{e}(i_2 = \langle w_{i1}, \mathbf{e} \cdot \top_{i1}, \bot_{i1}\rangle$ $\wedge\ speak.up_{\mathbf{d}\omega i1}(\mathbf{e}, \text{AGT}_{\mathbf{d}\omega i1}\ \mathbf{e}))$	A1, A2
$\equiv\ \exists \mathbf{e}(i_2 = \langle w_o, \langle \mathbf{e}, w_o\rangle, \langle\ \ \rangle\rangle$ $\wedge\ speak.up_{w0}(\mathbf{e}, \text{AGT}_{w0}\ \mathbf{e}))$	(7a), footnote 3, A1, Ax1–3

And finally, the time of the topical perspective point in the topical reality is set up as the default temporal topic. (Note that $\mathbf{d}\varepsilon_j = {}^{1}({}^{\varepsilon}(\mathbf{e} \cdot \langle w_o\rangle)) = {}^{1}\langle \mathbf{e}\rangle = \mathbf{e}$.) We thus arrive at the state i_3, as the final output of the start-up update (Stalnaker's "commonplace effect"):

[3] $\langle\ \ \rangle$ for $\iota z_\zeta\, \forall n({}^{n}(z) = \dagger)$
$\langle x_1, \ldots, x_n\rangle$ for $(x_1 \cdot \ldots (x_n \cdot \langle\ \rangle) \ldots)$

$$
\begin{array}{lll}
(7) & (c) & i_1([\mathbf{e}|\ \mathbf{e}\text{: AGT } speak.up_{\mathbf{d}\omega}];\ [\mathbf{t}|\ \mathbf{t} =_{\mathbf{d}\omega} \vartheta \mathbf{d}\varepsilon])i_3 \\
& & \equiv \exists j(\exists \mathbf{e}(j = \langle w_{i1}, \mathbf{e} \cdot \top_{i1}, \bot_{i1}\rangle \qquad \text{A1, A2} \\
& & \quad \wedge\ speak.up_{\mathbf{d}\omega i1}(\mathbf{e}, \text{AGT}_{\mathbf{d}\omega i1}\ \mathbf{e})) \\
& & \quad \wedge \exists \mathbf{t}(i_3 = \langle w_j, \mathbf{t} \cdot \top_j, \bot_j\rangle \\
& & \quad \wedge\ \mathbf{t} = \vartheta_{\mathbf{d}\omega j}\ \mathbf{d}\varepsilon_j)) \\
& & \equiv \exists \mathbf{e} \exists \mathbf{t}(i_3 = \langle w_o, \langle \mathbf{t,e}, w_o\rangle, \langle\ \ \rangle\rangle \qquad \text{(7a), footnote 3,} \\
& & \quad \wedge\ speak.up_{w0}(\mathbf{e}, \text{AGT}_{w0}\ \mathbf{e}) \qquad \text{A1, Ax1–5} \\
& & \quad \wedge\ \mathbf{t} = \vartheta_{w0}\ \mathbf{e})
\end{array}
$$

A model for i_3 is shown below. Indexed symbols stand for semantic values of unindexed variables, and currently topical semantic objects of various types are indicated by $^{\top}$-superscripts.

Model for i_3
i-reality: $^{\top}w_o$ • $^{\top}e_o$: e_o-agent speaks up
| $^{\top}t_o = \vartheta_{w0}e_o$: e_o-time

In this context sentence (5) can now be interpreted directly and online, by processing each morpheme in turn as in (8). (From now on new conditions are spelled out as they become relevant.)

(8) I

$[\mathbf{a}|\quad 1s_{\mathbf{d}\omega,\mathbf{d}\varepsilon}\ \mathbf{a}];$

$\equiv \lambda ij\ \exists \mathbf{a}(j = \langle w_i, (\mathbf{a} \cdot \top_i), \bot_i\rangle \wedge \text{AGT}_{\mathbf{d}\omega i}\ \mathbf{d}\varepsilon_i = \mathbf{a})$

be-

$[sk^a|\ \mathbf{d}\alpha =_{\mathbf{d}\omega} k^a\{s\}];$

$\equiv \lambda ij\ \exists s k^a(j = \langle w_i, \top_i, (s \cdot k^a \cdot \bot_i)\rangle \wedge \mathbf{d}\alpha_i = k^a \mathbf{d}\omega_i s)$

-PRS

$^{\mathrm{P}}[|\ \mathbf{d}\varepsilon \subseteq_{\mathbf{d}\omega} \mathbf{d}\tau];\ [|\ \mathbf{d}\tau \subseteq_{\mathbf{d}\omega} d\sigma];$

$\equiv \lambda ij(j = i \wedge \vartheta_{\mathbf{d}\omega i}\ \mathbf{d}\varepsilon_i \subseteq \mathbf{d}\tau_i)\ ;\ \lambda ij(j = i \wedge \mathbf{d}\tau_i \subseteq \vartheta_{\mathbf{d}\omega i} d\sigma_i)$

busy

$[\ |\ busy\ d\kappa^a]$

$\equiv \lambda ij(j = i \wedge \forall w \in \text{Dom}\ d\kappa^a{}_i \forall e^\bullet \in \text{Dom}\ d\kappa^a{}_i w \exists s:$
$\quad s = e^\bullet \wedge busy_w(s, d\kappa^a{}_i ws))$

The pronoun *I* refers to the agent of the topical speech act (e_o) in the topical world (w_o). In addition, since the pronoun *I* is the subject, it sets up its animate referent as the α-topic. Next, the verbal root *be-* introduces two background drefs: a state (s_1) and an α-kind ($k^a{}_1$). In the topical world the α-topic instantiates this α-kind in this state. The present tense then first of all tests that the input topic time (t_o) includes the topical perspective point (e_o). This presuppositional test is met by i_3 (since $\vartheta_{w0}e_o \subseteq t_o$). The new state evoked by *be-* is then located at the topic time in the topical world ($t_o \subseteq \vartheta_{w0} s_1$). Finally, the adjective *busy* elaborates the α-kind: in any world where this kind is instantiated, it is instantiated in states of business by the experiencer. So the content of (5) is that in the speech reality at the speech time the speaker is in a state of some kind of business. The degree of business, its nature, etc., are not specified. That is, the adjective *busy* refers to a kind in the same way as the non-specific indefinite *a man* refers to a person.

Formally, (8) updates the output i_3 of the speech start-up to encode the content of what is said, by further updating the stack structure and the associated conditions. A sample output of this update (Stalnaker's "essential effect") is spelled out in (8*a*), along with a model:

(8) (*a*) $i_4 = \langle w_o, \langle a_1, t_o, e_o, w_o \rangle, \langle s_1, k^\alpha{}_1 \rangle \rangle$
s.t. $speak.up_{w0}(e_o, \text{AGT}_{w0}\, e_o)$
$t_o = \vartheta_{w0}\, e_o \wedge t_o \subseteq \vartheta_{w0}\, s_1$
$a_1 = \text{AGT}_{w0}\, e_o \wedge a_1 = k^\alpha{}_1 w_o s_1$
$\forall w \in \text{Dom}\, k^\alpha{}_1 \forall e^\bullet \in \text{Dom}\, k^\alpha{}_1 w \exists s: e^\bullet = s \wedge busy_w(s, k^\alpha{}_1 ws)$

i_4-reality: $^\top w_o$ • $^\top e_o$: e_o-agent speaks up
| $^\top t_o = \vartheta_{w0}\, e_o$: e_o-time
—— s_1: e_o-agent $^\top a_1$ is $k^\alpha{}_1$-busy

The morpheme-by-morpheme analysis in (8) exemplifies direct composition by *online update*. In general, online update interprets the surface string as is, with each morpheme in turn updating the input state of information-and-attention. I assume that each morpheme may lexically contribute up to three updates: *presupposition*, *assertion*, and *implicature*. Presupposition is an anaphoric test on the input. The tested drefs should be familiar (*pace* van der Sandt 1992), but the test conditions need not be (*contra* Heim 1983). For instance, the presuppositions of tenses or pronouns often add new information about the antecedent topic time (*Today I am/was busy*) or about the nominal antecedent (*A doctor came in. He/She looked tired*). Assertion updates the state of attention and/or information by updating stacks and/or eliminating worlds. Implicature is a default extra update: it is defeated if it conflicts with either assertion or presupposition (cf. Gazdar 1979).

This basic conception gives rise to some fundamental questions. First of all, what is a possible lexical meaning? Second, adjacent morphemes often interact, that is the update by one morpheme is adapted to fit the next one (cf. assimilation of one phoneme to the next). In such cases what is an admissible adaptation? And since each morpheme is thus assigned a whole family of meanings (see Appendix), which of these related meanings is to be selected in any given local context? Last but not least, if sentences are composed by sequencing updates, as in discourse, why is compositional anaphora unambiguous? It is beyond the scope of this paper to answer these questions in full. But I can offer some partial answers, based on cross-linguistic text studies (see Bittner 2003 and http://www.rci.rutgers.edu/~mbittner).

Cross-linguistically, there is a limit of at most two new drefs per morpheme, and of these, at most one may be topical. Topical drefs cannot be introduced by open-class items (nouns, verbs, etc.), only by items from closed classes. Typical sources of topical drefs are particles, and grammatical markers forming closed paradigms (mood, tense, case, etc.). The highest dref of a verb (or noun) must be an eventuality (nominal object) or an eventuality-valued function (nominal object-valued function). These basic meaning constraints are cross-linguistically stable. No exceptions have been found in any language.

Meaning adaptations concern the level of abstraction. For instance, by default, an event-root evokes a real event. But this may be adapted to something more abstract—for example an event concept, to fit a modal suffix; an event-valued habit, to fit a habitual suffix; or a dependent event-concept, to fit a habitual report (see Appendix). The principles at work are difficult to formalize, but the basic idea is simple. By default, the simplest meaning is selected as long as it fits the next morpheme. But this morpheme may have a presupposition that forces a certain adaptation. Later morphemes may also require adaptations, but the likelihood drops off sharply with the distance. In actual texts most meaning adaptations involve only adjacent morphemes (see text studies at http://www.rci.rutgers.edu/~mbittner). Finally, any morpheme may either introduce or anaphorically retrieve its drefs—*ceteris paribus* anaphora is preferred—subject to the above morphological constraints on dref number, centering, and type, and subject to any local familiarity/novelty presuppositions (see e.g. *skakkir-* in Appendix).

The meanings thus selected are composed by one of the following two *linking rules* (adapted from Bittner 2001):

($^{\perp}$;) BACKGROUND-ELABORATION LINK
If A $\rightsquigarrow$ α and B $\rightsquigarrow$ β, then [A B] $\rightsquigarrow$ $(\alpha; \beta)$, provided that a demonstrative dR (:= $d\text{R}_0$) in β is anaphoric to an R-dref in α.

($^{\top}$;) TOPIC-COMMENT LINK
If *A* $\rightsquigarrow$ α and B $\rightsquigarrow$ β, then [A B] $\rightsquigarrow$ $(\alpha; \beta)$, provided that a demonstrative **d**R (:= $\mathbf{d}\text{R}_0$) in β is anaphoric to an R-dref in α.

These two linking rules account for assertion and implicature; presupposition may require less local links. Productive word building generally proceeds by Background-Elaboration: a non-initial morpheme elaborates a background dref from the last morpheme. That is, a suffix elaborates the last morpheme of the base, while a prefix is elaborated by the first morpheme of the base. Background-Elaboration may also link some words. Otherwise, words are linked by Topic-Comment. For instance, the inflection on one word may introduce a topical dref for comment by the next word or word group.

In terms of these two linking rules, the online update proposed in (8) can be analyzed as follows (ignoring presuppositions):

(9) I be- -PRS

$([\mathbf{a}|\ 1\ s_{\mathbf{d}\omega,\,\mathbf{d}\varepsilon}\ \mathbf{a}]^{\top};\ ([s k^{\alpha}|\ \mathbf{d}\alpha =_{\mathbf{d}\omega} k^{\alpha}\{s\}]^{\perp};\ (\ldots;\ [|\ \mathbf{d}\tau \subseteq_{\mathbf{d}\omega} d\sigma])))$

busy

$^{\perp};\ [|\ \mathit{busy}\ d\kappa^{\alpha}]$

Within the verb, the tense inflection (-PRS) elaborates the background state dref evoked by the verbal root (*be-*). The verb comments on the topical α-dref set up by the subject (I). And the postverbal adjective (*busy*) elaborates the background α-kind dref evoked by the verbal root (*be-*), which selects this adjectival complement.

I now turn to show how this simple example of online update in a tense-based analytic language naturally extends to the other extreme of the typological spectrum—mood-based polysynthesis.[4]

11.3 Kalaallisut Episodics Online

In episodic discourse in Kalaallisut temporal location depends on two factors: aspectual type (*state*, *event*, or *process*), and whether the topic time is a *discourse instant*—the time of an atomic event—or a *period*.

Discourse-initially, the topic time (start-up now) is the time of an atomic event, that is an *instant*. This yields the temporal pattern in (10).

(10) (*a*) *Anaana-ga* sinip-*pu-q*. — state
mum-1S.SG *asleep*-IND.IV-3S
My mum is asleep.

(*b*) *Anaana-ga* itir-*pu-q*. — event
mum-1S.SG *wake.up*-IND.IV-3S
My mum has woken up.

(*c*) Skakkir-*pu-gut*. — process
play.chess-IND.IV-1P
We are playing chess.

[4] In §§11.3–7 I gradually develop an account of (1)–(4), adding lexical meanings as needed. To get a sense of the lexical patterns, see the final list in the Appendix.

Relative to a topical instant, a state (e.g. sleep in (10*a*)) is understood to be current. An event (e.g. waking up in (10*b*)) is understood to have a current result state. And a process (e.g. playing chess in (10*c*)) is understood to have a current result state of the first stage. Depending on the context, the first stage of a chess game may be the first move, the opening gambit, or perhaps some larger chunk.

In (11) an initial factive clause updates the topic time to the time of the result state of a presupposed event (entry by the father). Unlike the time of an event, the time of a state is a (*discourse*) *period.*

(11) *Ullu-mi ataata-ga isir-m-at*...
day-sg.LOC dad-1s.sg enter-FCT$_{\perp}$-3S$_{\perp}$
Today when my dad came by, ...

(*a*) ...sinip-*pu-tit.* — state
...*asleep*-IND.IV-2S
...you were asleep.

(*b*) ...itir-*pu-nga.* — event
...*wake.up*-IND.IV-1S
...I woke up.

(*c*) ...skakkir-*pu-gut.* — process
...*play.chess*-IND.IV-1p
...we played chess.

This makes no difference if the matrix verb is stative: the state of (11*a*) is understood to be current, just like the state of (10*a*). Events, however, are located differently. Unlike an instant, a period can frame an event. Accordingly, the event of (11*b*), as well as the start event of the process of (11*c*), are located *within* the topical period (result time of the father's entry) evoked by the initial factive clause.

To analyze verbal roots and realis verbal inflections in episodic discourse I propose the conditions in A5 and A6. For states and events, these conditions are mostly standard (see Partee 1984; Webber 1988). But the paradigm in (10)–(11) further motivates a third aspectual type: *processes*, similar to events but with discourse-transparent stages. To model the discourse-transparent structure of processes I use functional drefs of type $\varepsilon\varepsilon$. As stated in A4, a process function sends each non-final stage to the next stage and locates the latter during the result state of the former. The process stages that are often referred to in discourse are the first stage (^{1}ee), the next stage (^{n+1}ee), and the end (^{f}ee).

A4 Processes and stages.

- $process_w\ ee$ for $\forall e \in \text{Dom}\ ee{:}\ \vartheta_w ee(e) \subseteq \vartheta_w\text{RES}_w e$
- $e \in ee$ for $e \in (\text{Dom}\ ee \cup \text{Ran}\ ee)$
  ^1ee for $\iota e.\ e \in (\text{Dom}\ ee - \text{Ran}\ ee)$
  ^{n+1}ee for $ee(^n ee)$
  $^f ee$ for $\iota e.\ e \in (\text{Ran}\ ee - \text{Dom}\ ee)$

A5 Episodic predicates.

- $s{:}\ \text{EXP}\ sleep_{\mathbf{d}\omega}$ for $\lambda i.\ sleep_{\mathbf{d}\omega i}(s, \text{EXP}_{\mathbf{d}\omega i}\ s)$
- $e{:}\ \text{EXP}\ wake.up_{\mathbf{d}\omega}$ for $\lambda i.\ wake.up_{\mathbf{d}\omega i}(e, \text{EXP}_{\mathbf{d}\omega i} e)$
- $ee{:}\ \text{AGT}\ play.chess_{\mathbf{d}\omega}$ for $\lambda i.\ process_{\mathbf{d}\omega i}\ ee$
  $\wedge \forall e \in ee : play.chess_{\mathbf{d}\omega i}(e, \text{AGT}_{\mathbf{d}\omega i} e)$
  $\wedge\ \text{AGT}_{\mathbf{d}\omega i} ee = \bigcup\{\text{AGT}_{\mathbf{d}\omega i}\ e{:}\ e \in ee\}$

A6 Episodic temporal anaphora and update.

- $\text{BEG}\ d\sigma <_{\mathbf{d}\omega} \mathbf{d}\varepsilon$ for $\lambda i.\ \vartheta_{\mathbf{d}\omega i}\ \text{BEG}_{\mathbf{d}\omega i}\ d\sigma_i < \vartheta_{\mathbf{d}\omega i}\ \mathbf{d}\varepsilon_i$
  $d\varepsilon <_{\mathbf{d}\omega} \mathbf{d}\varepsilon$ for $\lambda i.\ \vartheta_{\mathbf{d}\omega i}\ d\varepsilon_i < \vartheta_{\mathbf{d}\omega i}\ \mathbf{d}\varepsilon$
  $^1 d\varepsilon\varepsilon <_{\mathbf{d}\omega} \mathbf{d}\varepsilon$ for $\lambda i.\ \vartheta_{\mathbf{d}\omega i}\ ^1 d\varepsilon\varepsilon_i < \vartheta_{\mathbf{d}\omega i}\ \mathbf{d}\varepsilon$
- $\mathbf{d}\tau \subseteq_{\mathbf{d}\omega} d\sigma$ for $\lambda i.\ \mathbf{d}\tau_i \subseteq \vartheta_{\mathbf{d}\omega i}\ d\sigma_i$
  $d\varepsilon \subseteq_{\mathbf{d}\omega} \mathbf{d}\tau$ for $\lambda i.\ \vartheta_{\mathbf{d}\omega i}\ d\varepsilon_i \subseteq \mathbf{d}\tau_i$
  $^1 d\varepsilon\varepsilon \subseteq_{\mathbf{d}\omega} \mathbf{d}\tau$ for $\lambda i.\ \vartheta_{\mathbf{d}\omega i}\ ^1 d\varepsilon\varepsilon_i \subseteq \mathbf{d}\tau_i$
- $\mathbf{t} =_{\mathbf{d}\omega} \vartheta d\sigma$ for $\lambda i.\ \mathbf{t} = \vartheta_{\mathbf{d}\omega i}\ d\sigma_i$
  $\mathbf{t} =_{\mathbf{d}\omega} \vartheta\text{RES}\ d\varepsilon$ for $\lambda i.\ \mathbf{t} = \vartheta_{\mathbf{d}\omega i}\ \text{RES}_{\mathbf{d}\omega i}\ d\varepsilon_i$
  $\mathbf{t} =_{\mathbf{d}\omega} \vartheta\text{RES}\ ^1 d\varepsilon\varepsilon$ for $\lambda i.\ \mathbf{t} = \vartheta_{\mathbf{d}\omega i}\ \text{RES}_{\mathbf{d}\omega i}\ ^1 d\varepsilon\varepsilon_i$

The paradigm in (11)—with a topical period—can now be interpreted directly and online, as in (11′). First, "day-sg.LOC" updates the topic time to the day of the speech event ($^\top e_0$ in the model below). Kalaallisut factives are verbal definites: they presuppose familiar events. Here, the presupposed entry (e_1) by the speaker's father is located within the current topic time (t_{11}), which is then updated to the time of the result state (t_{12}). The background agreement ($3\text{s}_\perp$) indicates that the main clause is about some α-topic other than the backgrounded father.

(11′) day-[5] -sg.LOC
$[k^\tau | k^\tau day.of\, \varepsilon^\bullet];\ [\mathbf{t} |\ \mathbf{t} \subseteq_{\mathbf{d}\omega} d\kappa^\tau\{\mathbf{d}\varepsilon\}];$

dad-[6] -1s.sg ($\perp$-dref)[7]
$[k^a{}_a | k^a{}_a\ dad.of\, a];\ [a | 1s_{\mathbf{d}\omega,\mathbf{d}\varepsilon} a];\ [a | a =_{\mathbf{d}\omega} d\alpha\kappa^a\{d\alpha, \mathbf{d}\varepsilon\}];$

[5] Any k^τ-time is the day of the instantiating episode:
$k^\tau\ day.of\, \varepsilon^\bullet$ for $\lambda i.\ \forall w \in \text{Dom}\ k^\tau \forall e^\bullet \in \text{Dom}\ k^\tau w{:}\ day_w k^\tau we^\bullet \wedge \vartheta_w e^\bullet \subseteq k^\tau we^\bullet$

[6] For any animate $a \in \text{Dom}\ k^a{}_a$, $k^a{}_a awe^\bullet$ is a's dad in w at the time of $e^\bullet$:
$k^a{}_a\ dad.of\, a$ for $\lambda i.\ \forall a \in \text{Dom}\ k^a{}_a \forall w \in \text{Dom}\ k^a{}_a a \forall e^\bullet \in \text{Dom}\ k^a{}_a aw \exists t{:}$
$\vartheta_w e^\bullet \subseteq t \wedge dad.of_{w,t}(k^a{}_a awe^\bullet, a)$

[7] In $\mathbf{d}\omega$, a instantiates in $\mathbf{d}\varepsilon$ the kind $d\alpha\kappa^a$-of-$d\alpha$:
$a =_{\mathbf{d}\omega} d\alpha\kappa^a\{d\alpha, \mathbf{d}\varepsilon\}$ for $\lambda i.\ a = d\alpha\kappa^a{}_i d\alpha_i \mathbf{d}\omega_i \mathbf{d}\varepsilon_i$

enter-
$[l|d\varepsilon\text{: AGT } enter_{\mathbf{d}\omega}\, l];$

-FCT$_\perp$
$[|d\varepsilon <_{\mathbf{d}\omega} \mathbf{d}\varepsilon, \text{AGT } d\varepsilon =_{\mathbf{d}\omega} d\alpha]; [|d\varepsilon \subseteq_{\mathbf{d}\omega} \mathbf{d}\tau]; [\mathbf{t}|\ \mathbf{t} =_{\mathbf{d}\omega} \vartheta\text{RES } d\varepsilon];$

-3S$_\perp$
$[|3s_{\mathbf{d}\omega,\mathbf{d}\varepsilon} d\alpha]; [\mathbf{a}|\ \mathbf{a} \neq d\alpha]$

The main verb comments on these topics. Thus in (11′*a*) the comment is that in the topical world (w_o) during the topical period (t_{12}), the α-topic ("2s") is asleep:

(11′) (*a*) asleep-
$[s|s\text{: EXP } sleep_{\mathbf{d}\omega}];$

-IND. .IV
$[|\text{ BEG } d\sigma <_{\mathbf{d}\omega} \mathbf{d}\varepsilon]; [|\ \mathbf{d}\tau \subseteq_{\mathbf{d}\omega} d\sigma]; [|\text{EXP } d\sigma =_{\mathbf{d}\omega} \mathbf{d}\alpha];$

-2S
$[|\ 2s_{\mathbf{d}\omega,\mathbf{d}\varepsilon}\ \mathbf{d}\alpha]$

In (11′*b*), the α-topic ("1s") wakes up within the topical period:

(11′) (*b*) wake.up-
$[e|e\text{: EXP } wake.up_{\mathbf{d}\omega}];$

-IND. .IV -1S
$[|d\varepsilon <_{\mathbf{d}\omega} \mathbf{d}\varepsilon]; [|\ d\varepsilon \subseteq_{\mathbf{d}\omega} \mathbf{d}\tau]; [|\text{ EXP } d\varepsilon =_{\mathbf{d}\omega} \mathbf{d}\alpha]; [|\ 1s_{\mathbf{d}\omega,\mathbf{d}\varepsilon}\ \mathbf{d}\alpha]$

And in (11′*c*) the α-topic ("1p", e.g. the speaker and his father) start—and possibly finish—a chess game within the topical period:

(11′) (*c*) play.chess-
$[ee|ee\text{: AGT} play.chess_{\mathbf{d}\omega}];$

-IND. .IV
$[|^1 d\varepsilon\varepsilon <_{\mathbf{d}\omega} \mathbf{d}\varepsilon]; [|^1 d\varepsilon\varepsilon \subseteq_{\mathbf{d}\omega} \mathbf{d}\tau]; [|\text{ AGT } d\varepsilon\varepsilon =_{\mathbf{d}\omega} \mathbf{d}\alpha];$

-1p
$[|1p_{\mathbf{d}\omega,\mathbf{d}\varepsilon}\ \mathbf{d}\alpha]$

We thus predict the following models for (11′*a*, 11′*b*, 11′*c*), given an initial input of the form $\langle w_o, \langle\quad\rangle, \langle e_1\rangle\rangle$:

i-reality: $^{\top}w_o$	•	$^{\top}e_o$: e_o-agent speaks up
	|	$t_o = \vartheta_{w0} e_o$
	||||||||||||||||||||||||||||	$k^{\tau}{}_1 w_o e_o$: e_o-day
	||	$^{(\top)}t_{11} \subseteq k^{\tau}{}_1 w_o e_o$
	•	e_1: e_o-agent's dad enters l_1
	||	$^{\top}t_{12} = \vartheta_{w0}\ \text{RES}_{w0} e_1$
(11′*a*)	—	s_2: e_o-experiencer is asleep
(11′*b*)	•	e_2: e_o-agent wakes up
(11′*c*)	•••	ee_2: (e_o-agent + ?) play chess

The start-up update models Stalnaker's "commonplace effect", so the default topics which it sets should be universal: the speech world ($\mathbf{d}\omega$), the speech event ($\mathbf{d}\varepsilon$), and the speech time (initial $\mathbf{d}\tau$). Often, the speaker wants to talk about a past period, so he first updates the topic time—for example by means of an initial updating verb (as in (11′)). The new topic time then depends on the aspect of that verb, as stated in the last column of Table 11.3. That is, depending on whether the updating verb refers to a state, event, or process, the new topic time is the time of the state, the result time of the event, or the result time of stage one of the process.

TABLE 11.3 Real episodes ($\mathbf{d}\tau$ period)

Base	Reality presup.	Location test	Temporal update
$[s\|\ldots]$;	$[\|\ \text{BEG}\ d\sigma <_{\mathbf{d}\omega} \mathbf{d}\varepsilon]$;	$[\|\ \mathbf{d}\tau \subseteq_{\mathbf{d}\omega} d\sigma]$;	$[\mathbf{t}\|\ \mathbf{t} =_{\mathbf{d}\omega} \vartheta d\sigma]$
$[e\|\ldots]$;	$[\|d\varepsilon <_{\mathbf{d}\omega} \mathbf{d}\varepsilon]$;	$[\|d\varepsilon \subseteq_{\mathbf{d}\omega} \mathbf{d}\tau]$;	$[\mathbf{t}\ \|\mathbf{t} =_{\mathbf{d}\omega} \vartheta \text{RES} d\varepsilon]$
$[ee\|\ldots]$;	$[\|^1 d\varepsilon\varepsilon <_{\mathbf{d}\omega} \mathbf{d}\varepsilon]$;	$[\|^1 d\varepsilon\varepsilon \subseteq_{\mathbf{d}\omega} \mathbf{d}\tau]$;	$[\mathbf{t}\|\ \mathbf{t} =_{\mathbf{d}\omega} \vartheta \text{RES}\ ^1 d\varepsilon\varepsilon]$

In the updated context the episode of the next verb is located in relation to the current temporal and modal topics. The location tests too depend on the aspect, as stated in the penultimate column of Table 11.3 and illustrated in (8) (for English) and (11′*a*, 11′*b*, 11′*c*) (for Kalaallisut).

In Kalaallisut factual moods (IND and FCT) presuppose reality. That is, they test whether the episode qualifies as a fact in the topical world ($\mathbf{d}\omega$) from the topical perspective ($\mathbf{d}\varepsilon$). As stated in Table 11.3, reality presuppositions likewise depend on aspect. To be reported as a fact, an event (e.g. waking up in (11′*b*)) must have already happened, while a state or a process must, at the very least, have begun (e.g. sleep in (11′*a*), or chess playing in (11′*c*)). So all real episodes must, at the very least, begin in the past of the speech event ($\mathbf{d}\varepsilon$). Thus, the reality presuppositions of factual moods also contribute to temporal anaphora.

11.4 Kalaallisut Habituals Online

In Kalaallisut habitual aspect is explicitly marked by suffixes (e.g. *-tar*):

(12) *Ataata-ga sapaati-kkut isir-tar-pu-q.*
dad-1s.sg Sunday-VIA enter-*habit*-IND.IV-3s
My dad comes by on Sundays.

(13) *Ilaanni-kkut skakkir*-tar-*pu-gut.*
sometime-VIA play.chess-*habit*-IND.IV-1p
Sometimes we play chess.

Habits are understood to be current at the topic time, like states and processes. This might suggest that a habitual suffix evokes a state or a process. But in Kalaallisut episodic states and processes are morphologically unmarked (as in (10*a*, 10*c*)). Without a habitual suffix, a state or process verb is ungrammatical with temporal quantifiers, for example *ilaanni-kkut* "sometimes" in (13). It is also incompatible with other habitual modifiers, including *sapaatikkut* "on Sundays" in (12), and the habit-based reading of *siullirmik* "the first time" in (23). That is, Kalaallisut grammatically distinguishes episodic states and processes, on the one hand, from habits, on the other.

This can be understood if episodic verbs evoke discourse referents for episodes, that is particular states, events, or processes, while habitual verbs evoke referents for habits, that is modally and temporally distributed patterns. For example, (12) evokes a habit instantiated by events of the father coming by on a Sunday. Not necessarily every Sunday, just enough to call it a habit. Sentence (13) evokes another habit, instantiated by processes of playing chess. The quantifier "sometimes" correlates these two habits: some instances of the antecedent entering habit of (12) result in an instance of the chess-playing habit of (13).

More formally, a habit is (characterized by) a function that sends each world and time when the habit is instantiated to the episode that instantiates that habit in that world at that time. Any episodic predicate has a related habitual reading. A7 spells this out for a habitual state, habitual event, and habitual process. Note that an instance of a habitual state, event, or process relates to its instantiation time like an episodic state, event, or process, to the current topic time (cf. Table 11.3).

A7 Habitual predicates

- h^{σ}: EXP *sleep* for
  $\lambda i.\ \forall w \in \text{Dom}\ h^{\sigma} \forall t \in \text{Dom}\ h^{\sigma}w \exists s: s = h^{\sigma}wt \wedge t \subseteq \vartheta_w s$
  $\wedge$ (s: EXP $sleep_w$)

- h^{ε}: AGT *win* $\eta^{\varepsilon\varepsilon}$ for
  $\lambda i.\ \forall w \in \text{Dom } h^{\varepsilon} \forall t \in \text{Dom } h^{\varepsilon} w \exists e\text{: } e = h^{\varepsilon} wt \wedge \vartheta_w e \subseteq t$
  $\wedge \exists ee \in \text{Ran } d\eta^{\varepsilon\varepsilon}{}_i w\text{: } e = {}^f ee \wedge win_w(e, \text{AGT}_w e, ee)$
- $h^{\varepsilon\varepsilon}$: AGT *play.chess* for
  $\lambda i.\ \forall w \in \text{Dom } h^{\varepsilon\varepsilon} \forall t \in \text{Dom } h^{\varepsilon\varepsilon} w \exists ee\text{: } ee = h^{\varepsilon\varepsilon} wt$
  $\wedge \vartheta_w{}^1 ee \subseteq t \wedge (ee\text{: AGT } play.chess_w)$

Habitual modifiers like "on Sundays" evoke kinds of time, while temporal quantifiers evoke sub-kinds of antecedently given kinds.

A8 Temporal (sub-)kinds

- *sunday.time* k^{τ} for
  $\lambda i. \forall w \in \text{Dom } k^{\tau} \forall e^{\bullet} \in \text{Dom } k^{\tau} w \exists t\text{:}$
  $sunday.at_w(t, \Pi_w e^{\bullet}) \wedge k^{\tau} we^{\bullet} \subseteq t$
- $Q\{\vartheta\text{RES } d\eta^{\varepsilon}, k^{\tau}\}$ for
  $\lambda i. \forall w \in \text{Dom } k^{\tau}\text{: Ran } k^{\tau} w \subseteq \{\vartheta_w \text{ RES}_w e\text{: } e \in \text{Ran } d\eta^{\varepsilon}{}_i w\}$
  $\wedge Q(\{\vartheta_w \text{ RES}_w e\text{: } e \in \text{Ran } d\eta^{\varepsilon}{}_i w\}, \text{Ran } k^{\tau} w)$

Habitual aspect markers presuppose antecedent habits and, possibly, kinds of time. Antecedent habits are also required by descriptions like "the *n*th time", which evoke the *n*th instance of a habit.

A9 Habitual anaphora

- $\text{Dom } d\eta^{\nu} = \mathbf{d}\kappa^{\tau}$ for
  $\lambda i. \langle \text{Dom } d\eta^{\nu}{}_i w\text{: } w \in \text{Dom } d\eta_i{}^{\nu} \rangle$
  $= \langle \text{Ran } \mathbf{d}\kappa^{\tau}{}_i w\text{: } w \in \text{Dom } \mathbf{d}\kappa^{\tau}{}_i \rangle$
- $e = {}_{\mathbf{d}\omega}{}^n (d\eta^{\varepsilon})$ for
  $\lambda i.\ e = {}^n(\text{Ran } d\eta^{\varepsilon}{}_i \mathbf{d}\omega_i)$

Finally, to interpret verbal inflections, temporal anaphora and update must be extended from episodes (A6) to habits (A10). A habit can be reported as a fact as soon as it begins (cf. states and processes in A6). It is understood to be current at the topic time in the relevant modality (real or reported, cf. states in A6). If a habitual verb updates the temporal topic, it evokes a new kind of time rather than a particular time. But the dependence on the aspectual type of the instantiating episodes is the same as for episodic verbs (cf. A6).

A10 Habitual temporal anaphora and update.[8]

- ${}^1 d\eta^{\varepsilon} <_{\mathbf{d}\omega} \mathbf{d}\varepsilon$ for
  $\lambda i.\ \vartheta_{\mathbf{d}\omega}{}^1(\text{Ran } d\eta^{\varepsilon}{}_i \mathbf{d}\omega_i) < \vartheta_{\mathbf{d}\omega i}\ \mathbf{d}\varepsilon_i$

[8] The minimal period that includes every T-time:
$\cup_{\tau} T$ for $\min\{t \in D_{\tau} | \forall t' \in T\text{: } t' \subseteq t\}$

- $\mathbf{d}\tau \subseteq_{\mathbf{d}\omega} d\eta^{\varepsilon}$ for
  $\lambda i.\, \mathbf{d}\tau_i \subseteq \cup_{\tau}(\mathrm{Dom}\, d\eta^{\varepsilon}{}_i \mathbf{d}\omega_i)$
  $\mathbf{d}\tau \subseteq_{\mathbf{d}\Omega} d\eta^{\varepsilon}$ for
  $\lambda i.\, \forall w \in \mathbf{d}\Omega_i{:}\ \mathbf{d}\tau_i \subseteq \cup_{\tau}(\mathrm{Dom}\, d\eta^{\varepsilon}{}_i w)$
  $\vartheta e \subseteq_{p} d\eta^{\varepsilon}$ for
  $\lambda i.\, \forall w \in p{:}\ \vartheta_w e \subseteq \cup_{\tau}(\mathrm{Dom}\, d\eta^{\varepsilon}{}_i w)$
- $\mathbf{k}^{\tau} = \vartheta d\eta^{\sigma}$ for
  $\lambda i.\, \mathbf{k}^{\tau} = \langle\{\langle s, \vartheta_w s\rangle{:}\ s \in \mathrm{Ran}\, d\eta^{\sigma}{}_i w\}{:}\ w \in \mathrm{Dom}\, d\eta^{\sigma}{}_i\rangle$
  $\mathbf{k}^{\tau} = \vartheta\textsc{res}\, d\eta^{\varepsilon}$ for
  $\lambda i.\, \mathbf{k}^{\tau} = \langle\{\langle e, \vartheta_w \textsc{res}_w e\rangle{:}\ e \in \mathrm{Ran}\, d\eta^{\varepsilon}{}_i w\}{:}\ w \in \mathrm{Dom}\, d\eta^{\varepsilon}{}_i\rangle$
  $\mathbf{k}^{\tau} = \vartheta\textsc{res}\, {}^1 d\eta^{\varepsilon\varepsilon}$ for
  $\lambda i.\, \mathbf{k}^{\tau} = \langle\{\langle {}^1ee, \vartheta_w \textsc{res}_w {}^1ee\rangle{:}\ ee \in \mathrm{Ran}\, d\eta^{\varepsilon\varepsilon}{}_i w\}{:}\ w \in \mathrm{Dom}\, d\eta^{\varepsilon\varepsilon}{}_i\rangle$

The habitual discourse (12)–(13) can now be interpreted directly and online, as in (12′)–(13′). First, sentence (12) introduces a habitual pattern of events ($h^{\varepsilon}{}_1$ in the model below), instantiated by the speaker's father coming by on a Sunday. This habit is real and current (in $^{\top}w_0$ at $^{\top}t_0$), and its distribution is set up as a topical kind of time ($^{\top}k^{\tau}{}_1$):

(12′) dad- -1s.sg (⊤-dref)
$[k^{a}{}_{a} | k^{a}{}_{a} \mathit{dad.of}\ \alpha];\ [a | 1s_{\mathbf{d}\omega,\mathbf{d}\varepsilon} a];\ [\mathbf{a} |\ \mathbf{a} =_{\mathbf{d}\omega} d\alpha\kappa\{d\alpha, \mathbf{d}\varepsilon\}];$

Sunday- -VIA
$[k^{\tau} |\ \mathit{sunday.time}\ k^{\tau}];\ [\mathbf{k}^{\tau} |\ \mathbf{k}^{\tau} = d\kappa^{\tau}];$

enter- -habit(-*tar*)
$[h^{\varepsilon} l |\ h^{\varepsilon}{:}\ \textsc{agt}\ \mathit{enter}\ l];\ [\,|\ \mathbf{d}\varepsilon \subseteq_{\mathbf{d}\omega} d\pi];\ [\,|\ \mathrm{Dom}\, d\eta^{\varepsilon} = \mathbf{d}\kappa^{\tau}];$

-IND. .IV[9] -3S
$[\,|\ {}^1 d\eta^{\varepsilon} <_{\mathbf{d}\omega} \mathbf{d}\varepsilon];\ [\,|\ \mathbf{d}\tau \subseteq_{\mathbf{d}\omega} d\eta^{\varepsilon}];\ [\,|\ \textsc{agt}\ d\eta^{\varepsilon} =_{\mathbf{d}\omega} \mathbf{d}\alpha];\ [\,| 3s_{\mathbf{d}\omega,\mathbf{d}\varepsilon}\ \mathbf{d}\alpha]$

Next, in (13) the quantifier "sometimes" updates the topical kind of time to a new kind, instantiated by some of the result times of the father's entries ($^{\top}k^{\tau}{}_2$). This topical selection is then linked, by the habitual suffix *-tar*, to a chess playing habit ($h^{\varepsilon\varepsilon}{}_2$). That is, each of the selected result times frames the start of a chess game. The chess playing habit is likewise real and current (in $^{\top}w_0$ at $^{\top}t_0$):

(13′) sometimes- -VIA
$[k^{\tau} |\ \mathit{some}\{\vartheta\textsc{res}\, d\eta^{\varepsilon}, k^{\tau}\}];\ [\mathbf{k}^{\tau} |\ \mathbf{k}^{\tau} = d\kappa^{\tau}];$

play.chess- -habit (-*tar*)
$[h^{\varepsilon\varepsilon} |\ h^{\varepsilon\varepsilon}{:}\ \textsc{agt}\ \mathit{play.chess}];\ [\,|\ \mathrm{Dom}\, d\eta^{\varepsilon\varepsilon} = \mathbf{d}\kappa^{\tau}];$

-IND.
$[\,|\ {}^1 d\eta^{\varepsilon\varepsilon} <_{\mathbf{d}\omega} \mathbf{d}\varepsilon];\ [\,|\ \mathbf{d}\tau \subseteq_{\mathbf{d}\omega} d\eta^{\varepsilon\varepsilon}];$

[9] In $\mathbf{d}\omega$, $d\eta^{\varepsilon}$ is a habitual action by $\mathbf{d}\alpha$:
($\textsc{agt}\ d\eta^{\varepsilon} =_{\mathbf{d}\omega} \mathbf{d}\alpha$) for $\lambda i.\forall e \in \mathrm{Ran}\, d\eta^{\varepsilon}{}_i \mathbf{d}\omega_i{:}\ \textsc{agt}_{\mathbf{d}\omega i}\, e = \mathbf{d}\alpha_i$

.IV -1p

$$[\|\ \text{AGT}\ d\eta^{\varepsilon\varepsilon} =_{\mathbf{d}\omega} (\text{AGT}\ \mathbf{d}\varepsilon + \mathbf{d}\alpha)];\ [\|\ 1\,p_{\mathbf{d}\omega,\mathbf{d}\varepsilon}\ (\text{AGT}\ \mathbf{d}\varepsilon + \mathbf{d}\alpha)]$$

Model for (7); (12′); (13′)

i-reality: $^{\top}w_o$ •	$^{\top}e_o$: e_o-agent speaks up
|	$^{\top}t_o = \vartheta_{wo}e_o$
… |||||| |||||| |||||| …	Ran $^{(\top)}k^{\tau}{}_1w_o$ = Dom $h^{\varepsilon}w_o$ $k^{\tau}{}_1$-Sundays spanning $^{\top}t_o$
… • • • …	Ran $h^{\varepsilon}{}_1w_o$: e_o-speaker's dad a_1 enters e_o-here
… || || …	Ran $^{\top}k^{\tau}{}_2w_o$ = Dom $h^{\varepsilon\varepsilon}{}_2w_o$ *some*$(\{\vartheta_{wo}\ \text{RES}_{wo}e$: $e \in$ Ran $h^{\varepsilon}{}_1w_o\}$. Ran $k^{\tau}{}_2w_o)$
… •• •• …	Ran $h^{\varepsilon\varepsilon}{}_2w_o$: ($e_o$-spkr + a_1) play chess

According to this analysis, the habitual suffix *-tar* is not an operator. Instead, it has an anaphoric presupposition ($d\eta^{v}$) which defeats the default episodic reading of the base in favor of the habitual reading. The interpretation of the indicative mood on the habitual verbs of (12′)–(13′) illustrates more general patterns, spelled out in Table 11.4.

TABLE 11.4 Real habits

Base	Reality presup.	Location test	Temporal update
$[h^{\sigma}\|\ldots]$;	$[\|{}^1d\eta^{\sigma} <_{\mathbf{d}\omega} \mathbf{d}\varepsilon]$;	$[\|\ \mathbf{d}\tau \subseteq_{\mathbf{d}\omega} d\eta^{\sigma}]$	$[\mathbf{k}^{\tau}\|\ \mathbf{k}^{\tau} = \vartheta d\eta^{\sigma}]$
$[h^{\varepsilon}\|\ldots]$;	$[\|{}^1d\eta^{\varepsilon} <_{\mathbf{d}\omega} \mathbf{d}\varepsilon]$;	$[\|\ \mathbf{d}\tau \subseteq_{\mathbf{d}\omega} d\eta^{\varepsilon}]$	$[\mathbf{k}^{\tau}\|\ \mathbf{k}^{\tau} = \vartheta\text{RES}\ d\eta^{\varepsilon}]$
$[h^{\varepsilon\varepsilon}\|\ldots]$;	$[\|{}^1d\eta^{\varepsilon\varepsilon} <_{\mathbf{d}\omega} \mathbf{d}\varepsilon]$;	$[\|\ \mathbf{d}\tau \subseteq_{\mathbf{d}\omega} d\eta^{\varepsilon\varepsilon}]$	$[\mathbf{k}^{\tau}\|\ \mathbf{k}^{\tau} = \vartheta\text{RES}\ {}^1d\eta^{\varepsilon\varepsilon}]$

As already noted, these patterns of habitual temporal anaphora depend on aspect in much the same way as their episodic counterparts (recall Table 11.3). And both patterns generalize to *de se* reports, as I now proceed to show in §§11.5–11.7.

11.5 Reported Habits Online

Recall that, in the context of the habitual (1) the *de se* report in (2*a*), with the root verb *uqar-* and direct first person quote is equivalent to (2b), with the v\v suffix *-nirar*. The data are repeated in (14)–(15):

(14) *Ataata-ga skakkir-tar-pu-q.*
dad-1s.sg play.chess-habit-IND.IV-3s
My dad$_{\top}$ plays chess.

(15) *Siurna arna-mi uqaluqatigii-mm-ani,*
last.year mother-3s$_\top$.sg.ERG talk.with-FCT$_\bot$-3s$_\bot$.3s$_\top$
Last year when his$_\top$ mother talked with him$_\top$, ...

(*a*) uqar-*pu-q:* "*Amirlanir-tigut ajugaa-sar-pu-nga.*"
say-IND.IV-3s most-VIA win-habit-IND.IV-1s
... he$_\top$ said: "I mostly win."

(*b*) *amirlanir-tigut ajugaa-sar-*nirar*-pu-q.*
most-VIA win-habit-*say*-IND.IV-3s
... he$_\top$ said that he (= *se*) mostly won.

Since the surface forms are radically different, the equivalence of (14)–(15*a*) and (14)–(15*b*) is difficult to explain in LF-based semantics. In contrast, online update offers a natural account. The second habit is anaphorically linked to the first just as in (12)–(13). But in (15*a*, 15*b*) the second habit is only reported, not necessarily real. Therefore, it is not located in reality, but in the modality evoked by the report verb "say" (i.e. by *uqar-* or *-nirar*). In the reported modality, the second habit is current at the time of the report (temporal *de se*) and is instantiated by events in which the reporting agent wins (individual *de se*):

(14′) My dad plays chess.

dad- -1s.sg ($\top$-dref)
$[k^{\alpha}{}_{\alpha}|k^{\alpha}{}_{\alpha}\mathit{dad.of}\,\alpha]$; $[a|1s_{\mathbf{d}\omega,\mathbf{d}\varepsilon}a]$; $[\mathbf{a}|\ \mathbf{a} =_{\mathbf{d}\omega} d\alpha\kappa\{d\alpha, \mathbf{d}\varepsilon\}]$;

play.chess- -habit (*-tar*)
$[h^{\varepsilon\varepsilon}k^{\alpha}|\ h^{\varepsilon\varepsilon}\!: (\textsc{agt} + k^{\alpha})\mathit{play.chess}]$; $[k^{\tau}|\ \mathrm{Dom}\ d\eta^{\varepsilon\varepsilon} = k^{\tau}]$;

-IND. .IV
$[|{}^{1}d\eta^{\varepsilon\varepsilon} <_{\mathbf{d}\omega} \mathbf{d}\varepsilon]$; $[|\ \mathbf{d}\tau \subseteq_{\mathbf{d}\omega} d\eta^{\varepsilon\varepsilon}]$; $[|\ \textsc{agt}\ d\eta^{\varepsilon\varepsilon} =_{\mathbf{d}\omega} \mathbf{d}\alpha]$;

-3s
$[|3s_{\mathbf{d}\omega,\mathbf{d}\varepsilon}\ \mathbf{d}\alpha]$

(15′) Last year when his$_\top$ mother talked with him$_\top$...

last.year ($\top$-dref)
$[k^{\tau}|k^{\tau}\ \mathit{last.year.of}\ \varepsilon^{\bullet}]$; $[\mathbf{t}|\ \mathbf{t} =_{\mathbf{d}\omega} d\kappa^{\tau}\{\mathbf{d}\varepsilon\}]$;

mother- -3s$_\top$.sg .ERG ($\bot$-dref)
$[k^{\alpha}{}_{\alpha}|k^{\alpha}{}_{\alpha}\mathit{ma.of}\,\alpha]$; $[|3s_{\mathbf{d}\omega,\mathbf{d}\varepsilon}\ \mathbf{d}\alpha]$; $[a|a =_{\mathbf{d}\omega} d\alpha\kappa\{\mathbf{d}\alpha, \mathbf{d}\varepsilon\}]$;

talk.with-
$[ee\ k^{\alpha}|\ ee\!: \textsc{agt}\ \mathit{talk.with}_{\mathbf{d}\omega}\ k^{\alpha}]$;

-FCT$_\perp$
$[|\ ({}^1d\varepsilon\varepsilon <_{\mathbf{d}\omega} \mathbf{d}\varepsilon), (\text{AGT } d\varepsilon\varepsilon =_{\mathbf{d}\omega} d\alpha)];$
$[|{}^1d\varepsilon\varepsilon \subseteq_{\mathbf{d}\omega} \mathbf{d}\tau]; [\mathbf{t}|\ \mathbf{t} =_{\mathbf{d}\omega} \vartheta\text{RES } {}^1d\varepsilon\varepsilon];$

-3S$_\perp$. .3S$_\top$
$[|3s_{\mathbf{d}\omega,\mathbf{d}\varepsilon} d\alpha, d\alpha \neq \mathbf{d}\alpha]; [|3s_{\mathbf{d}\omega,\mathbf{d}\varepsilon}\ \mathbf{d}\alpha, \mathbf{d}\alpha =_{\mathbf{d}\omega} d\kappa^{a}\{d\varepsilon\varepsilon\}];$

(*a*) ...he$_\top$ said: "I mostly win."
say- (*uqar-*)
$[ep|e\text{: AGT } say_{\mathbf{d}\omega} p];$

-IND. .IV -3S
$[|d\varepsilon <_{\mathbf{d}\omega} \mathbf{d}\varepsilon]; [|\ d\varepsilon \subseteq_{\mathbf{d}\omega} \mathbf{d}\tau]; [|\text{AGT } d\varepsilon =_{\mathbf{d}\omega} \mathbf{d}\alpha]; [|3s_{\mathbf{d}\omega,\mathbf{d}\varepsilon}\ \mathbf{d}\alpha];$
"(quote start-up)
$[\mathbf{p}|\ \mathbf{p} = d\Omega]; [\mathbf{e}|\ \mathbf{e} = d\varepsilon]; [\mathbf{t}|\ \mathbf{t} =_{\mathbf{d}\omega} \vartheta\mathbf{d}\varepsilon];$

most- -VIA
$[k^\tau|\ most\{\vartheta\text{RES } {}^1d\eta^{\varepsilon\varepsilon}, k^\tau\}]; [\mathbf{k}^\tau|\mathbf{k}^\tau = d\kappa^\tau];$

win- -habit (-*tar*)
$[h^\varepsilon|h^\varepsilon\text{: AGT } win\ d\eta^{\varepsilon\varepsilon}]; [|\ \text{Dom } d\eta^\varepsilon = \mathbf{d}\kappa^\tau];$

-IND. .IV
$[|\ {}^1d\eta^\varepsilon <_{\mathbf{d}\Omega} \mathbf{d}\varepsilon]; [|\ \mathbf{d}\tau \subseteq_{\mathbf{d}\Omega} d\eta^\varepsilon]; [|\ \text{AGT } d\eta^\varepsilon =_{\mathbf{d}\Omega} \mathbf{d}\alpha];$
-1S
$[|1s_{\mathbf{d}\Omega,\mathbf{d}\varepsilon}\ \mathbf{d}\alpha];$
"(unquote)
$[\mathbf{w}|\ \mathbf{w} = \mathbf{d}\omega]; [\mathbf{e}|\ \mathbf{e} = \mathbf{d}\varepsilon_1];$

(*b*) ...he$_\top$ said that he (= *se*) mostly won.

most- -VIA
$[k^\tau|\ most\{\vartheta\text{RES } {}^1d\eta^{\varepsilon\varepsilon}, k^\tau\}]; [\mathbf{k}^\tau|\ \mathbf{k}^\tau = d\kappa^\tau];$

win- -habit (-*tar*)
$[h^\varepsilon|h^\varepsilon\text{: AGT } win\ d\eta^{\varepsilon\varepsilon}]; [|\ \text{Dom } d\eta^\varepsilon = \mathbf{d}\kappa^\tau];$

-say (-*nirar*)
$[ep|\ (e\text{: AGT } say_{\mathbf{d}\omega} p), (\vartheta e \subseteq_p d\eta^\varepsilon), (\text{AGT } e =_p \text{AGT } d\eta^\varepsilon)];$

-IND. .IV -3S
$[|d\varepsilon <_{\mathbf{d}\omega} \mathbf{d}\varepsilon]; [|\ d\varepsilon \subseteq_{\mathbf{d}\omega} \mathbf{d}\tau]; [|\ \text{AGT } d\varepsilon =_{\mathbf{d}\omega} \mathbf{d}\alpha]; [|\ 3s_{\mathbf{d}\omega,\mathbf{d}\varepsilon}\ \mathbf{d}\alpha]$

This analysis captures the equivalence of the two discourses, (14)–(15*a*) and (14)–(15*b*). They converge on the model shown below, but differ in centering. In (15′*a*) the quote begins with a start-up update that temporarily shifts the modal, perspectival, and temporal topics until the end of the quote. The shift of perspective means that within the quote "1s" refers to the quoted speaker.

Also, "IND" locates the winning habit at the time of the quoted report (current topic time) in the reported modality (current modal topic). So individual and temporal *de se* is due to a temporary topic shift by the quote. The suffixal report (15′*b*) does not involve any topic shift. Instead, the v\v suffix *-nirar* "say" lexically encodes temporal and individual *de se*. Thus, by different routes, (14)–(15*a*) and (14)–(15*b*) converge on the following model:

Model for (7); (14′); (15′*a*, 15′*b*)

i-reality: $^{\top}w_o$ • $^{\top}e_o$: e_o-agent speaks up
| $^{\top}t_o = \vartheta_{wo}e_o$
...•• •• •• •• ... Ran $h^{\varepsilon\varepsilon}{}_1w_o$: e_o-speaker's dad $^{\top}a_1$ plays chess with a $k^{\alpha}{}_1$-partner
...|| || || || ... Ran $k^{\tau}{}_1w_o$ = Dom $h^{\varepsilon\varepsilon}{}_1w_o$
|| $^{(\top)}t_{2.1}$: during last year of $^{\top}e_o$
••• ee_2: $^{\top}a_1$'s mother $^{\perp}a_2$ talks with $^{\top}a_1$
|| $^{\top}t_{2.2} = \vartheta_{wo}$ RES$_{wo}{}^{1}ee_2$
• e_3: $^{\top}a_1$ says p_3

~~~~~~

$w_3 \in p_3$ (e_3-report)
... •• •• •• ... Ran $h^{\varepsilon\varepsilon}{}_1w_3$: e_3-speaker plays chess with a $k^{\alpha}{}_1$-partner
... || || ... Ran $^{\top}k^{\tau}{}_3w_3$ = Dom $h^{\varepsilon}{}_3w_3$
most($\{\vartheta_{w3}$RES$_{w3}{}^{1}ee$: $ee \in$ Ran $h^{\varepsilon\varepsilon}{}_1w_3\}$, Ran $k^{\tau}{}_3w_3$)
... • • ... Ran $h^{\varepsilon}{}_3w_3$: e_3-speaker wins a $h^{\varepsilon\varepsilon}{}_1$-chess.game

Lexical *de se* anaphora is not peculiar to the v\v suffix *-nirar*. It instantiates a general pattern in Kalaallisut. Verbal moods relate the (last) eventuality of the v-base to the currently topical modality, perspective, time, and individual. In contrast, v\v suffixes—like *-nirar* "say", *-suri* "believe", *-ssa* "prospect", etc.—relate the base eventuality to their own perspective and a modality they evoke. Therefore, reports with v\v suffixes are temporally *de se* (like nonfinite reports in English, for example *claim to have won, expect to win, dread losing*). Intransitive v\v reports are also individually *de se*: the agent (or experiencer) of the v-base is identified with the reporting agent (or experiencer) of the v\v suffix—as we saw in (15′*b*) and will see again in §§11.6 and 11.7.

11.6 Reported Attitudes Online

Mutatis mutandis online update for reported habits generalizes to reported attitudes. Thus, for example, in the context of (14), (3*a*, 3*b*) (repeated as (16*a*, 16*b*)) can be interpreted online essentially like (15*a*, 15*b*):
~~~~~~

(16) *Ilaanni skakkir-a-mi,*
once play.chess-FCT$_{\top}$-3S$_{\top}$
Once when he$_{\top}$ played (chess), ...

(*a*) isuma-qa-*lir-pu-q:* "*Immaqa ajugaa-ssa-u-nga.*"
belief-have-begin-IND.IV-3S maybe win-prospect-IND.IV-1S
... he$_{\top}$ began to think: "I might win."

(*b*) *immaqa ajugaa-ssa*-suri-*lir-pu-q.*
maybe win-prospect-*believe*-begin-IND.IV-3S
... he$_{\top}$ began to think that he (= *se*) might win.

Reference to habitual events and their temporal domains (by "win-" and "-habit" in (15*a*, 15*b*)) is replaced with reference to concepts of prospective events and their modal domains (by "win-" and "-prospect" in (16*a*, 16*b*)). Quantification over temporal domains (by "mostly" in (15*a*, 15*b*)) is replaced with quantification over modal domains (by "maybe" in (16*a*, 16*b*)). In the context of (14), (16*a*) and (16*b*) thus converge on the following model, which is point for point parallel to the model that (15*a*) and (15*b*) converged on in the same context (see above):

Model for (7); (14′); (16′*a*, 16′*b*)

i-reality: $^{\top}w_0$ • $\quad$ $^{\top}e_0$: e_0-agent speaks up

| $\quad$ $^{\top}t_0 = \vartheta_{w0}e_0$

... •• • • •• •• ... $\quad$ Ran $h^{\varepsilon\varepsilon}{}_1w_0$: e_0-speaker's dad $^{\top}a_1$ plays chess with a $k^{a}{}_1$-partner

... || || || || ... $\quad$ Ran $k^{\tau}{}_1w_0$ = Dom $h^{\varepsilon\varepsilon}{}_1w_0$

|| $\quad$ $^{(\top)}t_{2.1} \in$ Dom $h^{\varepsilon\varepsilon}{}_1w_0$

• $\quad$ $[^1\underline{ee}_2]w_0 = {}^1h^{\varepsilon\varepsilon}{}_1w_0t_{2.1}$ 1st stage of $t_{2.1}$-instance of $h^{\varepsilon\varepsilon}{}_1$

||||| $\quad$ $^{\top}t_{2.2} = \vartheta_{w0}$ RES$_{w0}$ $[^1\underline{ee}_2]w_0$

— $\quad$ s_3: $^{\top}a_1$ believes p_3

• $\quad$ e_3 = BEG$_{w0}s_3$

~~~~~~

$w_3 \in$ Ran $^{\top}\underline{w_3} \subseteq p_3$ $\quad$ (s_3-believed possibility $^{\top}\underline{w_3}$)

• • $\quad$ $\langle[^1\underline{ee}_2]w_3, [^f\underline{ee}_2]w_3\rangle = \langle{}^1[h^{\varepsilon\varepsilon}{}_1w_3t_{1.2}], {}^f[h^{\varepsilon\varepsilon}{}_1w_3t_{1.2}]\rangle$

— $\quad$ $\underline{s_3}w_3$ = RES$_{w3}$ $[^1\underline{ee}_2]w_3$

• $\quad$ $\underline{e_3}w_3 = [^f\underline{ee}_2]w_3$: s_3-exp. wins $\underline{ee}_2$

The following online updates for (16*a*) and (16*b*) implement these ideas. The proposed adaptations are explicated in footnotes.
~~~~~~

(16′) Once when he$_{\top}$ was playing...

once[10]

$[\mathbf{t}\ \underline{ee}|\ \underline{ee} = d\eta^{\varepsilon\varepsilon}\{\mathbf{t}\}];$

play.chess-[11]

$[|\ d\underline{\varepsilon\varepsilon}\text{: (AGT} + d\kappa^{a})\textit{play.chess}];$

-FCT$_{\top}$[12]

$[|^{1}d\underline{\varepsilon\varepsilon} <_{\mathbf{d}\omega} \mathbf{d}\varepsilon,\ \text{AGT}\ d\underline{\varepsilon\varepsilon} = \mathbf{d}\alpha];$

$[|^{1}d\underline{\varepsilon\varepsilon} \subseteq_{\mathbf{d}\omega} \mathbf{d}\tau];\ [\mathbf{t}|\mathbf{t} =_{\mathbf{d}\omega} \vartheta\text{RES}\ ^{1}d\underline{\varepsilon\varepsilon}];$

-3s$_{\top}$

$[|3s_{\mathbf{d}\omega,\mathbf{d}\varepsilon}\ \mathbf{d}\alpha];$

(*a*) ...he$_{\top}$ began to think: "I might win."

belief.of- (*isuma-*) -have (*-qar*)[13]

$[k^{\Omega}{}_{a}|k^{\Omega}{}_{a}\ \textit{belief.of}\ \alpha];\ [s\,p|\,p =_{\mathbf{d}\omega} d\alpha\kappa^{\Omega}\{\text{EXP}, s\}];$

-begin

$[e|\ (e =_{\mathbf{d}\omega} \text{BEG}\ d\sigma),\ (\text{EXP}\ e =_{\mathbf{d}\omega} \text{EXP}\ d\sigma)];$

-IND. .IV -3s

$[|d\varepsilon <_{\mathbf{d}\omega} \mathbf{d}\varepsilon];\ [|\ d\varepsilon \subseteq_{\mathbf{d}\omega} \mathbf{d}\tau];\ [|\ \text{EXP}\ d\varepsilon =_{\mathbf{d}\omega} \mathbf{d}\alpha];\ [|3s_{\mathbf{d}\omega,\mathbf{d}\varepsilon}\ \mathbf{d}\alpha]$

"(quote start-up)

$[\mathbf{p}|\ \mathbf{p} = d\Omega];\ [\mathbf{s}|\ \mathbf{s} = d\sigma];\ [\mathbf{t}|\ \mathbf{t} =_{\mathbf{d}\omega} \vartheta\text{BEG}\ \mathbf{d}\sigma];$

---

10 $\underline{ee}$ is the chain of concepts of the stages of the $d\eta^{\varepsilon\varepsilon}$-process that begins at t

- $\underline{ee} = d\eta^{\varepsilon\varepsilon}\{\mathbf{t}\}$ for $\lambda i.\ \exists W, n(W = \{w \in \text{Dom}\ d\eta^{\varepsilon\varepsilon}{}_{i}: \mathbf{t} \in \text{Dom}\ d\eta^{\varepsilon\varepsilon}{}_{i}w\}$ $\wedge \forall w \in W(^{n}d\eta^{\varepsilon\varepsilon}{}_{i}w\mathbf{t} = {}^{f}d\eta^{\varepsilon\varepsilon}{}_{i}w\mathbf{t} = {}^{f}\underline{ee}w)$ $\wedge \forall m \leq n(^{m}\underline{ee} = \langle^{m}(d\eta^{\varepsilon\varepsilon}{}_{i}w\mathbf{t}): w \in W\rangle))$

11 $\underline{ee}$ is a process-chain of (contingent and causally linked) stage-concepts

- *process* $\underline{ee}$ for $\forall \underline{e} \in \text{Dom}\ \underline{ee}: (\emptyset \subset \text{Dom}\ \underline{ee}(\underline{e}) \subseteq \text{Dom}\ \underline{e}$ $\wedge \forall w \in \text{Dom}\ \underline{ee}(\underline{e}): \vartheta_{w}\ \underline{ee}(\underline{e})w \subseteq \vartheta_{w}\text{RES}_{w}\ \underline{e}w)$

  $\underline{ee}$ is a process s.t. at each stage the current agent and $d\kappa^{a}$-partner play chess

- $\underline{ee}$: (AGT + $d\kappa^{a}$) *play chess* for $\lambda i.\ \textit{process}\ \underline{ee} \wedge (\forall \underline{e} \in \underline{ee}\forall w \in \text{Dom}\ \underline{e}:$ $\textit{play.chess}_{w}(\underline{e}w, \text{AGT}_{w}\ \underline{e}w + d\kappa^{a}{}_{i}w\underline{e}w))$

12 In $\mathbf{d}\omega$, $d\underline{\varepsilon\varepsilon}$ is real from the perspective of $\mathbf{d}\varepsilon$ (i.e. stage one is real)

- $^{1}d\underline{\varepsilon\varepsilon} <_{\mathbf{d}\omega} \mathbf{d}\varepsilon$ for $\lambda i.\ \vartheta_{\mathbf{d}\omega i}{}^{1}[d\underline{\varepsilon\varepsilon}_{i}]\mathbf{d}\omega_{i} < \vartheta_{\mathbf{d}\omega i}\ \mathbf{d}\varepsilon_{i}$

Any realization of any stage of $d\underline{\varepsilon\varepsilon}$ is an action by $\mathbf{d}\alpha$

- AGT $d\underline{\varepsilon\varepsilon} = \mathbf{d}\alpha$ for $\lambda i.\ \forall \underline{e} \in d\underline{\varepsilon\varepsilon}_{i}\forall w \in \text{Dom}\ \underline{e}: \text{AGT}_{w}\ \underline{e}w = \mathbf{d}\alpha_{i}$

13 $\forall a \in \text{Dom}\ k^{\Omega}{}_{a}$, any instance of $k^{\Omega}{}_{a}a$ is a current belief of a

- $k^{\Omega}{}_{a}$ *belief.of* a for $\lambda i.\forall a \in \text{Dom}\ k^{\Omega}{}_{a}\forall w \in \text{Dom}\ k^{\Omega}{}_{a}a\forall e^{\bullet} \in \text{Dom}\ k^{\Omega}{}_{a}aw\exists s:$ $(s = e^{\bullet} \vee e^{\bullet} = \text{BEG}_{w}s) \wedge \textit{believe}_{w}(s, a, k^{\Omega}{}_{a}awe^{\bullet})$

In $\mathbf{d}\omega$, p instantiates in s the Ω-kind $d\alpha\kappa^{\Omega}$-of-the experiencer of s

- $p =_{\mathbf{d}\omega} d\alpha\kappa^{\Omega}\{\text{EXP}, s\}$ for $\lambda i.\ p = d\alpha\kappa^{\Omega}{}_{i}(\text{EXP}_{\mathbf{d}\omega i}s)\mathbf{d}\omega_{i}s$

maybe[14]
$[\underline{e}|\ can\{^f d\underline{\varepsilon\varepsilon}, \underline{e}\}]$; $[\underline{\mathbf{w}}|\ (poss\ \underline{\mathbf{w}}), (d\underline{\varepsilon} =_{\underline{\mathbf{w}}} {}^f d\underline{\varepsilon\varepsilon})]$;

win-[15]
$[|d\underline{\varepsilon}$: AGT $win\ d\underline{\varepsilon\varepsilon}]$;

-prospect[16]
$[|\ \mathbf{d}\Omega = \text{Dom}\ \mathbf{d}\underline{\omega}]$;
$[\underline{s}|\ (\underline{s} =_{\mathbf{d}\Omega} \text{RES}\ {}^1 d\underline{\varepsilon\varepsilon}), (d\underline{\varepsilon} \subseteq_{\mathbf{d}\underline{\omega}} \vartheta\underline{s}), (\text{AGT}\ d\underline{\varepsilon} =_{\mathbf{d}\underline{\omega}} \text{EXP}\ \underline{s})]$;

-IND. .IV
$[|\ \text{BEG}\ d\underline{\sigma} <_{\mathbf{d}\Omega} \mathbf{d}\sigma]$; $[|\ \mathbf{d}\mathcal{T} \subseteq_{\mathbf{d}\Omega} d\underline{\sigma}]$; $[|\ \text{EXP}\ d\underline{\sigma} =_{\mathbf{d}\Omega} \mathbf{d}\alpha]$;

-1s[17] " (unquote)
$[|1s_{\mathbf{d}\Omega, d\sigma}\ \mathbf{d}\alpha]$; $[\mathbf{w}|\ \mathbf{w} = \mathbf{d}\omega]$; $[\mathbf{e}|\ \mathbf{e} = \mathbf{d}\varepsilon]$;

(*b*) ...he$_{\top}$ began to think that he (= *se*) might win.
maybe
$[\underline{e}|\ can\{^f d\underline{\varepsilon\varepsilon}, \underline{e}\}]$; $[\underline{\mathbf{w}}|\ (poss\ \underline{\mathbf{w}}), (d\underline{\varepsilon} =_{\underline{\mathbf{w}}} {}^f d\underline{\varepsilon\varepsilon})]$;

win-
$[|d\underline{\varepsilon}$: AGT $win\ d\underline{\varepsilon\varepsilon}]$;

-prospect
$[p|p = \text{Dom}\ \mathbf{d}\underline{\omega}]$;
$[\underline{s}|\ (\underline{s} =_{\mathbf{d}\Omega} \text{RES}\ {}^1 d\underline{\varepsilon\varepsilon}), (d\underline{\varepsilon} \subseteq_{\mathbf{d}\underline{\omega}} \vartheta\underline{s}), (\text{AGT}\ d\underline{\varepsilon} =_{\mathbf{d}\underline{\omega}} \text{EXP}\ \underline{s})]$;

-believe (-*suri*)
$[s|\ (s\text{: EXP}\ believe_{\mathbf{d}\omega}\ d\Omega), (\vartheta s \subseteq_{d\Omega} d\underline{\sigma}), (\text{EXP}\ s =_{d\Omega} \text{EXP}\ d\underline{\sigma})]$;

-begin
$[e|\ (e =_{\mathbf{d}\omega} \text{BEG}\ d\sigma), (\text{EXP}\ e =_{\mathbf{d}\omega} \text{EXP}\ d\sigma)]$;

14 The end of $d\underline{\varepsilon\varepsilon}$ can be realized as $\underline{e}$

- $can\{^f d\underline{\varepsilon\varepsilon}, \underline{e}\}$ for $\lambda i.(\forall w \in \text{Dom}\ \underline{e}: \underline{e}w = {}^f d\underline{\varepsilon\varepsilon}_i w) \wedge some(\text{Dom}\ {}^f d\underline{\varepsilon\varepsilon}_i, \text{Dom}\ \underline{e})$
  Ran $\underline{\mathbf{w}}$ is a possibility within Dom $\underline{\mathbf{w}}$
- $poss\ \underline{\mathbf{w}}$ for $\lambda i.\ \emptyset \subset \text{Ran}\ \underline{\mathbf{w}} \subseteq \text{Dom}\ \underline{\mathbf{w}}$
  In Ran $\mathbf{d}\underline{\omega}$, $d\underline{\varepsilon}$ is the end of $d\underline{\varepsilon\varepsilon}$
- $d\underline{\varepsilon} =_{\underline{\mathbf{w}}} {}^f d\underline{\varepsilon\varepsilon}$ for $\lambda i.\ \forall w \in \text{Dom}\ \underline{\mathbf{w}} \exists w'\text{: } w' = \underline{\mathbf{w}}w \wedge d\underline{\varepsilon}_i w' = {}^f d\underline{\varepsilon\varepsilon}_i w'$

15 Any $d\underline{\varepsilon}$-event is the end of $d\underline{\varepsilon\varepsilon}$-(competition) and victory for $d\underline{\varepsilon}$-agent

- $d\underline{\varepsilon}$: AGT $win\ d\underline{\varepsilon\varepsilon}$ for $\lambda i.\ \forall w \in \text{Dom}\ d\underline{\varepsilon}_i \exists ee\text{: } (ee = \langle [^1 d\underline{\varepsilon\varepsilon}_i]w, \ldots [^f d\underline{\varepsilon\varepsilon}_i]w \rangle \wedge d\underline{\varepsilon}_i w = {}^f ee \wedge win_w(d\underline{\varepsilon}_i w, \text{AGT}_w d\underline{\varepsilon}_i w, ee))$

16 In $\mathbf{d}\Omega$, $\underline{s}$ is the result state of stage one of $d\underline{\varepsilon\varepsilon}$

- $\underline{s} =_{\mathbf{d}\Omega} \text{RES}\ {}^1 d\underline{\varepsilon\varepsilon}$ for $\lambda i.\ \forall w \in \mathbf{d}\Omega_i\text{: } \underline{s}w = {}^1 d\underline{\varepsilon\varepsilon}_i w$
  In Ran $\mathbf{d}\underline{\omega}$, $d\underline{\varepsilon}$ is realized during $\underline{s}$
- $d\underline{\varepsilon} \subseteq_{\mathbf{d}\underline{\omega}} \vartheta\underline{s}$ for $\lambda i.\ \forall w \in \text{Dom}\ \mathbf{d}\underline{\omega}_i \exists w'\text{: } w' = \mathbf{d}\underline{\omega}_i w \wedge \vartheta_{w'}\ d\underline{\varepsilon}_i w' \subseteq \vartheta_{w'}\ \underline{s}w'$

17 In $\mathbf{d}\Omega$, $\mathbf{d}\alpha$ is the experiencer of $\mathbf{d}\sigma$

- $1s_{\mathbf{d}\Omega, \mathbf{d}\sigma}\ \mathbf{d}\alpha$ for $\lambda i.\ \forall w \in \text{Dom}\ \mathbf{d}\Omega_i\text{: EXP}_w\ \mathbf{d}\sigma_i = \mathbf{d}\alpha_i$

-IND -IV -3S

$$[|d\varepsilon <_{\mathbf{d}\omega} \mathbf{d}\varepsilon]; [|\ d\varepsilon \subseteq_{\mathbf{d}\omega} \mathbf{d}\tau]; [|\ \text{EXP}\ d\varepsilon =_{\mathbf{d}\omega} \mathbf{d}\alpha]; [|\ 3s_{\mathbf{d}\omega,\mathbf{d}\varepsilon}\ \mathbf{d}\alpha]$$

As promised, the online updates in (16′*a*) and (16′*b*), for modally quantified *de se* belief, converge on the above model and are point for point parallel to the online updates in (15′*a*) and (15′*b*), respectively, for temporally quantified *de se* speech.

The analyses in (15′*a*, 15′*b*) and (16′*a*, 16′*b*) explicate the parallel between temporal and modal quantification in a new way. Traditionally, temporal and modal quantifiers have been analyzed as first-order operators that bind variables for times or worlds, respectively, in verb meanings that are also used for simple predication. Unfortunately, this simple and elegant first-order semantics is not transparently related to surface forms such as (15*a*, 15*b*) or (16*a*, 16*b*). Therefore, the interpretation of such sentences cannot proceed without transformations that are neither simple nor elegant. Indeed, even for English, there is still no formally explicit theory that would build all and only the requisite LFs.

In contrast, the direct online updates in (15′*a*, 15′*b*) and (16′*a*, 16′*b*) draw the semantic parallel directly, interpreting each surface form as is. On this neo-Fregean view, natural language quantifiers are higher-order predicates. They do not combine with ordinary verb meanings used for simple predication (A5). Instead, they presuppose adapted meanings that are distributed over a suitable domain (temporal in (15′), modal in (16′)). They presuppose distributed meanings because they restrict the domain of such distribution to a topical subdomain.

The analysis of the modal in (16′*a*, 16′*b*) can also be related to the ordering semantics developed, with varying details, by Stalnaker (1968), Lewis (1973), and Kratzer (1981). The common idea is that modals quantify over a subset of the "contextually salient" set of worlds (Kratzer's *modal base*)—to wit, the worlds ranked highest by the "contextually salient" order (Kratzer's *ordering source*). In (16*a*, 16*b*) the modal base is the set of worlds the experiencer currently believes he inhabits. The ordering source ranks these worlds according to what the experiencer believes to be the most likely future developments. A key problem, which remains unsolved (even in the dynamic implementation of Stone 1997), is just how the context determines the modal base and the ordering source. Online update in (16′*a*, 16′*b*) offers a surface-based solution, composing lexical meanings by prominence-guided anaphora.

More precisely, the predicate "believe" (*isuma-qar-* or *-suri*) evokes a belief state (in the above model, the belief state s_3, newly formed at ${}^{\top}t_{2.2}$). The experiencer of this state of *de se* belief is a habitual chess player (agent of $h^{\varepsilon\varepsilon}{}_1$). He has just completed the first stage of the current chess game ($[{}^1\underline{ee}_2]w_o$), so he locates himself in a set of worlds where this is the case (p_3). This set of worlds is the modal base for the modal *immaqa* "maybe". The modal quantifies only over the worlds with the most likely future developments—that is those worlds where the final stage (${}^f\underline{ee}_2$) of the current chess game accords with the aforementioned chess playing experience ($h^{\varepsilon\varepsilon}{}_1$). What the modal "maybe" asserts—and this is the content of this *de se* belief—is that these most likely futures include some (Ran ${}^\top\underline{w}_3$) where the anticipated final stage (${}^f\underline{ee}_2$) of this game is realized as a victory ($\underline{e}_3$) by the believer.

Compositionally, in (16′*a*, 16′*b*) the key dref for the current chess game ($\underline{ee}$) is set up by the very first word: *ilaanni* "once". This dref is not new. It is induced by the currently prominent chess playing habit ($d\eta^{\varepsilon\varepsilon}$), evoked in the last sentence (14′), and a topic time (**t**) selected from the temporal domain of this chess playing habit by *ilaanni* "once" itself. The subsequent factive verb, *skakkirami* "when he$_\top$ played", is a verbal definite. It tests that the induced dref ($d\underline{\varepsilon\varepsilon}$) is a game with a completed first stage (${}^1d\underline{\varepsilon\varepsilon}$) and updates the topic time to the result time of this stage. (Accordingly, *skakkirami* can be omitted without materially changing the meaning of (16′*a*, 16′*b*).) The modal *immaqa* "maybe" anaphorically retrieves the expected final stage of the current chess game (${}^f d\underline{\varepsilon\varepsilon}$). Based on this prospect, it evokes a possible realization ($\underline{e}$), along with a topical concept of a world where this possibility comes to pass ($\underline{\mathbf{w}}$). Both concepts, in turn, are anaphorically linked to the prospective suffix *-ssa*. This modal distributor requires a modally distributed meaning of its verbal base ("win-") and identifies the domain of this distribution by anaphora to salient modal drefs.

Thus, for episodic *de se* reports with temporal or modal quantifiers, online update makes more detailed predictions than previous analyses. The relation to prior discourse and to the surface form is also more transparent. Last but not least, surface-based online update generalizes to habitual *de se* reports, as I now proceed to show.

11.7 Habitual Reports Online

To complete the paradigm, consider the last semantically equivalent pair of discourses, (1)–(4*a*) and (1)–(4*b*). The data are repeated in (17)–(18*a*) and (17)–(18*b*).

(17) *Ataata-ga skakkir-tar-pu-q.*
dad-1s.sg play.chess-habit-IND.IV-3s
My dad$_\top$ plays chess.

(18) Aqagu-*ani*
next.day-3s$_{\perp}$.sg.LOC
The next day...

(*a*) *uqar*-ajut-*tar*-*pu*-*q*: "*Ajugaa-sima-vu-nga.*"
say-*often*-habit-IND.IV-3s: win-prf-IND.IV-1s
...he$_{\top}$ often says: "I won."

(*b*) *ajugaa-sima-nirar*-ajut-*tar*-*pu*-*q*.
win-prf-say-*often*-habit-IND.IV-3s
...he$_{\top}$ often says that he (= *se*) won.

In different speech events that instantiate this reporting habit the uttered sentence—quoted in (18*a*)—is the same. But the proposition expressed is not. Each report is about the outcome of the previous day's game. In addition, both (18*a*) and (18*b*) can mean either: (i) that many days directly after the day of a chess game are reporting days, or (ii) that, for each chess game, there are many reports the next day.

To encapsulate these quantificational patterns, I propose that habitual reports relate report-valued habits to proposition-valued kinds. A verb (e.g. "win-") in the scope of a habitual *de se* report evokes a report-dependent concept (of *se*'s victory reported on that occasion), and may induce other report-dependent concepts (e.g. the result state): habitual *de se* can then be captured by distributing such concepts over the reporting habit. Temporal quantification can also be distributed.

The online updates in (18′*a*, 18′*b*) implement these ideas. I assume that the opening sentence (17) (=(14)) is still interpreted as in (14′), and so again yields the following context for interpreting the next sentence:

i-reality: $^{\top}w_0$	•	$^{\top}e_0$: e_0-agent speaks up
	|	$^{\top}t_0 = \vartheta_{w0}e_0$
... •• •• •• •• ...		Ran $h^{\varepsilon\varepsilon}{}_1 w_0$: e_0-speaker's dad $^{\top}a_1$ plays chess with a $k^{\alpha}{}_1$-partner
... || || || || ...		Ran $k^{\tau}{}_1 w_0$ = Dom $h^{\varepsilon\varepsilon}{}_1 w_0$

(18′) The next day...

next.day- (*aqagu-*) -3s$_{\perp}$.sg.LOC[18]
$[k^{\tau}{}_{\eta}|k^{\tau}{}_{\eta}\mathit{day.after}\ \eta^{\varepsilon}]$; $[\mathbf{k}^{\tau}|\ \mathbf{k}^{\tau} \subseteq_{::} d\eta\kappa^{\tau}\{^{1}d\eta^{\varepsilon\varepsilon}\}]$;

[18] $\forall h^{\varepsilon} \in \mathrm{Dom}\ k^{\tau}{}_{\eta}$, $k^{\tau}{}_{\eta}h^{\varepsilon}$ is the τ-kind instantiated, for each h^{ε}-event, by the next day
• $k^{\tau}{}_{\eta}\ \mathit{day.after}\ \eta^{\varepsilon}$ for $\lambda i.\forall h^{\varepsilon} \in \mathrm{Dom}\ k^{\tau}{}_{\eta}\forall w \in \mathrm{Dom}\ k^{\tau}{}_{\eta}h^{\varepsilon}\forall e \in \mathrm{Dom}\ k^{\tau}{}_{\eta}h^{\varepsilon}w$:
$\mathrm{Dom}\ k^{\tau}{}_{\eta}h^{\varepsilon} = \mathrm{Dom}\ h^{\varepsilon} \wedge \mathrm{Dom}\ k^{\tau}{}_{\eta}h^{\varepsilon}w = \mathrm{Ran}\ h^{\varepsilon}w\ \wedge$
$k^{\tau}{}_{\eta}h^{\varepsilon}we = \mathit{day.after}_w(\mathit{day.of}_w e)$
$\mathbf{k}^{\tau}$-times are subintervals of the corresponding $d\eta\kappa^{\tau}$-of-$^{1}d\eta^{\varepsilon\varepsilon}$ times

(*a*) …he$_T$ often says: "I won."
say- (*uqar-*)[19]
$[h^{\varepsilon}k^{\Omega}|h^{\varepsilon}\text{: AGT } say\ k^{\Omega}]$;

-often (*-gajut*)[20] -habit (*-tar*)
$^1[|\ often\{\mathbf{d}\kappa^{\tau}, d\eta^{\varepsilon}\}]$; $[k^{\tau}|\ \text{Dom}\ d\eta^{\varepsilon} = k^{\tau}]$:
$^2[|\ \mathbf{d}\kappa^{\tau}{::}\ often\{d\kappa^{\Omega}, d\eta^{\varepsilon}\}]$; $[k^{\tau}|\ \text{Dom}\ d\eta^{\varepsilon} = k^{\tau}]$:

-IND. .IV
$^{\text{P}}[|^1 d\eta^{\varepsilon} <_{\mathbf{d}\omega} \mathbf{d}\varepsilon]$; $[|\ \mathbf{d}\tau \subseteq_{\mathbf{d}\omega} d\eta^{\varepsilon}]$; $[|\ \text{AGT } d\eta^{\varepsilon} =_{\mathbf{d}\omega} \mathbf{d}\alpha]$;
-3S
$^{\text{P}}[|3s_{\mathbf{d}\omega,\mathbf{d}\varepsilon}\ \mathbf{d}\alpha]$

"(quoted habitual speech)[21]
$[\mathbf{k}^{\Omega}|\ \mathbf{k}^{\Omega} = d\kappa^{\Omega}]$; $[\mathbf{h}^{\varepsilon}|\ \mathbf{h}^{\varepsilon} = (d\eta^{\varepsilon}|\mathbf{d}\omega)]$; $[\mathbf{k}^{\tau}|\ \mathbf{k}^{\tau} = \vartheta\mathbf{d}\eta^{\varepsilon}]$;

win-[22] -prf[23]
$[\underline{e}_{\varepsilon}|\ \underline{e}_{\varepsilon}\text{: AGT } win\ d\eta^{\varepsilon\varepsilon}]$; $[\underline{s}_{\varepsilon}|\ (\underline{s}_{\varepsilon} = \text{RES } d\varepsilon\underline{\varepsilon}), (\text{EXP } \underline{s}_{\varepsilon} = \text{AGT } d\varepsilon\underline{\varepsilon})]$;

- $\mathbf{k}^{\tau} \subseteq_{::} d\eta\kappa^{\tau}\{^1 d\eta^{\varepsilon\varepsilon}\}$ for $\lambda i.\ \text{Dom}\ \mathbf{k}^{\tau} = \text{Dom}\ d\eta\kappa^{\tau}{}_i{}^1 d\eta^{\varepsilon\varepsilon}{}_i$
  $\wedge\ \forall w \in \text{Dom}\ \mathbf{k}^{\tau}\text{: } (\text{Dom}\ \mathbf{k}^{\tau}w = \text{Dom}\ d\eta\kappa^{\tau}{}_i{}^1 d\eta^{\varepsilon\varepsilon}{}_i w$
  $\wedge\ \forall e^{\bullet} \in \text{Dom}\ \mathbf{k}^{\tau}w\text{: } \mathbf{k}^{\tau}we^{\bullet} \subseteq d\eta\kappa^{\tau}{}_i{}^1 d\eta^{\varepsilon\varepsilon}{}_i we^{\bullet})$

19 Any h^{ε}-event is a speech act whose agent expresses a k^{Ω}-proposition

- $h^{\varepsilon}\text{: AGT } say\ k^{\Omega}$ for $\lambda i.\forall w \in \text{Dom}\ h^{\varepsilon}\forall t \in \text{Dom}\ h^{\varepsilon}w\exists e\text{:}$
  $e = h^{\varepsilon}wt \wedge \vartheta_w e \subseteq t \wedge say_w(e, \text{AGT}_w e, k^{\Omega}we)$

20 $d\eta^{\varepsilon}$-times are $\mathbf{d}\kappa^{\tau}$-times, and $\mathbf{d}\kappa^{\tau}$-times are often $d\eta^{\varepsilon}$-times

- $often\{\mathbf{d}\kappa^{\tau}, d\eta^{\varepsilon}\}$ for $\lambda i.\forall w \in \text{Dom}\ d\eta^{\varepsilon}{}_i\text{: Dom}\ d\eta^{\varepsilon}{}_i w \subseteq \text{Dom}\ \mathbf{d}\kappa^{\tau}{}_i w$
  $\wedge\ often(\text{Ran}\ \mathbf{d}\kappa^{\tau}{}_i w, \text{Dom}\ d\eta^{\varepsilon}{}_i w)$

For any $\mathbf{d}\kappa^{\tau}$-time t, $d\eta^{\varepsilon}$-events in t are $d\kappa^{\Omega}$-events & $d\kappa^{\Omega}$-events in t are often $d\eta^{\varepsilon}$-events

- $\mathbf{d}\kappa^{\tau}{::}\ often\{d\kappa^{\Omega}, d\eta^{\varepsilon}\}$ for $\lambda i.\forall w \in \text{Dom}\ \mathbf{d}\kappa^{\tau}{}_i\forall t \in \text{Ran}\ \mathbf{d}\kappa^{\tau}{}_i\text{:}$
  $\{e \in \text{Ran}\ d\eta^{\varepsilon}{}_i w\text{: } \vartheta_w e \subseteq t\} \subseteq \text{Dom}\ d\kappa^{\Omega}{}_i w$
  $\wedge\ often(\{e \in \text{Dom}\ d\kappa^{\Omega}{}_i w\text{: } \vartheta_w e \subseteq t\}, \text{Ran}\ d\eta^{\varepsilon}{}_i w)$

21 $\mathbf{h}^{\varepsilon}$ is the restriction of $d\eta^{\varepsilon}$ to $\mathbf{d}\omega$; $\mathbf{k}^{\tau}$-times are times of $\mathbf{d}\eta^{\varepsilon}$-events

- $\mathbf{h}^{\varepsilon} = (d\eta^{\varepsilon}|\ \mathbf{d}\omega)$ for $\lambda i.\ \text{Dom}\ \mathbf{h}^{\varepsilon} = \{\mathbf{d}\omega_i\} \wedge \forall w \in \text{Dom}\ \mathbf{h}^{\varepsilon}\text{: } \mathbf{h}^{\varepsilon}w = d\eta^{\varepsilon}{}_i w$
- $\mathbf{k}^{\tau} = \vartheta\mathbf{d}\eta^{\varepsilon}$ for $\lambda i.\ \mathbf{k}^{\tau} = \langle\langle\vartheta_w e\text{: } e \in \text{Ran}\ \mathbf{d}\eta^{\varepsilon}{}_i w\rangle\text{: } w \in \text{Dom}\ \mathbf{d}\eta^{\varepsilon}{}_i\rangle$

22 For any $e \in \text{Dom}\ \underline{e}_{\varepsilon}$, any realization of $\underline{e}_{\varepsilon}e$ is an action of winning a $d\eta^{\varepsilon\varepsilon}$-(game)

- $\underline{e}_{\varepsilon}\text{: AGT } win\ d\eta^{\varepsilon\varepsilon}$ for $\lambda i.\forall e \in \text{Dom}\ \underline{e}_{\varepsilon}\forall w \in \text{Dom}\ \underline{e}_{\varepsilon}e\exists ee \in \text{Ran}\ d\eta^{\varepsilon\varepsilon}{}_i w\text{:}$
  $\underline{e}_{\varepsilon}ew =^f ee \wedge win_w(\underline{e}_{\varepsilon}ew, \text{AGT}_w\ \underline{e}_{\varepsilon}ew, ee)$

23 $\underline{s}_{\varepsilon}$ sends all $e \in \text{Dom}\ d\varepsilon\underline{\varepsilon}$ to the concept of the result state of $d\varepsilon\underline{\varepsilon}$-of-$e$

- $\underline{s}_{\varepsilon} = \text{RES } d\varepsilon\underline{\varepsilon}$ for $\lambda i.\ \underline{s}_{\varepsilon} = \langle\langle\text{RES}_w d\varepsilon\underline{\varepsilon}_i ew\text{: } w \in \text{Dom}\ d\varepsilon\underline{\varepsilon}_i e\rangle\text{: } e \in \text{Dom}\ d\varepsilon\underline{\varepsilon}_i\rangle$

-IND [24]
$^{P}[\,|\; \mathbf{d}\eta^{\varepsilon} :: \text{BEG}\; d\varepsilon\underline{\sigma} <_{\mathbf{d}\kappa\Omega} \varepsilon];\; [\,|\; \mathbf{d}\eta^{\varepsilon} :: \mathbf{d}\kappa^{\tau} \subseteq_{\mathbf{d}\kappa\Omega} d\varepsilon\underline{\sigma}];$

.IV -1S "(as in (16′*a*))
$[\,|\; \mathbf{d}\eta^{\varepsilon} :: \text{EXP}\; d\varepsilon\underline{\sigma} =_{\mathbf{d}\kappa\Omega} \mathbf{d}\alpha];\; [\,|\; \mathbf{d}\eta^{\varepsilon} :: 1s_{\mathbf{d}\kappa\Omega,\varepsilon}\; \mathbf{d}\alpha];\; [\mathbf{w}|\ldots];\; [\mathbf{e}|\ldots]$

(*b*) ...he$_{\top}$ often says that he (= *se*) won.

win- -prf
$[\underline{e}_{\varepsilon}|\; \underline{e}_{\varepsilon}\text{: AGT } win\; d\eta^{\varepsilon\varepsilon}];\; [\underline{s}_{\varepsilon}|\; (\underline{s}_{\varepsilon} = \text{RES}\; d\varepsilon\underline{\varepsilon}),\; (\text{EXP}\; \underline{s}_{\varepsilon} = \text{AGT}\; d\varepsilon\underline{\varepsilon})];$

-say (-*nirar*)
$[h^{\varepsilon}k^{\Omega}|\; (h^{\varepsilon}\text{: AGT } say\; k^{\Omega}),\; (h^{\varepsilon} :: \vartheta\varepsilon \subseteq_{k\Omega} d\varepsilon\underline{\sigma}),$
$(h^{\varepsilon} :: \text{AGT}\; \varepsilon \subseteq_{k\Omega} \text{EXP}\; d\varepsilon\underline{\sigma})];$

-often (-*gajut*) -habit (-*tar*)
$^{1}[\,|\; often\{\mathbf{d}\kappa^{\tau}, d\eta^{\varepsilon}\}];\quad [k^{\tau}|\; \text{Dom}\; d\eta^{\varepsilon} = k^{\tau}]:$
$^{2}[\,|\; \mathbf{d}\kappa^{\tau} :: often\{d\kappa^{\Omega}, d\eta^{\varepsilon}\}];\; [k^{\tau}|\; \text{Dom}\; d\eta^{\varepsilon} = k^{\tau}]:$

-IND. .IV
$^{P}[\,|^{1}d\eta^{\varepsilon} <_{\mathbf{d}\omega} \mathbf{d}\varepsilon];\; [\,|\; \mathbf{d}\tau \subseteq_{\mathbf{d}\omega} d\eta^{\varepsilon}];\; [\,|\; \text{AGT}\; d\eta^{\varepsilon} =_{\mathbf{d}\omega} \mathbf{d}\alpha];$

-3S
$^{P}[\,|3s_{\mathbf{d}\omega,\mathbf{d}\varepsilon}\; \mathbf{d}\alpha]$

The reader can verify that the online updates in (18′*a*) and (18′*b*) converge on the same model but differ in centering. That is, yet again, direct online update accounts for the semantic convergence of radically different surface forms. In this case, the convergence extends to the apparent scope interaction between the initial temporal description *aqagu-a-ni* "next.day-3s$_{\perp}$.sg-LOC" and the suffixal temporal quantifier *-gajut* "often". But according to the surface-based analysis in (18′*a*, 18′*b*), what is ambiguous is not structure, but an anaphoric presupposition.

The suffix "often" presupposes a salient domain of quantification. On one reading (^{1}), this domain is identified with the set of days after a chess game, evoked by "next.day-3s$_{\perp}$.sg-LOC". In effect, the suffix "often" takes wide scope: many days after a chess game are reporting days. More precisely, though, "next.day-3s$_{\perp}$.sg-LOC" evokes not just a set of days but a kind of day ($\mathbf{k}^{\tau}$): in each chess playing world, each game is mapped to the next day. This kind-level

24 For any $\mathbf{d}\eta^{\varepsilon}$-event *e*, in $\mathbf{d}\kappa^{\Omega}$-of-*e* the state $d\varepsilon\underline{\sigma}$-of-*e* is real from perspective of *e*

- $\mathbf{d}\eta^{\varepsilon} :: \text{BEG}\; d\varepsilon\underline{\sigma} <_{\mathbf{d}\kappa\Omega} \varepsilon$ for $\lambda i.\forall w \in \text{Dom}\; \mathbf{d}\eta^{\varepsilon}{}_{i} \forall e \in \text{Ran}\; \mathbf{d}\eta^{\varepsilon}{}_{i} \forall w' \in \mathbf{d}\kappa^{\Omega}{}_{i}\, we\text{:}$ $\vartheta_{w'}\, \text{BEG}_{w'}\, d\varepsilon\underline{\sigma}_{i}\, ew' < \vartheta_{w'} e$

For any $\mathbf{d}\eta^{\varepsilon}$-event *e*, in $\mathbf{d}\kappa^{\Omega}$-of-*e* the state $d\varepsilon\underline{\sigma}$-of-*e* holds at $\mathbf{d}\kappa^{\tau}$-of-*e*

- $\mathbf{d}\eta^{\varepsilon} :: \mathbf{d}\kappa^{\tau} \subseteq_{\mathbf{d}\kappa\Omega} d\varepsilon\underline{\sigma}$ for $\lambda i.\forall w \in \text{Dom}\; \mathbf{d}\eta^{\varepsilon}{}_{i} \forall e \in \text{Ran}\; \mathbf{d}\eta^{\varepsilon}{}_{i} \forall w' \in \mathbf{d}\kappa^{\Omega}{}_{i}\, we\text{:}$ $\mathbf{d}\kappa^{\tau}{}_{i}\, w' e \subseteq \vartheta_{w'}\, d\varepsilon\underline{\sigma}_{i}\, ew'$

referent supports a distributed reading (^{2}), with apparently reversed scope: for each chess game, many ($d\kappa^{\Omega}$-)events the next day are reporting events.

On either reading, each of these habitual reports is about the reporting agent (individual *de se*) at the time of the report (temporal *de se*). On each occasion the agent expresses a report-dependent proposition, claiming to be in the result state of winning one of the aforementioned chess games (anaphorically retrieved from (17′)).

So "scope ambiguities" do not require an LF-based account. Instead, we can attribute them to ambiguous lexical items, such as the suffixal quantifier *-gajut* "often". This lexical alternative maintains direct surface-based interpretation by online update.

The evidence presented so far shows that surface-based online update is a viable alternative to LF-based semantics. I now turn to two examples of compositionality puzzles where surface-based online anaphora has a clear advantage over variable binding at LF.

11.8 LF-Based Semantics vs. Online Update

One puzzle concerns a general characteristic of polysynthetic verbs, namely, that they can form sentences all by themselves. In particular, the Kalaallisut verbs of (15*b*) and (16*b*) can stand alone, as complete sentences, without any external quantifiers. The quantification is then understood to be universal, as in (19) and (20).

(19) [My father plays chess. Once when he came by we talked about it.]
Ajugaa-sar-*nirar*-*pu*-*q*.
win-*habit*-say-IND.IV-3S
He said that he (*always*) won.

(20) [My father plays chess. Once he started off well.]
Ajugaa-ssa-*suri*-*lir*-*pu*-*q*.
win-*prospect*-believe-begin-IND.IV-3S
He began to think that he *would* win.

The puzzle is how the meanings of such lone verbs relate to the meanings of the same verbs construed with external quantifiers.

If we assume the direct online analysis proposed in (15′*b*) and (16′*b*), then this question has a straightforward answer. The universal temporal or modal quantification characteristic of lone habitual or prospective verbs is the default case of pure distributivity. The domain of the distribution is determined by the antecedent, in prior discourse, of the verb-internal distributor. Thus, in (19) the habitual *-tar* is linked to the aforementioned habit ($d\eta^{\varepsilon\varepsilon}$), and in (20) the prospective *-ssa* is linked to the aforementioned chess game in progress ($d\underline{\varepsilon}\varepsilon$). These discourse-anaphoric readings are spelled out in (19′) and (20′).

(19′) win- -habit (*-tar*)

$[h^{\varepsilon}|h^{\varepsilon}\text{: AGT } win\ d\eta^{\varepsilon\varepsilon}]$; $[|\ \text{Dom}\ d\eta^{\varepsilon} = \vartheta\text{RES}\ {}^{1}d\eta^{\varepsilon\varepsilon}]$;

-say

$[ep|\ (e\text{: AGT } say_{\mathbf{d}\omega}\,p), (\vartheta e \subseteq_{p} d\eta^{\varepsilon}), (\text{AGT } e =_{p} \text{AGT } d\eta^{\varepsilon})]$;

-IND. .IV -3S

${}^{\mathrm{P}}[|d\varepsilon <_{\mathbf{d}\omega} \mathbf{d}\varepsilon]$; $[|d\varepsilon \subseteq_{\mathbf{d}\omega} \mathbf{d}\tau]$; $[|\ \text{AGT } d\varepsilon =_{\mathbf{d}\omega} \mathbf{d}\alpha]$; ${}^{\mathrm{P}}[|3s_{\mathbf{d}\omega,\mathbf{d}\varepsilon}\ \mathbf{d}\alpha]$

(20′) win-

$[\underline{e}|\ \underline{e}\text{: AGT } win\ d\underline{\varepsilon}\varepsilon]$;

-prospect (*-ssa*)

$[p|p\text{= Dom}\ {}^{f}d\underline{\varepsilon}\varepsilon]$;

$[\underline{s}|\ (\underline{s} =_{d\Omega} \text{RES}\ {}^{1}d\underline{\varepsilon}\varepsilon), (d\underline{\varepsilon} \subseteq_{d\Omega} \vartheta\underline{s}), (\text{AGT } d\underline{\varepsilon} =_{d\Omega} \text{EXP } \underline{s})]$;

-believe

$[s|\ (s\text{: EXP } believe_{\mathbf{d}\omega}\ d\Omega), (\vartheta\text{BEG } s \subseteq_{d\Omega} d\underline{\sigma}), (\text{EXP } s =_{d\Omega} \text{EXP } d\underline{\sigma})]$;

-begin

$[e|\ (e =_{\mathbf{d}\omega} \text{BEG } d\sigma), (\text{EXP } e =_{\mathbf{d}\omega} \text{EXP } d\sigma)]$;

-IND .IV -3S

${}^{\mathrm{P}}[|d\varepsilon <_{\mathbf{d}\omega} \mathbf{d}\varepsilon]$; $[|d\varepsilon \subseteq_{\mathbf{d}\omega} \mathbf{d}\tau]$; $[|\ \text{EXP } d\varepsilon =_{\mathbf{d}\omega} \mathbf{d}\alpha]$; ${}^{\mathrm{P}}[|3s_{\mathbf{d}\omega,\mathbf{d}\varepsilon}\ \mathbf{d}\alpha]$

What the optional external quantifier (e.g. "mostly" or "maybe") does is to restrict the domain of the verb-internal distributor by evoking a topical subdomain ($\mathbf{k}^{\tau}$, in (15′*b*) and (21); $\underline{\mathbf{w}}$, in (16′*b*) and (22)). The verb-internal distributor must then be anaphorically linked to this topical subdomain ($\mathbf{d}\kappa^{\tau}$ or $\mathbf{d}\underline{\omega}$). Otherwise, there would be a topic without a comment, which would be infelicitous.

(21) He said that he *mostly* won.

most- (*amirlanir-*) -VIA (*-tigut*)

$[k^{\tau}|\ most\{\vartheta\text{RES}\ {}^{1}d\eta^{\varepsilon\varepsilon}, k^{\tau}\}]$; $[\mathbf{k}^{\tau}|\ \mathbf{k}^{\tau} = d\kappa^{\tau}]$;

win- -habit (*-tar*)

$[h^{\varepsilon}|h^{\varepsilon}\text{: AGT } win\ d\eta^{\varepsilon\varepsilon}]$; $[|\ \text{Dom}\ d\eta^{\varepsilon} = \mathbf{d}\kappa^{\tau}]$;

-say

$[ep|\ (e\text{: AGT } say_{\mathbf{d}\omega}\,p), (\vartheta e \subseteq_{p} d\eta^{\varepsilon}), (\text{AGT } e =_{p} \text{AGT } d\eta^{\varepsilon})]$;

-IND. .IV -3S

$[|d\varepsilon <_{\mathbf{d}\omega} \mathbf{d}\varepsilon]$; $[|\ d\varepsilon \subseteq_{\mathbf{d}\omega} \mathbf{d}\tau]$; $[|\ \text{AGT } d\varepsilon =_{\mathbf{d}\omega} \mathbf{d}\alpha]$; $[|\ 3s_{\mathbf{d}\omega,\mathbf{d}\varepsilon}\ \mathbf{d}\alpha]$;

(22) He began to think that *maybe* he would win.
maybe (*immaqa*)
$[\underline{e}|\ can\{{}^{f}d\underline{\varepsilon\varepsilon}, \underline{e}\}]; [\underline{\mathbf{w}}|\ (poss\ \underline{\mathbf{w}}), (d\underline{\varepsilon} =_{\underline{\mathrm{w}}} {}^{f}d\underline{\varepsilon\varepsilon})];$

win-
$[|d\underline{\varepsilon}{:}\ \mathrm{AGT}\ win\ d\underline{\varepsilon\varepsilon}];$

-prospect (*-ssa*)
$[p|\,p = \mathrm{Dom}\ \mathbf{d}\underline{\omega}];$
$[\underline{s}|\ (\underline{s} =_{d\Omega} \mathrm{RES}\ {}^{1}d\underline{\varepsilon\varepsilon}), (d\underline{\varepsilon} \subseteq_{\mathbf{d}\underline{\omega}} \vartheta\underline{s}), (\mathrm{AGT}\ d\underline{\varepsilon} =_{\mathbf{d}\underline{\omega}} \mathrm{EXP}\ \underline{s})];$

-believe
$[s|\ (s{:}\ \mathrm{EXP}\ believe_{\mathbf{d}\omega} d\Omega), (\vartheta\mathrm{BEG}\ s \subseteq_{d\Omega} d\underline{\sigma}), (\mathrm{EXP}\ s =_{d\Omega} \mathrm{EXP}\ d\underline{\sigma})];$

-begin
$[e|\ (e =_{\mathbf{d}\omega} \mathrm{BEG}\ d\sigma), (\mathrm{EXP}\ e =_{\mathbf{d}\omega} \mathrm{EXP}\ d\sigma)];$

-IND .IV -3S
$[|d\varepsilon <_{\mathbf{d}\omega} \mathbf{d}\varepsilon]; [|\ d\varepsilon \subseteq_{\mathbf{d}\omega} \mathbf{d}\tau]; [|\ \mathrm{EXP}\ d\varepsilon =_{\mathbf{d}\omega} \mathbf{d}\alpha]; [|\ 3s_{\mathbf{d}\omega, \mathbf{d}\varepsilon}\ \mathbf{d}\alpha]$

In contrast, the standard LF theory (Heim 1982) makes a bizarre prediction. If this theory is applied to Kalaallisut, then (19) and (20) both involve a covert, habitual or modal, quantifier plus rebracketing at LF. But then the verb is no longer a constituent at LF and is therefore not assigned any meaning at all. So a Kalaallisut verb is predicted to be meaningful only if it does not contain any suffix, like the habitual *-tar* or prospective *-ssa*, which can be construed with an external quantifier. This is a bizarre result. It is comparable to predicting that an English noun is meaningful only if it does not contain the plural suffix *-s*.

The second puzzle is for a complete theory of semantics and pragmatics. Whatever the division of labor, the complete theory must be able to interpret heavily context-dependent sentences, since everyday talk is full of continuations such as (23):

(23) [(17) My father plays chess. (18b) The next day he often says that he won.]
Siullir-mik uanga tamanna qulara-a-ra.
first-sg.MOD 1S that$_{\Omega}$ doubt-IND.TV-1S.3S
The first time I doubted it.

Intuitively, this continuation is coherent: one has no sense of "something missing", characteristic of presuppositions in need of accommodation. The online update in (23′) is faithful to this intuition:

(23′) first- -MOD
$[e|e =_{\mathbf{d}\omega} {}^{1}d\eta^{\varepsilon}]; [\mathbf{t}|\ \mathbf{t} =_{\mathbf{d}\omega} \vartheta\mathrm{RES}\ e];$

1s   that$_{\Omega}$
$[\mathbf{a}|1s_{\mathbf{d}\omega,\mathbf{d}\varepsilon}\ \mathbf{a}];\ [p|p =_{\mathbf{d}\omega} d\kappa^{\Omega}\{d\varepsilon\}];$
doubt-
$[s|s\text{: EXP } doubt_{\mathbf{d}\omega}\ d\kappa^{\Omega}];$

-IND.   .TV
$[|\ \text{BEG}\ d\sigma <_{\mathbf{d}\omega} \mathbf{d}\varepsilon];\ [|\ \mathbf{d}\tau \subseteq_{\mathbf{d}\omega} d\sigma];\ [|\ \text{EXP}\ d\sigma =_{\mathbf{d}\omega} \mathbf{d}\alpha];$

-1s   .3s
$[|1s_{\mathbf{d}\omega,\mathbf{d}\varepsilon}\ \mathbf{d}\alpha];\ [|\ d\kappa^{\Omega}\{d\sigma\} =_{\mathbf{d}\omega} d\Omega]$

The initial modifier "first-MOD" retrieves the reporting habit ($d\eta^{\varepsilon}$) from (18′*b*). It evokes the first speech event that instantiates this habit, and updates the topic time to the result time. The verb comments on this topic ($\mathbf{d}\tau$), as usual. But in (23′) it also elaborates a background dref: the reported proposition ($d\Omega$). This is introduced by a propositional anaphor, "that$_{\Omega}$", as the proposition that instantiates, in that first reporting event, the aforementioned kind of proposition ($d\kappa^{\Omega}$).

In contrast, even the dynamic theory of Kamp and Reyle (1993) has no drefs to retrieve because it does not encapsulate habitual quantification. To interpret the continuation in (23), this LF-based theory appeals to *subordination*—a structure-building operation that copies LF constituents and may also insert other inaudibilia (Roberts 1989). So far nobody has succeeded in formalizing this operation, but let us suppose for the sake of argument that it could be done. What worries me is the best-case scenario. For instance, if we try to match the predictions of (23′), a subordination account would have to build the LF equivalent of something like:

(LF23) ~~There is a current period *t* such that~~ the first time ~~my father played chess during *t* and claimed the next day to have won~~ I doubted ~~the proposition he expressed when he claimed, for the first time, the day after playing chess during *t*, to have won~~.

So the best-case scenario for subordination is massive redundancy: endlessly rebuilding and recomposing LF constituents.[25] In contrast, direct online update simply retrieves familiar dref objects that are currently most prominent, given their type. So this puzzle too favors direct online update, which offers a cleaner and more intuitive account.

11.9 Conclusion

I have presented a new framework for direct composition: *online update*. The basic idea is that the surface string is interpreted as is, with each morpheme

[25] Some LF theories represent "missing material" as free variables. But since they do not say how these variables get their values, this is hardly a solution.

in turn updating the current state of information and attention. A formal representation language, *Logic of Centering*, with stack-based anaphora, was defined and some general constraints on basic meanings and compositional operations were formulated.

This framework was then used to analyze a series of mini-discourses in Kalaallisut, with increasingly more complex polysynthetic morphology. After some paradigm examples of episodic and habitual discourse, we analyzed three cases of semantic convergence across surface diversity—to wit, a pair of mini-discourses with reported habits, a pair with reported beliefs, and a pair with habitual reports. Each pair illustrated two patterns—morphosyntactically far apart but semantically equivalent—of interacting temporal, modal, and *de se* anaphora. Direct online update naturally accounted for the semantic convergence by positing parallel anaphoric links, within and across sentence boundaries.

In LF-based semantics temporal, modal, and *de se* dependencies are generally analyzed in terms of variable binding. Since variable binding is sentence-bound, it cannot match the present, more general, theory. In direct online update variable binding operations are "encapsulated" in the sense of Stone (1997). That is, they are recast as anaphora to discourse referents for entire patterns. The encapsulation strategy is viable even for highly complex dependencies. In the present analysis temporal quantification was encapsulated by means of discourse referents for habits and kinds of time; modal quantification, by means of discourse referents for analogous modal concepts; and *de se* dependencies in habitual reports, by means of discourse referents for report-dependent modal concepts. Parallel anaphoric links within and across sentence boundaries are then an automatic consequence of encapsulation. Once a discourse referent for a pattern has been introduced, it is available for anaphora. That is, it is possible to talk about that pattern, both later in that sentence and later in the discourse.

Appendix: From NL Lexicon to LC

Class	Kalaallisut	LC (basic meaning listed first)	Text example
<u>n-roots</u>			
α-cn	*angut-*	$[k^{\alpha}\vert\ man\ k^{\alpha}]$	
α-rn	*ataata-*	$[k^{\alpha}{}_{\alpha}\vert k^{\alpha}{}_{\alpha}\ dad.of\ \alpha]$	(11′)
τ-cn	*amirlanir-*	$[k^{\tau}\vert\ most\{\vartheta\text{RES}\ {}^{1}d\eta^{\varepsilon\varepsilon}, k^{\tau}\}]$	(15′*a*, *b*)
τ-rn	*aqagu-*	$[k^{\tau}{}_{\eta}\vert k^{\tau}{}_{\eta}\ day.after\ \eta^{\varepsilon}]$	(18′)
Ω-cn	*uqaluttualia-*	$[k^{\Omega}\vert\ story\ k^{\Omega}]$	
Ω-rn	*isuma-*	$[k^{\Omega}{}_{\alpha}\vert k^{\Omega}{}_{\alpha}\ belief.of\ \alpha]$	(16′*a*)

Class	Kalaallisut	LC (basic meaning listed first)	Text example
<u>v-roots</u>			
σ-iv	*sinig-*	$[s \mid s\!: \textsc{exp}\ asleep_{\mathbf{d}\omega}]$	(11′*a*)
σ-tv	*qulari-*	$[s \mid s\!: \textsc{exp}\ doubt_{\mathbf{d}\omega} d\kappa^{\Omega}]$	(23′)
ε-iv	*uqar-*	$[ep \mid e\!: \textsc{agt}\ say_{\mathbf{d}\omega}\, p]$	(15′*a*)
		$[h^{\varepsilon} k^{\Omega} \mid h^{\varepsilon}\!: \textsc{agt}\ say\ k^{\Omega}]$	(18′a)
	ajugaa-	$[e \mid e\!: \textsc{agt}\ win_{\mathbf{d}\omega} d\varepsilon\varepsilon]$	
		$[\underline{e} \mid \underline{e}\!: \textsc{agt}\ win\ d\underline{\varepsilon\varepsilon}]$	(16′*a*, *b*)
		$[h^{\varepsilon} \mid h^{\varepsilon}\!: \textsc{agt}\ win\ d\eta^{\varepsilon\varepsilon}]$	(15′*a*, *b*)
		$[\underline{e}_{\varepsilon} \mid \underline{e}_{\varepsilon}\!: \textsc{agt}\ win\ d\eta^{\varepsilon\varepsilon}]$	(18′*a*, *b*)
ε-tv	*tillug-*	$[e \mid e\!: \textsc{agt}\ hit_{\mathbf{d}\omega} d\kappa^{\alpha}]$	
εε-iv	*skakkir-*	$[ee\ k^{\alpha} \mid ee\!: (\textsc{agt} + k^{\alpha})\ play.chess_{\mathbf{d}\omega}]$	(12′)
		$[\underline{ee}\ k^{\alpha} \mid \underline{ee}\!: (\textsc{agt} + k^{\alpha})\ play.chess]$	
		$[\mid d\underline{\varepsilon\varepsilon}\!: (\textsc{agt} + d\kappa^{\alpha})\ play.chess]$	(16′)
		$[h^{\varepsilon\varepsilon} k^{\alpha} \mid h^{\varepsilon\varepsilon}\!: (\textsc{agt} + k^{\alpha})\ play.chess]$	(14′)
εε-tv	*uqaluqatigi-*	$[ee\ k^{\alpha} \mid ee\!: \textsc{agt}\ talk.with_{\mathbf{d}\omega} k^{\alpha}]$	(15′)
<u>derivational suffixes</u>			
•	*-qar* (n\v)	$[sp \mid p = {}_{\mathbf{d}\omega} d\alpha\kappa^{\Omega}\{\textsc{exp}, s\}]$	(16′*a*)
.	*-lir* (v\v)	$[e \mid (e = {}_{\mathbf{d}\omega}\ \textsc{beg}\ d\sigma), (\textsc{exp}\ e = {}_{\mathbf{d}\omega}\ \textsc{exp}\ d\sigma)]$	(16′*a*)
<•	*-sima* (v\v)	$[s \mid (s = {}_{\mathbf{d}\omega}\ \textsc{res}\ d\varepsilon), (\textsc{exp}\ s = {}_{\mathbf{d}\omega}\ \textsc{agt}\ d\varepsilon)]$	
		$[\underline{s}_{\varepsilon} \mid (\underline{s}_{\varepsilon} = \textsc{res}\ d\varepsilon\underline{\varepsilon}), (\textsc{exp}\ \underline{s}_{\varepsilon} = \textsc{agt}\ d\varepsilon\underline{\varepsilon})]$	(18′*a*, *b*)
se•	*-suri* (v\v)	$[sp \mid (s\!: \textsc{exp}\ believe_{\mathbf{d}\omega}\, p),$ $(\vartheta s \subseteq_{p} d\underline{\sigma}), (\textsc{exp}\ s =_{p} \textsc{exp}\ d\underline{\sigma})]$	(16′*b*)
	-nirar (v\v)	$[ep \mid (e\!: \textsc{agt}\ say_{\mathbf{d}\omega}\, p),$ $(\vartheta e \subseteq_{p} d\eta^{\varepsilon}), (\textsc{agt}\ e =_{p} \textsc{agt}\ d\eta^{\varepsilon})]$	(15′*b*), (19)
		$[h^{\varepsilon} k^{\Omega} \mid (h^{\varepsilon}\!: \textsc{agt}\ say\ k^{\Omega}),$ $(h^{\varepsilon}\!:: \vartheta\varepsilon \subseteq_{k\Omega} d\varepsilon\underline{\sigma}),$ $(h^{\varepsilon}\!:: \textsc{agt}\ \varepsilon =_{k\Omega} \textsc{exp}\ d\varepsilon\underline{\sigma})]$	(18′*b*)
se>	*-ssa* (v\v)	$[\mid \mathbf{d}\Omega = \text{Dom}\ \mathbf{d}\underline{\omega}]; [\underline{s} \mid \underline{s} =_{\mathbf{d}\Omega} \textsc{res}\ {}^{1}d\underline{\varepsilon\varepsilon}),$ $(d\underline{\varepsilon} \subseteq_{\mathbf{d}\underline{\omega}} \vartheta s), (\textsc{agt}\ d\underline{\varepsilon} =_{\mathbf{d}\underline{\omega}} \textsc{exp}\ \underline{s})]$	(16′*a*)
		$[p \mid p = \text{Dom}\ \mathbf{d}\underline{\omega}]; [\underline{s} \mid \underline{s} =_{\mathbf{d}\Omega} \textsc{res}\ {}^{1}d\underline{\varepsilon\varepsilon}),$ $(d\underline{\varepsilon} \subseteq_{\mathbf{d}\underline{\omega}} \vartheta s), (\textsc{agt}\ d\underline{\varepsilon} =_{\mathbf{d}\underline{\omega}} \textsc{exp}\ \underline{s})]$	(16′*b*)
		$[p \mid p = \text{Dom}\ {}^{f}d\underline{\varepsilon\varepsilon}]; [\underline{s} \mid \underline{s} =_{\mathbf{d}\Omega} \textsc{res}\ {}^{1}d\underline{\varepsilon\varepsilon}),$ $(d\underline{\varepsilon} \subseteq_{\mathbf{d}\Omega} \vartheta s), (\textsc{agt}\ d\underline{\varepsilon} =_{\mathbf{d}\Omega} \textsc{exp}\ \underline{s})]$	(20′)
••	*-tar* (v\v)	$[\mid \text{Dom}\ d\eta^{V} = \mathbf{d}\kappa^{\tau}]$	(12′), (13′)
		$[\mid \text{Dom}\ d\eta^{V} = \vartheta\textsc{res}\ {}^{1}d\eta^{\varepsilon\varepsilon}]$	(19′)
		$[k^{\tau} \mid \text{Dom}\ d\eta^{V} = k^{\tau}]$	(18′*a*, *b*)
	-gajut (v\v)	$[\mid often\{\mathbf{d}\kappa^{\tau}, d\eta^{V}\}]$	(18′*a*, *b*)
		$[\mid \mathbf{d}\kappa^{\tau}\!:: often\{d\kappa^{\Omega}, d\eta^{V}\}]$	(18′*a*, *b*)

Class	Kalaallisut	LC (basic meaning listed first)	Text example
<u>n-inflection</u>			
$\text{CN}^{\top}$	-(ERG)	$[\mathbf{t}\mid \mathbf{t} =_{\mathbf{d}\omega} d\kappa^{\tau}\{\mathbf{d}\varepsilon\}]$	(15′)
	-LOC	$[\mathbf{t}\mid \mathbf{t} \subseteq_{\mathbf{d}\omega} d\kappa^{\tau}\{\mathbf{d}\varepsilon\}]$	(11′)
	-VIA	$[\mathbf{k}^{\tau}\mid \mathbf{k}^{\tau} = d\kappa^{\tau}]$	(12′), (13′)
$\text{RN}^{\top}$	-LOC	$[\mathbf{k}^{\tau}\mid \mathbf{k}^{\tau} \subseteq_{::} d\eta\kappa^{\tau}\{{}^{1}d\eta^{\varepsilon\varepsilon}\}]$	(18′)
$\text{RN}^{\perp}$	-(ERG)	$[a\mid a =_{\mathbf{d}\omega} d\alpha\kappa^{a}\{d\alpha, \mathbf{d}\varepsilon\}]$	(15′)
<u>v-inflection</u>			
main	-IND	$[\mid \text{BEG}\ d\sigma <_{\mathbf{d}\omega} \mathbf{d}\varepsilon]; [\mid \mathbf{d}\tau \subseteq_{\mathbf{d}\omega} d\sigma]$	(11′*a*)
		$[\mid d\varepsilon <_{\mathbf{d}\omega} \mathbf{d}\varepsilon]; [\mid d\varepsilon \subseteq_{\mathbf{d}\omega} \mathbf{d}\tau]$	(11′*b*)
		$[\mid {}^{1}d\varepsilon\varepsilon <_{\mathbf{d}\omega} \mathbf{d}\varepsilon]; [\mid {}^{1}d\varepsilon\varepsilon \subseteq_{\mathbf{d}\omega} \mathbf{d}\tau]$	(11′*c*)
		$[\mid {}^{1}d\eta^{\varepsilon} <_{\mathbf{d}\omega} \mathbf{d}\varepsilon]; [\mid \mathbf{d}\tau \subseteq_{\mathbf{d}\omega} d\eta^{\varepsilon}]$	(12′)
		$[\mid {}^{1}d\eta^{\varepsilon} <_{\mathbf{d}\Omega} \mathbf{d}\varepsilon]; [\mid \mathbf{d}\tau \subseteq_{\mathbf{d}\Omega} d\eta^{\varepsilon}]$	(15′*a*)
		$[\mid \text{BEG}\ d\underline{\sigma} <_{\mathbf{d}\Omega} \mathbf{d}\sigma]; [\mid \mathbf{d}\tau \subseteq_{\mathbf{d}\Omega} d\underline{\sigma}]$	(16′*a*)
		$[\mid \mathbf{d}\eta^{\varepsilon}{::}\ \text{BEG}\ d\varepsilon\underline{\sigma} <_{\mathbf{d}\kappa\Omega} \varepsilon];$	(18′*a*)
		$\quad [\mid \mathbf{d}\eta^{\varepsilon}{::}\ \mathbf{d}\kappa^{\tau} \subseteq_{\mathbf{d}\kappa\Omega} d\varepsilon\underline{\sigma}]$	
	.IV	$[\mid \text{AGT}\ d\varepsilon =_{\mathbf{d}\omega} \mathbf{d}\alpha]$	(15′*a*)
dep	$\text{-FCT}_{\top}$	$[\mid ({}^{1}d\underline{\varepsilon\varepsilon} <_{\mathbf{d}\omega} \mathbf{d}\varepsilon), (\text{AGT}\ d\underline{\varepsilon\varepsilon} = \mathbf{d}\alpha)];$	(16′)
		$\quad [\mid {}^{1}d\underline{\varepsilon\varepsilon} \subseteq_{\mathbf{d}\omega} \mathbf{d}\tau]; [\mathbf{t}\mid \mathbf{t} =_{\mathbf{d}\omega} \vartheta\text{RES}\ {}^{1}d\underline{\varepsilon\varepsilon}];$	
	$\text{-FCT}_{\perp}$	$[\mid ({}^{1}d\varepsilon\varepsilon <_{\mathbf{d}\omega} \mathbf{d}\varepsilon), (\text{AGT}\ d\varepsilon\varepsilon =_{\mathbf{d}\omega} d\alpha)];$	(15′)
		$\quad [\mid {}^{1}d\varepsilon\varepsilon \subseteq_{\mathbf{d}\omega} \mathbf{d}\tau]; [\mathbf{t}\mid \mathbf{t} =_{\mathbf{d}\omega} \vartheta\text{RES}\ {}^{1}d\varepsilon\varepsilon];$	
agr	-1S	$[\mid 1s_{\,\mathbf{d}\omega,\mathbf{d}\varepsilon}\ \mathbf{d}\alpha]$	(11′*b*)
	$\text{-3S}_{\perp}.\text{3S}_{\top}$	$[\mid 3s_{\,\mathbf{d}\omega,\mathbf{d}\varepsilon} d\alpha,\ d\alpha \neq \mathbf{d}\alpha];$	(15′)
		$\quad [\mid 3s_{\,\mathbf{d}\omega,\mathbf{d}\varepsilon}\ \mathbf{d}\alpha,\ \mathbf{d}\alpha =_{\mathbf{d}\omega} d\kappa^{a}\{d\varepsilon\}]$	
<u>particle</u>			
$\Diamond$	*immaqa*	$[\underline{e}\mid can\{{}^{f}d\underline{\varepsilon\varepsilon}, \underline{e}\}]; [\underline{\mathbf{w}}\mid poss\ \underline{\mathbf{w}}, (d\underline{\varepsilon} =_{\underline{\mathrm{w}}} {}^{f}d\underline{\varepsilon\varepsilon})]$	(16′*a*, *b*)

References

BITTNER, M. 1994. *Case, Scope, and Binding*. Dordrecht: Kluwer.

—— 2001. 'Surface composition as bridging', *Journal of Semantics*, 18: 127–77.

—— 2003. 'Word order and incremental update', in *Proceedings from CLS* Chicago: Chicago Linguistic Society. 39–1.

CHIERCHIA, G. 1989. 'Anaphora and attitudes *de se*', in R. Bartsch, J. van Benthem, and P. van Emde Boas (eds), *Semantics and Contextual Expression*. Dordrecht: Foris. 1–31.

DEKKER, P. 1994. 'Predicate logic with anaphora', in *Proceedings from SALT* IV. CLC, Ithaca. 79–95.

GAZDAR, G. 1979. 'A solution to the projection problem', in C. K. (ed.), *Syntax and Semantics* 11. New York: Academic Press. 57–89.

Grosz, B., Joshi, A., and Weinstein, S. 1995. 'Centering: A framework for modeling the local coherence of discourse', *Computational Linguistics*, 21: 203–25.
Heim, I. 1982. The Semantics of Definite and Indefinite Noun Phrases. Ph.D. thesis, University of Massachusetts, Amherst.
—— 1983. 'On the projection problem for presuppositions', in *Proceedings of WCCFL* 2 Stanford University, CA. 114–25.
Kamp, H. and Reyle, U. 1993. *From Discourse to Logic*. Dordrecht: Kluwer.
Kaplan, D. 1978. 'On the logic of demonstratives', *Journal of Philosophical Logic*, 8: 81–98.
Karttunen, L. 1976. 'Discourse referents', in J. McCawley (ed.), *Syntax and Semantics*, 7. New York: Academic Press. 363–85.
Kratzer, A. 1981. 'The notional category of modality', in H. Eikmeyer and H. Rieser(eds), *Words, Worlds, and Contexts*. Berlin: de Gruyter. 38–74.
Lewis, D. 1973. *Counterfactuals*. Oxford: Blackwell.
—— 1975. 'Adverbs of quantification', in E. Keenan (ed.), *Formal Semantics of Natural Language*. Cambridge: Cambridge University Press. 3–15.
—— 1979. 'Attitudes *de dicto* and *de se*', *Philosophical Review*, 88: 513–43.
Muskens, R. 1995. 'Tense and the logic of change', in U. Egli, P. Pause, C. Schwarze, A. von Stechow, and G. Wienold (eds), *Lexical Knowledge in the Organization of Language*. Philadelphia: John Benjamins. 147–84.
Partee, B. 1984. 'Nominal and temporal anaphora', *Linguistics and Philosophy*, 7: 243–86.
Roberts, C. 1989. 'Modal subordination and pronominal anaphora in discourse', *Linguistics and Philosophy*, 12: 683–722.
Sandt, R. van der 1992. 'Presupposition projection as anaphora resolution', *Journal of Semantics*, 9: 333–77.
Sapir, E. 1922. *Language*. New York: Harcourt, Brace.
Schlenker, P. 2003. 'A plea for monsters', *Linguistics and Philosophy*, 26: 29–120.
Stalnaker, R. 1968. 'A theory of conditionals', in N. Rescher (ed.), *Studies in Logical Theory*, No. 2. Oxford: Blackwell. 98–112.
—— 1978. 'Assertion', in P. Cole (ed.), *Syntax and Semantics*, 9: 315–32. New York: Academic Press.
Stone, M. 1997. 'The anaphoric parallel between modality and tense', Technical Report IRCS 97–6. http://www.cs.rutgers.edu/~mdstone
—— and D. Hardt 1999. 'Dynamic discourse referents for tense and modals', in H. Bunt and R. Muskens (eds), *Computing Meaning*, i. Dordrecht: Kluwer. 301–20.
Webber, B. 1988. 'Tense as discourse anaphor', *Computational Linguistics*, 14: 61–73.

12

The Dimensions of Quotation*

CHRISTOPHER POTTS

12.1 Direct Compositionality Beyond the Sentence Level

This paper is geared towards compiling and motivating the objects and principles we need for a semantic analysis of subclausal quotations such as (1), in which the quoted expressions pick out linguistic objects but also have the usual semantics of their quotation-free counterparts (here, *apricot*).

(1) (*a*) When in Santa Cruz, Peter orders "[eɪ]pricots" at the local market.

(*b*) When in Amherst, Peter orders "[æ]pricots" at the local market.

The danger lurking around these examples is that we will derive a meaning that has Peter ordering up linguistic objects. We must avoid this pitfall, but we must also preserve the meaning difference: (1*a*) is true in a different class of situations than (1*b*). It will not do to strip off the quotation marks and gesture at a "metalinguistic" theory to explain why speakers easily find situations in which *Peter orders* "[eɪ]*pricots*" is semantically distinct from *Peter orders* "[æ]*pricots*". The two sentences have clearly contrasting entailments. This is therefore clearly a semantic issue.

My analysis capitalizes on the insight that "[eɪ]*pricots*" and "[æ]*pricots*" (with their quotation marks) have a dual semantics: they are natural language objects as well as properties. The sentences containing them in turn express two distinct propositions. In the case of (1*a*), we have at least the following:

* Maria Bittner's commentary on my presentation at the Brown Workshop on Direct Compositionality led to a complete overhaul of the original version of this chapter. I am indebted to her for the commentary and extensive conversation before and after it. My thanks also to Polly Jacobson for organizing the workshop and, through her work, helping me to see things afresh. For conversation and advice, I am grateful to Judith Aissen, Luis Alonso-Ovalle, Jan Anderssen, Ash Asudeh, Kent Bach, Chris Barker, Kai von Fintel, Lyn Frazier, James Isaacs, Angelika Kratzer, Bill Ladusaw, Helen Majewski, Line Mikkelsen, Barbara Partee, Geoff Pullum, Ken Shan, Peggy Speas, Tom Roeper, and Youri Zabbal.

(2) (*a*) *Regular meaning*: Peter orders apricots at the local market when in Santa Cruz

(*b*) *Speech-report meaning*: Peter utters [eɪ]*pricots* while in Santa Cruz

Two propositions, one sentence (Bach 1999).

But it would be a mistake to launch directly into an analysis of these difficult subclausal quotations. I first address the somewhat simpler class of *clausal quotations*, (3).

(3) (*a*) Lisa said "Maggie shot Burns".

(*b*) Lisa said "Burns was shot by Maggie".

Here again, we must capture the intuition that these examples have different truth conditions. Both examples denote, in part, the proposition that Lisa said Maggie shot Burns. But they differ with regard to what they say about the natural language objects to which Lisa stands in the utterance relation; *Maggie shot Burns* and *Burns was shot by Maggie* are different sentences. They might have the same semantic representations, but Lisa could rightly object if we inferred from the fact that (3*a*) obtained to the fact that (3*b*) obtained also. Our semantics should block this inference.

It sounds at first as though this talk of representations threatens the basic tenets of the directly compositional semantics that Jacobson (1999, 2000) pioneered. But this is not so. The discussion is entirely about model-theoretic objects. The only inaudibilia it countenances are type-shifting functions, which are part of the stock and trade of this approach. So my hope is that this paper will have a liberating effect: adopting a directly compositional semantics does not mean that we must eschew all talk of linguistic representations. Once it is recognized that linguistic objects have the same status as individuals like you and me, nothing stops us from appealing to their properties. See §§12.4 and 12.6 for additional details and examples.

Before beginning the analysis, it is worth briefly mapping out one of the roads that this paper does not take from examples (1) and (3), namely, the road that leads to a reanalysis of opacity in propositional attitude contexts. The paper does provide something like a framework for developing an analysis in which speech reports play a role in determining the truth of old chestnuts like *Jan believes that Mohammed Ali is Cassius Clay* (Davidson 1968). But I do not endorse such quotational theories, and in §12.5 I distinguish propositional attitude *say* from quotation-taking *say* by making only the latter sensitive to utterances. For evidence against quotational theories of propositional attitudes (evidence against extending the present proposal into that domain), I refer to Partee (1973).

12.2 The Utterance Relation

We should not tackle even clausal quotation head-on. It seems best to approach from the point suggested by (4), where we see the utterance relation at work in its most basic form.

(4) (*a*) Lisa: Homer is bald.

(*b*) Lisa entered into the utterance relation with the sentence *Homer is bald*.

(*c*) We were unsure whether Homer still had a few hairs on his head, but Lisa was confident in her assessment of the situation: "Homer is bald".

In (4*a*), the colon indicates who is responsible for uttering the sentence *Homer is bald*. Example (4*b*) is a somewhat ponderous statement with the same content. The colon appears again with an utterance-based semantics in (4*c*), although its contribution is more oblique there.

Most semantic theories are limited in their ability to describe systematically even simple cases of this form. Typically, we capture the notions of utterer and utterance as part of the interpretation procedure. For (4), we could fix Lisa as the speaker index on the interpretation function, either as an element in a context tuple (Kaplan 1989) or as a lone parameter, as in (5).

(5) $[\![\mathbf{bald(homer)}]\!]^{[\text{lisa}]}$

We could regard this speaker index not only as determining the meaning of first-person pronouns but also as an indication that interpretation is relative to Lisa's belief state. On this approach, *say* and *utter* have a much different sort of semantics. Whereas *say* denotes a function in our model, *utter* (and the colons in (4*a*, 4*c*)) has a more abstract, metalogical meaning, one that is wired into the interpretation brackets and our notion of which models count as admissible. The difference is suspicious. One would expect to find the denotations of both *say* and *utter* in the models for the semantic theory. More importantly, the treatment of *utter* is not flexible enough to provide the basis for a theory of quotation. Indeed, we lack the means even to capture the semantics of sentences such as (6).

(6) (*a*) When Lisa said "Burns is dead", Maggie was nowhere to be found.

(*b*) There is a past time **t** such that Lisa uttered the sentence *Burns is dead* at **t** and Maggie was nowhere to be found at **t**.

In order to describe such examples in anything like the above terms, we would need a highly flexible theory of the interpretation function. We would need a way to shift the speaker index in mid-discourse (for quotation), and we would need some way to keep track of the interpretations themselves, so that we could refer back to them later. In short, we would need a logic—that is, a grammar—of the interpretation brackets. In many ways, this is where the present paper heads.

12.3 Natural Language Expressions and Their Names

If we are going to discuss natural language objects, we need a precise view of what such objects are like. This is the question to which all of linguistics is addressed, so I will not try to settle the issue. I simply offer a small grammar which generates triples $\langle \Pi\ ;\ \Sigma\ ;\ \alpha : \sigma \rangle$, in which Π is a phonological representation, Σ is a syntactic representation, and α is a semantic representation of type σ. I call this grammar $\mathcal{G}_1$. It is preliminary; the appendix provides the complete grammar for this paper, which develops from $\mathcal{G}_1$ as the paper proceeds and which has $\mathcal{G}_1$ as a subgrammar.

The grammar $\mathcal{G}_1$ is defined as follows:

i. ⟨ [bɑrt] ; NP ; **bart** : e ⟩
⟨ [lisɑ] ; NP ; **lisa** : e ⟩
⟨ [mægi] ; NP ; **maggie** : e ⟩
⟨ [bərnz] ; NP ; **burns** : e ⟩

ii. ⟨ [wɛrwʊlf] ; $S/_L NP$; **werewolf** : $\langle e, t\rangle$ ⟩
⟨ [dɛd] ; $S/_L NP$; **dead** : $\langle e, t\rangle$ ⟩
⟨ [bɔld] ; $S/_L NP$; **bald** : $\langle e, t\rangle$ ⟩

iii. ⟨ [it] ; $(S/_L NP)/_R NP$; **eat** : $\langle e, \langle e, t\rangle\rangle$ ⟩
⟨ [si] ; $(S/_L NP)/_R NP$; **see** : $\langle e, \langle e, t\rangle\rangle$ ⟩
⟨ [skɛr] ; $(S/_L NP)/_R NP$; **scare** : $\langle e, \langle e, t\rangle\rangle$ ⟩

iv.
$$\begin{array}{c}\left\langle\begin{array}{c}[\Pi\ \Phi]\\ \mathrm{A}\\ (\alpha(\beta)) : \tau\end{array}\right\rangle\\ \left\langle\begin{array}{c}\Pi\\ \mathrm{A}/_{\mathrm{R}}\mathrm{B}\\ \alpha : \langle\sigma,\tau\rangle\end{array}\right\rangle \quad \left\langle\begin{array}{c}\Phi\\ \mathrm{B}\\ \beta : \sigma\end{array}\right\rangle\end{array} \qquad\qquad \begin{array}{c}\left\langle\begin{array}{c}[\Phi\ \Pi]\\ \mathrm{A}\\ (\alpha(\beta)) : \tau\end{array}\right\rangle\\ \left\langle\begin{array}{c}\Phi\\ \mathrm{B}\\ \beta : \sigma\end{array}\right\rangle \quad \left\langle\begin{array}{c}\Pi\\ \mathrm{A}/_{\mathrm{L}}\mathrm{B}\\ \alpha : \langle\sigma,\tau\rangle\end{array}\right\rangle\end{array}$$

v. If $\mathcal{P} = \langle \Pi\ ;\ \Sigma\ ;\ \alpha : \sigma \rangle$ is well-formed, then $\langle \Pi\ ;\ \Sigma\ ;\ \ulcorner\langle \Pi\ ;\ \Sigma\ ;\ \alpha : \sigma\rangle\urcorner : u \rangle$ is well-formed.

Clauses (i)–(iv) generate objects that are typical of the categorial grammar perspective on natural language grammars (Bach and Wheeler 1981; Oehrle *et al.* 1988). Jacobson (1992*b*, 1999, 2000) introduced the helpful subscripted slashes. The rules in (iv) are given as parsetree admissibility conditions. But we could as easily regard them as inference rules in a proof system. I opt for the look of parsetrees because these are familiar to the broadest range of linguists. On this proof-theoretic conception of natural language composition, the proofs might simply verify the well-formedness of the triple decorating the root node of the proof (as in Jacobson's work), or we might elevate them to the status of first-class objects of the theory and state linguistic generalizations in terms of their (normalized) forms (as in Glue semantics; Dalrymple 2001; Asudeh and Crouch 2002; Asudeh 2004*a*). Either view is compatible with the results of this paper, since the root node stores all the presently relevant information about the proof itself.

We can summarize the action of the proof rules as follows:

(7) (*a*) *Phonology*: concatenation (an oversimplification, but my focus is not on the phonology)

(*b*) *Syntax*: directional application

(*c*) *Semantics*: functional application, represented in a lambda calculus like that of Carpenter (1997: §2)

The twist in this grammar is its final clause, (v), which we can regard as a semantic quotation function. It takes any well-formed expression of the grammar and turns it into an object of type *u*, the type of linguistic expressions themselves. The output is itself a well-formed expression, so it too can be quoted. The definition leaves room for the addition of quoted expressions that do not correspond to well-formed phrases: the mock machine-gun barrage of Partee (1973) and the groans and gestures of Postal (2004), for example.

The raised corner brackets are conceptually just a particular typographic implementation of the common practice of distinguishing natural language objects when we wish to talk about them rather than use them. Most publications use italics or quotation marks. In this paper, I use raised corner brackets and, when I am being careful, display much more information about the object than the standard orthography is capable of expressing.

In many respects, the quotation function is like the nominalizing function of Chierchia (1982, 1984) and Chierchia and Turner (1988), which takes functional expressions to their entity-level correlates. Here, we take complex natural language expressions and turn them into entity-level expressions.

The idea is simply this: just as we can talk about entities and propositions and the like, we can also talk about linguistic objects. We can, for instance, say things like (8).

(8) (*a*) The sentence *Bart burped* is annoyingly alliterative.

(*b*) Ali's favorite word is *salmagundi.*

(*c*) [æ]*pricot* begins with a low-front vowel.

(*d*) George W. Bush uttered the sentence *I don't think our troops ought to be used for what's called nation building.*[1]

The final clause of the definition for $\mathcal{G}_1$ provides us with a way to turn the expressions of $\mathcal{G}_1$ into objects that we can talk about using $\mathcal{G}_1$.

In (9), I specify the objects that support the model-theoretic interpretation of the semantic representations for $\mathcal{G}_1$.

(9) (*a*) D_e is the domain of nonlinguistic entities. D_e is the domain of type e.

(*b*) $D_t = \wp(W)$, the power set of the set W of possible worlds. D_t is the domain of type t.

(*c*) D_u is the domain of well-formed linguistic entities. $D_u \cap D_e = \emptyset$. D_u is the domain of type u.

(*d*) For any types σ and τ, $D_{\langle\sigma,\tau\rangle}$ is the set of all functions from D_σ into D_τ. $D_{\langle\sigma,\tau\rangle}$ is the domain of type $\langle\sigma, \tau\rangle$.

I use $[\![\cdot]\!]$ to interpret semantic representations. This function is constrained so that if α is of type σ, then $[\![\alpha]\!] \in D_\sigma$. It works just as one would expect. For instance $[\![\textbf{homer}]\!]$ is the individual Homer, and $[\![\textbf{bald}]\!]$ is the property of baldness. Here is the action of the interpretation function $[\![\cdot]\!]$ on a type-u expression of $\mathcal{L}$:

(10) $[\![\ulcorner\big\langle$[hoʊmər ɪz bɔld] ; S ; $\textbf{bald}(\textbf{homer}) : t\big\rangle\urcorner]\!] =$
$\big\langle$[hoʊmər ɪz bɔld] ; S ; $\textbf{bald}(\textbf{homer}) : t\big\rangle$

In general, $[\![\ulcorner\langle\Pi\ ;\ \Sigma\ ;\ \alpha : \sigma\rangle\urcorner]\!] = \langle\Pi\ ;\ \Sigma\ ;\ \alpha : \sigma\rangle$. The type-$u$ terms are presently quite cumbersome. I thus adopt the abbreviatory convention of giving these terms in the form of the usual orthographic representation of their phonology, with raised corner brackets. For example:

(11) ⌜Homer is bald⌝ abbreviates
⌜$\big\langle$[hoʊmər ɪz bɔld] ; NP ; $\textbf{bald}(\textbf{homer}) : t\big\rangle$⌝

1 From Bush's second debate with Al Gore, Winston-Salem, North Carolina, October 11, 2000.

It seems to me that one can usefully think of ⌜Homer is bald⌝ as the name of the sentence in (10). One might worry, however, that this constitutes a philosophical blunder; Searle (1969) warns against such glosses:

(12) "It is generally claimed by philosophers and logicians that in a case like 2 [= *"Socrates" has eight letters*] the word "Socrates" does not occur at all, rather a completely new word occurs, the proper name of that word. [...] I find this account absurd." (Searle 1969: 74)

This seems to be an injunction against just the sort of interpretation procedure that $\mathcal{G}_1$ provides. The view that Searle recommends in its place is described in (13).

(13) "But how shall we characterize the utterance of the first word in 2? The answer is quite simple: a word is here uttered but not in its normal use. The word itself is *presented* and then talked about, and that it is to be taken as presented rather than used conventionally to refer is indicated by the quotes [...]" (Searle 1969: 74–5)

I believe that we can accept this view without changing the grammar; we can regard ⌜Homer is bald⌝ as the presentation of the sentence in (10). If there are differences between naming and presentation in this area, then the logic is not sensitive to them.

So, to take stock: we have structures that contain entities like you, me, and Homer, as well as linguistic objects like phrases and sentences. Thus, we can form ordered pairs like

$$\left\langle [\![\textbf{lisa}]\!], \langle[\text{hoʊmər ɪz bɔld}]\ ;\ \mathrm{S}\ ;\ \textbf{bald}(\textbf{homer}) : t\rangle\right\rangle.$$

Let's say that the collection of all such pairs at a world w is the utterance relation at w. It will prove useful to have a handle on this two-place relation, so I define a term in (14).

(14) (*a*) **utter** : $\langle u, \langle e, t\rangle\rangle$
(*b*) $[\![\textbf{utter}(\ulcorner \mathrm{S} \urcorner)(\textbf{b})]\!]$ = the set of worlds in which $[\![\textbf{b}]\!]$ utters $[\![\ulcorner \mathrm{S} \urcorner]\!]$

This meaning provides the basis for an analysis of examples such as those in (4). In (15*b*), I offer a semantic parsetree for (4*a*). If we regard **utter** as the translation of the colon in examples like (4*a*), then this structure is appropriate for that example as well.

(15) (*a*) Lisa uttered (the sentence) *Homer is bald.*

(*b*) **utter**($\ulcorner$Homer is bald$\urcorner$)(**lisa**) : t

    lisa : e **utter**($\ulcorner$Homer is bald$\urcorner$) : $\langle e, t \rangle$

        utter : $\langle u, \langle e, t \rangle\rangle$ $\ulcorner$Homer is bald$\urcorner$: u

(*c*) ⟦**utter**($\ulcorner$Homer is bald$\urcorner$)(**lisa**)⟧ =

⟦**utter**⟧(⟨[hoʊmər ɪz bɔld] ; S ; **bald**(**homer**) : t⟩)(⟦**lisa**⟧)

I stress that this is not a variant of the performative verb hypothesis (Ross 1970; Krifka 1999, 2001; Geurts and Maier 2003). The utterance relation is different from, and in a sense more basic than, the usual contribution of a speech-act operator. First, the utterance relation tells us nothing about the communicative intentions of the speaker. Second, the utterance relation is inherently linguistic: it contains only pairs $\langle d, \mathcal{S} \rangle$ where d is an individual and $\mathcal{S}$ is a natural language object. In contrast, as Searle (1969) and others have stressed, illocutionary force is not inherently linguistic. One can assert things in many nonlinguistic ways: by pointing, gesturing, and even by consciously remaining silent (Foer 2002).

12.4 Properties of Linguistic Objects

The presence of the type u and its associated domain D_u greatly increases the descriptive coverage of the usual type theory based in the entity and proposition types; the range of expressions in English for talking about expressions in English (and other languages) is truly enormous. Since we can define properties of linguistic objects (type $\langle u, t \rangle$) and modifiers of such expressions (type $\langle\langle u, t \rangle, \langle u, t \rangle\rangle$), among others, we have the means for talking about the compositional semantics of this realm.

We also have the ability to capture some subtle contrasts. Consider, for instance, the example in (16*b*), and its quotation-free counterpart (16*a*).

(16) (*a*) The answer is yes.

(*b*) The answer is "yes".

These seem to manifest contrasting kinds of copular clause. The first appears to be a predicational copular clause, equivalent to *The answer is affirmative* or something of that nature. In this case, we can assume that the semantics involves predicating **yes**, or **affirmative**, of the subject **the** (**answer**).

The second is of more interest. It appears to be a specificational copular clause, in particular the sort that predicates a property-denoting definite description in pre-copular position of some kind of proper name in post-copular position (Higgins 1973; Mikkelsen 2004). We find many parallels between this example and things like *The winner is Susan*. In the present theory, the parallel is nearly exact. Compare the following derivations, which are modeled on the proposal of Mikkelsen (2002, 2004):

(17) (*a*)

$$\mathbf{yes}(\mathbf{the}(\mathbf{answer})) : t$$

$$\mathbf{the}(\mathbf{answer}) : e \qquad \mathbf{yes} : \langle e, t\rangle$$

(*b*)

$$\mathbf{the}(\mathbf{answer})(\ulcorner \text{yes} \urcorner) : t$$

$$\mathbf{the}(\mathbf{answer}) : \langle u, t\rangle \qquad \ulcorner \text{yes} \urcorner : u$$

In many cases, these do not differ in truth conditions. But they can part company. Suppose, for instance, that we are taking a yes–no test. Suppose the correct answer to question 7 is *yes*. Then we would use (16*b*). In contrast, we use (16*a*) when we wish to answer a question positively. For instance, if someone asks me whether I am called Chris, I would reply with (16*a*). I sense that (16*b*) would actually be false in this situation.

12.5 Clausal Quotation

The above analysis is a useful abstraction, perhaps appropriate for the somewhat artificial examples such as *Lisa uttered the sentence Burns is dead* and the like. It is not, though, a complete semantics for sentences such as (18).

(18) Lisa said "Homer is bald".

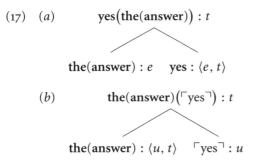

Direct quotation is effective in argumentation and in reporting because it tells us about the relevant individual's words *and* ascribes to him the content of those words. Missing from (15*a*) as a translation of *Lisa said "Homer is bald"* is the fact that a sentence like this also conveys that Lisa said that Homer is bald (no quotation). We require something like (19).

(19) Lisa said "Homer is bald".

(*a*) $[\![\textbf{utter}]\!]\left(\left\langle [\text{hoʊmər ɪz bɔld}]\ ;\ \text{S}\ ;\ \textbf{bald}(\textbf{homer}) : t\right\rangle\right)\left([\![\textbf{lisa}]\!]\right)$

(*b*) the set of worlds in which all of Lisa's utterance worlds w are such that Homer is bald in w

The first is the speech-report contribution. The second gets us to the content: it is what we would give as a semantics for *Lisa says Homer is bald* (no quotation marks). This is the sense in which quotative utterances are multidimensional. Let us call (19*b*) the *attitude dimension* of *Lisa said "Homer is bald"*. This dimension is, as noted, equivalent to the quotation-free counterpart, so we need a semantics for the propositional attitude verb *say*. I provide a standard view of that function in (20) (modeled on the propositional attitude operators of Hintikka 1971).

(20) (*a*) $\textbf{say} : \langle t, \langle e, t\rangle\rangle$

(*b*) $[\![\textbf{say}(\textbf{p})(\textbf{b})]\!]$ = the set of worlds w in which every utterance world w' for $[\![\textbf{b}]\!]$ in w is such that $w' \in [\![\textbf{p}]\!]$

This meaning will have to be, in a sense, embedded in the semantics we provide for the quotation-taking realization of *say*. The first step towards such a meaning is a tool for accessing the semantic representations in the triples that we take to reconstruct linguistic objects. I use *SEM* for this function. It is defined as in (21).

(21) $\mathit{SEM}(\langle \Pi\ ;\ \text{A}\ ;\ \alpha : \sigma\rangle) = \alpha$

So *SEM* takes an interpreted type u expression as its argument to return a semantic representation. This means that we can apply the interpretation function to the output as well. For example:

(22) (*a*) $\mathit{SEM}([\![\ulcorner\text{Homer is bald}\urcorner]\!]) = \textbf{bald}(\textbf{homer})$

(*b*) $[\![\textbf{bald}(\textbf{homer})]\!]$ = the set of worlds in which Homer is bald

(*c*) $\left[\!\!\left[\mathit{SEM}([\![\ulcorner\text{Homer is bald}\urcorner]\!])\right]\!\!\right]$ = the set of worlds in which Homer is bald

We now have the tools needed for specifying the meaning of the quotation-taking meaning for *say* that is employed in (18). I translate this *say* as $\textbf{say}_q$, to distinguish it from the propositional attitude operator **say** defined in (20).

(23) (*a*) $\textbf{say}_q : \langle u, \langle e, t{\times}t\rangle\rangle$

(*b*) $$[\![\textbf{say}_q(\ulcorner S \urcorner)(\textbf{b})]\!] = \left\langle \begin{array}{c} [\![\textbf{utter}(\ulcorner S \urcorner)(\textbf{b})]\!] \\ , \\ [\![\textbf{say}]\!]\big([\![\mathit{SEM}([\![\ulcorner S \urcorner]\!])]\!]\big)\big([\![\textbf{b}]\!]\big) \end{array} \right\rangle$$

The type $t{\times}t$ that is the output of $\textbf{say}_q$ is an addition to the type system presented in (9). It is a *product type*. The type constructor for product types is $\times$; their syntax and domains are as follows:

(24) (*a*) If σ and τ are types, then $\sigma{\times}\tau$ is a type.

(*b*) The domain of $\sigma{\times}\tau$ is $D_{\sigma\times\tau} = D_\sigma \times D_\tau$, the Cartesian product of D_σ and D_τ.

I often represent terms with product types by placing a centered dot between the two terms. That is, $\alpha \cdot \beta$ is a well-formed semantic representation of type $\sigma{\times}\tau$ if α is a well-formed expression of type σ and β is a well-formed expression of type τ.

It should be noted that (23) must represent only one of a handful of realizations of *say* when it takes a quotative complement. In examples like (25), the second dimension of meaning would be undefined if we used the meaning in (23).

(25) (*a*) Lisa said "Is Homer bald?".

(*b*) Lisa said "Read this book!".

The difficulty is that $\mathit{SEM}([\![\ulcorner \text{Is Homer bald} \urcorner]\!])$ is a representation that denotes a question meaning, not a proposition. Similarly, $\mathit{SEM}([\![\ulcorner \text{Read this book} \urcorner]\!])$ is a command, not a proposition, and hence cannot be the argument to the propositional attitude operator **say**. Thus, we must tolerate a degree of ambiguity: the operator in the second dimension of $\textbf{say}_q$ can be **ask**, **command**, and so forth, depending on the nature of the semantic representation in the quotative complement. I see no way to avoid this ambiguity; imperative denotations differ from declarative denotations, and this difference has to be retained, at some level, by their indirect quotative realizations. (My thanks to Chris Barker for bringing this issue to my attention.)

In (26), I provide the parsetree for (18), along with the interpretation of its root node in (26*c*).

(26) (*a*) Lisa said "Homer is bald".

(*b*) $\mathbf{say}_q(\ulcorner\text{Homer is bald}\urcorner)(\mathbf{lisa}) : t \times t$

$\mathbf{lisa} : e$ $\quad$ $\mathbf{say}_q(\ulcorner\text{Homer is bald}\urcorner) : \langle e, t \times t\rangle$

$\mathbf{say}_q : \langle u, \langle e, t \times t\rangle\rangle$ $\quad$ $\ulcorner\text{Homer is bald}\urcorner$

(*c*) $$\left\langle \begin{array}{c} [\![\mathbf{utter}]\!]\Big([\![\ulcorner\text{Homer is bald}\urcorner]\!]\Big)\Big([\![\mathbf{lisa}]\!]\Big) \\ , \\ [\![\mathbf{say}]\!]\Big([\![\mathbf{bald}(\mathbf{homer})]\!]\Big)\Big([\![\mathbf{lisa}]\!]\Big) \end{array} \right\rangle$$

This parsetree brings to the fore two important issues. The first is largely a technical matter concerning the way proofs in this system conclude. To ground the discussion, I provide in (27) a fuller picture of the final node in the proof suggested by (26*c*).

(27) $\Big\langle$[lisɑ sɛz hoʊmər ɪz bɔld] ; S ; $\mathbf{say}_q(\ulcorner\text{Homer is bald}\urcorner)(\mathbf{lisa}) : t \times t\Big\rangle$

It is typical, in approaches such as the one represented by $\mathcal{G}_1$ and my extensions of it, to assume that the syntactic category S appears with all and only the type *t* (i.e. propositional) meanings. The object in (27) represents a departure from this view, because the category is S but the meaning is a pair of propositions. I would like to suggest that this is not so much a departure from the standard view as a generalization of it. We can regard the standard view as associating the category S with 1-tuples of propositions. I merely generalize this: the category S associates with *n*-tuples of propositions.

We could of course mark the categories: S_1, S_2, and the like. But a change in the syntactic category leads one to expect that we will find distributional differences among the S_is. The expectation is not, as far as I know, borne out; for the most part, the multidimensional content explored in Bach (1999) and Potts (2005) yields sentences with the same distribution as those that terminate with a propositional denotation. So I opt for a minor deviation between category and type. I refer to Asudeh (2004*b*) for evidence that such departures are attested elsewhere. The second issue raised by (26) is more directly factual: How do these product-type meanings interact with higher scope-sensitive operators. What happens when we embed examples like (26), as in (28)?

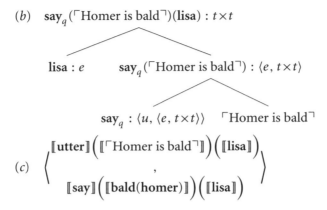

(28) (*a*) Bart believes that Lisa said "Homer is bald".

(*b*) Everyone in Springfield thinks that Lisa said "Homer is bald".

In these examples, the semantic judgments seem clear: both propositions in the final meaning for *Lisa said "Homer is bald"* are in the scope of the higher quantificational element (the attitude verb or the quantifier *everyone in Springfield*). Thus, for example, (28*a*) says that Bart believes both that Lisa uttered the sentence "Homer is bald" and that all of Lisa's utterance worlds are worlds in which Homer is bald. How should we ensure this result?

My answer is that we must generalize the meanings for attitude verbs and nominal quantifiers so that they can take product-type arguments. Since quotations can be embedded within other quotations, and since there is extensive evidence from other realms that clauses can have multidimensional content (Bach 1999; Potts 2005: §6), we should have general enough meanings to allow any finite *n*-tuple of meanings to form the arguments to these elements. To illustrate, I provide the semantics we need for *believe*:

(29) (*a*) **believe** : $\langle t \times t \times \cdots \times t, \langle e, t \rangle \rangle$

(*b*) $[\![\textbf{believe}([\textbf{p}_1 \cdot \ldots \cdot \textbf{p}_n])(\textbf{a})]\!] =$
$\left\{ w \;\middle|\; [\![\textbf{a}]\!] \text{ believes } [\![\textbf{p}_i]\!] \text{ in } w \text{, for all } 1 \leqslant i \leqslant n \right\}$

This semantics for *believe* takes any finite tuple of propositions as its first argument to return a regular property—a function from entities into the set of worlds in which the entity argument believes the conjunction of all the input propositions. The semantics for *every* and other nominal quantifiers should work in roughly this fashion, except with tuples of properties as their nuclear scope arguments. We will see below, in §12.8, that negation works somewhat differently, in that the members of product-typed arguments are kept separate.

One might be initially suspicious of the decision to treat *say* as ambiguous between a propositional attitude verb and a quotation-taking verb. But there is a genuine lexical ambiguity between *say* when it has a clausal complement and *say* when it has a quotative complement. The differences show up clearly when one looks at inversion. With quotation, inversion is possible, as seen in (30*a*); with indirect quotation, it is impossible, as seen in (30*b*).

(30) (*a*) "Ed fled", said Jed.

(*b*) * (That) Ed fled said Jed.

The lexical ambiguity claim is further supported by the many languages that employ different morphemes for the two kinds of construction. (My thanks to Judith Aissen for discussion of this point, May 30, 2003.)

I will close this section by addressing a contrast from Walker (1990), which was brought to my attention by Christine Gunlogson:

(31) Q: When the officer asked him how much he had to drink, what did he say?

A: Nothing

B: "Nothing."

In the A reply, we apparently have a claim that the officer's subject of interrogation made no reply in response to the question about his drinking. It is quite probable that he made no reply because he had in fact been drinking. In the second example, the subject of interrogation enters into the utterance relation with the word $[\![\ulcorner\text{Nothing}\urcorner]\!]$. Our semantics for *say* with a quotative complement reaches into the meaning of this expression and pulls out its semantic representation, which in this case seems to be something denoting the proposition that the speaker had had nothing to drink. Thus, the theory associates the two replies with different denotations. This would presumably be a useful point if one were called to testify as to the importance of knowing the nature of the reaction to the officer's query.

12.6 Engaging the Theory of Direct Compositionality

The fact that we can talk about natural language objects has potential ramifications for a directly compositional theory of ellipsis. Jacobson (1992*b*, 1992*a*, 2003) observes that some deletion theories of ellipsis have much to recommend them. Furthermore, a deletion operation is easy enough to define in a framework like the one suggested by $\mathcal{G}_1$ above:

(32)

$$\begin{array}{c} \big\langle\ ;\ \mathrm{S}/_{\mathrm{L}}\mathrm{NP}\ ;\ \mathbf{delete}(\alpha) : \langle e, t\rangle\big\rangle \\ \hline \big\langle\ ;\ (\mathrm{S}/_{\mathrm{L}}\mathrm{NP})/_{\mathrm{R}}(\mathrm{S}/_{\mathrm{L}}\mathrm{NP})\ ;\ \mathbf{delete} : \langle\langle e, t\rangle, \langle e, t\rangle\rangle\big\rangle \quad \big\langle \Pi\ ;\ \mathrm{S}/_{\mathrm{L}}\mathrm{NP}\ ;\ \alpha : \langle e, t\rangle\big\rangle \end{array}$$

But we cannot allow this operation to apply freely, because verb-phrase ellipsis is subject to contextual restrictions. Broadly speaking, the elided material must find some antecedent in the discourse. As Jacobson (2003) observes, this "is not a local property of the syntax/semantics" of the phrase in question. It is one determinable only "by looking globally at the discourse context".

Jacobson proposes to solve this problem by treating elided verb phrases in the same manner in which deictic pronouns are treated: just as a sentence such as (33*a*) denotes a property in virtue of its free pronoun, a sentence like (33*b*) denotes a function from properties to truth values (a property of properties) in virtue of its missing VP.

(33) (*a*) She giggled. $\rightsquigarrow \lambda x.\,\mathbf{giggle}(x)$
(*b*) Ellen did. $\rightsquigarrow \lambda f.\ f(\mathbf{ellen})$

Both expressions are then subject to the condition that we can find an appropriate argument for them somewhere in the discourse.

This analysis is in conflict with Hankamer and Sag's (1976) distinction between deep and surface anaphora. Deep anaphors require an antecedent somewhere in the discourse. It need not be an antecedent that rose to salience via a linguistic event. These anaphors can be, in their terms, pragmatically controlled. Regular pronouns such as *she* in (33*a*) are deep anaphors.

Surface anaphors are subject to the stricter condition that they have an antecedent in the discourse that rose to salience in virtue of some linguistic event. Thus, whereas *she giggled* can be felicitous if a female entity is salient (perhaps she has made a grand entrance at a party), Hankamer and Sag claim that (33*b*) is felicitous only if the context includes some act of someone uttering a verb phrase that can fill out its meaning.

So far, the direct-compositionality community, led by Jacobson, has responded to this tension by denying that the distinction between deep and surface anaphora is real, at least for verb-phrase ellipsis. There is evidence of this; I refer to Pullum (2000) for a useful summary and assessment of the known arguments for and against the classification of verb-phrase ellipsis as surface anaphoric. But we need not sacrifice the surface-anaphora classification of verb-phrase ellipsis, which seems very real for some speakers, for the sake of a directly compositional theory. The preceding sections of this paper show that the language has devices for talking about and referring anaphorically to utterance events. A statement enforcing surface anaphora is within reach of the resulting proposal, which is entirely model-theoretic. To be more specific, nothing prevents us from defining the requisite deletion operator as follows:

(34) (*a*) $[\![\mathbf{delete}(\alpha)]\!]$ is defined only if α is of type $\langle e, t\rangle$ and the context world w is such that $w \in [\![\mathbf{utter}]\!](\ulcorner \mathrm{A} \urcorner)(d)$ for some $d \in D_e$ and some $\ulcorner \mathrm{A} \urcorner$ such that $\mathit{SEM}(\ulcorner \mathrm{A} \urcorner) = \alpha$
(*b*) Where defined, $[\![\mathbf{delete}(\alpha)]\!] = \alpha$

This defines **delete**(α) as a surface anaphor in the sense of Hankamer and Sag (1976). Deep anaphoric verb-phrase pronouns might impose the weaker restriction that their referents merely be entailed by some element that precedes them in the discourse context (Schwarzschild 1999). But in terms of Jacobson's theory, the distinction can be made simply as follows: expressions containing deep anaphors are functional expressions that are felicitous only in contexts that contain suitable arguments for them; surface anaphors like **delete**(α) in (34) are felicitous only in contexts that contain suitable arguments for them *that have been mentioned linguistically.*

12.7 Subclausal Quotation

The theory of clausal quotation developed in §12.5 centers around the meaning for *say* when it takes a quotative complement. The functor is called $\mathbf{say}_q$. It has a dual semantics, in the sense that its output is a pair of propositions. Not all instances of quotation involve full clauses, however. I opened this paper with example (1), repeated in (35), and I now offer the slightly different example (36) (from Potts 2003).

(35) (*a*) When in Santa Cruz, Peter orders "[eɪ]pricots" at the local market.
(*b*) When in Amherst, Peter orders "[æ]pricots" at the local market.

(36) (*a*) Ellen: *The Godfather II* is a total snooze.
(*b*) Frank: Well, Pauline Kael said that this "total snooze" is a defining moment in America cinema.

These examples both make use of linguistic features of the items inside quotation marks, but at the same time those items have their usual semantics. Example (35*b*) involves the natural language object

$$\big\langle [\text{æprɛkɔts}] \; ; \text{NP} \; ; \textbf{apricots} : e \big\rangle$$

but we will also clearly need access to the semantic representation **apricots**. So far, this is quite like our theory of clausal quotation, where we used the linguistic object and its semantics. The function *SEM* is designed to reach into natural language expressions and pull out their semantic representations.

Similarly, (36*b*) makes use of

$$\big\langle [\text{toʊtl snuz}] \; ; \text{N} \; ; \textbf{total-snooze} : \langle e, t\rangle \big\rangle$$

but it combines with **that** to pick out the movie *Godfather II*. This example is useful because it is so clear that the phrase *total snooze* is quotative. One could not easily argue that the quotation marks were, for instance, merely a device for signalling that the phrase is evaluated at a particular, sentence-internal intensional index. Nothing external to the quotation gives us any reason to think that the intensional index associated with, say, Ellen's belief worlds is a part of the composition. Rather, we really do need a theory of quotation to understand how "*total snooze*" works.

Perhaps the most important feature of these examples is that they are anaphoric, in the sense that we need to find an entity in the discourse to whom we can attribute the quotation. Thus, for example, (36*b*) imposes the requirement that, in our context world w, we can find some contextually salient entity $d \in D_e$ such that

$$w \in [\![\textbf{utter}]\!](\langle[\text{toʊtl snuz}]\ ;\ \text{N}\ ;\ \textbf{total-snooze} : e\rangle)(d)$$

The requirement is rarely merely existential, though. In general, we attribute such quotations to specific individuals. For instance, it is overwhelmingly likely that Ellen is the source of "*total snooze*" in (36*b*).

The projection properties of these subclausal quotations are different from those of the complements to *say* (in its $\textbf{say}_q$ manifestation). Whereas both dimensions of those quotative complements seem to form the argument to higher operators, the speech-report dimension of subclausal quotations seems much freer in its scope-taking properties. This is useful additional evidence that the regular and speech-report meanings can be independent of one another, but it does place an additional burden on the compositional semantics, which must provide a mechanism for this variable scope behavior.

A look at the multidimensional denotations that these subclausal quotations have suggests an explanation for this point of contrast with direct clausal quotation. For instance, here is a reasonable first approximation of the meaning for "*apricots*" in (35*b*).

(37) $$\left\langle \begin{array}{c} \text{the } x \text{ such that } x = [\![\textbf{apricots}]\!] \text{ in all of Peter's utterance worlds} \\ , \\ [\![\textbf{utter}(\ulcorner[\text{æ}]\text{pricots}\urcorner)(\textbf{peter})]\!] \end{array} \right\rangle$$

The second meaning in the pair is a proposition, whereas the first is a plural entity. Only this plural entity is truly suited to the semantic environment it is in—that is, only it can be the argument to [[**order**]]. The proposition-denoting second member is ill-suited as a denotation for something in the object position of this transitive verb. Presumably, it must be passed along, either to become the argument to a higher predicate or to be interpreted at the root level. Thus, we require a version of the projection function of Karttunen and Peters (1979), which regulates how what they call "conventional implicatures" are inherited upwards in a semantic parsetree. I accomplish this with the addition of the term **project**, as in (38) (which we can assume has no phonological or syntactic effects).

(38) (*a*) **project** : $\langle \sigma, \langle \tau \times t, \rho \times t \rangle \rangle$

(*b*) $[\![\mathbf{project}(\alpha)(\beta \cdot \mathbf{p})]\!] =$

$\left\langle [\![\alpha(\beta)]\!], [\![\mathbf{p}]\!] \right\rangle$

or

$\left\langle [\![\beta(\alpha)]\!], [\![\mathbf{p}]\!] \right\rangle$

whichever is well-formed

The type is complex, but the action of **project** is easy to describe: it takes an expression α and a product expression $\beta \cdot \mathbf{p}$ as its arguments. It applies α to the first member of the product, or the reverse, depending on which is the functor. It outputs the result of that application paired with the second member of the product, which remains untouched (just along for the ride).

With these additions to the theory, we can now interpret subclausal quotation with the function in (39).

(39) (*a*) **quote-shift** : $\langle u, \langle e, \sigma \times t \rangle \rangle$

(*b*) $[\![\mathbf{quote\text{-}shift}]\!](\mathcal{P})(d) =$

$$\left\langle \begin{array}{c} \text{the } X \text{ such that } \mathbf{say}([\![X]\!] = [\![SEM(\mathcal{P})]\!])(d) \\ , \\ [\![\mathbf{utter}]\!](\mathcal{P})(d) \end{array} \right\rangle$$

for any $\mathcal{P} \in D_u$ and $d \in D_e$

Notice that the regular denotation, the first element in the tuple, is relativized to the utterance worlds of the entity argument. This is essential to the description of examples such as (36), in which the speaker, Frank, uses "*total snooze*" to pick out the *Godfather II*, despite the fact that he clearly does not endorse this as a description of that movie. The scenario strongly suggests that none of Frank's utterance worlds w is such that $w \in [\![\mathbf{total\text{-}snooze(godfather\text{-}II)}]\!]$. But reference to the movie goes through because the entity argument to "*total snooze*" can be Ellen.

Once we have fed **quote-shift** a natural language phrase, we are left with a function from entities into pairs of propositions. If there is no entity salient in the discourse to whom we can apply the function, then the example is infelicitous due to the fact that its final meaning components are not propositional; the reasoning here, which is due to Jacobson (1999: §2.2.2), is the same as that of §12.6.

In (40), I outline the composition for the phrase *orders* "[æ]*pricots*".

(40)

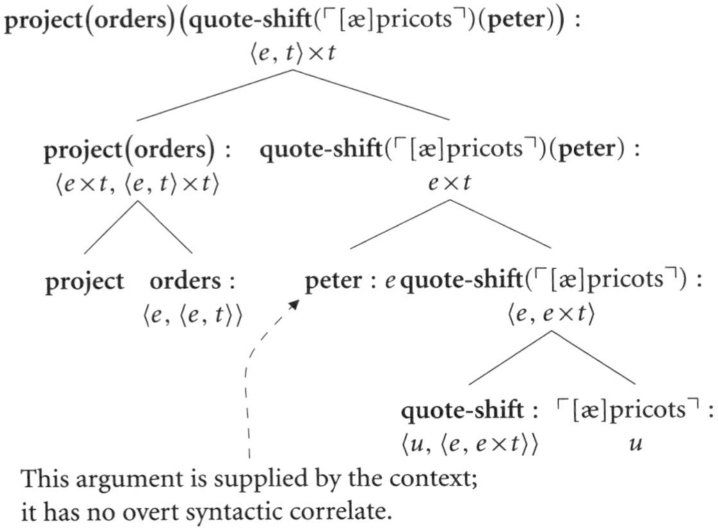

As noted above, subclausal quotation is essentially anaphoric. I have represented this by supplying it with the entity argument **peter**. In a framework like that of Jacobson (1999), this argument could be deferred until the final step in the computation, in exactly the way that pronouns and relational nouns are treated. This involves additional type-shifting functions, to pass on this argument slot unsaturated. Rather than complicate the semantics with these details, I have just supplied an argument as part of the well-formedness proof. In treatments that employ variables, this argument could be filled by a free variable, which would then be "discourse bound" in the sense that the context would supply an appropriate assignment function for it.

12.8 Metalinguistic Negation

As noted above, in §12.4, we can define properties of sentences that reference their phonology, their syntax, or their semantics. Here are some examples

(41) (*a*) **stress-initial** : $\langle u, t\rangle$ (a property of words and sentences)

(*b*) **composed-of-open-syllables** : $\langle u, t\rangle$ (a property of words and sentences)

(*c*) **deems-inappropriately-blunt** : $\langle u, \langle e, t\rangle\rangle$ (a function from sentences to functions from entities to truth values)

Predicates like these are helpful in formalizing and understanding existing observations about the way that so-called "metalinguistic" negation works. Consider, for instance the following example, from Horn (1989: 371).

(42) He didn't call the POlice, he called the poLICE.

The small capitals illustrate the stressed syllable. In the case at hand, we are dealing with the following two lexical items:

(43) (*a*) $[\![\ulcorner \text{POlice} \urcorner]\!] = \big\langle [\text{'po.lis}]\ ;\ \text{NP}\ ;\ \textbf{police} : \langle e, t\rangle \big\rangle$

(*b*) $[\![\ulcorner \text{poLICE} \urcorner]\!] = \big\langle [\text{po.'lis}]\ ;\ \text{NP}\ ;\ \textbf{police} : \langle e, t\rangle \big\rangle$

The first of these has the property defined by the meaning of **stress-initial**. The second does not.

The semantics explored in §12.7 derives a pair of propositions for each of the sentences in (42). For the sake of simplicity, let us factor the negation out of each of these pairs, as in (44)–(45).

(44) (*a*) **call**(**the**(**police**))(**charlie**)

(*b*) **utter**(⌜POlice⌝)(**the-speaker**)

(45) (*a*) **call**(**the**(**police**))(**charlie**)

(*b*) **utter**(⌜poLICE⌝)(**the-speaker**)

These examples differ in their truth conditions in virtue of having contrasting second dimensions of meaning.

How does negation act on such pairs? The continuation in (42) indicates that it can operate solely on the utterance dimension. On this reading, the first sentence in the example entails that Charlie called the police and that the speaker does not say PO*lice*.

Natural language negation can of course operate in a way that is insensitive to pronunciation. For instance, *He didn't call the police*, without any special intonation, says that Charlie did not call the police.

The most important observation is that there seems not to be a reading of (42) on which it is equivalent to either of the paraphrases in (46).

(46) (*a*) It is false that Charlie called the police, and it is false that the speaker uses the pronunciation PO*lice*. $[\neg p \wedge \neg q]$

(*b*) It is false that Charlie called the police and that the speaker uses the pronunciation PO*lice*. $[\neg(p \wedge q)]$

The generalization is that the negation can target one dimension of meaning but not both of them. This should resonate with people who work on categorial grammar and other *resource sensitive* logics for natural language. In such theories, it would be highly unnatural to have to derive readings such as (46*a*), in which we seem to use the negation twice.

The fact that we lack readings like (46*b*) is additional support for the idea that the theory of quotation should be multidimensional: when we have quotation, we generally have two independent propositions expressed, one contributed more or less directly by the quotation and the other contributed by the main clause content around it. The negation operator we need in order to describe these facts is given in (47).

(47) (*a*) $\mathbf{not}_i : \langle t{\times}t, t{\times}t\rangle$ where $1 \leqslant i \leqslant 2$

(*b*) $[\![\mathbf{not}_1(\mathbf{p} \cdot \mathbf{q})]\!] =$

$$\Big\langle \big\{w \mid w \notin [\![\mathbf{p}]\!]\big\}, [\![\mathbf{q}]\!]\Big\rangle$$

(*c*) $[\![\mathbf{not}_2(\mathbf{p} \cdot \mathbf{q})]\!] =$

$$\Big\langle [\![\mathbf{p}]\!], \big\{w \mid w \notin [\![\mathbf{q}]\!]\big\}\Big\rangle$$

If we choose the first interpretation, we obtain a regular propositional negation; the speech-act dimension remains untouched. If we choose the second meaning, we negate the speech-act dimension but leave the first untouched. This corresponds to the "metalinguistic negation". I suspect that this is as close as it is possible to come to a negation that can cover both regular and "metalinguistic" uses. The two denotations are naturally related, in that each is the usual sort of propositional negation (a set complementation operator) plus the addition of an identity function on propositions. The difference is just which of the argument's projections each of dimensions acts on.

12.9 Conclusion

Bart Geurts has done some of the most important and detailed work on quotation to date (Geurts 1998, 2001). It is thus somewhat surprising to read in Geurts (2001) the claim that "Quotation may not be a hugely important matter, but it is still of some interest". It seems clear to me that quotation *is* a hugely important matter for linguistic theory. It forces us to enrich our stock of basic entities, as we saw in §12.3, and this in turn sheds new light on what it means to refer to and manipulate representations (§12.6). What is more; quotation provides additional evidence for the theses of Bach (1999) and Potts (2005) that individual sentences can express multiple independent propositions; in the realm of quotation, we see this particularly clearly when we inspect the interactions between quotation and negation.

Moreover, this paper addresses only a handful of the types of quotation discussed by Jespersen (1992 [1924]: §21) and Fillmore (1974), and I have not attempted to foster connections between this realm and that of free indirect discourse (Jespersen 1992 [1924]: §21; Schlenker, 2004; Sharvit 2003). It seems clear also that a complete theory of quotation will reference specific intonation contours as the auditory equivalent of quotation marks (Partee 1973), making this a potentially important area for researchers on information structuring. And these new directions are likely to lead to additional ties with the rest of linguistic theory. My hope for the present paper is merely that it reveals a directly compositional semantics to be a fruitful setting in which to explore this class of meanings.

Appendix: The Full Grammar $\mathcal{G}$

The grammar $\mathcal{G}$ is defined as follows:

A.1 *Types*

(i) e, t, and u are types.
(ii) If σ and τ are types, then $\langle \sigma, \tau \rangle$ is a type.
(iii) If σ and τ are types, then $\sigma \times \tau$ is a type.
(iv) Nothing else is a type.

A.2 *Terms*

(i)	⟨	[bɑrt]	;	NP	;	**bart** : e	⟩
	⟨	[lisɑ]	;	NP	;	**lisa** : e	⟩
	⟨	[mægi]	;	NP	;	**maggie** : e	⟩
	⟨	[bərnz]	;	NP	;	**burns** : e	⟩
(ii)	⟨	[wɛrwʊlf]	;	$S/_{L}NP$	;	**werewolf** : $\langle e, t \rangle$	⟩
	⟨	[dɛd]	;	$S/_{L}NP$	;	**dead** : $\langle e, t \rangle$	⟩
	⟨	[bɔld]	;	$S/_{L}NP$	;	**bald** : $\langle e, t \rangle$	⟩
	⟨	[jəs]	;	$S/_{L}NP$	;	**yes** : $\langle e, t \rangle$	⟩
(iii)	⟨	[it]	;	$(S/_{L}NP)/_{R}NP$	;	**eat** : $\langle e, \langle e, t \rangle\rangle$	⟩
	⟨	[si]	;	$(S/_{L}NP)/_{R}NP$	;	**see** : $\langle e, \langle e, t \rangle\rangle$	⟩
	⟨	[skɛr]	;	$(S/_{L}NP)/_{R}NP$	;	**scare** : $\langle e, \langle e, t \rangle\rangle$	⟩

(iv)
$\langle$ [seɪ] ; $(S/_{L}NP)/_{R}S$; **say** $: \langle t, \langle e, t\rangle\rangle$ $\rangle$
$\langle$ [biliv] ; $(S/_{L}NP)/_{R}S$; **believe** $: \langle t \times t \times \cdots \times t, \langle e, t\rangle\rangle$ $\rangle$
$\langle$ [ʌtər] ; $(S/_{L}NP)/_{R}NP$; **utter** $: \langle u, \langle e, t\rangle\rangle$ $\rangle$
$\langle$ [seɪ] ; $(S/_{L}NP)/_{R}NP$; $\mathbf{say}_q : \langle u, \langle e, t \times t\rangle\rangle$ $\rangle$

(v) $\langle$ [nɑt] ; $S/_{R}S$; $\mathbf{not}_i : \langle t \times t, t \times t\rangle$ $\rangle$ where $1 \leqslant i \leqslant 2$

(vi)
$\langle$; $(S/_{L}NP)/_{R}(S/_{L}NP)$; **delete** $: \langle\langle e, t\rangle, \langle e, t\rangle\rangle$ $\rangle$
$\langle$; $(S/_{L}NP)/_{R}(S/_{L}NP)$; **project** $: \langle \sigma, \langle \tau \times t, \rho \times t\rangle\rangle$ $\rangle$
$\langle$; $(S/_{L}NP)/_{R}(S/_{L}NP)$; **quote-shift** $: \langle u, \langle e, \sigma \times t\rangle\rangle$ $\rangle$

(vii)

$$\dfrac{\left\langle \begin{array}{c} \Pi \\ A/_{R}B \\ \alpha : \langle \sigma, \tau\rangle \end{array} \right\rangle \quad \left\langle \begin{array}{c} \Phi \\ B \\ \beta : \sigma \end{array} \right\rangle}{\left\langle \begin{array}{c} [\Pi\ \Phi] \\ A \\ (\alpha(\beta)) : \tau \end{array} \right\rangle} \qquad \dfrac{\left\langle \begin{array}{c} \Phi \\ B \\ \beta : \sigma \end{array} \right\rangle \quad \left\langle \begin{array}{c} \Pi \\ A/_{L}B \\ \alpha : \langle \sigma, \tau\rangle \end{array} \right\rangle}{\left\langle \begin{array}{c} [\Phi\ \Pi] \\ A \\ (\alpha(\beta)) : \tau \end{array} \right\rangle}$$

(viii) If $\mathcal{P} = \langle \Pi ; \Sigma ; \alpha : \sigma \rangle$ is well-formed, then $\langle \Pi ; \Sigma ; \ulcorner\langle \Pi ; \Sigma ; \alpha : \sigma\rangle\urcorner : u\rangle$ is well-formed.

A.3 *Domains*

(i) The domain of type e is D_e, the domain of nonlinguistic entities.
(ii) The domain of type t is $D_t = \wp(W)$, the power set of the set W of possible worlds.
(iii) The domain of type t is D_u, the domain of well-formed linguistic entities. $D_u \cap D_e = \emptyset$.
(iv) The domain of type $\langle \sigma, \tau\rangle$ is $D_{\langle \sigma, \tau\rangle}$, the set of all functions from D_σ into D_τ.
(v) The domain of type $\sigma \times \tau$ is $D_{\sigma \times \tau} = D_\sigma \times D_\tau$, the Cartesian product of D_σ and D_τ.

A.4 *Interpretation*

$[\![\cdot]\!]$ is the interpretation function, taking semantic representations of $\mathcal{G}$ to elements in the set of domains specified in §A.3. It is constrained so that if α is of type σ, then $[\![\alpha]\!] \in D_\sigma$. Below, I provide the interpretations for the most important terms discussed in the paper. The terms that go unmentioned work as one would expect (e.g. $[\![$**homer**$]\!]$ is the individual Homer, and $[\![$**bald**$]\!]$ is the property of baldness).

(i) $[\![\mathbf{utter}(\ulcorner S \urcorner)(\mathbf{b})]\!]$ = the set of worlds in which $[\![\mathbf{b}]\!]$ utters $[\![\ulcorner S \urcorner]\!]$

(ii) $[\![\mathbf{say}(\mathbf{p})(\mathbf{b})]\!]$ = the set of world w in which every utterance world w' for $[\![\mathbf{b}]\!]$ is such that $w' \in [\![\mathbf{p}]\!]$

(iii) $SEM\Big(\big\langle \Pi \; ; \; \mathrm{A} \; ; \; \alpha : \sigma \big\rangle\Big) = \alpha$

(iv) $[\![\mathbf{say}_q(\ulcorner S \urcorner)(\mathbf{b})]\!] = \left\langle \begin{array}{c} [\![\mathbf{utter}(\ulcorner S \urcorner)(\mathbf{b})]\!] \\ , \\ [\![\mathbf{say}]\!]\big([\![SEM([\![\ulcorner S \urcorner]\!])]\!]\big)\big([\![\mathbf{b}]\!]\big) \end{array} \right\rangle$

(v) $[\![\mathbf{believe}\big([\mathbf{p}_1 \cdot \ldots \cdot \mathbf{p}_n]\rangle\big)(\mathbf{a})]\!] =$
$\Big\{ w \;\Big|\; [\![\mathbf{a}]\!] \text{ believes } [\![\mathbf{p}_i]\!] \text{ in } w \text{ , for all } 1 \leqslant i \leqslant n \Big\}$

(vi) $[\![\mathbf{delete}(\alpha)]\!]$ is defined only if α is of type $\langle e, t\rangle$ and the context world w is such that $w \in [\![\mathbf{utter}]\!](\ulcorner \mathrm{A} \urcorner)(d)$ for some $d \in D_e$ and some $\ulcorner \mathrm{A} \urcorner$ such that $SEM(\ulcorner \mathrm{A} \urcorner) = \alpha$
Where defined, $[\![\mathbf{delete}(\alpha)]\!] = \alpha$

(vii) $[\![\mathbf{project}(\alpha)(\beta \cdot \mathbf{p})]\!] =$
$\big\langle [\![\alpha(\beta)]\!], [\![\mathbf{p}]\!] \big\rangle$
or
$\big\langle [\![\beta(\alpha)]\!], [\![\mathbf{p}]\!] \big\rangle$
whichever is well-formed

(viii) $[\![\mathbf{quote\text{-}shift}]\!](\mathcal{P})(d) =$

$$\left\langle \begin{array}{c} \text{the } X \text{ such that } \mathbf{say}\big([\![X]\!] = [\![SEM(\mathcal{P})]\!]\big)(d) \\ , \\ [\![\mathbf{utter}]\!](\mathcal{P})(d) \end{array} \right\rangle$$

for any $\mathcal{P} \in D_u$ and $d \in D_e$

(ix) $[\![\mathbf{not}_1(\mathbf{p} \cdot \mathbf{q})]\!] =$
$\big\langle \{ w \mid w \notin [\![\mathbf{p}]\!] \}, [\![\mathbf{q}]\!] \big\rangle$

(x) $[\![\mathbf{not}_2(\mathbf{p} \cdot \mathbf{q})]\!] =$
$\big\langle [\![\mathbf{p}]\!], \{ w \mid w \notin [\![\mathbf{q}]\!] \} \big\rangle$

References

Asudeh, A. 2004*a*. Resumption as Resource Management. Ph.D. thesis, Stanford University.

——2004*b*. 'The resumptive puzzle of relational nouns', MS, Stanford University. URLhttp://semanticsarchive.net/Archive/WY0ODgxN/ .

—— and Crouch, R. 2002. 'Derivational parallelism and ellipsis parallelism', in L. Mikkelsen and C. Potts (eds), *Proceedings of WCCFL 21*. Somerville, MA: Cascadilla Press. 1–14.

Bach, E. and Wheeler, D. 1981. 'Montague phonology: A first approximation', in W. Chao and D. Wheeler (eds), *University of Massachusetts Occasional Papers, 7*. Amherst, MA: GLSA. 27–45.

Bach, K. 1999. 'The myth of conventional implicature', *Linguistics and Philosophy*, 22: 327–66.

Carpenter, B. 1997. *Type-Logical Semantics*. Cambridge, MA: MIT Press.

Chierchia, G. 1982. 'Nominalization and Montague grammar: A semantics without types for natural languages', *Linguistics and Philosophy*, 5: 303–54.

—— 1984. Topics in the Syntax and Semantics of Infinitives and Gerunds. Ph.D. thesis, University of Massachusetts, Amherst. (Distributed by GLSA).

—— and Turner, R. 1988. 'Semantics and property theory', *Linguistics and Philosophy*, 11: 261–302.

Dalrymple, M. (ed.) 2001. *Semantics and Syntax in Lexical Functional Grammar*. Cambridge, MA: MIT Press.

Davidson, D. 1968. 'On saying that', *Synthese*, 19: 130–46.

Fillmore, C. 1974. 'Pragmatics and the description of discourse', in C. J. Fillmore, G. Lakoff, and R. Lakoff (eds.), *Berkeley Studies in Syntax and Semantics*, Volume 1, V.1–21. Department of Linguistics, University of California, Berkeley: Institute of Human Learning.

Foer, J. S. 2002. 'A primer for the punctuation of heart disease', *The New Yorker*, June 10: 82–5.

Geurts, B. 1998. 'The mechanisms of denial', *Language*, 74: 274–307.

—— 2001. 'The pragmatics of quotation', MS, University of Nijmegen.

—— and Maier, E. 2003. 'Layered DRT', MS, University of Nijmegen.

Hankamer, J. and Sag, I. A. 1976. 'Deep and surface anaphora', *Linguistic Inquiry*, 7: 391–426.

Higgins, R. F. 1973. The Pseudo-Cleft Construction in English. Ph.D. thesis, MIT. (Published by Garland, 1979).

Hintikka, J. 1971. 'Semantics for propositional attitudes', in L. Linsky (ed.), *Reference and Modality*. Oxford: Oxford University Press. 145–67.

Horn, L. R. 1989. *A Natural History of Negation*. Chicago: University of Chicago Press. Reissued 2001 by CSLI.

Jacobson, P. 1992*a*. 'Antecedent-contained deletion in a variable-free semantics', in C. Barker and D. Dowty (eds.), *Proceedings of SALT II*, OSU Working Papers in Linguistics. Columbus, OH: Ohio State University. 193–213.

—— 1992*b*. 'Flexible categorial grammars: Questions and prospects', in R. Levine (ed.), *Formal Grammar: Theory and Implementation*. Oxford: Oxford University Press. 129–67.

—— 1999. 'Towards a variable-free semantics', *Linguistics and Philosophy*, 22: 117–84.

Jacobson, P. 2000. 'Paycheck pronouns, Bach–Peters sentences, and variable-free semantics', *Natural Language Semantics*, 8: 77–155.

—— 2003. 'Direct compositionality and ellipsis', paper presented at the UCSC Workshop on Ellipsis, 18 January.

Jespersen, O. 1992 [1924]. *The Philosophy of Grammar*. Chicago: University of Chicago Press. With a new introduction and index by James D. McCawley.

Kaplan, D. 1989. 'Demonstratives: An essay on the semantics, logic, metaphysics, and epistemology of demonstratives and other indexicals', in J. Almog, J. Perry, and H. Wettstein (eds), *Themes from Kaplan*. New York: Oxford University Press. 481–563. (Versions of this paper began circulating in 1971).

Karttunen, L. and Peters, S. 1979. 'Conventional implicature', in C.-K. Oh and D. A. Dinneen (eds), *Syntax and Semantics*, Volume 11: Presupposition. New York: Academic Press. 1–56.

Krifka, M. 1999. 'At least some determiners aren't determiners', in K. Turner (ed.), *The Semantics/Pragmatics Interface from Different Points of View*, Volume 1 of *Current Research in the Semantics/Pragmatics Interface*. Oxford: Elsevier. 257–91.

—— 2001. 'Quantifying into question acts', *Natural Language Semantics*, 9: 1–40.

Mikkelsen, L. 2002. 'Two types of definite description subjects', in M. Nissim (ed.), *Proceedings of the Student Session at ESSLLI 14*. Trento, Italy. 141–53.

—— 2004. Specifying Who: The Structure, Meaning, and Use of Specificational Clauses. Ph.D. thesis, University of California, Santa Cruz.

Oehrle, R. T., E. Bach, and D. Wheeler (eds.) 1988. *Categorial Grammars and Natural Language Structures*. Dordrecht: Reidel.

Partee, B. H. 1973. 'The syntax and semantics of quotation', in S. R. Anderson and P. Kiparsky (eds), *A Festschrift for Morris Hallle*. New York: Holt, Reinhart and Winston. 410–18.

Postal, P. M. 2004. 'The openness of natural languages', in *Skeptical Linguistic Essays*. Oxford: Oxford University Press. 173–201.

Potts, C. 2003. 'Expressive content as conventional implicature', in M. Kadowaki and S. Kawahara (eds), *Proceedings of the North East Linguistics Society 33*. Amherst, MA: GLSA.

—— 2005. *The Logic of Conventional Implicatures*. Oxford Studies in Theoretical Linguistics. Oxford: Oxford University Press.

Pullum, G. K. 2000. Hankamer does! URLhttp://ling.ucsc.edu//Jorge/ index.html, Jorge Hankamer's WebFest.

Ross, J. R. 1970. 'On declarative sentences', in R. Jacobs and P. Rosenbaum (eds), *Readings in English Transformational Grammar*. Waltham, MA: Ginn and Company. 222–72.

Schlenker, P. 2004. 'Context of thought and context of utterance: A note on free indirect discourse and the historical present', *Mind and Language*, 19: 279–304.

Schwarzschild, R. 1999. 'GIVENness, AvoidF and other constraints on the placement of accent', *Natural Language Semantics*, 7: 141–77.

SEARLE, J. 1969. *Speech Acts: An Essay in the Philosophy of Language*. Cambridge: Cambridge University Press.

SHARVIT, Y. 2003. 'Issues in the syntax and semantics of free indirect discourse', talk presented at University of Massachusetts, Amherst, November, and University of Connecticut, December.

WALKER, A. G. 1990. 'Language at work in the law: The customs, conventions, and appellate consequences of court reporting', in J. N. Levi and A. G. Walker (eds), *Language in the Judicial Process*. New York: Plenum Press. 203–45.

Index